PIETRO ARETINO

The First Modern

ALSO BY DANNY CHAPLIN

The Medici: Rise of a Parvenu Dynasty, 1360-1537

Strenuitas. The Life and Times of Robert Guiscard and Bohemond of
Taranto: Norman Power from the Mezzogiorno to Antioch
1016 – 1111 A.D.

PIETRO ARETINO

The First Modern

DANNY CHAPLIN

On the front cover: engraving of Pietro Aretino by Marcantonio Raimondi (Raimondi's engraved portrait of Aretino was probably designed by the Venetian painter Sebastiano del Piombo, although the name of Giulio Romano—with whom Marcantonio collaborated on I modi—has also been proposed. It probably dates from the early stages of his career, when Aretino was still an unknown newcomer to Rome and he and Giulio were working for the wealthy papal banker Agostino Chigi. An alternative view is that the print was executed around 1525 as an expression of gratitude by Marcantonio to Aretino, who had negotiated the engraver's release from prison after the scandal of I modi.)

Cover artwork credit: Chris Baker.

In loving memory of my mother
Sheila Anne Harris.

CONTENTS

Pietro Aretino by Titian (1545).

'Here is a similar portrayal of my own appearance, likewise the work of his [Titian's] paintbrush. Truly it breathes, its pulses beat, and it is animated with the same spirit with which I am in actual life, and if I had only counted out more crowns to him, the clothes I wore would likewise have been as shining and soft, yet firm to the touch as are actual satin, velvet and brocade.'

Veritas odium parit ('truth breeds hatred').
The motto of Pietro Aretino.

Riches, the dumb god, that giv'st all men tongues:
That canst do naught, and yet mak'st men do all things;
The price of souls; even hell, with thee to boot,
Is made worth heaven! Thou art virtue, fame,
Honour, and all things else! Who can get thee,
He shall be noble, valiant honest, wise.

Ben Johnson, Volpone 1.1.22-27

༄༅

Literary Innovator or 'Literary Ruffian?'

Base in character, coarse in mental fiber, unworthy to rank among real artists, notwithstanding his undoubted genius, Aretino was the typical ruffian of an age which brought ruffianism to perfection, welcomed it when successful, bowed to its insolence and viewed it with complacent toleration in the highest places of Church, State, and letters. He was the *condottiere* of the pen in a society which truckled to the Borgias. He embodied the infamy and cowardice which lurked beneath the braveries of Italian court-life–the coarseness of speech which contradicted literary purism–the cynicism and gross strength of appetite for which convention was a flimsy veil. The man himself incarnated the dissolution of Italian culture. His works, for the student of that period, are an anti-mask to the brilliant display of Ariosto's or of Tasso's puppets. It is the condemnation of Italy that we are forced to give this prominence to Aretino.

John Addington Symonds.

In 1492, the horizon of European men's minds was suddenly and dramatically expanded by the surprise discovery of a vast, unexplored continent situated on the far side of the largely uncharted western ocean. Despite what anyone might say to the contrary, things would never be quite the same ever again. If *any* year can lay claim to being the commencement date for the 'modern world' it was the year 1492. This, incidentally, was arguably also the same year in which the Florentine Renaissance drew to a close with the death of that great artistic patron Lorenzo de' Medici, known to the Florentines as *il Magnifico*. The great flourishing of humanist literature and of art and culture in this Tuscan mercantile city-state had been the means by which the old and outmoded medieval ways of thinking, philosophising, writing, painting, sculpting and

15

building had been forever swept away. The old ways had, as a result, been replaced with a new, more enlightened, era in which the new visual rules of perspective described the proportions of man's world more faithfully, and in which the wisdom of the ancients pierced the gloom of centuries of stultifying Christian scholasticism. How fitting, then, for 1492 to have been the birth year of a man who can, with every conceivable justification, lay claim to the title of 'the first modern'? The first man, that is to say, who though born into obscurity was able to flout the traditional, strictly-ordered social hierarchy of the *cinquecento*; the first to 'game' the established system of patronage to his own personal advantage and remake himself entirely in his own image as the foremost celebrity *literato* in all of Christendom.

The name of the man in question is Pietro Aretino and his story is remarkable if only for the fact that, although in many ways the inventor of the modern individualistic sensibility, he is practically unknown today in our so-called modern twenty-first century world. Although now practically forgotten outside of Italy beyond the odd, sparsely-attended postgraduate class on sixteenth-century Renaissance literary studies, Pietro Aretino was in fact a veritable giant in his own day who was known to both great and small alike. He was the first man to openly defy and contradict lords, kings, emperors and popes and survive unscathed to tell the tale to both his acolytes and his large European readership. Instead of being quietly done away with as a nuisance, on the contrary, he emerged triumphantly from these many public controversies, often with people in high places, each of which only seemed to add to his growing fame. Eschewing the need to please his social superiors, and making them beat a path to *his* doorstep instead, he evinced a distinctly modern sensibility in apparently not caring who he offended or, by the same token, who slandered him back (a challenge to which he was always equal). He was the first literary realist, the first cultural nihilist, the first (through both his life as well as his writings) to publicly and defiantly elevate (unChristian) amorality as a well-publicised and culturally-acceptable 'lifestyle choice'. He was a man who successfully detached society from its old Church-bound moralism and initiated the unabashed ethos of decadence which 'godly' monarchs like Louis XIV of France and Charles II of England would lustily embrace and, with gusto, make wholly their own. He was something entirely new and anomalous in the Italy of this time. In point of fact, Aretino was not merely a celebrity *literato* who was primus inter pares; he was arguably the world's first 'celebrity' as we today might understand that term, as being famous simply for being famous.[1]

Aretino achieved his fame, many might say notoriety, through being a kind of literary jack-of-all-trades, a so-called *poligrafo*. Known to all through his scabrous literary attacks on popes and other renowned men of the day, ultimately his controversies would bring him fame and recognition. In so doing, he became also the world's first well-publicised (or rather self-publicised) 'go-getter', the prototype of the modern man who, though not necessarily well-born, knows exactly what he wants in material terms and goes out there and pulls out all the stops to get it. Aretino was the infamous, best-selling, celebrity author who was able to pull down 'the big bucks' of his sixteenth-century era. Aretino was a poet, a dramatist, a prose essayist, a satirist, as well as a prodigious composer of published letters (or epistles). If blackmail may be said to figure amongst his array of literary skills, which it probably can, he was also a remarkably successful literary extortionist (the line between his letter writing and his extortionism was, if truth be told, often an extremely fine one). His catalogue of literary innovations is quite breathtaking. In eschewing the old classical forms inherited from the Greeks and Romans and by refusing to write in Latin (which he did not possess to any great extent due to lacunae in his own formal education), Aretino was the first to write in the vernacular Tuscan with a truly modern sensibility. This gives him claim to be the first modern literary realist in European literature. Through his *pasquinata* (sardonic 'editorials'), his *giudizi* (satirical, quasi-astrological almanacs of annual predictions on personalities and current affairs), and his *epistole/lettere* (collections of letters to famous and prominent people), Aretino also qualifies for recognition as the world's first modern journalist or columnist. Through his florid praise for the famous and wealthy people of the age, or for personal friends like the painter Titian, he was the first modern publicist. Through his writings, descriptions and *ekphrases* of the work of his artist friends (again, principally Titian but also others like Jacopo Sansovino and Tintoretto), he was the first modern art critic. When he published sixteen 'licentious sonnets' to accompany a collection of equally salacious engravings, Aretino acquired the dubious mantle of the first modern pornographer. Realist, journalist, publicist, art critic, and pornographer–during his life Aretino made all of these roles uniquely his own.

But if you go out into the streets of London, Hong Kong or New York City today and ask any passing stranger whether they have ever heard of the name Pietro Aretino you are more than likely to be met with a blank stare. This would certainly not be the case if were you to mention instead the name of Aretino's contemporary, Niccolò Machiavelli. But why is this so? Why would the memory of a man who played such an important pioneering and developmental role in so many literary and cultural genres be allowed to slide into virtual obscurity? A person's reputation and legacy can be ephemeral things at the best of times. In a flash of brilliance, the art historian Patricia Emison offers a possible answer to this question when she suggests that 'Pietro Aretino's posthumous lack of reputation is one indication that what was said while he was alive was not always what was thought'.[2]

It could also conceivably be argued too that Aretino was not particularly accomplished in any of the fields that he turned his hand to; that, once detached from his own larger-than-life persona with its bombastic tendency towards self-promotion, his work fails to stand by its own merits. Some would argue that his poems and sonnets were not particularly accomplished, though they were of course passable journeyman examples of the prevailing poetic forms of the day. His *pasquinata*, though often biting exhibitions of contemporary satire, were not really all that far removed from common street doggerel that unquestionably played to the lower-brow end of the gallery. His comedies, try as he might, never quite soared to the consummate brilliance of Machiavelli's *Mandragola*, which Aretino achingly emulated and paid homage to, or indeed that other masterful comedy of the era, Bernardo Dovizi da Bibbiena's *La Calandria*. Unable therefore to produce anything theatrically new or really leading-edge, Aretino's lazy characterisation was satisfied merely to bask in the shallows of the usual gross caricatures of the day—the aristocratic poltroon, the greedy and manipulative whore, the jealous husband, the lustful cleric, the braggart soldier, the sneaky and avaricious servant. None of these types were particularly original and so Aretino over-compensated with plots containing ever more transgressive varieties of sex.

One of the most astute summations of Aretino's theatrical characterisation has been given by his 1922 biographer Edward Hutton. In *Pietro Aretino, The Scourge of Princes* Hutton writes: 'In all these comedies there is no living character, no human being whom we know as an individual: never for a moment is Aretino within measurable distance of creating a Falstaff or a Jourdain, yet he had matter made to his hand. Consider what he makes of Marescalco and what Shakespeare made of Malvolio—a thing eternally living and exquisite: think what he made of Ipocrito and what Moliere made of Tartuffe. His work suffers with even the best Italian work of all ages in this, that it cannot build with character or create living human beings who live in and by themselves and endure for ever. He cannot create, he can only give us at his best what he sees and is able to understand.'[3] As for his epistolary correspondence, Aretino's voice is often so tortuously florid and long-winded as to make his offerings almost unbearable to read. He is far better, it should be added, when he is penning libellous insults than when he is conjuring insincere praise; clearly this was something that did not seem to come easy to the author unless he genuinely admired the subject on some personal level, as was the case with Titian. Even his pornography, with its giggling, ham-handed double entendres, tends to be vulgar and somewhat pedestrian ('And now, we enter a moist woodland dell, Whose scenery would leave me breathless quite, If I had any breath from that last kiss! Is this not better than the tales they tell around the fire upon a winter night? My tale, too, has a point you cannot miss').[4]

But despite his shortcomings as a writer it could nevertheless be argued too that Pietro Aretino has, over the past four centuries, seemingly been written out of history for reasons quite other than simple mediocrity of craft. This was, after all, a man who rode at the side of kings and emperors and who angered popes to the point of apoplexy. Someone who was so supremely well-known during his own lifetime as to become virtually a 'must-see' tourist attraction for all well-to-do visitors to Venice. A man of this stature would not ordinarily have been forgotten so quickly and so comprehensively by popular history. It is almost as if the literary and cultural establishment had closed ranks after Aretino's death and imposed an unspoken conspiracy of silence on his legacy. If and when they did speak of him at all the judgement was usually invariably harsh. Soon after his passing we find slanderous works like the *pseudo-Berni* which deliberately sought to blacken Aretino's reputation. Poetic luminaries of the seventeenth-century like John Donne satirised the vogue for Aretino. In *Ignatius His Conclave* (1611) Donne would characterise the Aretine as being 'erotically uninventive' and would chide those misguided and misinformed youths who regarded Aretino as an authority on the subject of eroticism.[5]

This disparagement of Pietro Aretino became, for several centuries, a common refrain amongst 'serious' writers, poets and *littérateurs*. There is, however, some relief in the opinions of Thomas Nashe who himself earned the soubriquet 'the English Aretine' because of his varied writing career which was similar in some respects to Aretino's own. In *The Unfortunate Traveller* (1594) Nashe offers a two-page encomium to Aretino, whom he describes as 'one of the wittiest knaues that ever God made. If out of so base a thing as inke there may bee extracted a spirite, hee writ with nought but the spirite of inke, and his stile was the spirituality of the artes, and nothing else.'[6] But Nashe's opinion, and his enthusiasm, seem on the whole to be quite rare amongst Aretino's fellow writers and, with the rise of Puritanism in the seventeenth-century, countries like England and the Spanish Netherlands would begin to overlook his scandalous and amoral works.

Even as recently as 1846 we find Michelangelo's biographer Richard Duppa writing: 'Of the abilities of Aretino, whether in prose or verse, whether sacred or profane, epic or dramatic, panegyrical or satirical, notwithstanding their number and variety, not one piece exists, which, in point of literary merit, is entitled to approbation; yet the commendations he received from his contemporaries are beyond example; and by his unblushing effrontery, and the artful intermixture of censure and adulation, he contrived to lay under contribution almost all the sovereigns and eminent men of his time.'[7] Similarly, in 1851, we find authors like James Dennistoun who leaves us in very little doubt as to his own rather low opinion of the poet, playwright, satirist and lampooner: 'He has been aptly compared to an ill-conditioned cur, ever ready to yelp and snap at all who do not feed or fondle him, but to such as do, the most fawning of his species'.[8] Dennistoun goes on to decry 'The popularity which his writings enjoyed among all ranks', which seemed to him like 'an infatuation, considering their very moderate merit, and must be viewed as symptomatic of a generally depraved taste, though no doubt his own ineffable conceit and insolence contributed to the delusion ... As to his manners, they are amply testified by his works, wherein, besides a prodigal sprinkling of obscenity, there are mentioned the women with whom he intrigues, and the children these bore him; they in fact prove him destitute of moral or religious principle; and if ever he makes a show of compunction or amendment, it is but to relapse speedily into his wonted profanity. Truly such a fellow, who ought hardly to have ventured to show himself in public, stands unequalled in presumptuous arrogance.'[9]

That giant of nineteenth-century Renaissance scholarship, Jacob Burckhardt, called Aretino 'the greatest railer of modern times', and concludes that 'A glance at his life and character will save us the trouble of noticing many less distinguished members of his class.'[10] Another Victorian literary critic John Addington Symonds is no less acerbic in his evaluation of Aretino's *oeuvre*. In his biographical essay on the poet in *Renaissance in Italy: Italian Literature* (1888), Symonds exclaims with exasperation: 'The miracle of Aretino's dictatorship is further enhanced by the fact that he played with cards upon the table. His epistles were continually being printed–in fact, were sent to the press as soon as written. Here all the world could see the workings of his mind, his hypocrisies, his contradictions, the clamorousness of his demands for gold, the grossness and universality of his flatteries, his cynical obscenity, his simulation of a superficial and disgusting piety. Yet the more he published of his correspondence, the louder was the acclamation of society. The charlatan of genius knew his public, and won their favour by effronteries that would have ruined a more cautious imposter.'[11] It is an all-too-familiar refrain: Aretino is greedy, insincere, obscene, incorrigible.

Neither are Aretino's own countrymen any kinder towards their fellow Italian author. Francesco de Sanctis, the celebrated author of the *Storia della Letteratura Italiana* and the foremost Italian literary critic of the nineteenth-century, opens his biographical monograph on Aretino with the following dismissive, throwaway statement: 'The theological-ethical world of the middle ages touched the extremity of its contradictions in the positive world of Guicciardini, a world purely human and natural, walled in by individual egoism, superior to all the moral chains that bind men together. The living portrait of this world, in its most cynical and depraved form, is Pietro Aretino.'[12] In contrast to de Sanctis, another nineteenth-century Italian critic, Eugenio Camerini, does however go so far as to grant Aretino a certain questionable vitality when he writes that 'It is notable that the influence of Aretino carried over into the sixteenth-century. When the other great writers of the *cinquecento* were being forgotten, his works were being travestied, disguised and read, *sotto mano*, on account of the attractions exercised by their obscenity, as well as because of the vivacious and original force.'[13]

Camerini's praise is a backhanded compliment at best though and Aretino's presence was usually felt to taint any aspects of high culture with which he had come into contact. The eighteenth-century art critic Ireneo Affò, for example, dismissed Parmigianino's 1530 painting *Madonna of the Rose* as having a licentious subject merely by virtue of the fact that the canvas was, according to Vasari, first destined for the art collection of Pietro Aretino, '*l'uomo più libertino de' giorni suoi*' ('the most libertine man of his day').[14] By Affò's prejudiced reasoning the entirety of Titian's artistic output should also therefore be suspect in light of the fact that Aretino had made it his business to position himself as the painter's foremost admirer, eulogiser, salesman and promoter. Yet Titian's reputation remains solid and intact, no better and no worse for his having been Aretino's long-time friend, companion and dinner guest. Indeed, Aretino's sweeter, more disarming nature is often revealed in his genuine and heartfelt tenderness towards Titian. His despondency when Titian has neglected to write to him from Augsburg, for example, is highly poignant and so his presence in Titian's life remains an inconvenient fact which censorious critics are forced to live with as best they can.

Other Italian critics reverted to type when discussing Aretino's merits. The anonymous *Introduzione* in the Giulio Bertoni edition of the *Ragionamenti* (Parma, 1923) states: '.. it is not for this reason to be believed that his cutting vivacity as a flaying polemic had any noble end, animated, as it was, by an expressive exuberance that frequently became vulgarity. Aretino was bent upon lucre, which he—euphemistically—called "the moving power of my ink." He adulated the powerful, making them pay profusely, and at times he would not keep still about their faults, even when he had received the highest sums. An inspired letter writer has said Aretino had for successors in the art of blackmail "certain journalists". And indeed, the system by which Aretino organised those speculations which procured him the money to live surrounded by a court of vicious men and women does anticipate that of certain libellists of our time.'[15] For the anonymous author of this assessment, therefore, Aretino is ultimately unable to transcend his career as Europe's most accomplished literary blackmailer and gentleman extortionist, surrounded by his small personal court of literary disreputables.

The vituperative moral outrage of Victorians like Duppa, Dennistoun, Symonds, de Sanctis and the anonymous author of the *Introduzione* is perhaps to be expected for all these writers are products of their era, just as Aretino was unquestionably a product of his. From the vantage point of our own modern epoch such sentiments seem quaint and unfamiliar. We no longer 'get our knickers in a twist' over the kinds of topics Aretino chose to write about; ours is an age in which pornography, to take just one of Aretino's chosen genres, flows in a constant, easily-accessible stream of 'bits and bytes'. As John Ralston Saul puts it in *Voltaire's Bastards: The Dictatorship of Reason in the West*: 'No longer respecting hypocritical public decorum, we can see naked bodies entwined on the advertising pages of mainstream magazines, as well as in various stages of copulation in mainstream films. By simply reaching a little higher on any magazine rack, we can buy concentrated sex images. For that matter, we can walk through a door in any city and pay a small sum to see females or males or both acting out live intercourse.'[16] We are habituated, satiated even, by the vast emporium of uncensored images of every conceivable kind of sex act that are just a mouse click away. And yet, even so, the 'moderns' are, in the words of Georges Bataille, still ready to admit that eroticism is 'the problem of problems. In that he is an erotic animal, man is a problem for himself. Eroticism is the problematic part of ourselves ... Of all problems eroticism is the most mysterious, the most general and the least straightforward'.[17]

Would Aretino have applauded our age's complete absence of censorship and its voyeuristic obsession with prurient imagery, force-fed to the general public seven days a week, three-hundred and sixty-five days a year through the medium of periodicals, advertisements, billboards, television, films and of course the ever-ubiquitous Internet? Uncomfortably, the answer to this question is perhaps 'yes'. We can safely assume this about Aretino because of his comments to Battista Zatti in 1537 in which he reviled what he described as 'the hoggish custom that forbids the eyes what most delights them'.[18] Today, the private sexuality of the wealthy and the famous, especially those ever-ubiquitous stars of Hollywood, is a matter of routine public record. Indeed, 'celebrity sex videos' are often circulated by famous personalities themselves as a bizarre species of self-promotion and attention-signalling. Today our culture is seemingly obsessed with prurience and voyeurism. Aretino himself was a voyeur in the most literal sense of the word. Through his collaboration in *I Modi: The Sixteen Pleasures* he pioneered the first modern European instance of mass-circulation pornography which had ever been seen in Europe ('pornography' here defined as comprising both lewd words *combined with* pictures). But he provides another critical link to the modern world through his innovation of making the courts and the private lives of some of the highest people in Europe subject to the 'voyeuristic' scrutiny of the common labouring masses as well as the middle classes.

By co-opting the technology of the printing press and moveable type to publish regularly updated folios of *Lettere* that gossiped about the peccadilloes of marquesses, dukes, cardinals, kings, popes and even emperors, Aretino created from scratch an entirely new genre which was perhaps an early precursor to the glossy celebrity magazines, periodicals and salacious 'scandal sheets' of today. For the first time in their lives, ordinary working people were able to purchase, for the price of a few days' labour, affordable books which purported to give them a peek into the private lives of Italy's great and powerful magnates. What they were wearing, what they were buying, how they were decorating their *castelli* and their *palazzi*, and—most important of all—who was sleeping with who. Today we dismiss this genre as 'gutter journalism' or 'celebrity gossip' and relegate it to the lower end of the tabloid spectrum. However in Aretino's day, the early sixteenth-century, it was completely and utterly unheard of and caused a publishing sensation. Unsurprisingly, Aretino's single-handed creation of this titillating new 'kiss and tell' genre established an almost insatiable hunger for news and gossip about the mighty lords and masters amongst the everyday people. For the first time, ordinary individuals living in the towns or the *contado* ('surrounding countryside') could laugh at the foibles of those 'of gentle blood', to use the popular expression of the day, who were set above them in the social pecking order. The Romans had for years enjoyed an embryonic form of this genre in the *pasquinata*, a harmless liberty which enabled the common man to chuckle at his social betters without endangering the entire social edifice. Aretino, as usual dominating everything around him, became during his early years in Rome not only the undisputed king of the *pasquinata* but also succeeded in transforming these libellous verses into a Europe-wide phenomenon, becoming one of the originators of mass-produced satire and lampoonery.

Aretino's skill at these new genres of satire and gossipy 'tabloid style' journalism remains undisputed. The lords and princes of the era did not at first know quite how to deal with these witty and well-crafted assaults on their person and their *dignitas*. In Rome, one outraged papal administrator was even driven to resort to deadly violence. But Aretino was by now far too well-known to be quietly put out of the way with an assassin's poisoned dagger and the attempt largely backfired. After this disconcerting incident, which took place in 1525, the high and mighty realised that any attempt to have so skilful a publicist-cum-propagandist killed could easily rebound on them, leaving them looking even worse off than before should the writer choose to mount a vengeful literary counter-attack upon them. Instead, they reasoned, it was far better to purchase Aretino's affections and encourage him to continue praising them whilst simultaneously condemning their enemies. As the literary scholar Richard Andrews has written: '[Aretino] was to deploy such devastating, and sometimes scurrilous verbal aggression that princely and even royal patrons recognized the necessity of keeping him on their side, or at least not on the side of their current adversary'.[19] In this way, Aretino was able to transform himself from a mere writer of satirical *pasquinata* into Italy's most celebrated pundit on the affairs of the greatest, most eminent men in Europe. This was real power through the pen and Pietro Aretino was arguably the person who invented this kind of journalistic power.

However, is it true to hypothesize that Aretino owes his public neglect in the modern world to his having been little more than a highly successful extortionist? As ugly as this side of his career incontrovertibly was, he was dangerous to society but not primarily for this reason alone. The reason why Pietro Aretino was regarded as such a threatening and subversive influence was because he did what he did so successfully and also quite openly and unapologetically. Aretino's editor and compiler Samuel Putnam perhaps sums it up best when he writes: 'Aretino has no illusions about himself or, above all, about humanity. He knows human lusts and meannesses and deprivations, and speculates in them; they are his stock in trade. He is a non-conformist. He lives his own life, amid his harem of beautiful women and his art treasures, and remarks with a sneer, "Who's going to keep me from it?" He prefers a talk with Titian or an interview with a lady of fortune to going to mass. When, on his death bed, he is given the holy oils, he bursts forth, to the horror of the pious ones about him, with "Now that I'm all greased up, don't let the rats get me".'[20] Pietro Aretino commits the unpardonable error of living a selfish and egotistical life and doing all the things which please him, but this is not his real offence. His real offence is in refusing to be apologetic about his lifestyle in any way, shape or form. Not only that, but of subversively publicising his self-interested lifestyle for the amusement and edification of the profane masses.

If Machiavelli's *The Prince* divulged the crafty techniques for getting what you want in life, conveniently cosmeticized as generalised lessons from classical history, its readers could nevertheless excuse themselves by arguing that Machiavelli's ideas were applicable mainly to the political sphere. This is how the rulers of city-states should behave if they wish to prevail in the complex world of government or international politics. It was self-interest but with a redemptive ulterior motive which could always be disguised as being 'for the good of the state'. Aretino was a man who, perhaps without even knowing it, put Machiavellian ideas into practice to obtain his material objectives on a purely personal level. There was no higher good, no balsamic ulterior political motive, merely honest, unalloyed self-interest. Furthermore, Aretino's application of practical psychological principles to his own private affairs left no room for any admission of guilt and hence there was no need for any act of contrition. The great and the mighty might well go through life serving their vast egos and regarding all the world as existing simply to cater to their own needs, but ordinary individuals were expected to conduct themselves with humility. The Church was there to remind them of this fact lest they forget it. Aretino transcended this process, this whole social ritual of admitting and paying penance for one's sinfulness, and therein lay his cardinal sin.

In truth, Aretino was quite simply a very honest, often highly jaded, realist who saw the world precisely for what it was: a place of resources inhabited by goal-oriented individuals with irrepressible natural needs. As Raymond Rosenthal writes in his 1971 Introduction to Aretino's *Dialogues*: 'His men are goaded to love-making by gross and vulgar lust; his women do not even have this excuse, but do so out of simple greed for the money ... lust and greed provide the basis for the deceptive, entrapping machinery of the social world, in which money, ambition, and cynical power rule ... Aretino, a nihilist before his time defines his age by showing it its own miserable and distorted face in the mirror of its most degraded characters and their acts.'[21] So, men driven by the fire in their loins and unchaste harlots hustling those same randy men for a *ducat*. This what men and women are like, this is what they *do*, would have been Aretino's stance. They are fundamentally selfish, they go after what they want, and so do I. Hinting at this publicly, then doing it, then refusing to be contrite about it like a good Christian, this was why the sixteenth-century establishment privately hated Pietro Aretino. This was why the post *cinquecento* Counter Reformation Jesuitical establishment ensured that his name would languish in obscurity.

What Aretino had done you were not supposed to be able to do in civilised society. He was nothing more than the son of a cobbler (*il figlio di un ciabattino*) and a lowborn man of obscure social origins was not supposed to take on the hierarchical system, flout its rules, manipulate its conventions, and then triumph spectacularly by ending one's life with wealth and universal acclaim. This was expressly to go against the divine order of things. Power and reputation came from lands and titles, which in turn derived from God, and not through 'the sweat of [one's] ink'. And for a maverick like Aretino to question and call to account his social superiors was not only an unpardonable social crime, worse still it was positively subversive. If a nobody like Aretino could get away with this, what was to stop others from similarly low birth from emulating his example? From censuring the great and the powerful? But on a broader level Aretino was nothing more than a litmus test for the upended consciousness of an entire era.

By 1500, Italian society was in a palpable state of crisis. The glue which held society together, the Roman Catholic Church, had on the one hand been impaired by a succession of self-seeking, nepotistic popes from Pope Sixtus IV onwards. The high level abuses of Church wealth and power by powerful papal dynasties like the della Rovere, the Borgia, the Medici and the Farnese had trickled down to the rest of the ecclesiastical hierarchy and manifested in widespread and all-pervasive clerical pluralism and absenteeism, not to mention a general laxity in moral standards. On the other hand, the increasingly lofty and autocratic ruling styles of the Italian court nobility and the distancing of this aristocratic élite from everyday society were producing all manner of social tensions. The widening, highly-visible gulf between the excessive luxury of the titled nobles and their splendid courts and the daily toil and hardship of the ordinary people, together with the shrill insistence on the primacy of noble breeding and 'gentle blood', were at this time provoking a mutual dislike between the classes which had seldom been more corrosive. But far worse even than these structural failures in the fabric of Italian society had been the successive invasions of the peninsula by powerful foreign interests such as France, Spain, Imperialist Germany and the Swiss cantons. These incursions had created a sense of panic, instability and uncertainty which were wholly alien and opposed to the earlier confidence and optimism of the mid-fifteenth-century Renaissance. Faced by these root causes of social upheaval and disquiet, the popular cultural consciousness fractured and bifurcated.

Some writers, poets and satirists like Pietro Aretino, Niccolò Franco, Anton Francesco Doni and Ortensio Lando opted to adopt a realist approach to this crisis by decrying and satirising the doleful state of affairs in Italy at this time, by calling attention, for example, to pompous nobles or fornicating clerics. Others, meanwhile, preferred to seek psychological sanctuary in flights of outlandish and magical idealism. Such was the case with Aretino's contemporary Ludovico Ariosto whose romantic epic *Orlando Furioso* would establish a deeply compensatory world of medieval heroism, chivalry and romance in place of the increasingly gritty and tawdry world of military adventurism which was now becoming the norm in Italy. (It is telling that Aretino's attempt to emulate *Orlando Furioso* in his own epic poem *La Marfisa* foundered after just two or three cantos; in spite of himself he was a realist and not a fantasist). In the sphere of painting, this bifurcation in consciousness can also be seen in the departure from early Renaissance realism and the descent into the more idealised Mannerism prefiguring the later Baroque era. In writing it may be glimpsed in the idealism of Sir Thomas Moore's *Utopia* or in the continued humanist championing of Platonism, which saw earthly life as but the dim and flickering reflection of the eternal realm of the forms. In romantic love it may be seen in the idealisation of the female in the form of courtly Platonic Love, as championed by the likes of Marsilio Ficino, Pietro Bembo and Baldassare Castiglione, as well as the Jewish poet and philosopher Leone Ebreo in his hugely popular philosophical disquisition on idealised love, *Dialoghi d'amore*.

Not so, however, in the extreme realism of Pietro Aretino, who inhabits an inverted world in which whores are transmogrified into enlightened fonts of philosophical wisdom who reason with the sophistication of a Socrates. A milieu in which panders play Plato! In a universe turned on its head, where priests behave no better than brothel-keepers, where monks squat in their confessionals learning wide-eyed about fashionable new sexual *posizioni* from their parishioners, where nuns pleasure themselves with engorged dildos fashioned from the finest Murano glass, and where every prince is out for what he can get through brute force and animal cunning, Aretino is the perfect moral foil for the age. Defying the ever more elitist social conventions of the day by having been spawned from obscure, humble stock, Aretino finds fault with the diseased institutions of his time: Church, state, courts, 'pedants' (learned 'classicising' humanists).[22] He unapologetically holds the cynically powerful to even more cynical ransom. He is the man who is able to say and publish exactly what he likes for, in the final analysis, nothing really matters anymore and quite literally anything goes. Aretino is just like everyone else in this uncertain world, out for what he can get and reliant on his natural talents to rob the world blind. He is the individualist par excellence; indeed, in the words of John Addington Symonds, 'He lived up to Guicciardini's conception of the final motive, which may be described as the cult of self. Sneering at all men less complete in purpose than himself, he disengaged his conduct from contemporary rules of fashion; dictated laws to his betters in birth, position, breeding, learning, morals, taste...'[23]

In a time when entire states like powerful Milan, prosperous Florence or divine Rome are being either conquered, toppled or sacked, Pietro Aretino affronts the established order simply through being alive, healthy, commenting, living, loving, and above all *prospering*. To our modern sensibilities he often comes across as an ogre, a blowhard, a walking caricature. An author who swanned through life with only a care for his own physical comforts might be looked at askance today, an *enfant terrible*. Authors are expected to be sensitive, liberal, empathetic and not gourmandising, fornicating mavens of the good life with one hand held perpetually out for donations. Aretino was never a monastic type of writer and to have starved in a garret for his art would have seemed completely absurd to him. Hence, even as he levelled accusations of moral hypocrisy against the wealthy and powerful men of his age, he strove to emulate their grand lives and stuck his hand deep into their pockets. This low-born man waged a lifelong literary war against his social betters and his targets meanwhile imagined they were being praised by him. The irony is delicious.

Aretino's crime therefore lay not in his incorrigible lewdness, nor in his irredeemable tendency towards serial blackmail, but in his subversive defiance for surviving so abundantly as a commoner during such troubled times, 'an age which brought ruffianism to perfection'[24] as John Addington Symonds priggishly describes it. As Aretino himself brazenly put it in one of his final letters towards the very end of his life: 'We poor citizens, ah? We boorish bumpkins, eh? But we have a right to be born, I have always said. We have a right to be born, I say now. We have a right to be born, I will keep on saying in a loud and disrespectful voice.'[25] But he was being disingenuous for merely existing was never enough for The Divine Aretino. It was every man's right not only to exist but to exist *well*. One suspects that Aretino knew that he was not making particularly great art, and that for much of the time his writing was simply a means to an ends. What he really craved was an income, a living, preferably a cardinal's benefice or a noble title with the estates that entailed. Many contemporaries of his ended their lives in abject poverty, despite having written and published hundreds of books. Pietro Aretino would die enjoying a good meal and good drink surrounded by a company of friends in a noisy tavern (the scholar Janet Sethre's judgement that 'he died in the odor of gluttony, profligacy, perhaps even sodomy' is perhaps a little too unkind).[26] Pietro Aretino's story is that of a virtuoso survivor in politically dark times.

CHAPTER 1

Madonna, Whore and Antichrist

I am,
indeed,
a king,
because I know how
to rule myself.

Pietro Aretino, 1537.

Ludovico Ariosto, the author of the best-selling romantic epic *Orlando Furioso*, called him *'il flagello dei principi'*, 'the scourge of princes', as well as *il divino*, 'the divine one'. He was the intimate friend of artists like Vasari, Cellini, Giulio Romano, Jacopo Sansovino, Tintoretto and Titian (who described him as 'the brigand chief of letters').[27] He was also a correspondent of Michelangelo, to whom he would impertinently write, 'But do not forget, I am one to whom kings and emperors reply',[28] and he was the constant companion *e grande amico* of Italy's first great patriot and last great *condottiere*, Giovanni delle Bande Nere. King François I of France fêted him and sent him a necklace of gold serpents tongues worth 600 crowns. Charles V craved the good publicity that he alone could summon almost at will and bade him ride at his side through the city streets of Padua. He grandiosely referred to himself as the 'Secretary of the World', by which he really meant 'he who knows the world's innermost secrets'.[29] He came from humble beginnings (quite literally and by his own admission *il figlio di puttana* or 'the son of a whore') and he knew little Latin or Greek yet, by the end of his life, he was an acknowledged member of the literary and cultural élite of sixteenth-century Italy. He did all this through 'the sweat of [his] ink'. He was by turns a poet, a playwright, a satirist, a proto-journalist, an art critic, a pioneer of pornography, a liar, an embellisher, a serial blackmailer of the rich and powerful, and he was the world's first celebrity. The name of this literary whirlwind and legendary scoundrel was Pietro Aretino.

If it is permissible to mix one's metaphors, Pietro Aretino lived his life as an open book wearing his heart on his sleeve. 'While none of my line share my glory in their own right, the fact that they are related to me brings them no small glory. The reason is that I can give nobility to others, even though I have received it from no one myself.'[30] This was the remark made by Aretino to Danese Cattaneo, the Tuscan sculptor and medallist who came to live and work in Venice in the aftermath of the tragic events of 1527 when the city of Rome was conquered and sacked by a rogue mercenary army belonging to the Emperor Charles V. When we consider this remark we must keep in mind that, beneath the obvious bombast and self-promotion of the speaker, there lies a mind which appreciated that when a career had generated as many enemies as his had done over the years, self-aggrandisement was a necessary counterweight to vilification and defamation by others. A man who made his living with his sharp (often poisoned) tongue and quill, was bound to create rivals and at least some of those rivals would be of the literary persuasion. Certain recollections of Aretino's life such as the Pseudo-Berni, erroneously attributed to Francesco Berni, maliciously plumb the depths of deliberate denigration and disparagement. Other enemies had formerly been friends or employees. Typical amongst the latter are men like Niccolò Franco (plausibly cited as the real author behind the libellous Pseudo-Berni) who had served as Aretino's secretary and protégé and whose first published work the Pistole vulgari had been plagiaristically inspired by Aretino's own correspondence and consequently earned the great man's wrath ('The sodomite, from the writer of my letters he becomes their emulator, from which he made a book that, with its failure to sell even one copy, has ruined the Frenchman Gardano, who lent him the money to print them', Aretino would later fulminate after the two mens' tumultuous falling out.)[31]

As the subject for a biography, Pietro Aretino is notoriously problematic. Like the goldsmith Benvenuto Cellini, Aretino was an accomplished and inveterate liar and therefore every utterance, each written account, every letter needs to be treated with a healthy and condign degree of scepticism. Titian's two famous portraits of Aretino, one painted in 1537, the other in 1545, both show a large man of massive bulk and imperial bearing festooned with heavy gold chains. The 1545 portrait, painted when Aretino was fifty-three, is more closely realised; the subject adopts a self-consciously belligerent pose and the painter manages to capture the 'aggressive, inflated arrogance'[32] of his subject who was, by this time, his close friend. Proudly, he wears the sumptuous trappings of his material success: a magnificent velvet coat with gold and silver lining and an olive green doublet. The ostentatious gold chain, there perhaps to purposefully remind people of chains of high office, confer a spurious nobility which, by Aretino's own admission, had never existed in his family but which Aretino is somehow able to invoke or manifest, with Nietzschean determination, solely through the force of his iron will. Characteristically, Aretino had accused Titian of deliberately leaving the 1545 canvas partially incomplete, adducing the painter's venality as the reason for this: 'And if only I should have counted out more *scudi* for him, the clothes would have been actually shining and soft and firm as are actual satin, velvet, and brocade'.[33] In reality, Aretino was making use of his own likeness as a means of leverage to extort more ducats from Cosimo I, on which more later.

He was born on the evening of 20 April in that watershed year of 1492[34] in the small Tuscan cathedral city of Arezzo in the Val di Chiana, that flat alluvial valley which borders the provinces of Arezzo and Siena in Tuscany and Perugia and Terni in Umbria. By his own later admission, the first utterances from his infant lungs echoed down the corridors of a common *ospedale* for the not particularly well-off citizens of Arezzo. He came from humble artisan stock. His name was a simple borrowing from the descriptor *Aretine*, the common-or-garden epithet for any wholly unremarkable person hailing from Arezzo. In the Renaissance era, anybody who attained fame might have been simply referred to by their town or city of origin, hence Pietro Vannucci from Perugia was known as Perugino, Giovanni Pisano was from Pisa, Ercole Ferrarese was from Ferrara and Leonardo da Vinci had been born in the small Tuscan hill town of Vinci. By the same token, people were often also known by the trades which their fathers had practised: Andrea del Sarto's father had for instance been a tailor (*sarto*), whilst Antonio del Pollaiolo's father had raised chickens (*pollo* being the Italian word for chicken). Tintoretto's father Giovanni had been a dyer (*tintore*) and so, with the addition of the suffix *etto*, Tintoretto became 'little dyer'. So little Pietro Aretino began life in a common people's hospital, the child of a common man, and bearing a generic name. What was this town from which he hailed like during this era?

Nestled in the foothills of the Apennines, Arezzo, which had its origins in the ancient Roman town of Arretium Fidens ('Faithful Arezzo'), was to be quite honest not so dissimilar from any other comparable town of its size and pedigree in Renaissance Italy. The historian and diarist Goro Dati described Arezzo as being 'very old, and according to ancient chronicles it was a noble city even before the Romans came to Tuscany. It is situated near the river Arno, which rises in the Casentino over Pratovecchio in a mountain called Falterona; the river Tiber, which flows to Rome, also originates in this mountain. The city of Arezzo is forty miles from Florence, a distance which can be travelled in one day. Its site is strong and well-placed, descending from the hill on which the citadel is located and spreading below onto a plain furnished with many springs of running water. The nearby countryside is flat rather than hilly and possesses more fine land than anywhere else in that region. For there is an abundance of grain, oats and fine game. The town is well situated and has good air, and it begets men of keen intellect.'[35] The town itself was rustic, picturesque but otherwise nondescript. Stone houses clustered along crooked medieval streets; a gothic cathedral built in 1278 overlooked Arezzo to the south and faced the Casentino Valley to the north; the Piazza Grande was the main town square. There were the usual abundant array of churches and the ruins of an old Roman amphitheatre silently mouldered on the town's periphery. Petrarch had been born here in the year 1304, his father having earlier been banished from Florence for some unspecified crime. His birthplace could still be seen in Aretino's day, and still can today, a pleasingly solid-looking stone edifice. But Petrarch would not remain here in Arezzo for his father, a former Florentine ambassador to Pisa, forced him quite against his will to study law at Montpellier and Bologna. It was perhaps just as well for had he stayed he might have become an otherwise routine victim of the town's lawlessness. The ubiquitous 'tower homes' of Arezzo, many soaring as high as 260 feet into the air, testified to the inherently violent nature of the town. Indeed, life in Arezzo could prove quite deadly; approximately 40 percent of the town's male inhabitants tended to die before the age of twenty-five from casual street violence. The White Guelph Dante Alighieri had once distastefully described the *Aretini* as *botoli ringhiosi* ('growling dogs') and Michelangelo, born in nearby Caprese, attributed his sharp wits to having been born in Aretine territory. Not only were they renowned as individuals for their short-temper, but the fiercely-independent *Aretini* also disliked any interference in their affairs by outsiders. It was unsurprising therefore that the city had revolted against Florentine rule no less than six times between the years 1409 and 1530.[36]

Yet at the same time, for all its rough edges, Arezzo was also a place of notable humanist learning as well as for thuggery. It boasted its own university and many of its wealthier citizens owned expensively produced works by the classical authors. In his funeral oration for the Florentine Chancellor Leonardo Bruni, the humanist Poggio Bracciolini had declared: 'All learned men owe the greatest debt to that city [of Arezzo], which seems to be the home of the muses in our times; indeed, they have cultivated and enhanced the study of the humanities and of wisdom'.[37] The Accolti family were the most illustrious citizens of the city. Benedetto Accolti the Elder, a man of prodigious recall capable of memorising entire speeches *ex tempore*, had been notable for his Latin history of the First Crusade *De Bello a Christianis contra Barbaros gesto pro Christi Sepulchro et Judaea recuperandis libri IV* (1464). He would become Chancellor of the Florentine Republic in 1458. His son Cardinal Pietro Accolti would, as abbreviator under Pope Leo X, draw up in the momentous year 1520 the historic papal bull *Exsurge Domine* denouncing Martin Luther as a heretic.[38] Yet another son, Bernardo Accolti, would become a celebrated reciter of impromptu verse, praised and enriched by the same Pope and known in his day as *l'Unico Aretino* ('the One Aretine'). Bernardo, already twenty-seven in the year 1492, would in time face competition from a new home-grown arrival on the literary scene, a man who would effectively give the lie to his name.

Pietro Aretino's father Andrea 'Luca' del Tura was a humble cobbler by profession, his mother an ordinary tradesman's wife named Margherita 'Tita' Bonci.[39] We know from his own letters that Aretino had two uncles, Nicolò and Fabiano, who were respectively a jurist and a canon,[40] however it is not wholly clear whether they were Luca's brothers or Tita's.[41] He also had two younger sisters, Francesca and another slightly older sister whose name has not come down to us. Francesca would later marry an impecunious *condottiere* named Orazio Vanotti and eventually die in childbirth after a largely bleak and penurious marriage. However, Francesca was evidently held in some esteem socially (probably because of her relation to Pietro) since 'Alessandro de' Medici, Duke of Florence and nephew of two popes, once came to her door, and saluted her with bare head in the presence of the people'.[42] This would have been counted as a great honour. Duke Alessandro de' Medici was the sixteenth-century equivalent of, for example, Tony Blair and Tom Cruise all rolled into one. Before her death in 1542, Aretino's sister gave birth to twins, which were subsequently cared for by Aretino's extended relatives. Little else, however, is known about his blood siblings or their progeny.

To be a shoemaker during the Renaissance was a good, honest trade and a fairly stable vocation: whatever the economic climate, the price of wool from the Low Countries or the going rate for marble from the quarries of Carrara and Pietrasanta (held in far higher esteem by Michelangelo than the cheaper marble from the quarries at Seravezza), people would always need *shoes*. Shoes moreover carried a man far from his place of birth. Armies also needed shoes to march, unless of course they were Swiss armies, in which case they often went barefoot. Shoes were not to be disregarded. Two popes had been sons of cobblers: John XXII and Urban IV (both were Frenchmen, one from Cahors, the other from Troyes, since this had been during the so-called 'Avignon Papacy' lasting from 1309 to 1377 when the papacy had become virtually a French institution).[43] No, shoes were good; craft itself was considered good. Besides, as the Renaissance gathered steam and the new learning led to the re-evaluation of all the old social and cultural prejudices, artisanal skills were no longer misprized as base mechanical arts poised awkwardly at the opposite end of the social spectrum from 'nobility'.

As the old gods stirred once more, one of their pantheon, Mercury, re-emerged to take Italy's unsung craftsmen under his protective wing. In 1460, the miniaturist Leonardo Dati included a plate in an edition of Johannes de Sacrobosco's popular Medieval introduction to the basic elements of astronomy *De sphaera mundi* ('On the Sphere of the World'). Dati's miniature depicted various craftsmen–a scribe, a painter, a clockmaker, a sculptor, an armourer, a musical instrument maker and a potter–all labouring under the benign influence of the Roman god Mercury.[44] But nonetheless, all things being equal, being the son of a shoemaker was still a modest, unassuming beginning to anyone's life. It was the kind of beginning that a man who in later life would move in the company of lords and princes and wealthy Roman bankers, and yes even popes, and who was at one time on a retainer with the Emperor Charles V, who paid him to say quite childishly flattering things about him, would naturally enough be eager to gloss over.

The shoemaker 'Luca' del Tura, though humble of trade, was nonetheless blessed with a ravishingly beautiful wife. So favoured was 'Tita' Bonci that she was much sought-after by local artists as a life model; it is said that the *Aretine* painter Matteo Lappoli used her serene likeness in his depiction of the Madonna in his fresco *Madonna col bambino tra due angeli reggicortina*, painted on the wall of Arezzo's Church of Sant'Agostino around 1475-80.[45] The Madonna survives to this day with its creamy complexion, long sleek nose, rosebud lips and disconcertingly come-hither expression. Many years later, Aretino would write to his artist friend Giorgio Vasari imploring him to send him a copy of his beloved mother's fresco portrait. When he received it in Venice he hung it proudly on his wall, causing the writer, editor and translator Anton Francesco Doni to accuse Aretino–who appeared to be claiming for himself the status of having been born of a virgin–of comparing himself to Jesus Christ, making him therefore by logical extension the Antichrist.[46] Perusing Vasari's portrait of Tita, the great Titian meanwhile had doubted the inherent 'virginal purity' of the subject, remarking that in all his long experience he had 'seen only one face less worldly'.[47] This was the sort of off-kilter comment about his mother that, given his disposition, Aretino would no doubt have enjoyed immensely, taking not the least offence.

So jealous were the *Aretines* of Tita's great beauty, however, that they sneered behind Luca's back that she was as 'commercially free' with her sexual favours as she was evidently willing to offer her spare time as a life model. The vulgar Italian word for 'a prostitute', *puttana*, implies a woman who sells her body for a little money, or even sometimes just for the carnal pleasure of sex itself. The Italians tend to use the word interchangeably with the English words 'whore' or 'bitch' or 'slut'. Its etymology is argued by some to derive from the Latin word for 'girl', *puella*; the transformation of the Latin term for girl into the vernacular Italian word for 'whore' follows the linguistic process known as euphemism. According to the town scuttlebutt, Tita, a real *puttana*, had prostituted herself out to a scurrilous local nobleman named Luigi Bacci. When Luca the boot maker learned of his wife's infidelity he was so heartbroken that he packed a bag and left Arezzo for good, never to be seen in the town again. Some said that in his misery he had joined a roving mercenary company, others speculated that Luigi Bacci had him done away with so that he could have the comely Tita all to himself. The conflation, in Aretino's ancestral story, of the Blessed Virgin Madonna with the common town whore invokes the eternal war between the sacred and the profane; how could the *Aretines* possibly have realised that in reproving the lusty Tita they would erect–pun wholeheartedly and unapologetically intended–the fundamental dichotomy of Pietro Aretino's life?

Following Luca's departure, Luigi Bacci appears to have taken Tita's family under his personal protection and Aretino more than likely received some form of rudimentary education from his new guardian, although by his own admission he was a negligible scholar ('I went to school only long enough to learn the Santa Croce ... conniving thievishly, calling for many excuses, not being one of those who pour over the art of the Greeks and Latins', he later shrugged.[48]) Aretino would never acquire any great facility in either Latin or Greek, which was the underlying reason why he would rail throughout his life against hidebound 'pedants' who slavishly copied the forms of the ancient literary classics ('A plague on them! Let them fall into a consumption and die!')[49] For many years afterwards, when he had already been established as Italy's most celebrated and successful satirist, Aretino would claim to be Luigi Bacci's bastard by the beautiful courtesan Tita Bonci.[50] It was, after all, far preferable in social circles–and also made for a better yarn–to be the illegitimate son of a nobleman and his alluring whore than the progeny of a humble cobbler. When he corresponded with Luigi Bacci's two legitimate sons Gualtiero and Francesco, treating them as brothers, the two were apparently more than happy to be condescended down to by such a famous 'celebrity'.[51] It was an artifice which had served him well, at least up until the year 1550.

In that year, Aretino had shown characteristic hospitality to a fellow *Aretine* named Medoro Nucci, allowing him and his wife Angelica to stay with him at his *palazzo* in Venice. But the acquaintances had subsequently fallen out over some matter (perhaps Aretino, not being able to help himself, had openly flirted with Nucci's wife, perhaps Nucci himself–a known sodomite–had rejected Aretino's advances) and Nucci repaid the writer's hospitality by publicly exposing his true origins.[52] Even the Florentine ambassador would become involved in the unseemly fracas which followed, and the news was destined ultimately to reach the ears of Duke Cosimo I (later the Grand Duke of Tuscany), who was the son of Aretino's late best friend Giovanni. Having been called out in this way, Aretino turned brazen, effortlessly transforming from an élitist into that even more irritating type, the inverted snob. To Florence's Duke Cosimo he crowed: 'I tell you, I glory in the title which he, to vilify, has given me; and may it teach the nobility to procreate sons like the one which a cobbler has born in Arezzo … Yes, I am the son of a maker of shoes.'[53] With good grace, the exalted Duke Cosimo wrote back telling Aretino to disregard Nucci's attempted character assassination and kindly assuaging the writer's ego by reassuring him that, despite his humble roots, he was nevertheless a man 'grown old in experience'.[54]

☉☾

For a span of 286 years, Pietro's birthplace, the commune of Arezzo, had enjoyed the status of an independent city-state. Arezzo had given Italy such luminaries as the poet Petrarch, the humanist Poggio Bracciolini[55]–a close friend and associate of Florence's great ruler Cosimo de' Medici–the historian Leonardo Bruni, and the painter and art historian Giorgio Vasari, who later became Aretino's close friend (they had also shared the same teacher, the writer Pollastra). But the town's location, trapped as it was between the twin spheres of influence of the rival cities of Florence and Siena, had ultimately doomed Arezzo's aspirations for self-determination. At the time of Aretino's birth, Arezzo was a Florentine possession and had been since the fateful year 1384, when the wealthy merchant *signoria* of Florence purchased the city for the sum of 40,000 golden *scudi* from the renowned *condottiere* Ingelram of Coucy, the son-in-law of King Edward III of England and Philippa of Hainault.[56] The *Aretines*, aligned traditionally with the imperial Ghibelline faction, had fought the Guelph Florentines intrepidly for decades prior to this transaction. However, ninety-five years earlier, at the Battle of Campaldino, Florence along with her Guelph allies Pistoia, Lucca, Siena and Prato had managed to encircle the *Aretine* army and completely destroy it.[57] After that, it was just a matter of time before the commune was absorbed into the ever-expanding Florentine *imperium*. As in the case of Florence's other possessions, Pisa and Pistoia for example, the inhabitants of Arezzo were denied full Florentine citizenship and the city was governed by a *podestà* or mayor who was appointed by Florence.

Just eleven days prior to Pietro Aretino's birth, Florence's greatest ruler Lorenzo de' Medici, son of Cosimo de' Medici, had died at his villa in the Tuscan countryside at Careggi. Arezzo's relationship with the Medici, and with Florence, was to say the least a somewhat complicated one. In the decade or so prior to Cosimo's political ascendancy in 1434, the *Aretines* had adopted a distinctly anti-Medicean stance, preferring to side with such conservative bipartisan politicians as Niccolò da Uzzano, or with their own countryman Leonardo Bruni, Chancellor of Florence from 1427 until his death in 1444. During the tumultuous year of 1433, when Cosimo de' Medici and his political *amici* were unceremoniously ousted from power and cast into brief exile at Venice, Arezzo had flaunted its affiliation with Cosimo's nemesis Rinaldo degli Albizzi.[58] Although, as a result of these allegiances, Cosimo de' Medici had subsequently kept aloof from the city (and also perhaps for the simple reason that he had no significant business interests there), Arezzo nevertheless later moved into the orbit of his grandson Lorenzo, who went out of his way to develop networks of Medici patronage within the commune. Thus it came to be affirmed that *il nome de' Medici* ('the name of Medici') was *molto amato dagli Aretini* ('much loved by the Aretines').[59]

Lorenzo's own son Piero di Lorenzo, less gloriously nicknamed by the unappreciative Florentines as *'lo Sfortunato'* ('the Unfortunate'), and sometimes even worse as *'il Fatuo'* ('the Fatuous'), would however prove a poor substitute as ruler. After misrepresenting himself to the comical and dwarfish French King Charles VIII as the voice of the Florentine government, and submissively handing over to him some of Florence's most valuable towns and fortifications including Pisa and Livorno, *lo Sfortunato* would eventually be run out of town together with his younger brothers Cardinal Giovanni de' Medici and Giuliano di Lorenzo de' Medici. Thereafter, Piero *lo Sfortunato* would sometimes appear in Arezzo, trying to stir up trouble for the Florentines amongst the inhabitants of one of their subject cities,[60] but just as quickly he would vanish again, lured by the siren song of the taverns, whorehouses and the easy living of Rome.[61] This, incidentally, was a world that the adult Pietro Aretino would understand and appreciate only too well, and he would certainly never judge men who were drawn to that milieu. But for Piero *lo Sfortunato* his self-indulgence would inevitably prove to be his downfall.

In June 1502, when Aretino was ten years old, the commune of Arezzo and the surrounding Val di Chiana was rocked by a fresh rebellion.[62] A long build-up of factors had contributed to the rising sense of discontentment within the subject city. For one thing, amidst imminent rumours of famine there was speculation that the Florentines planned to seize Arezzo's precious grain harvest and send it to their troops stationed at Borgo San Sepolcro, a move which would have left the Aretine population starving. For another thing, Florence was deeply preoccupied at this time, having lost control of Pisa some eight years earlier. Now she was in the midst of a military reconquest of her lost possession and had therefore taken her eye off day-to-day affairs in Arezzo. At the same time, Florence was also distracted by the looming threat posed by Cesare Borgia, the virile son of Pope Alexander VI, who was busily engaged in creating a hereditary fiefdom for himself throughout the Papal States. One of Borgia's captains happened to be a *condottiere* named Vitellozzo Vitelli, the homicidal lord of Città di Castello. Vitellozzo's equally psychopathic brother Paolo had been executed by the Florentines three years earlier for disobediently failing to press home an assault against Pisa.[63] As a result, Vitelli bore Florence a deep grudge and so, while Borgia was engaged elsewhere, Vitelli had brought his force of 3,500 soldiers into the Val di Chiana where he provided active military support and encouragement to the *Aretine* uprising.[64] Meanwhile, another intensely unpleasant lieutenant in Borgia's service, Gian Paolo Baglioni, had occupied the surrounding countryside of the Val di Chiana itself. Borgia's military engineer, Leonardo da Vinci, obligingly drew Vitelli and Baglioni a sketch map of all the major city-states in the vicinity: Arezzo, Borgo Sansepulcro, Perugia, Chiusi and Siena.[65] This useful visual aid helped them in enforcing their rule over the surrounding region.

The mere presence of these two renegade anti-Florentine *condottieri* was enough to prove incendiary to the locals. The natives of Arezzo rose up and butchered the Florentine garrison wholesale along with the *podestà*. Seeing an opportunity to make trouble for the Florentine republic, Piero *lo Sfortunato* dragged himself away from Rome's brothels long enough to put in an appearance at Arezzo as well. Many of the *Aretine* rebels had run through the streets of the town crying '*Palle! Palle!*' a call-to-arms which made reference to the balls which appeared on the Medici family's coat-of-arms, and which was the traditional rallying cry of the Medicean faction. As in the case of most popular uprisings there were the usual vendettas and ugly revenge killings were played out. The wealthier burghers who had supported Florence were especially singled out for righteous retribution. Many were murdered in cold blood and their *palazzi* were raised to the ground. Local priests suspected of pro-Florentine sympathies were also butchered, the preferred method of despatch being either stabbing to death or else defenestration from high buildings. The Florentine *castello* in Arezzo was slighted, a largely symbolic gesture. But freedom from Florence proved tantalisingly short and sweet and by the end of August that same year Arezzo's rebellion had been crushed by the sober, scarlet-robed men of the *signoria*.

Florence's most powerful ally was France and King Louis XII commanded his vassal Cesare Borgia to order his lieutenants out of Arezzo forthwith. Fearing the loss of the French King's favour, Borgia complied, threatening to sack the two *condottieri's* fiefs of Perugia and Città di

Castello if they refused to obey. Louis XII's general, Monsieur Imbalt, then rode to Arezzo with his troops and took possession of the town in the name of Florence. When the Florentines themselves regained control, bloody reprisals were meted out in short order. There was a minor sacking of the town and thirty citizens were carted off to Florence to be held as hostages, which was all pretty standard in the scheme of such things. Meanwhile, those pro-Medicean *Aretine* rebels who survived the bloodletting gingerly crossed over into Sienese territory.[66] Ruminating on the Arezzo uprising in his *Discourses on Livy*, Niccolò Machiavelli later recorded that the Florentines 'exiled part of the *Aretini*, and a part they condemned to death, and they deprived all of them of their honours and their ancient ranks in the city, but left the city entire'. This leniency, to Machiavelli's somewhat uncompromising way of thinking, had been a huge error. Arezzo, he argued, should by rights have been raised to the ground as an example to Florence's other troublesome possessions, but those in the *signoria* who appeared wiser ('*più savi*') had prevailed, affirming that 'it would do little honour to the [Florentine] republic to destroy Arezzo, because it would appear that Florence lacked the power to control the Aretines'.[67]

In his later career, Aretino would often be held up as the 'devils disciple' of the Florentine political strategist Machiavelli, the man who, in his writings, had advocated the destruction of Aretino's home city and justified it as a necessary object lesson in shrewd colonial government. Aretino would intervene many years later to spare Arezzo from sacking at the hands of an imperial army, and Arezzo would honour him for this compassionate act of mediation, but for now he was just another restless young man keen to break away from hearth and home and experience the wider world beyond the town walls. Besides which, the rebellion and its murderous consequences had made a deep and lasting impression on the boy's psyche. Most importantly, it helped lay the foundation for a lifelong distaste for naked physical violence. Pietro Aretino would never shrink from waging war but he would wage it on his terms and using the quill rather than the sword.

Around the age of nineteen, Aretino left Arezzo precipitately having purportedly stolen some valuables belonging to his mother Tita in order to finance his escape.[68] One reason often cited by biographers for his having to leave the city of his birth so impetuously is because he wrote a sonnet speaking out against the sale of indulgences. This act allegedly landed him in hot water with the local Church authorities and he had no recourse except to flee.[69] But when we stop to examine this claim, however, it is difficult to imagine how a few lines of doggerel by a green young man could have stirred up enough trouble to force him to leave town. More likely perhaps is that young Pietro had already grasped by this time that his talents would be better served not in this provincial backwater but in the more promising precincts of Rome, a city with which he would always have something of a love-hate relationship and which he would later thank by publicly describing it as 'the world's backside'.

⊙☾

Aretino made his way first, however, to nearby Perugia, that ancient and picturesque hilltop citadel that was the capital of Umbria. Here he found sanctuary employed as a domestic in the household of the humanist Francesco Bontempi.[70] Perugia by this time was under papal authority but had formerly been ruled by several generations of the Baglioni family, the current head of which was Cesare Borgia's *condottiere* Gian Paolo Baglioni. The Baglioni were that quintessential phenomenon of Renaissance Italy, which is to say, petty intergenerational tyrants who used cruelty, force and repression to cow their population into meek submission. Like similar families of the period they also fought viciously amongst themselves as well. On 3 July 1500, Gian Paolo's embittered cousins Carlo and Grifonetto Baglioni had staged a coup d'état and, in the process, had slaughtered most of Gian Paolo's relatives. The mercenary had only narrowly escaped from his murderous cousins by clambering over Perugia's rooftops and had fled to Marsciano where his colleague-in-arms Vitellozzo Vitelli loaned him troops with which to re-take the city.[71] Grifonetto Baglioni was confronted by Gian Paolo and butchered in the town square. Grifonetto's mother, Atalanta, experiencing such remorse at having refused her slain son sanctuary in her house, later commissioned the painter Raphael to capture Grifonetto's likeness in the painting now known as *The Entombment* (Grifonetto is believed to be the younger man on the right who holds Christ's legs in the painting).[72] By such brutal means, Gian Paolo was able to regain control of his fief. Nothing in this grim episode, it is worthwhile noting, had been outside of the social norm.

Earlier, before serving under Cesare Borgia, Gian Paolo had fought for Florence from 1493-1498[73]. When he had colluded in the Arezzo uprising in 1502 his colleague-in-arms Vitellozzo Vitelli appears to have taken him under his wing as a surrogate brother to replace the executed Paolo Vitelli. Now, however, Borgia's growing power caused several of his most senior *condottieri* to begin fearing for the safety of their own hereditary lordships. '[We will be] devoured one by one by the dragon',[74] Gian Paolo is reputed to have warned and so a conspiracy was hatched amongst Borgia's captains to have the Pope's rapacious son removed and killed. Borgia, however, was no ordinary warlord. As the inspiration for Machiavelli's best-known work *The Prince*, he was already thinking several moves ahead of them. Borgia had lured Vitelli and his confederate

Oliverotto Euffreducci to the Rocca di Senigallia where both men had been seized and garrotted with violin string by Borgia's henchman Don Miguel de Corella.[75] Luckily for him, Gian Paolo had remained aloof from Borgia's ploy and had therefore escaped with his life. Borgia's own sudden downfall had come not long afterwards and Gian Paolo was able therefore to continue ruling untroubled in Perugia.

Untroubled, that is, until Alexander VI's replacement, Pope Julius II, who was known as *il Pontifice terrible*, decided in the late summer of 1506 to reclaim Perugia in the name of Rome and the Papal States. With 500 mounted men-at-arms and several thousand Swiss pikemen (plus twenty-four somewhat reluctant cardinals of the Holy Roman Church following up the rear) he had advanced on Perugia. At this point Gian Paolo lost his nerve and, instead of waiting patiently for the Pope behind his stout hilltop citadel walls, he hastened instead to Orvieto where he promptly abased himself before Julius and capitulated. Pope Julius II entered Perugia on 13 September 1506. Feeling magnanimous at this bloodless victory he spared Baglioni's life, although his fief was now placed under papal authority, to be administered by the Florentine exile Cardinal Giovanni de' Medici. In return for his liberty, Baglioni obligingly supplied the Supreme Pontiff with 150 mounted Perugian soldiers for the next phase of his military campaign against the Bentivogli family of Bologna.[76] Niccolò Machiavelli, himself a diplomatic witness to these events, had evinced shocked surprise that Baglioni 'did not, to his perpetual fame, crush his enemy [Pope Julius II] at a stroke and enrich himself with booty, since with the Pope were all the cardinals and all their delights'.[77] Machiavelli had found it inconceivable that Baglioni, a man allegedly guilty of 'taking his sister for himself'[78] and who casually delighted in leaving the corpses of his hanged rivals piled up in Perugia's town square, had not had Julius put to death as soon as 'he [Julius] put himself with a single guard in the hands of the enemy'.[79] The political analyst was left to conclude that 'rarely do men know how to be altogether wicked or altogether good',[80] an aphorism that might well have pleased Pietro Aretino.

Although it had suffered for decades under the oppression of the vicious Baglioni, Perugia was nonetheless a cultured, scholarly town. It even had its own university, the *studium generale*, which had been granted by Clement V in a papal bull in 1308.[81] The city's most recent conqueror, the current reigning Pope Julius II, had himself been educated here by his doting Franciscan uncle Francesco della Rovere, who had risen to become Pope Sixtus IV. He had most likely studied civil or Roman law[82] before downing his quill and taking up the sword. (When, whilst working on a large bronze statue of Julius in Bologna, Michelangelo had asked whether he should place a book in the figure's left hand Pope Julius had purportedly answered 'Give me a sword! I am not a man of letters!')[83] In his youth, Julius's great rival Cesare Borgia had also been educated at the University of Perugia as well as at Pisa.

A warlike man like his great rival, *il Pontifice terrible*, Cesare Borgia preferred to go out with weapon in hand. Aged thirty-one, he would end his days skewered and stripped naked of his armour outside the Castilian-held town of Viana, his genitals obscured only by a strip of red cloth. At this time, the Perugian historian Francesco Matarazzo was State Chancellor and ambassador in the city, in addition to serving as a professor in the University (at a salary of 110 ducats, the surety for which was the taxes of two villages which were assigned to him.)[84] He was an enthusiastic partisan of the ruling Baglioni family and was an avid chronicler of his native city. Matarazzo's *Chronicles of the City of Perugia 1492-1503* leaves us with a lively account of the town's history from a contemporary eyewitness. Matarazzo writes: 'And I would also have you to know that in these days, notwithstanding the evil lives that men led, much money was given in charity both by the commonwealth and by private people', continuing, 'and such they say was of old the custom in the city of Perugia; and thus it was that many sacred buildings were built and enlarged'.[85]

In Perugia, the young Pietro Aretino met a student of the university one year younger than himself named Agnolo Firenzuola. As young men often do at that age, the pair formed a lifelong attachment and they would be friends in Perugia, Florence and also in Rome.[86] In later life, Firenzuola became a versatile man of letters who could turn his quill to any genre. He would become a teacher, scholar, humanist and cleric as well as an acknowledged poet and *literato* in his own right. Firenzuola's compendium of short tales, the *Ragionamenti amorosi*, would imitate the licentious style of Boccaccio. His adaptation of 'The Golden Ass' of Apuleius became something of a best-seller and was published in numerous editions. Like Aretino, Firenzuola would author burlesque satirical poems as well as comedies such as *I Lucidi* and *La Trinuzia* and several love poems and ballads, one of the most admired being *Orozza Pastorella*. Becoming a monk at Vallombrosa, Firenzuola later went to Florence, and finally settled at Prato. When he was abbot of San Salvatore in Prato, Firenzuola would still write longingly to his friend Aretino, addressing him as '*Divinissimo uomo*'. Given the predilection of the era for homosexual love, the relationship between the two men was most likely in some respects carnal. As a native of Florence, Firenzuola would have been used to the easy-going attitude of his native Florentines towards such matters. Although the official penalties for sodomy in Florence were fairly severe, especially under the puritanically-minded theocracy of Girolamo Savonarola, a man obsessed with eradicating buggery, certain areas of the mother city still remained notorious for roving catamites. The

Ponte Vecchio with its many butchers shops ('a meat market' both literally and figuratively) was one such dstrict and no self-respecting adolescent boy could venture there unless he wanted to 'have his cap stolen'.[87] Already, by the early sixteenth-century, at least one German dictionary defined *Florenzer* as 'buggerer' and its accompanying verb *Florenzen* as 'to bugger'.[88] The sense of official paranoia over sodomy eventually grew so bad that 'anyone found day or night in a vineyard or a locked room with a boy who was not a relative was suspect'.[89]

In a letter to Firenzuola dated 26 October 1541, Aretino would remind his friend of their '*giovenili piacevolezze*' or 'youthful pranks'. 'Indeed, I often whimsically recall examples of our youthful pranks', Aretino reminisced. 'Don't think I've forgotten about the time when that old woman created an uproar in the town, terrified by your rude words to her in broad daylight at the window—you in your shirt and me stark naked.'[90] Aretino goes on in the same letter to reference a famous courtesan of the era, Camilla Pisana who, as her name suggests, was probably from Pisa, and who was the mistress of the wealthy Florentine banker Filippo Strozzi the Younger (Piero *lo Sfortunato's* son-in-law). It is probable that Aretino and Firenzuola knew Camilla sometime later either at Florence or Rome or at both places. In his comedy *La Cortigiana*, Aretino would later have one of his characters, Messer Maco, describe Camilla as being 'softer than ricotta, cooler than ice, shinier than mandrake, sweeter than the full moon, and more beautiful than Fata Morgana or the Morning Star' and that, upon glancing at her, 'Cupid becomes stupid'.[91] Clearly the lads enjoyed a roistering lifestyle together with their fellow ne'er do wells and courtesan friends. In his 1541 letter, Aretino reminds his friend Firenzuola of the time when he once started a brawl at Camilla's house.

In Perugia, Aretino mixed around in the company of the university town's many resident painters, poets and artistic hangers on. It was a vibrant place to which many talented young men had gravitated to seek their fame and fortune. Aretino himself studied and dabbled in painting.[92] Here he also began his own lifelong commitment to humanism, that literary and cultural movement which advocated the study of man in the here and now, in all his flaws, as opposed to some distant eschatological man resurrected at some indeterminate point in the future after the Last Judgement. But for all its lofty pretensions humanism sometimes tended, when all was said and done, to sanctify the profane and profane the sanctified. One of Florence's most renowned humanists, Poggio Bracciolini, the man who had rediscovered Lucretius's verse poem *De Rerum Natura* ('On the Nature of Things'), was no great paragon of Christian saintly virtue. He was amused by jokes about farting and defecation (which he collected together in his scatologically-themed book of *Facetiae*) and by the age of fifty-six had sired fourteen bastards before settling down to marry a coltish eighteen-year-old beauty who would bear him six more.[93] Satyr-like, as the old Epicureans of antiquity, Bracciolini was a *bon vivant* who loved rich food, fine wine, and the company of pretty young women. Another well-known humanist Æneas Silvius Piccolomini, the late Pope Pius II, had declared in his correspondence, 'Venus is dearer to me than food' and had gone on to pen that highbrow work of smut entitled *Historia de duobus amantibus* ('The Tale of Two Lovers') which became a veritable Renaissance bestseller.[94] It was Piccolomini, not knowing that fourteen years later he would be the Supreme Pontiff of the Holy Roman Church, who in 1444 had unguardedly confessed in a letter to Piero da Noceto: 'I have seen and loved many women, and after possessing them, have grown extremely weary of them'.[95]

There would have been ample opportunity for Aretino in Perugia to become familiar with the writers who had gone before, not all of whom were entirely above the inclusion of smut in their work. Matteo Maria Boiardo's epic poem *Orlando innamorato* (1483), for example, contained allusions to necrophilia. Antonio Beccadelli's *L'Ermafrodito* (1419-1425) and Ruzante's *L'Anconitana* (early 1520s) both had references to male homosexuality. In particular, Boccaccio's 1353 masterpiece the *Decameron* catalogued the exploits of wayward friars, randy nuns, lovesick older men, impotent husbands, and wanton noblewomen. Although not sexually explicit per se, the book was nevertheless subversive in portraying the women characters as both sexually awakened *and* sexually available. For the male characters in Boccaccio the issue is not so much how to stimulate the ladies' passions–their lust is already aroused–it is the practical problem of how to gain access to their bedchamber or, in the case of wanton nuns, scale the convent walls and gain admittance to their holy of holies. When Boccaccio did descend to describing the sportive sex act it was usually in comedic terms, as in Panfilo's story concerning Friar Puccio, who 'thought he felt the floor of the house shake a little' because he was indulging in such a vigorous bout of lovemaking.

Aretino's later work, *The Secret Life of Nuns*, which constituted the first part of his dialogue the *Ragionamenti della Nanna e della Antonia*, would take as its jumping off point the assumption that convents and friaries were already a secret hotbed of sexual adventurism, a theme which echoes Boccaccio's earlier allegations of nuns and monks regularly throwing their vows of chastity to the four winds. Libidinous nuns and lustful monks were also a common theme of Masuccio Salernitano's posthumously published 1476 book *Il Novellino*. In the 'Thirty-Third Novel' of this collection of stories is perhaps the first published iteration of the tragic love story which would later become famous as Shakespeare's *Romeo and Juliet*, except for the fact that in Salernitano's telling of the tale the Juliet character, Giannozza, is a sexual aggressor who convinces the Romeo character, Mariotto, to marry her so that they may partake of 'love's sweetest fruits'. There is also an additional character who is not present in Shakespeare's play at all, an Augustine friar who marries the couple but who seems homosexually enamoured of the bridegroom Mariotto/Romeo. During this time Aretino himself was already reading, writing, experimenting with style and his first published work would soon see the light of day.

In 1512, Aretino gave birth to his literary debut, the *Opera Nova del Fecundissimo Giovene Pietro Pictore Aretino zoe Strambotti Sonetti Capitoli Epistole Barzellete et una desperate* which he paid from his own pocket to have published in Venice. The Cambridge History of Italian Literature refers to the *Opera Nova* as 'a collection of verse whose chief distinctions are its shameless self-advertisement, its prosodic omnivorousness, and the consummate cleverness with which it mimics current taste'.[96] In the words of one of his modern biographers James Cleugh, the work 'included folk songs and epigrams of a burlesque sort, sonnets, facetious compositions in *terza rima*, letters in rhyme and a *Disperata*–probably a lugubrious elegy of some kind in fashionable terms and a mere literary exercise'.[97] Writing to one of his correspondents Aretino was hardly self-deprecating: 'If the style does not please you at least the boldness will ... I dashed the stuff off almost in an instant'.[98] If the work was one of shameless self-advertisement then it would set the tone for the life of a man who, in later years, would announce his entry to the hallowed courts of lords and princes by booming at the top of his voice, 'I am Pietro Aretino!'[99]

By this time, Aretino was working in a book binding shop although he would spend more time ensconced reading the many free manuscripts than in the practice of learning his new trade. Inevitably, his work in the book binders became merely another of his short-lived experiments. Clearly he did not seem to evince any interest in the technical aspects of book-binding as a long term career. Neither did his labours there incline him towards scholarship or what Aretino himself referred to as 'pedantry'. Though he may have had a smattering picked up here and there, Aretino had never studied Latin and Greek and was therefore an outsider to formal humanist scholarship. Later on, in 1531, he would confess: 'It is a strange humour, mine–that of not having been willing to use the idiom of my native land. The reason for this is the dusty dissertations that every pedant has made upon the Tuscan speech. If the souls of Petrarch and Boccaccio are as tortured in the world where they now are as their works are in this world, they ought to forswear their baptism.'[100] So we can perhaps picture the youthful Aretino as an autodidact, pouring over the manuscripts after hours by candlelight, meticulously teaching himself the ropes of his future trade.

When he was not giving birth to his first faltering attempts at literature he was experimenting in painting. Aside from Perugino himself, the greatest living Tuscan painters of the time included Sandro Botticelli, Piero di Cosimo and Cosimo Rosselli. Another great Florentine painter, Domenico Ghirlandaio, had died in 1494 just two years after Aretino's birth. Brunelleschi had already laid down the revolutionary laws of linear perspective: his innovation, proportionally receding transversal lines, offered a completely new way of measuring and creating a three-dimensional space on a two-dimensional plane. The architect's new artistic framework for seeing 'in perspective' had been entirely appropriate to an awakening age of the intellect in which scholars, bankers and statesmen alike sought to discern more clearly how different elements existed in relation to each other. It was also appropriate in view of the epoch-making discoveries taking place in geography and navigation by men such as Vasco da Gama, Christopher Columbus and Ferdinand Magellan. This was an era of uncovering that which had previously been hidden or unknown. In the arts this impulse to depict the external world as accurately and faithfully as possible would lead eventually to realism, to photography, to cinematography and to 3D computer simulation.

It was natural that a gifted, expressive lad like Pietro Aretino should experiment with both literature as well as painting and the visual arts. During the Renaissance, one word perhaps more than any other expressed what all artists and humanists aspired to and that word was *virtù*. Although cognate with the English word 'virtue' it did not mean exactly the same thing. Instead it had its roots in the Latin word *vir* or 'man' and connoted a certain 'manly' engagement in meritorious pursuits. These accomplishments, be they poetry, scholarship, painting, architecture, sculpture or indeed different combinations of these activities, were to be conducted with *sprezzatura* which may be loosely translated as 'virtuosity'. The idea being conveyed was that the man of *virtù* (the 'virtuoso') went about his undertakings with a certain effortlessness.[101] This, however, required long years of training from early in one's youth. Experimentation in different disciplines was therefore to be expected. And yet, for the restless, impatient and quick-to-anger Aretino, painting would never be the chosen medium for him. It was far too painstaking an art for a glib, quicksilver temperament like his. This makes it all the more comically ironic that painting would be the reason for Aretino's final rushed departure from Arezzo.

According to the eighteenth-century historian Giammaria Mazzucchelli's telling of the story (taken in turn from the Perugian poet

Caporali's yarn), Aretino encountered in the Piazza Grande one afternoon a fresco of Mary Magdalen sitting at the feet of Christ, her arms held upward in supplication. Not being able to help himself, Aretino returned that night and used his artistic skills to paint the Madonna with a lute in her hands.[102] Since high class Renaissance courtesans often played the lute to entertain their customers, the implication was that Aretino had returned the Magdalen to her former professional state, that of a common prostitute. Sacrilege! Once again, the sombre Church authorities of Perugia were not amused and Aretino was forced to leave town rather precipitously. By this time, according to the popular legend, he had earned his living successively as a mule driver, tax collector, pimp and even as a hangman's mate.[103] But these 'facts' are unreliable at best since they were concocted by Aretino's detractor Niccolò Franco, who was concerned to depict Aretino as a wastrel in his youth. Whatever the truth of Aretino's subsequent activities, like many others seeking fame and fortune, he would eventually follow the inevitable trajectory to Rome. The city of the popes would therefore begin as his nursemaid, although by the time he was done he would end by denouncing her as a whore.

CHAPTER 2

Rome: Cortigiane alla Candela

Keep the money and let the offices go!
Benefices are better if you've cash.
Sixty per cent is what you ought to show.
A sound investment; nothing rash!

Pasquinade, Francesco Berni.

R ome in the first quarter of the *cinquecento* was no longer the filthy, neglected quasi-pastoral backwater which it had once been; a sparsely-populated, crime-ridden place where cows and sheep grazed peacefully amidst the Corinthian columns of the forum whilst the tempestuous *bravi* of rival baronial families fought for supremacy in the streets. Neither, admittedly, was it quite yet the pristine marble-hewn city of the High Renaissance, where Michelangelo's cupola soared above the newly-completed marvel of Bramante's and Raphael's magnificent new basilica of St. Peter's. Rome was a city still as yet evolving and successive generations of resident popes had over the decades invested their time, their attention, and their revenues in making improvements to the city's general living conditions.

Not long after the papacy's return from Avignon, Pope Martin V had signalled the need for civic improvements when he grumbled in 1425: 'many inhabitants of Rome have been throwing entrails, viscera, heads, feet, bones, blood and skins, besides rotten meat and fish, refuse, excrement, and other fetid and rotting cadavers into the streets'.[104] It was, however, under the tutelage of Pope Nicholas V that the papacy began to actually do something about Rome's pitiful condition. Pope Nicholas had hired Leon Battista Alberti and the Tuscan sculptor and architect Bernardo Rossellino to draw up plans for the rebuilding of the Vatican and St. Peter's basilica. Alberti duly prepared a master reconstruction plan whilst the Pope's contractors cleared streets, demolished slums and rescued the city's once life-giving aqueducts from centuries of accumulated waste. Rossellino meanwhile began the process of stabilising the walls of the old and decaying basilica which the first Christian Emperor Constantine had originally commissioned many centuries ago.

Successive popes like Sixtus IV (builder of the Sistine Chapel, named immodestly after himself), Innocent VIII and Alexander VI continued to improve and expand the Vatican palace on a grand scale. However, it was during the later reign of Pope Julius II that Donato d'Angelo Lazzari, popularly known as 'Bramante' (from the Italian word *bramare* meaning 'to yearn or solicit', presumably implying Lazzari's habit of constantly 'soliciting for business'), persuaded the pontiff to demolish the crumbling Constantinian basilica altogether and rebuild afresh in truly visionary scope. The first stone of this great new basilica had been laid by Pope Julius II on 18 April 1506, the same day that Michelangelo, who had been working on the Pope's tomb, had famously fled the city of Rome for Florence, furious that his own schemes had been eclipsed by Bramante's showy new project. On gaining the papal tiara in March 1513, Pope Leo X continued to employ Bramante in his capacity as *capomaestro* but when the latter died in 1514, Raphael was given the contract to take over as supervisor of works. Pope Leo further added to Rome's civic upgrading by building a new road, the Via di Ripetta, which provided a spacious new boulevard running north to the Piazza del Popolo and which was known as the Via Leonina after its sponsor. Other civic beautification works that the Medici Pope embarked upon included tasking the sculptor Andrea Sansovino with enhancing the façade portico of the Church of Santa Maria in Domnica with Tuscan columns and a fountain. The Rome of the High Renaissance was slowly starting to take shape.

By now, and not before time, the popes were also finally beginning to feel a great deal more secure in their theocratic city-state. The power of the ancient Roman baronial families had been–if not entirely shattered–at least curtailed by Leo X's predecessors. Sixtus IV and his nephew Girolamo Riario had attempted to contain the power of the Colonna, whilst Alexander VI and his son Cesare Borgia had meanwhile cowed the great Orsini. Under the warlike Julius II, the Roman nobles had sensibly kept a low profile and had not dared to make any trouble. All that changed again under the reign of Pope Leo X who was related to the Orsini. For the last two generations Pope Leo's family the Medici had intermarried with the Roman Orsini: the Pope's mother, the wife of Lorenzo the Magnificent, was Clarice Orsini whilst his sister-in-law (the wife of Piero the Unfortunate) was Alfonsina Orsini. By the time of Leo X's *possesso*, that traditional Roman ceremony which signified the Pope's taking possession of the spiritual and temporal aspects of the bishopric of Rome, the conditions had therefore been set for a less belligerent and altogether more peaceful and festive era in the city of Rome. The Pope, morbidly obese and sweating profusely, had rode through the streets of the city on a snow white Turkish horse as his equerries scattered gold coins to the cheering crowd. Doing his utmost to project an image of hieratic grandeur, Pope Leo was nevertheless compelled to sit side-saddle due to a painful bout of haemorrhoids. This, then, was the relieved, celebratory and self-indulgent Rome to which Pietro Aretino now came seeking his fortune.

Working backwards from 1525, the year he is known to have left Rome, one of Aretino's twentieth-century biographers, Edward Hutton, extrapolates from Aretino's rather ungracious throwaway comment that he had 'wasted seven years in the service of the two Medici popes'[105] that the satirist probably first came to Rome around the year 1516. By this time, Leo X had reigned for just three years but, through the extraordinary example of pluralism that he had set up to that point, it is perhaps fair to say that he might have been born to be Pope. Giovanni de' Medici first received the tonsure in 1482 at the tender age of six and at seven years old he was already abbot of Font Douce. King Louis XI of France next created the boy archbishop of Aix-en-Provence and Pope Sixtus IV made him an apostolic protonotary. Pope Innocent VIII allowed Giovanni to possess riches accrued at the Abbey of Passignano and, at the age of eleven, King Ferrante of Naples made him abbot of the historic and prestigious abbey of Montecassino. And these were not the only benefices which Giovanni scooped for he was also bishop of Aretino's own hometown of Arezzo. The Pope was, as much as anything, a product of the soaring ambition of his father Lorenzo *il Magnifico* who, although dedicated to keeping his son's feet firmly on the ground, could not have created otherwise than a spoiled, entitled, self-indulgent, pleasure-seeking adult. When he was elected as Pope, therefore, Rome became his grownup playground.

Leonine Rome was, in many respects, an eight-year-long party; under Leo's pontificate the city was—by the time that Aretino arrived—already enjoying a prosperous, hedonistic hiatus before the gathering imperial storm which would devastate Rome in the dismal year of 1527. Leo X remains notorious in papal history for his exclamation upon ascending the throne of St. Peter: 'God has given us the papacy, now let us enjoy it!' If other popes had done likewise, Pope Innocent VIII for instance, they had not been quite so embarrassingly open and frank in their enthusiasm. A morbidly obese *bon viveur*, Leo revelled in the sumptuous dinner parties thrown by wealthy friends like Agostini Chigi, parties which often culminated in Chigi encouraging his guests to toss the golden dinner service from which they had just dined into the river Tiber. This extravagant practise was just so that Chigi could demonstrate the sheer extent of his wealth. These parties, which were attended by the cream of Roman society and which set the general tone for the extravagant Leonine pontificate of Giovanni de' Medici, became perennial topics for awestruck public gossip. But the endless round of building, banqueting and hunting was, nonetheless, being financed by such infamous ecclesiastical shysters as Johann Tetzel; this notorious Church official hawked his papal indulgences all around devout Germany, offering fraudulent and undoctrinal remission from all sin–past, present and future–in return for the appropriate contribution of *specie* (defined by theologians as 'good works') to Holy Mother Church.

As a city, Rome during this time owed its prominence within Italy and its standing as an important city-state in its own right almost exclusively to the presence of the bishop of Rome and his papal court. Although this was ostensibly a theocratic state the Pope nevertheless governed as both spiritual and secular head of the patchwork of territories and fiefdoms known as the Papal States. The papal court itself comprised the College of Cardinals and the papal household or *famiglia palatine*, which comprised the pontiff's administrative officials and 'familiars'. By the time of Pope Leo's reign the papal familiars numbered 418 and were supported by a staff of some 265 servants.[106] The actual city itself was nothing more than a reflection of the pomp and circumstance of the papal court. Its civic traditions, however, and even its ceremonial, were of an appreciably inferior quality to that of a city like Florence for instance. Unlike Florence or Milan, Rome also possessed little home-grown industry of its own. What trades existed within the city were chiefly service industries catering to Rome's resident population of ecclesiastics, or else geared towards the burgeoning numbers of pilgrims who flocked there each year to pay homage to the many shrines and holy relics. Innkeeping, milling, baking and food supply, fine crafts such as goldsmithing and jewellery-selling, banking and moneylending, the purveyance of religious artefacts (*paternostari*), bookselling and fine arts and crafts–these tended to be foremost amongst Rome's offerings, although some native Lombard tanners and curriers did congregate in the artisanal Arenula district. Donna Vanozza dei Catanei, the former mistress of Pope Alexander VI and the mother of Cesare Borgia, had been both an innkeeper and an investor in hotels. One pilgrim who was less than enamoured of Rome's service-oriented focus was Martin Luther who visited the city some years before Aretino's arrival in 1510 during the time of Julius II's pontificate. Luther describes 'a state of affairs in Rome that beggars description. You can find there a buying and selling, a bartering and a bargaining, a lying and trickery, robbery and stealing, pomp, procuration, knavery, and all sorts of stratagems bringing God into contempt, till it would be impossible for the Antichrist to govern more wickedly.'[107]

Another Roman 'service industry' which Luther would have disapproved of, but one that would become intimately associated with

Aretino's craft as wordsmith, was that of prostitution. Leonine Rome was at this time home to some 750-1,000 prostitutes.[108] Strictly speaking, although the *avvisi* ('newsletters') of the day often made little distinction between them for the purposes of news or legal cases,[109] there was nevertheless a commonly-accepted social hierarchy of working girls. At the very top of the pecking order there was the *cortigiana onesta*, the so-called 'honest' or 'honoured' courtesan. These were the most exclusive courtesans who modelled themselves in similar vein to the refined and educated court ladies of Castiglione, and who made themselves sexually available only to the most worthy of men.[110] Indeed, the etymology of the word *cortigiana* was closely related to that of *cortigiano*, the word for a male courtier. The term connoted a certain degree of splendour, luxury, and expense which the courtier and high class prostitute both shared in common. Next down the pecking order came the *cortigiana di lume* (the 'lamp' or 'candle' courtesan), who was of a more lower class stripe and who usually carried out her illicit trade from inns, shops and even workshops, where she also lived.[111] Next came the common *Meretrice* ('prostitute') who was usually crowded into a low brothel for the plying of her trade and who differed from the *cortigiana* by her inferior economic status and infinitely less selective approach to her clientele.

Finally, right at the bottom of the scale, was the universally-despised *puttana* ('whore'), a mere slut who didn't necessarily always exchange her favours on a commercial basis but often simply for the carnal pleasure of sex itself. It was a common enough belief in the sixteenth-century that, as Michel de Montaigne puts it, women 'are, without comparison, more able and ardent in the practice of love than we [men]'.[112] This unsettling view of women as being fundamentally 'sexual beings' led to some remarkable rationalisations and extrapolations. In the *Ragionamenti di Zoppino ('The Reasoning of Zoppino')*, when Ludovico asks Zoppino to explain the meaning of the word *puttana*, Zoppino replies with the following risible pseudo-humanist etymology: '*Puttana* is a noun composed of both the vernacular and Latin: in Latin, that which we call *culo* [ass] in our language is called *ano* [anus], and thus [the word *puttana*] is composed of *potta* [cunt] and *ano*; and in our vernacular *puttana* means "a woman whose cave stinks" and *cortigiana* means "courteous with the anus."'[113] *Puttana* was one of the most derogatory words that a man could use about a woman at this time, as indeed it still is today in Italy. Its insinuation of the complete absence of womanly virtue, as well as its inference of transgressive sexuality (transgressive because it entailed that arch taboo the openly-displayed 'feminine enjoyment of orgasmic sex') combined with the indiscriminate sale of the woman's body to all and sundry, regardless of their social rank, generated deep fears and insecurities in the established male social order. The *cortigiane alla candela*, who restricted her customers only to the 'better sort' was therefore considerably less socially threatening and, because of this, more easily assimilated into polite society.

The more well-to-do *cortigiane alla candela* who, like the Geisha of feudal Japan or the *hetairai* of ancient Greece, preferred to classify themselves as high class cultural entertainers (lute and poetry recitals mandatory) rather than as mere whores. They were often distinguished by their intelligent and forceful personalities as much as for their physical allure. Tullia d'Aragona, whom Aretino had known in Perugia, and who had also by this time completed a grand tour of Venice, Ferrara, Siena, and Florence before subsequently reappearing triumphantly in her birthplace of Rome, was emblematic of this more refined category of prostitute. She was allegedly the natural daughter of Cardinal Luigi d'Aragona, a grandson of King Ferrante of Naples. The cardinal had reputedly sired the girl by the courtesan Giulia Campana and had taken pains to give Tullia a good upbringing, educating her in Latin, the classics and singing and had even permitted her to use his name. This did not prevent one of Aretino's Roman friends, a detractor of hers, from later dismissing her hereditary claims with the words: 'His Eminence's mule might have relieved itself from time to time in the courtyard of the house where Tullia was born'.[114] The humanist pretensions of this celebrated bluestocking courtesan were a constant source of mirth for the less couth and followed her wherever she went throughout Italy. Aretino himself condemned her, labelling her a hypocrite for striving to present herself as a muse or a princess. Though for those who could afford her services, important men such as Cardinal Ippolito de' Medici, Tullia was a goddess, a veritable nymph. The cardinal carried on a well-publicised affair with her, and also dedicated to her a sonnet which acclaimed her golden tresses and praised her sweet nature and engaging laugh. In these days, it was considered nothing amiss for a cardinal of Holy Mother Church to be dedicating sonnets to a celebrated prostitute.

Another bluestocking whore was Clarice Matrema-non-Vuole who, as evidence of her erudition, was able to recite, from memory, the works of Petrarch, Boccaccio and most of the works of Virgil, Horace and Ovid as well. Inevitably, in a chauvinistic male-dominated society such women had their detractors. The *Ragionamenti di Zoppino* expressed the opinion that all customers wanted from an expensive whore were 'a bottom, breasts, and a body that is firm and soft, from fifteen to sixteen years old, and not over twenty, and ... not [someone who would] affect Petrarchian rubbish'.[115] A contemporaneous *pasquinata* from Rome made much the same sort of point, lumping the pretentious and affected *cortigiane alla candela* in with ordinary whores and making the point that she differed from them only in her expensive price tag:

Lassa andare le cortesane
Se non voi disfarte al tutto;
Come l'altre son puttane;
Ma più caro vendon loro frutto[116]

('Leave the courtesans alone if you don't want to completely ruin yourself. They are whores, just like the others, but they sell their fruit at a higher price'.) Although he often entertained them, Aretino himself would evince a lifelong aversion for whores who sought to affect knowledge that was above their station. In this he was merely a product of his time. Indeed this misogynistic prejudice against female learning in general sometimes even extended to virtuous noblewomen too; in 1534, in a fit of pique, Aretino would speak out against the cultured poetess Veronica Gambara, unkindly labelling her as a *'meretrice laureata'* ('prostitute laureate').[117]

Tullia d'Aragona was of course at the more extreme end of the spectrum and although misogynists might try to lump them in with common whores they were to a large extent insulated, so long as their youth and their looks held. Unlike in the Medieval era, Roman prostitutes were permitted to peddle their trade from their own homes instead of being herded into brothels as in other cities such as Venice, and the streets of Rome often made for amusingly bawdy cameos as the ladies wolf-whistled and solicited prospective customers from their balconies. Others meanwhile plied their profession in the many *stufe*, or public baths, an early iteration of the massage parlour, conveniently combining ablutions with evacuations. Some were even fortunate enough to rent ground floor rooms in the private *palazzi* belonging to the cardinals of Holy Mother Church.[118] All classes of men patronised these ladies: noblemen, the lower orders, casual visitors from out of town, and especially–enjoined as they were to vows of celibacy–the city's numerous randy priests and clergymen.

⊙☾

With some measure of good fortune, shortly after arriving in Rome, Pietro Aretino fell within the orbit of the wealthiest man in Rome and was subsequently employed in his household. This was the renowned Sienese banker Agostino Chigi, close friend to the Pope. There are diverse theories on how this fortuitous meeting came about. It may have been that Pietro's uncle Niccolò Bonnci, who was *Lettore* at the *Studio di Siena*, could have arranged the introduction following an unrecorded early sojourn in that city by Aretino, who by the time he reached Rome was demonstrably familiar with Sienese customs.[119] Another possibility is that the uncle of Claudio Tolomei (a notable Sienese philologist) arranged for Aretino to be introduced to Chigi.[120] Yet another theory is that Raphael introduced Aretino to his patron, having heard of him from his associate Perugino who, in turn, could have come into contact with the young Aretino whilst the latter was living in Perugia.[121] By this time fifty years old, Chigi had first come to Rome himself around 1487 together with his banker father. He made his first independent fortune during the reign of the Borgia Pope Alexander VI and acquired highly lucrative monopolies in both salt as well as alum, the common name for hydrated potassium aluminium sulphate, which was the raw material essential in different manufacturing processes like dyeing, glaziery and armour-making. The papal alum came from the mines of Tolfa just north of Rome and was one of the papal court's prime assets as it broke the stranglehold which the Turks had imposed on eastern alum deposits since the fall of Constantinople.

Under Pope Julius II, Chigi further expanded his wealth by funding the new Pope's election, in gratitude for which Julius awarded him the position of notary of the Apostolic Camera and adopted him into his own family, according him the right to name himself 'Chigi della Rovere' and quarter his coat of arms with the Pope's own. To demonstrate his gratitude to Pope Julius, Chigi accompanied him on his glorious military campaigns in 1506 and 1510. Surprisingly, upon Pope Leo's succession to the tiara, the new Florentine pontiff had not used the opportunity to restore the Court of Rome's business to the Medici Bank (which was anyway virtually defunct since the death of his father Lorenzo, who had allowed the family banking business to run down during his lifetime), but instead kept the shrewd Sienese banker in his service. By 1516, when Aretino first came into his orbit, Chigi had made a phenomenal fortune, retained some 20,000 people in his employ, owned 100 merchant ships and 300 horses, had been awarded the honorific *il Magnifico* by his native Siena, and owned the sumptuous Villa Chigi in Trastevere on the banks of the river Tiber. Here, the Leonine Pope was his frequent house guest. Neither was the banker's fame limited to Europe either, for at the Sublime Porte he was known to the Turkish Sultan as *magnus mercator christianus*, 'the great Christian trader'. The Turk had even sent Chigi a personal gift of some rare hunting dogs and a superb horse.[122]

We do not know exactly what specific service Aretino performed for Chigi, and Aretino himself had always promoted the idea that he was never merely a lowly 'domestic' (Aretino alluded to his having been a '*quasi garzone*' or 'resembling an errand boy').[123] Nonetheless, his varied experiences at the Villa Chigi, moving amongst the banker's élitist circle of financiers, courtiers, poets and artists, would certainly prove transformative for the young aspirant from Arezzo. Writing much later,

Aretino would describe how he had 'always hated the poverty of their [the merchant class's] wealth; but my fate, to laugh at me, when I was little more than a youth, shoved me up against Agostino Chigi, where I might have died if he had been a mere merchant, but I revived my soul with the splendours, the banquets, the pomp which often amazed Leo the inventor of the grandeur of the Popes'.[124] The house itself was undoubtedly a luxurious setting; as one modern author writes: 'The "urban villa" with its flower parterres, groves, fruit trees, vines, fountains, ancient statues and grottoes was a civilised ambience whose object was to revive the "learned leisure" of the ancients, and also to conserve something which was essentially a transformation of the milieu of the courtly pastoral. In the villa the learned, the amorous and the frivolous all met.'[125]

Chigi had entrusted the design and building of his villa, intended to reinforce his image as a *ricchissimo*, to the largely untried and untested Sienese painter and architect Baldassare Peruzzi. Interior fresco work was supplied by such luminaries as Sebastiano del Piombo, Giovanni da Udine and Giulio Romano, all under the guidance and supervision of the great Raphael himself. However, sometimes the emotional lability of the hired help meant that their work ethic required a nudge. Vasari relates the story of how 'Raphael could not give his mind entirely to the work because of his infatuation for his mistress', whereupon 'Agostino ... in despair ... managed with the help of others to arrange for the woman to go and live with Raphael in the part of the house where he was working; and that was how the painting was finished.'[126] Another notable contributor to the villa's wealth of frescos, not to mention its decadent social life, was the homosexual Piedmontese artist Giovanni Antonio Bazzi who revelled in the provocative name of *Il Sodoma* and whose famous mural in Chigi's bedchamber, *Nuptials of the Conqueror with Roxanne*, an erotic episode in the life of Alexander the Great, was widely regarded as his life's great masterpiece.

The wealth of Croesus had its perks in other respects too. Agostini Chigi hardly lacked for beautiful women to accompany him in that splendid Alexandrian bedroom. The celebrated Roman courtesan Imperia Cognati, for instance, was one of his lovers. Acknowledged as Rome's most haunting and legendary beauty, Imperia was painted by Raphael successively as a Muse, as Galatea, and as a Sybil. Chigi had acknowledged Imperia's second daughter Marguerita as his natural daughter; her select group of well-heeled clients brought her wealth, security, her own *palazzo* in Rome and a pleasant cultivated lifestyle. In his *novella*, the friar and raconteur Matteo Bandello described her inhabiting a palace with cloth-of-gold wall hangings and tables strewn with expensive books and various musical instruments. The environment sometimes took her professional clients aback. According to one anecdote told by Bandello, when the Spanish ambassador paid her a visit one afternoon he found every inch of her abode so perfectly decorated that, upon feeling the urge to expectorate, he called for one of Imperia's servants and spat in his face, telling him: 'Don't be upset, for I do not see anything ugly in here at all except for your face!'[127] In his *Ragionamenti della Nanna e della Antonia* (1534-35), Aretino would later make Nanna, a whore, utter to her friend Antonia the line: '*Le Putane non sono donne, ma sono putane*' ('Tarts are tarts, not women'). Young, gorgeous but still emotionally immature, Imperia would forget this dictim and fall prey to romantic tragedy. When one of her longtime clients, the dashing Angelo del Bufalo, fell out of love with her she took poison and despite the ministrations of the very best doctors that Chigi's money could buy she died on 13 August 1512.

Chigi buried Imperia lavishly in a funeral which all of Rome turned out to watch and on her tombstone he left the inscription: 'Imperia, Roman courtesan, who, worthy of such a great name, gave the example of a beauty rare among humans'. Imperia was nevertheless soon replaced in Chigi's affections by another lovely young courtesan, the Venetian Francesca Ordeaschi, who soon replaced her predecessor as the toast of Rome. In August 1519, Pope Leo X, flanked by twelve cardinals of the Holy Roman Church, formerly married Chigi and his erstwhile concubine Francesca and legitimised their two existing sons. The wedding ceremony and festivities took place at the Villa Chigi beneath Giulio Romano and Raphael's mural of the *Story of Cupid and Psyche*, whose rich vegetable and plant festoons in the painted frame by Giovanni da Udine include the copulation of a flying *capriccio* (cucumber) with a fig (the fig being, of course, the common metaphor for a lady's secret part).[128] Thereafter, Chigi and Francesca held court at their home, either beneath the *trompe-l'œil* of the *saloni* with its vegetative innuendos or else in the pastoral setting of the gardens, to most of the great names of *cinquecento* Rome. These gatherings were sometimes (relatively-speaking) 'simple' banquets and sometimes they were elaborate masques but when staging them Chigi always tried to outdo his rival the powerful Florentine banker Lorenzo Strozzi, whose tastes in dinner parties ran to the distinctly macabre.[129]

During Leo X's *possesso* Chigi had inscribed an eight-columned triumphal arch that he commissioned for the occasion with elegiac couplets associating the reign of Alexander VI with Venus and that of Julius II with Mars; accordingly, for the reign of Leo X he predicted that this would be Minerva's era, a time of wisdom and learning.[130] And, indeed, during Leo's brief reign Rome flourished as a centre for learning and the arts, with Chigi's "urban villa" and Leo X's court being the twin stars around which this glittering artistic and intellectual firmament revolved. Perhaps Pope Leo's greatest contribution to learning was to revitalise Rome's pontifical university, the *Sapienza*. Established by Pope Boniface VIII as a *Studium* under the papacy's direct control, Pope Eugenius IV had (with no small sense of irony) used a tax on wine to raise funds for its reorganisation. Leo X brought in scores of new academics in a range of fresh disciplines including botany, mathematics, astronomy and medicine and established new chairs of Greek and Hebrew. He kept up a correspondence with the Dutch humanist Desiderius Erasmus, who dedicated his first Latin/Greek Bible, the *Novum Instrumentum*, to Pope Leo (by contrast, Erasmus's experience of witnessing Julius II's entry to Bologna in 1506 had led him to pen the anonymous satire *Julius Exclusus* in which a warlike Julius is locked out of heaven because of his bellicose and ungodly warmongering).

From around the year 1500, after his return from a tour of Europe, Cardinal Giovanni de' Medici, as he was then, had surrounded himself with some of the most diverting artistic talents and intellects of the age. Most of the celebrated Tuscan and Florentine artists were at Rome around this time. The great Michelangelo was still dithering on Leo's 1513 commission to reconstruct the façade of the Basilica of San Lorenzo in Florence and in July 1516 the sculptor returned to Rome to dither further on that longrunning undertaking, the tomb of Julius II. *'L'arte non è mai finita, ma solo abbandonata'* ('Art is never finished, only abandoned') Leonardo da Vinci had slyly epigrammatised in a thinly veiled stab at his great rival's equivocation. In terms of the literary arts, meanwhile, there was the irrepressible Pietro Bembo, the noted Venetian scholar, poet, linguist, literary theorist and lover who bragged of his seduction of Pope Alexander VI's daughter, Lucrezia Borgia. In 1525, Bembo would write his *Prose della volgar lingua* ('Writings in the vernacular tongue'), a prose treatise on writing poetry in Italian which would argue for the adoption of a standardized version of the Tuscan dialect, codified of course by Bembo himself, as the basis for a national language for the whole of Italy.[131] Bembo would also pen *Gli asolani*, a series of Neoplatonic dialogues whose setting was the bucolic court of the tragic Queen Caterina Cornaro of Cyprus, and which was located at Asolo in the foothills north of Venice.[132] Bembo was to become an important correspondent of Aretino's in later years, by which time he would be created a cardinal by Pope Paul III and be a resident of Padua. Possessing little Latin or Greek, Aretino would also further Bembo's project for a vibrant vernacular Tuscan literature.

Upon gaining the tiara, Leo X had taken Bembo as his Latin secretary alongside Jacopo Sadoleto, another noted poet-priest, whom Leo created bishop of Carpentras in 1517 and whose name had also been romantically tied to that of the courtesan Imperia Cognati. A humanist and a Church reformer, Sadoleto was most well-known for his *De Laocoöntis statua*, a poetic ode to the *Laocoön* group, the ancient statue of the mythical Trojan high priest believed to have been carved by Agesander Polydorus and Athenodorus of Rhodes during the first century B.C. The *Laocoön* had been randomly unearthed in a Roman vineyard in 1506 by a peasant who had been digging in that spot. Not to be outdone, in the *Ragionamenti* Aretino would later pay his own homage to the *Laocoön*, invoking the statue in the lurid tale of a prelate who reaches sexual climax whilst engaging in an orgy at a Roman convent.[133] There was also at Pope Leo's court one Paolo Giovio, a singular man of many talents. Giovio was a prelate, a physician, a historical essayist and would later become Leo X's biographer, eventually being knighted by his biographical subject.[134] Like many others whom Aretino came into contact with at this time, Giovio would escape neither the satirist's pen nor his talent for a crude epitaph: 'Here lies Paolo Giovio, hermaphrodite, / who knew how to play both husband and wife'.[135]

Another of Pope Leo's boon companions at this time was his former tutor (and his brother Piero's former secretary) Bernardo Dovizi da Bibbiena, a priest whose gifts as a polished courtier and ever-obliging witty servitor had endeared him to the former cardinal. In his *Il Libro del Cortegiano*, the Mantuan courtier, diplomat and author Baldassare Castiglione would later present Bibbiena as a worldly, facetious and urbane courtier-in-residence at the court of Urbino. And yet Bibbiena, who was also devastatingly successful with the ladies at court, was far more than mere courtier. As a *literato* in his own right, he was to distinguish himself by writing the first comedy of any literary significance to be written in Italian prose, *La Calandria*. Bibbiena himself was an avowed libertine who, despite his priestly vocation, openly flouted the Vatican's rules on celibacy by cohabiting with his favourite concubine. But since Pope Leo himself, like Pope Julius II before him, was a confirmed sodomite who had officiated at his good friend Chigi's wedding to his favourite courtesan beneath an erect *capriccio*, the Vatican was on thin ice even had it wanted to reprove Bibbiena for his lifestyle. These were generally laissez-faire times when it came to the morals of those set at the top of the hierarchical pyramid.

Castiglione himself was also resident in Rome and an active member of the Pope's circle. He had spent years at the refined and enlightened court of Urbino, first during the reign of Duke Guidobaldo da Montefeltro and then under his nephew and successor Duke Francesco Maria della Rovere. At Rome his official function was to serve as Urbino's ambassador to the papal court. The work by which Castiglione is best known, the *Libro del Cortegiano* ('The Book of the Courtier'), takes place over a span of four days in the year 1507, and features an elegant philosophical dialogue between Duke Guidobaldo's wife Elisabetta Gonzaga and her sister-in-law Emilia Pia on the question of what constitutes the ideal courtly gentleman. The book became the veritable guidebook and instructions manual on how to survive and flourish in the pluralistic and often chaotic court of Rome of this period. Aretino's own later work *La Cortigiana* ('The Courtesan') would be a bare-faced parody of Castiglione's work, as indeed would the *Ragionamenti* and the *Dialogo* between the whore Nanna and her daughter Pippa.[136]

Not long after Aretino came to Rome around 1516, the Pope initiated an expensive war against the duchy of Urbino and Castiglione's former patron Duke Francesco Maria della Rovere, with the Pope intending to place his own nephew Lorenzo de' Medici on the ducal throne. This was partly to fulfil the Medici ambition of creating a hereditary family dynasty in Urbino, and partly because Leo X bore Francesco Maria a grudge for refusing to show up for the Battle of Ravenna, an engagement in which Leo himself had been present and during which he had been taken prisoner by the French army. Hardly a sympathetic figure, however, the displaced Duke was a brutal man. He had, for instance, been the murderer of Julius II's alleged catamite Cardinal Francesco Alidosi, whom he had clubbed to death in a fit of rage in May 1511. The conquest of Urbino had eventually succeeded, but only after an enormous fiscal outlay (a reputed 800,000 ducats) and only after Lorenzo de' Medici had been badly wounded in the head by a harquebus ball. But for all that, Castiglione's relations with the papacy remained diplomatically cordial and Aretino would have encountered the great man often at the various gatherings held at the Villa Chigi.

Aretino himself was destined to outlive Giovio, Sadoleto, Bembo, Bibbiena and Baldassare Castiglione, who would die a broken man in Spain, having been unjustly accused by Pope Clement VII of conspiring against him with the Emperor Charles V. But, for the four brief years between 1516 and 1520, Pietro Aretino was mingling, honing his craft and starting to build his personal reputation in Rome. The anonymous author of a pastoral comedy which was doing the rounds at this time cites Aretino alongside both Bembo and Castiglione as being one of the poets of the papal court: '*L' altro Aretino el qual sol si cognomina / Fra pastor Toschi in cantar dolce e libero / Che il bene e il male in lingua sciolta domina*'[137] (the closing reference to 'good and evil predominating in a loose tongue' could not have been more apt and indicates that, even at this early stage, Aretino was recognised as having mastered the art of mingling both sacred and profane and inverting the conventional moral order). At the same time, since he was residing in snobbish and image-conscious Rome, Aretino would busy himself cultivating the pretence that he had come from an altogether more aristocratic pedigree than was in fact his to claim. Aretino also sometimes exaggerated the weight that he carried with the artistic geniuses amongst which he now readily moved, bragging on one occasion that he was by no means 'blind in regard to painting, and indeed Raphael, Fra Sebastiano and Titian often pay close attention to my judgements. I know in some part both the ancient and modern styles.'[138] By the end of his life, Aretino had clearly failed to curb his boasts, in which the name of Raphael still predominates. An especially egregious boast seems to have been taken up post-mortem by the early Italian arts theorist, Lodovico Dolce, in his *Dialogo della pittura* ('Dialogue on Painting'). In a *paragone* ('comparison') between Michelangelo and Raphael, Aretino is rolled out like a medium in a séance to speak on behalf of his late friend Raphael: 'Raphael's regard for me was even more considerable, as Agostino Chigi would bear out, supposing he were still alive. For the fact is that Raphael would almost invariably show me each painting of his before he made it public. And my influence was valuable in persuading him to decorate the ceiling of the Chigi palace.'[139] Clearly, since the Villa Chigi was already completed by 1506, Master Aretino (who only arrived around the year 1516) could have played no conceivable part in the plans for its adornment. But by that time Aretino's lies, fabrications and embellishments were indistinguishable from the truth and nobody held him to account for his statements.

Aretino was by now already crystallising his considerable talents as a satirical commentator on the social life of Rome. As early as 1513 when Leo X had been named Pope, Aretino was remarking on the veritable floodtide of Florentines who had arrived in Rome hoping for favours and emoluments from their new Florentine Medici *papa*. Not only had members of the Medici extended family such as Filippo Strozzi the Younger been part of Cardinal Giovanni de' Medici's retinue but Strozzi's wealthy banker brother Lorenzo had also arrived together with 'forty young men outfitted in elegant suits of clothing worth over 300 ducats apiece' as part of Giuliano de' Medici's entourage.[140] These initial arrivals were soon joined by other countrymen of the Pope's, all ecstatic and gleeful at the prospect of reward and good fortune. Aretino revealed his early scathing satirical ability when he penned the lines: 'Since the time of Constantine never have so many Florentines come to Rome. They travel from Florence shouting, "*Palle, Palle*," each a relative of the pope … There are those who think to capture the bark of St. Peter, others his fisherman's net or some great merchant venture. Among them are still more, willing to make themselves priests in order to obtain a benefice.'[141] Aretino's budding career as a satirist and social observer was by now well underway.

☉☾

Aretino's employer Agostino Chigi died in Rome on 11 April 1520 aged fifty-four. Serendipitously, Raphael and Chigi died within five days of each other (Raphael succumbing beforehand on 6 April). Commenting on the dual loss to Rome's cultural life, the Venetian cardinal Francesco Pisani admitted candidly: 'In my opinion, although the great mass of the people does not share my view, yesterday's death of Agostino Chigi will cause much less damage [than Raphael's death]'.[142] Nevertheless, as papal banker, Chigi was accorded the maximum respect in his final journey and his solemn funeral procession included the full complement of religious orders, priests of the various Roman churches and a large delegation of Sienese expatriates and businessmen carrying tall wax candles.[143] His body was deposited in the Chigi Chapel, an octagonal temple incorporating two pyramid-shaped tombs which Raphael had designed for his patron between 1513-16.[144] As for Raphael's own death at the young age of thirty-seven, Giorgio Vasari later sniffed that it had been precipitated by a night of carousing and gossiped that, before he expired, Raphael had summoned his current *innamorata* to his bedside and entrusted her future care to his friend Il Baviera, a print dealer. This mysterious sweetheart is traditionally identified with Margarita Luti, *La Fornarina* (the baker's daughter), whom Raphael had earlier painted bare breasted and wearing an oriental style hat.

At some point before Chigi's death, Aretino had found himself a member of Pope Leo X's court. Given his early predisposition to wit and *bon mots* and his familiarity with all the poet-scholar-priests of the day this was hardly a surprising transition. Furthermore, the court was perhaps the best place for a non-physical, literary-minded individual such as Aretino to gain favour and advancement. Patronage was a fundamental lynchpin of Renaissance culture; a great deal of energy was expended by great men in seeking the patronage of the most powerful figures in society–dukes, princes, kings, popes and emperors–as well as in obtaining additional prestige and merit by securing the allegiance and services of less important men such as artists, humanists and poets. There was an accepted way of going about this whole process. Leon Battista Alberti had devoted part of the fourth book of his 1430 work *della famiglia* ('On the Family') to a discussion of the techniques for securing the exalted patronage of popes and princes.[145] Alberti also highlighted the importance of socialising young boys at an early age to the company of older men, to whom they must be taught to be respectful and 'reverent' ('*essere a tutti riverenti*').[146] Similarly, Baldassare Castiglione writes to his mother in 1524 instructing her to have his four-year-old son Camillo sign his letters to his father formally as 'your respectful son and servant'. In this way, Castiglione reasons, his boy will be inculcated early on with the rules of his society's strictly hierarchical and relational culture.[147] For Castiglione, human beings define themselves in relation to this divinely-ordained social hierarchy and can only truly be considered as *humano* ('civilised' or 'mannerly') by operating within its context. Seeking the patronage of the great and powerful and in return according them respect and reverence is therefore a *condicio sine qua non* for operating within polite human society.[148] In its most extreme manifestation, patronage could take expression in such works as Filarete's 1464 *Treatise on Architecture* in which the author names his ideal city 'Sforzinda' after his patron Francesco Sforza, who is depicted as an inescapable ingredient and capstone of that imaginary Utopia.[149] These were the lengths to which the Renaissance client was prepared to go to please his more socially elevated benefactor. Seeking the patronage of great and powerful men would be a lesson in life which Aretino would now need to undergo and experience for himself. Arguably, this search for patronage would remain very much his true vocation for the rest of his days.

At this time the Pope's court differed little from the other courts of Italy and under Leo X it was extraordinarily secular in nature, given over to endless rounds of banqueting and gourmandising, the staging of amusing comedies and other theatrical confections. The Pope particularly loved to surround himself with dwarfs and jesters. The latter tended to fall into roughly two separate categories: there were those who specialised in the 'refined wit' known as *facezie*, and the rest were more or less equivalent with court *buffoni*, purveyors of inconsequential buffoonery. One of Leo's jesters, Fra Mariano, gorged himself one day on a whole pigeon, 20 chickens and 44 eggs, which the Pope found highly amusing.[150] Aretino soon became the familiar of another of the Pope's favourite court jesters, Serapica (one had to start somewhere), as well as Leo's hairdresser, who went by the jaunty name of il Rosso ('the Red').[151] It was a well known fact of life at Leo X's court that anyone who wanted to gain access to the Pope and secure his favour was enjoined to become a jester and make the Pope laugh. There was also, of course, the papal hunt. This pastime took place in the *bandita*, the rural area outside Rome designated by the Pope as a game preserve in 1514, as well as in the Campagna and the estates around the papal hunting lodge known as La Magliana.

Aretino's transfer most likely came about as a direct result of his satirising of Pope Leo's newest and greatest love, his pet elephant Hanno. If the pontiff's addiction to ribald comedy was occasion for askance glances and the odd lampoon, his love affair with the white elephant Hanno made him a prime target for Rome's unflinching satirists. The exotic four-year-old beast first arrived in Rome on 12 March 1514, a gift from King Manuel of Portugal, and was an immediate sensation for this was the first time that a live elephant had been witnessed in Rome since classical antiquity. Upon being presented to the Pope as part of a Portuguese homage under the direction of Manuel's ambassador, Tristão da Cunha, Hanno's Indian *mahout* made the animal bow thrice in succession, at which the Pope reportedly erupted in peals of delighted laughter. The elephant was thereafter housed in the Belvedere Palace, in a specially constructed house. Hanno made numerous appearances after this, usually as part of the regular round of Roman festivals, and was always the centre of attention. One of Hanno's most notorious appearances, however, came on 27 September 1514 when he was made to participate in the crowning of the poet Baraballo of Gaeta, who demanded to be publicly crowned as 'the new Petrarch'. Pope Leo merrily indulged Baraballo in this unseemly farce, making the poet ride on Hanno's back wearing a toga while the beast paraded around to the sound of trumpets, the boom of cannon fire and the jeers and laughter of the crowd. Eventually the cacophonous din upset the bewildered animal and the festivities came to an end as Hanno withdrew to his shed at the Belvedere.

Eventually, despite being absurdly cosseted by the Pope, Hanno died on 16 June 1516. Aretino, who had only arrived in Rome that same year, found occasion for a hilariously cheeky polemic called *The Last Will and Testament of the Elephant Hanno*. In this burlesque, which was immensely famous at the time, Aretino makes Hanno will his tusks to Cardinal San Giorgio on condition that the prelate's 'thirst, like that of Tantalus, for the papacy may be moderated'; his knees to Cardinal Santa Croce 'to enable him to imitate my genuflections' on the condition that 'he tells no more lies in council'; and his jaws to Cardinal Santi Quattro, 'so that he can devour more readily all of Christ's revenues.'[152] Cardinal Grassi, reputed to be the Sacred College's most notorious fornicator, was bequeathed Hanno's colossal genitals. Aretino delighted in the public adulation that the burlesque *Testamento del Elefante* had generated and he hastened to make capital from the mild notoriety it had brought him, writing: *'Fa sol che l' Aretino ti sia amico / Perchè gli è mal nemico a chi l' acquiste. / Io ho piu volte viste le sue rime ... / Dio ne guardi ciascun dalla sua lingua'* ('Take care that Aretino be your friend / for he's a bad enemy to wrong. / His words alone the Pope's high fame could rend, / so may God guard us all from such a tongue.')[153] Already we have a *soupçon*, just the barest trace, of the implied blackmail, the literary protection racket, that was to become so much a part of Pietro Aretino's later stock-in-trade.

Had Aretino attempted to lampoon the members of the Sacred College during the reign of Pope Sixtus IV, Alexander VI or Julius II he would almost certainly have found himself incarcerated, racked, and possibly even killed. The cardinals were great men, all drawn from the noblest families in all of Italy: the Colonna, della Rovere, Petrucci, Farnese, d'Aragona, Cybò, and Gonzaga; such proud lords and princes of the Church did not suffer humiliation lightly. The Pope was not unaware of Aretino's lampoonings but, being an expansive and forgiving personality, he chose to overlook any transgression on the part of the rising young writer. Being a Medici, a family which had suffered egregiously at the hands of past Roman pontiffs like Sixtus IV, an acknowledged conspirator in the Pazzi Conspiracy which had targeted his father Lorenzo and murdered his uncle Giulio, Leo X was glad to watch the discomfiture and public humiliation of his cardinals. When Aretino reported for service at the court of the Vicar of Christ, Pope Leo asked him if he'd prefer rather to be Virgil or else Camillo Querno[154] his poet laureate and 'Archipoeta'. Aretino immediately shot back: 'Your Holiness's laureate of course, for he can drink more good mulled wine in the Castello in July than old Virgil could have got from the Emperor Augustus for two thousand fawning Aeneids and a million Georgics.'[155] The response was perfect and Pope Leo X was delighted with the witty riposte. Aretino was now *in*.

Home and workplace for Aretino now became that warren-like network of buildings, palaces and chapels situated on the Vatican hill. In addition to the main Vatican palace and the Sistine Chapel built by Pope Sixtus IV, the complex also included the Belvedere villa which Pope Innocent VIII had built due north of the main palace. Pope Julius II had subsequently commanded Bramante to devise a huge courtyard by extending two long, three-storied loggias from the main palace to the Belvedere and due to the villa's being built on higher ground this resulted in three separate though interconnected *piazze*. The Belvedere itself was distinguished by its great hemispherical Roman nymphaeum and later, during the reign of Pope Paul III, the entire complex would be enclosed within its own fortified bastion. In terms of size the Cortile del Belvedere is at least comparable with the completed St. Peters and, during Aretino's day, would have been by far and away the most impressive structure on the Vatican hill, at least whilst the new basilica was still under construction. To underscore the somewhat secular nature of Leo's pontificate, the Belvedere courtyard and its *piazza* was the setting for recreational displays, bullfights, tournaments and military parades but little in the way of actual religious ceremonies. Attached to the southern portion of the Belvedere's immense courtyard was the official residence of the Pope and his 'curial' cardinals, the Apostolic Palace. This large complex had also been gradually improved upon by successive popes, sometimes for the sole reason that a pope refused to inhabit the rooms formerly occupied by a rival. This was so in the case of Julius II, who created an entirely new set of rooms known as the Stanze, famously decorated by Raphael, because he could not bring himself to occupy the Borgia apartments. Julius had also taken the trouble to install hot and cold running water throughout the entire building.

The Apostolic Palace was not home to all the members of the papal court and indeed many wealthy cardinals stayed in their own luxurious *palazzi* across the river Tiber. Cardinal Raffaele Sansoni-Riario, for example, had reputedly financed his own glorious *palazzo* (today known as the Palazzo della Cancelleria) with the winnings from a single evening's gambling with Pope Innocent VIII's son, Franceschetto Cybò. Key members of the Curia and secretariat such as Bernardo Dovizi da Bibbiena would, however, have had their abode within the Apostolic Palace itself. Taking advantage of Julius's innovations in apostolic plumbing, the worldly and wealthy Bibbiena commissioned Raphael in 1514 to decorate his heated *stufetta* (a combination of bathroom and sauna) with ribald pagan imagery inspired by classical Rome; the Stufetta della Bibbiena would feature lusting satyrs peeping at naked nymphs and, whether or not at Bibbiena's explicit instruction we don't know, Raphael would exclude no anatomical detail.[156]

Due to problems in the past with the Roman baronage, Julius II had initiated the practice of excluding their membership from those offices which brought them close to the Pope on a day-to-day basis. He tended instead to employ a surfeit of Germans and when Leo succeeded him he largely continued this security-conscious protocol. Aretino may have been given lodgings at the Apostolic Palace as one of the many 'familiars' of the papal household but we cannot know for certain; nonetheless the palace's complex of state rooms and *saloni* would become one of his main haunts when he was not otherwise engaged in the tavernas and bordellos located across the river.

The worldliness of the papal court had its champions just as much as it did its detractors. Tommaso Inghirami, Prefect of the Palatine Library, belonged unmistakably to the former. He was always known more for his acting ability and his powerful booming voice than for his curial duties; having played the role of Phaedra in a 1486 performance of Seneca's *Phaedra*, the character's name would become his nickname and Raphael would paint his evocative portrait in 1509. Aged forty-six at the time of his death in 1516, he was an obese man, like Pope Leo, and also like the homosexual Pope he enjoyed the company of handsome young courtiers. He died of injuries sustained eight years earlier when he had fallen from his mule and been run over by an oxcart. Inghirami would become the post-mortem mouthpiece and advocate for worldly court values in Sadoleto's *De laudibus philosophiae* ('Praise of Philosophy') which explores the lack of true humane wisdom (*sapientia*) at the Roman court and juxtaposes it with the counterfeit 'wisdom' espoused by the narcissistic papal courtiers. But Jacopo Sadoleto was not the only scholar-cleric who would ultimately turn his back on the papal court. Leo X's memoirist Paolo Giovio would, later in his life, find peace and tranquillity at his villa far away on the shores of Lake Como. Dubbed the *Museo*, Giovio's villa was his place of refuge from worldliness, home nevertheless to numerous portraits of some of the most famous and worldly personalities of the day. However, the ability of a member of the court to enjoy the pose of *otium liberale*, that is to say 'cultured retirement' (quite literally 'liberal leisure'), hinged largely upon his ability to build up his wealth through profitable court employment and for every former secretary or administrator who retired into peaceful seclusion there were ten new faces to take their place, all eager and hopeful for advancement.

To such *gente nuova* or 'new men' it made little odds that a court clustered around a single exalted, quasi-divine patron made for a capricious and highly arbitrary career path, nor that prior to Leo's reconquest in 1512 of his home state of Florence he had endeavoured to reintroduce a pre-Medicean system whereby talent and ability were justly and routinely rewarded with civic office. Such men were happy to play the eternal game of flattery and cajolery in their endless quest for papal emoluments. Looking back on his few brief years in Leo's service, Aretino would later write the *Ragionamento delle corti* (1538), a scathing rebuke on the callousness and petty place-seeking of the Roman court and its denizens. Having by this time broken free of the Court of Rome and having survived to make a healthy living for himself at Venice and elsewhere, Aretino could not help but snipe at artists, humanists and men of letters who could not survive, let alone flourish as he had done, away from the limelight of court; dismissively, he compared such people to soldiers who had never been to war. The Roman court, declared Aretino, was 'a hospital of hope, burial of life, ... market of lies, ... school of fraud, ... paradise of vices and hell of virtues, ... more wretched than the most horrid and bestial cave or tomb.'[157] This would not be the first time that Aretino would be found inverting and subverting the message of Castiglione's *Libro del Cortegiano*, that indispensable manual of mannered courtly life. The same criticism would come many times over, even as Aretino (who was ultimately a realist) would be grudgingly forced to admit that, without the largesse of the papal court, the sublime genius of a Raphael or a Michelangelo could not have found its fullest expression.

For writers and men-of-letters, the papal court still remained the best outlet for their talents and, for a few short years prior to the Counter Reformation of Pope Paul III, the Leonine court would play host to numerous privately-staged performances whose plots and themes were often self-referential in nature and certainly unsuitable for the strait-laced. Reputedly one of Leo's favourite works was Bibbiena's sophisticated sex comedy *La Calandria* (1506), which was first performed for Urbino's carnival season in 1513, and then subsequently in Rome in 1514 and 1515.[158] The play was, on one level, a complex farce involving the usual theatrical canards–a wager over a seduction and an exchange of identities–yet on another level entirely it was a sexually-subversive tract involving risqué references to cross-dressing and gender interchangeability. Not only do all the main characters of *La Calandria* swap clothes at some point or another, but they also swap their sexual parts between themselves as well. The basic underlying motivation of the main protagonist, Dr. Calandro, is sexual appetite.

La Calandria was typical of that style of play which came to be known as the *commedia erudite*, a more scholarly iteration of the *commedia dell' arte* or 'art comedy', which tended to be performed to more educated and cultured audiences and whose performance depended on a written script often derived from either Plautus or Terence. Giambattista della Porta and Lodovico Ariosto also wrote in this style, as did Niccolò Machiavelli in his satirical play *La Mandragola* ('The Mandrake') which was first performed during Florence's carnival season of 1518 and which Pope Leo X requested to be performed again in Rome in the spring of 1520. In *La Mandragola*, a lusty Callimaco uses the wile of a mandrake concoction combined with a series of disguises to convince an elderly fool, Nicia, to allow him to sleep with his beautiful, young yet 'infertile' wife Lucrezia. As in Bibbiena's *La Calandria*, adultery once more ultimately triumphs and fools are rendered as cuckolds. Machiavelli's sex comedy was performed much to Leo's delight, even though the work was quite obviously a thinly-veiled satirical critique of power politics in Medici Florence.

Perhaps the staging of Machiavelli's play was Pope Leo's way of making it up to the former republican secretary of Florence's second chancery for having ordered Machiavelli's torture by *strappado* in 1513 (the writer had been implicated in the anti-Medicean Boscoli Plot of that year and the severity of the Pope's reprisals had stunned even the sternest Vatican disciplinarians). Aretino's own dual *homage* to the genre would come later in the form of his own bawdy comedy *La Cortigiana* (1525 and 1534), itself a satire on the Roman court, and *Il Marescalco* (1533), which was loosely based on Plautus's *Cascina* and which therefore followed the rules of the *commedia erudite*. For the moment, however, Pietro Aretino would find his true voice and calling not in theatre or poetry but in satire. His medium would be a crumbling relic of Roman antiquity named Pasquino.

CHAPTER 3

A Statue Named Pasquino

You who want to live a holy life, leave Rome.
Here everything is allowed, but for honesty.

Anonymous *Pasquinata*.

In the first half of 1519, Europe was rocked by huge tectonic changes in the political landscape. In January of that year the Emperor Maximilian had died and, on 28 June 1519 at Frankfurt am Main, the electors of the Holy Roman Empire offered the Imperial Crown to his grandson King Charles of Castile and León, Aragon, Sicily and Naples. Barely even out of his teens, the son of the late Philip the Handsome and his wife Queen Juana *la Loca* ('the Mad'), now the Emperor Charles V, ruled a vast dominion extending to all four points of the compass. From the Baltic Sea to the Mediterranean, from Spain in the west to Germany and Austria in the east, Charles's new Empire was described at the time as '*el imperio en el que nunca se pone el sol*' ('the empire on which the sun never sets'). To consolidate his position further, Charles would also soon lay claim to the vast untapped wealth of the New World as his conquistadors began their epic drive inland to subjugate both Mexico and Peru. On February 1519, Hernán Cortés had already set out from Cuba on his voyage of conquest. In 1524 and 1526, meanwhile, Francisco Pizzaro would attempt to defeat the Incans. Finally, at the Battle of Cajamarca on 16 November 1532, Pizzaro would achieve victory over the indigenous people and the captive Incan King Atahualpa would be forced to fill an entire chamber with gold for the greedy Spanish adventurers. Soon, the fully-laden treasure galleons of Charles V would ply the Atlantic ocean between the New World and the Old, a source of unrivalled income.

Charles had not only inherited the realms of Castile and Aragon together with his hereditary Austrian lands, but also those territories that his grandfather Maximilian had managed to conserve belonging to his wife Mary of Burgundy. Charles's dominions therefore threatened to encircle France which, in turn, sought to impede the consolidation of the huge imperial dominions. Although Italy had to a certain extent already been prey to the international power plays of France, Spain and the Empire ever since Charles VIII's fateful invasion in 1494, the election of Charles V would lead wholeheartedly to that era of *preponderanza straniera* ('foreign preponderance') which would see the two major powers using Italy as a chessboard in their ongoing struggle for European supremacy. France at this time occupied Milan, Genoa, Parma and Piacenza. In so doing, she interfered in what Charles regarded as the *Regnum Italiae*, those lands in northern and central Italy which were traditionally considered as part of the Holy Roman Empire. As Charles VIII and Louis XII had done before him, François I also laid claim to the Kingdom of Naples, by this time under Charles's direct control. The drums of war were beating. Little could Pietro Aretino know at the time, but he would eventually be brought within the nexus of both of these mighty and adversarial European monarchs. Just as King François I and the Emperor Charles V fought over rulership of Italy, so in a sense would they also squabble over the right to patronise Pietro Aretino. On 2 May 1519, François had lost his maestro, Leonardo da Vinci, who died at the age of sixty-seven at Clos Lucé in Amboise, France. (The visionary genius Leonardo had been very much a man of the fifteenth-century, but men like Pietro Aretino and Leonardo's great artistic rival Michelangelo were unmistakably sixteenth-century individuals.) Aretino would in turn court the attention of both rulers. As things would turn out, Charles would ultimately become one of Aretino's staunchest supporters and patrons. So much so that when Aretino later sent the Emperor a portrait which Titian had painted of him (a portrait which Aretino had refused to part with 500 *scudi* to acquire for himself), Charles was so delighted with the gift that he sent the satirist 2,000 *scudi*.[159] Pope Leo X was also shopping around for new affiliations and saw certain definite advantages in abandoning his former French ally for the much more credible and powerful new Emperor.

When the war drums beat the call-to-arms, a certain kind of individual invariably answers the call. In 1515, there had arrived in Rome a young man of about seventeen years of age named Giovanni di Giovanni di Pierfrancesco de' Medici. He was a cousin of the Pope's from a minor cadet line of the Medici family which traced its lineage back to Cosimo de' Medici's younger brother Lorenzo the Elder. This brusque, assertive young hell-raiser, who also happened to be the natural son of Renaissance Italy's celebrated virago Caterina Sforza, had already been banished from Florence in 1511 by the republican government of Piero Soderini for his role in the sodomitical rape of a sixteen-year-old boy of the Neretti family. Giovanni himself had been just twelve or thirteen years old at the time of the offence and had been exiled for two years to beyond twenty miles of the city.[160] The second time he was exiled from Florence was for engaging in an illegal duel with the city's best swordsman, Boccaccino Alamanni. In Rome, Giovanni got drunk and frequented the bordellos. But most of all he fought. On one occasion a gang of Orsini *bravi* tried to take him captive on the Ponte Sant'Angelo so they could ransom him back to the wealthy Medici but Giovanni, who knew no fear, spurred his horse forward and together with his small bodyguard of Corsican *banditti* he cut his way free of his attackers. When Pope Leo learned of this daring exploit he knew immediately how best to employ the young Medici scion. The pontiff equipped Giovanni with a company of 100 mounted lancers and sent him and his Corsican scrappers to join his nephew Lorenzo de' Medici who, from 1516 to 1517, was preoccupied with the conquest of the duchy of Urbino from its rightful owner Francesco Maria della Rovere. Here, in the duchy's rugged foothills, Giovanni joined Lorenzo's sanguinary campaign and here he was forged in the white hot maelstrom of war.

To say that Giovanni de' Medici took to his military vocation with alacrity would be a monumental understatement. As it had been with his mother, a permanent sense of quarrel coursed through his veins and he took to soldiering as naturally as a Hawkwood, a Carmagnola, or a Montefeltro. Having been raised by the warlike Caterina, Giovanni had been trained in his youth by the best swordsmen that money could buy. He was also a quick study in the rudiments and art of battle and possessed an outstanding tactical and strategic mind. Quickly grasping all the factors which decided the outcome of modern engagements, he was able to adapt his military practices accordingly and provide nuanced leadership. He understood, for instance, how gunpowder had completely revolutionised the sixteenth-century battlefield and foresaw the need to change the use and purpose of cavalry in battle. Giovangirolamo de' Rossi, in his eulogy to Giovanni de' Medici, would later write that his half-uncle Giovanni was the first to equip all his horsemen with the sturdy metal helmets called burgonets and to mount them on smaller, more mobile 'Turkish' or 'Berber' horses instead of the traditional big, expensive but delicate warhorses.[161] In so doing he therefore capitalised on the two major strengths of the cavalry arm–'speed and mobility'–and began to specialise in fast but devastating skirmishing tactics and ambushes. Above all Giovanni was possessed of extraordinary levels of energy and endurance. He was brash, competitive and rarely out of the saddle whilst on campaign. He preferred to recruit those hardy and frighteningly wild rural Corsicans into his ranks and he pushed his men exceptionally hard, demanding from them their complete obedience. He led from the front and always displayed bravery in the face of the enemy. On one occasion he challenged a rival *condottiere*, Camillo degli Appiani, to a one-on-one duel over an imagined insult to his man, *Il Corsetto*.[162] He was a proud soldier but with good reason due to his unquestioned martial abilities. Aretino would later call Giovanni, by then his brotherly companion, *Sua Alterezza Giovanni* or 'His Haughtiness Giovanni'.[163]

Giovanni was still only eleven when his mother Caterina Sforza was taken from him in 1509. In 1516, he had married Maria Salviati, Lorenzo the Magnificent's granddaughter, with whom he had been raised as an orphan after his mother had died. Maria was a somewhat strait-laced girl who was nevertheless devoted to her dashing young husband. Three years later, Maria bore Giovanni a son whom they would name Cosimo after the most famous member of the Medici clan, Cosimo de' Medici–the great statesman who had been named *pater patriae* of Florence. Aretino had made Giovanni's acquaintance probably around the year 1517 when he had been his guide around the higher class bordellos of the city of Rome. Married life clearly failed to curtail the lustier side of Giovanni's nature and the erudite *cortigiana* Clarice Matrema-non-Vuole was one of his many lovers at this time. The fearless young soldier was six years Aretino's junior but the chemistry between the two men was immediate and palpable. Aside from the obvious commonality of leisure pursuits, Giovanni was neverthless a simple, uncomplicated man who loathed the artifice and superficiality of court life, preferring instead the honesty of campaigning and the hardness of a military cot. His readiness to ridicule the priests and courtiers surrounding his cousin the Pope made him instantly appealing and sympathetic in Aretino's eyes. Furthermore, given the direction in which Aretino's own career was developing, one which often incurred the wrath of influential figures, it was wise to cultivate a powerful man who could shelter and protect him should the need arise. His *Testamento del Elefante* had undeniably ruffled a few feathers here and there; Rome was still very much the sort of city in which the wealthy and influential could, and did, solve their problems through recourse to the assassin's dagger. But, if he were protected by Giovanni de' Medici, potential assassins might think twice before accepting such a dangerous commission from an affronted patron.

But the Roman idyll of Aretino and Giovanni was over all too soon as the King of France's general, Odet de Foix, Viscount de Lautrec, had recently entered Italy to take command of the French army in possession of Milan and François's other northern Italian cities. Lautrec had received his assignment (over the head of the far more capable and experienced Duke of Bourbon, Constable of France) for the sole reason that the King was currently sleeping with Lautrec's sister, Françoise, Comtesse de Châteaubriant. Lautrec was a capable enough soldier, having fought at the battle of Marignano, however he now found himself outclassed and outmatched by the Imperialist generals confronting him, and who aimed to seize Milan from French rule. Comprising the latter were Prospero

Colonna, who had overall command of the imperial, papal and Florentine forces, assisted by Fernando Francesco d'Ávalos, Marchese di Pescara. Giovanni de' Medici rode off to participate in the hostilities with his light horsemen, ostensibly under the command of the twenty-one-year-old captain-general of the Papal forces, Federico II Gonzaga, Marquess of Mantua. Giovanni earned distinction early on in the campaign in November 1521 by forging a passage across the river Adda on horseback and in full armour, thereby opening the way for the imperial advance towards French-occupied Milan, Parma and Piacenza. The French, who knew a genuine soldier when they saw one, dubbed Giovanni 'il Gran Diavolo' and were hugely impressed by his audacious brand of soldiering. Lautrec now pulled back, well behind the line of the Adda river. His Swiss mercenaries began deserting him for want of pay and a well-timed uprising within Milan itself gave the imperial forces control of the city. On 20 November 1521, the exiled twenty-six-year-old Francesco II Sforza was formally restored to the duchy under imperial protection. When he arrived to take up his rule, he would thank Giovanni de' Medici personally for the latter's heroic role in the triumphant campaign.

Not long after the imperial conquest of Milan, the city received an exalted visitor from Rome—Cardinal Giulio de' Medici. Garbed in the impressive robes of a Knight of Rhodes, the Pope's illegitimate cousin had come north as papal legate to call upon the joint imperial commanders Colonna and Pescara, both of whom were in the midst of a bitter dispute as to who should wear the laurel for Milan's capture. Born in that murderous year of 1478, Cardinal de' Medici was forty-three years old; handsome, swarthy of skin and with lugubrious, heavily-lidded eyes, he was an altogether more guarded and stern personality than his freewheeling cousin the Pope. More temperate in his appetites than the over-indulgent Leo X, Cardinal Giulio de' Medici wielded considerable influence at court. Marco Minio, the Venetian Ambassador to Rome, had reported to his masters in 1520 that 'Cardinal de' Medici, who is not legitimate, has great power with the Pope; he is a man of great competence and great authority; he resides with the Pope, and he [Leo] does nothing of importance without first consulting him'.[164] It had been Cardinal de' Medici whom, in the temporary absence of his boon companion and protector Giovanni de' Medici, Pietro Aretino had decided for the time being to cultivate in Rome. However, Aretino would never truly trust the cardinal, sensing perhaps his mercurial unpredictability and perceiving his troubling want of principle when it came to political affairs.

But the Pope was not getting any younger and he refused to look after his health and so it was with some justification, therefore, that Aretino regarded Giulio de' Medici as Leo's natural heir apparent on the throne of the fisherman. Aretino was astute to try to cultivate Leo's evident successor. In the event, Pope Leo X failed to live long enough to bask in his most recent policy victory, his alignment with the Emperor Charles and the Imperialist reconquest of Milan. The Pope was taking his ease at one of his favourite hunting lodges, the Villa Magliana, when news reached him of Milan's fall and the subsequent recovery of the papal fiefs of Parma and Piacenza from the French general Lautrec. He returned immediately to Rome, arriving back on Sunday, 24 November, with the intention of conferring with his war council and participating in the public festivities being planned to commemorate the great victory of the papal-imperial alliance he had orchestrated. However, not long afterwards, he succumbed to a chill and took to his bed. By 1 December 1521, mere days after achieving the victory he had so shrewdly envisaged, Christendom's first Medici pope was dead at the age of forty-six.

The usual post-mortem rumours of poisoning flew in the wind. The Pope's cup bearer Bernardo Malespina, then Francesco Maria della Rovere, then King François, and ultimately Alfonso d'Este of Ferrara were all placed under intense scrutiny. The duchies of Ferrara and Urbino stirred uneasily, and Venice also began to flex and unwind. There was an uncomfortable sense that with the Lion Pope's death there would be a sea-change in papal affairs that would not be for the better. A 1513 *pasquinata* had crowed: 'I used to be an exile, but I'm back in Leo's reign. / So burn your midnight oil, boys, and follow in my train. / For no one leaves my Leo without a handsome gain. / Bards will sing for prizes, and they'll not sing in vain.'[165] Leo's papacy had been a flowing river of largesse for some of the most talented artists and *letterati* of the age; but now the papal treasury was empty and the papal court groaned collectively at the prospect of straightened circumstances ahead. 'He ruled like a lion—well named for Leo, forsooth—and he died like a dog', sneered one contemporary versifier.[166] The judgement was an unworthy one, yet for a few fleeting months, Rome would be caught up in a whirlwind of free-speech, the like of which it had never experienced. The chief instigator of this would be none other than Pietro Aretino.

☉☾

I n the corner of the small, triangular space that is the Piazza Navona in the district of Parione stood, and still stands to this day, an ancient battered, defaced Roman statue believed to be the aging effigy of Menelaus holding the dead body of Patroclus, an episode from the Trojan Wars. It was known to the Romans as Pasquino and It was said that in 1501 Cardinal Oliviero Carafa had first propped the statue there, against the crumbling walls of the Orsini palace where he had his rooms.[167] In subsequent years Pasquino became the focus for an annual festival on 25

April (the 'Feast of Pasquino') during which the statue received papier-mâché limbs in replacement of its missing ones and was dressed up in mythological costume as for example Neptune or Janus. An annual competition was held to find the best examples of Latin epigrams and the winning entries were pasted on the statue's plinth.[168] In 1513, Pasquino appeared dressed as Apollo, to commemorate the election of Cardinal Giovanni de' Medici as Pope Leo X (Apollo being a reference to the pope's passion for music).[169] How the statue earned its name was the subject for much speculation. Some said that Maestro Pasquino had been a schoolmaster, others that he was an unusually forthright tailor who used to have his shop in the corner where Pasquino stood and that 'Pope, cardinals, nobles, all in turn were mocked, praised, and censured according to this merry man and his apprentices'. Over time this gave rise to an unusual insulation of both offender and offendee because '..as the epigrams uttered were those of plebeian mouths and spoken in a vulgar tongue, it never occurred to anyone to take vengeance of them, or in any way to molest the tailor. When, therefore, any nobleman, or doctor, or other considerable personage wished to relate an injurious anecdote upon someone in power, Pasquino and his men were quoted as the authors, and so made to serve as shields against the wrath and vindictiveness of the offended.'[170]

By now, the Romans had made a practice of attaching to Pasquino's base mostly anonymous–but also sometimes attributed–political critiques and tirades. These were the celebrated tracts known as *pasquinate*. Pasquino quickly became what one might anachronistically describe as a countercultural icon in early sixteenth-century Rome. The epigrams pasted haphazardly on the statue's base and on the surrounding walls were, at least prior to Aretino's adoption of the statue as his personal mouthpiece, a succession of largely undistinguished doggerel, the venting of subversive Roman humanists against the wealth and pretentions of their superiors in the divinely-wrought social order. Yet these rhymes and verses became, if you will, the unique voice of the statue itself, which subsequently developed an autonomous personality of its own thanks to those who used it as a ventriloquist's mannequin. If Pasquino's limbs and facial features had sadly crumbled then, in a satisfyingly compensatory sense, its voice remained clear and true–a mouthpiece of scurrilous invective and acerbic truth-telling in venal and corrupt times. Pasquino represented nothing less than what one modern author has called 'the diverse, unpredictable, and ephemeral noises of the street'.[171]

Pietro Aretino, 'the Chancellor of Maestro Pasquino', had finally found his medium. It was a match made in heaven, one in which the satirist could display his ventriloquial virtuosity. Together with another satirist, the Roman Anton Lelio, he invented the literary adumbrations and tropes by which future satirists would measure the effectiveness of their own *pasquinate*. A common narrative topos which Aretino would introduce was that of games of chance, especially card games, as arbiters of fortune in papal elections. Those cardinals regarded as the *papabili* or 'frontrunners' were sometimes depicted as playing common card games such as *tarocchi* and *trionfi* to determine who should receive the triple tiara. Another procedure which Aretino and Lelio would adopt would be to list down all the *papabili* together with an honest, more often than not scatalogical, assessment of their respective strengths and weaknesses. All too frequently such *pasquinate* made reference to their vices far more than to their virtues and proved embarrassing for many a high-living, gourmandising or fornicating prince of the Church.[172]

Upon his cousin's sudden death, Cardinal de' Medici, who was still serving with the imperial army as papal legate, hurried back to Rome for the ensuing conclave. As vice-chancellor of the Church he nurtured the not unreasonable hope that he would be elected as Pope Leo's replacement. As a candidate his qualifications were admittedly quite persuasive; as a Knight of Rhodes and a proven papal diplomat, Giulio had been a highly dependable adviser to the late pontiff. When the conclave went into session Giulio was certain of being able to command the support of at least fourteen out of a total of thirty-nine cardinals. During this period of *sede vacante*, Aretino threw his support behind his adopted Medici patron and night-after-night produced a constant slew of *pasquinate* supportive of Cardinal de' Medici's candidacy and dismissive of everybody else's. Aretino's campaign was, in effect, the first sustained, editorialising political commentary on an election process, the forerunner of all the commentaries by political pundits which have been produced ever since. The format of Aretino's commentary often took the style of a debate between Pasquino and another ancient statue excavated in the Campus Martius which was popularly known as Marforio. Commonly, Marforio would ask a question and Pasquino would provide the answer; the dialogue therefore took on the semblance of repartee.

In his *pasquinate* Aretino seldom flinched from one of his favourite themes, the sexual proclivities of prelates. In one cheeky *pasquinata* he versified: 'If Flisco's pope he'll go for a whole year / without a lawsuit and for that same time / Farnese will not talk and all of crime / Colonna Armellino sure will clear. / Mantua to small boys will not go near, / Ponzetta money lavishly will throw, / Campeggio'll be less civil and more slow, / and Grassi will desert his wife, poor dear.'[173] Worse was to come, however: 'We have a Pope! And each low hostelry, / each custom-house, each corner butcher's store, / blazes with light and sound and trumpet's roar / to see fulfilled Pasquino's prophecy / about the bleating, braying hierarchy / of geldings, sheep, slow oxen, bullocks, cows. / Lord of high-bellowed but of broken vows, / Armellino's Pope on fool's epiphany.[174] These witty and insolent *pasquinate* became so popular that they were circulated in the streets, avidly copied, sold regionally and overseas, and eventually made their way to all the courts of Italy and Europe. The name of Pietro Aretino, part editorialising journalist-cum-irreverent political pundit, part public relations man for the Medici family, quickly became a household name. In Mantua, Federico Gonzaga prevailed upon his aristocratic ambassador to Rome, Baldassare Castiglione, to send him as many *pasquinate* as possible for his reading pleasure.

Many years later, Aretino would still harbour the same jaundiced view of the clergy and their corruption that he held during the halcyon days of Messer Pasquino. He reserved his particular censure, it seems, for the various orders of friars who feigned holiness and asceticism yet lived easy lives of merry gluttony behind the walls of their great abbeys. In this regard, a letter which Aretino would later write to the Pisan soldier Gabriele Cesano in 1545 is perhaps worth quoting to show how little his view of the clergy would change over the years:

'They know when it is appropriate to eat pullets and when fowl: in what month boiled beef is good: and where the best veal comes from. There is not a fisherman who has as much knowledge of the habits of fish as does this tribe of hypocrites, and when it comes to knowing about the soundness of heavy wine, the flavour of light wine, the names of the different kinds of white wine, and the qualities of the different kinds of red, even Bacchus is an ignorant fellow in comparison ... In fine, these scoundrels, who would not give a thimbleful of water to a thousand who were dying of thirst, are revered, honoured, and adored by the greater part of the human race. They are maintained in their position, set forth in glory and conserved in riches, and this in despite of their "I do believe in disbelief" by means of which they prosper.'[175]

Despite the best efforts of Aretino on behalf of his chosen candidate, however, in the Sistine Chapel things were not going quite as Cardinal Giulio de' Medici had planned. For one thing, both Cardinal Francesco Soderini and Cardinal Pompeo Colonna stood firmly opposed to the election of a second Medici prelate as pope of Rome. Furthermore, fuming at Pope Leo X's recent betrayal, the king of France had let it be widely known that if another treacherous Medici were elected as pope 'neither he nor any man in his kingdom would obey the Church of Rome'[176] and he forbade all French cardinals from casting their votes for Cardinal de' Medici. This impasse left as *papabile* several other frontrunners that were nevertheless considered equally objectionable as candidates for Supreme Pontiff. One of these was Cardinal Alessandro Farnese, who had been affiliated with the hated Spanish Borgia family. His colleagues punningly referred to him as 'Cardinal Fregnese' or 'Cardinal Cunt'. It was a widely known fact that Pope Alexander VI had only awarded Farnese the red hat because he was sleeping with his sister Giulia at the time and he had done so as a favour for *La Bella*, as she was called in Rome.

Yet another candidate, with seven votes in his favour, was Cardinal Thomas Wolsey the lord chancellor of England and a man who was by now at the very height of his powers. But if the idea of a non-Italian pope was unpopular with the Latin cardinals then the prospect of an English pope was an abomination. The last (and only) English pope had been a certain Nicholas Breakspear, who ascended St. Peter's throne in 1154 as Pope Adrian IV and had shortly thereafter collapsed the local economy by placing the city of Rome itself under a papal interdict. As a result the Italian cardinals had come to an unspoken agreement to never again elect another Englishman as pope. Added to this was the natural Italian xenophobia towards the English in general. In 1500, the Venetian nobleman Andrea Trevisan had reported that 'the English are great lovers of themselves, and of everything belonging to them; they think that there are no other men than themselves, and no other world but England; and whenever they see a handsome foreigner, they say that "he looks like an Englishman!"' Trevisan had continued in like vein: 'when they partake of any delicacy with a foreigner, they ask him, "whether such a thing is made in *their* country?" ... [T]hey think that no greater honour can be conferred, or received, than to invite others to eat with them, or be invited themselves; and they would sooner give five or six ducats to provide an entertainment for a person, than a groat to assist him in any distress...'[177]

To block the election of either of these two cardinals, Giulio de' Medici persuaded his colleagues to throw their support behind a complete outsider in the hope that he himself would garner more votes in succeeding rounds. This nonentity was the Emperor Charles V's former schoolmaster, the puritanical sixty-three-year-old Fleming, Adrian Florensz of Utrecht, Cardinal of Tortosa. Florensz was not even physically present in Rome at this time but serving as Charles V's regent in Spain. The only problem with this scheme was that the other voting blocs who were opposed to Cardinal de' Medici tried the exact same gambit with the result that on 9 January 1522 the Dutch cardinal of Tortosa garnered sufficient votes for election. Inadvertently, the College of Cardinals had essentially elected their latest pontiff by accident. When the cardinals emerged ashen-faced from the Sistine Chapel, incredulous at their own folly, they were very nearly lynched by an angry Roman mob waiting for them in the *piazza* outside. Cardinal Gonzaga alone summoned the courage to try to placate the crowd, telling them: 'We deserve the most rigorous punishment. I am glad you do not avenge your wrongs with stones.'[178] Aretino nevertheless upped the ante in his rhetorical campaign, even though the battle was essentially already lost. But Aretino and Anton Lelio were not the only ones making enemies in high places. For they were soon joined by yet another writer of *pasquinata* named Francesco Berni.

One morning, one of Berni's *pasquinata* appeared which violently excoriated the Romans for 'having lost the papacy [to gain] a bastard renegade tyrant'.[179] As was by now customary, Berni's tract offered little in the way of self-censorship: 'O vile rabble, O asses [good only] for beating, beasts without learning, without intellect, born only to stuff your faces and go to bed with whores, boys, and buggerers!'[180] The pestiferous ritual satire of Pasquino continued relentlessly. Rome herself was lampooned as a harlot who called after a fleeing Saint Peter: 'Come back! I've freed myself from the moneylenders [meaning the Medici]; but now I'm in thrall to the Jews!' [meaning the new Pope Adrian VI, an imperialist]. In contrast to the many new cardinals created by Pope Leo X, Adrian would create only one. This was Wilhem van Enckevoirt, whom the Romans irreverently renamed 'Trincaforte' or Big Drinker.[181] It seemed that the Dutchman's papacy was a rich vein of gold for the city's enterprising lampooners and satirists. Nonetheless, Aretino knew in his heart that, despite what Pasquino might say to the contrary, both he and Cardinal de' Medici had failed and the conclave's decision could not be rescinded.

One of his own final lampoons betrays his bitterness at the members of the Sacred College: 'O cardinals, if you were changed to us - / and not for anything would we be you - / and we had done the same bad things as you, / tell us quite frankly, what would you do to us? / We are most certain that you would hang us, / as we should like to hack to pieces you. / Indeed, had we the same power as you, / you would be crucified at once by us.[182] Aretino by this time was a man already accustomed to getting his own way, convinced of his ability to bend people to his will through the power and persuasiveness of his words. He knew that with the replacement of the epicurean Pope Leo X with the abstemious Pope Adrian VI he could anticipate little future employment at the papal court. It was a moment of clarity. Aretino therefore did not wait around to see his position evaporate in the new order of things; before Pope Adrian VI had even made landfall at Portofino, Aretino took himself off two hundred miles to the north. By the summer of 1522 he was comfortably ensconced at Bologna. Rome, 'the world's posterior', could go hang.

☉☾

Situated in the Emilia-Romagna Region of Northern Italy, the city of Bologna had–up until late 1506–been controlled by the Bentivoglio family, another family of vicious tyrants very much akin to the Baglioni and the Vitelli. However, following his victory in the summer of 1506 over Perugia and the Baglioni, Pope Julius II had subsequently marched on Bologna and Giovanni II Bentivoglio (having first been excommunicated by Julius) fled in panic to Milan. Aside from a brief intermission in 1511 when Annibale II Bentivoglio reconquered his father's city with French assistance, Bologna had remained a possession of the Papal States ever since. Bologna was therefore the setting when Pope Leo X met with the King of France in December 1515, when he was newly victorious over the Swiss at the battle of Marignano. During that conference, and to honour both the Pope and King François, the late Leonardo da Vinci had created an astonishing mechanical lion which walked and opened and closed its jaws and from whose chest had burst a clutch of French lilies. Although Bologna was still controlled by the papacy, Aretino felt that it was sufficiently distant from Rome to provide him with shelter and protection, at least for the time being.

Aretino's painter friend Andrea del Sarto wrote from Rome to the famous lampooner, humorously trying out a variety of honorific titles such as 'Respected Sir' and 'Your Excellency', and informing Aretino how sorely he was missed in Rome and how 'Master Pasquino has not spoken a word since you left. He is wearing deep mourning'.[183] This was in July 1522, 'a thieving traitor of a year'. The *Pasquinate del Conclave* as they became known (and which would only be published centuries later in 1891),[184] had already made Aretino a household name. The following month Pope-elect Adrian arrived in Rome and on 31 August 1522 the sixty-three-year-old was crowned as Supreme Pontiff. Aretino's Roman friends kept him abreast of the new Pope's ever growing litany of *faux pas*. Adrian VI proved every inch the poetaster that the satirist had predicted he would be. Having dismissed the majority of his papal household he opted instead to exist modestly on just one ducat per day; simple homespun meals eaten in solitude and prepared by Adrian's lone Flemish cook now replaced the sumptuous and convivial banquets of Pope Leo X. Moreover, in ever more unseemly displays of self-abnegation, Pope Adrian insisted on abasing himself before the poor of Rome, telling them consolingly but somewhat pointlessly: 'I love poverty'.[185] When he was not engaged in displays of poverty he scoured the gardens of the Vatican and the Apostolic palace on a mission to uncover 'indecent' classical statues, ordering that they be removed from sight. Not even the venerable *Laocoön* group, housed in the Villa Belvedere and the former subject for

Jacopo Sadoleto's lewd versifying, escaped his censure and Sadoleto's orgasmic treatment of *Laocoön* certainly cannot have helped matters. Even worse, Aretino also learned how upon his arrival in Rome Adrian had floated the idea of casting the mouldering statue of Pasquino into the river Tiber. In Aretino's absence his chief imitator, the vicious Tuscan satirist Francesco Berni, had taken up the mantle of truth-telling and in his *Capitolo di papa Adriano* was hawking such tirades as the following: '*O poveri infelici cortigiani, / Usciti della man de i Fiorentini, / E dati in preda a Tedeschi, e marrani*' ('O poor unhappy courtiers, / Out of the hands of the Florentines, / Now you are given up to the Germans, and Marranos (Jews)'.[186] The Church authorities were nevertheless inclined to tolerate Pasquino's tirades; the headless torso was rightly regarded as a kind of safety valve for public opinion and whilst Pasquino complained it tended at least to occupy and entertain the fickle mind of the mob. But Adrian would have none of it and he sought to rid himself of this quaint Roman institution which he neither understood nor appreciated. Only the quick thinking of one of the Pope's courtiers, Ludovico Suessano, had saved the statue. If we toss Pasquino into the Tiber, Suessano had suggested, might we not instead create an entire army of frogs who croaked *pasquinate*? The witty objection dissuaded Pope Adrian from his course of action and Pasquino received a stay of execution.

Years later, Pasquino would enjoy a brief resurgence under the auspices of one of Aretino's protégés Niccolò Franco, who would take an almost savage delight in bastinadoing the dead Pope Paul IV. Dead popes were customarily addressed by the Church authorities with the prefix '*santa memoria*' or else '*felice memoria*' and so, by attacking a late pope's name with the scatalogical language of the Roman streets, writers of pasquinades like Aretino, Lelio and Niccolò Franco besmirched their memory and stained their reputation.[187] The conservative reaction against such liberties would, however, be much more powerful during Franco's time than it had been during Aretino's and Franco would suffer dire consequences for his defamations. On 19 March 1572, Pope Pius V would issue the bull *Romani Pontifices* directed in part against writers of pasquinades.[188] Pasquino nevertheless survived to continue issuing his amusing satirical vitriol for another couple of centuries until the practise of posting *pasquinata* gradually died off. Fernando and Renato Silenzi date Pasquino's demise to 18 July 1870, which was the date when Italy was finally unified and the papacy's political power was therefore eclipsed.[189] Pasquino and Marforio would lapse into silence, rising Phoenix-like from time to time, as they did the year Adolf Hitler visited Rome, when Pasquino boldly declared: 'Rome of travertine / now dressed in cardboard / salutes the pale one / her future boss'.[190]

Meanwhile, there was little to hold Aretino in his temporary refuge of Bologna any longer. Sebastiano Serlio (who had worked in the *atelier* of Baldassare Peruzzi, the architect of the Villa Chigi) was there, working on the facade of the Church of San Petronio between July 1522 and April 1523[191] but otherwise this provincial backwater was not particularly interesting to Aretino and not especially secure for a satirist who had deeply offended the incumbent pope. Aretino continued pouring his invective upon Adrian VI, whom Berni had recently called a *'bestiaccia'*, but he began to wonder how safe he really was. He knew that his erstwhile patron Cardinal Giulio de' Medici was currently in Florence settling important affairs of state and he decided to ride to the city of the Medici and petition the cardinal to help clear the air between him and the new Pope. It was by now either late 1522 or early 1523 and Aretino left Bologna and set out to ride the short distance to Florence.

CHAPTER 4

Florence & Mantua

But do not forget, I am one to whom kings and emperors reply.

Pietro Aretino to Michelangelo.

Upon seeking out Cardinal de' Medici in his Florentine city-state, Pietro Aretino found his erstwhile sponsor preoccupied with putting Florence's government back into some semblance of order. Piero *lo Sfortunato's* legitimate son Lorenzo, Duke of Urbino, had recently died in 1519. He had succumbed not from the harquebus wound that he had sustained earlier in the war to secure his duchy, but from syphilis, the *sive morbus gallicus* as the *Veronese* poet-physician Girolamo Fracastoro christened it – 'the French disease'. Problematically, it had been Duke Lorenzo whom the Medici family had counted on to rule in Florence as the city-state's secular lord. Lorenzo did have a son, a mixed-race boy named Alessandro but he was only twelve-years old in 1522 and moreover he was not only illegitimate but his natural mother had been a common household slave of either negroid or Moorish origin. It had not taken long for the young Alessandro to be disparagingly nicknamed *il Moro*. Admittedly, there was also another boy, one year younger, named Ippolito de' Medici who was the bastard of the late Giuliano di Lorenzo de' Medici, Duke of Nemours, but he was still schooling and, like Alessandro, he was as yet too young to carry the weight of the state. Besides which, Pope Leo X had earmarked Ippolito for an ecclesiastical career (even though like Cesare Borgia before him he evinced little inclination towards holy orders and instead strutted around the city like a diminutive *bravo*). As for the dead Duke Lorenzo's infant daughter Caterina Maria Romula (Catherine de' Medici, the future Queen of France), she was being raised by family members as an orphan since her mother had also died mere days before her father, having most likely been infected with the deadly syphilis by Lorenzo.

In the absence of any obvious Medici candidate for rule, Niccolò Machiavelli, former secretary to the second chancery of Republican Florence, now semi-retired political theorist and rustic scribbler, had attempted to persuade Cardinal de' Medici to transition Florence back to an essentially republican system of government whilst at the same time preserving the property and dignities of the two young Medici scions Alessandro and Ippolito. Machiavelli, himself long out of favour with the Medici for his role in Florence's Republican interlude of 1494-1512, had been introduced to Giulio through the good offices of Lorenzo Strozzi, brother to the wealthy papal banker Filippo Strozzi the Younger.[192] It had been to Lorenzo that he had dedicated his most recent book *Dell'arte della guerra* ('On the Art of War') which he had churned out amidst scratching chickens at his country villa. Machiavelli was in a sense a kindred spirit to Aretino, though not an obvious one. Machiavelli sought to change the way that government was carried out, whereas Aretino's diatribes sought to change nothing, but merely shame those whose failings made them deserving of humiliation. Machiavelli had previously rolled his sleeves up and attempted to create Florence's first quasi-professional militia, the *Ordinanza*, but Aretino–despite his affinity with Giovanni de' Medici–would never be interested in the profession of arms on any personal level. And yet, having said that, both men were industrious to a fault, both came from humble beginnings and both were largely self-made, self-created men. Like Aretino, Machiavelli detested idleness and one of his pronouncements on the subject even sounds vaguely Aretine in its vehemence: '[those men] who are ... enemies of the virtues, of letters, and of every other art that brings utility and honour to the human race, as are the impious, the violent, the ignorant, the worthless, the idle, the cowardly.'[193]

Cardinal de' Medici was reluctant to agree to Machiavelli's proposal of a diminishment of Medici political power and the suggestion had ultimately gone nowhere. In June that same year, the cardinal had been further troubled by the discovery of a republican conspiracy to have him assassinated on Corpus Christi Day, the 19 June. Two of the conspirators had been beheaded but another two had managed to slip away. It was with these weighty affairs on his mind that the newly arrived Pietro Aretino sought an audience with the Medici cardinal with whom he had earlier aligned himself. The meeting did not go entirely as Aretino had hoped. Cardinal de' Medici was in a somewhat delicate position viz-a-viz the new Pope and therefore rather ambiguous in his reception of the lampooner. Anybody would have to question the wisdom of offering sanctuary to a man who had gone so far out of his way to insult Pope Adrian. Giulio himself still harboured the ambition of mounting St. Peter's throne himself someday, and yet to have as his client a writer of such lewd and scurrilous anti-papal tirades called his suitability for the role into question. In short, Cardinal de' Medici could not really afford to have Pietro Aretino around.

As tactfully as he was able to, he suggested to the satirist that other equally worthy lords might be eager to patronise him instead. He assured Pietro that he had many admirers the length and breadth of Italy who enjoyed his wit and sagacity and who would profit from Aretino's facility with a quill. The name of the young marquess of Mantua, Federico Gonzaga, was bruited as one possible patron. Federico was still only twenty-two at this time, whilst Aretino at thirty-one was not so old as to be unable to establish a rapport with the young Marquess. Federico had ruled Mantua since 1519 and his mother was the esteemed Isabella d'Este, one of the most remarkable and most cultured women of her age. As for Mantua itself, it was unusually secure, having been built on the banks of three great artificial lakes which helped keep the city safe from attack. Surely, this was a place where Aretino could feel both secure and more adequately appreciated. Aretino had kept his peace throughout this clever attempt at deflection on the cardinal's part. Perhaps the cardinal had a point and Mantua would be a relatively safe court from which to practice his art. Furthermore, the Marquess himself sounded like the sort of man whom Aretino would be able to bond with; for one thing he was known to be a pleasure-loving individual who indulged in rampant womanising. Indeed, despite his relative youth, Federico's priapism was already legendary throughout Italy. Knowing that he was not wanted in Florence, Aretino therefore bowed to Cardinal de' Medici's suggestion and resolved to seek Federico's favour. Mantua would be the satirist's next port-of-call.

☉☾

B idding Florence and Cardinal de' Medici adieu, Aretino rode north for the swampy lands just north of the river Po where it meets its tributary, the river Mincio, winding lazily down from Lake Garda. In his saddlebag was a personal letter of introduction from Cardinal de' Medici to the lord of Mantua, Federico Gonzaga. By February 1523, Aretino had arrived at the moated city of Mantua. Facing out across the Lago di Mezzo, the Castello di San Giorgio where, on the ground floor, Federico kept his living apartments, was impressive enough on first appearance and certainly appeared to be a safe haven to the tired and travel-weary satirist. Built in 1406 by Bartolino of Novara, the Castello was a stout, square building comprising four towers surrounded by a moat with three gates. Each of these gates had a drawbridge which could be drawn up in the event of an attack, although by Federico's time the structure had largely lost its earlier defensive function. Federico's parents, the *condottiere* Francesco Gonzaga and his wife Isabella d'Este, the marchioness of Mantua, were acknowledged patrons of many prominent artists and humanists of their day such as Andrea Mantegna, Antonio da Correggio, Perugino and Leonardo da Vinci. During their reign they had acquired many paintings and classical sculptures which graced the Mantuan court and its associated *studioli*. Isabella, in particular, had established for herself a remarkable level of Europe-wide celebrity for a woman of the period. Mantegna's 1502 painting of *Minerva Expelling the Vices from the Garden of Virtue* depicts, amongst other things, the rescue of Diana, goddess of chastity, from the act of rape by a concupiscent Centaur; it was an allegory of Isabella's many virtues, which in addition to Chastity also included Justice, Temperance and Fortitude.[194]

Federico had inherited his parents' passion for art, having by this time acquired his own equally impressive collection of portraits by various masters which he proudly displayed throughout his castle.[195] The court painter Lorenzo Leonbruno had gaily festooned the Castello's militaristic halls and rooms with Gonzaga family heraldry.[196] Family lineage was a crucial component of men's and women's social identity and also took expression through genealogies, ancestral portraiture, family chapels and family crypts. The Sala dei Soli ('Hall of Suns') on the *Piano Terreno* (ground floor) incorporated numerous fifteenth-century frescoes whilst the Sala dello Zodiaco ('Zodiac Room') featured paintings by the court artist, Giulio Romano. Federico's court was the locus for an appreciable degree of humanist activity and was frequented by several notable scholars and poets also actively patronised by the cultivated Isabella d'Este and the late Pope Leo X. These included Matteo Bandello, Paolo Giovio, Pietro Bembo, Niccolò d'Arco, Ludovico Ariosto, Baldassare Castiglione and Niccolò da Correggio.

And then of course there was Federico Gonzaga himself. In his 1527 portrait of the young marquess, the Venetian painter Titian pays the subject many compliments. An attractive, heavily bearded man stares out from the canvas, clearly a carnal man from the set of the sensuous, amused, slightly flippant mouth as well as the languorous eyes. Federico's deep blue costume is opulent; engagingly he places his right hand on the back of a small, pampered dog. It is a portrait of ease and privilege. But nothing in Federico's childhood had been particularly easy. To secure his father Francesco Gonzaga's loyalty to Rome, Federico had spent much of his youth as a hostage, initially to the court of Pope Julius II where, according to the author Julia Cartwright, he had been exposed to 'orgies of cardinals and monkish buffoons'.[197] On a rather more cultural note, in July 1511, Federico is recorded as having recited an *Eclogue* of Virgil's during a night banquet at the Villa Chigi[198] and his condition seems by all accounts to have been comfortable despite the trauma of being removed at such a young age from his parents' care. Following his captivity in Rome, Federico was later sent to the court of King François from 1515 to 1517. As a condition of being able to return to Mantua, Federico had undertaken to marry Maria Paleologa, daughter to the French king's ally the marquess of Monferrato. Federico, however, had later reneged on the arrangement, having accused Maria of attempting to poison his mistress Isabella Boschetti. Somewhat scandalously, Isabella herself was a married woman, the wife of Count Giovanni Calvisano and the niece to Federico's gifted Mantuan ambassador Baldassarre Castiglione. In his writings, Paolo Giovio decried the fact that Isabella swanned haughtily around Mantua with her entourage, casting shame on Federico's mother Isabella d'Este.[199] When, in later years, Federico's romantic interest in Maria Paleologa was reignited for the sake of siring heirs to Mantua, their long-awaited matrimony would end unexpectedly in September 1530 with Maria's death.

Due to the conditions of his gilded confinement, Federico's had been a distinctly courtly rather than an avowedly humanist upbringing. His ambassador Castiglione would pay flattering homage to him in *Il Libro del Cortegiano*: 'In addition to the fine manners and discretion he shows at so tender an age, those who have charge of him tell wonderful things about his talent, his thirst for honour, his magnanimity, courtesy, generosity and love of justice'.[200] Here was a cultured man who, while in Rome, had watched Michelangelo complete the ceiling of the Sistine Chapel for Pope Julius II and had witnessed Raphael finish the Stanze for Pope Leo X. He was also a devotee of theatrical performances, having recently been inducted into the Company of the *Immortali* whose activities are recorded by the Venetian historian Marino Sanudo. The *Immortali* were one of a number of fraternities of young Venetian noblemen known as the *Compagnie della Calza* ('Companies of the Hose'), the Company of the *Hortolani* being another notable example. These companies were named for their colourful stockings and their members got together to organise site-specific 'pop-up' plays and carnivalesque 'happenings' staged in the canal city's innumerable atmospheric backdrops. On 13 February 1520, Federico had been the recipient of a *momaria*–that uniquely Venetian concept–entitled *la edification di Troja* ('the construction/edification of Troy') which had been staged specially in Federico's honour to celebrate his joining their ranks.[201] These different brotherhoods, which often had racy undertones, were extremely popular around this time and had their antecedents in such clubs as Poggio Bracciolini's *Bugiale*, or 'Liar's Club', in which well educated, sophisticated young men gathered to amuse themselves, often with lewd and ribald jokes and stories.[202] Another such example was Siena's Accademia degli Intronati ('The Academy of the

Stupefied'), the Sienese literary society made notorious by Antonio Vignali's homoerotic work *La Cazzaria*, in which two of its members discuss the manifold advantages of sodomy. It would be through Federico's good offices that Aretino would himself, in later years, become acquainted with the Companies of the Hose, an association which would ripen into the 1542 production of Aretino's comedy *La Talanta*.[203]

Cardinal de' Medici had earlier written Aretino an introduction to the twenty-three-year-old marquess which, somewhat disingenuously, pretended regret at the loss of Aretino's services. 'Messer Pietro, the bearer of the present, for his rare virtues, is so grateful and acceptable to me, that for no other person than your Excellence should I have deprived myself of him. However, having sought leave from me to come to you I have conceded it to him freely. Pray excuse both him and me if his coming has been tardy, for neither of us is in fault: but two not little infirmities which have come upon him ... I am sure that Messer Pietro is not wanting in the desire to serve your Excellence as myself.'[204] Federico replied with enthusiasm and good grace: 'I do not doubt that the presence of Messer Pietro Aretino is an honour to the Court of Your Excellence and a delight ... The charm that I find so copiously in the aforesaid Messer Pietro constrains me to retain him...'[205] According to a letter which Aretino wrote to Gualtiero Bacci soon after his arrival, the Marquess quickly installed Aretino in 'the very apartment occupied by Francesco Maria, Duke of Urbino, when he was driven from his dominions' [by Lorenzo de' Medici] and gave the writer his own personal steward, 'to take charge of my meals'.[206] He also promised Aretino an income of 300 *scudi* a year if he remained with him and kept him and his small but sophisticated court suitably entertained.

Clearly, Aretino had found a confirmed admirer in Federico Gonzaga, who declared: 'Our Pietro Aretino is like a festival of joy and pleasure to me ... for being with him is like being in a whole crowd and his conversation takes the place of many talented men.'[207] Federico moreover vowed to 'decorate my court permanently with this precious jewel'.[208] Aretino, for his own part, enjoyed the masquerade of living like a noble lord ('at my table there are always great gentlemen')[209] whilst at the same time allowing himself to take the measure of his new master and patron. The Marquess was clearly a sybaritic womaniser, though probably not quite on the same predatory scale as for example Galeazzo Maria Sforza, one of the late dukes of Milan, who had even gone to the considerable lengths of setting up a state fund to discreetly pay off the reluctant victims of his lechery. It is possible that Federico himself was influenced in his libertinism by the French King François, who had kept him captive for several years, following which he had elected to remain at the French court for a while longer, presumably to continue his enjoyment of the court's spirit of debauchery. François's womanising was legendary even for this dissolute era; it was alleged that the King had had his first mistress by the age of ten and that he had incestuous relations with his own sister. By August 1524, he was said to have already contracted syphilis and so it was jokingly said that he was 'sick of his own French disease'.[210]

Federico Gonzaga's obsession with sex was hardly surprising: the House of Gonzaga had been practically decimated by the scourge of incurable sexual disease.[211] Federico's father, Francesco I Gonzaga, the hero of the Battle of Fornovo, had suffered from syphilis since 1508,[212] having probably acquired the malady from his regular patronage of Mantuan prostitutes. Earlier, from 1503 onwards, Francesco had also carried on a torrid and well-publicised affair with Lucrezia Borgia (who was by then married to her third husband Alfonso d'Este) which was reportedly mostly sexual in nature.[213] On 29 March 1519, Francesco had died at the age of fifty-two from complications arising from his syphilis, surrounded by his wife and children whom he had also unwittingly infected. Unfortunately, as syphilis can be spread during pregnancy from a mother to her foetus, Federico inherited the then incurable malady from his father and his mother Isabella. Federico's son, Francesco III, born in 1533, would in turn also be 'ruined by syphilis', which would leave him 'morose and difficult' and he was fated to die at the tender age of sixteen.[214]

Due to this position as lord of one of the key Papal States, Federico was, at least ostensibly, a fighter as well as a lover. Despite his youth and relative military inexperience, the Marquess had been appointed *gonfalonier* and captain-general of the Church by the late Medici Pope Leo X. It was an exceptionally high honour since the recumbent essentially commanded the armies of the reigning Pope. Furthermore, the role would under normal circumstances have been a heavy obligation for the young marquess because, by the year 1523, the so-called 'Italian Wars' had already been raging for exactly twenty-nine long years and showed no sign of abating. In truth, Federico's appointment as gonfalonier and captain-general had been a papal bribe to detach him from his allegiance to his legitimate sovereign the Emperor, from whom he held his marquessate in fee, and make the Marquess 'a good Italian'. As an additional sweetener, Pope Leo had given Federico's younger brother Ercole control of the diocese of Mantua.[215] Later that year, in August 1523, Federico would finally be confirmed in his role as commander-in-chief of the Pope's armies with a *condotta* of 10,000 ducats for three years.

In 1521, when he had fought initially under the command of Prospero Colonna he had proven himself fairly reliable and by-and-large amenable to taking orders from his superior officer. Federico's passion for war would soon dim, however, and his dual allegiance to both Pope and

Emperor would become a major problem for the Church. After Pope Leo X's death, Mantuan agents at liberty in the Vatican archives would track down the document signifying that Federico had agreed to take service against his legal sovereign Charles V. His mother, Isabella d'Este would then destroy the document personally.[216] Conveniently for Federico, this now made papal accessibility to the papal *gonfalonier's* contracted services somewhat problematic to say the least. But Federico also had other ways of evading his military responsibilities. He was not above such sly deceptions as adulterating urine samples with pig's blood so as to obtain a medical excuse for not taking the field.[217] Federico had no such qualms, however, about taking the field in pursuit of the hunt. Hunting, along with horses and attractive women, remained his foremost pastime and Aretino no doubt joined him in this pursuit during his brief stay in Mantua. But already, Aretino would begin to tire of his new patron's company and the stifling court of refined yet remote Mantua. Years later, he would lampoon Federico in the following lines: 'Sardanapalus, I mean Federico, is capable of making a hundred herds of swine citizens and after offering up his sword in the temple of Venue, the pleasure-giver, he will announce that the greatest good is Petrarch's "sloth, gluttony and lazy lassitude"'.[218] The familiarity extended to Aretino by the Marquess had seemingly bred only contempt.

Having discussed his possible return to Florence with Federico, overtures were then made to Cardinal de' Medici. The results however were disappointing. A herald returned to Mantua with the disconcerting statement that the good cardinal regarded his former client as 'a loud-mouthed and unreliable trouble-maker'[219] and informed the Marquess that he was free to dismiss Aretino from his service any time he wished. Cardinal de' Medici had by this time regained some of his lost stock in the eyes of the Dutch Pope and was loathe to see his prospects ruined by being seen to associate openly with Adrian's worst critic, Pietro Aretino. The herald also made it known that some of Aretino's more recent scribblings had made their way to Rome, where they had come to the attention of Pope Adrian. The Pope had subsequently sent a brief to Florence for the cardinal to seek the arrest and detention of the satirist and to send him under armed guard to Rome, where he was presumably to stand trial. Disconcerted by this news, Aretino dictated a reply for Federico to send in his name to Cardinal de' Medici. In his reply the Marquess asserted: 'I desired the excellent Messer Pietro even before Your Eminence allowed me to have him and I shall do so still more after his departure, which will take place soon'.[220] The letter then went on to somewhat sarcastically add: 'I thank you infinitely for the gift you have made me [of Aretino]. It is a favour among the greatest that I have ever been granted'.[221] Finally, on 15 April, Federico wrote to Cardinal de'

Medici that Aretino had left Mantua and was making his way back to Florence.

Federico was genuinely sorry to see him go. He had already expressed his wish to the cardinal that Aretino should stay with him as long as possible, and had even offered the satirist a pension of 300 gold crowns a year to settle permanently in Mantua. It wasn't always easy to obtain a salaried position at Mantua's court, as Federico's old tutor Francesco Vigilio had found out late in life, when his appointment as tax superintendent was suddenly whipped away again as soon as Federico made a brief journey outside of Mantua. Aretino, however, was determined to seek a better living for himself elsewhere.

☉☾

I n the Autumn of 1523, a plague would strike Florence with such fury that the *lazzaretti*, those specialised 'plague hospitals' which looked after the contaminated, would have insufficient beds to accommodate all the victims and huts would be erected along the length of the city walls to house the overspill.[222] Fortunately, Aretino would evade the plague which, along with a second outbreak in 1527 would denude the city's population by as much as 20 percent in a mere matter of months[223]. Upon arrival at the Medici *palazzo*, he is reputed to have barged his way into Cardinal de' Medici's presence bellowing 'I AM PIETRO ARETINO!' This sort of bombastic theatricality was by now *de rigeur* with the writer. Unmoved, the Medici cardinal bloodlessly asked the impolite blackguard whether he had tired so soon of Mantuan court life? Unctuously, Aretino retorted that he had missed being in the cardinal's service and could not keep away. Mollified perhaps by Aretino's irresistible glamour, Giulio de' Medici was reluctant to offer his client up into the hands of Pope Adrian, which would almost certainly have entailed either imprisonment or worse. But neither, however, was he prepared to accept the risk of keeping Aretino close to his person, having worked long and hard to rebuild his bridges with the Dutch Pope. He therefore sidestepped the problem by sending Aretino to the camp of his young kinsman, Giovanni de' Medici.

Despite his affiliation with the Emperor Charles V, Pope Adrian VI had—unlike his predecessor Leo X, who had backed Charles—bravely attempted to maintain a position of neutrality between the countervailing forces of France and the Empire. Charles had meanwhile quartered his imperial troops in the papal cities of Parma and Piacenza and had stubbornly refused to move them. Furthermore, the Emperor was also claiming suzerainty over Modena and Reggio, both of which he was offering to sell to Alfonso d'Este of Ferrara to raise the much-needed funds with which to pay his army of occupation. In the face of this imperial hegemony there was little that Adrian's impoverished and pacifist papacy could do. On the other hand, the papacy was also hampered by King François who, amidst a blizzard of recriminatory insults, had withheld from Adrian VI all French Church tithes as punishment for the late Pope Leo's support for Charles. Consequently, the unmilitaristic Adrian had little use for the expertise of the *condottiere* Giovanni de' Medici, who was left more or less free to choose his own employer. Switching allegiance away from the Empire, he chose the French since his troops needed to be paid and French ducats were just as serviceable as German or Spanish coin. In his freedom of action he was still at heart a *condottiere* in the traditional fifteen-century mould.

According to the *Mémoires* of Martin du Bellay, Giovanni de' Medici rode into the French army's camp one afternoon to offer his services to the King.[224] In commemoration of his late cousin Pope Leo X, he had made his soldiers burnish their armour to a black 'mourning' finish and tear off black strips of cloth and attach them to their banners and their armour. For this, he soon acquired the *nom de guerre* of Giovanni delle Bande Nere or 'Giovanni of the Black Bands'. The light horsemen and well-drilled infantry of the *Bande Nere* now joined France in its bid to reconquer Milan which, ironically, Giovanni had helped capture just one year before for the Imperialist marionette Francesco II Sforza. However, when the French forces under the vicomte de Lautrec had advanced optimistically against Milan they were effectively rebuffed by Giovanni's former commander-in-chief, Prospero Colonna, who had made the city impregnable from attack. Worse had followed shortly afterwards when the French had suffered a crushing defeat at the little village of Bicocca just north of Milan at the hands of the imperial forces of Colonna and Francesco Sforza. Afterwards, the disenchanted French commander Lautrec left for Lyons to make his report to the King. His departure heralded a complete collapse of the French position in northern Italy.

Giovanni himself had retired on the city of Cremona together with Lautrec's brother, Thomas de Foix-Lescun, who now assumed overall command of the French army in Italy. From here, the pair mounted guerrilla-style attacks on both Colonna and Pescara who were stationed nearby. However, for three weeks the men of the *Bande Nere* remained unpaid by the French and it did not take long for their enthusiasm for French service to wane. It was around this time that Giovanni was called upon to go to the assistance of his half-sister, Bianca Riario, who—following the death of her husband Troilo I de' Rossi—was at that time acting as regent of the marquessate and county of San Secondo on behalf of her young son Pier Maria Rossi. Surrounded by hostile neighbours and numerous enemies which included relatives of her late husband Troilo, Giovanni had rode to her aid and occupied her enemies' lands and fortifications. Pier Maria, whose lands had been saved, was so impressed with Giovanni's skill at the profession of arms that he later joined the Black Bands himself.[225]

One year later, Giovanni found himself and his men still unemployed and consequently living an existence of good natured brigandage. Arriving at Giovanni's encampment at Reggio Emilia, Aretino found his rough Corsican and Italian troops in a festive mood for their commander had given them a night of liberty: 'Torches were blazing everywhere. The whores of the city had come to the camp in great numbers. Some of the troopers were leaping from their horses, having just returned from a foraging expedition. Bottles of wine, well cured hams, baskets of fruit and even bleating lambs were slung across their saddle-bows. Such provisions had cost them nothing, for they had robbed everyone for ten miles around'.[226]

Reggio Emilia was the seat of Azzo di Gaspare da Correggio, Count of Casalpò. His nickname was 'Contazzo' and Giovanni frequently used his lands as a base of operations for his troops. Aretino always referred to him as the *'buon Contazzo da Casal Po'* and later relished telling the story of how the Count had one day startled the exhausted *'condottiere* of letters' as he lay sleeping on the same bed as his wife, the 'Contessa Madrina', of whom Pietro had been taking care. After waking him up very loudly, *Contazzo* drolly invited the poet to undress and climb under the covers. On another occasion, Aretino recounted how the flirtatious lady Madrina had invited him to join her again in bed, because her husband had written to her from Milan 'that she should do for Aretino the same things she would do for him'.[227] *Il Gran Diavolo* himself was at this time preoccupied with his courtesans, one of whom was the incomparable Paola, about whom Aretino wrote: '*Insomma, Iddio permesse tal cosa acciò la gentile Paola che gli infiammò l'anima con le sue divine grazie, gloificasse la sua riguardata onestà.*' ('the good Paola, who inflamed him with her divine graces, could take glory from his respecting her chastity').[228]

Despite their hugely different callings, Aretino and Giovanni had–in Rome and during their time together at Reggio Emilia–found themselves, to use that indispensable Italian expression, *simpatico*. In fact their relationship was by now closer to that of brothers than mere friends. Aretino appreciated Giovanni's drive and vitality; Giovanni meanwhile reciprocated the attraction by glorying in Aretino's ready wit. Both men enjoyed the diverting pleasures of women, drinking and having adventures. Reggio Emilia was a supremely happy time for Aretino, a dissolute time which he would reminisce about in later life ('For although jests will not keep us from growing old and dying, it is true that thinking continually about the wild recklessness of youth makes time walk with a slow pace. Thus memory drives ruthlessly away the thought of the death sentence which every man carries in his head').[229] He devoted his days chasing a young woman named Laura, a cooks maid. When not engaged in this diverting pastime he amused himself watching the romantic antics of his friend. With suggestive *double entendre*, Aretino described his friend's activities thus: 'Did you ever see a more continent or timid lover than Giovanni? … Often enough Orlando wished to carry away Angelica. But our youthful great one never even thought of eloping with his lady-love. Owing to the grandeur of his soul he was able to quench the fire that was truly burning up his heart in festivals, banquets and jousts, when he shattered with lustful thrusts of his lance the very columns which supported her portico.'[230]

Aretino himself was no warrior. As he would later caution Battista Strozzi in 1537, 'you would not get any praise for killing and wounding people … you are not one of the men-in-armour boys.'[231] As an individual, he seemed to disapprove of the military life, or at least he acknowledged that he himself was unsuited to it. But the military camp in the late springtime nevertheless offered tremendous fellowship for a man like Aretino, of whom the celebrated Italian literary critic Francesco De Sanctis remarked: 'Among so many adventurers and *condottieri*, with whom Italy was infected, a vagabond race, without profession and in search of fortune at any cost, the prince, the model, was he'.[232] There were many colourful characters serving under Giovanni, men such as Lucantonio Cuppano and Pasquino Corso. The former, Lucantonio, had been with Giovanni since the very beginning when he had first taken up the profession of arms and rode out against the displaced Duke of Urbino with his 100 men-at-arms. He would ultimately become the *condottiere's* most trustworthy commander and Giovanni himself would refer to him as his '*occhio dritto*' (right eye).[233] Pasquino Corso, meanwhile, was the captain of the largest of the two Corsican companies incorporated into the Black Bands. Throughout his career, Giovanni continued to surround himself with these hardy and belligerent islanders. Corsican bodyguards had protected him during his contentious days in Rome and their national characteristics made them the best possible soldiers and guerrilla fighters.[234] As Gustave Flaubert would later write of them: 'One must not judge Corsican customs with our petty European ideas', by which Flaubert was implying that a Corsican bandit with his wandering 'life of laziness, pride and grandeur' was generally 'the most honest man in the region.'[235]

Despite the attractions of the camp, however, Aretino still did not neglect his art. When Pietro Aretino was nearby, few could escape his slurs unscathed. At Reggio Emilia, Aretino now turned his diamond sharp spotlight onto Francesco II Sforza who, thanks to the capable military reorganisation of his chancellor Girolamo Morone, had managed to organise the *Milanese* into a reasonably effective militia that Machiavelli himself would have been proud of. Following the imperial victory at Bicocca in April 1522, public support for Sforza remained appreciably high in Milan, although in more general terms the city had still remained divided between imperial supporters on the one hand and the vestiges of the city's French faction on the other. The humble *Milanese* observer and diarist Gianmarco Burigozzo recorded that on Advent Sunday in 1523 political tensions erupted into violence when a friar spoke out against the French during a sermon at the city's Duomo and was assaulted by a group of pro-French townspeople.[236] At this time the French forces of Lautrec were still encamped all along the Ticino river and continued to pose a credible threat to the city and its domestic stability.

Aretino went out of his way to pay tribute to Sforza's ineffectuality by citing the story of how, in his absence one day, the Duke's soldiers succeeded in capturing a solitary Frenchman and taking him prisoner back to Milan. 'The Duke sounded his trumpets and went round and round the city as if he had routed the whole French army. All the women rushed to the windows with lights in their hands and screamed "Victory! Victory!" Next morning, in the cathedral, a sermon was delivered celebrating the ducal prowess. A solemn and villainous procession, robed in white, was then organised and little Sforza paraded the streets in a triumphal chariot drawn by four German lancers. He had the prisoner in front of him with a sign reading VENI, VIDI, VICI...'[237] Aretino's lampoon was, for those with an eye for Milan's recent history, wholly defensible. The House of Sforza was by now a far cry from the days of its first Duke, Francesco I Sforza, who had been Francesco's grandfather. When, on 20 March 1450, Francesco I had made his triumphal *ingresso* to the newly-conquered Golden Ambrosian republic of Milan, he at least had declined to ride in the chariot which the vanquished and humbled signory had prepared specially for him. Sforza had modestly demurred, believing this to be a dignity more properly belonging to a monarch than a mere duke.

The closing months of Adrian VI's pontificate in 1523 witnessed a new French expedition under the command of Guillaume Gouffier, seigneur de Bonnivet and Admiral of France. An enigmatic figure, Bonnivet was a reputed libertine who had competed (reputedly with some success) with King François for the affections of the Comtesse de Châteaubriant. When Bonnivet had crossed the River Ticino into Italy with 36,000 infantry and over 2,000 mounted men-at-arms, Giovanni delle Bande Nere, turning weather vane, had wasted no time in seeking employment with the Imperialist side once again.

⊙☾

On 14 September 1523, whilst the plague raged unchecked in a stricken Florence, Pope Adrian VI fulfilled the unspoken wishes of the papal court by doing them the good deed of dying. In his brief pontificate he had presided over at least one appalling disaster, the fall of Rhodes and the expulsion of the Knights Hospitallers by the Sultan Süleyman the Magnificent. The least militaristic of popes, he had also allowed himself, shortly before his death, to be browbeaten into a new alliance with Charles V. This Pope gives few audiences, complained the Venetian ambassador, who also added that 'when he does consent to see anyone he says little except the same answer, we shall see'. Francesco Berni had stolen this morsel of censure when he raged: 'A papacy composed of compliment, / Debate, consideration, complaisance, / Of 'furthermore', 'then', 'but', 'yet', 'well', 'perchance', / 'Haply', and such like terms … / Of feet of lead, of tame neutrality… / To speak the truth, you will live to see / Pope Adrian sainted through this papacy'.[238] Somewhat unfairly, Pope Adrian VI would later be immortalised by the fiercely Protestant playwright Christopher Marlowe in *Doctor Faustus*. In the play, Pope Adrian is found disputing with a schismatic antipope named Bruno and invokes the principle of papal infallibility to prove that his arguments are correct versus those of a former pope who, one presumes, is equally 'infallible'. In short he was made to embody all those illogical and sophistical tendencies which Marlowe's by then well-entrenched, breakaway Protestant Church believed contaminated the Roman Catholic communion. It was unfair since Adrian himself had been a pious man who devoted more time in personal prayer than to running the affairs of the Church and compared to Pope Leo X he was a positively saintly individual.

Amongst the elated multitudes celebrating the Pope's demise was Pietro Aretino. Not to be outdone, 'the Chancellor of Maestro Pasquino' penned an epitaph to the late Pope in which he seized upon a common punning witticism of the time by quipping that Adrian had been made '*divino*', by which he meant—not that he was in any way celestially transfigured—but that he had become 'drunk' (*di vino*) on the strong Italian wine:

> Here lies poor Adrian, made by the wine divine.
> He was a Dutchman, a shipbuilder's son.
> To be a cardinal he surely won
> By teaching Charles the alphabet to whine.
> He was a pedant and he used to hold
> A school for janitors. This makes me weep.
> He was named shepherd, though himself a sheep,
> And he chased Soderini from his fold…[239]

Thirty-five cardinals went into seclusion in the Sistine Chapel on 1 October 1523 to elect the late Pope Adrian's successor. Cardinal Giulio de' Medici, with the backing of the Emperor and his Spanish cardinals, soon emerged as the frontrunner with Cardinal Pompeo Colonna trailing a close second. But when the French cardinals threatened to vote for Colonna's great rival Cardinal Franciotto Orsini it was time for Colonna to capitulate and make a compromise; he now swung his bloc of four votes behind Cardinal de' Medici and, with a majority of twenty-seven votes, the bastard son of Giuliano de' Medici inherited the sandals of the fisherman on 19 November 1523. He assumed the name Clement VII. There had already been a foreshadowing of his victory when, at the beginning of conclave, Cardinal de' Medici had drawn the partitioned cell which lay directly beneath Perugino's painting of *Christ Giving the Keys of heaven to Saint Peter*. Hardly a superstitious man, Pietro Aretino would not have cared about this auspice. The main thing was that his Medici patron was now the Supreme Pontiff and Vicar of Christ and therefore it was finally time for his long-awaited, triumphant return to Rome.

It would have been imprudent, not to mention fairly bad form, for Aretino to have merely shown up on the new Pope's doorstep uninvited. What he needed was an appropriate segue back into court favour; in other words he needed a suitable intermediary. Aretino identified such a person in the figure of the venerated noblewoman and poetess Vittoria Colonna. Vittoria was the wife of Fernando Francesco d'Ávalos, Marchese di Pescara, the celebrated *Napoletano* general who had been instrumental in such imperial victories as the battle of La Motta and the more recent triumph at Bicocca. Although Pescara himself had been betrothed to Vittoria at the tender age of six, his wife had had scant pleasure of his company since he was perpetually away at the wars. At the battle of Ravenna, however, he had been taken prisoner by the French and had to be ransomed back. To compensate for her husband's long periods of absence the neglected young wife had turned to poetry and letter-writing, maintaining an avid correspondence with many of the luminaries and intellectuals of the age including Pietro Bembo, Luigi Alamanni, Baldassare Castiglione and the historian Paolo Giovio, She was also on friendly terms with Ambrogio Politi, the fanatical Dominican heresy hunter known as *Il Caterino*, who would later accuse Michelangelo's *The Last Judgement* of being a sacrilegious work of art (despite his own amatory sensibilities Aretino, in a sudden and uncharacteristic attack of prudery, would strangely agree, dismissing the fresco as 'obscene and lascivious').[240]

Exemplary women of scholarship and learning were widely regarded by their cities and communities as a kind of civic asset. Local humanists sung their praises and when important international dignitaries paid visits or passed through such learned women were paraded out to give speeches or declaim the classics, something which reflected the exemplary nature of the community as a whole. Vittoria Colonna would have been viewed as one such 'exemplary' woman.[241] It was to Vittoria Colonna that Aretino now sent his greetings together with some epistolary sonnets in praise both of herself as well as the new papal *datarius* Gian Matteo Giberti. These verses were the *Canzone in Laude del Datario*, which reached Vittoria in Rome in February 1524.[242] As *datarius*, Giberti–the son of a *Genovese* sea captain–had been created bishop of Verona the year before by Pope Clement. As Giberti controlled all papal appointments, and much of the court's official channels of funding as well, he would be an important potential friend to have at court. Giberti was also known to be the leading papal Francophile at the Roman court. Nevertheless, ever eager to cover all possible bases, Aretino also wrote at the same time to Giberti's Saxon-born rival, Nicholas Schomberg, Archbishop of Capua. Imprudently, he included in his letter some versified invective aimed at the *datarius* designed to appeal to Schomberg's Germanic sense of humour. Aretino hoped to play both ends against the middle for his own benefit. In truth, neither man was an optimistic prospect for someone like Aretino to hope to cultivate. Giberti, on the one hand, was a reforming prig whilst Schomberg on the other was a former Dominican who had been inspired to enter the order after hearing the puritanical friar Girolamo Savonarola preach in Florence. But the two men detested each other and so Aretino was forced to adopt a strategic position somewhere between the two.

By this time the German reformation under the German friar Martin Luther was steadily gathering steam and papal administrators such as Giberti and Schomberg were desperately concerned to sanitize the image of the Vatican in response to steadily growing criticism from the breakaway Protestant states situated to the north. More worrying still, the Lutherans had shown themselves capable of employing the still relatively recent innovation of the printing press to further their cause. Printed tracts, pamphlets and woodcut prints were circulated avidly throughout the heretical German states. Just recently, in 1522, Martin Luther and Philippe Melanchthon had produced a polemical pamphlet featuring an engraving of a monstrous 'papal ass' standing in front of the Castel Sant'Angelo; the outrageous imagery was clearly intended to portray the Pope as the Antichrist, visualised in this case as a bestial chimera. As a result of these Lutheran attacks, the month of April 1524 had seen the creation of the Congregation of Divine Providence, later known as the 'Theatines', whose avowed objective was papal reform of the Holy See. Although Giberti was not himself a member, he facilitated the administrative permissions which its fellowship needed to establish themselves as a legitimate body within the Curia.[243] It was into this climate of moral transformation and reform, a milieu which the profane Aretino was poorly-equipped to navigate at the best of times, that he now hopefully returned. Brushing aside the inherent difficulties of his situation, he once more set foot in Rome in either late February or early March of 1524. He had been away from the city for little under two years.

By April 1524, Aretino had by and large found himself welcomed back to the bosom of the papal court. His earlier support for Pope Clement VII (then merely Cardinal Giulio de' Medici) in his 1521-22 bid for the papacy could not in the scheme of things go entirely unrewarded. Aretino's pasting of slanderous doggerel criticising Medici's rivals on that famous ancient statue Pasquino had, it was true, failed to forestall the election of the unpopular Dutchman Adrian VI; nevertheless, his propagandising efforts on Clement's behalf led the latter to gladly take him back 'with favour and appreciation'[244] This bankable goodwill on the Pope's part now paved the way for his successful return. He also persevered in seeking the goodwill of both Giberti and Schomberg. For the time being at least, Pasquino remained obligingly mute. A pasted verse on the statue's counterpart, Marforio, now posed the question: 'Marforio, what have you to say now that thy Pasquino, from the day this Pope was created, is become almost completely silent, nor any longer does Aretino resume his old ways, ... Pietro Aretino who now is in such favour...'[245]

Aretino also used his newfound influence at court to praise his recently-acquired patron Federico Gonzaga to the Pope. Around this time Aretino could feel that his fame was growing and he meant to use this to his advantage in advancing the fortunes of those who had supported him. The lord thanked him from Mantua most sincerely in a letter dated 13 November 1524. The momentary vaccum for novelty created by Aretino's departure was being filled at this time by the arrival of a singular character from a world far different from the satirist's, Antonio Pigafetta. Pigafetta had sailed with Ferdinand Magellan on his great circumnavigation of the globe and was now back in Italy writing his account of the arduous and dangerous expedition from which Magellan himself had failed to return. Initially Pigafetta had gone to Mantua in January 1523, where Federico had given him a commission to write the book. Castiglione had assisted him in gaining the Marquess's attention. He then drifted to Rome to continue the project, and perhaps pick up some additional papal sponsorship. However, by April 1524, his failure to garner any financial support led him to cast his eye back towards Mantua. On 2 February he had already written to Federico promising him the first copy of the book off the printing press and Pigafetta now applied to enter Mantuan service. This does not seem to have been granted however because by August he went to Venice.[246]

Had Aretino, meanwhile, played his cards differently at this point, he might well have secured for himself an unassailable place back in the bosom of Pope Clement VII's court. The new Pope owed him a not inconsiderable debt of gratitude after all. But in the year 1524-25, Aretino would blot his copybook so monumentally with a publication so unacceptable to Roman society that one can only wonder at his apparent lack of judgement. 1524 would be the scandalous summer of the *Sixteen Pleasures*.

CHAPTER 5

❦

The Sixteen Pleasures

> It was about the year 1525 that Giulio Romano, the most celebrated painter of his time, instigated by the Enemy of Mankind, invented twenty designs, whose subjects were so scandalously lewd, that they cannot be modestly named.
>
> The Reverend Charles Lamotte,
> *An Essay Upon Poetry and Painting, with Relation to the Sacred and profane History with an Appendix Concerning Obscenity in Writing and Painting* (1730).

The story of the most scandalous publication of the sixteenth-century and Pietro Aretino's subsequent brush with death at the hands of an assassin's dagger all began with a sprawling pleasure palace that Federico Gonzaga decided to build for himself on the outskirts of his city around the year 1524, the Palazzo Te.[247] Federico called in his court painter and architect Giulio Pippi, better known as Giulio Romano, who as his name indicates hailed originally from Rome. Romano had formerly been Raphael's principal student in Rome for close to a decade and had inherited the master's studio upon the latter's death in 1520. He had previously distinguished himself by painting the frescoes at Rome's celebrated Palazzo Medici which Raphael had designed for Pope Leo X in 1518.[248] The biographer Vasari describes Romano as being 'very pleasant in his conversation, gay, amiable, gracious, and supremely excellent in character'.[249] His artistry had made such a deep impression on Federico that he had urged his ambassador in Rome, Baldassare Castiglione, to prevail upon Romano to leave Rome and come to work for him in Mantua. The artist was enticed from the splendours of the eternal city for a trial visit and Federico had seduced him further with 'several canne of velvet, satin, and other kinds of silk and cloth wherewith to clothe himself', in addition to sending him 'a favourite horse of his own, called Luggieri' with which to make the journey north.[250] Romano's initial visit to Mantua was made in the year 1522 but two years later, liking what he had seen, he had permanently relocated to the city. The young artist now set his mind to his new patron's flagship commission, the construction of the suburban *palazzo* which Federico had decided to build as a fitting upgrade from his existing apartments at the Castello di San Giorgio.

At twenty-five, Romano was at the time just one year older than his master Federico and was seemingly able to translate his new patron's wishes effortlessly: 'no sooner had [his patron] opened his mouth to explain to him his conception than he had understood it and drawn it', wrote Vasari.[251] This former star pupil of the great Raphael now swept into the parochial little court of Mantua like a force of nature. Up until this time, Federico's court had depended upon the expertise of mostly local Mantuan artists supplemented by impresarios from other cities as and when needed. The Mantuan court style in the arts was still somewhat archaic, a relic more of the fifteenth-century than of the newly emerging Mannerist style of the sixteenth-century. Giulio Romano, about whom we really know relatively little on a personal level, did not so much reform or revolutionise Mantua's court artistry around this time as completely ignore it. But not everybody was as satisfied as the Marquess to have Romano at court as his towering ability soon eclipsed those court artists who were already comfortably established in Mantua. Two of them, Giovan Francesco Tura and Antonio da Pavia, would ultimately capitulate and go to work in Romano's new atelier whilst a third, Lorenzo Leonbruno, would grumble that his reduced position at court 'gnaws at and torments my heart and consumes my mind'.[252]

The *palazzo* that Romano was assigned to create was to be erected just outside Mantua's city walls on the periphery of a patch of marshland. Indeed, much of Mantua outside of the walls was marshy, a result of the city being surrounded on three sides by three large lakes. The site was an existing stable yard, one of Federico's chief pursuits being, as we have noted, equestrianism and hunting. Collecting superb horses was a pastime only the wealthy could partake in. Ercole I d'Este of Ferrara had owned 500 horses and in his palace he had even created a special ramp so that men on horseback could ride up to the *piano nobile* without having to dismount.[253] The Marquess of Mantua, according to Vasari, declared to his assembled architects and painters that he wished 'to have some sort of place arranged to which he might resort at times for dinner or supper, as a recreation'.[254] The building was conceived as a single-storey Roman house incorporating a vestibule and a large atrium, something which Romano had created earlier for the Villa Medici in Rome. Its style would be Mannerist; that is to say, a structure incorporating balanced classical proportions, graceful Palladian loggias and flat pilasters which would be combined with heavily rusticated masonry. Access to the villa would be via an archway to the square central courtyard. The main living area or *piano nobile* was to be on the ground floor of the building. Federico's married mistress Isabella Boschetti was to have her very own suite of apartments for when they 'hunted' together. Federico brought in a landscape gardener who had previously worked in the Vatican's Cortile del Belvedere and together they planned to plant grapevines and lemon trees in the villa's grounds.

Federico begged Michelangelo to contribute one of his own sculptures to beautify the project, hoping in vain for *the Battle of the Centaurs*, an early work which the artist swore that he would never part with.[255] Needless to say, the work was not forthcoming. Giulio Romano worked fast, throwing up the outer shell of the *palazzo* and then moving indoors to plaster the interiors so that work could then begin without delay on the painstaking business of covering every square inch of the halls and *saloni* in comprehensive, if not always the finest, cycles of thematic fresco work. The many frescoes at the Palazzo Te are typified by those which are to be found in one of its more famous rooms, the Sala dei Giganti or 'Hall of the Giants', whose decorations the Enlightenment thinker Francesco Algarotti disparagingly compared in 1744 to 'a magic lantern show' (*di lanterna magica*).[256] Ovid's version of the story of Zeus overcoming the giants with lightning bolts is given an exhausting mural treatment on both walls as well as on the ceiling dome. However the Sala dei Giganti itself would not be finished until six years later in 1530 and its completion would coincide with a visit by the Emperor Charles V to his loyal ally the lord of Mantua, whom he would create Duke.

From 1524-25, however, Giulio Romano and his fellow frescoists Benedetto Pagni and Rinaldo Mantovano[257] worked feverishly on other fresco cycles. These included a series of frescoes painted on the walls of the main banqueting hall which depicted stories from the tale of Cupid and Psyche as documented by the Roman writer Apuleius in his *Metamorphoses*. As one modern scholar, Courtney Quaintance, describes the general tenor of the cycle: 'On one wall, Cupid reclines with a languid Psyche, her buttocks and breasts turned invitingly towards the viewer. The daughter born from their union, Voluptas (Pleasure), peeks out from between her mother's legs.'[258] Other racy depictions include '..a voluptuous Venus [who] is shown bathing with a heroic Mars. In the next scene, Venus restrains Mars, who brandishes his sword as he pursues Adonis.'[259] The Palazzo Te also supposedly featured a series of sixteen erotic murals depicting male and female subjects engaged in various positions of copulation. Federico's marked preference for profane over sacred art is revealed by his instructions in May 1524 to Castiglione in Rome to source from Sebastiano del Piombo some paintings '*vaghe et belle da veder'* ('vague and beautiful to the eye') which were however not *'cose di sancti'* (about 'sanctified things/subjects').[260]

Erotic art was nothing exceptional in and of itself during the early-to-mid Renaissance period, nor indeed well into the *cinquecento*. The ancients had seemingly been obsessed with sex in all its myriad and pullulating forms and had decorated their villas, their bath houses and even their manufactured daily objects like drinking goblets with images and scenes of frantic copulation. When in Giulio Romano's era the art and literature of the Greeks and Romans had resurfaced a century or so earlier, erotica was one subject which genuinely came into its own in a society long enjoined to observe a repressed Christian morality which was perennially obsessed with sin, which—when all was said and done—usually equated with fornication. The art of the ancients had, by contrast, celebrated the endless priapism of the gods of the pagan pantheons: Isis impregnating herself on the golden phallus of Osiris, for example, or Bacchus, the god of wine, and his love of the abandoned princess Ariadne, or the many amorous conquests of Zeus which were often craftily attained through guile and disguise.

Neither were the Olympians' tastes always of the purely heterosexual variety either. In the guise of an eagle, Zeus had famously abducted the beautiful Trojan shepherd boy Ganymede, whose Latin name Catamitus would become synonymous with the passive partner in male homosexual sex. Aphrodite and her Roman equivalent Venus, meanwhile, was the divine embodiment of love and sexuality; indeed, the pages of ancient myth were rife with examples of goddesses who allowed themselves to be transported with wanton lust for the beautiful sons of men. And on it went. In addition to the great sexual deeds of the main members of the Greek/Roman pantheon, the pagan erotic tradition could also call upon a whole cast of supporting characters who were equally concupiscent: the Greek god Pan and his Roman counterpart Faunus, for example, both related to ever-popular fertility rites, not to mention the numberless satyrs, nymphs, fauns and dryads which swell the pages of the ancient classics.

Although the pagans had also at times taken a slightly more voyeuristic attitude by occasionally celebrating the copulation of ordinary mortals, during the Renaissance era the Christian artists generally confined themselves to depicting the sex acts of the gods. This was done from simple propriety. It set up a necessary mental barrier if you will because the sexual deeds of the gods, being the stuff of legend and far removed from the deeds of mere humans, could not be so easily reduced in the viewer's mind to simple titillation. Towards the end of the sixteenth-century, for instance, Annibale Carracci would deliver a series of intricate frescoes known as the *Loves of the Gods* for the Palazzo Farnese in Rome. Carracci's imagery would be lifted unashamedly from Ovid's *Metamorphoses* and would include pneumatic nudes in great profusion; but Carracci's work would neglect to manifest truly explicit sex acts, being content merely to insinuate the act of lovemaking. Where Giulio Romano revolutionised this convention was in reverting to the ancient practice of memorialising the coitus of common mortals in all their wonderful rutting glory.[261]

The Romano cycle of sixteen erotically-themed frescoes, correlating with the traditional significance of the number sixteen in classical sexual compendiums, would come to be known as *I Modi*, a direct translation of which might be 'The Ways' but which is perhaps served better by the name 'The Postures' or even more explicitly, 'The Positions'. In the unblushing mundaneness of the catalogue-like exposition of these various techniques of the *Ars amatoria*, Giulio Romano embraced the spirit of Ovid who wrote:

> The petite should ride horse (Andromache, Hector's Theban)
> Bride, was too tall for these games: no jockey she);
> If you're built like a fashion model, with willowy figure,
> Then kneel on the bed, your neck
> A little arched; the girl who has perfect legs and bosom
> Should lie sideways on, and make her lover stand.
> Don't blush to unbind your hair like some ecstatic maenad
> And tumble long tresses about
> Your up curved throat. If a childbirth's seamed your belly
> With wrinkles, then offer a rear
> Engagement, Parthian style.[262]

Romano would make no claim on classical mythology or pagan legend as a distancing insulator for his images. His murals would feature highly aroused men and women enjoying full penetrative sex whilst standing up, whilst lying down, lying side by side, with the man carrying the woman, with the woman on top, with the woman on top but facing in the reverse direction and so on and henceforth.[263]

☉☾

Giulio Romano was a prolific draftsman, leaving preparatory drawings for a wide range of projects encompassing architecture and the decorative arts, religious works, frescoes and stuccoes. One of the main reasons why he was able to so heavily influence the outgrowth of the Mannerist movement away from the High Renaissance style of his former master Raphael is due in large part to the sheer number of preparatory sketches that he generated, which were subsequently reproduced as engravings and widely disseminated throughout Italy and the rest of Europe. One of Romano's main collaborators and enablers in this process was the *Bolognese* engraver Marcantonio Raimondi. Raimondi at this time was aged around forty-two or forty-four (his precise date of birth remains unknown) and he had been making engravings since the age of twenty-six, beginning with copies of woodcuts by the likes of the renowned German painter and printmaker Albrecht Dürer. Indeed, so successful had Raimondi's copyist business become that poor Dürer was forced to seek legal redress from the government of Venice, who subsequently upheld that he was entitled to have protection for his famous monogram (which Raimondi had been shamelessly forging) but not his actual compositions.[264] It was one of the first high profile cases in history concerning questions of intellectual copyright.

Raimondi had also used Michelangelo's celebrated mural *The Battle of Cascina* on the wall of the Sala del Gran Consiglio in Florence as the basis for his engraving called *The Climbers*, which depicts three naked men, one seen from behind, clambering hurriedly onto a river-bank to don their armour as enemy soldiers emerge threateningly from the forest in the background. Painters and other artists were just beginning to shrug off their long-time image as 'mere artisans' and win recognition and acclaim for themselves within society at-large as individuals and as geniuses in their own right. Michelangelo and Leonardo da Vinci had been leading the charge in this cultural revolution but arguably the process had already begun in the early fifteenth-century in Florence. At the same time, however, the emergence of personal artistic virtuosity would now collide with the mass production technologies of printing and engraving. If the artist was now recognised as being the paramount author of his images, then it was just as easy for artistic 'pirates' such as Marcantonio Raimondi to swoop down, steal and mass-produce those same images for widespread distribution, often merely for cynical personal gain.[265]

Conversely, the relationship between artist and engraver was not always an illicit or unwelcome one. In the case of Giulio Romano and Marcantonio Raimondi the association appears to have been both consensual, reciprocal and indeed beneficial to both parties. Raimondi was freely able to sell his engraved reproductions of Romano's paintings with the artist's blessing, whilst the artist was able to popularise his accomplishments widely throughout Europe through Raimondi's engraving methods. It was a marriage of convenience between the two craftsmen which certainly already had its antecedent. In 1512, Raimondi had actively collaborated with Romano's former master Raphael in the engraving known as *The Massacre of the Innocents*. However, Romano only began his own association with Raimondi in the aftermath of Raphael's death 'lest he should seem to wish to compete with him' as Vasari hastens to clarify. The first collaboration between the two men was on 'two most beautiful battles of horsemen on plates of some size, and all the stories of Venus, Apollo, and Hyacinthus, which he had painted in the bathroom that is at the villa of Messer Baldassarre Turini da Pescia'.[266]

Raimondi did not work by viewing the finished paintings but instead worked mostly from the preparatory drawings and sketches from which artists worked up their final painted image. Romano produced an abundance of such sketches and cartoons and this became critical to the engraver's methodology. The engraving process itself was essentially a simple one which drew on the techniques already being used in intricate crafts like goldsmithing and Niello work. The image would first be sketched on a copper plate and then incised using a sharp chisel-like instrument called a burin, which came in several shapes such as flat, round, square, bevel or oval depending on the kind of incision required. When the plate was completed, printers ink would be forced into the grooves etched by the burin and the surface of the plate wiped clean. When the plate came into contact with paper in the printing press, the pressure would force the paper slightly into the grooves thus picking up the ink and creating a printed image.[267] Shadow and fill effects were created by the engravers through skilful use of the technique known as 'cross-hatching'.

Having first completed certain, more edifying, works including 'four stories of the Magdalene and the four Evangelists that are in the vaulting of the chapel of the Trinita', Raimondi now commenced his reproductions of Romano's erotic 'Postures'. Vasari seems to give the impression that Romano was the primary instigator of the project: 'Giulio Romano caused Marc' Antonio to engrave twenty plates showing all the various ways, attitudes, and positions in which licentious men have intercourse with women..'[268] Here there was no distancing through the opaque screen of mythology. The subjects of the erotic engravings went about their love making with explicit and businesslike purpose. In the words of B. J. Sokol: 'Their resolute faces, laborious postures and intense activities are given stunningly direct expression'.[269] Since Romano evidently made free with his preparatory drawings and Raimondi had sufficient access to the art to complete the sixteen reproductions, we can safely conclude that Romano gave his blessing to the reproduction and subsequent publication of *I Modi*. Back in Rome, when he heard about it, Aretino simply had to become involved in this cutting edge project which seemed to test the very limits of public acceptability for visual erotica.

Aretino proceeded to pen a poetic companion piece, a literary pendant, to the sixteen pornographic engravings entitled the *Sonetti lussuriosi sopra i XVI modi* ('Lustful sonnets on the Sixteen Postures'), sometimes also known as the *sonetti licenziosi*. Both the poems, written in the manner of *ekphraseis*,[270] and the engravings were published together in a single manuscript volume which became widely circulated throughout Europe at the time.[271] The 'positions' and their accompanying amatory lines echo a later disquisition by Aretino's fictional *puttana* Nanna in the *Dialogo*, in which she matter-of-factly itemises all the different sexual positions that her clients routinely ask her to perform: 'One likes his meat rare and another likes it well done, and they come up with the "horizontal shuffle", "legs in the air", "side-saddle", the "crane", the "tortoise", the "church steeple", the "relay", the "grazing sheep" and other postures stranger than the gestures of a mime'.[272] The sonnets/*ekphraseis* were intended to magnify the arousing effect of the explicit images by recreating the pillow talk of the couples depicted in the engravings in all their ecstatic and transgressive 'heat'.[273] In consequence, Aretino's imagery, often deliberately vulgar, left very little to the imagination:

> Open your thighs so that I can look straight
> At your beautiful *culo* and *potta* before my face-
> Paradisical *culo* to be enjoyed,
> *Potta* that melts hearts through the kidneys.

> While I contemplate these things,
> Suddenly I desire you, and I seem
> To myself more handsome than Narcissus
> In the Mirror that keeps my *cazzo* erect.

> Ah, shameless pair! I spy you
> On that mattress pulled down to the floor.
> You whore, you'd better defend yourself.
> I'm going to break a rib or two!

> Shit on you, syphilis-ridden hag!
> In order to enjoy this superb pleasure
> I'd throw myself into a well.

> I'm greedier
> For a noble *cazzo* than bees are for flowers.
> Even just looking at it tickles me.[274]

Although he could not possibly know it at the time, Pietro Aretino–poet/voyeur–had, through his involvement in giving poetic narrative voice to the *I Modi* cycle, stepped out of the pages of common literary doings and into the enduring pages of literary notoriety. His was an era which frowned upon sexual experimentation. The woman especially was required to simply lay on her back while the man went about his exertions with missionary zeal. Indeed, sexual intercourse with a woman in any position other than the church-endorsed 'missionary position' were technically considered to be 'instances of sodomy' that were on a par with [male] homosexual sex, sex with the ordained clergy, and acts of bestiality.[275] Raimondi and Aretino, perhaps for the first time in recent centuries, had drawn public attention to the existence of sexual acrobatics as a viable procreative option. It was quite possibly this sudden broadening of the boundaries of sexual possibility which was so incredibly subversive, and not the simple eroticism of the actual images themselves. Perhaps even Aretino failed to grasp this at the time, or indeed for some years afterwards. In 1537, he would thunder to his friend Battista Zatti that he rejected 'the hoggish custom that forbids the eyes what most delights them'.[276] But revealing those sights and embellishing them with poetry had not been his or Raimondi's gravest offence. What had most upset the authorities was the awakening of people to the possibility of sexual experimentation. The Church had laid down the officially mandated routines for copulation; anything which intruded on this prerogative was necessarily sinful. There was also the suspicion that if a woman enjoyed sex too much she actually ran the risk of transforming into a biological male, or at the very least a hermaphrodite. The Dominican philosopher Tommaso Campanella would caution women to use sex for strictly procreative reasons lest their self-arousal turn them into men.[277] Given the right conditions even the opposite could happen, if only in the humorous mind of someone like Boccaccio. In one of his tales the simpleton Calandrino is persuaded by his friends that he is pregnant; the fool goes home and assigns the blame to his wife for having insisted on 'making love on top'.[278]

The *Lustful Sonnets* also detracted from the traditional bias of classical humanist study in a highly indecorous and improper way. Simply put, they reminded a late Renaissance audience somewhat uncomfortably that the Greeks and Romans had been every bit as interested in fucking as in philosophy, grammar, logic or rhetoric. In ancient Greece, sodomitical rape was deemed a normal rite of passage for young men and women were routinely raped in order to assert patriarchal domination—both political and physical—over them. Rape in general, both male and female, was furthermore an integral aspect of many classical Greek myths.[279] The *Lustful Sonnets* also harkened uncomfortably back to some of the most degraded days of the Roman Empire, the activities of the Emperor Tiberius on the island of Capri being naturally one long-repressed classical narrative which sprang to mind. Tiberius was said by Suetonius to have brought with him to Capri a complete set of the notorious sex manuals written by the Greek poet-courtesan Elephantis. One of the poems of the ancient erotic poetic collection the *Priapeia* refers to this sex manual in terms which seem to vividly prefigure *I Modi*:

Obscenas rigido deo tabellas
dicans ex Elephantidos libellis
dat donum Lalage rogatque, temptes,
si pictas opus edat ad figuras.[280]

('Lalage dedicates a votive offering to the God of the erect penis, bringing shameless pictures from the books of Elephantis, and begs him to try and imitate with her the variety of intercourse of the figures in the illustrations'.) At Capri, Tiberius had enthusiastically set about establishing a kind of sexual research institute replete with love gardens, sexually explicit mosaics and half-naked young boys and girls kitted out like fauns and dryads. Aretino's comment to Zatti concerning 'hoggish customs' that forbid the eye satiation with their natural 'delights' was taken to its *reductio ad absurdum* in the case of Tiberius who, old and impotent, surrounded himself with every conceivable variety of erotic experimentation 'so that', according at least to Suetonius, 'the sight might excite his flagging desires' (*'ut aspectu deficientis libidines excitaret'*).[281]

Academic humanists were not, of course, wholly aloof from this awareness of classical smut. Aretino, a non-humanist who was deeply entangled in the world of politics and commerce, might write such lines as: 'Put a finger in my asshole, dear old man, and push the cock in little by little, lift up this leg, and make a good game...'[282] but the learned scholars of classical rhetoric and poetic forms also got together after hours to regale each other with similarly vulgar jokes and stories over *vino*. This humanist side-interest in smut, or else in general bodily functions, is quite evident for example in Poggio Bracciolini's scatalogical work the *Facetiae*. Renaissance humanists were fully aware of the erotica of Ovid, Sappho and Martial. The Socratic relationship embodied in Platonic Love meanwhile carried with it discomforting overtones of epheberasty, that is to say, physical love between older teachers and their youthful students which found its contemporary correlation in the sexual relationships between priests and their teenage seminarians. Scholars were by no means ignorant of these matters and often, privately, found them grounds for shared humour. It also had its slightly darker side in the development of justifications for unwholesome activities like pederasty 'on classical grounds'.

If Aretino had succeeded in opening the public's minds to the sheer variety of sex acts on offer, over and above those officially sanctioned by the Church, and if he brought classical Ovidian sexuality out of the 'closet' of private after-hours gatherings of humanist scholars, history would not judge him kindly for it. In subsequent centuries the *Sonetti lussuriosi* would become a *cause célèbre* for the prim exponents of censorship who exist in every era. In his *Sculptura, or, The History, and Art of Chalcography and Engraving in Copper* (1662), John Evelyn would recall 'those twenty vile designs of *Julio* cut by M. Antonio, and celebrated with the impure verses of Peter Aretino, which he so dishonour'd this excellent art'.[283] With appropriate rectitude, the Reverend Charles Lamotte, in *An Essay Upon Poetry and Painting, with Relation to the Sacred and profane History with an Appendix Concerning Obscenity in Writing and Painting* (1730), gives us his judgement of *I Modi*: 'It was about the year 1525 that Giulio Romano, the most celebrated painter of his time, instigated by the Enemy of Mankind, invented twenty designs, whose subjects were so scandalously lewd, that they cannot be modestly named'. During Aretino's own age, even his friend Giorgio Vasari disapproved of *I Modi*, describing them as '*disonestissimi*' or 'extremely dishonest/dishonourable'. Though it is worth remembering that Vasari always had a tendency to be rather selective about where he applied his praise or censure; in his *Vita* of Antonio da Correggio, for instance, he fulsomely praised the artist's painting of Leda enjoying pleasurable intercourse with Zeus in the form of a swan. The painting had been commissioned by Federico Gonzaga for Charles V and Vasari judged it as being 'a gift truly worthy of such a Prince'[284]

☉☾

When, sometime in 1524, probably around summer time, the sixteen erotic engravings of men and women engaging in sexual intercourse together with their accompanying Aretine sonnets began circulating in Rome, the result was absolutely incendiary. All of Rome was in total uproar at the indecency of the images on display. Disturbingly to many contemporary sensibilities, the engravings showed women not only passively giving pleasure but also wantonly seeking pleasure from the sexual act. In response to the discomforting reality that women too were sexual beings, many donned the cloak of prudishness. Vasari himself would later confess: 'I know not which was the greater, the offence to the eye from the drawings of Giulio, or the outrage to the ear from the words of Aretino'.[285] Having said this, Vasari does nevertheless subtly imply that *I Modi* found a ready audience amongst many enthusiastic cognoscenti of lewd art, which (he hints) included amongst its ranks numerous high-ranking clerics: '...*ne furono trovati di questi disegni in luoghi dove meno si sarebbe pensato*' ('these sheets were found in places where they were least expected').[286] He stops short of naming the furtive consumers explicitly as being priests but this was unquestionably what he was driving at.

With so many members of the public now talking about the risqué *I Modi* engravings, not to mention so many appreciative ecclesiastics being fully aware of the edition's existence, it did not take long for news of the lascivious pictures to reach the priggish ears of Pope Clement VII. The popular rumour doing the rounds at the time was that Clement himself was no saint. Many speculated that he was in fact the natural father of Alessandro de' Medici, who was born three years before Clement had been created a cardinal by his cousin Pope Leo X. Unlike Pope Alexander VI or Pope Julius II, however, two recent pontiffs who had actually sired children after having been created cardinals, it was suggested that Pope Clement had baulked at the idea of openly admitting his paternity of the half-Moorish Alessandro. As a result, so it was claimed, the child had been pawned off as the bastard of the late Lorenzo de' Medici, Duke of Urbino. Instead of cultivating the studied rascality of his jocular forebear Leo X, Pope Clement VII at least kept up the pretence of moral propriety whilst he was in office. (This, it must be said, was one of his good points, although he did show a marked tendency later on to favour the fortunes of Alessandro.) With the mood in Rome turning ugly, and sensing which way the wind was blowing, Giulio Romano now promptly fled back home to Mantua; however his engraver Raimondi was not quite so fortunate. Vasari details what happened next: 'This work was much censured by Pope Clement; and if, when it was published, Giulio [Romano] had not already left for Mantua, he would have been sharply punished for it by the anger of the Pope ... not only were they [copies of *I Modi*] prohibited, but Marc' Antonio was taken and thrown into prison'.

Prison in the early *cinquecento* was certainly no laughing matter. One of the most feared gaols in Rome at this time was the Torre dell'Annona, the dilapidated medieval tower in the rione of Ponte which was owned by the Orsini family and which served as Rome's notorious pontifical prison. It may well have been here that the unfortunate Marcantonio Raimondi now languished. For the *I Modi* manuscript's combination of verse and engravings to have been printed together at all would naturally have entailed an active collaboration between Raimondi and Aretino himself. However, for some strange reason, Aretino escaped being sent to prison alongside Raimondi. The explanation for Aretino's being let off was probably due quite simply to his 'special relationship' with Pope Clement VII. The fact of the matter was that, however much Aretino may have transgressed, he had after all served Clement's interests faithfully in the past and had always refrained from attacking him personally. Moreover, the instigator behind Raimondi's arrest was the lugubrious figure of Pope Clement's secretary and *datarius*, Gian Matteo Giberti. This was the papal functionary whose favour Aretino had earlier sought through verse and, once again, it is quite possible that his credit in Giberti's eyes was sufficient to allow him to escape imprisonment.

Twenty-nine years old at the time, Giberti was, as we have seen, engaged in a battle to clean up the image of the Church and the bearing of its priestly brethren in response to the scathing criticisms of Martin Luther's reformist followers in Germany, Austria, Hungary and the lands of the Czechs. The year that the *I Modi* engravings were published, Giberti was busy enforcing the decrees of the Fifth Lateran Council of 1515, which had sought to police matters such as clerical dress, comportment and the wearing of beards (Pope Clement VII himself would soon flout these rules by going hirsute, as Julius II had done before him). Because of this, the supervision and regulation of both sacred and profane art also fell within his remit and, as *datarius*, Giberti held the purse strings to papal financing for artists and other prospective clients. Formally at least, the order to prohibit the distribution of the *I Modi* prints and send Raimondi to prison would have come from the *maestro del sacro palazzo*, Silvestro Mazzolini da Prierio, the curial official who was accountable for all matters of orthodoxy and censorship. In reality, as head of the court appeals process, the *datarius* Giberti would have been responsible for denying Raimondi his appeal and keeping him imprisoned. It had all been a simple question of monumentally poor timing. With Giberti desperately trying to shore up the growing Lutheran schism within the Church, and especially concerned to address matters pertaining to morality, Raimondi had picked the worst possible moment to release his erotic prints on the scandalised Roman public.[287]

Whilst Aretino savoured his freedom, officials of the Curia were vigorously engaged in rounding up every copy of *I Modi* they could find and destroying them. They were industrious in this pursuit. So thorough and so systematic were the papal officials in their efforts, in fact, that only nine solitary fragments of *I Modi*, and those printed from later 'replacement plates' made by Raimondi's erstwhile collaborator Agostino Veneziano, survive to this day.[288] This nonetheless seems unusual in view of the work's wide distribution throughout the continent. For instance, in the later part of the century Pierre de Bourdeille, seigneur de Brantôme, reports that a '*bella e onesta donna*' ('beautiful and honest woman') that he knew kept, with her husband's tacit permission, an illustrated copy of the lewd Aretino manuscript. He also gossips that a Venetian printer named Bernardino Torresani sold in his Paris shop 'in less than a year more than fifty sets of the two volume Aretino to many men, married and unmarried, and also to some women'.[289] Therefore there must have been a great many copies of *I Modi* in private hands despite the prohibition and censorship of the Church. *I Modi* also had its imitators. *The Loves of the Gods* (1527), engraved by Gian Giacomo Caraglio after drawings by Perino del Vaga and Rosso Fiorentino, sought to cash in on the newly-discovered appetite for the pornographic genre. However, although such imitations were better preserved and more widely circulated than the Giulio-Marcantonio engravings, the latter still achieved the greatest literary prominence because of the unique textual contribution of Pietro Aretino.

Considerately, Aretino used his own liberty to lobby for the release of his friend Raimondi. He later writes, in a letter to Battista Zatti, that it was he who managed to secure Marcantonio's freedom.[290] Presumably he appealed to Pope Clement VII directly. Vasari does not corroborate this account as such but merely affirms that 'he [Raimondi] would have fared very badly if Cardinal de' Medici and Baccio Bandinelli [the sculptor, draughtsman and painter], who was then at Rome in the service of the Pope, had not obtained his release'. Raimondi, having been newly released, promptly went to work for his sponsor Baccio Bandinelli, creating a large engraved plate of a less sexual and altogether more edifying subject: 'a great number of nude figures engaged in roasting S. Laurence on the gridiron, which was held to be truly beautiful').[291]

In his own somewhat revisionist recollection of the *I Modi* affair, Aretino would later insinuate that he had not in fact been Raimondi's accomplice in the initial 1524 publishing but that his poems had been a *post facto* response to the engravings. According to Aretino's retelling of these events to Zatti, Raimondi published the engravings *first* and was thrown into gaol. Afterwards, when Aretino had obtained Raimondi's freedom, the desire came over him 'to see the figures which had caused the querulous followers of Giberti to exclaim that this good craftsman ought to be crucified'.[292] Journeying to Mantua to view the original murals by Giulio Romano, Aretino confesses: 'I was overcome by the spirit that caused Giulio Romano to design them. And since the poets and sculptors, ancient as well as modern, used to write and sculpture sometimes, to give vein to their genius, lascivious things, even as in Palazzo Chigi the Satyr of marble bears witness—the Satyr who is attempting to violate a boy, I amused myself by writing the sonnets that are seen beneath the figures, the wanton memory of which I dedicate by leave to the hypocrites, out of patience with their villainous judgment'.[293] Aretino then famously concludes his remarks to Zatti by affirming that 'The beasts are more free than we!' His lurid *poésie* was purportedly then appended to a later printing of *I Modi*, perhaps a 1525 or 1527 (woodcut) edition and that this was done from Aretino's usual motivation to want to thumb his nose at officially-sanctioned moral rectitude and test the bounds of censorship.

Aretino's revisionism and selective remembrance pose a problem for historians attempting to piece together the chain of causality in the whole *I Modi* affair. However, it is probably the case that his later account deliberately garbled the events so as to make him appear all the more bold in the eyes of his reading public (the letter to Zatti would be published in his collection of *Lettere*). To his credit, Aretino did use his influence with Pope Clement VII to have Raimondi released. However, in his 1537 letter to Zatti, Aretino would sincerely have us believe that, having engineered Raimondi's release from prison, he would then run the risk of imprisonment himself just in order to further the cause of 'free speech' and thumb his nose at the papal establishment. Given what we know of Aretino's instinct for self-preservation, the idea is essentially preposterous. Aretino was all for freedom of expression, admittedly, although the publication of *I Modi* in that year had perhaps been the worst possible timing and hence a huge error of judgement on his and Raimondi's part. But whether he was willing to run the risk of arrest and possible torture by rubbing salt into an already open wound is highly questionable. At heart Aretino, for all his bluster, was a physical coward. He may have accompanied Giovanni delle Bande Nere on campaign but battles of the bedside were the only martial activities which he felt secure in engaging in, endeavours where he could 'break a lance' as many times as he wished in the course of one night without actually placing his person in mortal jeopardy. We must therefore conclude that Aretino and Raimondi had collaborated together on *I Modi* from the very beginning and that Aretino had only evaded punishment thanks to his special relationship with the Pope.

Although Aretino's subsequent falling out with Giberti coincided with the *I Modi* débâcle there is evidence to suggest that, by the time of the work's publication, relations between the two men had already cooled considerably for other reasons. For one thing, by this time we find Aretino now writing in fulsome praise of the pro-French Giberti's sworn enemy the pro-Imperialist archbishop of Capua, Nicholas Schomberg.[294] The rift with Giberti may have been primarily caused by Aretino's authorship of the *Sonetti lussuriosi*, however the deterioration in the relationship between the two men can only have been exacerbated by Aretino's contravening of Giberti's authority by having appealed over Giberti's head to Pope Clement VII for clemency for Raimondi.

Prudently, Aretino fled to his hometown of Arezzo in August 1524. We have no record of what Aretino got up to in Arezzo. Quite probably he paid a visit to his relatives and stayed with them. He was by no means financially established yet, or even secure, but he was already famous throughout Italy due to his satirical, anti-papal *pasquinate*. After Arezzo he then rejoined his close friend, Giovanni delle Bande Nere, possibly at the town of Aulla in the Lunigiana.[295] This was a small mountaintop town that Giovanni had purchased, as opposed to conquered, and somewhere around this time he was busily employed with the construction of the Brunella Fortress.[296] Earlier that year he had, as usual, been covering himself in the usual military glory. On 30 April 1524, the Imperialist forces under Pescara (with whom Giovanni was now serving) had delivered a crushing defeat to Admiral Bonnivet and his Frenchmen as they attempted to ford the river Sesia near Romagnano. Amongst the fallen that day was the Chevalier de Bayard, Pierre Terrail, a knight worthy of an epic by Ariosto, who had participated in most of the major engagements of the Italian Wars and who was widely regarded as the foremost French knight in chivalry. Pope Clement VII had grudgingly congratulated his cousin on his role in this latest triumph and had assisted in the purchase of Aulla as Giovanni's reward for his role at the battle of Romagnano.

But although the arrival of his friend Aretino cheered him, the peaceful life of a lord of the *contado* sat uncomfortably with the restless warrior Giovanni, as well as with his men. Inevitably, it had not taken long for the unruly Corsicans of the Black Bands to become embroiled in petty quarrels with their neighbouring lords, chief amongst whom were the Malespini. At Aulla, Giovanni had begun—consciously or unconsciously—to build a power base which Pope Clement privately feared might eventually threaten nearby Florence's security. Regretting his earlier decision to make his relative a gift of Aulla, the Pope now arranged for the family of Cardinal Cybò to purchase the town together with its imposing new citadel for a huge sum. The ever-impecunious Giovanni took the offer and agreed to retire once more to his old stamping ground of Reggio Emilia pending the Pope's providing him with a new fief. The replacement lordship, when it came sometime later in 1525, would be the town of Fano on the Adriatic. For anyone with a basic grasp of geography it was obvious that this was be about as far as Pope Clement VII could possibly put Giovanni and the Black Bands without actually placing them across the waters in Hungary.

☉☾

That October of 1524, King François had taken advantage of a failed Imperialist summer invasion of southern France by counter-invading northern Italy at the head of his army. So swift and unopposed was his march that he entered Milan practically unopposed. Wearily, the *Milanese* watched as their city changed hands yet again for the umpteenth time. With Francesco Sforza and his Chancellor Girolamo Morone shut up inside Milan's fortified *castello*, François next moved rapidly to lay siege to the nearby imperial-held city of Pavia. France was back in the ascendant once more. By December, the Venetians would conclude a mutual non-aggression pact with François, while both sides conducted negotiations for a renewal of their alliance. The Duke of Ferrara had, at least for the moment, also fallen in line with the French king. During his days as a cardinal, Pope Clement VII had been the acknowledged leader of the pro-Imperial faction at the Roman court. Indeed, it had only been through Charles V's help in influencing the votes of the German and Spanish cardinals that Clement had secured his election. Now however, like Adrian VI before him, the new pope sought neutrality and held off from evincing support for either side.

Giovanni delle Bande Nere, however, had no such compunction. *Il mestiere delle armi* (the profession of arms) called inevitably for the taking of sides. This was something that Clement VII would always agonise over, but for the Medici *condottiere* one side was as good as the other provided that it paid, and that it paid well. He now arrived at the French siege lines at the head of four thousand well-drilled infantry and four hundred lances of his superb crack cavalry. François, hugely impressed with the cut of his Corsicans, embraced his arrival and rushed to offer *il Gran Diavolo* the highest honour that France could bestow, the Order of St. Michel. Politely, Giovanni refused the chivalrous investiture, explaining as delicately as he could that as an 'Italian' *condottiere* he was free to offer his sword in battle but not his undying fealty. Watching these events suspiciously from Rome, Pope Clement by now privately nursed a festering grudge against his far more dynamic cousin. The reasons for this were many.

On a purely personal basis, Giovanni was a fully legitimate scion of the House of Medici, albeit that house's cadet branch, and he was also the son of the great Caterina Sforza. Clement on the other hand had been born illegitimate because his father, Giuliano de' Medici, had spilled his seed into a woman of humble means named Fioretta Gorini, said by many to be from the poorer quarter of Florence known as the Borgo Pinti.[297] Clement was fully cognizant that, although of the younger branch, Giovanni was in reality the sole legitimate heir to the Medici name. Even more nauseating, Giovanni was by now earning the plaudits of all of Italy as its greatest living patriot and its potential liberator from the *preponderanza straniera*. This effectively gave him, as it were, a double claim upon the esteem of the Florentines. Giovanni's long-suffering wife Maria Salviati, who was by this time preoccupied raising their five-year-old son Cosimo, had recognised the Pope's animus for what it was and quietly pleaded with her reckless husband to stop putting himself in harm's way, something which ultimately only served Clement's interests. But her entreaties fell on deaf ears for Giovanni was not the kind of person who believed in leading his men from the rear. He was above all a soldier and fighting was his profession. Unlike his kinsman Pope Clement VII, there was very little guile about him.

A rumour doing the rounds in Florence at this time was that Giovanni intended to raise a *Bandiera di Ventura* or company of soldiers-of-fortune with which, like Cesare Borgia, he intended to wage war for personal profit whenever and wherever it suited him. But instead of instilling fear in the mind of Florence's Niccolò Machiavelli, this prospect had instead made Machiavelli realise that Giovanni of the Black Bands could well be the answer to Italy's problems. He wrote to his friend Francesco Guicciardini: 'This rumour set me thinking whether the popular voice had not suggested the right course. I believe everyone is of the opinion that in all Italy there is no leader the soldiers would more willingly follow than Giovanni de' Medici, nor any one of whom the Spaniards have a greater awe. Then everyone knows Il Signor Giovanni to be a man of undaunted courage, large ideas, and ready for any great enterprise. Would it not be well secretly to increase his power by giving him the command of as many horse and foot as can be supplied, so as to induce him to raise his banner?'[298] In recognition of this insight, Niccolò Machiavelli and Giovanni's friend Pietro Aretino were already by now both openly referring to Giovanni as 'Giovanni d'Italia'.

During the latter half of 1524, Aretino paid two consecutive visits to Giovanni's camp, both visits punctuated by a fleeting return to Rome which Aretino still longed for since his recent, albeit brief, self-imposed exile. It was probably on the initial visit that Aretino met his future royal sponsor François I. This was in the somewhat halcyon days prior to the later events of February 1525 when the French king was basking in his more or less bloodless conquest of Milan. Arriving in the French camp together with Giovanni and his troops, Aretino made a distinct impression on the King during this their first meeting; he had, it seems, an uncanny knack of being able to charm all the socially-exalted personages of the time. But the association was all too brief and Aretino would experience a foretaste of the French king's parsimoniousness in dispensing largesse. Aretino would later write of François: 'I adored him but never to get money from the stirring of his liberality is enough to cool the furnaces of Murano'.[299] (Murano of course was the suburb of Venice where the city's famous glass was produced.) Aretino could not linger with François, needing desperately to repair his reputation in Rome. By now it was already November and four months had elapsed. Aretino felt that the brouhaha had died down sufficiently for him to chance a permanent reappearance at court. The fact that he was now in good standing with the king of France, whose presence in Italy was backed by Giberti and the papacy, earned him a passport back to the eternal city.

Back in Rome, Aretino's first task was to make good his differences with Giberti by whatever means were available to him; this chiefly involved penning the *datarius* a sycophantic new sonnet.[300] Just for good measure, he had also written a pair of laudatory sonnets for his two patrons Federico Gonzaga and Pope Clement as well, the latter being published that same year under the title *Laude di Clemente VII*. The verses seemingly had the desired effect. Giberti, as yet perhaps unaware of the deprecating verses which had earlier been sent to Schomberg, had warmed once more to Aretino in spite of his past transgressions. Although a puritanical sort, Giberti was not above seduction by flattery and Aretino's recent sonnets in his praise seem therefore to have had the desired effect. As for the Pope, Aretino's relationship with Clement had not appeared to have suffered unduly. In November, Clement created the cobbler's son a Knight Hospitaller of the Order of Rhodes, thus technically elevating him to the nobility. Since their eviction from the island of Rhodes in 1522, Aretino's new brotherhood had effectively been rendered homeless. This situation lasted one year until 1523, when Clement made the Knights a gift of the city of Viterbo, roughly forty miles from Rome, as a temporary asylum (seven years later Charles V would grant them the island of Malta where they remain to this day). With the knighthood came a modest knight's pension, which temporarily alleviated Aretino's ever-precarious financial situation.

Miraculously, Aretino's rehabilitation in Rome now seemed to be complete. In September 1524, Giberti had taken into his service as secretary the scabrous poet/satirist Francesco Berni who was Aretino's potential competitor as the authentic voice of Messer Pasquino. Writing from the vantage of a resentful onlooker, Berni described Aretino's swagger at this time: 'He walks through Rome dressed like a duke. He takes part in all the wild doings of the lords. He pays his way with insults couched in tricked up words. He talks well, and he knows every libellous anecdote in the city. The Estes and the Gonzagas walk arm in arm with him, and listen to his prattle. He treats them with respect, and is haughty to everyone else. He lives on what they give him. His gifts as a satirist make people afraid of him, and he revels in hearing himself called a cynical, impudent slanderer. All that he needed was a fixed pension. He got one by dedicating to the Pope a second-rate poem.'[301] In Rome, although his alter-ego Pasquino remained for the time being silent, Aretino felt restored to that former situation to which he felt ideally suited–a man of importance whose words were sufficient to make popes and princes quail.

Berni's word portrait of the poet during 1524 conveys the newly-resurgent confidence that Aretino must have been experiencing at this time. Pietro Aretino, the newly-minted Knight of Rhodes, now exercised his newfound voice as self-appointed intermediary and arbitrator between kings. That year he published his *Esortazione de la pace tra l'Imperatore e il Re di Francia*. The piece was a *canzone d'occasione*, basically a carnival song, urging Charles and François to make peace with each other, something which the latter was palpably unlikely to do while he was in such a strong position holding Milan and laying siege to Lombardy's second most important city, Pavia.

With this newfound self-assurance came a return of the old Aretino, capable of rounding on his former patrons and protectors if they displeased him in any way. Federico Gonzaga, all too often the butt of Aretino's private jokes for his aristocratic self-indulgence and excess, could expect to feel the potential sting of his client's words if the latter did not get his way. One anecdote is worth citing as evidence of Aretino's tendency to turn scorpion on those who had once offered him a roof and an audience. Raphael had, in 1517, completed a portrait of Pope Leo X flanked by his two relatives Cardinal Giulo de' Medici and Cardinal Luigi de' Rossi. Federico longed to own this famous painting and he sent word to Pope Clement through his representative and cousin Francesco Gonzaga begging the pontiff to part with it. Clement replied, through Pietro Aretino, that he would gladly send it to him. After some weeks the painting still had not arrived on Mantua, however, and Federico sent word once more through Francesco inquiring after its whereabouts. Aretino apologised on behalf of the Pope, informing Francesco that the delay was caused by the fact that Clement—not wishing to be parted from the likeness of his beloved relative—had commissioned 'a certain excellent painter in Florence' to make a copy for him. This painter was Andrea del Sarto, whom Ottaviano de' Medici had engaged on behalf of his relative the Pope. Aretino meanwhile promised to send Federico an ode which he had lately composed in his honour.

The guileless Federico Gonzaga was overjoyed at hearing that Raphael's painting would soon be in his possession and remained completely oblivious of the Pope's intention to fraudulently pass him del Sarto's canvas whilst retaining Raphael's original in his safe-keeping.[302] Flattered at the same time by Aretino's attentions, Gonzaga instructed Francesco to accede to the poet's demand to be sent 'two pairs of shirts worked with gold in the style now in use and two other pairs of shirts worked in silk, together with two golden caps'.[303] Some weeks passed, however, and the promised gifts of the gold and silk shirts failed to arrive. Through Francesco, Aretino sent word that more gifts would be forthcoming from Rome in addition to Raphael's as yet undelivered painting: a full-size plaster replica of the *Laocoön* together some more Aretine poetry in praise of the papal *datarius*. But Aretino's gesture failed to have the desired effect of making the longed-for shirts materialise in

Rome. Several days later Aretino burst into Francesco Gonzaga's apartments, blaspheming that he would deny God's very existence if the shirts were further withheld from him. Francesco managed somehow to mollify the furious poet, persuading him that the oversight was not the Marquess's but some court servant's and Aretino then departed, still in high dudgeon. Soon afterwards, however, Federico received a letter from his cousin in Rome notifying him that Aretino 'does not want to make peace, since the Carnival has passed without his having them [the shirts]. Your Excellency knows his tongue. Therefore I will say no more.'[304] Federico knew only too well the harm that Aretino's pen might well do him if he unleashed his dissatisfaction publicly. Federico would have been aware how much dirt on him the writer had managed to accumulate from their days carousing and womanising in Mantua. He acted swiftly, writing to Francesco that he enclosed the promised shirts ('four shirts worked in gold and four of silk–twice the number, therefore, which the Scourge has demanded') and assigning the blame to 'The Holy sisters [who] will not work except at their own hours and convenience'.[305]

Aretino's response was not overly effusive, considering it *infra dignitatem* to grovel before sovereign power; he merely replied back with the following somewhat cool and non-committal lines: 'I have had the ancient *Laocoön* of the Belvedere copied in stucco ... in the opinion of the Pope and of all the sculptors in Rome nothing was ever better copied. It was done by a certain Jacopo Sansovino, and your painter Master Giulio Romano can tell you who he is ... it took him all the winter and the Pope often went to the Belvedere to watch him at work ... I will send it to you within ten days, accompanied by many other new things ... The Pope told me yesterday that the painting by Raphael is almost copied. He will send it to Your Excellency soon.' Aretino added, with a final menacing twist in the tail, 'They are going to celebrate Master Pasquino in my name this year and he will make a fortune. God protect every faithful Christian from the evil tongues of poets!'[306] It was not Aretino's way to be obsequious, except in the occasional ode, and only if he was being well paid. His adamant refusal to play the role of grovelling client seemed wilful but it was also original. Even in these early years, he refused to adhere to society's well-rehearsed rules. Increasingly, the great men of Italy and later Europe would beat a path to *his* door, and not the other way round. Aretino was learning his trade, feeling his way as he went. What he learned concerning simple human psychology from his dealings with Federico Gonzaga would stand him in good stead in the years to come.

CHAPTER 6

꙰

Daggers of the Datarius

Well, gang, if this story has been a long one, I'll remind you that here in Rome everything tends to drag on a bit; and if you don't like it, that's fine by me, because I didn't ask you to come in the first place. Anyway, if you wait there until next year, you'll hear an even sillier story. But if you can't wait that long, I'll see you all at Ponte Sisto.

Valerio's lines in *La Cortigiana* (1534),
Act V, Scene 22.

Pope Clement VII was unable to remain neutral in the ongoing standoff between Charles V and François I and before long the latter forced Clement's hand with an audacious play. John Stewart, the exiled Scots Duke of Albany, was sent by François with one third of the French army across the Apennines and down into Tuscany. His orders were to recruit fresh new men on the march and that necessarily included Florentines as well. The gambit was a thinly-veiled threat against Clement's home city-state of Florence which the Medici once more ruled, at least for the time being. Swayed by an overriding concern for Florence's safety the Pope capitulated. Reluctantly, he signed a secret treaty with François on 12 December 1524. Having signed the treaty document he blustered to his court officials: 'What would you have me do? The French are strong, and I cannot resist them. The imperial army needs money, and I have none to give. The Emperor is far off and cannot help me.'[307] If Clement's earlier stance of neutrality had irritated the Emperor Charles, the Pope's defection to France now infuriated him. He swore vengeance on Rome.

To the north, meanwhile, the French army of King François was dug in around the city of Pavia. To the north of the city was a great hunting park which the dukes of Milan had built for their leisure and enjoyment and it was here, at the ducal hunting lodge known as the Castello di Mirabello, that the king of France made his campaign headquarters. All throughout the winter, as the ground hardened and ice began to form on the many streams and rivulets which criss-crossed the game park, the investing troops settled into their miserable existence in the trenches. Their only consolation was that they were well-supplied with provisions from the surrounding countryside, whilst by contrast Pavia's occupants ate through their siege provisions and slowly began to starve. Commanding Pavia's garrison was the gout-ridden yet valiant forty-four-year-old Don Antonio de Leyva, by now celebrated for his brave habit of being carried into the thick of battle on a sedan chair. Leyva, who hailed originally from Spanish Navarre, had fought under Pescara in the recent botched Provence campaign and was one of Charles V's best, though perhaps least-recognised and most under-appreciated, senior captains.

From time to time, the boredom of the besieging troops was alleviated by the appearance on the walls of a *Pavese* noblewoman, the Marchesa Ippolita Fioramonda. She would appear in plain sight of the besieging army, doing the rounds of the battlements, hurling scorn at the French and encouraging the imperial defenders with kind and solicitous words. When making her rounds, she always wore a heavenly blue satin dress sprinkled with moths stitched in gold. This was intended as a metaphor for her 'fatal attraction' and was meant to dissuade unwanted potential suitors who hovered around her like moths around a flame. Aretino for one would have appreciated her show of virginal aloofness before a veritable army of lascivious would-be French rapists. Baldassare Castiglione was one of her greatest admirers. He wrote to her encouragingly from overseas: 'your ladyship has shown to the entire world, in addition to her other qualities, to be a valiant lady in arms, and not only beautiful, but still bellicose'.[308] Boccaccio, in his *De mulieribus claris* ('On Famous Women') had argued that remarkable women should be celebrated when and wherever they were encountered because the limitations of their sex made their achievements all the more admirable. Out of courtly respect, therefore, the French troops were forbidden to fire upon the Marchesa Ippolita whenever she made her regular appearances at the walls for the purpose of taunting them.

French-Papal relations improved slightly as the weeks wore on. Although he had essentially been dragooned into his alliance with France, discreetly Pope Clement was pleased to see a balance of power restored to the Italian peninsula. It was not healthy for Charles V to rule the roost without any check or balance to his growing power in Italy. Furthermore, when Charles had controlled Lombardy his constant demands for the cities of the plain to finance his army of occupation had been voracious. Furthermore, the Medici (and also Florence) were the traditional allies of the French; indeed, Louis XI of France had earlier granted the Medici the considerable honour of being allowed to emblazon one of the Medici *Palle* on the family's coat of arms with the royal *fleur-de-lis* of the House of Valois. If Leo X's pro-Imperialist interlude had been a deviation from this traditional Franco-Florentine alignment, then Clement VII was determined to leverage French military prowess to constrain the growing power of Spain and Germany on the peninsula. The Spaniards and their country cousins the *Napoletani* had never been especially liked in Italy if the truth be told. To the Italians they seemed extremely uncouth, not to mention rapacious (had not Pope Alexander VI been especially demonstrative of their rapacity?) The *compañías* of Spaniards were comprised of rough, simple fellows who seldom bathed and who enjoyed the pungent delights of chopped garlic and onions soused in vinegar. Many of their most talented generals also tended to be Spanish chauvinists who regarded Italy as nothing more than a resource to be pillaged, just as the *conquistadores* were at this time mercilessly conquering and plundering the Americas. The Spaniards, for all their coarseness, nevertheless ranked amongst the best soldiers of their era, but most ordinary Italians longed to see them expunged from Italy. Sadly, however, for the long-suffering Italians this was not to be.

As so often occurred during the course of this protracted and confusing series of wars, disaster now struck and the French and papal cause would experience a sudden and catastrophic reversal of fortune. On 24 February 1525, all of Europe gasped in bemused astonishment as an imperial relief force advanced on Pavia and defeated the mighty French army within the grounds of the ducal game park where the French monarch had made his winter camp. The terrain of the park had proven injurious to the customary French tactic of massed heavy cavalry charges. At the same time, swarms of imperial pike men and harquebusiers had converged on the French king's position. An unhorsed King François had watched his loyal Swiss bodyguard cut down one-by-one until, unprotected, he was surrounded and taken prisoner by the imperial mercenary *landsknechts*.[309] Serendipitously, the defeat had come on the same day as the Emperor Charles V's birthday. Just days before, Giovanni delle Bande Nere had been struck in the leg by a harquebus ball and had been removed from the field, preventing him from participating in the battle. He was subsequently sent to Piacenza to recuperate from the surgery on his leg. Pope Clement VII was disconsolate; François had seemed at the top of his game, so how could he have lost to Charles's poorly-paid Spanish mercenaries? It was widely speculated at the time that, had Giovanni of the Black Bands been present that day at Pavia, the French would never have lost the engagement. The question is moot, something for military historians to agonise over, for we can never really know whether his presence might have tipped the balance. Meanwhile, a miserable and defeated King François sat under imperial confinement and scribbled a letter to his mother, Louise of Savoy, which contained the iconic words: 'To inform you of how my ill-fortune is proceeding, all is lost to me save honour and life, which remain safe'.[310]

Despite his intense concern for his wounded friend Giovanni de' Medici, Aretino busied himself with composing a consoling letter to the King of France. It remains, even today, one of the most vivid expositions of the exultation of triumphant victory contrasted with the drawbacks and vagaries of blind *Fortuna*. Full of rich philosophical advice and seeking to place the vicissitudes of life into a wider, more stoical perspective, Aretino wrote to François: 'Although your loss has been another man's gain, I do not know, most Christian Sire, who deserves the greatest congratulations, the conquered or the conqueror. For after the treacherous trick played upon you by Fate, you, François, can now free your mind from any doubt that she can take a king prisoner, whereas Charles, as he thinks over the prize which Chance has given him, must find his mind a prey to the realisation that she could do the same thing to an Emperor'.[311] Warming to his theme, Aretino then urges the King not to curse Lady Luck, who cannot do any more harm, having already done her worst. Rather, she 'has made all your good qualities shine forth resplendently'.[312] Hitting his stride, Aretino continues, waxing even more philosophical: 'Victory is the downfall of the man who wins it and the salvation of the loser, for the conqueror, made blind with insolence and pride, forgets God and remembers himself, but the vanquished, his mind lighted with modesty and humility, forgets himself and thinks about the Deity ... And let whatever misfortune you have found to be a bridle which keeps you from never even contemplating, not to say essaying any rash adventure. Then, in truth, a day will come when remembering your present plight will be both sweet and useful to you.'[313] These comforting words were written on 24 April 1525. They might seem strange and somewhat ironic in light of Aretino's personal tribulations the year before. The reference to 'rash thoughts and enterprises undertaken without due prudence' could so easily have been applied to the recklessness of publishing *I Modi* and the lascivious sonnets.

In the aftermath of the battle of Pavia, Pope Clement's heart grew even more hardened towards his former ally Charles V and, despite the dangers, he was determined to continue supporting the French at all costs, even though François himself was now held captive. However, the Pope's *gonfalonier* and captain-general, Federico Gonzaga, would be of little use to him in this. The pro-Imperialist marquess of Mantua was still heavily preoccupied with the designing and building of his Palazzo Te, whose erotic decorations had precipitated so many difficulties for Aretino, Romano and Raimondi. Many now openly criticised the Pope for his tendency to continually change his mind and shift his strategic allegiances at the drop of a hat. Francesco Berni would later lampoon Clement's by now famous tergiversations in four lines of *poesie bernesche*:

Un papato composto di rispetti,
Di considerazioni e di discordi,
Di piu, di poi, di ma, di si, di forsi,
Di pur, di assai parole senze affetti...[314]

('A papacy made up of respects, / Of considerations and of talk, / Of yets, and then, of buts and ifs and maybes, / Of words without end that have no effect at all.')[315] Rome was meanwhile cast into a mild case of shock and panic. After a lengthy interval of obedient silence, that traditional outlet for plebeian criticism and discontent, the statue of Pasquino, awoke once more and began voicing its discontent with the political status quo.

Following the tragedy of Pavia, Aretino's quill hand began to twitch with epigrammatic zeal. His comeback had been astonishing by anyone's reckoning. Despite his narrow escape over the whole *I Modi* imbroglio he was once more in the good graces of both the Pope and his *datarius*; he had also been made a pensioned Knight of Rhodes. Any sensible man would perhaps have rejoiced in his blessings but not Aretino, whose temperament was seemingly incapable of letting sleeping dogs lie. If he had had tasted humility, that same humility which he had urged on François, he might well have remained in Rome for the rest of his life and subsequent history may well have been quite different. But Aretino was incorrigible, Pasquino/Aretino had to speak out again! Even if he could not criticise the Pope directly he could still find fault with Clement's two principal advisors, the pro-French *datarius* Giberti and the pro-Imperialist advisor Nicholas Schomberg, who was now urging reconciliation with Charles V. Aretino's chief quarry, however, was the hapless *datarius*. Although he admired the French king and commiserated with him, Aretino saw absolutely no contradiction in criticising Giberti as being the chief architect of the Pope's calamitous pro-French policy. This notwithstanding the fact that his friend Giovanni de' Medici had fought on the French side. He also continued to bear the *datarius* a grudge for having censored *I Modi* and the *Sonetti lussuriosi* and having burned all the copies which the Church had collected. To Aretino, men like Giberti were parsimonious hypocrites; they were perfectly aware that all sorts of erotic images routinely adorned the halls and *saloni* of the extremely well-to-do, but when erotica was made accessible to the lumpen masses these dissemblers protested that such images were 'immoral and corrupting'.[316]

Aretino now launched a series of exquisite written attacks on this detestable clerical élitist through his old friend Pasquino. These began on

Messer Pasquino's Day in April and lasted right through till May and June of 1525. Aretino was back on form and enjoying himself immensely in his natural satirical element. In addition to these brand new *pasquinate* he also took pains to modify some of the *Sonetti lussuriosi* to more closely reflect current political events. Sonnet number four in particular, entitled *Light Arms Practice*, was re-written to reflect a 'royal French' theme:

Then, light arms practice, dear! Yet not so light!
You must learn to hold a broadsword in your hand –
I need not tell you more; you'll understand:
We'll leave the rest to instinct and the night.
But there's one lesson which you must not slight,
To be a member of our valiant band:
A lesson that is known throughout the land,
And one that even horses can recite.
I'll help you learn it, though I know it's hard,
And, dear, you must not let it slip away,
For you're a backward pupil if you do!
To lances, then! For I would not retard
Your progress or the pleasure of the fray:
The Queen of France tonight might envy you.[317]

Giberti alone was the recipient of this fresh Aretine onslaught; Giberti, who glowered at *I Modi* and the *Sonetti lussuriosi*, which had overstepped all bounds of decorum: a volume in which, to coin one modern critic's words: 'The men all have over-sized penises; the women hairless groins and prominent vulvas' and where 'Aretino's accompanying poems describe the action with lines such as "Let's fuck, my love, let's fuck quickly"'.[318] Giberti, for his part, had decided that enough was enough. Aretino had already escaped with his life and liberty once but instead of wisely adopting a low profile he was once again cocking a snook at papal authority. Not only that but, astonishingly, he was actually going on the offensive. In his own mind, Gian Matteo had decided what needed to be done. Yet there was a time to wait and a time to act. Several more weeks would elapse before the *datarius* would make his move.

☉☽

Pietro Aretino would later pen this well-known epigram: 'Angry men are blind and foolish, for reason at such time takes flight and in her absence; wrath plunders all the riches of the intellect, while the judgement remains the prisoner of its own pride'. In the late summer of 1525, Aretino would become all-too acquainted with the truth of his own maxim for he would be placed at the mercy of one whose reason had 'taken flight'. Yet it had been his own insufferable arrogance which would lead him down this path, and the fatal conviction that he, Pietro Aretino, the 'Scourge', was virtually untouchable. As events would subsequently prove, he was anything but.

On the night of 28 July 1525, as the satirist was riding home that evening through the dark streets of Trastevere, he was set upon by one of Gian Matteo Giberti's creatures, a ruffian named Achille della Volta, who was joined in the assault by his brother Marcantonio. In the scuffle which ensued in the dimly-lit streets, the two assailants inflicted several knife wounds on Aretino's person, including a fairly serious laceration to the breast (which the writer feared at the time would prove fatal) and a particularly bad injury to the right hand which would leave him permanently lame in that limb. 'Five wounds in the breast and right hand', cites one later source.[319] Unlike Giovanni delle Bande Nere, Aretino was no fighter and it was only through sheer luck, brute strength and force of will that he was able to survive the assault and make his escape from the clutches of the della Volta brothers.

The following morning the news of this vicious attack on so well-known a public figure spread like wildfire throughout the entire city. The Romans were hardly a stupid people and speculation was rife that, since della Volta was a known associate of Giberti's, it had in fact been the *datarius* himself who was behind the assassination attempt. All echelons of society were soon acquainted with the scandalous incident and word reached Aretino's erstwhile patron, Federico Gonzaga. The marquess of Mantua wrote to the Florentine diplomat Francesco Guicciardini expressing his opinion that 'the cause of the quarrel is ugly and known to everyone'.[320] The allegation that Pope Clement's *datarius* was implicated in such an unseemly assassination attempt required an immediate rebuttal. Giberti asked his secretary, the Tuscan poet/satirist Francesco Berni, to concoct and publish a cover story. Berni, predictably, sought to deflect the responsibility for the attack onto Aretino himself. According to Berni's explanation the attack had been a simple unpremeditated crime of passion. Following his usual amoral ways, Aretino had been in the process of seducing Giberti's cook and had written her a sonnet, claimed Berni, however Achille della Volta was equally enamoured of the woman and when he came across Aretino's sonnet he flew into a rage: '..finding him [Aretino] alone, he gave him with a dagger five wounds in the chest, and even crippled his hands'.[321]

Giberti himself had pulled out all the stops to cast himself in a sympathetic light ever since the night of the attack. Not only had he instructed Berni to put out the cover story but he had also ordered della Volta to pay a very public call on Aretino at his house not long after the attack. Since a potential murderer with malice aforethought would never do such a thing, therefore his move was intended to convey the impression that the assailant had acted rashly that night, attacking Aretino on the spur of the moment, but was nonetheless experiencing genuine Christian remorse for his actions.[322] The culprit della Volta did not get off completely scot free and a legal case seems to have been brought against both Achille and Marcantonio della Volta for attempted murder, although for some reason this only came to fruition many years later in 1542 when Aretino was no longer living in Rome.[323] Berni's account probably fooled nobody at the time and Giberti certainly lacked no end of motive for wanting to see Aretino put out of the way. When Aretino's friend Federico Gonzaga wrote to Gian Matteo himself commenting 'although one might think you have not done what you have done against him without cause', Giberti's disingenuous reply came back: 'It is true that what was done was without my orders, without my consent and without my knowledge', a remark which seems to try too hard in its protestation of innocence, and at least acknowledges that both men implicitly understand the specific topic under discussion, namely a *premeditated* assassination attempt.[324] Least fooled of all was Aretino himself. For the rest of his life he would maintain that the *datarius* had instigated the attack and in a letter composed many years after the event (*Lettere*, VI, 8) he is still to be found declaring: 'Shame on the Gibertis of the Roman Court who would have been my executioners'.

It would take Aretino three months to heal his wounds and recover and until then he was in no fit condition to leave Rome. He was also arguably still in some considerable danger from his powerful ecclesiastical enemy. Meanwhile, Giberti's pretence of innocence annoyed Aretino intensely. Having little to lose he now publicly named the *datarius* as the instigator of the attack. At the same time, Aretino also began to nurse a grudge against Pope Clement VII for declining to arbitrate the dispute or become involved in any way. Caught in the middle of a quarrel between two allies Clement reacted in his usual characteristic manner, which was to do absolutely nothing. In Aretino's eyes the Pope was refusing to sully his hands by intervening in (what he saw as) an ignoble quarrel. Given all that Aretino had done for Clement in the past, his inactivity was considerable cause for offence and disappointment.

Meanwhile, Aretino's public denunciation of Giberti had caused the *datarius* to lash out at his accuser; at Giberti's likely instruction Francesco Berni now came up with a wretched piece of doggerel calumniating Aretino in the crudest possible terms. In Berni's sonnet, the infamous XVIII. *Sonetti contro a Pietro Aretino*, the satirist is described–amongst other things–as being *'ignorante ed arrogante'* and as *'prosuntuoso, porco, mostro infame'* ('conceited, a pig, an infamous monster').[325] Not unsurprisingly, this scabrous sonnet succeeded in ruining whatever vestigial friendship Berni and Aretino may have had up until that point. Besides, Berni himself was too similar in character to the man he was slandering for the pair to be able to coexist peacefully in a hothouse city like Rome. Like Aretino himself, Berni had lampooned the Dutch Pope Adrian VI and had also been obliged to leave Rome for the duration. Like Aretino, he too was a sybarite and an Epicurean who found his obligations to his social betters an inconvenient impediment to his enjoyment of life. In truth, Berni was a somewhat lazy and venal man. His main claim to literary fame would be his celebrated 'Rifacimento' ('recasting') of Matteo Maria Boiardo's late Medieval epic Orlando Innamorato into more nuanced Tuscan verse to better suit a contemporary sixteenth-century audience. When Aretino finally struck back at Berni it would be through this work, the Rifacimento, whose reputation Aretino would spitefully sabotage. Yet all this lay, for now, in the future.

⊙☾

Though he had been rendered temporarily *hors de combat*, Aretino spent his time recuperating and slowly mastering the difficult task of learning how to write with his left hand. Two fingers of his writing hand had been rendered lame, perhaps even severed right through (the precise extent of these wounds remains unclear), and as a writer he had no choice but to rely upon his remaining good limb (it is entirely conceivable, given the lyrical origins of Aretino's crime, that della Volta may have received instructions from his paymaster to sever the offending fingers of Aretino's writing hand). Nevertheless, while he was still recovering, he made appreciable progress on his latest work. This was a first version of the play which he had begun earlier that same spring, namely the five act prose comedy entitled La Cortigiana or 'The Courtesan'. The play is problematic for a modern audience not least because of the dearth of contemporary references to ephemeral people and events which only the Roman court of 1525 would have known, understood, or indeed appreciated. The work is also crammed full of the sort of Roman street argot and slang which only a contemporary Roman audience would have comprehended. Many of Aretino's cast of characters were based on real-life people, the courtesan Camilla Pisana for example, who was well-known to Aretino personally. La Cortigiana was significant in that it would be Aretino's first dramatic work. It drew together two unconnected plotlines into a single play.

The dual-plot hinges on a pair of intertwined pranks or practical jokes known in Italian as *beffa*. In the first plotline a stupendously foolish Sienese named Messer Maco, having arrived in Rome to become a cardinal, learns that as a precondition he must first become the perfect courtier. This was clearly a blatant dig at Castiglione's *Il Libro del Cortegiano*, a work which was not yet published at this time but which had been circulated in manuscript form by the author while he was resident in Rome during the early 1520s. Messer Maco, in need of a tutor, finds himself ensnared in the wiles of the unscrupulous Roman painter, Maestro Andrea. On the pretext that the would-be courtier needs to be melted down by steam and remade into his new 'courtly' identify, the latter proceeds to subject Messer Maco to a series of cruel physical ordeals which often result in his (comedic) humiliation. When Messer Maco subsequently falls in a love with 'a pretty lady', the Camilla Pisana character, whom he has glimpsed through an open window, this then opens the field to further uproarious pranks by the streetwise Maestro Andrea. The second plotline involves a *Napoletano* gentleman named Messer Parabolano who has recently come into a fortune and been made a lord through sheer blind luck and who now has a complex household of dependents comprising various individuals in descending order of social rank. Messer Parabolano is in love with a Roman matron named Laura (shades of Petrarch here) but is cruelly deceived by a pair of cunning servants, Rosso and the former prostitute-turned-procuress, Aloigia. The pair promise to bring Parabolano together with his beloved Laura but instead conspire to place the guileless man in a darkened bedroom with a common woman named Togna, the wife of a plebeian baker. Both plots concern the transposition of power. The wealthy Messer Maco and even wealthier Messer Parabolano come to be controlled by their devious servants, who proceed to make fools of them both.

Beyond its obvious farcical elements, *La Cortigiana* specifically held a mirror up to the Leonine Rome of *Papa Janni*, Pope Leo X, a period very much regarded by now as an untroubled golden age. It derided men who, like the guileless Messer Maco, seek the pointless and superficial attractions of the papal court whilst casting a spotlight on those others, like Messer Parabolano, whose new wealth makes them haughty, arrogant, and ignorant of the injustices perpetrated on their social inferiors. The title *Cortigiana* is itself ambiguous for as an adjective it implied that something was being done 'in courtly fashion' whilst as a noun it simply meant 'a courtesan'. Aside from Camilla Pisana's brief appearance as a tangential love interest, the play is not actually about a courtesan. Instead, Aretino was implying that the work of a polished courtier is little different from the work of a courtesan: both are no more than whores prostituting themselves at the corrupt Roman court. Indeed, this would soon become a recurring theme in the breakaway heretical preaching of the northern Protestants. That same year of 1525, Martin Luther published his ninety-five theses in Wittenberg, which would spark endless rhetoric comparing Rome to the Whore of Babylon of Revelation. Luther himself declared that Rome was 'more corrupt than either Babylon or Sodom'.[326] Aretino sought to critique a Rome of which he was still very much an integral part; he wished to lampoon the many faults of Roman society and in particular the system of patronage which existed at the papal court at this time, a system which made 'whores' of all who came into contact with it.

Yet Aretino himself was still uncomfortably close to his subject matter, close to powerful individuals at court, too entangled in the power plays, the jockeying for influence and (in Aretino's case quite literally) the backstabbing. Because of this he sometimes had to pull his punches when writing his characters' lines. The play, which was first written sometime between February and July of 1525, was destined to remain in manuscript form for almost a decade and would only come to be published years later in Venice, in 1534, in a revised version in which many of his attacks upon life in Rome would be heightened and intensified.[327] For example, in the 1525 version, Aretino writes that Rome is the '*capus mundi*' or 'head of the world' whereas in the 1534 version we find that Rome has become the '*coda mundi*'–the 'bottom of the world'. Aretino's comedy owed a debt to three other satirical comedies which had preceded his own: Ariosto's *I suppositi* (1508), Bibbiena's *La Calandria* (1513) and Machiavelli's *La Mandragola* (1518).

This year when Aretino was composing *La Cortigiana*, Niccolò Machiavelli was producing his final comedy. This was *Clizia*, a work loosely based on an interpretation of Plautus's *Casina*. The work was written specifically for Jacopo di Filippo Falconetti, to celebrate the expiry of his earlier ban from Florence. Sebastian Sangallo created the sets and Philippe Verdelot composed the madrigals which were sung by Barbara Raffacani Salutati, a famous singer at that time. Machiavelli was fifty-six years old and just two years away from his own death. In his Prologue to *Clizia*, Machiavelli opened the kimono and disclosed the following telling piece of comedic theory which is as remarkable for its didactic motivations as for its pseudo-moralising overtones: 'Comedies are composed to instruct and to entertain their audience. It is very instructive for anyone, especially for young people, to be shown the avarice of an old man, the frenzy of a lover, the deceits of a servant, the gluttony of a parasite, the wretchedness of a poor man, the ambition of a rich one, the flatteries of a prostitute, and the faithlessness of men at large: and comedies are full of examples of all these things, all of which can be shown on stage with perfect propriety'. Machiavelli then continues: 'But in order to entertain people, one has to be able to make them laugh, which cannot be done by keeping one's speeches solemn and decorous; because the words that make people laugh have to be either silly or insulting or amorous.'[328]

The satirist Aretino would have embraced such a theory. Above all, Aretino's writings in all their myriad forms sought to entertain and delight their intended audience, whether it be the recipient of a private letter or the audience of a theatrical performance. But above all, as well as entertain, Aretino also wanted to inculcate in his audience certain truths, often social or political in nature, at other times more theoretical or else concerned with the vagaries of human nature. Above all, despite its satirising of Roman court society, *La Cortigiana* still betrayed a wistful longing for the lost Rome of Pope Leo X. In Act II, scene v the characters Sempronio (an old man) and Flamminio (a worldly servant) discuss the perennial nostalgia felt by the older generation for things of the past. Sempronio expresses his desire to send his son, Camillio, to court in order to learn all the traditional courtly skills so that he may earn his reputation. Flamminio, however, makes it a point to disabuse him of this outmoded aspiration, telling him that 'Once he's a courtier, he'll become an envious, ambitious, wretched, ungrateful flatterer, a wicked, unjust, heretical hypocrite, a thief, an insolent lying glutton'.[329] Flamminio explains that such men spend their days waiting for those above to die and make room for them, adding 'it's a cruel thing to wish for the death of someone who never did you any harm'.[330] The inference in Aretino's writing is clear: the court, specifically the court of Rome, is a nest of vipers, even possibly of would-be murderers and assassins. On 13 October 1525, his wounds having healed sufficiently to permit him to travel, Aretino left Rome and made his way north to Mantua.[331]

CHAPTER 7

⌒⌒⌒

Giovanni d'Italia

Father, inasmuch as I have followed the profession of
arms, I have lived in the manner of a soldier. If I had put
on the habit that you wear, I would have lived in the
manner of a priest. I am sorry that it is not lawful for I
would gladly confess in front of everybody. I have never
done anything unworthy of myself.

Pietro Aretino records the last testament
of his friend Giovanni de' Medici.

Federigo Gonzaga welcomed Aretino back to Mantua and he spent a
miserable winter there in what he was now coming to regard,
despite the city's friendship towards him, as a dull provincial
backwater. There were few people of interest to him here. The Marquess
himself was already by now utterly transparent to Aretino, a two-
dimensional cypher and a predictable slave to his sensual appetites who
now bored the intellectually restless Aretino. Giulio Romano was the only
other cosmopolitan artist and intellectual of any real note at court but he
was by now deeply preoccupied with the completion of the Palazzo Te
and probably would not have been able to devote much time to keeping
Aretino company. Perhaps Aretino crunched his way through the Mantuan
winter snow and toured the half-finished villa, inspecting the dazzling
frescos being created by local artists under Romano's finicky direction.
The Palazzo Te would not be fully completed for another nine or ten
years. Perhaps other days were spent hunting in bleak snowscapes
together with the Marquess and his married mistress Isabella Boschetti
(Federico meanwhile had his favourite hunting horses immortalised in the
Palazzo Te's 'Rooms of the Horses'). The days were short, the nights long.
The brothels of Mantua may have alleviated Aretino's loneliness
somewhat. Despite everything he had been through, and despite his
mordant criticism of the papal court in La Cortigiana, Pietro could not help
himself; he still longed for the forbidden excitement of Rome.

Backed by the Spanish, Francesco Sforza had by this time been restored to the dukedom of Milan while King François now languished as a prisoner in Spain, held captive under imperial guard. But the main scuttlebutt that winter was the arrest of Sforza's chancellor Girolamo Morone. An Italian patriot who disliked his Sforza lord's reliance upon the Imperialists, whom he felt held Milan in a stranglehold, Morone had attempted to suborn Charles's man, Fernando Francesco d'Ávalos, Marchese di Pescara. Morone tried to persuade Pescara to seize the crown of Naples for himself and declare an end to imperial domination. The latter had played along but was ultimately loyal to the Emperor and had been keeping Charles regularly updated on the progress of Morone's plot. When d'Ávalos had learned all he could about the conspiracy, Morone was placed under arrest. Threatened with torture Sforza's Chancellor broke down and agreed to implicate the Duke of Milan in the plot in exchange for his liberty. Francesco's fortress in the centre of Milan was duly surrounded and cordoned off by imperial troops. Until Charles could reach a clear decision as to what should be done with him the duke of Milan would remain under house arrest. Worse still, Pope Clement VII was also implicated in the Morone plot because Morone had informed Pescara that the Pope was ready to invest him as King of Naples once he agreed to come on board. For once in his life, Clement did not lapse into his usual indecisive ways. With the threat of imperial reprisals hanging over him the Pope now opened feverish diplomatic channels with the Venetians as well as secret communications with Duke Francesco in Milan for the creation of a new papal league designed to oust Charles V from Italy for good.

On 14 January 1526, however, Clement learned that the French king had concluded the Treaty of Madrid with the Emperor. The news threw him into a fresh tailspin since, on the surface at least, François seemed to have capitulated to all the Emperor's conditions in exchange for his freedom. Crucially, François had agreed that the French Crown would relinquish the all-important duchy of Burgundy and as a guarantee of his continued good faith the French king surrendered his two young sons, the Dauphin and brother, into the Emperor's hands as hostages. It was a hard decision for any father to make yet, at the river Bidassoa which separated France from Spain, François had glided past the barque carrying his two vulnerable young boys into Spanish captivity. By February 1527, Paolo Giovio would be quipping to Ludovico Domenici that '... to have his sons back the king of France would drop his breeches, and leave the world turned into a brothel' ('... per aver li figliosi si calerebbe le brache el Re francese, e lasciarebe el mondo in bordello').[332] If the Pope's nose was initially put out of joint by these worrying developments he need not have worried. As soon as the French monarch was safely back on the French side of the river bank he exclaimed 'I am free!' and gleefully reneged on his agreement with Charles. The French army began mobilising once again.

The Florentine diplomat, statesman and historian Francesco Guicciardini was summoned to Rome in early 1526 to lend Clement his knowledgeable advice and counsel on international affairs. Born in 1483 into a distinguished pro-Medicean family, Guicciardini had served the Florentine *signoria* with distinction as one of the republic's youngest ever ambassadors to King Ferdinand of Aragon. Following the elevation of Pope Leo X this ambassadorial prodigy was taken under the new Medici Pope's wing and given a fast-tracked career in papal diplomacy. His latest appointment had been as papal vice-regent of the Romagna where he enjoyed a considerable degree of autonomy. With a somewhat cold, austere and aloof disposition, Guicciardini was, in spite of the vast differences in their social backgrounds, a good friend of Niccolò Machiavelli, or '*il Machia*' as he was known to his associates. Their mutual admiration was based on that best of all possible foundations, mutual respect for one another's intellect. But where they differed as individuals was that, unlike Machiavelli, Guicciardini the empiricist did not favour using ancient history as the standard for contemporary political decision-making and he had little patience for theory. His was sound advice, drawing on his immense diplomatic experience and offered in a practical way.

Upon entering the papal apartments at the Vatican, Guicciardini found the Pope beset by self-doubt and utterly incapable of making any clear decision either way. As Guicciardini later observed, 'Everything is done haphazard, and often today's action is contrary to and ruins yesterday's'.[333] Like his friend Machiavelli, Guicciardini was however a realist and agreed that war, though disruptive and destructive, was often unavoidable. Machiavelli had written to Guicciardini on 3 January 1526: 'For as long as I can remember, people have always been either making war or talking about going to war; it is now being talked about and in a short while it will be declared; when it is over, people will start talking about it again'.[334] To Guicciardini's way of thinking, the Treaty of Madrid, made as it was under duress, was automatically invalidated. Consequently, Guicciardini now advised His Holiness to throw his weight unequivocally behind the newly-released and remobilising French monarch. Accordingly, on 22 May 1526, Pope Clement VII concluded the Holy League of Cognac with Rome and the Papal States, Medici-controlled Florence, Venice, England and Francesco Sforza of Milan as co-signatories. François had also meanwhile signed for France and Pope Clement duly released him from his holy oath to the Emperor to abide by the terms of Madrid.

The goal of the 'Holy League', somewhat nebulously stated, was to 'safeguard the peace of Italy' yet the Emperor was put in little doubt as to the true nature of the alliance, or its anti-Imperialist intentions. The Holy League of Cognac was Clement's second great act of treachery towards Charles V and his latest blunder in a chain of steadily unfolding errors of judgement. In August 1526, the Turkish Sultan Süleyman would win a decisive victory over Louis II, the Christian king of Hungary, Croatia and Bohemia at the battle of Mohács. The eastern borders of Christendom were in grave peril. Even Aretino's character, the bawd Aloigia in *La Cortigiana*, is portrayed as seeking solace from a priest because she is afraid of 'all that impaling! Impaling! Oooh!' at the hands of the Turk, a clearly sexual innuendo if ever there was one.[335] But Pope Clement and the Emperor were now locked in a fatal dance and neither man was prepared to give the Turkish threat the attention it so obviously deserved.

Pietro Aretino left Mantua two months before the news of Mohács in June 1526 and journeyed to the camp of his friend Giovanni delle Bande Nere at Marignano. The town, which was a stone's throw from Milan, had in 1515 been the setting for François's great victory over a formidable army of determined Swiss pike infantry. He found Giovanni in good spirits and more or less recovered from the leg wound sustained the year previously at Pavia. Aretino strolled around the vast encampment taking stock of the martial sights and sounds: horses being stabled and shoed, swords being sharpened on the grindstone, armour plate being hammered back into shape by the blacksmiths, the customary clang and din of any sixteenth-century military encampment. The army of the Pope's Holy League of Cognac which had assembled that summer at Marignano was a complex and unwieldy beast. It comprised two main elements: the Venetian army, whose commander-in-chief was the duke of Urbino, Francesco Maria della Rovere, and the 'ecclesiastical' army whose commander-in-chief was the *condottiere* Guido Rangone, a captain who had served with distinction under Pope Leo X. Rangone's army was further subdivided into the papal forces commanded by Giovanni delle Bande Nere and the Florentine forces commanded by the republic's *condottiere* Vitello Vitelli, who was related to Giovanni by marriage.[336] Francesco Guicciardini had meanwhile been assigned by Clement as lieutenant-general with a mandate to act as the eyes and ears of His Holiness. Additionally, other contingents under the command of Renzo da Ceri and the Marquess of Saluzzo were also on their way to rendezvous with the main League force.

The League had already won first blood with the recent capture of Lodi when a disgruntled Italian officer serving with the imperial garrison had opened the gates to the League's army. But when, buoyed by the rumours of an anti-Imperialist uprising within the city, the League's forces advanced towards Milan, the gates had remained resolutely closed in their face and the duke of Urbino retired to Marignano, citing the need to await the arrival of 6,000 Swiss reinforcements which the Pope had recently summoned from the cantons. When the Swiss mercenaries finally deigned to arrive (*'point d'argent, point de Suisses'*—'no money, no Swiss' as the poet Racine had written),[337] the Duke marched the League army back to Milan for a second attempt. On 7 July, they came within sight of the enemy entrenchments. At this point a strong sally-in-force by Milan's German and Spanish garrison sent the Duke reeling back in confusion and he immediately sounded the retreat. Watching these dispiriting events, Francesco Guicciardini commented wryly of Francesco Maria della Rovere's conduct: *'Veni, vidi, fugit'* ('I came, I saw, I fled').[338] Outraged at Urbino's spinelessness it had been left to Giovanni delle Bande Nere alone to preserve the League's honour by mounting a tenacious attack on the city's Porta Romana. When it was clear his assault was making no headway the irascible commander of the Black Bands ordered that his men stand-to-arms until daybreak, at which point they turned their backs on their adversaries on the walls of Milan and slowly and proudly marched away with their dignity intact. Lacking relief from the army of the League, Milan's fortress fell on 24 July and Francesco Sforza was captured by the imperial forces after a brave eight-month-long resistance. He emerged from the *castello* thin and haggard, little more than skin and bone.

Sometime after this crushing humiliation for the League's army, the aging armchair strategist Niccolò Machiavelli arrived in camp. That August, Florence's *signoria* assigned him to report on the dispositions and discipline of the Florentine militia serving with the League's forces and he now met up with Aretino and Giovanni as well as his good friend Guicciardini. Machiavelli was by now fifty-seven, considered an old man by the standards of the age, and he was tired out by a life which had ended largely in personal and professional failure. In one more year he would be dead, but for now, for this one last time, he marched to the sound of the drum together with the younger men. Having studied the political arts his entire life he yearned to see Italy liberated from outside interference. He had come to observe in action that one man in all the peninsula who seemed to have both the drive and the raw talent to make this dream a reality, the celebrated 'Giovanni *d'Italia*'. Giovanni and Aretino were of course fully aware of Machiavelli's personal stature. Such works as *The Art of War*, *Discourses on Livy*, *The Prince*, and *Florentine Histories* had been illicitly circulated for years in pamphlet form and yet, instead of earning Machiavelli a well-deserved reputation as Italy's leading political philosopher, his writings had instead afforded him the unwholesome image of a manipulative cynic and 'an adviser to tyrants'. Aretino too, given time, would be reviled, partly because of his lifestyle and partly thanks to the enduring notoriety of the *I Modi* scandal. But like Machiavelli, Aretino was a fellow outsider. Perhaps he felt *simpatico* with Machiavelli on account of this, who knows?

Because this small, slight man with the twinkling, intelligent black eyes had written copiously on military matters, Giovanni regarded him as any 'doer' regards a mere 'theoriser'. Mischievously, the leader of the Black Bands now offered Machiavelli an opportunity to drill 3,000 of his veteran infantrymen. Having created Florence's militia the *Ordinanza*, Machiavelli felt confident of his abilities as a drill master and accepted the challenge enthusiastically. The Dominican friar and novella writer Matteo Bandello, who happened to be serving in the ranks at the time, describes what happened next: 'Niccolò kept us under the hot sun for more than two hours that day while he tried to parade [us] in the way he had described in writing, and he was having a very difficult time in so doing'. Bandello then went on to conclude that 'It became clear then how big the difference is between he who knows and never applied what he knows, and he who–besides the knowledge–gets his hands dirty, as it is customary to say'.[339] The poor men of the Bande Nere were left in a complete and utter shambles by Machiavelli's amateurish drilling and Giovanni had to step in and restore order to the ranks. Giovanni's prank had the desired effect of humbling the more theoretically-inclined Machiavelli but the latter, ever the diplomat, took his comedown in good part and the three men laughed over the incident that evening over supper. (Unlike Machiavelli, Aretino would never aspire to command military men. In 1537, he would write to the king of France: 'For I too am a captain, but my soldiery does not steal pay bags, cause people to revolt, or capture citadels. Instead, with its regiments of ink bottles and with truth painted on its banners, it brings more glory to the prince it serves than armed men take away from him.')[340]

It was perhaps over a warm meal and some much-needed goblets of wine that Machiavelli shared his own views on the future direction that Italy's affairs ought to take. Both Machiavelli and Guicciardini had discussed and corresponded about this topic previously. Niccolò had lately mooted to his friend that, instead of depending on the alliance with the king of France, a far better strategy would be to place Giovanni delle Bande Nere at the head of a great Italian army, which he himself had trained, and then send him to expel both the Imperialists *and* the French from Italy. In all likelihood Giovanni of the Black Bands would probably have been more than equal to the task. Giovanni was an immeasurably better soldier than the League's supreme commander, the Duke of Urbino. The pair of diplomats had even attempted to broach the subject with Pope Clement. Guicciardini had already laid the groundwork, writing with great frankness to Rome: 'Is it my fault if the Lord Giovanni keeps his infantry at work while Rangone lets his sleep? Is it my fault if the Lord Giovanni, who hourly exposes himself to danger, wishes his companies to be commanded by captains who really fight like soldiers? And if that other fellow has only, with one or two exceptions, men under him of no military capacity, with neither creditable reputation nor valour? Or that he employs them not as commanders but rather as courtiers to adorn his table and crowd after him wherever he goes in the camp? Or if the Lord Giovanni is ever with his foot-soldiers, seeing to their weapons, clothing and good discipline? And if that other fellow never sees his own troops or thinks of their comfort, arms of control, so that his men are worth more the first time that he pays them than every afterwards? If he doesn't rob them himself, and I don't know that he does, he lets his captains rob them without the slightest compunction, so openly that it is a perfect scandal.'[341] Before the idea could be seriously discussed with His Holiness, however, the Pope's Florentine banker and relative, Filippo Strozzi, had intervened to quash the proposal, reaffirming the paramount importance of the Pope's strategic alliance with King François.

Machiavelli and Guicciardini both felt that a valuable opportunity had been missed. The League's army was in the hands of Francesco Maria della Rovere, a blatantly incompetent poltroon. By November a disgruntled Machiavelli was writing from Imola to Bartolomeo Cavalcanti in Florence concerning the strategic errors of the Pope and the tactical shortcomings which he had observed on the part of the duke of Urbino: 'We have then on our side lost this war twice: once when we went to Milan and did not stay there; the second time when we sent and did not go to Cremona. The reason for the first was the timidity of the Duke [of Urbino]; for the second, the vanity of us all, because, feeling disgraced by the first retreat, nobody dared advise the second...'[342] He then went on in a similar vein: 'Many leaders, of many opinions, are left, but all ambitious and unbearable; and lacking anybody who knows how to assuage their factions and keep them united, they will be a chorus of dogs'.[343] Worst of all he expressed the very real fear that Giovanni d'Italia would desert them altogether for lack of payment for his troops and take service instead with the Germans and Spanish: 'From this results a confusion in our doings that is very great, and already Lord Giovanni [de' Medici] does not intend to remain there; I believe that today he will leave'.[344]

Aretino too was one of Giovanni's staunchest advocates. Unlike either Machiavelli or Guicciardini, he had actually watched Giovanni closely as a soldier and was intimately familiar with his many virtues as a leader of men. Aretino would write: 'He was so expert in the details of war that when his advance guard lost its way in the dark, he could lead them back to the right path again. He was a genius at patching up the quarrels between his men, and he knew just when to keep them at their task by love, when by fear, when by punishment, and when by rewards. No one knew better than he when to use deception and when force in attacking the enemy.'[345] Aretino also recorded Giovanni's care for his men: 'Laziness was his prime enemy. He was the first man to use Turkish steeds. He was the first man to insist on comfortable equipment for his soldiers. He was delighted when he had good meat and drink for them. As for himself, however, he cared for none of these things. He quenched his own thirst with water merely coloured with wine.'[346]

☉☾

Just after the League's failure to reconquer Milan in July and before Machiavelli's arrival in camp in August, Aretino had absented himself from the ranks for several weeks. He could feel proud that he had acquitted himself well in the military campaign, enduring many of the same hardships as Giovanni de' Medici and his men, and he had even shown personal courage, so far as this was possible for Aretino. But nevertheless he found the constant cheerless grind of army life a drain on his vitality and sought relief at Reggio, where he had previously spent such an engaging time with the men of the *Bande Nere*. At Milan, Giovanni had joked with him, 'Pietro, if I come through this war by the grace of God and good luck, it's my wish to make you the lord of your own country!'[347] It was a seductive prospect–Maestro Pietro Aretino a lord, following his noble inclinations and ignoble appetites like some more immanent version of Federico Gonzaga. But Aretino, ever the realist, refused to allow himself to get carried away by dreams of glory. Anything could happen to prevent a man from fulfilling his promises. Indeed, much later on in life Aretino himself acknowledged: 'However, it pleased that rogue named destiny that instead [of becoming a lord] I should be poor and old and he [Giovanni] dead and underground'.[348] These two brothers, *L'ultimo dei condottieri e il condottiere della penna*, would be separated from each other for just a short while.

Giovanni, for his own part, departed for Mantua were he lost little time in seeking out his mistress Paola. Soon afterwards a hyperbole-laden letter arrived from Aretino making certain anonymous references to yet another of the *condottiere's* unspecified casual lady-loves: 'Your long absence has widowed the town. Your unhappy feminine slave mourns you so greatly that I'm sure you will hear some terrible news about her. My lord … I don't believe any woman in the world could be so devoted to you. Her state of mind would arouse pity, I don't say in any man, but in cruelty itself. By God, the very women who used to envy her for having the invincible Giovanni de' Medici for a lover now feel something more than compassion for the wretched and comfortless life she leads. You're getting a reputation for pig-headedness, almost for ingratitude. For you alone awakened love in that chilly heart of hers, which had formerly yielded up to no other. Her angelic face is no longer that of a woman, but more like that of a buried corpse.'[349] The satirist was also writing once more. In 1526, Aretino would publish *Dubbi amorosi* ('Amorous doubts') a collection of raunchy short poems which drew on the popular courtly tradition of asking 'fashionable questions about love and sexuality'[350] but which were, in reality, little more than the versification of well-known dirty jokes.[351] True to form, Aretino's treatment of the genre would focus rather more on the sexual and somewhat less on the 'courtly' and 'romantic' element. Thirty-one sonnets written about husbands, wives, clergymen, nuns and prostitutes raised 'doubts' to each of which Aretino then provides a suitable 'resolution' in mock Renaissance Latin legalese. *Dubbio XXV* for example posits a hermit who, chancing upon a naïve abbess, asks her for a loaf of bread. In reply the abbess lifts her habit and shows the hermit her *bianca e bella potta* ('beautiful white cunt'). The sonnet then poses the question/doubt: 'whether [for the hermit] this was to accept charity?' The *risoluzione* that followed punningly answered 'no' since 'charity is *made in the box*' and it therefore advised the hermit to 'jump on the abbess and give her a good fuck' ('*saltarle addosso e darle una chiavata*') so as to express his true appreciation for her generosity.[352]

So popular was this collection of lewd jokes masquerading loosely as moralistic object lessons that Aretino published another seventeen of them under the title *Other amorous doubts*. One drawn from this fresh batch, the final one *Dubbio XVII*, displays the contemporary fondness for anti-Semitic jokes which was popular at the time: 'Of having fucked up the ass a Jew dog / Jimmy accused himself with great contrition: / But for absolution his holy confessor denied his ambition. / Does this mean really the sin my still his conscience clog?' The *risoluzione* of the question cites the usual Christ-killing rationale by means of which Jews were marginalised and maltreated during the Renaissance: 'Bartolo then tells this man of vice / about Chapter six and the Papal derriere code as well / that tells how he was bound to break and bust up that ass as well / to avenge the death of Christ'. The humour arose out of Aretino's conflation of the words *deretano* (derriere) and *decretali*, a canon law decree, to produce the bastardised expression 'deretali' (derriere code) by means of which the moral and legal judgement is then cast.[353] It is a good example of the witty and often vulgar word play which made Aretino so incredibly popular with his readership, not to mention his willingness to pander to low Jew jokes, which he frequently does throughout his canon of work.[354] In his antipathy to the Jews he was merely a product of his time and we should not rush to judgement. To Bernardo Tasso he writes in October

1537 commiserating that 'our good friend Molza'[355] had ran afoul of the charms of a woman of the tribe: 'I was astonished to see this cultivated soul who has access to the temples of God and to the palaces of the great, find what he sought for amid the synagogues. He had fallen in love with a Jewess and one known to the immortal fellow as such.'[356] Whilst he was admittedly guilty of conforming to the blind prejudices of the age, Aretino nonetheless tended to judge individuals on their own merits regardless of their race or religion. In July 1542 he would write to his Jewish physician Messer Elias Alfan: '..although you are a Jew, men could learn how to be a Christian from you. After all, fearing God and loving your neighbour are inherent to your nature. What else does a Christian have to do?'[357]

On returning to Giovanni's camp, Aretino busied himself by completing the play which he had begun whilst convalescing in Rome, La Cortigiana, a copy of which he now forwarded to the Marquess of Mantua. 'Your learned comedy has now arrived and is filling me with delight', Federico enthused, 'It is the true mirror of the modern court and of present-day life'.[358] (Aretino had made one of his characters, Flaminio, who is always on the lookout for a generous new master, say the line: 'I'll go to Mantua. His Excellency the Marquess Federico sees that everyone gets the bread he needs', which surely must have flattered Federico's ego.)[359] But Aretino was right perhaps to be critical of the corruption at the papal court. By this time in Rome, Pope Clement's chamberlain, Cardinal Francesco Armellino, camerlengo of the Holy Roman Church, had succeeded in making himself perhaps the most hated man in all of Rome. A confirmed simoniac, he enriched both the Church and himself by openly selling positions within the Curia, by inflating wheat prices, and by imposing a hugely unpopular tax on wine consumption. He demolished countless supposedly 'unsafe' structures in the city, chiefly the homes of the poor, so that he could cynically profit from the subsequent redistribution of land parcels. In consequence the disaffected Roman mob was unlikely to put up much of a struggle on behalf of the Curia should Rome be threatened by the forces of the Empire. Meanwhile, Charles V's agent in Naples, Don Ugo de Moncada, had met with Pope Clement and persuaded him through guile and cajolery to reduce the garrison of Rome to no more than 200 to 500 guardsmen supported by 100 horse. The Pope had effectively been talked into disarming himself. Political observers could not believe how he could be so foolish and trusting.

On 17 September, Charles V published an open letter to the Pope cataloguing the latter's many misdeeds towards himself. The letter took the form of a manifesto, reminding the Pope that Christ had exhorted Peter to put away his sword and censured Clement for furthering the Lutheran heresy by taking up arms against the Emperor; the letter was published in Spain, Germany and the Netherlands. Aretino and Giovanni watched dumbfounded from the chilly north as, on the early morning of 20 September, some 3,000 infantry and 800 horse led by Cardinal Pompeo Colonna and Don Ugo de Moncada swept into Rome, sacked the Vatican and sent Clement fleeing along the Passetto di Borgo to the Castel Sant'Angelo for safety. But what looked like conquest was merely a bluff by the Emperor. If Colonna had cherished hopes that Charles would place the triple tiara on his own head he was to be sadly disappointed. Having used the brief occupation of Rome to pressure Clement VII to sign a fresh agreement with the Emperor disavowing any involvement with the Holy League, Moncada and his forces then departed Rome on 22 September. Colonna, with his *bravi et capitani*, were left to bear most of the blame for this shameful outrage to the Pope's dignity and sovereignty. In the weeks that followed, units of papal troops were pulled out of Lombardy and repositioned in Florence to enforce Medici hegemony there. Other troops, including the Black Bands of Giovanni delle Bande Nere, were permitted to remain close to Milan under the pretext that they were in the French king's pay (the reality was that Giovanni's men had probably still not been paid by either French or papal paymaster). Thousands of papal troops, some under the command of Vitello Vitelli, now returned from the front and poured back into Rome, bolstering the Pope's desire for revenge upon the Colonna. The ink on Ugo de Moncada's treaty was barely dry, therefore, before the slippery Pope Clement had reneged on it.

In early September, Francesco Maria della Rovere moved to invest the Lombard city of Cremona which was under the control of its imperial governor, Thomas Sanchez de Baeça. Morale within the city had been high. On 7 September, Sanchez had written to Don Antonio de Leyva at Milan. 'To-day, at noon, we sent 100 cavalry and 300 infantry by the gates Ogni Santi and Sant Michele, and numerous prisoners have been brought in', reported Sanchez. 'The loss of the enemy is estimated at 200 men at least, besides the three above-mentioned captains, and upwards of 50 peasants they had engaged as pioneers. They had four guns with them, and expect to receive 16 more soon. I cannot imagine what they mean by having so much artillery, unless they want to frighten us with the noise.'[360] Despite Sanchez's Stoic optimism, however, Cremona fell to the League's forces later that same month.

The forces of the Holy League were not permitted to rest on their laurels for long. By November, an army of 16,000 fanatical Lutheran *landsknechts* under the able command of Georg von Frundsburg, a veteran of the battle of Pavia, had stumbled over the freezing cold Alps and down onto the icy Plain of Lombardy. In their leader's saddle bags was a length of embroidered silk chord with which he vowed to hang the pope of Rome and the entire membership of the Sacred College. The Lutherans had been summoned to Italy by the imperial commander-in-chief, the

Duke of Bourbon. The latter's orders were dismayingly vague, the Emperor's less so. 'Tell them, that they are to go against the Turks; they will know what Turks are meant', Charles had reputedly instructed.[361] By 'Turks' he of course meant the disobedient forces of Pope Clement VII. The nine day journey across the high Alpine precipices and gorges at the onset of winter had been a harrowing experience for the Germans. Cold, shivering and exhausted, they had been unable to find any wood above the Alpine tree line with which to light their cooking fires and by the time that they descended onto the Lombard plain they had degenerated into a half-starved and pitiful rabble. Only the sheer force of personality of their commanding general the prince of Mindelheim fired their determination. Now at last finding themselves on flat and level ground, the vast column of vagabond soldiers snaked its way down beside Lake Garda until they came to the marshy terrain around Mantua.

On 14 November, Guicciardini wrote to Aretino expressing his joy that Giovanni delle Bande Nere had opted to remain with the army of the League: 'Del Caccia and the man I sent down to the camp to appease the wrath of the Lord Giovanni, have told me that you have persuaded him not to go to Milan. If he had done so it would have made him most unhappy. For he would have inflicted injury on his ranks, his renown, his duty and all he holds dear.'[362] Guicciardini continued in similarly uncharacteristic tone: 'It would be well for him if he always had such a man as Pietro Aretino at his side. I don't write this to encourage you to go on representing yourself as what the whole world knows you to be. I merely express the pleasure I feel at so laudable a service, which I have reported to the benevolence of his holiness so warmly and sincerely that I trust in God I shall soon see you reconciled with him to the extent that your talents deserve. I greet you as a brother.'[363] Yes, Giovanni of the Black Bands had fulfilled Guicciardini's and *il Machia's* notions of patriotism and right conduct, this was indeed true, but honour would now lead Giovanni to his premature apotheosis and deprive Aretino of perhaps the greatest friend he would ever know. Giovanni's nemesis would be the steely prince of Mindelheim, Georg von Frundsburg, and the agency of his fate would be the new technology: cannon, foundries, ballistics, the dark arts of Tubal Cain. The glorious era of the *condottiere* was about to come to a rudely abrupt ending.

☉☾

When in 1523 the artist Titian had been commissioned to paint the portrait of Alfonso d'Este the duke of Ferrara, he had chosen to do so depicting Alfonso leaning against the muzzle of a cannon. It was a fitting tribute for this lord whose guiding deity was

Mars, just as surely as Federico Gonzaga's was Venus. Indeed, the Duke's *impresa* famously consisted of a blazing cannonball accompanied by the inscrutable maxim *loco et tempore* ('at the right time and place'), which suggested his somewhat explosive and unpredictable temperament. The Este, who took their name from the town of Este near Padua, were one of Italy's oldest and noblest families. They had ruled in Ferrara as vicars of the papacy since the year 1242. Later, they acquired the cities of Modena and Reggio as imperial fiefs. The Emperor Frederick III had made Borso d'Este, the half-brother of Alfonso's father Ercole, Duke of those two cities and in 1471 Pope Paul II created Borso Duke of Ferrara. The family was exceedingly well-connected. Alfonso's mother was the daughter of King Ferrante of Naples, whilst his sisters Isabella and Beatrice had been married to Francesco II Gonzaga and Ludovico Sforza respectively. Borso d'Este had not been an especially educated or cultured duke, but his successor Ercole initiated the Este trend in arts patronage which would be continued especially by his two highly cultivated daughters. He was responsible for bringing the poet Matteo Maria Boiardo, author of *Orlando Innamorato*, to the court of Ferrara where he was employed as a high functionary, Ercole later making him governor of Reggio. Ercole also inducted the promising young poet Ludovico Ariosto into his household. But it was in the military and mechanical arts that Ercole really excelled.

Ercole had established a cannon foundry at the city of Ferrara which pioneered the manufacture of high quality artillery in Italy. When Ercole died in 1505, Alfonso took the foundry over and keenly continued his father's passion. By the time of his own death in 1534, Alfonso would by then have acquired some 300 cannon, the casting of some of which he had personally supervised.[364] Although published sometime later in 1540, Vannoccio Biringuccio's technical manual on metallurgy, smelting and military casting known as *De la pirotechnia* gives a good overview of the technological capabilities of the era, of which Alfonso would have availed himself. This new technology could prove devastating in battle. In 1512, at the battle of Ravenna, a small imperial army had dug themselves in behind a defensive network of ditches, stakes and bladed wagons hoping to draw a considerably larger French force into their static killing zone. It had been Alfonso d'Este's artillery which had turned the tables. Instead of advancing to meet the entrenched Spaniards, Este's batteries had targeted them from a distance, a strategy which had resulted in truly appalling levels of slaughter. Jacopo Guicciardini, a witness to the day's events, would later write to his brother Francesco: 'It was a horrible and terrible thing to see how every shot of the artillery made a lane through those men-at-arms [the Spanish cavalry], and how helmets with the heads inside them, scattered limbs, halves of men, a vast quantity, were sent flying through the air'.[365] Ariosto had paid tribute to his master's triumph in *Orlando Furioso* ('Mad Orlando') when he wrote: 'There are victories so bloody that they bring little joy to the victors. And if I may compare modern things to ancient, unbeaten Alfonso, the great victory, the glory of which can be given to your acts of power, for which Ravenna must always have tearful eyelids, is like this one.'[366]

Traditionally, Ferrara–a key buffer state lying between the lands of the Veneto, the Papal States and Milan–had always leaned towards France rather than the Empire. Louis XII of France had protected Ferrara against the warrior Pope Julius II, and when Alfonso d'Este inherited his duchy in 1505, Ferrara was still allied with France. Furthermore, Charles's agreement with Pope Leo X on 8 May 1521 had offered Imperial support to recover wayward Ferrara for the Pope. But the French defeat at Bicocca in 1522 had changed all that and Alfonso had been forced to agree to accept the imperial ambassador at his court.[367] Charles's ambassador to the Pope, Don Ugo de Moncada, had then subsequently enlisted Ferrara as an imperial ally with the enticement that the Emperor would help return the lost cities of Modena and Reggio to the *Ferrarese* duchy. As a further inducement Alfonso d'Este was appointed as captain-general of the imperial army. As the prince of Mindelheim's *landsknechts* trudged towards the river Po, Alfonso secretly sent him several of his small-calibre 'falconets' made at his foundry. In the freezing conditions they were loaded onto rafts and floated downriver to Frundsburg's regiments. Relatively light and mobile, this new kind of ordnance derived its name from the flight of birds of prey in the aristocratic pastime of falconry–the cannon's projectiles, curving in a gentle arc, were said to resemble the graceful flight of falcons. Having received this discreet gift of light artillery from the duke of Ferrara, the Germans now searched for a viable crossing point over the Po. Thinly strung out along a line roughly corresponding to the length of the Po river were the Venetians and papal troops of the Holy League of Cognac under the overall command of the duke of Urbino.

As for Federico Gonzaga, even though Pope Clement VII had renewed his *condotta* as *gonfaloniere* and captain-general following the death of Adrian VI, his troops remained neutral and aloof from the coming showdown. Despite the fact that the fight was now well inside Mantuan territory, Federico had regressed into that well-known Gonzaga practice of fighting only when it suited Mantua's best interests. In this case, Federico and his mother Isabella did not believe that it served their interests to antagonise Federico's feudal sovereign, the Emperor. Neither, apparently, was Francesco Maria della Rovere keen on making a concerted stand against Frundsburg. Ever since Pope Leo X had attempted to steal Urbino for his nephew Lorenzo de' Medici, Francesco Maria nurtured little affection and even less loyalty towards any Medici occupying St. Peter's chair. Biding his time, he was content to stand aside rather than present Frundsburg with any real military obstacle. By chance, design or coincidence it is hard to know which, the nearest League units to Frundsburg's *landsknechts* at this time were the Black Bands of Giovanni delle Bande Nere, who–together with Pietro Aretino–were at that time encamped in the vicinity of the hamlet of Curtatone near Mantua. Giovanni now asked permission of the duke of Urbino to engage the enemy and the latter assented, more than happy perhaps to see a son of the House of Medici place himself in harm's way. It was drawing towards late November and the weather was already freezing. Wearing plate metal in such cold conditions was torture but, as he had done many times before, Giovanni stoically donned his burnished black armour and his dented, pock-marked burgonet, buckled on his sword, bade farewell to his friend and 'brother' Pietro Aretino, and rode off into the pages of Italian legend.

Giovanni intercepted a column of Frundsburg's men as they were attempting to ford the River Po near the village of Borgoforte. The light cavalry of the Black Bands repeatedly harassed the Swabian mercenaries with surprise mounted charges followed just as rapidly with timely feints and withdrawals. Giovanni had repeatedly stressed to his commanding officer the duke of Urbino the importance of these kinds of harrying tactics when engaging the Imperialist pike which, being highly professional and well-motivated, tended to stand 'with their pikes and halberds like a wall'. He had advocated that instead of confronting the pike squares of the enemy head-on it was more effective to interdict the army's lines of communications, in particular their slow-moving baggage trains. Eventually, as Giovanni knew it would, the repeated cavalry onslaughts and feints took their inevitable toll, forcing the Imperialists to withdraw a few miles downriver to another small village named Governolo, which is the point where the rivers Po and Mincio converge. In his now famous letter dated 10 December 1526 to Francesco degli Albizzi, Aretino tells us that 'His Lordship [Giovanni] moved with his well-known impetuousness toward the town of Governolo, in the outskirts of which the enemy had fortified a half-circle of strong points'.[368]

On 25 November 1526, on the freezing banks of the Mincio, Giovanni delle Bande Nere engaged the *landsknecht* rear-guard with strength and determination. But as the Black Bands charged towards the German pike men, who had occupied some limekilns as a defensive position, the enemy pushed over a low brick wall which had been part of their frontage revealing several of Alfonso d'Este's deadly falconets. The gunners unleashed a salvo. Instantly, Giovanni experienced a searing pain in his leg, as he fought desperately to remain in the saddle. Looking down he saw that a cast iron falconet ball had struck him in the same leg he had been wounded in at Pavia. The flesh and bone had been utterly shattered.

Seeing that their commander was seriously injured, the Black Bands withdrew from the field, allowing the Germans to continue their river crossing unmolested. 'No sooner was he thus struck down, than panic and demoralisation swept through the army. All hearts sank. Ardour and joy died in every one of us', records Aretino.

Giovanni was carried from the field on a litter and sent a little way back downriver to San Nicolò Po where no doctor could be found to treat him. Thereupon he was sent by stretcher to Mantua, to the *palazzo* owned by one of Federico Gonzaga's relatives, Luigi Alessandro Gonzaga, Lord of Castelgoffredo. Here, surrounded by his bodyguards, Maestro Abraham Arié, the Jewish surgeon who had treated his earlier wound, dressed and attended to Giovanni's appalling injury. Aretino's letter to Francesco degli Albizzi continued to record what happened next for posterity. Aretino himself, upon learning of his friend's wounding, rushed to Mantua to be at Giovanni's side. According to Aretino, the duke of Urbino called on him that same evening, asking Giovanni if he had considered making his last confession, for 'It is not enough that you are renowned and glorious in war. You must add to your good name by celebrating the rites of your religion. That religion christened you when you came into this world.' To this, Giovanni simply replied: 'I have always done my duty ... If needs be, I will do it in this matter too.'[369] After hearing this, Urbino left and Aretino was able to spend time talking quietly with his friend, who was concerned about who should take command of the Black Bands. Aretino offered to send for his second-in-command Lucantonio Cuppano however Giovanni objected that it would be a gross dereliction to deprive the army of Lucantonio's experienced leadership at this moment of crisis. Then Giovanni wished for his late brother-in-law the Count of San Secondo to be present.

But Aretino was politely interrupted by Maestro Abraham. If they did not act quickly the wound would fester and become gangrenous, it had to come off as soon as possible. Aretino turned to his friend and told him: 'I would wrong your immortal soul, if I convinced you with lying words that death is the cure of all ills, and that it is far more feared than it is really evil. It is best to do what is necessary willingly. Give, then, these sawbones your permission to cut away the wreckage made by that field-piece. In a week you can make Italy Queen again. She is now a slave. Your lost leg will be a medal for valour. It will take the place of the one given you by the King which you refused to wear.' Giovanni replied simply 'Let them set to work forthwith'.[370] In the sixteenth-century amputation of a lower limb technically consisted in the surgeon making guillotine-like incisions below the knee using a crescent-shaped knife and saw; but the surgical arts were primitive by today's standards and in reality little better than butchery. Aretino continues his account, telling us that when the doctors came in

'They praised the courage of his decision, and said that they would operate on him that evening. Then they gave him a soporific draught, and went out to make ready their instruments ... At last the time came, and the worthy surgeons appeared. They had with them assistants who were trained for this sort of business. "Send for eight or ten people," they directed me, "to hold him during the pain of the sawing." "Not even twenty would be enough," he said, smiling. Then he sat up with face as resolute as could be, and took in his own hands the candle that was to give light for the operation.' As the surgeons began their grim work sawing off the condottiere's lower leg, the squeamish Aretino could bear the scene no longer: 'I fled from the room, and thrust my hands into my ears'.[371]

Upon returning some time later, Aretino found the patient both lucid and in surprisingly good spirits, announcing "I am cured" and ordering the surgeons to bring 'the foot with a piece of his leg still hanging to it'. The Duke of Urbino prevented this grisly cameo however. But the agony of his surgery soon return to plague him and 'subjected him to every kind of torment'.[372] Giovanni's wound was neither closed nor adequately disinfected. Within a matter of days gangrene set in. Knowing that death was close at hand, Giovanni sought to forget his predicament by making idle conversation with his friend. Even now he seemed more concerned with Pietro's plight than his own. He confided in Aretino that: 'the thought of the poltroons [meaning Pope Clement VII and the *datarius*] causes me more agony than my wound!' Federico Gonzaga came to visit him and told him: 'Since your proud nature never allowed you to use anything of mine, ask me now—so that it may not seem that I did not want you to have anything—for a favour that is worthy of us both', to which Giovanni replied the Marquess, 'Love me when I am dead'. The Marquess of Mantua replied back, 'The heroism with which you have acquired so much glory ... will make you not merely loved, but adored by me and by all others'.[373] After making out his last will and testament, the by now delirious *condottiere* presently asked to be moved from the bed to his military cot crying: 'I am a soldier and will not die amidst these sheets and bandages'. As with many dying men, there were some final fleeting moments of lucidity and upon waking at one point, Giovanni told Aretino: 'I dreamt I was making my will and here I am healed. I no longer feel any pain; if I keep on getting better like this I will show the Germans how to fight and how I avenge myself.'[374] The final words of Aretino's account are both supremely poetic and descriptive: '*Mentre il suo animo dormiva, fu occupato da la morte*' ('while his mind slept he was occupied by death'.) Thus, on 30 November 1526, perished Italy's last great hope for independence and Pietro's friend and boon companion Giovanni delle Bande Nere.

He left behind his widow Maria Salviati and their infant son Cosimo. The widow wrote sometime afterwards to Aretino, addressing him as 'the brother and soul of him who had no equal in this world'. Giulio Romano took a death mask of Giovanni's features for Aretino with the intention of having the painter Titian create a portrait as a keepsake for the late *condottiere's* wife and young son. However these thoughtful plans came to nothing and the death mask languished amongst Aretino's belongings for many years before the poet was ultimately able to forward it to Florence in 1545. Here, the artist Gian Paolo Pace finally painted it between October and November 1545, after which it was presented to Giovanni's son Cosimo, who was by now the absolute ruler of Florence. Aretino would praise the portrait, stating that Pace's brush 'rendered life through colours, so he [Giovanni] is no less similar to himself than to your [Pace's] painting'.[375] Paolo Giovio would later opine in his 1557 work *Gli elogi: Vite brevemente scritte d'huomini illustri di guerra antichi et moderna* that Giovanni *d'Italia* had been the living embodiment of Pope Clement's own father Giuliano de' Medici. Perhaps the Pope was privately gratified to have relieved himself of a more popular cultural icon than himself; Clement's jealously of the folk-hero was well-known. If Paolo was comparing Giovanni to the beloved Giuliano de' Medici in 1557 it is not unreasonable to suppose that people were making the same observation in the year 1526-27. The Pope had never known his own father. But Giovanni's death, tragic as it undoubtedly was, would pave the way for an immeasurably greater tragedy to follow.

CHAPTER 8

La Serenissima

She embraces you, where others scorn you. She rules you, where others chastise you. She nourishes you, where others starve you. She receives you, where others hunt you down. And she cheers you in charity and love ... She is Rome's reproach because here there are no minds that could or would tyrannise over her liberty, or make her a slave in the minds of her people.

Pietro Aretino to Doge Andrea Gritti, 1530.

n his letter to Francesco degli Albizzi on the subject of Giovanni delle Bande Nere's final hours, Pietro Aretino had included a sullen barb aimed at Pope Clement VII: 'Would to God I lied, but Florence and Rome will soon find out what it means not to have this man among the living. Yet I can already hear the Pope's exclamations of joy. He thinks that he is better off for having lost such a man.'[376] Aretino quite explicitly infers that Pope Clement regarded his warlike relative Giovanni de' Medici as his potential rival and was glad to be rid of him. It is an extraordinary accusation for a private individual to publicly make against the Supreme Pontiff, one of the two most powerful men in all Christendom. Any other person might have thought twice about levelling such a bold allegation, especially given the personal difficulties he had previously experienced in Rome. Not Pietro Aretino. To him, he had just lost a man who was as close to him as a blood brother. Clement's failure to govern his supreme commander, the duke of Urbino, made the Pope at least indirectly responsible for Giovanni's death. The Black Bands had been practically the only military unit to engage Frundsburg's army as they attempted to cross the river Po. Francesco Maria, as usual, had hung back out of harm's way from either caution or cowardice, there was always a blurred line between the two when it came to the Duke's military endeavours.

Always the chivalrous knight deferring to his commander, Giovanni himself had reverenced the duke of Urbino. As Aretino informs us: 'For the Duke loved Giovanni. But Giovanni worshipped the Duke too. He reverenced him so greatly that he was almost afraid to speak in his presence and that was because of the Duke's great merit.'[377] But Giovanni was a junior commander and he was bound to unquestioning loyalty to the chain of command. This was not so of the Pope. Any other rational person might have seen that Francesco Maria della Rovere could not be counted on to have the Medici papacy's best interests at heart. Perhaps even Clement himself realised this, yet still he did nothing. There was always the possibility that had Clement replaced the Duke with someone more capable and committed he might have incurred Francesco Maria's wrath. His anger, once roused, was widely accepted to be homicidal. The latter, suitably aggrieved, might conceivably even have defected to the Emperor. But Clement's failure to address the problem of his commander-in-chief was nevertheless an egregious oversight. Francesco Guicciardini had occasion to be extremely critical of the Duke's passive strategy, and this judgement would only grow worse as the weeks progressed. Guicciardini, however, lacked the rank, both military *and* social, to effectively bring the Duke into line.

As for Aretino he now found himself, within the space of several brief days, with neither friend nor powerful protector. After Giovanni's funeral in late November, the satirist lingered bereft and ghostlike in Mantua. Federico Gonzaga, although by now ranking quite low in Aretino's private estimation, would have to serve as Giovanni's replacement for the time being. Mantua was still sufficiently remote from Rome to be reasonably safe and secure. Even the Lutheran threat posed by the Imperialist army had by now subsided since Federico, loyal to Charles V, had permitted Frundsburg and his men to pass unhindered through his Mantuan estates on their march south. Frundsburg's ultimate objective was not at this point known, even to him. His immediate aim was to effect a conjunction with the troops of the duke of Bourbon. After this he could advance either on Florence or else Rome and fulfil his vow to hang the Pope and the members of the Sacred College. Nervously, the duke of Urbino shadowed Frundsburg's march from a prudent distance. Francesco Maria della Rovere had no desire to risk an open confrontation with these ragged, unpredictable and half-starved Germans.

Initially, Aretino played it safe with regard to Pope Clement. He did not attempt to contact the Pope directly. Instead, he induced Federico Gonzaga to pen an unctuous letter, probably dictated by Aretino himself, to Francesco Guicciardini. The letter sought Guicciardini's help as an intermediary between Aretino and Pope Clement and began: 'I would be very ungrateful to the devotion which Messer Pietro Aretino has always shown me and I would scarcely act as a friend of genius if I did not in every way try to make the world pleasant for this unique man'.[378] It then went on to state its avowed hope: 'The object of my application is the restoration of Pietro to the Pope's goodwill and that of his respected Datary. Such an event would be as important to me as the appointment of my brother to be a cardinal.[379] Messer Pietro does not ask to be allowed to return to Rome but only for proof that his services to His Holiness have not been wasted.'[380] However, ill-advisedly perhaps, Federico had touched on a slightly censorious note as the letter continued: 'The ignoring of his petition can reflect little credit upon either the Pope or his Datary. In present circumstances general approval of their policy is more than ever necessary and everyone knows that the Aretine has good grounds for his feelings of resentment..'[381] The letter was bold, unapologetic and Aretino himself was almost certainly the author. It is strange to imagine how either the satirist or his sponsor Federico could have imagined that such a petition could have had the desired outcome. Both Clement and Guicciardini had far more important concerns at this time as Frundsburg might attack either Florence or Rome in the coming weeks. Aretino's hopes were dashed shortly thereafter by Guicciardini himself who replied that he could not be of any assistance and who affirmed tartly that 'The mere memory of one of the Aretine's offences will outweigh any argument I can offer'.[382] To be perfectly fair to Guicciardini, this business between the Pope and Aretino was hardly his fight.

With the Black Bands effectively neutralised by the death of their leader, Frundsburg's army of *landsknechts* had crossed the Po at Ostiglia and marched south to threaten first Parma and then Piacenza. In a terse communiqué to the duke of Bourbon in Milan, Frundsburg had stated: 'In the face of great dangers I have crossed the high mountains and deep waters, have spent two months in the country, enduring poverty, hunger and frost: that owing to the great patience of my soldiers and with the help of God I have divided and driven back the enemy. I now lay here in the enemy's country, attacked every day, and desire further instructions.'[383] Bourbon pulled out all the stops in Milan to settle arrears of pay with his own Spanish mercenaries and the two imperial armies were ultimately able to link up at Piacenza on 30 January 1527. By this time, Pope Clement VII was under pressure from the viceroy of Naples, Charles de Lannoy, to bribe Frundsburg's *landsknechts* with the sum of 200,000 ducats to send them home to Germany. The Pope's inquiries to Venice asking whether they would help raise this sum met with a stone wall and, at his wits end, on 31 January Clement signed a treaty with Lannoy agreeing to abandon his allies in the Holy League of Cognac and pay the *landsknechts* and Spaniards massing in Lombardy the sum they were demanding to disperse.

The following month, however, Clement had turned weathercock again and had abandoned the treaty with Lannoy. Shortly before his death, Giovanni delle Bande Nere had despatched five companies of the Black Bands, around 1,500 of his most seasoned veterans, under the command of his trusted lieutenant Lucantonio Cuppano and ordered them to march south and block the advance of Lannoy's Spanish troops advancing towards Rome from Naples. Lannoy's column was the other half of the pincer by which Charles V proposed to squeeze the Pope. Cuppano and his men reached the small hilltop hamlet of Frosinone which commanded the road to Rome and barricaded themselves inside the town. Bolstered by the unexpected, though immensely welcome, discovery of a thousand barrels of wine which had been stored in Frosinone, the men of the Black Bands had repulsed the Imperialist troops until the arrival of a sizable relief force from Rome on 1 February 1527, at which point the Spaniards abandoned the field. All of Rome was ecstatic at this unexpected victory by the late Giovanni's Black Bands. Believing himself to be holding the upper hand, Clement quickly abandoned his agreement with Lannoy. He now sent fresh word to King François through his papal nuncio of his eternal and undying loyalty to the crown of France. Upon hearing this, François remarked candidly to his amused court, expressing the wish that the Holy Father 'would make up his mind' whose side he was on. The panegyrists meanwhile had a veritable field day over the triumph of Frosinone. Paolo Giovio declared that the men of the Black Bands resembled '8,000 *morti*' [ghosts] and that Lucantonio Cuppano himself, who resembled the Greek hero Patroclus, had displayed an appearance '*da far saltare Venere fora del bagno e Volcano fora di fucina*' ('that would make Venus jump out of her bathtub and Vulcan out of his forge').[384]

Meanwhile, however, in Mantua an embittered Pietro Aretino was adding to Pope Clement's woes by applying his mordant wit to the composition of a new and devastating sonnet:

> Seven false and futile years I've flung away,
> Four with Pope Leo, with Messer Clement three.
> And if I thus made an enemy,
> Their fault it surely was, not mine, I say.
> And for all this I've had so little pay
> That poor as threadbare mountebank I be.
> Ay, just as so much wind have blown away all hopes I had of any papacy.
> Scars I still bear upon my hands and face
> Because five times a day I did defend
> The honour of my patrons and their fame.
> But rank and benefice and salary and place
> To bastards only come and men of shame.

Clement rewards but those who Clement rend.[385]

As if this was not enough, Aretino further compounded his provocation of Clement by publishing what he called *The Prophecy of Messer Pasquino, the Fifth Evangelist* which was dedicated to Federico Gonzaga. This latest tirade was composed in the form of a *giudizio*, which was a highly popular form of astrological almanac or 'prognostication' in the early sixteenth-century. Monarchs and other important personages often felt themselves to be at the mercy of blind fate and they regularly employed the services of court astrologers to guide them through turbulent current events. One notable who had made extensive use of court astrologers had been Filippo Maria Visconti, a former duke of Milan, who actively consulted his astrologers on all important political decisions. In his *Life of Filippo Maria Visconti* the Duke's private secretary Pier Candid Decembrio had written that his master 'Gave so much credit to astrologers as a *scientia* that he attracted the most experienced practitioners of this discipline, and he almost never took any initiative without first consulting them: among those who were held in the highest esteem were Pietro from Siena and Stefano from Faenza, both very experienced in the art, while towards the end of his time as lord of Milan he drew actively from the advice of Antonio Bernareggi, sometimes Luigi Terzaghi, and often Lanfranco from Parma. Among his physicians he counted also Elia, the Jew, a famous soothsayer.'[386] Another lord who had made it his regular practice to consult court astrologers was Giovanni Bentivoglio, the cruel tyrant of Bologna. In 1504, Bentivoglio had consulted his court astrologer, the *Napoletano* seer Luca Gaurico, about the destiny of his son Annibale. Disliking the astrologer's prediction, however, Bentivoglio had subjected Gaurico to the torture known as *Mancuerda*. This involved the tying of a thin cord around the victim's arm and tightening it until it cut right through to the bone (despite the dreadful injury, Gaurico went on to enjoy a renowned career, accurately predicting both the elevation of Pope Paul III and the death of Henry II of France in a joust).

But the passion for such *giudizi*, which were similar to the common almanacs of the lower classes, were in truth favoured by all sections of the community both high and low. *Giudizi* were usually published at the beginning of the year and set down the author's predictions for the year ahead. Aretino had already adopted this genre for himself as early as 1524, predicting a grand conjunction of all the planets in Libra; however the presence of Saturn in this conjunction would lead to 'storms, earthquakes and floods together with wars, apostasies, heresies and the conversion of infidels'.[387] The satirist turned his *giudizi* into witty divinations relative to men and events of the time, but they were no longer based on the observation of the stars but instead his knowledge of the world, posing as a prophet. Aretino hence transformed the *giudizio* genre from a homespun, superstitious catalogue of forecasts into a biting satirical tract which spared no person, however powerful, from Aretino's considerable powers of mockery and derision. This included the astrologer Luca Gaurico himself, of whom Aretino was jealous since he was a former favourite of the Gonzagas.[388] Aretino had first met Gaurico in 1526 when he had been in Mantua and had described disparagingly him as '*il Gaurico profeta dopo il fatto*' ('Gaurico the prophet after the fact').[389]

Of Aretino's *giudizio* of early 1527, only a bare fragment remains unfortunately,[390] however from his later letters it is possible to reconstruct many of the writer's 'astrological prognostications' (*pronostici*) for that year. Most tellingly, the 1527 tract poured scorn upon Pope Clement VII and his minions in the Curia. Furthermore, it openly censured them for the pitiful state in which Italy now found itself, at the mercy of Frundsburg and the duke of Bourbon's Imperialist army. *The Prophecy of Messer Pasquino, the Fifth Evangelist* even went so far as to predict the impending subjection of Rome to the imperial hordes, although this may have had more to do with Aretino's vengeful wishful thinking than with any real supernatural foresight. Understandably the Pope was not amused. Although Aretino would later be acclaimed as a *Propheta divino*, Clement VII still sat–albeit unsteadily–upon his throne in St. Peter's and shot back his reply courtesy of Federico's ambassador in Rome. 'A Little book by Pietro Aretino has just appeared in Rome', wrote the ambassador to Federico, continuing that 'It is full of slander and deals principally with the Pope, the cardinals and the other prelates of this court. It is dedicated to Your Lordship. This fact has caused a great deal of scandal among the persons concerned. It is thought strange that in view of your relations with the Pope and his cardinals as a captain-general of the Church you should allow such a book to be brought out in Mantua under your auspices and name.'[391] The Pope's emissary, a Franciscan friar, finished this harangue with the express wish that the Marquess of Mantua 'dismiss the Aretine from Mantua and deprive him of your grace'.[392] If Federico consented to do this the Pope indicated that he and his court would overlook his role in the whole affair.

Federico found that he had very little wiggle room. Called to account by Pope Clement, if he continued to shelter Aretino at the Mantuan court he risked incurring Clement's wrath. Obsequiously he replied back to the pontiff feigning ignorance of Aretino's dedication of the work to him and vowing solemnly that the writer would be dismissed from Mantua. Not only did he promise to send Aretino away but he also hinted that he was willing to have the satirist assassinated should the Pope so wish it. Tantalisingly, Pope Clement VII's response to this offer has not survived. One would like to imagine that, for all his faults, Pope Clement would have had the strength of character to recoil from such an ignoble proposal but lacking evidence either way we simply cannot know. Was Federico himself sincere about the offer? The consensus of Aretino's biographers is perhaps not. It has even been suggested that the proposal probably even came from Aretino himself and that both men had included it in the letter as some sort of private joke. Although it might have served Federico's interests to have had a potential blackmailer done in, the fact was that he felt too fond of Aretino to have been likely to carry it through. Unlike Francesco Maria della Rovere, a maniac who had beaten his rival cardinal Francesco Alidosi to death with his own bare hands in the street, Federico Gonzaga was a lover and not a cold-blooded killer.

Both patron and client parted therefore on good terms. In answer to the Marquess's question 'whither shall you now go?' Aretino shrugged. To him at this point 'a gondolier there was to be preferred to a chamberlain there', *there* meaning of course Rome.[393] He then quoted some lines of the character Flaminio from his own play *La Cortigiana*: 'I shall go to Venice. I shall enrich my poverty with her liberty. For there at least poor men are not ruined at the whim of any male or female favourite. Only in Venice does justice hold the scales with an even balance. There only fear of disgrace does not force you to adore someone who was in the gutter only yesterday. Surely Venice is a holy city and the earthly paradise'.[394] Aretino was once more a fugitive, out of favour with the Pope, and there were few cities in Italy that he could flee to that the papal authorities would not be able to track him down and drag him back in chains. Venice was the traditional place of refuge for such souls. No state could be found in history 'that may bee paragond with this of ours, for institutions & lawes prudently decreed' Gasparo Contarini would write in 1543 in *De magistratibus et republica venetorum* ('The Commonwealth and Government of Venice').[395] If you were an outsider, Venice would take you in and give you shelter. Venice herself had begun life as a place of sanctuary and the city had always been regarded as Italy's outcast, a place which was more eastward-looking than western, slightly oriental, and proudly independent. From the quiet, mist-shrouded lakes of Mantua, Aretino now prepared to make the seventy-seven mile horse ride east to the sheltering lagoons of Venice.

⊙☾

To the east, squatting on oak and larch wood piles driven deep into the mud of her coastal lagoons, lay *La Serenissima*, the Most Serene Republic of Venice. For Aretino, it was simply the city-state which knew nothing of 'the evils of courts'. Venice's citizens were descended from Latin refugees who, beginning in the tumultuous fifth-century C.E., had fled the Roman settlements of Padua, Aquileia, Treviso, Altino and Concordia in the wake of successive waves of invasions by Huns, Goths, Lombards and Franks. In their swampy lowland coastal lagoons, where their enemies had always lacked both the means as well as the inclination to pursue them, the Venetians felt safe. In the centuries that followed, they had taken naturally to the sea where their abilities as a traditionally coastal people served them well as they learned to combine trading with seamanship. Perched precariously on the waters of the Adriatic and ruled by her elected lifetime monarch the doge, Venice had traditionally eschewed the expansionism of the mainland Italian city-states such as Milan or Rome for a shrewd internationalist policy of merchant maritime development. This trans nationalist mercantile policy, a unique product of Venice's own lack of natural mainland resources, which were largely restricted to fish, white building stone from Istria, and sand for glassmaking, had led to the creation of a giant overseas trading empire that extended as far afield as Acre, Alexandria, Cherson, Constantinople, Sardinia, Sicily and Tunis.

Following a period of consolidation during the ninth-century during which Venice had exerted its iron will on the other islands of the lagoon and wrestled control of the mouths of the rivers Po and Adige, Venice had embarked upon its great overseas mercantile adventure. Coastal settlements all along the Dalmatian littoral were the first to either fall or agree, for the purposes of security against inland Balkan aggressors, to come under Venetian dominion. The mighty Byzantine Empire meanwhile cooperated with this growing sea power, granting Venice unprecedented trading privileges at Constantinople. Participation in the crusade of 1096 and then later in 1108 successfully opened the way to Venetian trade with the important Mediterranean seaports of the Levant. But then disaster struck in 1119 when the *basileus* John II Komnenos abruptly withdrew Venice's trading privileges. These were promptly restored again after Venice retaliated against Byzantine interests in the Aegean. But in 1171 the Empire struck back and John's son, Manuel I Komnenos, ordered that 20,000 Venetians resident on imperial territory were to be arrested and their property confiscated. An incensed Venice had despatched another fleet on a fresh punitive expedition but this time, decimated by the plague, it failed in its objectives.

The Venetians would have to wait thirty-three years for their revenge but when it came it was nothing short of devastating. In 1204, Constantinople was sacked by a rapacious Latin army of over 30,000 Crusaders—an army which had been transported in Venetian galleys—and Venice herself used the chaos which ensued to seize Crete, Corfu and numerous other strategic territories in the Ionians whilst solidifying her control over coastal Dalmatia. Venice's dominance of her seaways along the Adriatic were guaranteed and Constantinople's subjection was complete. The Venetians then rubbed salt into the Greeks' wounds; they carried off the four magnificent bronze horses formerly displayed at Constantinople's Hippodrome. Also stolen were the valuable porphyry sculptures of the Four Roman Tetrarchs that had previously adorned the pillars of the Philadelphion; they were reinstalled in a corner of the façade of the Basilica of San Marco where they remain to this day.

Numbering fewer more than 100,000 inhabitants in the year 1300, the Venetians' intelligence, their canny aptitude for survival and their unsurpassed ability to build fast, light, sea-going galleys in huge volumes led to their reputation as the acknowledged masters of the sea lanes. At Venice's state-of-the-art shipbuilding facility, the Arsenal, one ship could be assembled from a prefabricated 'kit' every few hours. No other state had this capability in maritime technology. Given their aggressive mercantile policies it was perhaps inevitable that they would clash with that other great Italian sea power Genoa, but by June 1380, having watched their proud fleet bottled up and destroyed by the Venetians at Chioggia, the *Genovesi* had bowed out of the confrontation having finally realised they had been outmatched and outclassed. In the aftermath of the War of Chioggia, Venice turned her attentions landwards and a period of territorial expansion ensued under the doges Tommaso Mocenigo and Francesco Foscari. Under Mocenigo, Venice neutralised the powerful Carraresi family by 1405 and seized their possessions of Padua and then Este, the ancestral home of Ferrara's rulers, following which Venice extended its possessions all the way to Verona and Lake Garda. The 1418 war that Mocenigo fought against the patriarch of Aquileia, meanwhile, had secured for Venice the whole of the region of Friuli including the capital city of Udine.

With the Adriatic Sea by now in effect a Venetian lake, by the early fifteenth-century Venice's huge trade income, combined with her tough and uncompromising inhabitants, stood her in good stead to face down the growing expansionist threat from Milan, with whom she shared a common frontier. This next phase of Venetian expansionism, chiefly against the Milanese House of Visconti for domination of the cities of the Lombard plain, took place under the auspices of the warlike and belligerent doge, Francesco Foscari. The war proceeded well and by 1428, Milan had been obliged to relinquish certain key cities in the Lombard Plain such as Bergamo, Brescia and Cremona to Venice. Venice and Milan finally came together in the Peace of Lodi on 9 April 1454, an accord which ended the hostilities between the two city-states and whose architect was Florence's ruler Cosimo de' Medici. But although this peace was further upgraded into the twenty-five-year-long truce known as the Most Holy League this failed to end further conflict and, up until the Treaty of

Bagnolo of August 1484, Venice continued to fight with Ferrara, Naples and Urbino over various fractious issues. 1484 marked the year that Venice reached the maximum historical extent of her territorial possessions on *terraferma*. Alliance with King Louis XII of France against Ludovico Sforza of Milan in the 1499 Treaty of Blois brought Venice additional possessions such as the Ghiara d'Adda.

Success inevitably brought envy and suspicion, however, and Venice now found herself opposed by a concerted front of Italian and European powers. In a cynical land-grab of Venice's possessions in the Romagna, Pope Julius II launched the Wars of the League of Cambrai in 1508 which saw *La Serenissima* facing the combined power of Rome, Germany, Spain and France. A French army led by King Louis XII crossed the river Adda, which served as the boundary between Venice's possessions on the *terraferma* and the duchy of Milan. On 14 May 1509, the vanguard of that same French army pounced upon the rear-guard of a Venetian army under the command of Bartolomeo d'Alviano at a town called Agnadello. The French king gave the order that no Venetian prisoners were to be taken. When the smoke of battle finally lifted thousands of Venetian corpses from the 30,000-strong Venetian army littered the battlefield. Agnadello and its aftermath had signalled the loss of virtually the entirety of Venice's territorial acquisitions during the preceding century. It was an absolutely devastating blow to the maritime republic and ended forever Venice's aspiration to become a formidable land power in Lombardy and the Romagna. The French invasion had overrun the entire Venetian *terraferma* except for Treviso and reached as far as Mestre, from where the bombardment was disconcertingly audible in the Venetian lagoon itself. As always, Venice's shallow creeks, coves and inlets protected the city from invasion and conquest and for the next eight years Venice endured a long, hard slog to regain her territory. In 1517, the Venetian diarist Marino Sanudo recorded the sense of elation as Venetian forces re-occupied Verona.

By the time of the Peace of Bologna of 1530, Venice's mainland empire—though truncated—nonetheless still encompassed Verona, Vicenza, Feltre, Bassano, Padua, Udine, Friuli, Brescia, Bergamo, Ravenna, Crema, Rovigo and the Polesine. In addition, Venice's fabled Arsenal continued to dominate military shipbuilding in the Adriatic. However, by this time, Venice's mercantile and seafaring might was under growing threat from the oceanic trade of the Americas and the Indies. Essentially a Mediterranean power, Venice's shallow-bottomed, oar-dependent galleys were ill-suited to the oceanic voyages which Columbus's discovery had opened up to the Americas in 1492 or those of Vasco da Gama from Portugal to India from 1497-99. Matters were hardly helped when the headquarters of the German merchants' union, the Fondaco die Tedeschi, burned to the ground in 1505, drastically affecting Venice's access to northern European markets for her eastern trade goods. The burning of the Rialto market in 1514 was another unwelcome blow to Venice's commercial life, as were the plague epidemics of 1503 and 1510. Although Venice would have one final moment of military glory at Lepanto in 1571, by the time that Pietro Aretino arrived in the city-state it was already by now a declining sea power and soon to be a declining mercantile power too. By the eighteenth-century Venice would devolve into little more than a tourist destination, the precursor of the Venice of today in fact–a city of shops, luxuries, good living and high-end prostitution for those who had wealth enough to enjoy it.

By the year 1527, *La Serenissima* was governed by its seventy-two-year-old Doge Andrea Gritti. Gritti was a former merchant and trade representative in Turkish Constantinople, where he served time in prison on charges of spying. He was also a martial man, having served as *proveditor* to the Venetian army during the Wars of Cambrai, as well as later its commander-in-chief. Palma il Giovane would depict Gritti in a fresco in the Great Council Chamber wearing a suit of armour and leading the reconquest of Padua in June 1509. Titian would paint Gritti in 1546 as a man of elderly girth, his leather belt fastened at the very last possible hole. But Gritti was also a shrewd diplomat as well as a formidable soldier; shortly after his election as doge in 1523 he brokered a treaty with Charles V which ensured Venice's neutrality in the ongoing wars between Charles and François. This guaranteed Venice a modicum of peace and stability which the rest of Italy would not enjoy until the cessation of the Italian Wars in 1559. As with his predecessors, Gritti's election had entailed that tortuously long and complex process by which doges were selected in the republic, a procedure which involved a sequence of committees appointing numerous other committees in their turn until the final committees–the Eleven and the Forty-one–ultimately selected the nobleman who would be doge.

Maintaining her neutrality had been the making of Venice during this quarrelsome period. Inevitably, however, a fierce rivalry had sprung up between Venice and that other great mercantile republic, Florence. This enmity occasionally took shape in popular literature; in his Second Tale of the Fourth Day, the Florentine Boccaccio wrote that Berto della Massa of Imola 'lived a wicked, corrupt life and the *Imolese* were so well acquainted with his despicable conduct that eventually not a soul believed a word he said, even when he was telling the truth. Realising that he couldn't get away with his mischief here any longer, he was driven to move to Venice, sink of all iniquity, as he expected that there he should be able to pursue his nefarious activities along fresh lines'.[396] Whilst other city-states lay bankrupt or devastated or else continually changed hands at a bewildering rate, as was certainly the case with Milan, Venice remained peaceful and prosperous, a natural haven for Italy's many political exiles who recognised in the maritime state a place where their freedom of speech would be upheld and their liberty as individuals safeguarded. During much of the fifteenth-century, Venice had been fiercely independent from Rome, with whom the republic had frequently been on poor terms throughout much of that tumultuous century. Laws had, for example, been set in place which expressly excluded from political office any Venetian nobleman who was endowed with ecclesiastical benefices. This was intended to counter the perceived growing problem of 'Romanism' within the state, as families such as the Foscari, Barbaro, Badoer, Corner, Emo, Grimani and Pisano sought to corner the market on Roman clerical appointments whilst continuing to have a significant say in the state's secular government.[397] Under Doge Gritti, however, there had ensued a period of rapprochement and rapport between Venice and Rome mostly fuelled by the former's suspicions of the Emperor Charles V's growing power on the Italian mainland. Treaties in 1524 and 1525 culminating ultimately in the 1526 League of Cognac installed a joint Roman-Venetian bulwark against the Empire.

Around the same time, printing and free speech blossomed in Venice throughout this period. Venice was especially fertile ground for the burgeoning post-Gutenberg printing industry, with the first printed editions appearing in the republic in 1469. Soon afterwards, Venice quickly emerged as the largest producer of printed material in Europe, a position it would maintain for the next 100 years thanks to the republic's extensive maritime networks, which provided a wide-ranging distribution system for print editions. The Aldine Press founded by Aldus Manutius, the inventor of Italic type and the semicolon, quickly established itself as the specialist in Greek volumes–the fictional protagonist of Thomas More's *Utopia* was proud of his books by the Aldine Press. Later, when cheap, vernacular printings of ephemera began to assume even greater importance than the Greek and Latin classics, Venice's printing industry really came into its own and, as such, the city might have been created with Aretino specifically in mind. The city was also home to the *cerretani*, who partly filled the role of street vendors and partly booksellers and sometimes even acted as publishers in their own right.[398]

During this time, Venice's most renowned living artists included the great Titian, as well as his much younger rival Tintoretto. Titian's two greatest influences, Giorgione and Giovanni Bellini were by now both dead, Giorgione in 1510, a victim of the plague, and Bellini in 1516. Their style of painting had revolutionised the arts in Venice during this time and helped lay the foundation for later Venetian masters of great repute. It had been Bellini who had painted the famous portrait of Doge Leonardo

Loredan, a canvas which was almost surreally photo-realistic and which captured every facet of the man's essence, character and *gravitas*. Another great Venetian painter, Sebastiano del Piombo, had already left Venice to seek his fortune in Rome; Agostino Chigi had filched del Piombo and enticed him back with him to Rome when he visited Venice on an official diplomatic mission in 1511. Del Piombo painted for Chigi and also for Aretino's nemesis Pope Clement VII and in Rome Aretino had known him well. Another notable Venetian painter, Giovanni di Niccolò Mansueti, had only just died the year previous in 1526. Like del Piombo, Aretino was already familiar with the Florentine architect and sculptor Jacopo Sansovino from his years in Rome, however Sansovino would soon flee to Venice due to the awful events later that same year. The freedom of self-expression, the more transparent system of government and of law, and the flourishing of the humanities, publishing and painting led Aretino to declare that in this metropolis of Venice 'the sun warms all men alike, the moon gives them light and for all the stars shine forth; our true fatherland is that which welcomes us'.[399]

Indeed Venice might have been made for a man like Aretino. Did the city not have its very origins as a haven for exiles and a place of refuge, first from the Huns and later the Lombards and Franks? There had of course existed other open cities in the course of history. In *The History of the Peloponnesian War* Thucydides had made Pericles boast in his Funeral Oration: 'We keep our city open, not expelling foreigners to prevent their seeing something whose exposure could be useful to an enemy'.[400] As in the case of Athens many centuries before, Venice also professed that outsiders were warmly welcome and this openness to foreigners was the city's unmistakable *genius loci*. Even as late as the fifteenth-century, one visitor to the city blandly recorded that 'most of the people are foreigners'.[401] Amongst the Venetians themselves this sentiment had been echoed by the diarist Girolamo Priuli who wrote that Venice 'was open to foreigners, and all could come and go everywhere without any obstacle'.[402] Like Athens, Venice tapped the skills, knowledge and expertise of those migrants and outcasts who came to dwell within the safety of her lagoons. Amongst the many ethnic groups which flocked to Venice were the French, Slavs, Greeks and Flemings, Germans, Spaniards and Turks. There was even a sizable Jewish community and, in the aftermath of the Turkish conquest of Constantinople in 1453, many Byzantine Greeks had also sought sanctuary here too, feeling quite at home in Venice's hybrid western-oriental culture.

The rights of immigrants to domicile were respected and enshrined in Venetian law. Selected foreigners, known as *forestieri*, were permitted to become *cittadini* (the middle classes) which actually even gave them higher rank than many of the local *popolani* or working class inhabitants.

167

Others of a less important stripe who were not granted citizenship were nevertheless permitted to conduct business in the city, work at one of the many trades, fight aboard Venice's galleys and establish their own fraternal clubs (*scuole*).[403] Beyond this superficial freedom to settle and become productive members of the community, however, the Venetian authorities kept these migrant alien populations under close observation; this was abetted by the fact that the national or ethnic groups themselves tended to congregate in their own specific areas. The Byzantines and Greeks had their neighbourhood clustered around their Orthodox churches, the Albanians likewise had their national quarter. The Jews were tolerated for the wealth which they brought (Marino Sanudo had described Jews as being 'as necessary in a country as bakers')[404] but were otherwise held at arm's length socially. Confined to the densely populated Cannaregio district to the north, specifically to the *Ghetto Nuovo* near the local iron foundry, Jews were only permitted to leave the ghetto at the tolling of the *marangona* bell in the morning and were locked in at night when the authorities raised the drawbridge which separated the self-contained island from San Polo and Venice's other *sestieri*. During the daytime they tended to congregate along the left bank of the Grand Canal, near the Rialto bridge[405] where they conducted their moneylending businesses, one of the few legal trades allowed to them by the authorities, and the pursuit of which caused them sadly to be reviled by the Venetians and other Christian communities. Aside from moneylending, Jews also engaged in second-hand goods dealing and were employed as medical doctors.[406] The German community meanwhile kept their distance from the Jews of the Rialto, generally adhering to the other side of the Grand Canal.[407]

Harmonising the needs of foreign communities with the overall good of the state was a delicate balancing act. Which is not to say that Venice was any less protectionist when it came down to brass tacks and the observance of particular trades. Merchants and even artists were required to register for a license before being permitted to engage in trade or crafts, and such licenses required fairly frequent renewal. In an April 1506 letter to Wilibald Pirkheimer, Burgher of Nürberg, Albrecht Dürer complained after his visit to Venice that same year that he had been summoned before the magistrate no less than three times and been forced to pay four florins to the arts guild in return for the work he was doing. Dürer had bitterly criticized the intolerance of the Venetian artists towards outside competition who, he complained, 'are very unfriendly to me'.[408] Florence, by contrast, was more welcoming towards visiting or migrant craft labour and refrained from pressuring artisans from joining the local *arti* or guilds.

⊙☾

Pietro Aretino made landfall at a jetty adjacent to the Ducal Palace in the Venetian republic on 27 March 1527. He was accompanied by a solitary groom, a former soldier from the Black Bands. He stepped off his boat onto the Molo, the stone-paved dock directly in front of the Doge's Palace. Here stood the two towering granite columns which paid homage to Venice's patrons, St. Mark and St. Teodoro of Amasea. Condemned men were traditional executed between these two great pillars. It had been on the Molo that the legendary *condottiere* Francesco Bussone da Carmagnola had been beheaded for treachery in the year 1432. Aretino stood and surveyed the scene which now greeted his eyes.

To his right stood the Palazzo Ducale, built in the mid 1300s and extended by Doge Francesco Foscari several years before his ordering of Carmagnola's execution. Immediately in front of him was the famous Piazza San Marco with its renowned church of St Mark's, an exotic-looking confection with its oriental domes in the Byzantine style and its soaring Campanile. Here were the four bronze horses looted from Constantinople in the year 1204 when Venice's blind Doge Enrico Dandolo and his Latin allies had brutally sacked the seat of Eastern Orthodoxy. Here too, under the church's gable, was the fabled Lion of St. Mark with its paw placed upon a book (in earlier, more expansionist decades, the lion had often been depicted carrying a sword instead). At this time the *piazza* was not yet fully enclosed by the three Procuratie buildings. Only the Procuratie Vecchie, the 'Old Procuratie', stood on the far side of the square, having been built just seven years before by Bartolomeo Bon the Younger. A 'new' Procuratie, the Procuratie Nuove, would shortly be designed by Aretino's friend Jacopo Sansovino, who would play an important role in the civic revitalisation of Venice. The Procuratie Vecchie itself terminated at its eastern end with the Clocktower of San Marco, the Torre dell' Orologio, which had been completed in 1499. Sansovino would also later sweep away some revolting open air public latrines which Giorgio Vasari described as 'something foul and shameful for the dignity of the palace and the public square, as well as for foreigners, who coming to Venice by way of San Giorgio saw all that filthiness first'.[409] Though he did not know it at the time, Pietro Aretino had finally come *home*.

No sooner than Aretino had landed than a non-stop stream of praise for his new home began flowing from his pen. Here in Venice Aretino knew that at last he was freed from the slavish subservience of courtly dependency and sycophancy; here at last was a city where men of merit were listened to and taken seriously on account of their own talents and not simply because of who they happened to know at court. Aretino's sense of delight was infectious. 'Believe me that those who have never seen either Rome or Venice have deprived themselves of two things that are marvellous sights. But in quite different ways!' he wrote to his half-brother Francesco Bacci, 'For in one, you see the insolence of undeserved fortune strutting up and down, and in the other, you see the grave march of rule and dominion. It is a strange thing to see the confusion of the papal court. But a beautiful sight to see the unity of purpose of this republic. Indeed, if you could let your imagination, so to speak, fly as high as the sky, you would never be able to picture in your mind the twisting and shifting of the first, and the straightforward progress of the second. For they are twin edifices of turmoil and of quiet.'[410] Aretino went on to describe to Bacci how one day a Mantuan citizen wanted to show him how Venice stands in the sea: 'He filled a basin of water with half shells of walnuts and exclaimed: "Behold! That's what it's like!"'.[411] Another time, said Aretino, a certain Venetian preacher wanted to describe the papal court without tiring himself out too much. He therefore simply held up a painting of Hell. (Aretino was not so transported by the joy of finding himself in such congenial surroundings as to forget to pass a wicked judgement on Rome at the same time that he was complimenting Venice.) Other cities, in comparison to Venice, seemed like mere paupers' settlements. Indeed, 'the Lord God Himself would be glad to stay here for eleven months of the year. For here your head is never splitting, nor do you think you are about to die, and here Liberty moves about with banners flying, and nobody to say to her "Haul them down!"'[412]

The same day that he arrived in Venice, Andreas Osiander's *A Wondrous Prophecy of the Papacy*, a work which spoke out about the creeping corruption of the court of Rome, was being banned by the city council of Nuremberg.[413] It was the shape of things to come. In his panegyrics Aretino himself often veered too far, being prepared to overlook any shortcomings in his new home since the contrast with Rome appeared to him so stark. It was the classic mindset of the fresh immigrant who fails to see anything amiss in the state which has granted him refuge. In its own way, Venice was just as socially ossified as Rome. Venice was a monumentally class-conscious society and the Venetian aristocracy had effectively been 'closed' since its *serrata* (closure or 'lock-out') in the year 1297. At the summit of Venetian society was the Venetian patriciate, which was restricted to a group of about 2,000 old aristocratic families. Next came the more bourgeois *cittadini originari* ('original citizens'), a hereditary caste which provided Venice with its civil service bureaucrats. The *cittadini originari* were demarcated from the patriciate by the *Libri d'Oro* (Golden Books), a register of all aristocratic births in the republic. Formal endogamy was practised by the patriciate; those nobles who married the daughters of wealthy *cittadini*, to perhaps give a fillip to their dwindling fortunes, were deprived of their noble status. The different social classes were also strictly delineated by dress.

None of this impinged on Aretino's newfound admiration for the republic. He would later write publicly to the doge, enthusing: 'For here treachery has no place. Here favour does no wrong to be set right. Here the cruelty of harlots does not reign. Here the insolence of Ganymedes does not command. Here there is no robbery. Here there are no rapes. Here no one is murdered ... O universal fatherland! O sanctuary for all! O Inn of the dispersed people! How much greater would be the woes of Italy if your goodness were any the less! Here is a refuge for her nations! Here is security for her riches! Here all her honours are preserved! Venice embraces you, where others scorn you. She rules you, where others chastise you. She nourishes you, where others starve you. She receives you, where others hunt you down. And as she cheers you in your tribulations, she preserves you in charity and love. So let us bow before her, and let us offer our prayers on her behalf to God ... She is Rome's reproach, because here there are no minds that could or would tyrannize over her liberty, or make her a slave in the minds of her people.'[414]

To one of his correspondents, a priest, Aretino wrote: 'I am now in carefree, liberal and just Venice, where neither sickness, death, hunger nor war oppresses the citizens. It is my opinion that if Eden, where Adam dwelt with Eve, had resembled Venice she would have had a hard time trying to tempt him out of that earthly paradise with her fruit. For to lose a place like Venice, where so much is lovely, would be a very different matter from losing the Garden of Eden, for all its figs, melons and grapes. For my part, as I have said before, I should wish God to change me into a gondola when I die, or else into its canopy, or if that is considered beyond my deserts into one of its oars, rowlocks or cleaning rags. Even a baling scoop would do. A sponge would be still more appropriate. And I would love, just so as not to have to leave Venice, to become one of those little copper coins with which people here pay the ferryman. If I were a rat that feeds in the Venetian Treasury I would feel like one of heaven's cherubim. Nor would I change my condition for that which popes are said to have in paradise, though I doubt whether any are really there, if I could only be the door leading into the Tower of St. Mark. For, to sum up, Venice is not only more eternal than or rather as eternal as the world itself but also the refuge, the delight and the consolation of all who live there.'[415]

CHAPTER 9

෧ᢂ෧

Il Sacco di Roma

In Rome, the chief city of Christendom, no bells ring, no churches are open, no masses are said. Sundays and feast days have ceased. Many houses are burned to the ground; in others the doors and windows are broken and carried away; the streets are changed into dunghills. The stench of dead bodies is terrible; men and beasts have a common grave and in the churches I have seen corpses that dogs have gnawed. In the public places, tables are set close together at which thousands of ducats are gambled for. The air rings with blasphemies fit to make good men–if such there be– wish that they were deaf. I know nothing wherewith I can compare it, except it be the destruction of Jerusalem. I do not believe that if I live for two thousand years I should see the like again.

Anonymous Spanish eye-witness
to the sack of Rome

At dawn on Monday, 6 May 1527 ('*Il dì sexto di Maggio, ohimè l'orrendo giorno infelice*', '..alas the ugly unhappy day', as Aretino would later write),[416] the ragged and starving army of the duke of Bourbon stormed the city walls of Rome in the vicinity of the Janiculum and Vatican Hill. The Imperialist troops concentrated their efforts on the small, vulnerable stretch of wall which lay between the Porta San Spirito and the Porta del Torrione. Opposing them were just 2,000 men of the Pontifical Swiss Guard and less than 1,500 remnants of the Black Bands. The latter comprised the five companies which had earlier triumphed at Frosinone; they had subsequently returned to be billeted in Rome whereupon an unappreciative Pope Clement VII neglected to settle their arrears of pay, a situation which had generated considerable friction between the Black Bands and the slightly more cosseted Papal Swiss

Guard.[417] Despite a stiff show of resistance, during which Lucantonio Cuppano's men repulsed the Imperialists' initial assault, the hard-pressed harquebusiers of the Black Bands were eventually overwhelmed and massacred at the end of a desperate mêlée. Lucantonio, wrote Aretino, *'combattendo con una sconcia ferita, dimostrò che pure in lui s'era trasferito lo spirto di chi lo allevò'* ('fighting with a ghastly wound, showed that the spirit of the man who had nurtured him [Giovanni de' Medici] had been transferred into him too'.)[418] For all his Herculean efforts, however, Lucantonio was taken prisoner. The Duke of Bourbon, meanwhile, was dead, shot supposedly by Pope Clement's friend the boastful silversmith Benvenuto Cellini. With Rome quickly overrun the Pope, along with several of his cardinals, fled for the second time that year along the elevated Passetto di Borgo and sought sanctuary inside the Castel Sant'Angelo. Aretino's bone-chilling prediction at the beginning of 1527 concerning Rome's impending fate had, it seemed, come chillingly true.

At Mantua, Federico Gonzaga, supposedly the Pope's captain-general, sat on his rear end whilst receiving communiqués and updates from his ambassador Francesco Gonzaga. On 7 May, Francesco would describe in unvarnished terms the *'exterminio et total ruina de Roma'*, lamenting the 'cruel spectacle that would move stones to pity', and adding for good measure that 'one could very well say that Our Lord God wishes to apply the lash to Christendom, which will not forget this for many years'.[419] Federico himself would be exonerated by a supportive post-facto pasquinade which stated 'The marquess of Mantua was embarrassed to have to be a captain to a church thus shamed, disgraced, slandered and abused' (*'Ho detto che è vergogna al marchese di Mantua a esser capitano della Chiesa sfacciata, amorbata, affamata e vituperata'*).[420] The streets of Rome teemed with rough Spanish and Lutheran soldiers who casually lay waste to the city. One of the participants in the sacking, the renowned German mercenary commander Sebastian Schertlin Burtenbach, would later write matter-of-factly in his autobiography: 'In the year 1527, on 6 May, we took Rome by storm, put over 6,000 men to the sword, seized all that we could find in the churches and elsewhere, burned down a great part of the city, tearing and destroying all copyists work, all registers, letters and state documents'.[421] On 8 June, Cardinal Salviati would write to Baldassare Castiglione, who was at this time in Madrid on a fool's errand trying to build goodwill with the Emperor, telling him: 'The impiety and knavery which have been done [are] such [as] I am not able to write. Dead are all the innocent boys of Santo Spirito [Hospital], all the infirm are thrown in the Tiber, profaned and violated are all the monasteries … Burned is the great chapel of St Peter and of Sixtus … Stolen are the heads of the Apostles and the other relics … The Sacrament is trampled on and thrown in the mud.' Salviati concluded dolefully with the words 'I shudder to contemplate this for Christians are doing what the Turk never did'.[422]

Acts of desecration seemed to come first, promulgated chiefly by the Lutheran Germans who had come to deal *Der Römische Antichrist* a righteous death blow. Throughout the city the Catholic churches were a principal target of the Lutheran soldiers. As roving bands of *landsknechts* wound their way through Rome's streets and *piazze*, church doors were torn from their hinges and their contents tossed into the streets. Chalices, sacred vessels, candlesticks, monstrances, all were swept from their altars into the bags of the soldiers. This was loot which the Lutherans maintained had been unlawfully stolen by the Church 'from the godly nations of the earth' and it was destined to be either melted down or sold. 'Why does not the pope, whose wealth is today greater than the wealth of the richest Crassus, build this one basilica of St. Peter with his own money rather than with the money of poor believers?' Martin Luther had asked in thesis number 86. Meanwhile, any documents, manuscripts or parchments from the various church archives were either destroyed, thrown to the horses for stabling, used as bedding or else cast to the four winds. After they had looted what they could the soldiers then laid fires in an orgy of senseless destruction. In the vicinity of the Vatican, where some of the most precious possessions of the Church lay, the holy relics were turned out of their hiding places and paraded through the streets. The skulls of saints were meanwhile used as target practice and blasted to fragments by bored harquebusiers. The golden Cross of Constantine the Great was unearthed and carried triumphantly through the streets to the jeers of the men; later it was broken down into smaller pieces, shared out, and subsequently lost to history.

One *landsknecht* had recovered the purported Holy Lance of Longinus which Sultan Bayezid II had presented to Pope Innocent VIII some years earlier. The German soldier affixed the Holy Lance to the tip of his pike and mockingly jabbed it skyward. The busts of the Apostles stolen from St. John Lateran were carried through the streets to the collective jeers of the Germans. The handkerchief of Veronica, once used to wipe the brow of Christ, was passed round by soldiers in a tavern to wipe their grimy necks as they drank themselves into a stupor. Nor did the sacrilegious outrages end here. In St. Peter's Basilica the soldiers lolled around the High Altar playing dice while drunken Roman *meretrici* blasphemously paraded around in the Pope's ecclesiastical vestments. When they grew tired of dice and whores the soldiers went in search of Catholic priests, forcing them to strip naked and perform the High Mass with braying donkeys for their communicants. When one such priest refused the indignity of performing this ritual he was butchered on the spot. In the Stanze di Raffaello, the soldiers went from fresco to fresco etching random graffiti with their weapons. On Raphael's work known as the *Disputation of the Holy Sacrament* the name of Martin Luther was rudely scratched. On another fresco Charles V was hailed as Emperor. Other Raphael tapestries were torn from their hangings and bartered in the city streets for coin. Michelangelo's ceiling, painted for Pope Julius II almost at the cost of the master's eyesight, was saved only by the fact that its sheer height (68ft) prevented the soldiers from doing it any serious damage.

Outside the Castel Sant'Angelo, soldiers gathered in drunken crowds beneath the ramparts, jeering and cat-calling, taunting Pope Clement with the words: '*Vivat Lutherus pontifex!*' Clearly this Pope was a monster. If not, why then did he not 'liberate everyone from purgatory for the sake of love (a most holy thing) and because of the supreme necessity of their souls?' as Luther had argued in his 95 theses. However, although the Germans were intolerable, it was the ardent Roman Catholics who displayed the worst conduct of all. The judgement of the Prior of the Canons of St. Augustine at the time was: '*Mali fuere Germani, pejores Itali, Hispani vero pessimi*' ('the Germans were bad, the Italians were worse, the Spaniards were the worst of all').[423] But greed for plunder remained, more than religious zeal, the prime motivation for most of these common soldiers. Anything remotely of any value was lifted, extracted, prised or hefted. Precious statues and other *objects d'art* had their jewels picked out by the men's daggers and precious gems were roughly apportioned on the marble floor of St. Peter's by men with shovels. The heads of St. Andrew and St. John were kicked around the streets like footballs. The grave of St. Peter itself was profaned. The tombs of Julius II and Alexander VI were smashed open, their mouldering remains desecrated. The Sistine Chapel and the Vatican Library founded by Pope Nicholas V were only spared through the intercession of Prince Philibert of Orange, who had laid out the duke of Bourbon's corpse on his bier in the chapel and ordered that the area be rendered off limits to the common soldiers. But his authority as head of the army did not save him from being harassed by his own troops; his secretary later recorded that whilst making his rounds Philibert had been 'robbed by *landsknechts* in the porch of Saint Mark'.

If the most senior commander of the imperial army was not impervious to extortion then the citizens of Rome were monumentally less so. Over the coming days and weeks the asset-stripping of both the city and its inhabitants assumed a grim and coldly systematic quality. Inhabitants of many of the wealthier *palazzi* were forced to pay huge ransoms in order to be left in peace by the soldiers. After the Germans had called to collect their ransom money the Spaniards in their turn would call and the hapless owners would be forced to cough up further large bribes. After that, the Italians would come calling too and the process would be repeated a third time, by which point there was frankly little left to give. Others were considerably less fortunate, despite their great wealth. Rome's richest citizen, the millionaire Domenico Massimi was forced to watch as his sons were put to the sword, his daughter raped and his *palazzo* burned to the ground before his eyes. Having suffered these unspeakable horrors he too was slain. Only those managing to gain sanctuary within some of the city's Ghibelline, Spanish, German or Dutch residences were spared and sometimes not even then.

To the imperial troops, every inhabitant of Rome was thought to have sequestered a small fortune in specie and no method was considered too harsh for prising its location out of them. Wrote Luigi Guicciardini: 'Many were suspended for hours by the arms; many were cruelly bound by the private parts; many were suspended by the feet high above the road, or over water, while their tormentors threatened to cut the cord. Some were half buried in the cellars; others were nailed up in casks while many were villainously beaten and wounded.'[424] Neither were the young and innocent spared. Children were flung from windows or else had their heads dashed against walls; anything to induce the Romans to reveal their secret treasure troves. 'In the whole of Rome not a living soul above the age of three years old was exempt from having to pay a ransom', wrote one observer.[425] Luigi Guicciardini took pains to emphasize that the cardinals especially were a favourite target for the soldiers. Some cardinals, so he recorded, 'were set upon by scrubby beasts, riding with their faces backwards, in the habits and ensigns of their dignity, and some were led about all Rome with the greatest derision and contempt. Some, unable to raise all the ransom demanded, were so tortured that they died there and then, or within a few days.'[426] Other cardinals were subjected, whilst still alive, to their own mock funerals. Guicciardini writes: 'For the sake of ridicule and punishments, they carried Cardinal Aracoeli one day on a bier through every street of Rome as if he were dead continually chanting his eulogy. They finally carried his "body" to a church where ... about half of his unusual (out of reverence I will avoid saying "criminal") habits were detailed in a funeral oration ... They returned to his palace and drank his wine.'[427]

As for the high class noblewomen of Rome, many of these were abducted and forced to work in impromptu brothels serving the unwashed common soldiery. The Sieur de Brantôme sneered that 'Marchionesses, countesses and baronesses served the unruly troops and for long afterwards the patrician women of the city were known as "the relics of the Sack of Rome."'[428] Very often convents were transformed into such brothels and the nuns repeatedly raped, being passed round amongst the men like sacks of wine. The inhabitants of the convent of Santa Rufina put up a remarkable resistance with any weapons that came to hand; knives, meat cleavers, kettles of scalding water. Nevertheless despite the fortitude of its defenders the convent was stormed, the inhabitants slaughtered and those who survived were tortured and raped in the most savage fashion imaginable. Many noble women were afforded protection from the troops by Isabella d'Este. Federico Gonzaga's mother had come to Rome, at least ostensibly, to accept the cardinal's red hat which had recently been granted to Federico's twenty-two-year-old brother Ercole Gonzaga. The real reason for her stay in Rome, however, was because she was at this time at cross-purposes with her son the Marquess, whose immoral affairs with married women had affronted her sense of decency. Federico had attempted to warn his mother of the looming danger of Frundsburg's army, writing that 'They already see Florence and Rome thrown down, and Rome pillaged'[429] but she had ignored the forewarnings and was now trapped in Rome by the imperial attack. Holed up in the Palazzo Colonna with sundry other gentlewomen, the only thing which stood between her and the marauding soldiers was her younger son, Ferrante, who was at that time serving in the rampaging imperial army.

On 8 May, when the city was being to subjected to its third agonising day of sacking, the duke of Urbino and the marquess of Saluzzo were encamped at Cortona a full 100 miles from Rome. Francesco Maria della Rovere was by this time fully informed of events inside the city. Not only had ample intelligence reached him from fleeing papal soldiers but the bishop of Motula had sent him a clear and unambiguous situation report which stated that the Borgo had fallen and that the Pope was a prisoner inside Sant'Angelo. If anything this information seemed to deter Urbino rather than galvanise him into action. If the Borgo had already fallen then surely all was lost? Francesco Guicciardini strongly disagreed and made the counter-argument: if the League were to march with all haste on Rome while the Imperialists within were still running amok, fragmented into small disorganised companies of looters, they might be able to carry the day and bring the sack to an abrupt end. But Francesco Maria, who had already suffered so grievously at the hands of one Medici pope, was privately enjoying watching his successor twist in the wind. Besides, the very idea of taking orders from a mere lawyer like Guicciardini deeply offended his noble sensibilities. Neither did he seem very greatly concerned about the plight of his mother-in-law, Isabella d'Este.[430] Frustrated at Urbino's wilful tardiness, Guicciardini was moved to write that 'the Pope remains in the *castello*, begging for help so earnestly that his entreaties would melt the very stones, and in so abject a state of misery that even the Turks are filled with pity'.[431]

⊙☾

I t would be a full ten months before the remaining Imperialist troops
would wearily withdraw from Rome, on 17 February 1528, leaving the
city devastated, plague-ridden and depopulated. Those Romans who
survived would by this time be consigned to a feral and almost
subterranean existence amidst the ruins, tunnels and cisterns of the city.
Rome would be transformed into a city of ghosts and ghouls. The Sack of
Rome would become the subject for a large outpouring of writing in each
of the four main genres which Renaissance humanists had revived from
classical antiquity: oratory, poetry, letters and dialogue. 'This is not the
ruin of one city but of the whole world', declared even the reformist-
minded Erasmus gloomily.[432] By now Pope Clement had already made his
escape to Orvieto, a small citadel town where he tried, with questionable
success, to reconstitute his papal court. The Mantuan ambassador
Francesco Gonzaga wrote to his cousin Federico estimating that fully four-
fifths of the city were by now uninhabited. Most of Rome's painters,
architects and humanist scholars had long since departed the city and
would remain absent for years, bringing Rome's own blossoming High
Renaissance period to an abrupt halt.

Polidoro da Caravaggio, a pupil of Raphael who specialised in painting
delightful frescos on the exteriors of Roman palaces, fled to Naples only to
be tragically murdered later in Messina. His close friend and collaborator
Maturino da Firenze is said to have perished during the sack. Giovanni da
Udine, the discoverer of the art of stucco, who had assisted Raphael in
commissions such as the Vatican Loggie, returned to his hometown of
Udine. The eccentric Florentine Mannerist painter Rosso Fiorentino fled
Rome after suffering torture at the soldiers' hands. Pietro Aretino's friend,
Jacopo Sansovino, fled to Venice in May 1527 whereupon, shortly
afterwards in 1529, he was appointed *protomaestro* of the *Procuratia de
supra* or supervising architect and superintendent of properties to the
republic. The appointment, which was in effect one of the most senior
civic-artistic positions in the entire city, came with a salary of 80 ducats
per annum and an apartment near the clocktower in San Marco, a salary
which would be raised to 180 ducats within one year.[433] The doge, Andrea
Gritti, who had embarked upon a deliberate drive to renovate and
beautiful the maritime city, gave him a commission to remodel the area
around San Marco. Sansovino would become associated with the design
and building of three principal new buildings in this area, the Mint, the
Library and the Loggetta. Red bearded, pale skinned and immodest,
Sansovino had a huge appetite for life and also for women. Even Cellini,
himself a legendary self-aggrandising braggadocio, was taken aback by the
architect's chutzpa. Another Mannerist artist, Parmigianino, escaped to
Bologna and later Parma. Here he was joined by the philosopher Lodovico

Boccadifferro and the engraver Marcantonio Raimondi, the infamous creator of the pornographic *I Modi: The Sixteen Pleasures.*

Sebastiano del Piombo, who had painted Aretino's portrait sometime in 1526, had sought refuge in the Castel Sant'Angelo together with his master the Pope. Vasari later praised del Piombo's depiction of the satirist, reporting that del Piombo 'made it such that, besides being a good likeness, it is an astounding piece of painting, for there may be seen in it five or six different kinds of black in the clothes that he is wearing–velvet, satin, ormuzine, damask, and cloth–and, over and above those blacks, a beard of the deepest black, painted in such beautiful detail, that the real beard could not be more natural. This figure holds in the hand a branch of laurel and a scroll, on which is written the name of Clement VII; and in front are two masks, one of *Virtue*, which is beautiful, and another of *Vice*, which is hideous.'[434] The artist had inscribed in the bottom left corner of the painting the Latin motto '*In utrumque paratus*' ('Ready for anything') taken from Virgil's Aeneid (II, 61) and Aretino had donated the work to his native city of Arezzo in the summer in which it had been painted.[435] Del Piombo's painting of his employer Pope Clement meanwhile depicted a swarthy, youthful and still clean shaven pontiff glancing sideways in a mood of glum Machiavellian melancholy, the famous canvas remaining amongst the artist's possessions until the time of his death decades later.

It would be the last time that Clement was depicted clean shaven; as part of the outer show of his inner contrition for the dreadful events that had overtaken both him and Rome, Clement followed Julius II's lead and refused to shave, growing his beard long for the remainder of his papacy. Obligingly, the humanist Pierio Valeriano, tutor to Alessandro and Ippolito de' Medici, quickly penned the treatise *Pro sacerdotum barbis* which advocated the wearing of beards for priests, a practice hitherto frowned upon.[436] While locked up with Pope Clement, Sebastiano del Piombo whiled away the long hours of inactivity penning letters that were subsequently smuggled to Pietro Aretino in Venice. In a gratifying twist of fortune, del Piombo informed Aretino that the Pope was missing his services. Clement had expressed to del Piombo only Pietro Aretino's pen had any chance of influencing the Emperor Charles to call off his troops. 'If Pietro Aretino had been with us we should not be here worse than a prisoner', Clement had allegedly lamented to the painter.[437]

Aretino's new home Venice did not–as might be imagined–exult in the destruction of her political and cultural rival; rather there was a sense of alarm and sympathy for the plight of the Romans and their bishop as well as an uneasy feeling of peril that Venice could well be next if Charles V could not somehow be bridled. As has been seen, there was a sizable influx of refugees from Rome, some of them artists but also many merchants and priests as well. The reforming order of Theatines for example had managed to escape Rome just before the sack; they had sailed here on a Venetian ship along with their leader Gianpietro Caraffa, the bishop of Chieti.[438] Venetian geography did little to assuage its inhabitants' sense of exposure. The republic was in effect surrounded on all sides by enemies: in the east were the Turks, who threatened Venice's sea trade, to the north and north-east lay the Habsburg dominions of Germany, Austria and Hungary, the Spanish were to the far west and Spain's dependencies (Mantua, Ferrara and Naples) lay to the immediate south.[439] In the immediate aftermath the events of May 1527, Venice's diplomat Gasparo Contarini had been despatched to Ferrara to try to win over Alfonso d'Este to the League of Cognac. But the dire situation did not of course prevent Venice from making capital out of Rome's predicament. Venice lost no time in annexing the two papal cities of Ravenna and Cervia on the flimsy pretext that she was 'protecting their inhabitants'. Venice also wrested back the right to determine her own ecclesiastical appointments within the republic.[440] As the sack of Rome became a sad fact of history, the rest of Italy had little alternative but to return to the usual day-to-day business of survival. For Pietro Aretino this meant settling into his adopted home.

☉☾

Although Pietro Aretino had arrived in Venice in March 1527 essentially as a refugee and an asylum-seeker it did not take him long to become established and well integrated into the cultural life of the republic. His friend Jacopo Sansovino had, as we have seen, already preceded him and the doge would shortly appoint him to improve and beautify the city. Aretino also renewed his acquaintance with the Venetian artist Tiziano Vecelli, better known to posterity as Titian. Aretino had known Titian from his days in Mantua. The painter, a student of Giovanni Bellini's who hailed from a family of minor bureaucrats in the Pieve di Cadore, had recently come to prominence during the 1520s. Impressed by Aretino's impressive appearance and bearing, Titian lost little time in painting the writer's portrait in June 1527. Having done so, the silver tongued Aretino then persuaded Titian to forward the canvas free-of-charge to his patron Federico Gonzaga in Mantua.[441] Always a generous gift-giver, Aretino made this gesture as an investment in the Marquess's continued goodwill and benevolence, although the actual painting itself however has since been lost to history. The portrait was despatched together with a second work by Titian, today known as *Man with a Glove*, which depicted one of Federico's deceased friends, a gentleman named Girolamo Adorno, who had served as an imperial envoy and who died in 1523 at the age of either thirty-three or forty.[442] The gesture seems to have worked wonders for shortly afterwards Aretino received an acknowledgement from Federico which gushed that the paintings 'are dear to me not only because I have always wanted to have a picture by that excellent painter, but also because one of them is a portrait of your talented self and the other of Signor Adorno, whom I loved much while he was alive'.[443] Through these two commissions both Titian and Aretino had benefitted; the former had found an appreciative new aristocratic client in Mantua whilst the satirist had pleased an existing patron. The win-win nature of this relationship would be the hallmark of their future association going forward.

We know that Federico had continued as Aretino's benefactor, even after Aretino departed from Mantua, for in April 1527 Aretino had already written to Vincenzo da Fermo concerning the 'splendid bounty of the Marquess of Mantua'[444] Furthermore, in August of that same year Aretino had written personally to the Marquess warmly expressing his gratitude to Federico for a gratuity of 50 *scudi* and a robe made from cloth-of-gold.[445] Aretino informs Federico in this letter that he has, furthermore, not only made arrangements for his new friend Titian to paint the Marquess's portrait, but has also arranged for Sebastiano del Piombo (at that time still incarcerated alongside Pope Clement VII in Rome but able to correspond with Aretino) to 'make you a painting of anything that pleases him just so long as it is not some hypocritical religious subject'.[446] He also apprises Federico that 'the most rare Messer Jacopo Sansovino is about to embellish your bedchamber with a statue of Venus so true to life and so living that it will fill with lustful thoughts the mind of anyone who looks at it'.[447] Ever appreciative of erotic art in all its forms and manifestations, Federico would reply back on 26 February 1528: 'I had been awaiting the Venus with devotion, but now that I hear she is as praised there as you have written to me, I am waiting for her with even greater desire'.[448] Neither did Aretino pause here in his charm offensive. Further gifts were soon forthcoming including some delicate Venetian glassware, a leather saddle and a decorative dagger exhibiting particularly fine workmanship.

When Aretino learned that the son of the dagger-maker was at that moment incarcerated in a Mantuan prison on a charge of wool smuggling, he intervened with the Marquess to have the young man released and restored to the bosom of his family in Venice. Consequently the craftsman made a gift of the piece to Aretino out of gratitude.[449] Having pleasantly found that his word carried significant weight with his Mantuan patron, Aretino was tempted to spread his largesse around and buy himself further goodwill through similar acts of vicarious clemency. Taddeo Boccaccio from Fano, one of Giovanni de' Medici's former soldiers of the Bande Nere, who had been charged in Mantua with murder, was acquitted and released when Aretino interceded with the Marquess on his behalf. And when the Imperialist troops, having sated themselves on the prostrate corpse of Rome, looked set to advance on Aretino's hometown of Arezzo, Federico wrote to his younger brother Ferrante, by now the new imperial commander-in-chief in Italy, asking him to divert his soldiers from the city 'so that Pietro Aretino can have the necessary peace of mind to go on with his writings and studies'.[450] In gratitude for his timely intervention, Aretino's hometown honoured the poet by naming him *Servator della Patria* in 1530.[451] The town which he had left under a cloud so many years earlier now regarded the libertine prodigal as their official hero and saviour. It was all quite a turnaround for the books.

So obliging was Federico with these many requests that he was sometimes almost in danger of becoming Aretino's panderer. At Mantua, Aretino had become besotted with a certain Isabella Sforza who, so it was said, had cured him of homosexuality (although a seducer of married women, Aretino was also a known chaser of boys).[452] Aretino had celebrated his infatuation with *La bella* Madonna Isabella by publishing two obscene sonnets, one of which unashamedly declared: 'Let it be clearly made known to everyone / How Isabella Sforza has converted / Aretino from that which he was born, a sodomite' ('*Sia noto a ogni persona et manifesto / Come Isabella Sforza ha convertito / L'Aretin da ch'ei nacque sodomito*'.)[453] While he was in far distant Venice, Aretino now asked Federico to intercede on his behalf with the lady. We do not know what specific message was passed by Federico to Isabella; it might have been a request for Isabella to join Aretino in Venice, it might have been an entreaty for her to stay put, there is no way of telling. Nonetheless, the good-natured Federico told his client that he would speak to the lady and see what he could do concerning the matter.

There was, however, a line which Federico would not cross no matter how much it might please his satirist-poet. When Aretino asked his patron to impose his lordly authority upon a contrary youth named Bianchino, who had coyly resisted Aretino's sexual advances in Mantua, Federico drew the line. The Marquess, an avowedly heterosexual pervert, interceded in Aretino's private pederasty but only up to a certain point. The topic incurred no small amount of correspondence between the two. On 3 January 1528, Federico wrote to Aretino: 'I very much regret your pain, torment and afflictions; ... [but] I cannot do what you would not gladly consent to; how much I can do to cure your grand passions, wanting very much to be capable of abolishing all your troubles and of consoling you, depends on your intentions. And as for what will occur, I was very happy to command that it be done..'[454] One month later, Federico wrote again to Aretino on the same subject: '.. I have had [a letter] written to Father di Carlo da Fano about your business ... such that he should certainly seek you out, and I wanted to send one of my grooms for the purpose of delivering it had it not happened that one of my gentlemen had to go there at that time and I gave the letter to him; I have as yet had no answer, which surprises me, but perhaps it will not be very long in coming. I would willingly satisfy your wishes regarding this kept boy who you write could remedy your trouble, if I knew who it was, but I do not know this boy..'[455]

A few weeks later, on 24 February Federico wrote Aretino yet another letter on the subject, telling him, 'I have not forgotten to have [a letter] written on your behalf to the Most Reverend Monsignor my brother [Cardinal Ercole Gonzaga], and I ordered it to be written well. If I have thus been able to satisfy you in your desire for Bianchino I will also have done it gladly. But having understood his reluctance when Roberto spoke to him on your behalf, and as it seemed to me that I was unable to do justice to the work that I wanted to do in this regard, I did not think it fitting to plead with him or otherwise to exhort him, nor to have him exhorted in my name and I failed to think that I should command him, IT NOT BEING EITHER JUST OR HONEST TO COMMAND HIM IN THIS CASE. But pardon me if in this case I have not pleased you; if I can please you in any other way, as you know very well I am only too glad to do it and you will always find me ready..'[456]

☉☾

Two months after moving to Venice news reached Aretino of Rome's tumultuous sacking at the hands of 'the Lanzknechte and braggadocios of Spain who were coming in pitiless bands to render Rome the arse end of the world'.[457] It is perhaps all too easy to imagine Aretino's private sense of satisfaction that the nettlesome Pope Clement had at last received his just comeuppance and was reduced to cowering in the Castel Sant'Angelo from the Lutheran hordes. Aretino might have proclaimed through the character Flaminio in La Cortigiana: 'The virtuous are there. At Venice there is personal gentility and at Rome rudeness and envy', but we should not be too quick to presuppose Aretino's sentiments concerning Rome. Whatever his differences with the present pope, Rome had still nurtured Aretino and given him his professional start. It was in Rome that he had found fame, if not fortune. Neither did Aretino share common cause with the Lutheran rabble who had carried out the sack; the German heretics had been responsible for Giovanni delle Bande Nere's untimely death and this he could never forgive.

The death of his friend and the sacking of Rome mingled to produce a common sense of revulsion. Aretino was no soldier. He could never personally identify with the motivation which took men off to war and to plunder by lawless brute force. 'The art of war is like the art of the courtesan', he would write; 'indeed they might be called sisters, since both are slaves of desperation'.[458] Thomas More had said much the same thing in *Utopia* when he wrote of the fearsome Swiss mercenaries: 'They go forth of their country in great companies together, and whosoever lacketh soldiers, there they proffer their service for small wages. This is the only craft they have to get their living by. They maintain their life by seeking their death.'[459] Aretino may have flirted with the military lifestyle in his youth through his association with Giovanni delle Bande Nere but it is probably true to say that Aretino's experience of war had always been somewhat vicarious, experienced through the eyes of his friend, 'my sometimes easy-going, sometimes hard-to-handle lord'.[460]

And though Aretino might write pornographic sonnets to accompany lewd engravings, or find diversion in a *Ragionamenti* in which a mother instructs her innocent daughter in the ways of whoredom, Aretino would never have endorsed the wanton rapine of the Imperial soldiers or the violation and butchering of entire communities of nuns. The painted Roman harlots who lolled around the altar of St. Peter with the Lutheran troops might have been a familiar enough trope of Aretino's, but the forceful 'taking' of women—many of them extremely well-born Roman noblewomen—on such a scale as had been witnessed in the prostrate city was simply beyond even Aretino's vivid imagination. Whoredom for Aretino would always be a straight two-way commercial transaction in which the whore invariably held the upper hand and the customer received his comeuppance. Mass gang rape, however, would have been repugnant even to such a ready purveyor of broken taboos and forbidden smut as Aretino. This is a distinction which must be made for Aretino's later detractors would certainly never go out of their way to make it. Aretino may not have been the paragon of saintly morality, he may have modelled his image after that of a corpulent and priapic satyr, but he was certainly no mindless beast. Neither was he a precursor to the Marquis de Sade, a deviant who took pleasure in inflicting pain and suffering on women. Aretino's sexual cosmos is not that of rape but a transactional world determined by good-natured paid access.

Indeed, it was Aretino who makes his character Togna, a baker's wife, utter this proto-feminist litany of the evils of being born a woman: 'Oh God, why wasn't I born a man? How do I look in these clothes? It is a great misfortune to be born a woman, and after all, what are we women good for? To cook, to sew, and to stay locked up in the house all year, and for what? To be beaten and insulted every day, and by whom? By a big drunkard and a lazy dolt like this old sport of mine. Oh poor we, what a lot is ours! If your man is a gambler and loses, it is you who are out of luck; if he has no money, it falls on you; if wine takes him off his pegs, it is you who bear the blame; and they are so jealous they think every fly is making or talking love. And if it wasn't that we have brains enough to make sport of them, we might as well go hang ourselves. It is a great sin that the preacher doesn't put in a word for us with the Lord, for it is not right that one like me should go to hell simply for having a husband like the one God has given me. And if the confessor gives me a penance for what I am doing, I hope I die if I don't say to him, for once: "Would you give a penance to a poor unfortunate woman who has for a husband a brute, a gambler, a tavern-hound, a jealous fool and a dog of a gardener?"'[461] Aretino genuinely feels for the plight of many women, whose lives are kerbed by society's rules. This is no mere pose or imposture on his part.

The satirist would include an account of Rome's defilement in his writings as told in the words of a woman. Nanna, the mother figure in the *Ragionamenti*, would later be made to recount the events of the sack of Rome in no small detail. The many word pictures which Aretino paints of the petrified inhabitants 'hiding their money, their silver, their jewels, their necklaces and their garments, everything of value' certainly rings true. Quite possibly this knowledge was derived from actual eye witness accounts which Aretino was privy to. He pulls no punches in Nanna's description of the sheer terror of being trapped inside the city as the imperial troops ran riot: 'The lunkheads guarding the Sisto Bridge were routed, and the army dropped back from the Trastevere and scattered all through Rome. Screams were heard; gates were broken down; everyone ran, everyone hid, everyone lamented and wept. Meanwhile blood poured over the ground, people were massacred, the tortured howled, prisoners prayed, women tore their hair, old men shuddered and shook, and the entire city was turned upside down. Blessed was the man who died quickly, or while lingering on, found someone to finish him off. But who could possibly tell all the terrible events of such a night? The friars, monks, chaplains, and all the other rabble, armed and unarmed, huddled in the tombs more dead than alive. Nor was there a cave, hole, well, tower, cellar, or any other secret hiding place which was not immediately jammed with all sorts of people.'[462]

Although Nanna's dialogue obviously harbours more sympathy for the common people caught up in the sacking than for the Pope and his ecclesiastical hangers-on, Aretino was not slow in recognising a possible opening back into favour when he saw one. When Aretino heard, through Piombino and other sources, that the Pope had claimed to miss both his pen and his counsel, the satirist was greatly heartened by the turnaround in his fortunes. He had even learned that Clement had finally reprimanded his *datarius* Gian Matteo Giberti for having made quarrel with Aretino, thus depriving the Pope of the writer's useful services when he needed them most. He was quick to try to make capital out of the Pope's change of heart. On 20 May 1527, Aretino composed a supplicatory missive to

Charles V in which he reminded the Emperor that, just as he had shown 'clemency' (clearly a pun on the Pope's name) to King François, so he now also held the fate of the Pope in his hand too. 'It is now plain to all that you have some of God's own qualities', Aretino wrote, 'You alone have a soul which is capable of emulating the greatness of His forgiving nature which is the scourge with which He humbles the pride of the contumacious who are punished by His acts of loving kindness.'[463] The satirist referred to the 'power [and] the generosity' in Charles's heart which is 'protected by his military might'.[464] He then ended with a call-to-action: 'It would not do for the justice of your contempt to turn into cruelty. Let it please you, therefore, to bid the destruction [of Rome] to proceed no further. In your hands are two things—religious devotion and the Pope. Keep your devotion and set the Pope free. Give back to Christ his Vicar. It was His favour who brought you to victory.'[465]

Imperially, Charles ignored Aretino's letter and so the poet applied himself instead to a one-off *pasquinata* specially composed for the sacking in which Pasquino recounts to Marforio the wretched afternoon that he had spent in Rome while the sack was in progress. The *pasquinata* came to Clement's attention after it had been published in Siena and the Pope was said (as reported to Aretino by Sebastiano del Piombo) to have been much moved and affected by it. But admittedly, the events of that year had contributed to a certain emotional lability on Clement's part and these days he was quick to evince a sentimental reaction to most things that were brought to his attention. On 30 May 1527, having written to the Emperor Charles, Aretino now turned his attention to the Pope. The letter he wrote to Clement managed to strike just the right note of sanctimony mixed with pompous effrontery for the recipient to recoil in proud repugnance. The writer reassured the Pope that he himself was not to blame but that it was God's will which had intervened to make him a prisoner in Rome, and not the Fates. 'It was inevitable that the Vicar of Christ should pay off, with his own woe and downfall, the debts which had been piled up by others in his name'.[466] God, Aretino informed Clement, had brought about his 'downfall' due to 'the lewd doings of your priests' only to 'permit you to mount higher than you have ever before!'[467] Indelicately, Aretino asked the Pope 'to turn your mind to forgiveness and not to revenge, for only by truly wishing to pardon and not to avenge, can you fit yourself for a role which is worthy of the high office which you hold'.[468] Aretino went on to school Clement on the need to make peace with his jailer, the Emperor, and redirect his passions against the Turk: 'His Majesty has no false pride. Embrace him, therefore, in the arms of that power which comes from above, and turning his Catholic sword against the haughty East, make him do the thing you ought to want him to do'.[469]

Though well-meaning, such classic Aretine bombast, commending Clement to forgiveness, were hardly calculated to please a pontiff whose nose was assailed by the foul odour of vast acres of decomposing flesh beyond the safety of Sant'Angelo. The Pope's response was to unleash the portentously dull blade that was Francesco Berni, the versifying secretary of the *datarius*. Berni was only too glad to oblige, churning out such unimaginative doggerel as the following to hurl in distant Aretino's direction:

> You say so much and do so many things
> with your foul tongue that has no salt of wit
> that in the end a blade will silence it
> sharper than that of Achille, with more stings.
> The Pope's still Pope and you are a vile thief
> Nourished by others' bread and words of scorn.
> You live in a brothel, in the slums you were born,
> O cripple ignorant and proud beyond belief![470]

The scurrilous sonnets did not unduly dismay Aretino. Their artistry was to say the least mundane, the sentiments expressed entirely pedestrian, plebeian. In his own mind at least, Aretino had sought to adopt the role of go-between for both Caesar and Supreme Pontiff in this their time of variance. That nobody had especially gone out of their way to appoint this cobbler's son, this *poseur*, to serve as intermediary between the two most exalted figures in Christendom had not occurred to him in the slightest.

CHAPTER 10

The Search for Patronage

Scoundrels say that I have an evil tongue, but my tongue only seems evil because I never flatter. To hurt my reputation, they point out that I am poor. They really honour me. The poor man is always good. All I want is this: I don't want to have so much that I am hated, and I don't want so little that men pity me. And that is sure to be my state. At least I hope so, and my hope is reasonable since it is based on what I deserve.

Pietro Aretino to Agostino Ricchi, 16 May 1537.

Of greater import than Berni's pathetic attempts to ruffle Aretino's armour-clad insouciance and God-given sense of purpose was the news of Niccolò Machiavelli's death on 21 June 1527. He at least had lived just long enough to enjoy the Medici pope's comeuppance at the hands of the Lutheran plague. The Medici had not been especially kind to *il Machia*. Previously they had imprisoned him and then they had tortured him with the agonising technique of the *strappado*.[471] When the Florentines had once again thrown off the Medici yoke in the wake of Rome's sacking, Machiavelli had been confidently optimistic that there would be a place for him in the new republic. To his disenchantment, however, his old post of secretary of the second chancery was given instead to the former Medici functionary Francesco Tarugi. It was a final, crushing disappointment from which Machiavelli never really recovered. On 10 June, not long after learning of his disheartening rejection by the republic, Machiavelli took sick and eleven days later he was dead at the age of fifty-eight.

Machiavelli had lived the final years of his life as a virtual social pariah. The political methods which he disclosed in his writings were considered ignoble and underhand even though they often drew heavily on classical precedent. His idolising of Cesare Borgia, never a friend to Florence, had also contributed to placing him well beyond the pale. Like

Aretino, Machiavelli had committed the cardinal sin of speaking openly of certain prohibited matters; in Aretino's case it was sexuality but in Machiavelli's he touched upon those matters which those engaged in the solemn business of government were obliged to know yet remain silent about. His ideal prince was no idealised, virtuous and quasi-divine being as in the writings of Castiglione; for Machiavelli the effective prince was instead a master of simulation and dissimulation, a man equally capable of soaring with the angels or descending to the level of a beast when occasion required it. Machiavelli's model ruler was a centaur, a combination of man and beast.[472] Italy's princely rulers, however, had shown themselves all too bestial, all too lacking in humanity; their pernicious tendency to use foreign invaders to leverage their own parochial advantage had left the peninsula in servitude to these odious and powerful outsiders. Machiavelli's diagnoses of Italy's ills were simply too uncomfortable a truth for Renaissance minds to accept.

Like Aretino, Machiavelli's collection of private correspondence would shine an illuminating spotlight on the era in which these men lived, creating in effect a new, modern and updated epistolary genre. His comedy *Mandragola* had meanwhile set the bar for the *commedia erudite* which Aretino himself was trying to emulate with his ongoing rewrites and polishing of *La Cortigiana*. Pietro and Niccolò were in a sense kindred spirits, both able to see through the vanities of their era and with a talent for penetrating the surface of men's affairs to the clandestine underlying motivations beneath. Both saw men through a glass darkly, but whereas *il Machia* saw humanity as a being of political appetites, *uomo politico*, Aretino saw mankind even more nakedly through the lens of *uomo sensuale*. Where Castiglione applied layer upon layer of courtly sheen to his subjects, Aretino and Machiavelli systematically stripped away all artifice so that man could operate according to his truest, most honest essence. For *il Machia* this was politics, for *il Divino Aretino* it was sexuality. Both believed they were simply being honest.

Where both men could nevertheless agree was in their recognition of the moral canker of conventional religion and the existing social hierarchy as it stood. For Machiavelli, as for Aretino, neither the Church nor the nobility, and most definitely not the *condottieri*, were able to provide a lasting foundation for the *patria* ('country'). Only the masses of the common people could provide this foundation and here the two men differed only in their specific approach, for whereas the republican Machiavelli sought to elevate the lumpen masses to the status of civic participants, the equally 'democratising' Aretino concentrated on his own private agenda of raising the son of a cobbler to a level which was on a par with kings, popes and emperors. Democracy for Aretino was bending great men to *his* will. For both writers, though, the Church was the worst offender. But since the Church was, in essence, itself a highly élite aristocratic institution, its failure had indicated the wider failure of the upper echelons of Italian society as a whole. It would later be said of Aretino after his death that he never spoke ill of God since 'he never knew him during his life' and indeed, Machiavelli too had confessed before his own death that he wanted none of religion in the afterlife:

> 'The evil example of the court of Rome has destroyed all piety and religion in Italy, resulting in infinite mischief and disorders, which keep our country divided and are the cause of our ruin ... This barbarous domination stinks in the nostrils of everyone.'[473]

Machiavelli's final joke with his friends on his deathbed had been that he'd much rather join the ancients in Hell for an engaging discussion on politics than go to Heaven and be with the blessed and the saintly for an eternity.[474] Aretino would no doubt have laughed uproariously had he been there at Niccolò's bedside. He would also have smiled to learn that both himself and Niccolò were the only two Italian authors being read at that time in Germany, great swathes of which had already given itself over to the Lutheran heresy.[475]

On 7 July, we find Aretino writing once more to Federico Gonzaga enclosing both a *frottola* and a *canzone* both of whose themes were the still current topic of the ongoing sack of Rome. The *frottola*, popular during the period from 1470 to 1530, was the predominant form of polyphonic secular Italian song in the late fifteenth- and early sixteenth-century and was a precursor to the madrigal which largely replaced it in fashionability after 1530. It was a composition for three or four voices, with the uppermost voice carrying the melody, a style that had been pioneered and would reach its zenith at the court of the Gonzaga. The *canzone* was the most unrestricted type of the *frottola* genre, with a variable number of stanzas and alternation of seven- and eleven-syllable lines.[476] Aretino's two lyrical compositions pulled no metaphorical punches, comparing Rome to Troy, Carthage and Jerusalem in her abject wretchedness and describing how the women of Rome, 'those universally beloved women', were prey to the 'tremendously reckless and daring Germans and Spaniards' and had found themselves 'in the hands of dogs and ruthless monsters' ('*In preda al temerario ardir tremendo / D'Alemagna et di Spagna, a gli occhi nostril / In man di cani et de spietati mostri / De l'universo la diletta donna / Trovossi inerme di consigli et d'armi*').[477] Chillingly, Aretino went on to describe how the beautiful river Tiber had run red with blood ('*Sangue è corso il bel Tebro, è corso sangue*').[478]

His writing should leave us in no doubt as to Aretino's genuine sorrow for Rome, however neither his vocalising of that grief nor the recent passing of Machiavelli excused or absolved Aretino from his own ongoing problems with the incarcerated Pope. Whether he recognised his latest error in hectoring the pontiff we cannot say. Certainly the effort had proved counterproductive, something he should perhaps have foreseen. That Aretino still sought Clement's approval is nonetheless certain for by September 1527 he set his mind to the completion of an epic verse poem, *La Marfisa*, with which he hoped to rehabilitate his public image and pave the way for a grand reconciliation with His Holiness, who was still trapped in the Castel Sant'Angelo and who would not escape Rome until 8 December that same year. *La Marfisa* was predicated upon Ludovico Ariosto's *Orlando Furioso* and developed the story that Ariosto had, in his turn, continued from Matteo Maria Boiardo's *Orlando Innamorato*. *La Marfisa* had originally been conceived as a eulogy to the House of Gonzaga and Aretino had begun the manuscript whilst lingering at Mantua following the death of Giovanni delle Bande Nere in late 1526.[479] Marfisa herself is based on the same character in Ariosto and Boiardo's poem. She is the sister of the heroic Ruggiero but becomes separated from him in childhood. A classic warrioress and virago in the mould perhaps of Giovanni delle Bande Nere's mother Caterina Sforza, she becomes queen of India and fights as a warrior for the Saracens before falling in love with Ruggiero without realising that he is her brother. Marfisa is very much an enabled woman but because she is also a knight she is still trapped within a world of male conventions and natural social bonds.

In conceiving of this bold new literary enterprise, Aretino assured himself that the poem, providing he could complete it, would be so accomplished that not even Clement could begrudge him the admiration he deserved. That Aretino believed the power of art capable of elevating an aggrieved man above his grievances was quite astonishing, perhaps endearing even. That he was able to polish off the requisite number of verses to proceed towards publishing a first edition through his Venetian printer Francesco Marcolini perhaps less so given his ability to write at speed. But what *is* remarkable is the fact that, having embarked upon the initial cantos of his epic, he now overstretched himself once more by writing to both Emperor and Pope requesting them to guarantee copyright over his (as yet unfinished) work by granting him a *privilegio*. This legal injunction would have effectively disallowed anyone within the imperial or papal domains from publishing the work for a period of ten years, thus giving Aretino a monopoly over printing and distribution. The satirist was optimistic that publishing *La Marfisa* would prove a profitable enterprise and he therefore sought to safeguard his interests, informing

His Holiness 'I have hopes that the printing will reward me'.[480] The application for a *privilegio* was undeniably fairly commonplace amongst writers seeking to protect the profits from their published work. During his visit to Venice in 1523, the chronicler of Ferdinand Magellan's circumnavigation, Antonio Pigafetta, applied to the doge for a similar *privilegio* for a proposed printing of his *Relazione del primo viaggio intorno al mondo* ('Report on the First Voyage Around the World'). In his application, Pigafetta had petitioned 'that no one may print it for twenty years, except myself, under penalty to him who should print it, or who should bring it here if printed elsewhere, of a fine of three lires per copy, besides the loss of the books'.[481]

Charles V had ignored Aretino's earlier letter importuning him for release of the Pope and he did the same to this second pushy and impertinent request. Regarding Aretino by now as *persona non grata* in Rome, Pope Clement followed the Emperor's lead and ignored the petition too. In today's parlance we would perhaps say that Aretino lacked not talent or artistic/literary ability but 'emotional intelligence'. The epitome of the proverbial bull in a china shop, he simply had no conception of when to speak out and when to simply stay silent and let time heal festering open wounds. He felt the world owed him his due and by god he had no compunction in writing to its god-anointed representatives demanding that due. His incorrigible lack of insight into how to manage people (when he was not threatening to blackmail them) is possibly his least attractive quality. In truth, few people love a blowhard. However Aretino had by now made a career out of this urge to try to bend others to *his* will. His will and his pen combined had become positively Nietzschean. Together, they would storm the established hierarchical order.

☉☾

By the beginning of 1528, Pope Clement VII had been permitted by the Imperialists, subject to his promising to pay the appropriate fines and ransoms, to leave Rome in disguise and re-establish his papal court at the small hilltop citadel of Orvieto. Watched closely by Charles V's agents, he expressed his dissatisfaction at the performance of the Duke of Urbino as well as the vicomte de Lautrec, whose large French army had neglected to come south to his aid from Parma. Now, that same French army was preparing to descend into Italy to enforce France's renewed claim to Naples. Since he had already regained his liberty, the Pope was irritated and questioned the usefulness of such a campaign. It would merely stir things up again with the Emperor and further endanger the interests of the Papal States. Nonetheless, on 22 January, citing a litany of grievances against the Emperor, the kings of England and France declared fresh war on Charles and by early February Lautrec had marched down the Adriatic coastline from Bologna to Fano and was poised to enter the Kingdom of Naples.

By now forty-three years old, Lautrec was still a formidable looking man; as the Calabrian noble Leonardo Santoro describes him: 'He was tall and well built, of light complexion, with the blue eyes and broad brow of a prince. He had a black beard a bit long, with a large moustache, and scars on his face. He spoke in Italian, which he understood very well, having served from his youth on long campaigns in Italy.'[482] All told Lautrec had around 22,000 mercenaries under his command, including 3,000 *landsknechts*, 1,000 more Germans in Venetian pay, the Italian troops of Michele Antonio, Marquess of Saluzzo, and the capable Spanish turncoat Pedro Navarro, together with thousands more *aventuriers* who flocked to his ranks. The Venetians supported the venture in the hope of regaining certain fiefs which they had lost to Charles in Apulia. The Florentine republic sent two envoys to travel with the army and Federico Gonzaga was also keeping close tabs on its progress through his envoy Girolamo Ceresari.[483]

Pedro Navarro's troops opened the ball by seizing Aquila and the Franco-Venetian army then invaded Apulia, moving into position around the old Byzantine hill fortress of Troia. Facing the French host was Philibert of Orange and Alfonso d'Ávalos, the new marchese di Pescara and del Vasto, together with the 10,000 or so remnants of the imperial army which had sacked Rome the previous summer. These men had finally been pulled out of Rome on 17 February 1528 when it became clear that Lautrec intended to march south from Parma. As a fighting force they were no longer at their best. Not liking the odds, and learning that Florence was planning to support Lautrec by sending him several companies of the by now legendary Bande Nere, Orange was convinced by d'Ávalos to fall back on Naples and make a stand there. After mopping up most of the rest of Apulia, Lautrec pursued the retreating imperial army to Naples and dug in on the heights surrounding the city whilst the League's *Genovese* admiral Andrea Doria blockaded Naples harbour with a small fleet of galleys. With Orange and his dwindling forces pent up inside Naples all the pieces on the chessboard seemed to be moving rapidly towards checkmate for the Emperor Charles's forces in Italy. But now the fortunes of war swung back once more, as they so often do, this time through the foolhardiness of the French king whose poor treatment of Doria drove him into the bosom of the Emperor.

On 4 July, Doria withdrew his fleet from Naples and by August he had concluded a separate deal with Charles V. Naples's besieged army now took heart. Imperial light horse were despatched from the city to scour the countryside for supplies, some of which were being brought in from the nearby port of Gaeta. Caught in the open on malarial marshlands and without Doria's naval support the League's army found itself whittled down by sickness and desertion. Lautrec himself succumbed and died on 16 August, as did his second-in-command, as did the Venetian war commissioner. The marquess of Saluzzo led what remained of the once formidable League army ('not so much an army as a walking pestilence') away from Naples on 29 August. They got as far as the old Norman hilltop town of Aversa in Apulia when the imperial army fell upon them. They had no more fight left in them and surrendered. The League's remaining captain, the marquess of Saluzzo, was taken prisoner only to expire not long afterwards in the dungeons of Naples. The Spanish turncoat Pedro Navarro, who had given long years of loyal service to the French king, and who had helped Machiavelli rebuild the city defences of Florence, was sentenced to be executed on the orders of the Emperor, but before this could happen he too was quietly murdered in prison at the ripe old age of sixty-eight. Charles's forces had ultimately prevailed, but this was by no means the final act of the play.

In Venice, Pietro Aretino too was engaged in his own admittedly smaller battles. The year 1528 brought a fresh *giudizio* from the pen of Aretino which was much appreciated by the Marquess of Mantua.[484] However, the writer now was feeling the pinch from lack of funds. Helpfully, Federico Gonzaga granted him the patent for a lottery which was held in Venice but unfortunately this scheme, which had been calculated to bring a windfall of several thousand ducats, somehow failed to meet its target and Aretino seems to have held the Marquess responsible for this. The two men suspended their correspondence for a while allowing a sensible period in which to cool off. When Aretino sent Gonzaga an initial draft of *La Marfisa* the Marquess was for the time being won over again, expressing his delight with the new work: 'I have read the fine stanzas you have sent me and I know that you have completed them in less time than most people would have taken to begin them. Yet they could not be more fair and learned than if you had worked on them for twenty-five years.'[485]

But despite the polite compliment, and although Aretino hoped that this new masterpiece would be dedicated—for the right pecuniary consideration—to Federico's posterity, the two men subsequently lapsed into their former frigid relations, probably for the same old reason that Federico was unwilling to come forward with a fresh monetary subsidy. Aretino's begging process was nothing if not predictable. As one of Aretino's harshest Victorian critics John Addington Symonds puts it: 'There is a hint here and there that the benefactor had better loosen his purse strings, if he wishes the stream of sycophancy to continue ... But no sooner has the gift been sent, than the fawning process recommences. In this way, by terrorism and toad-eating, by wheedling and bullying, by impudent demands for money and no less impudent assertions of his power to confer disgrace or fame, the rascal held society at his disposal.'[486]

Flabbergasted that he could make no headway with the Marquess, Aretino put out feelers to the French monarch, François I. Although François had already met Aretino and was aware of his existence, the satirist was nevertheless assisted in this endeavour by the papal *condottiere* Guido Rangone. The French ambassador to Venice, Ludovico Canossa, the bishop of Bayeux, was replaced in August 1528 by Jean Langeac, the bishop of Avranches. The new French diplomatic mission warmed to the idea of having a man of Aretino's obvious talents relocate to France to serve the promotional interests of the French crown. François, for his part, was also eager to appoint useful Italian agents into his service. The Florentine Battista della Palla, for example, was the French king's unofficial arts procurement agent in Florence; della Palla's remit was to syphon off as many notable artistic works as possible and send them to François at Fontainebleau. This was done in the hope of luring the King to republican Florence's military aid in their struggle to remain independent from the Pope and the Emperor. Florence was essentially trying to bribe the French king with fine art. Unfortunately for the Florentines, however, della Palla had gone about his commission with rather too much alacrity and many accomplished works had already vanished from the city including the 8 feet high statue of Hercules which Michelangelo had carved in 1493. Della Palla would end up shipping some forty crates of precious paintings and sculptures by various Florentine masters to François by way of Marseilles.[487] When Margherita Acciaiuoli, the wife of Pierfrancesco Borgherini, learned that della Palla planned to ship her marriage bed to France, because it contained some exquisite panels painted by Pontormo, she had dug her heels in, excoriating della Palla publicly as 'a vile salesman, a little tradesman who sells for pennies'.[488] From 1529 until the French king's death in 1547 Aretino would, like della Palla, keep François well-supplied with art from the Venetian masters like Titian, some of which would be personal gifts from the satirist commissioned at his own expense. But for the time being he was simply content to lend the support of his famous pen to an appreciative French crown.

In his *giudizio* of 1529, Aretino reflected this new French orientation by heaping praise on both King François as well as his new ambassador Jean Langeac whilst at the same time passing snide and indelicate remarks on certain friends of Federico Gonzaga's. This was the notorious barb for which Aretino would soon become widely feared. But he did not allow matters to rest there. The uptick in his fortunes caused by the new French sponsorship led to Aretino adopting an increasingly contemptuous, combative attitude towards the Mantuan agent in Venice, Jacopo Malatesta. Federico responded to this provocation by cutting off what little remained of Aretino's Mantuan allowance. To Aretino he pleaded poverty, disingenuously citing the ruinous expenses incurred by his ongoing duties as papal captain-general. In a tit-for-tat Aretino responded, arranging for Malatesta to be within earshot when he declaimed some insulting sonnets about Federico to an audience of diplomats which included the French and Florentine ambassadors. Malatesta had confronted the satirist, suavely informing him that his master Federico was accustomed to ignoring calumnies from far greater men than Aretino. There the matter ought to have rested. However, in the presence of the shocked French ambassador, the matter quickly escalated into an open altercation and words were spoken by Aretino which perhaps in hindsight should not have been. With Malatesta's dander up, a duel was now proposed, satisfaction vigorously demanded. Being essentially a coward in any physical confrontation, Aretino had backed down, effusively begging Malatesta's pardon.

Word of this damaging altercation with his personal envoy would, however, reach Federico in Mantua and so the satirist needed to act quickly to defuse the matter. Aretino scribbled to Federico his usual bold and unapologetic excuses: 'For ten years, with the greatest ardour, I have advertised, exalted and celebrated the name of your Excellency. For but one hour, moved by over-impulsive love for you, I have assailed what you hold dear. Since I have not been rewarded with your usual royal generosity for my best efforts on your behalf, I surely do not deserve to be punished for my worst indiscretions with such severity as would reflect upon your honour.'[489] By December 1529, however, Aretino's tone was no longer quite so brassy but instead had become markedly plangent: 'When did I receive my last crust from you? After my death you will regret that you permitted a work celebrating the glory of your house to be pawned for a paltry 200 crowns. Are you so anxious to punish me for a couple of words spoken in criticism of you that you do not reward me for a whole book composed in your honour?'[490]

Once again, the manuscript of La Marfisa was trotted out to order and dangled beneath the nose of the Marquess of Mantua who, tempted by the prospect of being immortalised in its heroic pages, tried, vainly as it turned out, to intervene with Clement to grant Aretino the requested privilegio. By January 1530, Aretino had sent Federico another peace offering, the draft of an as yet unpublished piece entitled Il Marescalco ('The Stablemaster'). This new work was a rather vulgar comedy which lampooned a real-life figure at Federico's court who was a well-known homosexual. In the play, the protagonist is mortified to find himself obliged to marry, but later is considerably relieved to learn that his prospective 'wife' is in fact a young boy in drag. Aretino importuned Federico for 50 *scudi* as payment for the lewd comedy and thanked him unctuously for the money when it arrived, but just a short while later he relapsed into his usual refrain. Why was it that his years of loyal service to the Marquess were not being adequately rewarded? Federico's own fortunes were on the rise. That same year he would be created Duke of Mantua by the Emperor Charles V. Under the onus of *noblesse oblige*, Federico capitulated, sending the whingeing poet a robe of 'night-hued velvet'. Appeased, Aretino replied on 2 June 1531: 'I have just received the black velvet cloak and the 50 scudi, which were personally counted out to me in my house by Signor Benedetto Agnelli, your Excellency's ambassador and my most honoured brother'[491] and he dutifully dashed off the usual bombastic stanzas in praise of the House of Gonzaga. The damage, however, had already been done thanks to the earlier unpleasant business with Jacopo Malatesta and Aretino would find his erstwhile patron increasingly distancing himself from the satirist to the point where a complete break would eventually become inevitable.

This break was forestalled for the time being by yet another racy work which Aretino had despatched to Mantua sometime in 1530. This was *La puttana errante* ('The Wandering Whore' or 'The Errant Whore'), a lewd poem which had been written by a young man named Lorenzo Veniero, whom Aretino describes to Federico with Svengalian glee as '*mio creato*' (my creation). To Federico he writes: 'But since I can sniff out a trend, I send you a small work which deals with that courtly exchange in a mischievous and perfidious style. It is entitled *The Wandering Whore*, and was written by Veniero, a creature of mine, who when it comes to a vicious tongue, runs four days ahead of me.'[492] The author was a patrician youth of about twenty years old who had recently become the first in a long line of amanuenses to the poet, and who—like so many of the young protégés that Aretino took under his wing—would eventually turn out to be a scoundrel and a traitor. In Veniero's obscene poem, a wanton woman of Venice, Maddalena, sets out on a vulgar odyssey of unabashed sexual indulgence following a licentious education in the transgressive, often same-sex, carnal activities in her own household. Her catalogue of lewd experiences commences with a menage à trois between a handsome young gallant and a church canon who insists on sodomising the young woman ('never did that traitor of a canon want to put it in my cunt' she exclaims at one point).[493] Maddalena's peregrinations lead her eventually to Rome, both the literal and figurative 'city of whores', where she enters the metropolis in triumph proudly wearing a *corona di cazzi* ('crown of cocks') on her head. The work was directed against a certain Venetian courtesan named Elena Ballerina, whom Veniero describes unchivalrously as being, '...pretty and dear, but her foolish featherweight brain is a great handicap ... If truth be told, this is the gentle wandering whore, who having a voracious appetite for pricks, already has despoiled this hemisphere and the other one.'[494]

Veniero was by now already notorious in Venice for having published the deeply misogynist text *Il trentuno della Zaffetta* which was directed against another renowned courtesan named Angela del Moro (known by her trade name of Angela Zaffetta), the notorious daughter of a *procuratore* of San Marco.[495] *Il trentuno* tells the story of *La Zaffetta's* gang rape on the island of Chioggia at the hands of a procession of eighty peasants, gondoliers, porters, fishermen, priests, servants and other men of low social standing. The mass rape, which subjects the courtesan not only to humiliation but to the possibility of infection by sexual disease, has been organised by her scorned lover in return for her 'crime' of having earlier refused him entry to her home. The fictionality or historicity of the lewd events that are recounted are not so important as the fact that the piece highlighted a depressing fact of life in Venice at this time, namely that the crime of rape bore few repercussions for the perpetrators, especially if they happened to come from one of the old, Venetian patrician families.[496] Neither was there any recourse to law by those unfortunate courtesans who suffered the crime of gang rape, which was known to Venetians as '*Il trentuno*' or 'the thirty-one'. It was a common enough reprisal against those prostitutes who were choosy enough to reject the advances of certain potential customers for pecuniary or other reasons. Often the courtesan in question would be enticed to the offended gentleman's (or a friend's) *palazzo* with the promise of supper; having eaten and drunk her fill she would then be assaulted by the host, his fellow dinner guests, and very often the household servants as well. Magistrates of the day looked askance at professional courtesans who came before them complaining of sexual assault in the aftermath of a sumptuous meal. Such were the occasional hazards of the trade. By contrast, those who perpetrated crimes against children (*puellae*) were, however, treated very severely indeed.

It is an unfortunate fact that, following Aretino's 1527 arrival in Venice, the public appetite for such misogynistic writings seems, through the influence of the satirist's own well-publicised libertinism, to have increased. The two scurrilous invectives *Il trentuno della Zaffetta* and *La puttana errante* were, after their previewing by Federico in Mantua, subsequently published in Venice together in a single volume in 1531 to a hugely appreciative audience. For his own part, Aretino endeavoured to remain the consummate gentleman when it came to his own personal treatment of working ladies, the most beautiful or talented of whom he entertained regularly in his home together with his friend Titian. In 1537, he would write to *La Zaffetta* telling her: 'I confer on you the greatest palm of victory since, more than any other, you have managed to cover the face of lust with the mask of honesty, gaining through wisdom and discretion, material goods and praise … So well do you distribute kisses, the touch of hands, laughter and slumber, that no one is ever heard to quarrel or blaspheme, or complain … You caress prowess and honour those who possess it.'[497] One year later, *La Zaffetta* would be the model for Titian's celebrated painting the *Venus of Urbino*, commissioned by Guidobaldo II della Rovere to commemorate his marriage to the child bride Giulia Varano, Duchess of Camerino. Reclining on her couch, as nude as the day that she was born, the Venus offers the viewer a come hither look which is both coy and yet enticing. The facial expression, however, belongs unmistakably to a high class Venetian courtesan rather than a classical Greek goddess.

☉☾

On the war front, the Empire had finally broken the back of Franco-Venetian power in Italy. Following Lautrec's reversal and death at Naples, the Emperor and his brother the Archduke Ferdinand had sent Henry, Duke of Brunswick, into Lombardy with 20,000 troops and 1,700 cavalry to reinforce the city of Milan. The French king responded by despatching Francis de Bourbon the Comte de Saint-Pol with around 10,000 men and 400 lances. Linking up with the Venetian troops of the duke of Urbino, Saint-Pol conquered and sacked Pavia on 19 September. As revenge for the capture of the French king in 1527, the unfortunate German and Spanish garrison was neither offered nor given any quarter. After spending winter in camp, Saint-Pol, Urbino and Francesco Sforza decided to exact further revenge on the newly-independent republic of Genoa, which was now ruled by the turncoat Andrea Doria. When the imperial governor of Milan, Don Antonio de Leyva, learned of this he led his men out of the city and after a forced night march he attacked the League's forces at the town on Landriano on 21 June 1529. The result was a crushing defeat for the French and the League which ended with Saint-Pol's capture, Francesco Sforza's flight to Crema, and around 3,000 League soldiers being taken prisoner.

With little else to do at this point but to make peace, France's Queen Mother Louise of Savoy and the Empire's Margaret of Austria came together in person at the border town of Cambrai on 3 August to broker a truce, sealed with a woman's touch, which was subsequently dubbed 'the Peace of the Ladies' (the *Paix des Dames*). 'Look!' wrote the Dutch poet Johannes Secundus soon afterwards, 'the treaty has been concluded through women's efforts' ('*En per femineas foedera pacta manus*').[498] Officially, although the Empire was now at peace with France, a state of war still technically existed between Charles V and the three League states of Venice, Florence and Rome. But Landriano had precipitated a powerful epiphany in the mind of Pope Clement. Declaring to his court: 'I have quite made up my mind to become an Imperialist, and to live and die as such',[499] he promptly made his own treaty with the Empire on 29 June 1529, agreeing to absolve Charles of any responsibility for the sack of Rome and promising to crown him Holy Roman Emperor in Italy. For Clement it was an astonishing climb down after all he had endured at the hands of Charles V. For his part, Charles undertook to provide the military muscle for an imperial reconquest of Florence, which had used the opening of Roman's sack of 1527 to once more declare its republican independence from Rome and the Medici family.

For his coronation, Charles had been sensibly advised not to hold it in Rome, which was still in a parlous condition due to the conduct of his own imperial troops. Süleyman the Magnificent was also by this time on the march again in the Balkans and it was prudent for Charles and his troops to remain as far north in Italy as possible, just in case the Turk should decide to strike at his brother Ferdinand's possessions in Austria and Hungary. It was decided therefore that the Emperor would instead meet the Pope on neutral ground at Bologna. Charles V arrived in Bologna *la Grassa* ('Fat Bologna') on 15 November 1529. The coronation was scheduled to take place sometime later on 24 February 1530 (the Emperor's birthday) in Bologna's Basilica of San Petronio.[500] In the meantime, Pope Clement VII and the Emperor Charles would spend the intervening period engaged in discussions designed to build bridges between the former adversaries and reformulate their renewed spirit of cooperation. Around the time that these grand affairs on the world stage were in train, Pietro Aretino received word from Federico Gonzaga's ambassador at Bologna that 'the Aretine is in worse grace than ever, for in addition to his former offences he has just written a "Last Will and Testament" in which he speaks very scornfully of Charles and Clement'.[501]

Whether some reprobate was masquerading under Aretino's name by publishing this offensive tract, or whether it was a carefully calculated attempt by an enemy to deliberately blacken his reputation we can only guess. For Aretino, however, the news could not have been more unwelcome nor more inopportune. The Pope and the Emperor were in the middle of their grand reconciliation at Bologna and could no longer be played off one against the other; it would do a great deal of damage if both figures were alienated together and presented a united front to their 'critic' Aretino. He acted quickly, shooting back a terse reply to Duke Federico in Mantua claiming: 'As to the "Testament", I never saw it, nor has anyone here. You can tell your nuncio that it is not mine'.[502] Instead, Aretino notified Federico that he had composed 'a series of eight sonnets on the coming of the Emperor to Italy and this year's *giudizio* in favour of both the Pope and the Emperor'. He then went on, somewhat immodestly, to assert that 'The works of genius are not subject to the favour or disfavour of princes'.[503]

But as Aretino was deftly fending off this latest controversy in Bologna, the past caught up with him in the guise of Gian Matteo Giberti, who was scheduled to pay a visit to Venice. Since Clement had now mended fences with the Emperor the francophile Giberti had decided to leave the still-devastated city of Rome and devote himself instead to his diocese of Verona in the Veneto, a city which at this time was in a deplorable state and needed his reforming proclivities. When Giberti arrived in Venice for a state visit, Aretino presented himself obsequiously to the *datarius*. Afterwards, in a letter to Federico, he reported that he had 'made peace with his reverence the datary', and noted that, 'If I have correctly interpreted the expression of his features they indicated cordiality and affection'.[504] For his part, Giberti courteously replied to the intermediary Federico Gonzaga that 'if anything was undertaken against Messer Pietro I gave no order for it and knew nothing of it. I was so much displeased, in fact, by what occurred that only repeated requests prevented me from taking more drastic steps than I did.'[505]

At this time, Aretino was still essentially living the life of an asylum-seeker and his status in Venice was by no means secure. His annual *giudizio*, not to mention his *pasquinata*, were nonetheless by now famous throughout the Venetian republic and Aretino himself was already arguably the city's most celebrated foreign resident. This placed the doge, Andrea Gritti, in a somewhat delicate position. Despite the uncompromising independence which Venice had traditionally maintained in her often stormy relations with the papacy and the Empire, with peace newly declared between France, Spain and Rome, Venice could not afford to remain an outsider to this new détente. At the same time, harbouring one of the Pope's enemies could prove injurious to Venice's diplomatic relations with Rome. Gritti summoned Aretino to the doge's Palace and laid his cards on the table. The two well-known portraits of Gritti by Titian (1540) and by Vincenzo Catena (1523-31) give some impression of the imposing majesty of His Serenity. White bearded and stern-eyed, Gritti would probably have been dressed that day in crimson satin with modified ducal sleeves and an oriental-inspired doge cap of crimson silk in the French style.[506] Like many successful former military commanders Gritti had a tendency towards arrogance, a trait which was decried by the contemporary Venetian historian Marino Sanudo. Gritti was not a man that one would consciously wish to cross. In the quiet splendour of the doge's audience chamber, Gritti candidly informed Aretino that he would write to Pope Clement urging him to forgive the satirist his past transgressions and petitioning him to grant the requested *privilegio* so as to safeguard the poet's income. By way of a quid pro quo, Aretino for his part would consent to cease and desist from waging paper warfare on His Holiness and would instead transform himself into the Pope's greatest eulogist.

For Aretino, the fact that the doge had agreed to be his advocate was a joyous indication that his presence in Venice was no longer simply tolerated but was in fact endorsed and welcomed by the Venetian Signoria. He was elated at this personal triumph and wasted no time in letting everyone around him know it. The Mantuan envoy to Venice wrote to Federico Gonzaga how 'Yesterday I saw Messer Pietro Aretino with a written confession in his hand and tears in his eyes. He told me that he knew God would never forsake him, but would treat him better than he deserved, though hitherto he had been a great sinner.'[507] The envoy then went on to relate how the satirist had told him 'he was determined now to live a different sort of life altogether, that he was going to lay aside rancour and hate and all the other wickedness people so gossiped about. He repented of it with all his heart, he said, and was now going to confession and mass with his entire household, a thing he had not done for many years.'[508] The idea of Aretino and his liveried grooms trotting off dutifully to celebrate mass is an engaging cameo to say the least, and as always with Pietro Aretino it would more than likely prove to be a short-lived reformation. But indeed, Doge Gritti's engagement with the writer was genuine cause for merriment.

With his image at least partially rehabilitated thanks to Gritti's timely intervention, Aretino was able to return to his role as 'fixer' amongst the high and mighty. It was at Bologna, in the aftermath of his imperial coronation, that the painter Titian would first meet Charles V and paint his full-length portrait wearing a suit of armour. Whether Titian's historic first association with the Emperor was arranged through the artist's patron Federico Gonzaga or whether his friend Aretino had somehow been the catalyst is not entirely clear to historians. Vasari, however, feels confident enough to assert that 'In 1530, when the Emperor Charles V was in Bologna, Titian, by the intervention of Pietro Aretino, was invited to that city by the Cardinal Ippolito de' Medici, and there he made a magnificent portrait of his Majesty in full armour'.[509] Cardinal Ippolito was at this time on friendly terms with the satirist, as well as being on good terms with the Emperor, so Vasari's account could well have been the case. Charles, however, paid an astonished Titian just one ducat for the painting, which has since been lost. He had been an impatient sitter during the painting process, his worried mind ranging over the many problems confronting him in his attempt to reorganise the Italian peninsula.

Three years later in 1533, Titian would meet Charles once more and paint him standing beside what Marino Sanudo later described to the Venetian senate in November 1530 as 'a large racing dog'.[510] What is certain is that these initial meetings with the Emperor Charles would catapult Titian to instantaneous international celebrity and fortune. So pleased in fact was Charles with Titian's masterly expertise that he ennobled the painter as Count Palatine, paid him 1,000 crowns and, in 1533, created him a Knight of the Golden Spur, which gave the painter various perquisites, including the right to attend on the Emperor at court.[511] From now on it was understood that Titian and Charles had a special relationship. It was even said abroad that when, on one occasion, Titian had dropped his brush whilst painting, the Emperor himself had stooped down to pick it up, telling his courtiers that such a man as Titian was worthy of having an emperor serve him.

Aretino continued to advise and serve as mentor to his artist friend in the wise conduct of his client-patron relationships, especially as they related to Charles V. Titian, for his part, was glad to have access to the financial savvy of a man like Aretino. When, not long after the painting of the first Bologna portrait, Titian completed an altar-piece painting of the Annunciation for the Church of S. Maria degli Angeli and Murano, he found to his dismay that the client who had commissioned the work was now reluctant to part with the 500 crown fee, Aretino advised Titian to instead send the painting as a gift to Charles's consort, the Empress Isabella of Portugal. It was a shrewd piece of advice for the Empress subsequently paid Titian four times the original amount for the altar-piece.[512] But when Charles persisted in pressuring Titian to leave Venice and come to Spain to paint for him full-time, the artist dug his heels in and politely resisted. In Madrid, Titian would have been reduced to the status of a court painter, beholden to Charles to paint to-order any subject that the Emperor so decreed. As a Venetian in Venice, Titian was by contrast a free man. He had no need to bend the knee to haughty, uncultivated and uncouth Spanish courtiers and aristocrats. Like Aretino, Titian treasured his precious independence above all other things. Aretino, the man who had begun his career as a courtier and a supplicant, and who was now starting out on his new career of bending princes to his own stupendous will, would surely have sympathised with his friend.

Thanks to Doge Gritti's intervention, the papal *privilegio* for *La Marfisa* meanwhile arrived in due course from Pope Clement. It was delivered personally around the middle of September 1530 by the Pope's envoy Monsignor Girolamo da Vicenza, the bishop of Vaison, as he passed through Venice on his way to the imperial court in Germany. The bishop had been assigned to accompany the Pope's grand-nephew Alessandro de Medici to Germany. The month before, on 10 August 1530, an Imperialist army had succeeded in re-conquering republican Florence for the Medici Pope and Alessandro was being quietly positioned by Charles to rule the city as its duke. The handover of the long-awaited *privilegio* document took place at the Venetian *palazzo* of the late Queen of Cyprus, a tragic figure named Catherine Cornaro who had been forced by Venice to abdicate her crown. In return for surrendering the throne of Cyprus in the aftermath of her husband's death, Queen Catherine had instead been given the tiny hillside fief of Asolo in the Veneto. Like Catherine, Aretino too felt short-changed.

In an earlier letter from Rome dated 5 May 1530, the Pope had promised to send him as a peace offering-cum-bribe the much-needed sum of 500 *scudi*. Instead of the much-needed *lucre*, however, His Holiness had sent Aretino a gold collar and the offer to raise him to the imperial rank of *cavaliere*. Grudgingly, the writer took to his pen on 20 September to acknowledge the Pope's gesture although his tone was hardly servile and appreciative: 'In accordance with your instructions he [Monsignor Girolamo da Vicenza, the Pope's envoy] told me that neither your elevation from the rank of a mere Knight of Rhodes to the papacy nor your transfer from that office to a prison has astonished you so much as my attacks upon you in writing, especially since I knew why you did not punish anyone for the attempt made upon my life'.[513] Here it was once again, Aretino's old grudge against Clement for protecting his *datarius*. The satirist then went on to assure Clement that 'in all the things that I have said or written, my heart was always in accord with my tongue'. Aretino concludes this impertinent letter by professing to be the Pope's 'good servant' and indelicately reminding His Holiness of his former service 'when my talents, fed by your appreciation, armed themselves against all Rome during the vacancy of the throne of Leo'. To the bishop of Vaison, Aretino meanwhile wrote three days earlier to thank him for the gold collar but declining the offer to be named *cavaliere*, replying boorishly that 'a *cavaliere* without entrée [revenue] is a wall without crosses, that everyone wets [pisses] against. Leave such dignities to those citizens who swell up over them..'[514]

Privately, Aretino had hoped to be granted a fitting benefice in his home town of Arezzo, one which was worth at least 400 ducats a year, an amount that he could live handsomely on. His efforts to secure this through Federico Gonzaga's good offices had unfortunately come to nought, however, despite the fact that Gonzaga, by now a full blown duke, ought correspondingly to have carried more clout with His Holiness. By way of cold comfort, Aretino was informed by Federico merely that his application had come too late and had been otherwise filled, but that

Pope Clement would otherwise have been glad to grant his request.[515] Aretino's failure was likely due at least in part to Federico's lacklustre efforts on his behalf, or else was a result of the Pope's resistance to the petition, or indeed a combination of both factors. Aretino wrote to Federico on 2 June 1531, acknowledging and thanking the Duke for his gift of a 'robe of black velvet and the fifty crowns. Signor Benedetto Agnello, your ambassador and my honoured friend, counted out the latter out to me in my own house with his own hands.'[516] But in the months that followed Gonzaga's gift-giving would dwindle and then stop. The two would not be properly reconciled again until 1540, the year of Federico Gonzaga's death.

Despite his want of graciousness in victory, a battle of sorts had nevertheless been won and Aretino rushed to publish what would be a highly public expression of gratitude to the doge, Andrea Gritti, for his part in the papal reconciliation. The florid and effusive document, which saw Aretino indulging in his usual extravagant fondness for overcooked metaphor and gushing polemic, gave the Aretine's golden seal of approval for his adopted home: 'The credence which I always had given to the reports of this land, and to the fame of its worthy doge, has now tasted the fruits of its own just hope. And so, I ought to celebrate the city and revere you: the former for having taken me in; you for having defended me against the persecutions of others, leading me back to the grace of Clement by appeasing the wrath of His Holiness, to the satisfaction of my own reason, which is very good and which, in the failure of the papal promises, observes that silence which your Serene Highness has imposed on me'.[517] This extraordinary letter then went on to eulogise Venice as only Aretino knew how. But the satirist did not stop there for he also went to some lengths afterwards to write and publish some supplementary stanzas praising the republic. For all his public disregard for the pedants and for past masters like Petrarch, Aretino seemed eager to outdo the former's pronouncement that Venice was 'the sole shelter in our days of liberty, justice and peace, the sole refuge of the good'.[518]

☉☾

Filled with *joi de vivre*, Aretino continued to seek a patron for his epic poem *La Marfisa* but in the wake of recent events his frosty relations with Mantua meant that Federico was unlikely to sponsor the work in return for a personal dedication. Perhaps he was still leery from Aretino's earlier dedication of that scurrilous tract which had got him into hot water with the Pope. Just as probably he was still simmering over Aretino's inability to accept periodic largesse gratefully without his continual complaining and pestering for ever more funds. The business over the Arezzo benefice had ended their last communication on a sour note and besides, his attention was now preoccupied with his impending marriage to Margherita Paleologa, which take place at Casale in Monferrato on 3 October 1531. A man like Aretino, who knew your deepest, darkest secrets and indeed had had fed and nourished them, was not a person you would especially want to have anywhere near a new wife. Predictably, Aretino took to his pen and threatened Federico with the exposure of his dark secrets if he did not receive his due from him. Federico's response was uncompromising. If the Aretine kept up his threats of blackmail the Duke would arrange to have him stabbed in the middle of Venice's most public place, the Rialto. Not long after this letter was delivered a Mantuan nobleman received a public beating for no apparent reason from a gang of Venetian *bravi*. When they left the scene of the assault they called after the unfortunate man that his walloping had come courtesy of Messer Pietro Aretino.

Revenge may have been sweet but even so, 'The Muses need money', as Aretino later confided to Giovan Battista Dragoncino.[519] With Federico Gonzaga and Mantua thus suitably alienated, Aretino turned instead to Florence and Alessandro de' Medici for patronage. At this time Alessandro's star was very much in the ascendant. In July 1531, Charles informed a vanquished, formerly republican Florence that Alessandro would be named duke of that city; indeed, he would be married to Charles's daughter Margaret of Parma and would rule Florence as the Emperor's vassal. By this time a tense rivalry had developed between Alessandro and Ippolito de' Medici, whom Clement had created Cardinal and archbishop of Avignon in January 1529. Although his ecclesiastical benefices made him an enviably wealthy man, Ippolito hankered after a secular career and saw himself as the senior and more legitimate Medici son. Alessandro's mother had been a freed Moorish slave from the town of Collevecchio, a woman of extremely low birth indeed. 'Viva Alessandro da Collevecchio!' was the graffiti scrawled on the side of his *palazzo* in Rome when he paid the city a visit. Alessandro was unfazed: 'I owe the writer a debt of gratitude for informing me where I was from, for I didn't know until now!' had been his good-natured response according to the historian Benedetto Varchi.[520] But his rival Cardinal Ippolito was a scandalously inflammable and unstable young man. At Bologna, while awaiting the Emperor's coronation, a bored Ippolito and his lawless *bravi* had become embroiled in a scuffle with some Spanish soldiers. The altercation had turned nasty and had resulted in several of the Spaniards' deaths. The rivalry between the two Medici scions was well-known to the Venetians, of course, and the republic's ambassador Gasparo Contarini had updated the Signoria to the effect that 'His Holiness is more content with Alessandro's cleverness and manners than those of the Cardinal'.[521]

In reality, though, there was actually very little to choose between the two fiery young men. Alessandro was as spoiled, imperious and often as brutal as Ippolito was already acknowledged to be. During a tour of Germany and the Low Countries with his prospective father-in-Law Charles V, Alessandro would become involved in an incident in which he slashed a steward named Panonto with one of his ornate, decorative daggers. Federico Gonzaga's agent Sigismondo della Torre informed the duke of Mantua of the distasteful episode and Venice's Signoria then got word of it from della Torre's report.[522] When he assumed the rulership of Florence, Alessandro came off as both haughty and distant, a trait which intensely annoyed the Florentines. Aretino's friend Giorgi Vasari had grown up together with Alessandro and Ippolito, having been taken under the wing of a Medici *amici* named Giovanni di Bardo Corsi and been taught by Pierio Valeriano in the same schoolroom as the two privileged Medici sons. Perhaps it had been at Vasari's suggestion, or perhaps Aretino had met Alessandro earlier when the Bishop of Vaison passed him his *privilegio*, but Aretino now made an approach to the young Duke Alessandro of Florence to agree to become La Marfisa's patron.

Aretino's nineteenth-century biographer Luzio suggests that the poet petitioned Alessandro in a letter dated 16 April 1531 and comments that it was only natural that Aretino should try 'to latch onto the bastard of the House of Medici since Gonzaga had very obviously left him in the lurch' ('*è naturale che l'Aretino cercasse anzi tutto di attaccarsi al bastardo di casa Medici, al quale possibilmente rivendere il poema infelice che il Gonzaga gli aveva piantato lì in asso'.)*[523] Courteously, Alessandro declined Aretino's entreaty and the 'honour' of Aretino's proposed dedication in the frontispiece of *La Marfisa*. This was a young man who had travelled at the Emperor's side for several months and was on the cusp of becoming his imperial son-in-law. The prospect of making an enemy of Aretino through this rejection clearly had not occurred to him or, if it had, it did not bother him. Aretino could take solace that Francesco Berni had at last found himself a new subject worthy of his admittedly limited talents when he compared Alessandro's nature with that of his dead hunting dog:

Here lies buried in this dark hole
A rebel traitor dirty dog
He was Spite, and called Love
There was naught good about him –
He was the Duke's dog[524]

As a third and final alternative, Aretino now sought out Alfonso d'Ávalos, the marchese of Pescara and del Vasto. This was the cousin of the illustrious imperial captain Fernando Francesco d'Ávalos, the man who had declined to be tempted by Girolamo Morone and Pope Clement's offer of the throne of Naples and stayed loyal to the Emperor, who had died in December 1525 at the age of thirty-six. His twenty-three-year-old cousin Alfonso was an orphan who had been brought up on the island of Ischia by Costanza d'Ávalos and who remained exceedingly close to his surrogate family. Upon the death of Fernando Francesco, Alfonso had inherited all his titles. He had fought at the battle of Pavia, commanding 3,000 harquebusiers who had played havoc with the French heavy cavalry and Swiss pike men. At the climax of the battle, he had been amongst those imperial captains who had captured the French king. During the French siege of Naples in 1528, Alfonso d'Ávalos had sailed out together with his superior officer Don Ugo de Moncada to challenge the *Genovese* admiral Andrea Doria in Naples harbour. Moncada had been killed and Alfonso had been taken prisoner by Doria. He had subsequently been ransomed and released. Alfonso was acknowledged to be a haughty and self-engrossed man who was arrogant, cruel and extremely powerful. He was also a rather vain man who wore extravagantly costly dress and was in the habit of sprinkling his horse's saddle with expensive perfume.[525] Like many well-to-do knights of that era, however, he was also a cultivated individual. An avid art collector as well as a politician and captain in Charles V's army, Alfonso acquired works by Andrea del Sarto, Michelangelo and Pontormo and also commissioned paintings from Titian, who would paint his standing portrait in 1533.

Alfonso was also fairly well placed in literary circles beyond Naples.[526] He had become a member of the Accademia degli Intronati in Siena in 1525, the year in which the institution had been founded, along with a number of other literate and cultured *Napoletano* noblemen.[527] He was the author of a volume in Latin about his military feats and was also reputed to have assisted his predecessor's widow, now his adoptive mother, the poetess Vittoria Colonna, in breaking onto the Italian literary scene. Castiglione had eulogised him thus: 'I'm telling you, a son might be born *semini eius* who would bring from the maternal womb some of the *pulcherrima gratia* like that possessed by Alfonso d'Ávalos, whose bearing both martial and Apollonian makes the rest of us appear like tailed apes'.[528] In 1531, Alfonso d'Ávalos had awarded Ludovico Ariosto an annual pension of 100 ducats in return for the poet's including some magnificent eulogies to the Marchese in the final 1532 edition of *Orlando Furioso*. He bestowed the pension by means of 'a deed which sets forth in its preamble the duty of princes to recompense poets who immortalize the acts of heroes'.[529] The following year, Alfonso introduced Ariosto to the Emperor Charles V.

Both generous acts of patronage would have highlighted Alfonso, in Aretino's eyes, as a promising potential benefactor.[530] In 1540, Alfonso could still be found shelling out hard cash for the privilege of a literary dedication; in that year the Mannerist architect Sebastiano Serlio would reprint his 1537 edition of the *Regole generali della architettura* replacing the earlier dedication to Hercules II d'Este, Duke of Ferrara, with a new one addressed to Alfonso, who had rewarded him with a 'tidy sum of crowns'. Being publicly associated with Aretino's new epic poem, a continuation of Ariosto's precursor, could do his literary and artistic accomplishments no harm and help stimulate talk for his personal exploits. Thus it was that an unfinished version of *La Marfisa* comprising just two cantos finally found its patron and the manuscript was duly published with Aretino's dedication to Alfonso d'Ávalos in 1532.[531]

When not busy seeking patronage for a work which would offer, at most, three cantos to Ariosto's prodigious output of forty-six cantos,[532] Aretino was busy embroiling himself like a busybody in quarrels which weren't even his own. In 1530, the young Venetian scholar and minor poet Antonio Broccardo[533] had mounted an attack on his fellow countryman Pietro Bembo. Preferring Padua to Venice and having been resident there since 1521, Bembo had like Aretino himself long since put the court of Rome behind him. Having prospered under Pope Leo X, following his patron's death Bembo had retired due to ill-health from his former ecclesiastical duties in Rome. In so doing he had luckily evaded the sack of the city in 1527. The Palazzo Bembo in Venice was a symbol of the Bembo family's illustrious history in the city but—despite the best efforts of his father—Pietro himself had been cold-shouldered by the city's government during his fledgling career, which was the main reason why he had moved to Rome to seek a name for himself there. Having earlier been rejected by Venice, Bembo was finally accorded status and recognition by his home state, accepting in 1530 an appointment to the office of official historian of the Republic as well as the librarianship of the Basilica of San Marco. Like Isabella d'Este, he was one of the most well-known cultural celebrities of his age. When Castiglione published *Il Cortegiano* in Venice in 1528, Pietro Bembo had been mentioned as one of the real-life characters in the book. Despite his status as an ordained priest he cohabited with his lover, the former courtesan Faustina Morosina della Torre, a relationship that would produce three natural children before her eventual death in 1535. His delightful property in Padua was filled with his collections of Roman coins, precious library books and classical statues. One statue was inscribed with epigrams in praise of the male erection, something which could only serve to commended him to the satyr-like Aretino.[534] He spent much of his time cultivating his orchards and gardens which cascaded pleasantly down to the riverside.

Broccardo, who had in 1508 been painted as a fey youth by the artist Giorgione, attacked Bembo's literary supremacy and Bembo, feeling he no longer had anything to prove, and considering it beneath his dignity to respond to Broccardo directly, had his acquaintance Lodovico Dolce make an approach to Aretino to take up the cudgels on his behalf. Ever eager to inveigle his way into the affections of 'serious' *letterati* like the esteemed Bembo, Aretino avidly accepted the assignment. Broccardo was then subjected throughout 1531 to sustained broadside of Aretino's choicest slanders. Reeling from the master's onslaught, Broccardo cast around for supporters of his own. Trying, but failing, to co-opt the sympathy of Aretino's friend the Venetian courtier Bernardo Tasso, he did however manage to co-opt Aretino's sworn enemy Francesco Berni onto his side without too much persuasion. According to various versions of the story, Broccardo was so mortified, however, by the withering storm of retribution rained down upon him by Venetian and Paduan pedants, all at Aretino's instigation, that he promptly took to his bed and died of grief. Whatever the case, his death had almost certainly been hastened by the razor-sharp calumnies of Pietro Aretino (the satirist himself boasted of having vanquished Broccardo, Cyrano-like, with a sonnet). But what happened next was even more astonishing. Having precipitated Broccardo's death, Aretino forgave him everything and penned no less than four touching sonnets in praise of the late poet.[535]

Aretino's championing of Bembo had succeeded in gaining the latter's friendship. It was a relationship which the intellectual snob Aretino treasured and from this time onwards he continued to serve on occasion as Bembo's go-between in various personal matters. In November 1536, for example, Aretino writes to Veronica Gambara, the poetess and widowed ruler of Correggio, making reference to his having acted as a courier between herself and Bembo.[536] When Bembo was considering publishing his correspondence, Aretino (who had this time already published the first edition of his own *Lettere* in vernacular Italian) felt free in a letter dated 7 October 1538 to express to Bembo his scorn for the classicising forms in Latin epistles. All those imitative classical or Tuscan writers: Virgil, Plautus, Terence, Petrarch, Boccaccio, none are spared Aretino's bile. The ever-tolerant Bembo, who would the following year be named a cardinal and prince of the Holy Roman Church by Pope Paul III, expressed good-natured forbearance at being lectured on the evils of Petrarchan Latin by a poet who possessed no classical languages (a serious classicist, Bembo himself had devoted two years of his life to learning Greek on the island of Sicily). Bembo's common law partner *La Morosina* died at the age of thirty-eight, leaving him struggling to raise his three children alone, including his young son Torquato and surviving daughter Elena, whilst still continuing to juggle his ecclesiastical and civic duties.

Aretino, by 1537 the father of a daughter, Adria, would naturally have sympathised with Bembo's predicament of being father to an illegitimate daughter. Like Bembo, he would have understood the need to leverage both his social connections and his wealth to ensure a socially advantageous marriage for the child.[537]

Despite these domestic anxieties, however, until the time came when he departed to resume his duties in Rome, Bembo endeavoured to make his idyllic villa in Padua a haven for Venetian and Paduan *letterati*, which included amongst its frequent guests Pietro Aretino. In his funerary oration to Bembo, his close friend Benedetto Varchi would later describe how 'The house of Bembo was like a public, worldly temple dedicated to Minerva: a family of pure and most chaste clergymen, where all who entered and presented themselves to pose questions to the science professors from the university, and with humility and much glory he [Bembo] sat, almost a new Apollo giving responses.'[538] Bembo, an avid collector of portraits, medals and figurines, displayed his collections for his guests' diversion and particular objects frequently became talking pieces. His delightful botanical garden contained antique sculptures of Juno and Apollo. Referring to the many classical antiquities that graced Bembo's home, Aretino would write brimming with praise to Bembo's son Torquato: 'It certainly appears that Rome itself has been transferred to Padua'.[539] Aretino too would seek to put down some roots now that he was established in Venice. Like Pietro Bembo he would stamp his unique personality on his home.

CHAPTER 11

Il Palazzo sul Canal Grande

In short, if I could feed the touch and the other senses as I feed the sight, this house which I am praising would be to me a paradise, for I content my vision with all the amusement which the objects it loves can give. Nor am I at all put out by the great foreign masters of the earth who frequently enter my door, nor by the respect which elevates me to the skies, nor by the coming and going of the bucentaur, nor by the regattas and the feast days, which give the Canal a continuously triumphal appearance, all of which the view from my windows commands. And what of the lights, which at night are like twinkling stars, on the boats that bring us the necessities for our luncheons and our dinners? What of the music which by night ravishes my ears? It would be easier to express the profound judgment which you show in letters and in public office than to make an end of enumerating all the delights my eyes enjoy.

Pietro Aretino to his landlord Domenico Bollani,
27 October 1537.

By the year 1529, Pietro Aretino's often parlous finances had resolved themselves sufficiently for him to take a long lease on a fine *palazzo* on the east bank of the Grand Canal (that *'più bella strada del mondo'*–'the most beautiful street in the world'), where he could at last settle down, create a permanent home for himself, and design his surroundings to his liking. His new residence, which still survives to this day in the form of the Palazzo Bolani-Erizzo,[540] was a four storey brick-built palace sandwiched between another building, known today as the Palazzo Dolfin Manin, and a narrow canal named the Rio San Giovanni Cristostomo (which would soon come to be known as the Rio dell'Aretino thanks to its illustrious neighbour).[541] In terms of its specific location, the house was situated almost mid-way between the Ca d'Oro and the Rialto bridge, just at that point where the Grand Canal bends gracefully around in a gentle curve to the north-west. Just 160 meters away to the south, the Rialto could clearly be seen from Aretino's windows, a fact which is later attested by the eighteenth-century painter Francesco Guardi's landscapes depicting the self same outlook that Aretino himself would have seen in the sixteenth-century. All in all, it was quite a lovely spot whose frontage looked out over one of the most vibrant stretches of the Grand Canal. Aretino would occupy this rented palace for the next 23 years from 1529 to 1552. Here the poet would establish his *salon*. Here he would establish his *court*.

The *palazzo* was given to him to rent by a wealthy patrician named Domenico Bollani and Aretino allegedly paid his way for the better part of a decade with sonnets rather than ducats, certainly an expedient arrangement for a writer as prolific as he could be. Bolani, who had grown up in the house now occupied by his new tenant, would later go on to become the bishop of Brescia in 1559. A stern prince of the Church and a participant in the latter stages of the counter-reformist Council of Trent, his moral outlook was not exactly on a par with Aretino's own but for the ensuing years at least Bolani was glad to make his property available to this celebrated novelty. On 27 October 1527, Aretino would write a letter to Bolani eulogising the sights and sounds that could be seen and heard from his balcony on the Grand Canal. The *palazzo* overlooked the Pescheria di Rialto (Fish Market) on the far side of the canal and Aretino appears to have spent many hours relaxing at his window surveying the hustle and bustle of the traders and the fishwives as they came and went: 'Here we have the grapes in barges, the game and pheasants in shops, the vegetables on the pavement. Nor do I long for meadow streams, when at dawn I wonder at the waters covered with every kind of thing in its season. It is a good sport to watch those who bring in the great stores of fruit and vegetables passing them out to those who carry them to their appointed places! All is bustle, except the spectacle of the twenty or twenty-five sail boats, filled with melons, which, huddled together, make as it were, an island in the middle of the multitude; but then comes the business of counting, sniffing and weighing them, to judge their perfection. Of the beautiful housewives, shining in silk and superbly resplendent in gold and jewels, not to appear to be indulging in an anti-climax, I refrain from speaking.'[542]

Occasionally, the local environment provided Aretino with some engaging comedy. Aretino recounts in his letter to Messer Bolani how 'I nearly cracked my jaws with laughter when the cries, hoots and uproar from the boats was drowned in that of grooms at seeing a bark-load of

214

Germans, who had just come out of the tavern, capsized in the cold waters of the canal, a sight that the famous Giulio Camilo and I saw one day'.[543] Aretino recounted, in another piece of vivid *reportage*, how he never grew tired of hearing the insults of the boatmen outside his palace, chuckling 'at the hoots, whistles and catcalls which the gondoliers hurled at those who had themselves rowed about by servants without scarlet breeches'.[544] The insolence of the gondoliers was by now legendary in Venice and indeed no small problem for the city's magistracy. Like Aretino in his correspondence, gondoliers tended to be outspoken and opinionated and often hurled profanities at state officials, for which they were routinely punished. In his 1585 tract *Piazza universale*, Tomaso Garzoni would describe Venice's boatmen as being 'always in the public square with some lie, blasphemy, buffoonery, scandalous bad word, curse, [or] boast ... and all of them are the lowest people ... They always have dirty words and vain oaths of every kind in their mouth.'[545] And yet the poor gondoliers would find a supporter and a benefactor in Aretino who appreciated their uncompromising outlook on life as well as their frank, earthy and outspoken sense of humour.

If Aretino had one criticism of his new residence it was the poky little 'entrance to my house from the land-side, being a dark one and with a beastly stair, [which] was like the terrible name I had acquired by revealing the truth. And then, he [Giulio Camillo] would add that anyone who came to know me would find in my pure, plain and natural friendship the same tranquil contentment that was felt on reaching the portico and coming out on the balconies above.'[546] The *palazzo*, therefore, was similar in nature to its new occupant–it had a disturbing dual aspect to it. The one side [if you found yourself on Aretino's wrong side] was dark and treacherous, whilst the other side [if you could find it with gifts and generosity] was light and expansive and generous to a fault. Aretino's house, a metaphor therefore for his own two-fold personality, was a popular port-of-call to his many friends and acquaintances, becoming in effect like an inn. Indeed, this was the theme of a letter which Aretino wrote to Messer Girolamo Agnello in November 1529 in which he thanks Agnello for 'the excellent fine wine that you sent me', adding, 'thanks to it, there is not an innkeeper who is kept on the jump the way my servants are. At daybreak, they have to begin filling the flasks of the lackeys of every ambassador in the city. These fellows have heard about it from the gracious praises bestowed by the French ambassador. He says that it would be good enough for his king'.[547]

Six years later visitors were still beating a path to his door. To Francesco Alunno he would write in November 1537: 'my stairs are worn out with the tramping of their feet, even as the pavement of Campidoglio is with the wheels of triumphal chariots. Nor do I believe that Rome, in a manner of speaking, ever saw so great an admixture of the nations as is to be met within my house. To me come Turks, Jews, Indians, French, Germans and Spaniards; and then, think of what our own Italians do to me. Of the smaller fry I do not speak, but I tell you, it would be an easier thing to break your devotion to the emperor than to find me for a moment alone, and without a throng of scholars, friars and priests about me.'[548] He himself became both father confessor and agony aunt to his numerous visitors: 'I have become the oracle of truth, since everyone comes to tell me the wrong that has been done to him by this prince and that prelate.'[549] A visit to Venice was no longer complete without a courtesy call on poor Pietro Aretino at his gracious *palazzo sul Canal Grande*.

Often, the crush of callers became so great that Aretino was forced to flee to the home of his friend Titian, or else to that of his friend and printer Francesco Marcolini da Forlì who, like his famous client Aretino, had arrived in Venice in 1527 and thereafter established his printing press in the Santo Apostolo precinct of the city.[550] To here Aretino sped when he needed some peace and quiet from all the comings and goings. Over the years, Aretino's many artist friends contributed to the decoration of his *palazzo*, which he would come to describe as his 'terrestrial paradise'.[551] In 1545, Jacopo Robusti, known as Tintoretto, painted the poet a ceiling in an unspecified room, probably his 'camera' or bedroom, which featured an allegory of the mythical contest between Apollo and Marsyas. In Greek mythology Marsyas, an expert at the *aulos*, a double-piped reed oboe, challenged the god Apollo to a musical competition which would be judged by the Muses. Because Marsyas had agreed to the condition that the winner could do what he liked with the defeated party, when he lost the competition to Apollo the latter flayed him alive and nailed his skin to a pine tree. The story was taken to be a fairly straightforward allegory on the dangers of hubris, since Marsyas had arrogantly challenged a god. The implied parallel with Aretino's own endeavours in browbeating 'godlike' kings, popes and emperors was only too obvious. Tintoretto placed Aretino himself within the ceiling fresco, depicting him as the standing man on the right of the painting with a fiery orange beard.[552] We know that Tintoretto also painted a now lost companion piece to the *Contest between Apollo and Marsyas* and that this had featured the story of Mercury and Argus. We know of this lost work because Aretino wrote to the artist in February 1545 praising his work and acknowledging the existence of this second piece.[553]

Over the years, Aretino's other friends such as Sansovino, Titian, Vasari and Sebastiano del Piombo (when he could get leave from his official duties as keeper of the papal seal in Rome)[554] contributed to the gradual adornment of the rented *palazzo* on the Grand Canal. Sansovino's son Francesco, at this time only eight years old, would later go on to become a noted and versatile Venetian scholar, *literato* and publisher. In his *Venetia città nobilissima* he would comment upon the Venetians' tendency to display status through the height or opulence of their *palazzi*: 'One reads that in early times, our citizens, wishing to show union and equality in all their things, built, in accordance with the Daula law, all houses of equal height. But once the riches had grown for the commerce that was always the nerve of this Republic, they went up and down according to the builders' appetite.'[555] Since Aretino's *palazzo* was rented he was prohibited from making any structural alterations and so he expressed his status through his interior decorations and furnishings. Throughout his stay here rich gifts continued to turn up unbidden from his small army of aristocratic admirers: 'chains, jewels, horses, pictures, costly stuffs, cups, mirrors, delicacies of the table, wines–nothing came amiss to him'.[556] The assortment of expensive tapestries, chairs, beds and bureaux which complimented his home evinced different styles from all over sixteenth-century Europe. By the front door Aretino placed a heavy marble bust of himself by his friend Jacopo Sansovino[557] which was designed no doubt to impress walk-in visitors with his physical omnipresence as it was the first sight anyone saw upon entering. At the centre of his *palazzo*, in the long *portego* or main hall, Aretino created a large *salon* overlooked by a bright dome of Murrano glass. In addition to this main hall the *palazzo* consisted of three other rooms.

When he could not pay his friends in cash for their services he paid them in kind, in glowing letters of praise, which was easy currency for him. To Titian, he describes a day spent under the baleful influence of 'the quartan fever which serves me as an eternal escort and which does not allow me to taste any food I eat'.[558] Bored, Aretino walks over to the window to indulge his pastime of gazing out on the Grand Canal and its ceaseless marvels. Having grown tired, however, of the usual sights of people going about their daily lives his attention turns to the painterly ambience of the panorama: 'Indeed, since that day when God created the heavens, never have they been so fair, so full of light, so fair with clouds. It was a sky for the despair of painters, at least for all those who envy you, gossip mine! And the houses, the houses of stone seemed like fairy palaces, here reflecting the pure clear light, there fading away into mist.'[559] At this point Aretino cannot help himself and launches upon a touching panegyric to his artist friend: 'Nature, mistress of all masters! How miraculous is her brush, how wonderful her pencil! I know that your pencil, my Titian, is the rival of Nature and you her most well beloved son: so I cried out three times, "Titian, Titian, Titian, where art thou?"'[560] Titian himself had a deep appreciation for Aretino's house, which he often appropriated for use as a studio since the domed glass ceiling made the room wonderfully light for painting. This was in spite of the painters messy method of working, which saw him foul his hands and very often his clothes with oil paints, something the fastidious Aretino privately abjured but kept silent about.[561]

It was here that the poet entertained and feasted his cosmopolitan array of guests with the superb repasts and viands for which he had become legendary thanks to his superb cook Marietta d'Oro. He disliked venturing into town to eat since he considered the venetians had much to learn about the Epicurean arts, preferring instead to hold his own sumptuous banquets where no expense was spared. Aretino's dining table served such delicacies as fresh thrush, the taste and fragrance of which he mentions in an October 1532 letter to the papal official Count Manfredo di Collaltino, drove Titian to transports of delirium when 'boiled with a bit of dried beef, two laurel leaves, and a pinch of pepper'.[562] Aretino also served 'ortolans, figpeckers, pheasants, peacocks and lampreys' to his guests, which included the bishop of Troia and his associates, whom the satirist describes as 'heirs apparent to every kind of drunken excess..'[563] Often the satirist's dining table groaned under the heavier cuts and joints of meat like beef and pork which were expensive to residents of the lagoon. Game birds like partridge, coot, capon and curlew were also a firm favourite with the poet who generally disliked the varied but unimaginative fish diet of the sea-dwelling Venetians.[564]

His friends and acquaintances kept him well victualed. The aforementioned Count di Collaltino and his wife Madonna Bianca (who are both mentioned in Aretino's play *Il Marescalco*) sent the poet sides of the celebrated and delicious *prosciutto* made in Friuli, whilst a particular *signora* who Aretino knew in Correggio kept the poet supplied with the fruity and acidic trebbiano wine. Brother Vitruvio dei Rossi sent him mushrooms from Treviso ('in Nero's opinion, they are the antipasto of the Gods!')[565] Maddalena Bartolina sent him olives ('I have decided to beg you to send me a few more. The two batches barely tickled the palates of my friends').[566] Captain Giovanni Tiepolo sent him 'a mess of hares torn by the dogs'.[567] His printer Francesco Marcolini kept him well supplied with orange blossom (used as an appetizer), artichokes, cucumbers, cherries, strawberries, as well the gift of 'gleaming goblets, fashioned in the newest of styles'.[568] Vittoria Colonna sent him lemons, truffles and carp from the waters of Lake Garda.[569] Count Ludovico Rangone, the brother of the *condottiere* Guido Rangone, sent him massive cheeses.[570] Girolamo Sarra sent him 'lush salads' with 'bee mint'.[571] Aretino himself enjoyed slathering vinegar all over his salads.[572] Occasionally, his many wealthy admirers even sent him meat on the hoof, as was the case one Easter with Lord Ranieri of the Marchesi dal Monte:

'It was the first day of the Easter season, and I had just returned from church and was withdrawn into a corner of my room, all filled with the sort of devoted contrition into which the sacrament of communion plunges every man who lives who is not forever impious and a wrong doer. I stood there, I say, with one of my cheeks resting in the palm of my left hand, when all at once there appeared a group of people who brought before me a goodly number of cattle and sheep, so that the place was filled with a confusion of bleatings and mooings ... They were your gift, O affable and courteous youth and cavalier!'[573]

Where Aretino housed this generous donation of livestock he neglects to say!

It was here too that Aretino began hosting his popular literary salons, the antecedent of other influential *salons* organised in the homes of such *letterati* as the historian Andrea Morosini and Domenico Venier, an aristocrat who held an influential weekly literary gathering at his private residence, Ca' Venier.[574] Venier would later become the friend and patron to the famous bluestocking courtesan Veronica Franco who, like Aretino's character Pippa, had been inducted into the courtesan's trade by her mother. Access to aristocratic *saloni* like Venier's was important for social climbers like Aretino and his fellow bourgeois friend Girolamo Parabosco, who were afforded the opportunity to mingle with such Venetian patricians as Federico Badoer, son of a prominent Venetian senator, career diplomat and founder of the *Accademia della Fama*, as well as other notables like Girolamo Molino or the poet Giacomo Zane.[575] Aretino would later rush to publicly signal his association with Venier in his published correspondence. In a letter to Parabosco he writes that 'He, the magnificent Domenico, who knows and understands so much (since he introduced me to you), will, in testifying to the talent that you demonstrated even as a babe in arms, prove it by believing in it himself, since cultured men listen to what he says and respect his taste'.[576] For the right people who could open high-level doors for him, Aretino always reserved the most nuanced flattery.

When Aretino was not throwing parties, feasts and literary gatherings he worked on his plays, dialogues, sonnets, and begging letters. His own needs in this respect were simple enough–a wooden desk, a stout chair and his writing materials comprising ink and goose feather quills, increasingly more for his secretary's use than his own since writing continued to be an ongoing problem for his crippled right hand. Surprisingly, the house was relatively free of books and other literary clutter and paraphernalia. Aretino loved to boast to house guests that he was 'free of Petrarca or Boccaccio' and that 'My own genius is enough. Let others worry themselves about style, and so cease to be themselves. Without a master, without a model, without a guide, I go to work and earn my living, my well-being and my fame.'[577] That said, he nevertheless kept himself privately up to speed on all the latest work from Bembo, Bibbiena and other 'serious' writers. All his papers were filed neatly away in several ebony cabinets, with different drawers and compartments set aside for his correspondence with this king or that prince. His one concession to ostentation was that he enjoyed displaying the many gifts which great and important people were continually sending him. Gift-giving and receiving became an important social marker in the lives of men of this era and explains Aretino's sometimes strange and needy habit of pleading for tokens of esteem from patrons and notable personages.[578] Aretino's request for a drawing from Michelangelo would lead to a celebrated decade-long feud between the two men, of which more later.

Of the nature of the kitchen arrangements at the 'Casa dell'Aretino' we can perhaps hazard a guess at the poet's priorities (not necessarily of a culinary nature) from a letter that Aretino would write in September 1549 to Giulia Bigolina. Bigolina was a married woman of the minor nobility residing in Padua and was renowned in her day as a writer of novellas and other works of prose fiction dealing with love, a potentially scandalous subject seldom touched upon by female writers of the era. In a misconceived attempt to curry favour with the great man, Bigolina had sent Aretino some household help but the gift had not been up to his expectations and he wrote to Bigolina: 'The country girl whom, in your kindness, you have sent to me has more need of being looked after herself than she is capable of looking after others ... Her mother made me laugh when she said that the girl is twelve years old, but she has not yet turned eleven. Perhaps Messer Titian will take her into his house to join the servants of his daughter and sister; if so, she will be well lodged and situated. In addition to the three I have already, I need a servant who can train them, not one who requires training from them. I told His Reverence Brother Giulio that I desired girls from fourteen to sixteen years of age, or up to eighteen; and not too unattractive, inasmuch as where beauty resides, good may almost always be found as well.'[579] Aretino then goes on to compare women to fresh fruits: 'what man, wishing to buy something, fails to require his purchaser to see to it that he buys, for example, a beautiful head of lettuce, a beautiful squash, or a beautiful watermelon? "O what beautiful peaches, what beautiful melons, what beautiful figs!" one calls to another in the market square ... After all, if upon seeing different kinds of women, one shouts out, "What a beautiful maid, what a beautiful bride!" or "What a beautiful widow!" or "What a beautiful housewife!" it is all quite appropriate.'[580] It is worth mentioning that Aretino himself made no secret of his practice of seducing his household servants and so inevitably his aesthetic sense necessarily extended to who was cooking his meals, doing his laundry or scrubbing his floors.

After having been given the nod of approval for his continued residence by the doge, Aretino threw caution to the wind and hired several more household grooms and attired them in expensive liveries designed by himself. His banquets, meanwhile, became, if anything, even more extravagant. Sansovino and Titian sometimes cautioned their egomaniacal friend over his dissipation and conspicuous displays of wealth, not wishing to see their friend squander the appreciable fortune he had tirelessly acquired through his pen. They also cautioned him that his over-indulged servants were turning impertinent and robbing him blind behind his back. Aretino dismissed their concerns, telling them 'I enjoy being abused by dull people, for if they praise me it would look as if I were like them!'[581] His argument turned on the fact that like Philip of Macedon he enjoyed a little humility in the midst of his triumphs and being hoodwinked by his servants provided this necessary grounding.[582] He was also by now on something of a social mission to prove a point about the stinginess of the aristocracy. His character Flaminio in *La Cortigiana*, who was often trotted out as Aretino's alter ego to declaim on a variety of topics, would comment in Act III, scene 7: 'Yes, Lords are Lords, and men are men. They take pleasure in seeing those who serve them die of hunger, and they rejoice at the sight as much as a good man would suffer. It is a triumph to me to tell of their poltrooneries.'[583] In his generosity of spirit, Aretino was determined to be *other*.

By now the Casa dell'Aretino was the centre of a veritable river of charitable largesse.[584] Aretino's publisher Marcolini produced at this time a hilariously immodest letter, to be used as shameless self-publicity for his books. The tract catalogued the poet's seemingly boundless generosity: 'If a poor man or woman of your acquaintance falls sick, you send a doctor to him or her at once. You pay for the drugs required and provide enough food for both the invalid and those in charge of him. Often you even pay the rent of his lodging. Even if you don't know him and he is merely recommended to you, you do the same. If a brat is born in poverty, the family come to you for help in attending both mother and child. If some needy person dies in the street you live in or even elsewhere, your charity will often bear the cost of his burial … You pay travelling expenses for traders, come to the assistance of unmarried mothers who have been deserted, advise and help women whose husbands ill-treat them and see to it that orphans are placed in suitable asylums. You clothe the destitute beggars who come to you, taking the hose off your legs, the shirt off your back and your very doublet to fit them out decently. I've seen you even give them shoes. I was told by Dragoncino that he actually did not have an old pair from you, but new ones, which you took off your own feet. You aid even the poor gondoliers. It is a fact that I know fifty to whose children you have stood godfather, giving each of them a handful not of coppers but of silver *scudi*. You are so well-known for this habit that, when your gondola passes, the embankments and bridges are packed with boys, girls and elderly people who owe their daily bread to you.'[585]

Aretino would later reiterate Marcolini's portrayal of him as generous to a fault when he wrote to Don Lope de Soria in 1542: 'For it so happens that everybody runs to me just as if I were the heir apparent of a royal treasure. If a poor woman gives birth to a child, it is my house that pays the bills for her. If a rogue is clapped in prison, I have to provide him with everything. Soldiers whose equipment needs repair, holy pilgrims in dire need, and in fact every kind of vagabond knight errant repairs to me. Nobody falls ill of any ailment that they do not send him to my medicine chest for drugs or to my doctor to be cured of it. It was, indeed, not more than two months ago that a young fellow was wounded near my house. He had himself carried into one of my chambers. Hearing the uproar, I rushed to his side only to find that he was already half dead. "I am glad to pay the host," I roared, "but I do not run a hospital." Is it any wonder, then, that I am always crying out: "I die of hunger!" Nor do the hundreds, nay even thousands, filched from me by my gallows bird servants, help me out any. I am not duped, but what can I do about it? For that reason I say: "Let those who have the taste for it acquire worldly goods. For my part I am content to live without the care of riches."'[586]

Another of his friends and protégés, Anton Francesco Doni, meanwhile described Aretino as 'the banker of the wretched'.[587] At some point the Venetians had created their own version of Pasquino on the Rialto. Initially this was located at the Campo di Rialto Buca di segrete denuncie, the mail slot where the ever-paranoid Venetians denounced their neighbours for suspected treason against the state. Here, members of the public could read official announcements, proclamations and sentences. Eventually, people began pasting their own notices and *pasquinata* on an adjacent pillar, the Colonna de Bando. By 1541, these often anonymous posters were using the stone hunchback carving known as Gobbo di Rialto who, Hercules-like, supported a stone staircase. In 1532, Marino Sanudo recorded that the Colonna de Bando had been plastered with the verses 'There is no bank, there is no shop to give thee credit' ('*Non é banca / Non é botiga a farti credenza*') as well as the additional lament 'Who has no wood to warm himself at the fire?' ('*Chi non ha legna da scaldarsi al focho*').[588] The two verses, whether placed there by Aretino himself or by some social commentator, unquestionably referred to the unstinting liberality of the satirist. By his own admission he had spent 10,000 *scudi* between the years 1527 and 1537 (*'Ho speso dieci milia scudi dal xxvii a questo giorno'*).[589]

☉☾

By 1533, despite his cooled relations with the Duke of Mantua, Aretino was very much in demand with the Italian and European nobility. His munificence of spirit was not confined merely to the common people whom he encountered in his day-to-day life but extended to potential patrons whom he often courted with the most lavish gifts. When the marquess of Monferrato sent him a bounty of 600 *scudi*, Aretino reciprocated with a fine mirror made of Oriental crystal worth 300 *scudi*. He also sent a medal featuring an effigy of Mars by the *Ferrarese* engraver Luigi Anichini as well as a picture by Titian.[590] Aretino's bounteousness, underwritten by the sound belief that you need to spend money in order to accumulate money, was famously reciprocated in November 1533 when King François sent the poet a magnificent gold chain weighing five pounds[591] and worth at least 600 crowns. 'Your gifts are so late in coming', sniffed Aretino, 'that they affect those who receive them as food does a man who has not eaten for three days'.[592]

The king of France's magnificent gift comprised many interlinked gold pendants, fashioned in the shape of serpents tongues, and dipped in vermillion enamel to represent poison–an unsubtle allusion to Aretino's own poison tongue. The chain was inscribed with a Biblical verse in Latin: 'His tongue uttereth great lies' (*'LINGUA EIUS LOQUETUR MENDACIUM'*).[593] François betrayed, through his gift and this particular inscription, his wickedly learned and witty disposition because he was making an oblique reference to Jeremiah ix, 4-6: 'Take ye heed every one of his neighbour, and trust ye not in any brother: for every brother will utterly supplant, and every neighbour will walk with slanders. And they will deceive everyone his neighbour, and will not speak the truth: they have taught their tongue to speak lies, and weary themselves to commit iniquity. Thine habitation is in the midst of deceit; through deceit they refuse to know me, saith the Lord.' No offence was taken at the King's learned yet equivocal metaphor and from this point forward Aretino would never be seen in public without this splendid gold chain draped around his neck and shoulders. A quick survey will reveal that it is unmistakably present in all of his portraits by Titian and several others.

Seizing upon the reference to his mendacity, Aretino wrote back to François: 'By God! If a lie does not sit better in my mouth than the truth in the mouth of a cleric. I suppose, if I were to tell you that you are to your people what God is to the world, and that you are father to your little sons, I should be telling a lie? If I told you that you have all the rare virtues, bravery and justice and clemency and gravity and magnanimity and a knowledge of things, I should be a liar? If I told you that you know how to rule yourself to the amazement of all, should I not be speaking the truth? If I told you that your subjects feel your power more in the benefits they receive than in the injuries they suffer, should I be speaking evil?'[594] It was a masterful return of volley and Aretino closed his epistle with the promise to turn from employing his pen in the scorn of others and instead 'always be the humble prattler of the ineffable benignity of Your Majesty'.[595] François was doubtless briefly diverted by the delightful tit-for-tat but the busy king still refused to be drawn by Aretino's blandishments into the trap of becoming the satirist's full-time sponsor and keeper.

Feeling slighted by the King's brushoff, petulantly Aretino threatened to relocate from Italy to Constantinople. The doge's illegitimate son by a Greek woman of the islands, Luigi Gritti, had made a career for himself in Transylvania and was at this time serving as the king of Hungary's ambassador to the court of Sultan Süleyman the Magnificent. Luigi, 'who spoke their barbarous tongue ... [and had] bolstered his cynical pride by going among the Turks who made no difference between a bastard and a lawful son',[596] had recently sent word to Venice introducing himself to Aretino. He invited the poet to join him at Constantinople where, if he made him 'happy with his delightful conversation' Gritti promised: 'I will satisfy you with such a *premio* as no prince will offer you'.[597] Aretino's customary open-handedness had by now left him hard-up for money around this time and he was sorely tempted by Gritti's offer, writing mordantly to Cardinal Ippolito de' Medici in December 1533: 'This miserable old man now goes to earn his bread in Turkey' ('*Misero e vecchio se ne va a procacciarsi il pane in Turchia*'), following with the remark that he was content 'leaving to the happy Christians the pimps, flatterers and hermaphrodites..'[598]

In the end, Aretino dishonestly accepted a cash advance from Luigi Gritti but failed, however, to make the journey to Constantinople where he might otherwise have been able to enjoy 'venison flavoured by Chian wine, with stuffed pheasants, rare swordfish from the White Sea, lobster from the Bosporus, dainty truffles and sweetmeats to go with the Oporto'.[599] Additionally, the legendary frequenter of brothels had missed his opportunity to freely partake in the renowned Turkish seraglios. His reasons? We have a hint as to why he declined Luigi's offer in Act III, scene 7 of *La Cortigiana* when the courtier Flaminio (Aretino's mouthpiece) tells his counterpart Valerio: 'If it were not for this [the munificence of the King of France], I should go to Constantinople to serve the Signor Alvigi Gritti, in whom is to be found the courtesy which has fled from those plebeian Lords who are Princes only in name. To him Pietro Aretino would go, if it were not that King François had bound him with chains of gold.'[600] Aretino still no doubt held out hope that the king of France would come to his aid and become his permanent patron.

Aretino's forlorn hope for French patronage led him to ignore seemingly good offers much closer to home. In both 1533 and 1535, Duke Alessandro de' Medici–who had earlier rebuffed Aretino's advances– offered to make a gift of the Palazzo Strozzi to Aretino provided he agreed to resettle in Florence.[601] The republican Strozzi family were by this time self-declared exiles from the Medici city-state; after having attended the October 1533 marriage in Marseilles of Pope Clement's grandniece Catherine de' Medici to King François's son Prince Henry, the Strozzi family patriarch Filippo the Younger failed to return home. Instead, his differences with Alessandro and family disputes with certain of the Duke's loutish *bravi* and other hangers-on, led him, together with his fiery and tempestuous son Piero, to become one of the many exiled political dissidents or *fuoriusciti*. The Strozzi family *palazzo*, a massive rusticated structure located just north of the Ponte Santa Trinita bridge, would certainly have been a far more prestigious home than the Casa Bolani, but there were certain hazards in accepting the gesture, of which Aretino would have been acutely aware. Not only were the Strozzi powerful, wealthy and extremely vicious (Piero was a notorious duellist who took offence at literally everything), but as exiles they were now politically aligned with Cardinal Ippolito de' Medici against Duke Alessandro.

The cardinal had in the past been friendly towards Aretino, having (according to Vasari) arranged at Aretino's behest for Titian to be introduced to the Emperor. Titian had painted Ippolito in Hungarian costume in 1532-33 and, when the cardinal had attended the wedding of Catherine de' Medici in Marseilles, he and his *bravi* had frightened the French onlookers by brandishing the curved Turkish scimitars which they had acquired during their months in the Balkans. Titian had depicted Ippolito grasping the haft of the oriental scimitar in an almost phallic way. Although a prince of the Church he saw himself, as Cardinal Cesare Borgia had done, as a secular and warlike prince and like the rambunctious and vindictive Strozzi, Cardinal Ippolito was clearly not a man to be crossed. Who, therefore, could honestly tell whether he or Alessandro would ultimately come out on top in their little quarrel? In December 1533, Aretino had confessed to Ippolito: 'I am not Pietro but a miraculous monster among men.[602] In this faith, I alone wear my heart on my forehead,[603] where all the world may see the respect I bear you.'[604] Prudently, Aretino decided to stay out of the disagreement between the two Medicis and therefore declined Alessandro's generous but somewhat problematic offer.

Aretino's *giudizio* of spring 1534 was published to more public demand than ever before. It was dedicated to the king of France and, as usual, spared nobody of importance in the public spotlight and took Aretino's literary impertinence to whole new levels. The recent high-level summit between the Pope and the Emperor at Marseilles was ridiculed. Pope Clement was labelled a liar through an unsubtle pun on his name– *Chi mente* ('He who lies'). Henry VIII's much-publicised romantic entanglement with Mistress Anne Boleyn led Aretino to assign him the motto *Omnia vincit amor* ('Love conquers all'). The same motto was, by the by, also said to be fitting for both the duke of Mantua as well as various assorted priests and friars of the Church. The *datarius* Gian Matteo Giberti was referred to as 'Madonna Gian Matteo', an obliquely insulting homosexual reference. The Emperor Charles, Aretino predicted, would 'turn Protestant'. Only King François escaped the almanac's humorous prognostications unscathed entirely. On the monarch who had awarded him the golden tongues of the habitual liar, Aretino heaped his usual clumsy and overblown praise: 'And if the king of France has followed such men in committing the sins of avarice and stupidity, either his gilding of my tongue nor the gold chains he put upon me will prevent me from saying the same of His Majesty–whose liberal hands I kiss–as I have said of all the lords and prelates who imitate Catholic and Apostolic stinginess instead of the generosity of Cardinals Lorraine and Medici, who shame their colleagues by being too good for this scurvy century, which suits the duke of Ferrara as well as the Golden Age suited Saturn...'[605]

However Aretino was no astrologer and his 'almanac' had no science or divination behind it, being purely a literary device for the poet to publish his usual smears and vilifications. His 1527 prediction of the chastisement of Rome had been nothing more than a lucky guess. When he forecast that the Dauphin, François III the duke of Brittany, would this year 'follow in his father's footsteps ... in the field of Venus [as in benevolence, courtesy and valour]' he could not have picked a worst subject to comment upon. Thanks to his three year confinement in a Spanish prison cell, the Dauphin's disposition was Saturnine, melancholy and bookish and his physical health delicate. He could not, in fact, have been any *less* like his father the King. By August 1536 he was dead and his brother Henry became next in line to the throne. This placed Princess Catherine de' Medici, Pope Clement's grand-niece, in the unenviable position of being the future queen of France.

Perhaps most remarkable of all, considering his earlier refusal to join Luigi Gritti in Constantinople, Aretino ended his almanac on a note of regret that 'to the infinite discredit of their most excellent and reverend lordships, Pietro Aretino will then turn his steps towards Constantinople. And at every step he takes he will preach the charity of Christian princes who, in order to exalt the seven deadly sins, constrain poor men of merit to go to Turkey, where they will find more courtesy and more piety than they find cruelty and asininities here. Thus the Aretinos of this world are forced to worship pashas and janissaries.'[606] The Venetian ambassador to Constantinople was this time calling upon him. The Grand Vizier had seen his portrait and asked where this magnificent-looking individual came from. Even the feared Barbary Corsair, Khair ed-Din or 'Barbarossa', whom the French called 'Barberousse', who was the Dey of Algiers and a vassal of the Ottoman Empire, had asked inquisitively after this poet who had 'the head of a captain, rather than that of a writer'.

In light of the politics of the era it was an odd attraction, not least because in the year 1534 Barbarossa would raid the commerce of all Christian southern Italy. Aretino's idol *du jour* King François had cut a strategic deal with Süleyman for the latter to assist him in impeding the designs of the Emperor. That the Christian king of France should enlist the aid of an infidel Turk to wage war upon a fellow Christian Emperor was an irony lost on François, who had never forgiven Charles for imprisoning him after the battle of Pavia. The Sultan had ordered the Barbary Corsair to sail up and down the western coast of Italy raiding and pillaging at leisure. Amongst other atrocities he had perpetrated, Barbarossa had stormed the gates of the town of Fondi. There resided one of the most beautiful women in all of Italy, the lovely twenty-two-year-old Giulia Gonzaga, the widow of the *condottiere* Vespasiano Colonna and the lady of the town. Giulia was a woman of renown: she had been eulogised by both Ariosto and Bernardo Tasso and painted by Raphael and Sebastiano. Barbarossa planned to carry her off to the Sublime Porte as an offering for the Sultan's harem but this was not to be. Cardinal Ippolito de' Medici had to come to her rescue with a detachment of papal troops and shortly thereafter the cardinal had become the grateful young woman's lover. Barbarossa meanwhile had been chased back out to sea. Aretino himself was no great admirer of pirates, at least not the Christian ones. Of the antipope John XXIII, a *Napoletano* named Baldassare Cossa who had begun his long and chequered career as a pirate, Aretino had remarked that his spiritual standing ought to be 'zero, or minus zero' since he favoured 'preying' to 'praying'.[607]

Barbarossa's work was by no means done. He next sailed his fleet to Tunis and in August 1534 succeeded in capturing the city from its ruler Muley Hasan, a vassal of the Spanish. Aretino had corresponded with the Corsair, entreating him to show clemency towards his Christian captives, which included some 1,200 Christian oarsmen. To Aretino, the feared Barbarossa had replied:

'To the first of Christian writers, Pietro Aretino ... Ariadin Bassa Barbarossa, general on the seas and of the armies of their Imperial Lordships, the Sultan Salim and the King of England, salutes you. Aretino Pietro, the Magnificent and circumspect. I would tell you that I have received your head in silver, along with the letter which you wrote me. Surely, you have the head of a captain, rather than of a writer. I have heard the fame of your name throughout the world and have asked after you a number of times of some of my Genoan and Roman slaves, who know you by sight; and I have been pleased with the report of your virtue, to which I feel indebted for the praise you have given me, as well as for the faith you have put in my valour, which makes me dear to the Turks as to the French. I should like to see one of those images which are in the likeness of my face, and which are common throughout Italy. I have instructed Bailo of Venice to tell you that you should excuse me if I have not yet rewarded you, for the great Signore commands me to be about his business in distant parts, but when I come back, I shall not be found lacking in courtesy, I promise you.'[608]

In the event, Aretino refused for a second time to be seduced by the myriad enticements of Constantinople. This was in spite of the fact that in all probability he could have done extremely well for himself there. Poised between east and west, Venice itself was as oriental as Aretino cared to get. Besides which, Europe still presented the best prospects for winning new patrons and sponsors and who could say how much of Aretino's native Italian wit would simply be lost in translation if he were to shift his base of operations to the lands of the 'barbarous, heathen Turks'? The latter did have an uncomfortable habit of occasionally sawing in half those Christians who offended them.

☉☾

The date, 6 July 1533, saw the death, at age fifty-nine, of the fabled poet Ludovico Ariosto. In September of the previous year was published the third and final version of his inestimable epic *Orlando Furioso* in 46 cantos. Soon afterwards, the congestion problems which had always plagued his enfeebled lungs returned with a vengeance and brought on the fatal consumption which killed him. Much of Ariosto's time when not working on or tinkering with the *Furioso* had been spent in service to his patrons the Este family of Ferrara and he had nimbly criss-crossed Italy in their service. In April and May of 1519 he had been despatched as goodwill ambassador to Lorenzo de' Medici, then the

Medicean duke of Urbino, to condole on Lorenzo's wife's recent death. He had arrived only to find that Lorenzo himself had already died several days after his wife. On another occasion, Alfonso d'Este–then embroiled in a bitter conflict with Pope Julius–had sent Ariosto to Rome as Ferrara's ambassador. However the Pope's welcome at Ostia had been so sullen and hostile that Ariosto had been forced to flee his presence and immediately fell sick as a result of stress. Then, from 1522 to 1525, the Este had sent him to be their representative in the rough and hilly Garfagnana region of northern Tuscany and a good deal of the 213 letters which Ariosto left for posterity shed light on his profound sense of fatigue at having to deal, as Ferrara's regional magistrate, with all the petty disputes between the uncouth inhabitants of that region.

He was married to a woman named Alessandra Benucci but had wed in secret so as not to deprive himself of the income from his various ecclesiastical benefices. For many years he had been at the epicentre of the court of the Este family and bore witness to, and what is more wrote poems about, some of its most tumultuous events including the Duchess Eleonora's death in 1493, Alfonso d'Este's marriage to Lucrezia Borgia in 1502, and the failed conspiracy against Duke Alfonso by his two brothers Ferrante and Giulio in 1505.[609] In the 1532 edition of *Orlando Furioso*, Ariosto paid generous homage to Pietro Aretino, assigning him in Canto 46, 14 the following appellation:

'…. Ecco il, flagello
De' Principi, il divin Pietro Aretino.'

Contained within these lines was not one but two discrete titles, '*flagellum principum*' (scourge of princes) and '*il divino*' (the divine) by which the greatest recognised poet of the era publicly sanctified for Aretino his reputation as a divine poet of Italy and an immortal scoundrel. Aretino had of course been referred to as 'divine' by many of his correspondents prior to 1532. The moniker 'scourge of princes', meanwhile, was said to have originally come from Giovanni delle Bande Nere, a man who was nevertheless admitted to have been poorly educated ('*non aveva lettere*').[610]

Ariosto's generous dual epithet was, however, the best possible memorialising tribute that he had received to-date. Ariosto's gesture would later inspire Aretino to create his own *impresa* or official emblem in the form of two separate bronze medals. On the first of these medals would be inscribed: '*Divus Petrus Aretinus, Flagellum, Principum*' ('the Divine Pietro Aretino, Scourge of Princes'). The second medal would chide the great men of the day, memorialising his extortion with the words: '*I Principi tributati dai popoli il Servo loro tributano*' ('I place under the obligation to pay tribute those to whom other men pay tribute'). It would depict the seated figure of Pietro Aretino on a dais receiving tributes from a procession of aristocratic figures, much like Caesar receiving tributes from the barbarian chieftains.

In 1535, Lodovico Dolce paid Aretino his own honour by dedicating his translation of the *Ars Poetica* to the satirist. The two men had been in correspondence since 1530 and would collaborate on a number of joint projects.[611] Dolce would eventually go on to publish a post-mortem compilation of Aretino's comments and remarks about painting in 1557, the *Dialogo della Pittura, intitolato l'Aretino*, which would also serve to incorporate his biography of Titian. In this work, Aretino assumes the role of advocate and defender of the Venetian school of painting, his arguments and remarks being juxtaposed to those of Giovanni Francesco Fabrini, who is made to represent the Florentine school. The *Dialogo della Pittura* would become one of the most important sources for Aretino's views on painting and the visual arts. There was already another similarly titled work by Paolo Pino, another minor art critic, which was published in 1548. Like Dolce's later book, Pino's *Dialogo di Pittura* also presented ideas originating from the numerous dinner parties of Aretino, Titian and Sansovino; these were, in effect, a kind of small court where Aretino invariably held court on art and any other subject under the sun. However, as one modern scholar has pointed out, although Dolce's and Pino's books filled certain lacunae in Venetian artistic literature at the time, there was nothing of the calibre of Leon Battista Alberti's *Della pittura* (1436) as regards artistic theory. In comparison with more conceptually minded Florence, in Venice 'critical theory about painting lagged behind execution; painters painted without the benefits and constraints of written guidelines'.[612]

In Rome, Pope Clement VII was by this time losing his tenuous grip on life. By now in his mid-fifties he had become visibly changed since the sacking of his city several years earlier. Stomach complaints had plagued him ever since his return from France in December 1533, where he had lately officiated at Catherine de' Medici's marriage to Henry, Duke of Orléans. By July 1534, the situation was looking serious and, as July progressed into August, the prognosis for the Pope looked grim. The final years of Clement's pontificate had witnessed the explosion of the Lutheran heresy north of the Alps. Furthermore, as a direct result of Clement's mishandling of King Henry VIII's divorce from Catherine of Aragon Rome had also lost the loyalty of the entire English congregation. On 3 November 1534 the English king forced through the first Act of Supremacy which made him the secular head of the English Church. Clement, however, was mercifully spared this final crushing humiliation because by 25 September 1534 he was pronounced dead at the age of fifty-six. The Pope had eaten a meal containing the highly poisonous 'death cap' mushroom known as *Amanita phalloides* and his already enfeebled constitution succumbed to the deadly toxins.

As was customary, many speculated that the Pope had been poisoned. Nobody wanted Clement around any longer, or so it seemed. In the words of Francesco Guicciardini, Clement *'morí odioso alla corte'* ('died odious to the court'). Paolo Giovio was considerably less circumspect, accusing Clement of '… divers abominations … He was a bastard, a poisoner, a sodomite, a geomancer, a church robber.'[613] The late Pope's body would never again return to Florence but was instead interred at St. Peter's where person or persons unknown desecrated the tomb's inscription *Clemens Pontifex Maximus* by scrawling the pun *Inclemens Pontifex Minimus*. His corpse had also at some point been transfixed by someone's sword, the final degradation in a pontificate which had been marked by failure, disillusionment, a devastating Sack of Rome, colossal doctrinal defeats for the Roman Catholic Church and the corresponding growth of heresy, as well as the final ascendancy of Spanish and German imperial power throughout Italy.

Aretino shed few tears. He had had few words of praise for Clement in his final months. One of Aretino's friends, the Venetian lawyer Pier Paolo Vergerio, had recently suffered the early death of his young wife and had accepted a position as papal nuncio to King Ferdinand in Germany. He set about attempting to secure Ferdinand's and Bernardo Clesio, Cardinal of Trent's patronage for Aretino and the satirist had despatched a copy of *I sette salmi della penitentia di David* which Vergerio duly reported had impressed the cardinal.[614] On 20 January 1534, Aretino wrote to Vergerio contrasting the 'avarice' of Pope Clement with the 'liberality' of King François which 'if only the pontiff could see it, it would convert even his innate misery and incomprehensible avarice into prodigality'.[615] In Clement's place came Cardinal Alessandro Farnese, the prelate so often derided in the past by his peers as 'Cardinal Petticoat' or rather less kindly 'Cardinal Cunt', who had rode his beautiful sister Giulia's skirts all the way to the pontifical throne.

The sixty-seven-year-old Cardinal Farnese accepted the papal tiara after a single solitary day of deliberation in conclave and was elected on 12 October, taking for himself the name Pope Paul III. Writing to Monsignor Guidiccione, Aretino explained how he was ill in bed 'prey to a most malignant fever' when he learned of a request from Monsignor Giovanbattista in Rome exhorting the satirist 'to proclaim the merits of His Holiness, who had been made pontiff by divine will and not by human favour'.[616] Aretino, it appeared, was suddenly back in the good graces of the papal court and under instructions to resume his duties as the new pope's eulogist, albeit from far off Venice. In the same letter Aretino quickly quashed any hint of his returning to Rome to serve Pope Paul. To Guidiccione he confessed that he had written to the new pope's illegitimate son Pier Luigi Farnese, a wild, brutal and amoral mercenary captain: 'God knows, I have always been his [Pier Luigi's] servant and when the devil takes me and makes me a servant out of a free man, I would sooner serve him than the Father, because I am used to camps; from soldiers I have had honours and money, and from priests insults and robberies. And I would sooner be confined in a prison for ten years than in a palace with [the papal favourites] Accursio, Sarapica and Troiano ... please put a stop to any movement that may have been started to bring me back to Rome, for I would not live there with St. Peter himself, much less with his successor.'[617]

Pope Paul III was welcomed by the city's inhabitants, who saw him as one of them, a fellow Roman. But Paul III's pontificate would nevertheless follow the same dreary nepotistic trajectory as that of his corrupt predecessors: Sixtus IV, Alexander VI, Leo X and Clement VII. One of Paul's first acts was to advance the fortunes of his natural son Pier Luigi, who would be granted title over Novara and the newly-created duchy of Castro, and who was also created captain-general of the Church in January 1537. Like Cesare Borgia before him, this fortunate son quickly embarked upon a campaign of pacifying the Papal States so as to pave the way for their planned absorption and assimilation by the House of Farnese. Pier Luigi's own son Alessandro was meanwhile created a cardinal. Aretino's praise for Pier Luigi Farnese had no basis in morality and was not in any way to the satirist's credit. A notorious sodomite, the Pope had already had cause to write Pier Luigi a letter reprimanding him for his numerous love affairs with younger men. But the act for which Pier Luigi would become infamous throughout all of Italy would be his rape of the twenty-four-year-old Bishop of Fano, Cosimo Gheri, during a visit to the town of Fano in May 1537, a notoriously brutal act which resulted in the death of the young bishop not long afterwards. By the following year, the Fano scandal had reached Germany and printed Latin and *volgare* pamphlets regarding the incident were widely available in Nuremberg. Eventually the gossip reached as far as England.[618] How, people wondered, could the papacy conceivably seek to reform itself whilst still under the control of such an amoral family as the Farnese?

Astonishingly, in view of Pier Luigi's unbridled brutality, Aretino would later change his tune and lash out at him years later in verse when his father displeased him by coming up short on an implied promise to make him a cardinal. However, as Jacob Burckhardt writes, 'As this gentleman had probably renounced altogether the pleasures of a good reputation, it was not easy to cause him any annoyance; Aretino tried to do so by comparing his personal appearance to that of a constable, a miller, and a baker'.[619] But Aretino's track record in handling feuds with other military figures was hardly an inspiring one. The satirist would incur the wrath of the powerful Florentine exile Battista Strozzi thanks to a letter dated 16 November 1537 in which he begs Strozzi not to go to war. The letter finds Aretino recounting an embarrassing anecdote whereby, during the capture of Prato by Spanish troops, Strozzi had allegedly hidden himself in a bale of hay. When a Spanish cavalry horse, unattended by its rider, approached to take a nibble from the haystack Strozzi had piped up from within the hay bale, meekly offering his surrender to the horse. As if this insinuation of cowardice and tomfoolery wasn't bad enough, Aretino then went on to suggest that Battista was not, by nature, 'armorum' (was ill-suited to the profession of arms) and further rubbed salt in the wound by suggesting that 'if Your Lordship is killed, everyone will say: "Served him right!" ... If worst comes to worst, lose no time in getting out, take to your legs, fly away, for it is better for your hide that they should say: "What coward is fleeing there?" than "What corpse is lying there?"'[620] Aretino's impudent letter angered the proud Strozzi. An unprincipled nonentity in Strozzi's eyes, Aretino was forced to apologise to the high born aspiring soldier.

Failing utterly to learn his lesson, Aretino next fell afoul of Battista's more formidable and exceptionally dangerous kinsman, Piero Strozzi. At the beginning of 1542, Piero Strozzi seized the small port of Marano, near Aquileia in the Republic of Venice. The move had been pro-French and anti-Habsburg in motivation and the satirist had issued a pasquinade lampooning Piero to the Venetians. This had caused Piero to coolly issue his own threat to slit Aretino's throat while he was asleep in his bed one night. Aretino's paranoid response had been to shut himself up inside his Venetian *palazzo* and trust no one for several weeks, and this behaviour persisted until Piero Strozzi had departed from Venetian territory. Why Aretino went out of his way to pick fights with intensely proud and often homicidal aristocrats we can only speculate. Could it possibly be that he had forgotten how to distinguish the literary persona from the flesh and blood person?

Aretino was always better off employing military metaphors to describe his true calling, the arts of love. This was where Aretino best focused his energies for he was always a slave to his emotions. 'For certain it is that the power to cease at one's pleasure from loving lies not in any lover's hands, and although the pathways of love are treacherous beyond measure, we perforce must keep to them', he would write to Messer Ferraguto di Lazzara. 'For the heart of a lover, when ravaged by the face and by the eyes of his beloved, is like a town offered to the licence and the cruelty of the foe. When it sees the fires which destroy it and the ruins which tumble down its walls, it is intent only on praying and

233

weeping, thinking that it will win from its tears and its prayers, if not mercy, at any rate pity'.[621]

CHAPTER 12

ᾧᾤ

Aretino's Ladies

Here is a second affair following the first, and a fourth
the third. They are jostling one upon the other just like
the debts which I run up with my extravagant life.
There is no doubt of it. In my eyes there dwells a tender
fury which draws to me every beauty. Yet at that I can
never sate myself with the fair sex.

Pietro Aretino to Bernardo Tasso,
21 October 1537.

The Medici Pope Clement VII was dead, thus bringing closure to a whole sordid chapter in Pietro Aretino's life, yet life still went on regardless. The two years from 1533 to 1534 witnessed an especially prolific period in Aretino's life. The lewd homosexual comedy *Il Marescalco* was published in 1533 to be followed in 1534 by the publication of the revised 'Venetian' edition of *La Cortigiana*. His poetic output during this period is also represented by *D'Angelica due primi canti* (1535). As though feeling the need to balance his two supremely lascivious plays with something more spiritually edifying, Aretino then published in 1534 two religious works, *La passione di Gesù con due canzoni* and *I sette salmi della penitentia di David*. These two works, being classic examples of cloyingly insincere and overblown Aretine piety, are perhaps left uncommented. In all honesty, he was compelled to churn them out just to make some money—there was always a ready market amongst *jejune* minds for these kinds of devotional subjects. John Addington Symonds, with characteristic malevolence, dismisses Aretino's imposture with the verdict that 'Aretino's religious works, it need hardly be said, are worthless or worse'.[622] Coloured by his opprobrium for Aretino's pornographic writings, Symonds's judgement is overly harsh perhaps. The fact of the matter was that the David *Psalmi* proved extremely popular at the time, with eleven different printings in Italian along with two French and two English translations, one of which was Thomas Wyatt's *Certayne*

psalms chosen out of the psalter of David, commonlye called thee vii.
Penytentiall psalms (1549).[623] Aretino knew how to produce pot-boilers
and religious themes worked just as well as secular ones.

Far more characteristic of Aretino's own literary tastes and
proclivities that year, however, was the first and most indecent of
Aretino's *Ragionamenti* ('Reasonings' or 'Conversations'), *Il Ragionamento
della Nanna e della Antonia*. The first *Ragionamento* (1534) is divided into
three 'days' of conversations between an aging prostitute, Nanna, and her
good friend Antonia. The question which lies at the heart of this extended
conversation is which occupation Nanna should choose for her young
daughter Pippa. She comes up with just three options for the girl, each of
which is examined and compared–in an analytical *faux* Platonic/Socratic
fashion–throughout the course of three consecutive days. The three
occupations in question are the lives of nuns, the lives of married women,
and the lives of courtesans. Conveniently, Nanna herself has prior
experience of all three occupations and so is well qualified to give the
reader the benefit of her considerable wisdom. The sex lives of nuns in
particular, and general conventual deviancy in general, had come under
the spotlight around this time; the Venetian government having held up
for scrutiny no less than fifteen convent-brothels. In the wake of these
allegations, the Venetian diarist Girolamo Priuli had even recommended
that these convents be burned down with the risqué nuns still inside 'for
the sake of the Venetian state' which had been brought to the brink of
ruin by the sisters' moral laxity.[624] Having scrutinised all three roles in no
small detail Nanna comes to the conclusion that the life of the whore is
infinitely preferable to that of the other two. As Nanna herself frames it:

'The nun betrays her sacred vows and the married woman
murders the holy bond of matrimony, but the whore violates
neither her monastery nor her husband; indeed she acts like the
soldier who is paid to do evil, and when doing it, she does not
realise that she is, for her shop sells what it has to sell. The first
day that a tavern keeper opens his tavern, he does not have to
put up a sign, for everyone knows that there one drinks, one
eats, one gambles, one screws, betrays, and cheats, and anyone
who would go there to say his prayers or start a fast would find
neither altars nor Lent. Gardeners sell vegetables, druggists sell
drugs, and the bordellos sell curses, lies, sluttish behaviour,
scandals, dishonesty, thievery, filth, hatred, cruelty, deaths, the
French pox, betrayals, a bad name and poverty; but since the
confessor is like a doctor who would rather cure the disease he
can see on the palm of your hand rather than the one which is
hidden from him, go there freely with Pippa and make a whore

of her right off; and afterward, with the petition of a little penance and two drops of holy water, all whorishness will leave her soul.'[625]

Accordingly, motivated by the logic of Nanna's reasoning, Antonia closes the work by urging Nanna to teach her daughter Pippa how to become a professional prostitute skilled in all the arts of both pleasure and deception. Two years later in 1536, Aretino would publish a further three days of 'reasonings' entitled *Dialogo nel quale la Nanna insegna alla Pippa sua figliuola* ('Dialogue in which Nanna teaches her daughter Pippa how to be a whore'). The printing was bankrolled by Bernardo Valdaura to the tune of 40 scudi and Aretino dedicated the work to him.[626] This second 'reasoning' is where Pippa is carefully schooled in the ways of the courtesan and is taught all the tricks of the trade by her courtesan mother. This includes, for instance, how to understand the intrinsic nature of men and their sexual desires, and how to deceive them and cheat them out of their hard-earned ducats, two skill sets which—depending as they do on an astute understanding of male psychology—go hand in hand. The total of six days' worth of conversations are often presented together for the purposes of discussion and published as precisely that—*Sei giornate* ('Six Days'). However, it is important to remember that the discussions were originally published in two separate instalments, two years apart.

The very idea of a mother teaching her own daughter in the ways and means of whoredom seems doubly offensive to anyone living in our modern era. On the first score it is offensive because of the advent of women's liberation, which has enabled females to define themselves with a more empowering self-image and with full and equal access to all the different opportunities that are open to men. On the second score it is also offensive because the very notion of a mother corrupting and sexualising her own naive daughter is arguably offensive in a prima facie sense, even though this was often how sixteenth-century Venetian courtesans were inducted into the trade. Because of the offensive and taboo nature of the subject matter, the *Ragionamento* and *Dialogo* are seldom read these days outside of classes on obscure Renaissance literature. But we should remember that when they were first published there was no political correctness as we understand it today; instead there was a seemingly insatiable appetite for literature of a lewd and entertaining stripe. The author of the *Ragionamento* and the *Dialogo* was, it should also be remembered, the notorious creator of the 'Lustful Sonnets' and the 'Amorous Doubts' which spoke so freely of sexual acrobatics and palpitating generative organs. He was a man renowned for seducing his kitchen staff and carrying on liaisons with multiple mistresses at once. Aretino merely saw himself and his considerable appetites in an honest light. Never one to hide his sins, he lived his life as an open book and this included his love life. God Almighty had made him this way and he was just following the nature that the Lord had given him. Nanna, the experienced and world weary whore-mother, is like Aretino himself–sexual, sardonic, and brutally honest. 'The world is in ruins', Nanna declares, 'Everything is going headlong. There is no faith, divine or earthly, no faith among the brides of Christ or those who are supposed to give faith to men; and I prefer my liberty. I am free, but I am loyal; I live with an open face. I sell openly my merchandise, while others pretend and simulate. Not I.'[627]

Nanna can be considered a modern 'liberated' woman in her very open and frank acceptance of her own sexual appetites. For her the ability to watch and indulge in orgies behind the walls of her convent is seen as more than adequate compensation for having taken her vows of poverty, if not chastity. As a nun she has her own lover, who is only know as The Bachelor who, on one occasion, 'made me sit on his lap, put one arm around my neck, and with the other hand fondled now my cheeks, now my tits, mixing his caresses with great tasty kisses, so that I was inwardly blessing the hour and minute I had become a nun and thinking that sisters lived in a true paradise'.[628] The discussion which Nanna then has concerning wives takes it for granted that wives will take lovers out of lust. 'I remind you of the conduct of the ladies who have pearls, necklaces, and rings to throw away and who behave like that beggar woman who would rather find a stud-lover on the road to Ravenna than a polished diamond. For each woman pleased with her husband there are five thousand disgusted with theirs.'[629] Her sensual passions lead the unhappily married Nanna to a life of unbridled promiscuity: 'I began to satisfy all my passing whims and desires, doing it with all sorts, from porters to great lords, with especial favour extended to the religious orders–friars, monks, and priests. And I revelled in the fact that not only did my husband know about it but that he saw it too.'[630]

Aretino, the honest literary craftsman striving to meet a genuine need in the marketplace for diversion, gossip and entertainment, catered to the male demand for titillation. And yet, in his male-dominated sixteenth-century world, Aretino breaks all the taboos by depicting women as struggling (rather successfully) against misogynistic constraints on their sexual self-realisation. Often, when the information imparted also fulfilled the demand for practical sexual 'instruction' as well as titillation, the benefits could be advantageous to both the sexes. In the dialogue between Nanna and Pippa the former offers some applied wisdom on how to how to stimulate a man's erection, counselling that a woman 'must be as patient as the man who trains a dog, parrot, starling, or magpie. Indeed, juggling with little balls is much less difficult to master than learning how to stroke a prick so that, even if the desire is not there, it stands up straight and stiff.'[631] Characteristically, Aretino could not resist including a self-referential nod to his own patronage of courtesans and, through the mouthpiece of Nanna, advises all neophyte whores not to spurn the advances of poets and writers: 'Why all you need is for someone to write a book against you and bandy about the dreadful things they say about us women; and it would serve you right if your life were published as some scoundrel published mine as if there were a lack of whores worse than myself: and if one brings into the open the doing of you know who, the sun would go into eclipse; but just look at the hue and uproar about my affairs!'[632] Aretino's disquisitions on the secrets of successful whoredom–though famously lewd as only Aretino could be– seldom veer into the mean spirited and chauvinistic vindictiveness characterised, for example, by the deeply misogynistic Lorenzo Veniero. The allusion to not refusing the custom of poets is humorous, playful and done with a light touch.

In the Cortigiana, Aretino had parodied courtiers as being akin to courtesans (whores who hire themselves out for advancement essentially). In the Ragionamenti he performs the same trick but this time the other way round: by examining the life of a woman who wholeheartedly accepts her commoditisation within the economic marketplace, Aretino holds a mirror up to the aspiring courtiers, poets, cardinals and condottieri who all commoditise themselves within the stratospheric atmosphere of the court environment. At the same time, Aretino also holds the same mirror up to himself too. Aretino came from a poor and undistinguished background. Beholden to nobody, earning ducats as he mentioned to Gabriele Cesano in December 1538 'by the sweat of my ink',[633] Aretino was at the same time willing, at the drop of a hat, to whore himself out to wealthy and powerful patrons if the price for his overblown flattery was right. And he cut an extremely fine line between cultivating an independent self-image and blatantly prostituting himself out. Even so, priests and monks and abbesses might be hypocrites and secret fornicators, and married men and women might break their sacred marriage vows in secret, but by embracing the simple need to earn money whilst gratifying one's immediate and impending physical urges, Aretino himself could hardly be accused of hypocrisy. The Ragionamento and Dialogo should therefore both be viewed as works of triumphant honesty rather than as merely six obscene discourses by fallen women.[634]

☉☾

The census of 1509 recorded a total of 11,654 prostitutes in a Venetian population of 100,000 people.[635] The government deemed them a necessary evil in what was still essentially a maritime port city. Through Venice each year flowed thousands of travellers, merchants, ships crews, and pilgrims bound for the Holy Land. In those days the tides determined embarkation times; the itinerant who was stuck in Venice awaiting favourable tides had little to do except perhaps drink or patronage the city's numerous working ladies. One foreigner passing through in the early sixteenth-century claimed to have been drawn there by sexual tourism itself, and he claimed to satiate his 'famine of fornication' with the great diversity of prostitutes who lived there, 'some of whom live in grand houses and some of whom live in whorehouses'.[636] The vast majority of working girls were drawn from the more ordinary sort of *meretrice* and *puttane*, those inevitable girls from impoverished backgrounds who, in the words of Bernardine of Siena, had been allowed to slip through society's cracks, whereupon they became 'the scum and vomit of the world'.[637] Others were quite simply the ordinary marriageable daughters of local artisans who could ill-afford the inflated dowries being extorted from fathers at this time. For many it was a straightforward economic decision: either become a whore or else work in one of the grim sweatshops of the Arsenal, stitching sails for a pittance.[638] Those who opted for whoredom were forced to identify themselves with a yellow scarf around the neck. On Sundays they went to St. Mark's basilica to find redemption.

Unlike in Rome, in Venice working girls were restricted to designated red-light districts. Firstly there were the city-licensed brothel-inns confined to red-light districts such as the 'Carampane' or the 'Castelletto' ('Little Castle') situated near the Rialto. Here was where the average *cortigiana di lume* might live and ply her trade. One of the most notorious areas was the Ponte delle Tette, the so-called 'Bridge of Tits' in the Carampane di Rialto which was reached by means of the Rio terrà delle Carampane. Here, as the name graphically suggests, the sex workers would drape themselves uncovered from adjacent windows and balconies or else loiter on the small bridge flashing their wares to passers-by. Another precinct was the speciously-named Calle della donna onesta or 'Alley of the Honest Woman'. North-east along the Rio di San Cassiano was another designated red-light area where *meretrice* and *puttane* operated from the *palazzi* of the aristocratic Trapani family. Tariffs for services were set by the authorities and the whores also served the useful social function of wheedling out the occasional closet homosexual and so earned additional money as police informers. They were tightly monitored by the official body set up for this purpose, the Provveditori alla Sanità or 'Overseers of Health' and were prohibited from attending church at the same hours as women of 'good and honest condition'.[639] Satirical price lists of the whores of Venice such as the 1535 *La tariffa delle puttane di Vinegia* itemised the various girls' attractions and specialties. No potential customer, however, is likely to have seriously made his selection based on such a catalogue. Aretino himself possibly needed no such list. As one modern writer asserts: 'Aretino claimed to be so fond of brothels that it almost killed him to be elsewhere'.[640]

At the opposite end of the spectrum was the more exclusive *cortigiana onesta* (sometimes referred to in Venice as a *meretrice sumptuosa* or 'luxury prostitute')[641] who was distinguished from the other fallen women by her good manners and refined education. Such courtesans often had literary or intellectual pretensions, something which Aretino generally reviled in this category of woman. Nevertheless, like the more common *meretrice* and *cortigiana di lume*, such prestigious and higher class prostitutes were basically still compelled, *mutatis mutandis*, to transact their intimate favours in order to feed, clothe and house themselves. The archetypical intellectual *cortigiana onesta* was a lady by the name of Veronica Franco, who was born in 1546.[642] Like some real-life version of Aretino's Pippa, Veronica's mother Paola Fracassa, a former *cortigiana onesta*, had inducted her into the high class courtesan's art as a means of snagging a well-heeled husband. By the age of twenty she was already listed in the register of prostitutes known as the *Catalogo de tutte le principal et più honorate cortigiane di Venetia* with her mother Paola listed as Veronica's go-between or procuress. Thanks to her mother's strategy she married a doctor by the name of Paolo Panizza in an arranged union in the early 1560s, however Veronica and Paolo separated not long afterwards as her will in 1564 requests for her dowry to be returned.[643] She turned once more to prostitution to earn her livelihood and by all accounts her abilities in this sphere enabled her to live quite splendidly.

Veronica's family were fairly well-to-do, coming from the native-born professional class known as the *cittadini originari*.[644] As the family's only daughter, the girl had been educated by private tutors alongside her three brothers and it was from this early beginning that her intellectual career had sprung. In the 1570s, Veronica became associated with Domenico Venier's celebrated literary salon which took place at his home Ca' Venier where, mingling with thinkers, artists, politicians and poets, she acted as a kind of literary mentor to emerging writers, both male and female, from around the Veneto. She became especially accomplished at the authorship of *capitoli* and even began receiving sonnet commissions for anthologies. In 1575, she published a volume of her own poetry, the *Terze rime*, of which seventeen out of twenty-five poems were authored by Franco herself.[645] Like Aretino, she was a natural and gifted self-publicist. Her poems advertised her many refined accomplishments, including an ability to play the lute and the spinet as well her familiarity with the literature of ancient Greece and Rome; this served to elevate her above less educated women who were merely selling sex. That said, many of her *capitoli* were openly sexual and erotic in nature, as well as often being addressed to specific clients and designed to elicit a desired response. In some of her poetry she openly advertises her sexual proficiency and her accomplishments as a professional courtesan and promises to satisfy her interlocutor's desires.

Another area where she shared common ground with Aretino was in the 1580 publication of her correspondence, the fifty *Lettere familiari a diversi* (*Familiar Letters to Various People*). These letters, which have immeasurable biographical value, depict Veronica in a range of everyday activities common to a woman of her profession - playing music, sitting for her portrait, preparing a dinner for friends, asking for a loan of a wheelchair, engaged in sundry literary projects. They also comment on the events and situations represented in her *capitoli*. The first letter was written to Henry III, the last French monarch of the Valois dynasty, and the twenty first is addressed to Tintoretto, thanking him for the portrait he painted of her. One letter 'Advising a young man that intellectuals win her affection' finds her disarmingly admitting her preference for brains over beauty: 'You know full well that of all the men who count on being able to win my love, the ones dearest to me are those who work in the practice of the liberal arts and disciplines, of which (though a woman on little knowledge, especially compared to my inclination and interest) I am so fond'.[646]

Aretino's ventriloquizing attitude behind the six 'Nanna and Antonia' and 'Nanna and Pippa' dialogues was, it must be remembered, essentially that of a male who, like most men of his era, patronised prostitutes and courtesans on a fairly regular basis. The practical, down-to-earth and matter-of-fact 'reasonings' which he therefore placed into Nanna's mouth were understandably self-serving. The wider social context was certainly never taken into account and Aretino himself would not have unduly gone out of his way to either flag or criticise negative social factors like dowry-inflation as contributing to the ever-rising numbers of prostitutes in Venice. Veronica Franco's *Letters* are consequently a far more valuable insight into the general situation and plight of many unfortunate Venetian women during this time. In selected letters, she adopts a firmly moral stance, openly disapproving of mothers who, like her own, initiated their daughters into the courtesan's trade. She advised such daughters to take full advantage of public institutions like the Zitelle or the Convertite, the monastery of repentant prostitutes, which provided at least some basic alleviation for their imperilled situation. She was also instrumental in helping to establish a new fund for such women, the *Pia Casa del Soccorso* in 1577.[647] Above all, Veronica advised mothers that by alleviating their daughters of their chastity by pushing them into a life of prostitution, they were tragically depriving them of the right to 'marry honestly' ('*onestamente maritare*').[648]

Where Aretino's plays and writings habitually celebrated the scheming, conniving and meretricious nature of prostitutes, who were usually portrayed as emerging on top in any given situation, Franco's own published output served to counterbalance this male-centric view. Her work emphasised instead that the courtesan was, despite her lowly profession, often a person of reason, wisdom and fairness who was entitled to be treated respectfully by men. Her characterisation of women is not as the cynical stereotyped *puttane* of Aretino the satirist but instead as human beings in their own right; one of the ways in which she bridged this divide was to try to dispel the dichotomy of women being depicted either as Madonna or whore. She therefore challenged the idealizing clichés of Petrarchan love poetry in which the beloved is viewed as silent, unattainable and, more often than not, ultimately cruel. Instead, Veronica's writings emphasised engagement and dialogue between men and women. She often had cause to respond to personal literary attacks made upon her, most notably on one occasion by Maffio Venier. In her *capitolo 16*, she fiercely rebuffs the three obscene poems which Maffio had penned against her in the Venetian dialect, taking the opportunity to defend all women who are verbally or physically abused by men.

In 1580, Veronica was arraigned on various charges including those of sorcery and casting magical incantations thanks to the allegations of her son's tutor, Ridolfo Vannitelli. Necromancy and the casting of spells was a fairly common practise amongst courtesans and prostitutes of the era. As Jacob Burckhardt explains: 'The Roman prostitutes ... tried to enhance their personal attractions by charms of another description in the style of the Horatian Canidia. Aretino may not only have known, but have also told the truth about them in this particular. He gives a list of the loathsome messes which were to be found in their boxes - hair, skulls, ribs, teeth, dead men's eyes, human skin, the navels of little children, the soles of shoes and pieces of clothing from tombs. They even went themselves to the graveyard and fetched bits of rotten flesh, which they slyly gave their lovers to eat - with more that is still worse. Pieces of the hair and nails of the lover were boiled in oil stolen from the ever-burning lamps in the church.'[649] Veronica's association with the wealthy and influential patrician Domenico Venier helped her to evade prosecution on that occasion but her career suffered as a result of the adverse publicity and, no longer a courtesan to the élite of Venice, she began a slow descent into poverty.

Domenico Venier, her faithful patron and friend of many years, died in 1582 and by the time of her own death at the age of forty-five in 1591, Veronica was living near the church of San Samuele, an area of Venice well-known as a refuge for destitute prostitutes. In one of her *Lettere*, Veronica herself had lamented, 'Vain and foolish is the man who thinks he can pass without troubles through this mortal life, into which we are first born crying, signifying that we have entered upon a demanding and difficult pilgrimage, full of miseries and afflictions, which is wrongly called life but actually leads to life or death, according to whether we lean to the right of the left ... There's no question of goodness in this worldly exile.'[650] She had given birth to six children from different men, though only three survived beyond infancy and for much of her life she had supported herself and her large household in sumptuous luxury. Her ultimate fate, sad as it was, nevertheless typified the many difficulties, dangers and losses which even the high class *cortigiana onesta* faced once her looks and marketability began to fade.

☉☾

Throughout the 1530s, while Aretino wrote about courtesans and whores, his own household had taken on the appearance of an eastern seraglio. Not only did he and Titian entertain such professional beauties as Angela Zaffetta, reputed to be one of the most beautiful courtesans in Venice, but also a prodigious number of other *puttane*, many of whom he accepted into his household 'from charity' and whom he happily dubbed his 'Aretines'. Always a slave to his senses, this chattering harem of fallen women nevertheless made for a complicated life. 'Anyone who has ever seen a crust of bread pecked at by a whole brood of hens', he wrote to Biagio Spina in 1544, 'has seen me as I was pulled this way and that way by the ladies of my household'.[651] Often, in addition to enchanting and enslaving him, they also satisfied him; sometimes the relationship was strictly Platonic. He maintained relationships too with women who did not dwell under his own roof and often wrote letters to his bevvy of lady admirers letters. To the prudish beauty Maria Basciadonna he would write in April 1548: 'My lady Marina, ... There is no need to tell you that you are a goddess, but rather to adore you as one.'[652] He frequently fell in love and lamented love's tendency to interfere with a man's sangfroid and curtail his productivity. 'O brother, this Love is an evil beast, and he who tags along at its tail can neither write verses nor carve intaglios' and 'a man in love is like one of those raging bulls which are tormented by a gadfly', he would write to the engraver Luigi Anichini.[653]

244

Lucrezia Squarcia, one of Aretino's many female admirers, was a bluestocking and a regular at literate social gatherings; she was especially well-known for walking around reading Petrarch and for discussing Homer and Virgil.[654] Virginia Violante, the daughter of the painter Palma Vecchio and supposedly Titian's long-time love interest (he had painted her in 1515 in the bloom of her youth) would join other renowned beauties such as Paola Sansovino, Giulia da Ponte and La Franceschina in becoming adornments at Titian's and Aretino's lively dinners and supper parties which were much talked about in Venice. La Franceschina (Franceschina Bellamano) was, in addition to being a courtesan, also an accomplished lutenist and Aretino would praise her in a letter to Abbot Vassallo: 'There is no doubt, Lord Abbott, that pleasures are the pimps of desire. To tell truth, the things that Lady Franceschina sang yesterday with the lute entered my heart in such a sweet musical manner that it must surely constitute the essence of amorous union. Certainly the three kinds of beauty are present in her, more than any other woman: beauty of the body, beauty of the soul, and beauty of the voice.'[655]

As for the Pistoian courtesan La Zufolina, whom Aretino described as 'my she-chatterbox' and whose conversation was 'like pine-nut tartlets, like honey on the comb, like marchpane, to those who find it amusing',[656] she indulged the poet's latent taste for transvestitism, as revealed in his letter to her in 1548: 'Twice my good fortune has sent your fair person into that house which is mine and others—the first time as a woman dressed like a man and the next time, as a man dressed like a woman. You are a man when you are chanced on from behind and a woman when seen from in front ... For look you, you talk like a fair lady and act like a pageboy. Anybody who did know you would think that you are now the rider and now the steed–i.e. now a nymph and now a shepherd; that is, now active and now passive.'[657] In the same letter, Aretino accuses Duke Alessandro de' Medici of having begun an affair with La Zufolina merely out of curiosity in order to discover for himself whether or not she was 'a hermaphrodite in reality or merely in jest' for 'certain it is that nature has so compounded you of both sexes that in one moment you show yourself a male and in the next a female'.[658] La Zufolina's liminal position betwixt and between the two gender roles would have rendered her uncomfortable for some contemporary clients and indeed Aretino himself hints at this sense of danger when he infers that her amalgamation of feminine speech with male dress and demeanour makes her, in the poet's words, a 'wolf that devours both hens and roosters'.[659]

And there were of course other women, many other women. There was his splendid cook and bed mate Marietta d'Oro who also titillated Titian and Sansovino's taste buds with her superb culinary skills. More on her in due course. There was Angela Sara who 'burned Aretino with her beauty' as she passed beneath his balcony in a gondola one fine day. There was also Cecelia Tina, *La Pocofila*, Cassandra, Cecilia, Tina and Chiara. Yet other names, some of whom Aretino may well have been on intimate terms with are mentioned in Marco Bandarini's 1535 work *Stanze del poeta in lode delle piu famose cortegiane di Venegia alla larghissima et nobilissima signora Lucretia Ruberta Marco Bandarin per sempre seruitore* ('Lines of the poet in praise of the most famous courtesans of Venice...') which was dedicated to the popular courtesan Lucretia Ruberta. These were such women as Cornelia Griffo, Cornelia da Santo Aluigi, Andriana Ziauatina, Iulia Riniera, Isabeta Griega, Marieta Bernardo and Cornelia Dolphina.[660] They were an incongruous assortment of streetwalkers and *puttane*, renowned courtesans, noble ladies and middle-class spouses. All found their way to Aretino's doorstep and many of them stayed.

To this veritable flood tide of ladies Aretino was always more than equal. In later life, in Book 4 of the *Lettere* (4.295) Aretino brags of his sexual prowess, even in middle age: '*ma io per me se stessi senza acoccarla quaranta volte il mese a questa e a quella ancilla, mi terrei arcispacciato*' ('but for my part, if I went without losing a shaft forty times a month at this or that maidservant, I would consider myself quite done for').[661] The ladies were kept happy and pliant with frequent gifts of expensive items of clothing, sometimes cash and jewellery. Often, as already mentioned, the 'Aretines' were drawn from the poet's own hired help; his *Lettere* of November 1552 for instance alludes to a tryst with his servant Lucietta Saraceno.[662] Neither was he apparently above having affairs with the wives of his friends; it was widely rumoured for instance that he had conquered the wife of the architect Sebastiano Serlio.[663]

In addition to these ladies, there were three women in particular who held a special place in Aretino's heart. The first of these was the auburn-haired beauty Caterina Sandella who for ten years managed his household and was somehow capable of keeping this legion, or perhaps gaggle, of chattering women in line. Titian later painted her portrait; it's the canvas with a rainbow arching in the background. So too would Tintoretto. Neither painter shows us some delicate or ethereal waif but instead a voluptuous, homely, forthright-looking woman, which perhaps gives us an insight into Aretino's particular tastes. The satirist was always considerate to a fault towards his 'Aretines' and he went out of his way to find many of them husbands, including Caterina herself, whilst often continuing to retain their services as lovers even after their marriage. But Caterina's arranged marriage to Polo Bartolo was not an especially happy one thanks to Polo's philandering and so Aretino merely continued to claim the buxom charms of *La Sandella* as his own.

In 1537, Caterina would bear Aretino a daughter who he named Adria 'and she is well-called, for was she not, by divine grace, born close to the Adriatic waves?' The name was Aretino's way of signalling his gratitude towards the maritime republic, perched on the edge of the Adriatic Sea, which had given him sanctuary. He wrote to Sebastiano del Piombo asking him to act as the child's godfather, expressing his gratitude that his first child was a girl since 'at about his twelfth or thirteenth year, a boy begins to strain at the parental bridle. He runs away from school and refuses to obey, making those who begot him very unhappy. What is worse is the abusive language and the threats which he showers day and night upon his father and mother.'[664] He expressed unalloyed joy at seeing a child 'created in my own image' whilst at the same time admitting that she also bore a marked resemblance to his mother Tita: 'in her forehead, her eyes, and her nose, so strikingly resembles Tita ... that she seems rather her daughter than to have been fathered by me'.[665] Aretino decided to have Adria baptised at his house rather than at church 'because I was afraid that she might die before she had even crossed the threshold of life',[666] although she did indeed survive into adulthood and 'Christ has preserved her to be the pleasure of my later years and a symbol of the life which I received from others and which in turn I pass on to her'.[667] Unkindly, one of the interlocutors in the *pseudo-Berni*, one Mauro, questions whether the child is really Aretino's ('*la dev' essere di più albumi che le frittate de frati*'.[668]

La Sandella would bear the poet a second daughter a decade later in 1547 who would be given the name Austria in honour of one of the Habsburg dominions of the Emperor Charles V, who was by this time an important patron of the satirist. Upon the birth of his second child Aretino would become even more the professional parent, endlessly solicitous in his advice to the long-suffering Caterina: 'I, Caterina, pray to you that you do not pray me, and enjoin you that you do not enjoin me, and counsel you that you do not counsel me to give Austria to the nurse we used to have and Adria to the one we have now. The former is dry of milk and the latter is a wench in her habits. Let my two daughters be brought up in our own house. Then the elder will be fed upon endearments and the younger will be taught with love.'[669] He also offered this advice concerning his eldest daughter's upbringing and disciplining: 'Since it is well to take faults in hand before they grow too deep-rooted, please use your sweet admonitions to break our daughter Adria of the obstinacy which at present makes her so difficult. For she who is by nature tractable and who is affectionate of disposition is now taking advantage of the fatherly and motherly kindness with which we bring her up.'[670] Despite his obvious devotion to his two daughters Aretino steadfastly refused to wed Caterina or indeed anyone else.

His own views on the subject of matrimony are expressed in an illuminating and forthright letter to his secretary, Ambrogio degli Eusebi, in which he urges Ambrogio against taking a wife lest 'your carefree bed will become a slave to arguments and a charity ward for quarrels'.[671] Aretino counsels the bachelor to 'Leave the heavy burden of a wife to those who have the shoulders of an Atlas. Leave her nagging to the ears of tradesmen. Leave her notions to someone who knows how to beat her or can put up with them.'[672] Ultimately, when a man has reached a sufficient age to be free of the allure of woman he can turn his mind to more eternal things: 'When the day comes when continence has mastered all your lusts, then I will really praise your sense and urge you to take comfort in poetry ... Are you not ashamed, then, even to think of losing your eternal glory for the sensual pleasures of Woman, whose beauty only lasts a day?'[673] Ambrogio did not, in the event, heed Aretino's advice and married anyway. This was to Aretino's housekeeper Marietta dell'Oro and only because she threatened to leave his household if the poet refused to find her a respectable husband.

The second great love of Aretino's life was the waifish Pierina Riccia. This was the niece of Monsignor Zicotto, a priest whom Aretino had known in his younger years prior to Zicotto's moving to Verona.[674] Aretino's first allusion to the fourteen-year-old Pierina appears in a letter dated March 1537 to Barbara Rangone, the wife of the *condottiere* Ludovico Rangone,[675] in which he thanks her for the present of a doublet and declares that he intends 'to give it to Pierina Riccia, the wife of one of my young men', and describing her as, 'no less virtuous than if she had been brought up by angels in paradise. She calls me her father and mother and in truth I am both to her.' He declares to Barbara that he has 'adopted her' and intends to 'keep her to care for me in my old age, for which there is no cure'.[676] Pierina had been married at fourteen to a young merchant in pepper and cotton, Polo Bartolini (not to be confused with *La Sandella's* husband Polo Bartolo, a different man), who was the son of Madonna Maddalena Bartolini. At this time his daughter Adria had yet to be born and Aretino's parental instincts were nevertheless in full bloom, for he saw in Pierina a kind of temporary surrogate daughter. But in reality his feelings for Pierina were anything but paternal. Pietro Aretino was head over heels in love with the girl.

To her uncle Monsignor Zicotto he wrote: 'Nor is she like other women. Her head is not turned when she discovers that she is mistress of all that I have and all that I am'.[677] Aretino sings the girl's praises: 'Her courteous kindness is so dear to my heart that I do not know what pain is; and so I rejoice when I see her sporting with Polo, the most discreet of consorts and my own dear creature'. He describes the girl to her uncle as his 'second daughter' and then, somewhat mystifyingly since his correspondent is supposedly a priest, drops a hint at his pleasure and enjoyment at watching the two ladies embrace: 'It is nothing less than a miracle to me to see her and Caterina with their arms always about each other's neck...'[678] Then, he writes to Pierina's mother-in-law, Madonna Maddalena Bartolini in much the same adulatory vein: 'Messer Polo, your son and mine, is playing the gentleman and only lives when he is with Madonna Pierina, his wife and your daughter-in-law. Nor would you recognise the latter, so greatly has she grown in beauty and manners, which makes her more esteemed. You should be glad that, thanks to God, she is a vessel of gold, holding all the virtues which are to be desired in a young girl. If you could see the timorous prudence she exhibits in her relations to her husband, you would love her.'[679]

But as with all unrequited lovers his adulation soon turned to morose longing. On 24 June 1537, the satirist wrote to the Count of San Secondo: 'I feel more sorry for those who are tormented by love, than I do for those who die of hunger or who go unjustly to the gallows. For if you die of hunger, it is through your own shiftless ways, and if you are wrongly executed it is the work of unkind fate, but the cruelty which assails a lover comes from his own soft-hearted gullibility, and from his wilful submission unto slavery.'[680] He then followed this observation with the most remarkable admission: 'I have always been, am, and—by God's grace and my own—I always will be without money. I have lost patrons, friends, and relatives. I have been near dying, laden with debts, and in a thousand other difficulties. But I have come to the conclusion that the above-named woes are as sweet as sugar when compared to the tortures of jealousy, and the certainty of lies and deceit, with which you are crucified both day and night when you fall in love.'[681]

Shortly afterwards, having given birth, *La Sandella* retired in August 1537 to Aretino's second home the Villa alla Gambarare which was situated on the mainland along the banks of the river Brenta. The new mother took Pierina and her young husband along with her for some companionship during her recuperative excursion. Ten days later, however, Aretino was already pining for Pierina ('I have cut my diet in half so as to grow thin', he wrote, 'although it is not the food but the lazy life of this city that has made me so fat, and I live in a continual rage at myself. But it does me no good. For it has come to pass that I have lost first one of my lady loves and then another. For this reason, I have become like one of those who, wasted by pestilence or famine, are about to depart from this life. They are now but the shadows of themselves.')[682] The satirist wrote Pierina a firm letter requesting that she return to Venice as soon as possible: 'I am happy that your mother—as she wanted to—could show those country folk what a fine-looking and well-mannered son-in-law she has ... But now everyone out there has seen the fine raiment you disport, and they know that you deserve all the splendour which I have bestowed on you. And you yourself have had time to find out whether Gamberare should be more sought after than this city, and whether the Brenta is more gay to look on than the Grand Canal.' Aretino then adds how 'In my opinion, no one should stay in the country longer than a week, for in that short time the freshness of the air, the wildness of the place, the country habits of the people, and the novelty of it all, will give you plenty of subjects to regale others with pleasant conversation. After that, the primitiveness of the site and the yokel ways of the inhabitants, will convert every pleasure into an annoyance.'[683]

Messer Polo, however, was not the attentive lover and consort that Aretino had made him out to be. Soon enough he disappeared from Aretino's household, abandoning his young wife to the older man, whose tender feelings for Pierina were only intensified by her predicament. When she fell sick from consumption[684] he moved her from Venice back to the Villa alla Gambarare where he hoped the pure country air would aid in her recovery. During the bitter winter of 1539/40, Aretino made constant trips from the Grand Canal across the lagoon to the mouth of the Brenta and upriver by gondola in order to be with her and nurse her in person. Before this poor, frail, suffering young girl this Scourge of Princes was as mere putty. When she was finally pronounced cured, Aretino brought her back again to Venice. By this time she was aged nineteen and he was forty-eight years old and he was by now completely and irrevocably besotted. She would repay the love-struck poet with faithlessness. For a year and a half he enjoyed her company and her revivified spirits but suddenly, one day in July 1541, she took off with a handsome young gondolier named Marco who often ferried the poet about the city. Bereft, immune even to the sting of his wounded pride, Aretino pined for the loss of his beloved. The very caricature of a foolish and lovesick old man, a stereotypical character from a comedy, the bearded old poet admitted: 'I blush at my own stupidity just as she should blush for her iniquity'.[685] He wished he had the water to quench her passion for Marco but then resigned himself to the forlorn hope that Pierina would eventually see through her handsome young lover's superficiality and return to he who loved her.

One of his friends, the *capitano* Adriano da Perugia, a capable military man, offered to track the fugitive girl and her lover down and chastise the latter. Aretino did the right thing for once and declined the offer on both counts, telling da Perugia 'I refuse the first because the departure of this misguided young woman has brought me to my senses and I refuse the second because he who keeps Pierina away from me frees me not only from a strumpet and a thief but also from expense, shame and sin'.[686] Instead, he vouched safe that Pierina's punishment would come in the form of the return of her consumption, words he would later live to regret. Some days later, still wallowing in sentimentality, Aretino was writing despondently to a friend named Ferraguta: 'as I had no water with which to quench so destructive a flame I waited for it to die down of its own accord. To have acted otherwise would have done violence to my own soul, as greedy boys twist the branches of a young tree in plucking down its fruit ... fruit which is not yet even ripe. Those who truly love cannot cease to do so whenever they wish. Though love betrays us, we must endure its perfidies. The soul deprived of the presence and attention of what it loves is like a land devastated by the cruel violence of its enemies..'[687]

When, to the entire household's surprise, the wandering truant returned after four years, prematurely aged from her life of hardship on the road with her irresponsible and dissolute lover, Aretino took her back in without question. The old flame for Pierina was still unquestionably there. She told the poet that Marco had caught syphilis during their travels and she almost immediately fell sick herself with a recurrence of the consumption. Just as he had done before, Aretino moved the frail invalid to the country villa on the Brenta and nursed her personally but in 1545, while he was away on a brief business visit to Venice, she died, 'utterly wasted and like a skeleton in the sepulchre'.[688] Upon learning of the news the poet stoically wrote to the girl's mother, Marietta Riccia, expressing his gladness that in her last hours Pierina was at least able to read the letter which he had sent her. Thus she was able to understand what Aretino truly felt in his heart for her. However, he wished that death had come more swiftly and added: 'The place where her body and my soul is to be buried will be worthy of her qualities and my gratitude, who have loved her, do love her, and will love her until the judgement of the Last Day passes sentence upon the vanity of our senses and the virtue of our spirit'.[689] Pierina was just twenty years old. Aretino would confess that a piece of him also died that day.

The third young woman who had meant everything to Aretino was Angela Serena, a raven-haired Sienese beauty who was married to one Giovanni Antonio Serena. As in the case of Pierina Riccia, Angela Serena had been unfortunate in her choice of husband. Giovanni was a reputed homosexual to whom Aretino gave a lecture on decorum: 'If you can only keep your vices in check you will lead a long and happy life. Get rid of your false friends and cleave to those who truly care for you. Associate with honourable persons, not with scoundrels. For the former will give you a good reputation and the latter will deprive you of whatever good reputation you may have. But I know I am talking to the wind!'[690] Where *La Sandella* had appealed to his paternal instincts, and Pierina had evoked his avuncular and protective side, the mercurial Angela Serena delighted

Aretino's questing intellect. The pair had embarked upon a largely Platonic relationship involving poetry readings and philosophy as well as the lofty discussion of similar noble ideas. She inspired him to neglect his bawdy verse for a while and instead compose mediocre love poetry. He did so, playing word games on her name 'Serena', which was an archaic spelling of the Italian for 'siren', *sirena*:

> *Stelle, vostra mercé l'eccelse sfere*
> *dette del Ciel Sirene hanno concesso*
> *a lei non solo in belle note altere,*
> *come titol gradito, il nome istesso,*
> *ma de le lor perfette armonie vere*
> *con suprema dolcezza il suono impresso*
> *ne le sue chiare e nette voci: ond'ella*
> *quasi in lingua de gli Angioli favella*

('It is thanks to you, stars, that the lofty spheres, called the heavenly Sirens, not only granted her their name itself as an agreeable title, with beautiful proud notes; they even imprinted the sound of their perfect true harmonies on her clear and neat voice, with sublime sweetness, so that she speaks almost in the language of angels.')[691] The collection of poems was published in 1537 under the title *Stanze in lode di madonna Angela Sirena* and Titian honoured his friend with a woodcut frontispiece which depicted a bearded shepherd, who is obviously intended to be Aretino himself, kneeling in rapt worship of a two-tailed siren, or Melusine, who represents Angelica.

The affair, such as it was however, was to be an abortive one. Perhaps not unreasonably, Giovanni Antonio Serena resented the amount of attention that Aretino was paying to his wife, which was an unseemly degree of respect to his considerably more strait-laced Sienese eyes. Angela was given a stern talking to by the extended family. After receiving her spousal reprimand she cut Aretino dead, returned his letters unopened, and even ignored him whenever they passed each other on the street. The husband's 'effrontery' in denying the poet access to his wife incensed Aretino and he sent Giovanni Antonio a rather rude letter informing him that both he and his wife would be obscure unknowns had it not been for his writing. He then added for good measure how '..popes, kings and emperors are happy when they are merely not vituperated by my pen..' and bragged that the duke of Ferrara had sent him 'a pocketful on money merely to induce me to visit him'.[692] The jealous husband was unimpressed and Angela remained off limits. By 1540, she had died, by which time Aretino—preoccupied with his many other women—had lost interest anyway.

In November 1547, we find Aretino writing to Dr. Francesco Macasola, possibly one of his personal physicians, admitting to being unhappily in love. By this time the satirist was 55 years old and still showing no signs of curtailing his romantic activities. The doctor has been pestering Aretino to find out how the satirist felt about the gallivanting of his latest lady love. Aretino replied to him tersely: 'But since all lovers live bitterly though their longings are sweet, I urge you to spend your time gibing those who love their youth, and not those, who, like me, fall into its snares in old age. For those who are in their fifties–ah me, they might just as well go to the wars in France, for at that age men think of nothing but death. But from then on until they reach 70, they think only of life which at this point is renewed in all its vigour. Then long live Cupid and death to Mars!'[693]

CHAPTER 13

New Enemies and Old Scores Settled

Love me if you don't want me to hate you; and appreciate me if you don't want me to despise you; because when Pasquino's spirit sends me into a poetic frenzy, I am more terrifying than the devil.

Pietro Aretino,
14 June 1537.

F rancesco Berni, so long a thorn in Aretino's side, eventually received his comeuppance. He would die in May 1535, some said at Aretino's hands, though this is doubtful, others claiming that it was at the hand of Duke Alessandro de' Medici. Aretino would later collaborate with the *Milanese* poet Giovanni Alberto Albicante in publishing, in both Venice and Milan in 1541, a deliberately garbled version of Berni's *Rifacimento* which was maliciously designed to ruin Berni's literary reputation.[694] How Aretino and Albicante gained possession of Berni's private, unpublished manuscript had long been a mystery in literary circles until it was suggested in 1554 by Aretino's Venetian friend, by now a wanted heretic, Pier Paolo Vergerio, that Berni, a private Lutheran sympathiser, had secretly used the *Rifacimento* to diffuse Protestant doctrines in an unobtrusive form. Vergerio cited as evidence of his theory some eighteen stanzas of Berni taken from the induction to the twentieth Canto.[695] This hypothesis does at least explain why Berni's friends failed to intervene in preventing Aretino and Albicante from mutilating Berni's life's work (their fear of the Holy Inquisition!) and even suggests a degree of complicity on the part of the Church. As for the eighteen stanzas adduced by Vergerio, they are reduced in Aretino and Albicante's version to a mere seven stanzas which are mostly a mangled and distorted assemblage of vulgarities. It is fascinating nonetheless to imagine Aretino assuming the unlikely role as righteous instrument of Holy Mother Church in this whole affair, however the opportunity to do mischief to the legacy of one of his sworn enemies would surely have been far too good to pass up.

The same month and year of Berni's death found the Emperor Charles V at Barcelona where, together with his *Genovese* admiral Andrea Doria, he was busy assembling a fleet of 400 ships and an army of 30,000 men with which to re-capture Tunis from the pirate Barbarossa. Just two months later, Charles had destroyed the Corsair's fleet and conquered the city. It had been the first time that Charles had personally led his army into battle. Anticipating that the Emperor would return to his domains via Naples and travel up the length of Italy, Cardinal Ippolito de' Medici had travelled south to meet him and planned to raise the subject of his candidacy for dukedom of Florence in Alessandro de' Medici's place. Combining this quest with a pleasurable visit to the town of Fondi to see his lover Giulia Gonzaga, Ippolito was at Itri on 10 August 1535 when he suddenly took sick and died. Notwithstanding the fact that two of the Cardinal's traveling companions, Dante da Castiglione and Berlinghere Berlingheri, had also fallen sick and died the following day of similar symptoms to Ippolito's, not to mention the pronouncements of the attending doctors that all their deaths were due to the pestilential marsh air of the region, suspicion now fell on the Cardinal's unfortunate major-domo, Giovanni Andrea.

At the same time, Francesco Berni's name was also resurrected in connection with Ippolito's 'murder'. Although Berni had already died on 26 May 1535 and Cardinal Ippolito had died more than two months later it was put about that the burlesque poet had been solicited by Duke Alessandro to poison Ippolito and by Ippolito to poison Alessandro, but that he had declined to be involved in either of the two counter-plots. For his non-compliance, so the rumour went, Berni himself had been poisoned by Alessandro. The story was typical of the sensational scuttlebutt of the era and probably had precious little basis in fact. As Aretino himself knew, perhaps more than anyone else, the pleasure-loving Francesco Berni would hardly have made for a reliable or an especially deadly assassin. The loss of yet another erstwhile Medici patron was the occasion for one of Aretino's turgid encomiums. Writing to Cardinal Ippolito's secretary 'the Divine Molza', Aretino mused 'For if I had not known him, or the taste of his liberality, his countenance, which shall always remain fixed in my mind, would not afflict me as it now does ... I am amazed at the method of Death in outraging an immortal personality.'[696]

By this time, storm clouds were once more gathering over Italy. The French King's diplomacy with Sultan Süleyman the Magnificent had ripened with the departure of France's ambassador Jean de La Forêt to Istanbul. By February 1536, the French were granted the rights of an official embassy in the town of Galata across the Golden horn and commercial privileges were accorded to all French merchants within the Turkish Empire. A 27,000-strong French army under the command of Philippe de Chabot invaded Piedmont and Savoy in March 1536. The Duke of Savoy fled to Vercelli on the border with Lombardy, a city which Chabot had been instructed by François to keep his distance from. Aretino, resenting François's niggardliness of the past few years, wrote to Charles V on 10 March prophesying his triumph in the coming conflict: 'I, O Caesar, should liken you to a torrent, swollen with rains, snows and sun-melted ice, swallowed by the fields that think they are drinking, while your own superb course is making a bed of them. I tell you that this new onslaught shall disappear, as every one that is made upon you always does disappear, and as every race, every banner and every name that contends with you shall disappear, for who fights with Caesar fights with God, and who fights with God confounds himself.'[697] Nevertheless, despite Aretino's encouraging words, it was the imperial side which this time looked set to be deluged by the numberless French. Charles had ordered the governor of Milan, Don Antonio de Leyva, to march to Vercelli with a paltry 1,000 troops, far too few for the Imperialists to realistically take on the French invaders.

Aretino wrote a separate letter of encouragement, this time to Don Antonio, informing him: 'You make the banners of pertinacity and terror tremble, you move peoples with your prudence and your valour, and you open a path through difficulties by the virtue of your arms'. That was on 4 June and it was in Aretino's interests to remain in de Leyva's good books since it was well-known that the wily old soldier was keen to detach Charles from this bothersome satirist and letter-writer who constantly held out his greedy hand. By 25 July, Charles had mounted a counter-attack on François by crossing over into Provence. The campaign was a complete and utter fiasco. By 11 September, Charles began withdrawing from southern France and Don Antonio de Leyva finally died of his gout and the rigours of campaigning. Aretino, who in later life shied away from all military endeavours, wrote expansively to Don Luigi de Leyva, 'What life was ever more deserving of the death that the great Antonio met, who spent himself in the sight of Augustus and in the bosom of the most famous and most glorious of armies that the sun of our day ever saw?'[698] While the land campaigns were ongoing, a small Franco-Turkish fleet comprising twelve French galleys and a single Ottoman galley plus 6 galiotes, commanded by Admiral Baron de Saint-Blancard and Barbarossa himself, conducted operations up and down the Spanish coast from Tortosa to Collioure. By the end of 1536, a considerably augmented fleet of 30 French and Turkish galleys was wintering in Marseilles harbour; it was the first time in history that a Turkish fleet had laid up for the winter in a Western European port.

All of Christian Europe was scandalised by this. Aretino saw a golden opportunity for some self-publicity. Returning to his occasional bailiwick of outraged spokesperson for Christendom, Aretino remonstrated with François: 'Now I lament—and as your servant, I regret this—that I can call you neither King of France nor François, for one cannot truthfully be called either King or Free (which last is what François and France means) if he goes about begging the aid of those barbarians who are both enemies of his race and rebels against his God.' Aretino continued with his remonstrance: 'My lord—for so I still name you—you have thrust the Ottoman sword into the heart of Christendom, and by doing this you have gravely wounded the glory of your hitherto unconquered excellence'. The satirist held up the example of Henry VIII who had been estranged from both Pope and Emperor on account of his divorce from Catherine of Aragon, but who nevertheless rallied to Christendom's aid when he realised that the 'Turkish fury was directed against the West'. Continuing, Aretino then went on to express his doubts that the Ottoman Sultan was sincere in his pact of brotherhood and alliance and suggested instead that Süleyman intended to use the Christian powers against each other, before closing in for the kill on the weakened remnants. 'Cast aside, then O Sire, break and cut to pieces this treacherous so-called brotherhood—that is if you want to be called a Christian. For we cannot all be brothers in Christ together, if you at the same time are the brother of Christ's most potent enemy.'[699]

The maestro's rebuke, once published, resonated throughout all of Europe. Once more, the satirist had held the mirror up to an erring monarch. François was horrified. French agents were despatched to Venice to make contact with Aretino and win him back over to France's side by any means possible. Rumours abounded that the King would pay the satirist as much as 400 *scudi* annually to guarantee his future loyalty and his acquiescence to French foreign policy. This was double the pension that Charles V was already paying Aretino, but was a sum which Charles had by now allowed to fall into arrears due to the ongoing expense of the war. Getting wind of France's offer, Charles responded by making it common knowledge that he might be prepared to double his enemy's bid provided that the satirist continued writing in the same vein, in support of Imperialist policy. Aretino's well-timed letter had not only hit a nerve, it had also sparked off a veritable bidding war between two sixteenth-century superpowers.

But at this point Aretino nearly sabotaged his own interests, something he had done many times before through his simple inability to keep his mouth shut when it mattered most. Here is how it happened.

Aretino's sometime literary collaborator, Giovanni Alberto Albicante, had lately published in Milan a history of the recent Piedmontese war (the *Historia de la guerra del Piedmonte*). Dedicating it to the Duke of Mantua, he sent a copy of the work to Aretino expecting good-natured praise. Poems in vernacular octaves that celebrated contemporary battles were Albicante's stock-in-trade and he at least expected a flattering word or two from his acknowledged literary superior. Instead, Aretino replied back with a *capitolo* of his own ridiculing Albicante's latest work. Taking umbrage, Albicante himself replied with another poem in *terza rima*, the *Apologia del bestiale Albicante contra il Divino Pietro Aretino*, signing himself as *furibondo e bestiale* ('furious and beastly').[700] Aretino was unimpressed. Tartly he responded: 'My brother, the rage of poets is but a frenzy of stupidity'. Nursing his grudge, Albicante now accepted bribes from French agents to compose some scurrilous attacks on the Emperor and maliciously signed them in the name of 'the Divine Aretino'. Having worked closely with Aretino before, this was a relatively easy task since Albicante was already somewhat familiar with his writing style and so the forgeries were duly put into general public circulation.

The verses, once he learned of their existence, fortunately caused Aretino a few sleepless nights but nothing more. A hastily written letter from the satirist to Cardinal Marino Caracciolo, the temporary governor of Milan, straightened things out with the Emperor. To Caracciolo, Aretino unburdened himself: '..although many foolish things come out in Milan under my name, practically everyone knows that they are not mine; which goes to show that the people are better judges than the senators'.[701] The spat with Albicante was subsequently smoothed over with the assistance of the Academy of the Intronati in Siena, who evidently thought the writerly squabble was of sufficient importance to produce a volume on the subject, the *Combattimento poetico del divino Aretino e del bestiale Albicante occorso sopra la Guerra di Piedmonte, e la pace loro celebrata nella Accademia degli Intronati a Siena*. Neither did the affair seem to unduly impinge upon the ongoing bidding war for Aretino's propaganda services. In 1538, François let it be known to the satirist that he was now prepared to pay him 600 *scudi* for his public support.

☉☾

In 1537, all of Italy was shaken by a fresh new scandal, the assassination of Duke Alessandro de' Medici by his own cousin Lorenzino de' Medici, a listless youth who was also widely known as 'Lorenzaccio' or 'Bad Lorenzo' for his habit when he lived in Rome of drunkenly striking off the heads of classical statues. Lorenzino had served as a member of the Duke's entourage and frequently acted as a pimp and procurer for the priapic Alessandro, whose rule had increasingly devolved into that of a sex-crazed tyrant. On the evening of 6 January 1537, the Duke had retired to Lorenzino's house situated behind the Palazzo Medici in the expectation of an enjoyable tryst with a married lady, Caterina Soderini Ginori, whose famously unobtainable favours Lorenzino had purportedly procured for his master. The assignation was bogus, however, a charade and a trap, for the Duke's boon companion Lorenzino had returned with a rough fellow named *l'Unghero* ('The Hungarian') and together they had repeatedly stabbed the Duke to death. After the assassination Lorenzino fled to Venice to escape the clutches of the Duke's father-in-law the Emperor Charles V as well as the public furore and the wrath of the Florentine authorities.

Numerous republican minded Florentines had already left Florence since Alessandro had come to power and many of them had made their home in Venice. As exiles and political dissidents, impartial Venice had welcomed them with open arms, just as they had welcomed Aretino in 1527. The leader of the exiles, Filippo Strozzi, commented: 'I had resolved to live in Venice, because the place and its customs entirely satisfied me, and I was as well regarded and affectionately treated there as I could wish'[702] Strozzi's sentiments recalled Aretino's own gushing enthusiasm as a fugitive who had found in Venice (quite literally) a safe harbour. Upon his arrival in the republic on the evening of 8 January, a tired and travel-weary Lorenzino found himself fêted by the dead Duke's enemies. These were the Florentine diaspora, a group which included such republicans and humanists as Benedetto Varchi, Girolamo Borgia, Francesco Maria Molza and others, who now tripped over themselves to memorialise and eulogise the assassin's deed. Filippo Strozzi compared Lorenzino with Caesar's killer, Marcus Junius Brutus, whilst conveniently overlooking the fact that Dante had placed Brutus in the bottommost pit of Hell, a placement later vindicated by Coluccio Salutati in his work *De tyranno*. Pietro Aretino's friend, the sculptor Jacopo Sansovino, promised meanwhile to dedicate a statue to Lorenzino.[703] In Rome, Michelangelo completed a bust of Brutus in commemoration of the assassin which was destined for the house of the exiled former republican war secretary Donato Giannotti.

Aretino's own attitude towards Lorenzino de' Medici was unequivocal. The satirist was one of those filo-Mediceans resident in Venice who had aligned their interests with Duke Alessandro and his father-in-law the Emperor. As we have already seen, Aretino had at one time tried, though unsuccessfully, to secure Alessandro's patronage and the latter had even honoured his sister Francesca by paying her a visit. But when Alessandro changed his mind and offered to give Aretino the Palazzo Strozzi for his home, the satirist had already decided not to become a resident of Florence. Taking up residence in the Strozzi ancestral home would hardly have endeared Aretino to the powerful Strozzi clan, some of whom—including Filippo the patriarch—were now exiles residing in Venice and so, to all intents and purposes, his neighbours. So towards Lorenzino, Aretino remained unsupportive and unsympathetic. 'For ambition and the worst heat of envy soil their sword in the generosity of others' blood, and these are the more audacious in their attempts, the more eager they are for position', the satirist fulminated in a thinly veiled reference to Lorenzino, adding 'But since others are not ashamed to follow the ambitious and envious counsels, vileness has given the name of "glorious" to disgrace.'[704] As late as 1544, we still find Aretino describing the assassin as 'an inhuman monster'[705] and when Lorenzino was himself assassinated by agents of Charles V on 26 February 1548, Aretino would write: 'Now, whether a man has put an end to his [Lorenzino's] days in order to get the reward or for some other reason, I care not' whilst observing that Lorenzino had lived twelve years more than he should have in light of his foul crime.[706] It was perhaps ironic that Aretino, the 'character assassin' *par excellence*, should have so thoroughly excoriated the actions of the real-life assassin Lorenzino de' Medici. But surely this attitude was not wholly to do with his affinity for the late Duke and his political non-alignment with the Florentine exiles. We can probably trace Aretino's general distaste for the underhand business of assassination to his own attempted assassination at the hands of Achille della Volta in 1525, a traumatic act which unquestionably left a deep, lifelong scar on the satirist's psyche.

As for the Florentine exiles, their own time in the sun would be preposterously short-lived. Failing to promptly galvanise themselves into action in the immediate aftermath of the tyrant's slaying, Alessandro's place was soon filled, with the Emperor's tacit blessing, by the eighteen-year-old Cosimo de' Medici. This was the young son of Giovanni delle Bande Nere and Maria Salviati. Since her husband's death, Maria had devoted herself untiringly to raising Cosimo as a fully-fledged scion of the House of Medici, someone who could one day expect to rule Florence in his own right. In this, and in her motherly duties, Maria had shown as much confidence and resolve as the late Giovanni had shown in the heat of battle. Her single-minded ambition for her only son may be glimpsed in a letter which she sent to a 'Giovanni' in Rome dated May 1531 in which she confides 'As soon as the blessed soul of my lord husband had departed, in that instant I decided to live forever with my son for many reasons that would be too long to relate by letter; and for a very special consideration that my son, having been born above all of those fortunate ancestors, was not to be abandoned by me, since it will be much more useful to him to remain with him rather than leave him, the self-same purpose I held until this time and principally hold [now]'.[707]

This new development was of course a positive windfall for Aretino. Giovanni of the Black Bands had been his closest friend and now his closest friend's son had gained power in wealthy Florence. It was especially timely news for in March that year one of Aretino's servants had planned to rob him of some 'cambric shirts finely embroidered with black silk' and other goods worth 200 crowns before absconding to his home city of Lucca. Leaving the booty in a gondola while 'he disembarked to get a pair of velvet breeches of his which were still at the tailors', the fellow had himself been robbed as the crafty gondolier rowed off with the ill-gotten gains 'as everyone now knows in every canal of this whole city'.[708] Here, therefore, was a chance to perhaps make good his recent losses. 'I don't want to have so much that I am hated, and I don't want so little that men pity me', he wrote to Agostino Ricchi on 16 May, but as usual he protested too much.[709] Not only did Aretino hold high hopes for future patronage from Cosimo, but you could hear the clinking of ducats as the satirist sat down at his desk to write to the powerful young ruler of Florence.

Aretino's letter to the city's new duke on 5 May 1537 was embarrassingly transparent in its pell mell rush to remind Cosimo how close he and Giovanni had once been, and how much Giovanni owed to the writer. 'For I am he who served that great father of yours living and buried him when he was dead', Aretino wrote, 'I am he who in Mantua caused him to be honoured and wept by those who perhaps would not have honoured or wept for him. I am he who took his praises out of the mouths of those who blamed him from envy. I am he who has placed in the hands of the incredulous the torches of his glory. I am he who loved and celebrated him more than all others..'[710] In the words of Jacob Burckhardt, 'He praised the beauty of the then youthful prince, who in fact did share this quality with Augustus in no ordinary degree; he praised his moral conduct, with an oblique reference to the financial pursuits of Cosimo's mother, Maria Salviati, and concluded with a mendicant whine about the bad times and so forth'.[711] Burckhardt goes on to suggest that when Cosimo consented to provide Aretino with a pension of 160 ducats a year, he did so based on his suspicions that the satirist was by this time an imperial agent. Unlike his predecessor Duke Alessandro, Cosimo was concerned to preserve his independence from the Emperor and he would not be overly eager to hear that Aretino had been circulating drolleries about him at the Spanish court.

Aretino had closed his thinly-veiled begging letter to Cosimo by offering the thought: 'That ferocity with which your tremendous sire fought for you should make you feared, even as you are loved'. Cosimo's first test of ducal ferocity was not long in coming. When Filippo Strozzi and his warlike sons led their army of Florentine exiles against Cosimo's new regime they were decisively defeated in August 1537 outside the little village of Montemurlo, not far from Florence. Unlike his father, Cosimo had declined to lead his troops in person, instead entrusting command of his army to his captain Alessandro Vitelli. Vitelli, a capable and experienced soldier, had gone about his trade quickly and professionally. Filippo the Younger was taken prisoner along with many senior exiles, some of whom were executed. His son Piero managed to evade capture and escaped to France. By December 1538, Filippo Strozzi himself was dead, either murdered or else by his own hand in his jail cell in Florence's grim and imposing Fortezza da Basso. His last words had been to bid his enemies make a sausage out of his blood and consume it. In September 1537, following the triumph at Montemurlo, Aretino wrote joyously to Maria Salviati expressing the thought that 'God, who never opposes what he has willed to be, has seen to it that he [Cosimo] was placed in that seat which was his from the day he was born, so that he might establish peace and union everywhere, reigning in justice and continence'.[712]

Aretino must have held out high hopes of winning Cosimo's favour and perhaps expected some easy ducats to wing their way to him in Venice. He was struggling with both his work and his personal finances by now. That same month he was complaining to Francesco dal' Arme of writer's block and cited his age for making his talents 'grow lazy' (he was forty-five, fairly old for the period). 'I used to write forty stanzas of a morning. Now I can scarcely put together one. I composed the "Psalms" in seven days, the *Cortigiana* and the *Marescalco* in ten, my two "Dialogues" in forty, and the "Life of Christ" in thirty,' he complained and admitted that he was 'in anguish for six months composing my "Lines to la Sirena", and I swear to you by the truth which is my guide, that except for a few letters, I now write nothing.'[713] The letters came easily to him and were his stock-in-trade because in his line maintaining networks of friendships from whom gifts and cash could be begged, wheedled and coaxed was everything. Around this time, in early-to-mid 1537, Aretino decided to embark upon a bold new literary project, the publication of his private correspondence to various prominent personages of the day. This had not really been attempted since the era of Petrarch. Aretino's project would, as with many of his other undertakings, revolutionise the art of letter-writing and publishing.

☉☾

On 22 June 1537, the satirist sent his printer Francesco Marcolini a letter in which he declined to accept any sales profits that his new and innovative letter-publishing project might generate. His pose in offering to forego his royalties was grounded in the assumption that his printed works existed merely as bait to attract more lucrative patronage in the form of regular courtly retainers and allowances. This was where the real money lay, in the milking of *noblesse oblige* for all it was worth. 'I hope God will grant that the courtesy of princes rewards me for the labour of writing and not the small change of book buyers; for I would rather endure every hardship than to prostitute my genius by making it a day labourer of the liberal arts … It is obvious that those who write for money become hosts to, and even porters of their own infamy, and so if you want the advantage of profit, become a merchant. Frankly call yourself a pedlar, and lay the name of poet aside'.[714] Aretino disliked the idea of paying for a print run at his own expense and then selling the run to paying customers.[715] He conjured a grisly metaphor to describe this process as he himself saw it: 'As for having printed at one's own expense and one's own urging the books that a man has drawn forth from his imagination, that seems to me to be like feasting on one's own limbs, and he who every evening visits the bookstore to pick up the money earned by the day's sales, to be like a pimp who empties the purse of his woman before he retires to bed.'[716] Five years on, however, when the soaring success of Aretino's *Lettere* had spawned a second, updated, edition and demand for the book had grown brisk, Aretino conveniently withdrew his letter to Marcolini from subsequent editions so he could enjoy the income that was by now being generated.[717]

The epistolary genre of publishing one's private letters, though rare at this time, was nevertheless not an altogether entirely new or novel one. During classical times 'familiar letters', that is to say, letters written to a friend but intended for eventual publication, had their origin in Cicero and Seneca's correspondence. The brevity and plain speech of Cicero had been especially admired in contrast to the verbose and stylised voice used by less adept writers, whom Quintilian had denounced as being the literary equivalent of a 'dressed up whore'.[718] Petrarch had also published his own collection of familiar letters, the *Familiari*, and therefore Aretino distinguished his correspondence from Petrarch's by crowing that his were the first letters which had been printed in the vernacular. Both men, it was true, sought through this particular endeavour to self-consciously aggrandise and possibly even immortalise themselves, sealing their future renown with selective recollections heavily embellished for their readership. The collections of both writers are effectively therefore the chapters of an implied autobiography of sorts. Also, as in Petrarch's case, Aretino's letters often take the form of 'essays' in which the writer expounds and pontificates on all manner of topics, from his meetings with all the most exalted personages of his era, to his tastes in food, women, wine and travel.

Both Aretino and Petrarch may therefore be seen in essentially the same tradition as their successor and inheritor Michel de Montaigne, author of the *Essais* (Montaigne, incidentally, had little regard for Aretino's own writings, which was no doubt due to the lewd element which was repugnant to Montaigne's prim sensibilities.) Machiavelli too had published his letters and had an engaging attitude towards his *oeuvre*. To his close friend Francesco Vettori he had written on 31 January 1515: 'Anyone who might see our letters, my dear friend, and might note their diversity would be very amazed, for at one point he would think that we were very serious men, involved in weighty matters, and that we never entertained a thought which was not lofty and honest. But then, turning the page, he would discover that these same serious men were frivolous, inconstant, lustful, and occupied with trifles.'[719]

There were some initial hurdles for Aretino in that the writer had not retained copies of all the letters he had sent out over the years. He therefore wrote to Vasari, begging him for a copy of the letter Aretino had written him describing the entry of Charles V to Florence in April 1536, 'For I am now having trouble amassing even two hundred letters for the printer. Yet there would be more than two thousand, if I, who have never attached any importance to them, had not sent them to the persons they were addressed to without troubling to keep any copies.'[720] Vasari obliged him by replying with the letter he had requested for his collection. For this initial first edition Aretino assigned his two secretaries Niccolò Franco from Benevento and Ambrogio degli Eusebi to compile the letters for publication. It was, however, a laborious and fatiguing task in the long, hot summer of 1537; 'the frenzy of this heat wave ... which is so trying to our patience and our poor frames', as he grumbled on 10 July to Agostino Richi.[721] By way of an incentive to his flagging helpers, both of whom were also fledgling writers in their own right, Aretino agreed to publish some of their rather run-of-the-mill sonnets. He also offered Franco a letter of his own, a disquisition *Against Rhetoric*, by which he meant 'against intellectual theft' and the tendency of dry humanists lacking all original inspiration of their own to plunder the classics for material. Aretino's views on plagiarism versus *homage* are perhaps worth pausing and reflecting on for a moment.

'There is a great difference between being "influenced by", and plagiarising', he tells Franco in his letter dated 25 June 1537. He then deploys a metaphor. 'Gardeners', he argues, 'complain about those who trample down their plants so as to make quack medicines, not of those who gather garlands in the name of beauty. They scowl at those who break all the branches of a tree to get its fruit, not at those who pick two or three plums and scarcely disturb a twig,' and he concludes that 'there are more today who steal than who emulate'. Humorously, he cites an anecdote about how the humanist Sperone Speroni's *Dialoghi* was read by Il Grazi who commented afterwards 'It seems to me that here and there Plato has imitated him'. Aretino then used another metaphor, of the nanny who teaches the infant in her charge just enough of her mannerisms to get him started in life as a unique individual in his own right; by the same token, 'the man who is influenced by this poet or the other poet … should take from them spiritual inspiration only, but the music that he plays should have the sound of his own instruments.' The best way to pay homage to Petrarch or Boccaccio, Aretino tells Franco, is to express his own ideas with the same beauty and skill with which they expressed theirs. 'And if the Devil so blinds us that we must make off with someone else's thoughts, let us force ourselves to be like Virgil who stole from Homer, or Sanazaro who used the bow of Virgil. They at least paid the debt with interest.' Above all, says Aretino, don't be like 'the pedants [who] sweat blood, and when they want to play the poet, they would rather drop dead than stop. They cackle the stuff written in their notebooks. They turn it into rhetoric. They embroider it with the moribund words which they have learned by heart.' Above all, he emphasises, be original and 'strive to be a sculptor of the things you feel'.[722]

Franco hailed from Benevento and was about twenty-two years old at the time. Prior to arriving in Venice he had already distinguished himself by composing some Latin epigrams in praise of Isabella di Capua, the wife of the imperial captain Ferrante Gonzaga and sister-in-law to Federico Gonzaga. In 1538, he would release perhaps his most engaging work, *Il Petrarchista*, an amusing parody of Petrarchian Platonic love in which a party of pilgrims unearth some lost letters by Petrarch to his beloved Laura which reveal him to be foolish and her to be rather silly and vain. In line with Aretino's advice on plagiarism, the work was whimsically original and paid homage to Petrarch's legacy but not slavishly so. The preparation of 'copy' meanwhile continued through the final months of 1537 but fortunately Aretino was not entirely low on manpower for, in addition to his two amanuenses Franco and Ambrogio, he was also assisted by several others. In his 22 June letter to Marcolini, Aretino speaks of the *lettere* being 'collected by my young men out of their love for the things that I do'.[723]

The *editio princeps* of the *Lettere* early in 1538 (published by Marcolini immediately after his printing of Sebastiano Serlio's *Regole generali della architettura*) was a resounding success. The first edition was presented in a luxuriously large format of 106 leaves in folio which created an instant impression of the writer's wealth, prestige, and social standing.[724] The frontispiece featured an engraving of Aretino in profile attired in rich clothing and wearing his by now famous trademark heavy gold chain. The author was enclosed within a frame of monumental classicising architecture of the kind published by Serlio and the trappings of his material wealth were prominently on display to his readers. Here was a man who was rich, potent and unafraid of flattering (or insulting) other, considerably more powerful men. The following year, a new imprint of the first edition would be published by Federico Torresani and Venturino Ruffinelli, but this may well have been without Aretino or Marcolini's express consent, and we do know that in the years 1534, 1541 and 1542 Marcolini was trying to obtain copyright privileges for the Venetian market similar to what Aretino had obtained from Rome for *La Marfisa*.[725]

As was often the case with Aretino, however, he had badly miscalculated in his sponsorship and encouragement of Niccolò Franco, whom he looked upon as one of his many promising young protégés. By overpraising the young poet's somewhat mediocre sonnets the master's blandishments had gone straight to Franco's head. In his mind's eye Franco now saw himself as Aretino's heir apparent and felt he could surpass his teacher in both skill and fame. The man whom Aretino had advised against becoming one of those 'who stand there begging a penny's worth of fame with the genius of a highwayman'[726] was now privately bent on imitation of the kind which Aretino had cautioned against in his letter. But even worse was to follow. Sometime in the spring of 1538, Aretino was denounced as a sodomite by Giovanni Antonio Serena. This was the same Sienese aristocrat who had taken exception to Aretino's earlier infatuation with his young wife Angela. The irony of course was that Giovanni himself was a known sodomite but nevertheless Aretino considered discretion to be the better part of valour and lost no time in bolting to his country retreat on the river Brenta.

He could have stayed and faced the charges in the Venetian courts but by this time he had made too many enemies to place himself in such a compromising position. Had he not himself published how Isabella Sforza had 'saved' him from a life of sodomy? Had he not written to Federico Gonzaga asking him to put in a good word for him with the ambivalent youth named Bianchino? Did he not indulge in merry pederasty as and when the occasion presented itself? Had not his own plays and poems touched repeatedly upon buggery, notably *Il Marescalco*, which had been forwarded to a man who was no longer even his friend or his patron? Even the great Ariosto, who had eulogised the Aretine in *Orlando Furioso*, admitted that 'Few humanists are without that vice that did not so much persuade as force God to lay waste Gomorrah and its neighbour! ... The vulgar laugh when they hear of someone who possesses a vein of poetry and then they say "It is a great peril to turn your back if you sleep next to him"'.[727] In a letter to Giovanni delle bande Nere written in 1524, Aretino had enclosed a satirical poem telling his late friend that due to a sudden aberration he had fallen in love with a female cook and temporarily switched his appetites from boys to girls. That said, he then concluded his letter by merrily reaffirming the sodomite's credo: 'My Illustrious Lord, be absolutely certain that we all return to the ancient great mother, and if I escape with my honour from this madness, will bugger as much as much and as much for me as for my friends.'[728]

In fact, although his works often touched upon sodomy, and he unquestionably practised it himself, Aretino had been careful never to openly advocate it. This was certainly not so in the case of the Sienese nobleman Antonio Vignali, whose homoerotic *faux* Platonic dialogue known as *La Cazzaria* ('The Book of the Prick') openly advocated the benefits and advantages of sodomitical coupling. *La Cazzaria*, which had been written in 1525 the same year as the *Sonetti lussuriosi*, was discreetly (but widely) circulated at the time. Its author Vignali posed as the character 'Arsiccio' ('an enemy to women in all his affairs') whilst his friend and fellow member of the Accademia degli Intronati, Marcantonio Piccolomini, posed as the character 'Sodo'. Much of its content was childishly scatological: why people fart when urinating, why peoples' genitals smell, why people have pubic hair, why women have periods and why monks invented confession (it was, so Vignali insisted, in order to ascertain the latest 'secrets in the art of screwing' from the lay world). In one epigram, Arsiccio/Vignali argues that 'No matter how ugly and vulgar a thing is [meaning sodomy], it is more ugly and vulgar not to be knowledgeable about it', a witticism calculated to scandalise since it deliberately confused enlightenment with sexual corruption.[729] *La Cazzaria* remained a popular underground work and would later be cited as evidence of blasphemy, heresy and sodomy in the notorious case of the Franciscan friar Francesco Calcagno, who was burned at the stake in 1550 for buggering a different boy almost every night and for maintaining that Jesus practised anal sex. In mitigation, Calcagno had confessed to possessing an illicit copy of *La Cazzaria* which he claimed had influenced his actions.[730]

In Venice, sodomy laws were notoriously harsh, harsher for example than those in Florence, which was widely regarded as the buggery capital of Italy. This was a direct result of Venice's origins as the God-given sanctuary for good Christians who had fled the depredations of the godless pillaging heathen Attila the Hun. Any form of deviant sexual behaviour that wilfully contravened God's law (anal sex, pederasty, bestiality or general debauchery) was construed as being prejudicial to the spiritual good standing of the state. Punishing those who practiced sodomy was thought to be a necessary precondition for saving the city from God's wrathful vengeance at some indeterminate point in the future. This 'wrath of the Almighty' commonly came in the form of the visitation of plagues which was of course a fairly common occurrence at this time, not because the Almighty was displeased but due to poor hygiene and sanitation. On Christmas Day of 1497, the Bishop of the Church of San Marco had issued a public plea to the Doge of Venice to prevent 'the blaspheming of God and the saints, the societies of sodomy, the infinite usurious contracts made at the Rialto...' so as to eliminate the spiritual causes that lead to the plague.[731]

In Florence, grown men convicted as sodomites might be subject to castration, procurers of boys might pay with a fine or else the loss of a hand (repetition with the loss of a foot), the fathers of boys accused of sodomy were considered as having been procurers and liable to prosecution themselves, and the houses in which acts of sodomy had taken place were quite literally torn down to their foundations.[732] In Venice, punishment was at a whole different level. The usual technique of execution was burning at the stake. This of course was the traditional Christian method of cleansing the individual and achieving grace and salvation for the eternal soul of those unfortunate enough to be convicted. Henceforth, because Venice's penalties for this crime were so severe the judicial Council of Ten tried in every case they heard to determine if there were any mitigating factors, such as whether for instance the sex act had been penetrative or merely confined to mutual masturbation, whether any of the participants had been fully aware of what was happening (were they awake or asleep?), and furthermore whether the accused were considered to be sufficiently young and immature as to be forgiven the charge (if they were for example the young, passive partners in an act of pederasty).

Venice's Council of Ten adjudicated its first sodomy case in 1348, which had involved a sexual relationship between two servants, Pietro di Ferarra and Giacornello di Bologna. The two servants had shared a bed and Pietro had unwisely boasted that the pair had on numerous occasions enjoyed non-penetrative sex. After the men's denunciation, Giacornello refused under torture to corroborate his sexual partner's assertions. In the absence of any admission of guilt, Giacornello was subsequently acquitted of the charge whilst the unfortunate Pietro was burned at the stake for having indulged in 'unnatural intercourse.'[733] Another noteworthy case involved a boat owner named Niccolo Marmagna and his servant Giovanni Braganza. Following their denunciation, Niccolo had selflessly tried to protect his lover by denying that Giovanni was even aware that he had had sex with him since he had been asleep each time.

This probably would have been sufficient for the Council to absolve Giovanni and perhaps even let Niccolo off with a non-capital conviction, but when questioned under torture Giovanni stated not only that he was aware what was going on but that the two men had swapped roles as penetrator and passive catamite. The admission of penetrative sex, where Giovanni had earlier denied this, was enough to seal the men's fate. Both were sentenced to death and burned at the stake.[734]

☉☾

At his villa on the river Brenta, Aretino watched and waited for word of the all-clear. Help, when it arrived, came from the unlikeliest of sources, Francesco Maria della Rovere the duke of Urbino. Although the latters' inaction in 1526 had more or less indirectly contributed to the death of Aretino's friend and patron Giovanni de' Medici, the Duke had been the recipient of one of the poet's treacly letters on 18 September 1537. Francesco Maria, who had served as captain-general of the Venetian army from 1523-1538, had recently been appointed *gonfalonier* of the Church. The Duke, 'who is a manifest example of religion, of merit and of experience', was lauded by Aretino for 'bringing peace to all the princes and putting an end to all wars, as if peace and war had consulted with your own admirable genius..'[735] The duke of Urbino's crowning contribution to peace, as Aretino well knew, was the fact that he never seemed to lead his men into battle, but this was neither here nor there. Titian was also busy painting the forty-eight-year-old duke's portrait in 1538, a commission which would be the crowning achievement in a patronage relationship dating back to the year 1532, from which date the Duke would be the recipient of no less than three Titian canvases: *Hannibal*, the *Nativity*, and the *Saviour*.[736]

Francesco Maria made a point to intercede on behalf of Titian's close friend with his former Venetian employers to have the sodomy charges quashed. Aretino's other influential protector, Doge Andrea Gritti, probably played a part in the backroom horse trading as well. The case more than likely did not even come to trial and certainly no records of any court case survive in Venice's meticulously-maintained government archives. It fell to Benedetto Agnello, the Mantuan ambassador, to break the news to the relieved satirist. By May 1538, Aretino was safely back in the Casa d'Aretino, having made a narrow escape from Venice's stern brand of spiritual justice. By October, the man responsible for securing his exoneration, the duke of Urbino, was himself dead, assassinated by his barber-surgeon, who poured a poisoned unction into his ears. Francesco Maria della Rovere's demise would later be immortalised in William Shakespeare's play Hamlet, Prince of Denmark.[737] Aretino composed his own lengthy *terza rima* in honour of the dead duke who, often to the exasperation of his employers the Venetians, seldom seemed inclined to commit to battle:

Oh Caesar, he is dead, the faithful duke
Of whom the esteem and the honour
Will live for ever in the common outcry.

In August 1538 there appeared in Perugia an alleged 'Life of Aretino' purportedly written by the late Francesco Berni, his final calumny from beyond the grave as it were. This work later became known as the *Pseudo-Berni*, a scabrous *faux* biography of Aretino's early life blatantly intended to ruin the satirist's legacy and reputation. Strangely, however, the *Vita* asserted in passing that the letters of Niccolò Franco were far superior to those of Aretino, revealing both a hidden agenda as well as its probable true author. Franco was still living and working under the poet's roof at this time and Aretino, who was no fool when it came to underhand dealings like this, did nothing for the time being. The second printing of the *Lettere* was published in September with no redactions made to Aretino's solicitous and avuncular letter to Franco. Being a shrewd man he must have nevertheless suspected something was by now afoot. Then, in November, came the final breach. Franco published his own compilation of letters entitled the *Pistole Vulgari*.

Aretino now allowed himself the luxury of being openly incensed. A writer whom he had sheltered, taught, encouraged and even publicly flattered in his *Lettere* was now attempting to compete with him in this potentially lucrative new genre which Aretino had singlehandedly created in the marketplace. His publisher, Antonio Gardano, printed the *Pistole Vulgari* in November 1538 in large folio, reserved only for the most deluxe publications.[738] Emulating Aretino, Franco addressed a range of important personages in his collection of letters, from the French king to the Duke and Duchess of Urbino and the Cardinal of Lorraine. Most, however, were directed to his Venetian friends, many of whom like Domenico Venier, Speroni Sperone, Jacopo Sansovino and Titian were also members of Aretino's inner circle. Worse still, Franco had openly attacked Aretino in the final letter of the collection. In a prophetic foreshadowing of the rift with Franco, Aretino had written in one of his *Lettere* of 1537 (1.280) of his attitude towards upstart writers who strove for fame regardless of their obvious lack of talent. In an allegory called the 'Dream of Parnassus' he denounces hack writers who aspire to ascend Mount Parnassus (by which he means 'attach themselves to publishers') only to end up drowning in a river of their own futile ink.[739] In light of this, Franco's betrayal was unforgivable and Aretino unceremoniously threw him out of the house.

Once dismissed from the Aretine's service, Franco wrote to his literary friends attempting to enlist them in his cause against *'L' Ignorante Aretino ciurmatore'* ('the ignorant charlatan Aretino'). To the grammarian and Petrarch scholar Francesco Alunno he wrote: 'The Aretine cannot say I am ungrateful for even though I admit he sometimes fed me, he cannot deny that I repaid his courtesy sevenfold by the work I did for him'.[740] Franco then went on to insinuate that Aretino's three recent devotional tracts produced between 1534 and 1538 had only been written thanks to Franco's indispensable labour in translating the original Latin sources on which they were based. These works, which were Aretino's cynical efforts to pass himself off as truly 'divine' and plug a gaping lacuna in his spiritual writings, were *I sette salmi della penitentia di David* (1534), *I tre libri de la humanità di Cristo* (1535), and *Il Genesi con la visione di Noè* (1538).[741] These were not in themselves especially well executed works or *exempla in bono* of the Renaissance devotional genre, being the usual insincere mish-mash of Aretine conceits, however the allegation that they could not have been written without Franco's assistance was palpably untrue. The first two works in particular had been written before Niccolò Franco had even arrived in Venice in August 1536 and taken up his post as amanuensis.

When Franco unwisely involved Aretino's other secretary, Ambrogio degli Eusebi, in the dispute by naming him as the poet's lover and accusing him of having pimped out his wife to Aretino, the infuriated Ambrogio stormed to the house where Franco had been staying and loudly called him down into the street for a private discussion. When Franco came down to face his challenger, Ambrogio pulled a hidden blade from his clothing and sliced it across Franco's face cutting him down to the bone. As Franco reeled backwards in horror and surprise Ambrogio then set about cutting his expensive clothing to ribbons with his dagger before storming off, leaving the victim bloody and whimpering in the middle of the street. Upon his return to the Casa d'Aretino, his employer went through the motions of reprimanding Ambrogio for the assault and hastened to the Magistrate's office to explain the matter away as a private affair in which the blackguard Franco had basically got what was coming to him. With clemency assured for Ambrogio in any criminal tribunal, Aretino then released him once more into the streets, whereupon he returned to Franco's lodgings and read aloud some abusive sonnets which Aretino had dashed off specially for the occasion. Bandaged and lying in his bed, Franco was forced to put up with insult being added to injury. Aretino later confided in a lengthy letter to Lodovici

Dolce that he was 'not surprised that Ambrogio carved on his phiz with his dagger a permanent memento..'[742]

Disheartened by the experience, Franco soon left Venice altogether in 1540 and took himself off to Padua where he was sheltered by the humanist scholar Sperone Speroni degli Alvarotti who, quickly tiring of Franco's malicious tongue, kicked him out not long afterwards. He then drifted to Milan and worked briefly as a schoolmaster before moving on to Casal Monferrato in Piedmont where Sigismondo Franzino gave him the job of principal of a literary academy there. Monferrato was by now merged with Mantua as a dependency. Federico Gonzaga had died in August 1540, aged forty and because his eldest son Francesco was still only a minor Mantua was ruled by a regency comprising the late Duke's spouse Margherita Paleologa as well as his two brothers Cardinal Ercole Gonzaga and Ferrante Gonzaga, Lord of Guastalla. Since Franzino was a client of the late Federico, Aretino's ire therefore fell squarely on Mantua's three regents. Franco was dismissed as a being 'like a cur that is kicked around by everybody and despised by everybody, and then when he sees a bone into which he cannot get his teeth, begins to growl so loudly that it is plain to all that he is starving to death'.[743] Aretino seems to have had a fixation on the metaphor of starving poets as growling dogs.

The Duchessa Margherita was able to experience how changeable her late husband's plaything and fool could be. Only in January 1541, Aretino had sent her in condolence for Federico's death a devotional work, the *Vita di Catherina vergine*, a life of Saint Catherine. Margherita wrote back to the poet appreciatively: 'I am grateful for the letter that you have written me and extremely grateful for your composition on the life of St. Catherine which you have also sent me, being an excellent subject and, having been recounted by you, I know that the book could be nothing less than excellent'.[744] In July 1541, however, there were rumblings that Aretino was preparing to publish damaging secrets of the Gonzagas as retribution for having indirectly protected Franco. This was smoothly dispelled by Mantua's good-natured and consummately even-tempered ambassador to Venice, Benedetto Agnello, who had himself been on friendly terms with Franco, having earlier accommodated him at his house for one year after he showed up in Venice in 1536.[745] Aretino had written in 1539 to Lodovico Dolce complaining that Franco had filled the head of Agnello's housekeeper with revolting ideas about him.[746] It was as well that Agnello was able to defuse the crisis since at that time Monferrato was chaffing against Gonzaga influence; a release of Aretine dirt on the late duke could not therefore have come at a more inopportune time.

Franco would remain one of Aretino's most implacable enemies and the mission of traducing Aretino's name and reputation remained his bitter occupation for the rest of his life. While under the protection of

Franzino and the Gonzagas, Franco started churning out a steady and prodigious stream of shockingly sexualised polemical invectives against Aretino, some two hundred and ninety-eight in all, which were later collected together in 1545 and published under the title *Rime contro Pietro Aretino* ('Rhymes against Pietro Aretino'). His hatred led him to also attack some of the most powerful and well-known names of the time including Pope Paul III, the Emperor Charles V, Jacopo and Francesco Sansovino and even poor Vittoria Colonna, the widow of Fernando Francesco d'Ávalos. Aretino could not take this attack lying down. In Marcolini's second edition of the *Lettere* in 1542 he had included forty-four new letters including personally addressed correspondence from the likes of Pietro Bembo, Sperone Speroni degli Alvarotti, Michelangelo and Vittoria Colonna, all of which were calculated to endorse his genius and refute Franco's slanders as baseless. Despite the high-stakes onslaught on his personal reputation, Aretino himself by now tended to look upon Franco with pity and scarcely-concealed contempt. He found time to write personally to him: 'because I once rescued you from starvation I cannot be bothered hating you. If you want to be as famous as I am, write against vice, not against virtue, tell the truth instead of lying and stop shaming your talents by attacking a man who is as good as you are evil.'[747] At the same time he also threatened Cardinal Gonzaga and Margherita Paleologa with the wrath of Charles V, whom Franco had been incautious enough to criticise for subsidising Aretino. Unperturbed, Ercole Gonzaga ignored the threat.

When Franco fell ill in 1545, as had occurred earlier in the case of Antonio Broccardo, Aretino the sentimentalist forgot all the former secretary's past wrongdoings and rushed to console him.[748] 'It would be right for me to rejoice at your misfortune, just as you lament my welfare. But I am so generous by nature that I feel very sorry for you. Take good care of yourself and hope for the best. The true doctor is God. Fortify your conscience and trust in Him. Then you will recover from your fever,' Aretino wrote to the ailing man.[749] But at the same time the poet's magnanimity, though clearly genuine, was also tinged with an element of dissatisfaction at being cheated of his sweet victory and he wrote to a friend, 'I am sick to my very soul to think that this fellow, whom I need not name, may be dying. I want him to live and suffer from the envy that gnaws him. If he dies, how can I look forward to my sweet revenge when he at last realised what a miserable villain he is?'[750] Alas, Aretino would not live long enough to enjoy the unravelling of the life of his old nemesis.

Moving around a lot in a constant bid to find a patron, Franco eventually arrived in Rome in 1558. Rome, however, proved no kinder to Franco than it had to Aretino. Shortly after his arrival there, on 15 July 1558, he was arrested at the home of Bartholomew Camerario, the general commissioner for Annona, who had been taken into custody and arraigned on charges of embezzlement. Franco then languished in prison for eight months. Franco's own erotic work, the *Priapea* of 1546,[751] a commentary on the *Priapeia* (ninety-five poems pertaining to the phallic god Priapus attributed to Virgil), was hardly less calculated to edify the papal authorities than Aretino's own *Sonetti lussuriosi* of 1525. In a familiar echo of Aretino's own earlier brush with clerical censorship, copies of this work were ordered suppressed and burned by Pope Paul IV, an act which generated considerable resentment on the poet's part. Franco had even managed to insert some well-aimed insults in the *Priapeia* at Aretino, implying that the only thing stopping Aretino's tongue was the act of fellatio: 'You know how to eat a prick raw and cooked, ... / Praise be to God that for now / The prick in your mouth prevents you from speaking.'[752]

Franco's subsequent *pasquinata* against the Pope were no worse than Aretino had penned at the height of his fame against both Adrian VI and Clement VII, as well as his *datarius*. The level of Franco's daring may be gauged from one of his earlier sonnets in the *Priapeia* in which he described the Pope's cardinals as being '*tutti i visi di cazzo*' ('all prick-faces').[753] However, Franco would overstep the mark. Eleven years later in 1569 he would be implicated together with the corrupt Apostolic tax attorney Alessandro Pallantieri and accused of having concocted a libellous and heretical tract against Pope Paul IV, the *Commento sopra la vita et costumi di Gio. Pietro Carafa che fu Paolo IV chiamato et sopra le qualità de tutti i suoi et di coloro che con lui governaro in pontificato.* Franco was tortured and eventually hanged by Pope Pius V on 11 March 1570 on the Ponte Sant'Angelo. Although Aretino himself was by this time long dead, he had left the following evocative account of his befriending of Niccolò Franco and the latter's subsequent betrayal: 'Most excellent ladies, I had occasion in Venice, to deal with a similar creature, namely a certain Niccolò Franco, whom I lifted out of that city's dregs. When my housekeeper–I tell you–saw that the same Franco had been let into my house, she cried out, saying: "I'll be damned! Thus the master who, to this day, was a host of great notables now becomes a hospital warden of rascals?" The cur happened to fall into my hands with nothing on him, in the same way this other wretch [Paluzzi] ended up, undressed, in the hands of the Jewess. I clothed him, and when he saw that I had provided him with a hat and shoes of velvet, he confessed to not being worthy of what I, in giving, did not make anything of, as one noticed. But after recovering his spirits somewhat and finding warmth in the fire of my courtesy, he spit his venom on me and publicly revealed himself as my enemy.'[754]

Niccolò Franco's end, some years after Aretino's own, could so easily have been Pietro's fate had he remained in Rome all those years ago. Franco's error perhaps had been to fall in with those men, far more powerful than himself, whose lives ran afoul of the ecclesiastical establishment; first Camerario and then Pallantieri and, despite having equally powerful protectors like Cardinal Giovanni Morone and Giovanni Carafa, Duke of Paliano, this proved insufficient to save him in the end. Admittedly, Rome and indeed Italy were in the full throes of the Counter Reformation by this time and the scurrilous writers of questionable tracts and *pasquinata* could not have expected the range of freedom which Pietro Aretino had formerly enjoyed, but one still has to ask whether it wasn't the case that an imitator of Aretino also required the intelligence, resourcefulness, guile and survival instincts of an Aretino. Alas, Niccolò Franco, a poor copy of the Aretine, embodied few of these traits if we are forced to be honest. Unfortunately, however, Franco's prodigious legacy of libels against Aretino have been one of the main reasons for the latter's poor personal reputation since his death.

To conclude the other half of this story, in 1538 Aretino had sent his other secretary Ambrogio degli Eusebi on a mission to the court of King François to collect 600 crowns that were owed to him. This was done at least ostensibly to place Ambrogio beyond the reach of any retaliation by Niccolò Franco. It was probably also done to get him out of the way so that Aretino could once more enjoy the favours of Ambrogio's wife, Marietta d'Oro. This young woman had formerly been a member of Aretino's swelling seraglio but had recently threatened to leave his household; to induce her to stay he'd promised to marry her off and had found the lovelorn Ambrogio degli Eusebi more than willing to take her on. This was despite his earlier strictures to Ambrogio against getting married unless he wanted 'to become like Job, for by suffering their [wives'] perfidy at home, a man is bound to suffer away from home and so become the monarch of patience' and in spite of his exhortation 'Blessed are those who marry by word and refrain from marrying in fact!'[755] Aretino rode with him part of the way towards France to ensure he would make the journey but unfortunately upon his return he found that Marietta d'Oro had robbed him blind and fled to Cyprus with one of his attractive young grooms. This made Aretino for a short time the butt of Venice's jokes. Worse still, having collected the French king's payment in Paris, Ambrogio foolishly lost it all again playing cards with Leone Strozzi, Filippo Strozzi's son, who was at this time an admiral in the Order of Malta's fleet of galleys.[756]

Ambrogio now tried to extricate himself from the situation in which he found himself by sailing for London and presenting himself to Thomas Cromwell, who was at this time Lord Privy Seal. He arrived at the English court claiming he was in England to collect the 200 crowns promised earlier to Aretino by King Henry VIII. The staunchly Protestant Cromwell, who was by now preoccupied with a fanatical campaign against Roman Catholic idolatry in England's churches, brusquely informed Ambrogio that the payment had already been forwarded to the poet in Italy. He nevertheless gave the secretary 80 crowns for his trouble so as to get rid of him. With coin in hand, Ambrogio did not return to Italy but instead made his way to Lisbon whereupon he set sail for Brazil. Writing to Aretino, Ambrogio informed the satirist somewhat improbably that he intended to carry the international renown of the Scourge of Princes to the New World. The last time that Aretino ever heard of his foolish former amanuensis, he had landed in Brazil and got as far inland as Paraguay, perhaps making his way to the settlement of Asunción in the Rio de la Plata Basin, which had been founded by the Spanish explorer Juan de Salazar de Espinosa in August 1537. After that, succumbing perhaps to disease, robbery, death by native indigenous Indians, or the myriad other perils of the 'green hell' of the Brazilian rainforest, Ambrogio degli Eusebi was never heard of again.

CHAPTER 14

Aretino and the Painters

Remember that even the pagans in their statues, I
won't say of Diana clothed but Venus naked, covered
with a gesture of the hands the parts that may not be
revealed, whereas our prudent genius, valuing art more
than faith, not only does not observe decorative
decorum in the martyrs and the virgins, but throws the
genitals and organs of those in ecstasy into such relief
that even in the whore-houses they couldn't fail to
make one close one's eyes: his work would be more
permissible on the walls of a voluptuous brothel than
on the surface of the walls of a choir.

Pietro Aretino to Alessandro Corvino,
On The 'Last Judgement' of Michelangelo
July 1547

One of the most remarkable 'duels' that Aretino ever fought was
with the artist Michelangelo. The latter had received a
commission from Pope Clement VII just days before the pontiff's
death to paint a new mural on the altar wall of the Sistine Chapel
featuring the subject of the Resurrection. Upon Pope Paul III's accession
he reconfirmed Michelangelo's commission but changed the subject to
that of the Last Judgement instead, a theme which the new pontiff felt to
be more in keeping with the gathering momentum of the Roman Catholic
reform movement which he was spearheading. The artist made his
preparations to the chapel wall throughout 1535, before commencing his
painting in 1536.

After Michelangelo had already been working on the fresco for well
over a year, Pietro Aretino wrote to him chummily on 15 September 1537.
The communication began promisingly enough with the satirist's
customary turgid flattery: 'Sir, just as it is disgraceful and sinful to be
unmindful of God so it is reprehensible and dishonourable for any man of

discerning judgement not to honour you as a brilliant and venerable artist whom the very stars use as a target at which to shoot the rival arrows of their favour'. So far, so good. Aretino next went on to vouchsafe to the artist that since 'my name is now acceptable to all our rulers and so it has shed a great deal of its ill-repute' the writer felt that it was his duty to 'honour you with this salutation, since the world has many kings but only one Michelangelo'.[757] From these largely inoffensive beginnings the letter then took a sharp dip into something of an allocution. Why, Aretino asked, was Michelangelo not content to rest content on the ample glory he had already acquired in his lifetime? Why should he seek to outdo himself by painting a rival masterpiece to the celebrated fresco which the artist had already painted on the ceiling of the Sistine Chapel some quarter of a century earlier?

This in itself could still be dismissed as the satirist's unsubtle rhetoric, for in seeking to surmount his own work, the *Creation of the World*, Michelangelo is depicted as having already 'vanquished the others'. But what Aretino now continued to address in his letter could only be viewed as the greatest impertinence by the proud and devout artist: in effect, Aretino proceeded to instruct the genius in his own baroque vision of how the fresco should be painted. He pointed out how he conceived of the Antichrist, Life and Death, Hope and Despair, 'the guardians of the infernal pit', Fame 'with her crowns and her palms scattered beneath her feet, crushed under the wheels of her own chariots', as well as the 'lights of Paradise and the furnaces of the abyss'. Aretino then signed off by informing Buonarroti that 'the vow I made never to see Rome again will have to be broken because of my desire to see this great painting'.[758] The letter is as astonishing for Aretino's descriptive foreshadowing of the artistic styles of Rubens and Bernini as it is for its colossal and unabashed impudence. That the writer should see nothing amiss in his instructing the foremost artistic genius of his age on how *he* envisaged Michelangelo's work-in-progress speaks volumes about Aretino's self-confidence, which simultaneously borders on the grossest arrogance.

Surprisingly, in view of Aretino's heavy-handed and impertinent iconographical suggestions for his fresco, Michelangelo reserved his usual tempestuous fury. Perhaps he was wary of openly insulting this famous serial blackmailer by hurling direct insults back at him as a reward for his presumptuousness. Perhaps he was even somewhat amused at Aretino's cheeky insolence in writing to him in this manner. That same month, Buonarroti graciously rebuffed Aretino with the following brief reply: 'Magnificent Messer Pietro, my lord and brother—The receipt of your letter has caused me at once both pleasure and regret. I was exceedingly pleased because it came from you, who are uniquely gifted among men, and yet I was also very regretful, because, having completed a large part of the composition, I cannot put your conception in hand, which is so perfect that, if the Day of Judgement were passed and you had seen it in person, your words could not have described it better. Now as to your writing about me, I not only say in reply that I should welcome it, but I entreat you to do so, since kings and emperors deem it the highest honour to be mentioned by your pen. In the meantime, should I have anything that might be to your taste, I offer it to you with all my heart. In conclusion, do not, for the sake of seeing the painting I am doing, break your resolve not to come to Rome, because that would be too much. I commend me to you.'[759] Buonarroti had kept his best for the final sting in the tail when he drolly informed Aretino that there was no real need for him to come to Rome. The first broadside had been fired in what would eventually become a decade-long feud.

The *Last Judgement* was unveiled on Halloween, 1541. Michelangelo was sixty-six and, by now, twenty-nine years had passed since the unveiling of the ceiling frescos. The mural created an uproar amongst the Church establishment. The Dominican preacher Ambrogio Politi, known as *Il Caterino*, attacked the fresco's nudity which he even went so far as to label heretical.[760] Wrote *Il Caterino*: 'I commend the art used in the matter, but I vehemently vituperate and detest the matter itself. For this nudity of limbs appears most indecent on altars and in the most important of God's chapels.'[761] Not only were there certain thematic deviations from the norms of Last Judgement iconography, but the prodigality of nude figures led Pope Paul III's Vatican protocol chief, Biagio da Cesena, to complain that the mural was 'more appropriate to a public bath or a roadside tavern' than the Pope's private chapel.[762] Biagio da Cesena had perhaps good reason to whine for Michelangelo had depicted him in the fresco with a snake coiled around his midriff whose head was firmly attached to his genitals, presumably in the act of taking an excruciating bite.

Neither had the artist forgotten Aretino or his insolent lecture on how to compose and paint a masterpiece. He painted the figure of St. Bartholomew with Pietro Aretino's likeness, balding with a magnificent flowing white beard. St. Bartholomew/Aretino holds in one hand a knife and in the other his own flayed skin. The skin bears the drooping facial resemblance of Michelangelo himself. This was the artist's humorous way of indicating to the satirist *not* to flay him alive in his subsequent writings. Unperturbed, Aretino wrote back, addressing Buonarroti 'certamente voi siète persona divina' ('certainly you are a divine person') and asking whether the artist could spare one or two drawings sketched with his own hand that might otherwise be destroyed anyway. In making this request, Aretino was as always operating firmly within the prestigious gift-giving culture of the time. Besides, a drawing by the incomparable genius

Michelangelo would be a real coup for Aretino, something which he could show off to all his friends in Venice. At this point he still mistakenly believed himself to be in the artist's good books. This time, however, the artist simply ignored the writer's solicitations. Aretino wrote to him again on numerous other occasions, but the artist ignored these letters too. Feeling in ill humour, Aretino then wrote instead to Titian, who was at this time painting in Rome, telling him 'remember not to lose yourself in contemplating The Last Judgement in the Sistine Chapel that you forget to return here'.[763]

Eventually, in the spring of 1545, Michelangelo sent Aretino some sub-par copies of his sketches which had been completed by his unknown apprentices. Indignantly, Aretino replied to the great Buonarroti: 'So now fulfil my expectation with the reward which it has vowed to long forever—not because you believe me to be what I have boasted that I am, nor for the audacity of my having dared to speak to you, but because of my overweening desire to have one of those marvels which are continually given birth to by the divinity which your genius makes pregnant'.[764] Still, the originals by Michelangelo's own hand failed to arrive. Aretino's ire was now sufficiently aroused at this direct slight. The impertinence of his original request was forgotten entirely as the satirist cleared the decks to lambast the latest person foolish enough to have offended him. He knew exactly what to target for greatest effect: Michelangelo's liberal use of nudity in the great altar fresco.

In a public letter written in November 1545 he opined that the sort of nudity which Michelangelo had depicted would not be wholly incongruous in a decorative loggia but was definitely inappropriate in the central chapel of Christianity, and he fulminated to the artist: 'Your work belongs in a sordid bathhouse, not in an exalted chapel! Your vice would be less if you yourself were an unbeliever, than that you should so determinedly undermine the faith of others.'[765] Aretino then went on to grumble that if Michelangelo had furnished him with a piece of his artwork, as he had earlier promised, he would have disproven the 'invidious reports that you can only give things to Gherardi and Tomai'.[766] This of course was an insinuating reference to Gherardo Perini and Tommaso de' Cavalieri, two young Roman men whom Michelangelo had favoured with drawings and with whom he was rumoured to be homosexually enamoured.

Writing in July 1547 to Alessandro Corvino, Aretino confessed that upon seeing an engraving of the *Last Judgement* 'I was able to perceive the noble grace of Raphael in the lovely beauty of its invention; but as regards its being Christian, I can only shrug my shoulders amiably at the licentiousness of his brush'.[767] A decade had already elapsed since Aretino's first letter to Michelangelo and here the writer was, reduced to little more than 'a deranged fan who felt snubbed by his idol'.[768] Worse was to come. 'Is it possible for a man who is more divine than human to have done this in the foremost church of God, above the main altar of Jesus, in the most excellent chapel in the world, where the cardinals of the Church, where the reverend priests, where the vicar of Christ, in Catholic devotions, with sacred rites and holy prayers, bear witness to, contemplate and adore His body, His blood and His flesh?'[769] Aretino then went on to compare his own 'honesty' in writing Nanna and Pippa's *Dialogo* to Michelangelo's 'outrageousness' in executing his fresco, the point being that, unlike the painter, Aretino had been the very model of decorous reserve: 'If the comparison were not wicked, I should boast of the judgement shown in my treatise on Nanna, preferring the modesty of my discernment to the outrageousness of his learning: for I with my obscene and lascivious subject-matter not only use restrained and polite words, but tell my story in a pure and blameless style; whereas he, with such an exalted story as his subject is, shows the saints and angels, the former without any of the decency proper to this world, and the latter lacking any of the loveliness of heaven.'[770]

Aretino's creature and acolyte, Lodovico Dolce, would record for posterity many of Aretino's pontifications about art and in his *Dialogo della Pittura* (1557) he would represent the satirist towards the close of his life still as acerbic as ever about the Sistine fresco and its disobliging artist:

> Fabrini: I hear it said that in the design of his stupendous Last Judgement there are some allegorical senses of great profundity which are understood only by a few.

> Aretino: In this he would deserve praise because it would appear that he had imitated those great philosophers who concealed under the veil of poetry the deepest philosophical mysteries both human and divine so that they might not be understood by the vulgar: not wishing as it were to throw pearls before swine. And this I would also believe was Michelangelo's intention ... [Yet] to me it does not seem so very praiseworthy that the eyes of children, matrons, and maids should openly see in these figures the improprieties which they exhibit, and only the learned understand the profundity of the allegories which they conceal.[771]

Lodovico Dolce goes on to make Aretino say of the figures in Michelangelo's *Last Judgement* that they 'display their backs and fronts in an immodest way'.[772] Dolce would ultimate make Aretino conclude that 'If Michelangelo wishes that his pictures be understood only by the learned few, I, who am not one of them, leave his thoughts to him'.[773] As a detractor of the *Last Judgement*, Dolce would line up alongside some truly formidable names who, like Aretino, had also found fault with the fresco including Gilio, Bellarmino, Pope Pius IV and Galileo. Ten years after its unveiling the Last Judgement was still being publicly attacked. In 1564, the decision would be taken to have the painter Daniele da Volterra drape Michelangelo's nude figures in modest loincloths, a meticulous and arduous assignment that earned the artist the nickname *Braghettano* (meaning 'Pantymaker' or 'breeches maker'). Nevertheless, by this time the gesture represented what one modern scholar has described as little more than the 'stern resolve of the Counter Reformation to contain and render harmless the exuberant and therefore dangerous potentialities of man'.[774]

There is considerable justification for supposing that Aretino cynically viewed the *Last Judgement* as an opportunity to rehabilitate his own reputation at Michelangelo's expense, whilst discharging the unquestionable grudge he felt towards the artist for having snubbed him so resoundingly over the years. The reification of the fresco into a moral and ecclesiastical *cause célèbre* was unquestionably far too good an opportunity for Aretino to remain uninvolved in the public controversy which attended its initial unveiling. Here was his chance to mend his relationship with a papacy which he had made an entire career out of censuring and criticising. There was also the issue that Aretino by this time cherished sincere though perhaps improbable hopes of being made a cardinal. There is little doubt that when he initially wrote to Michelangelo, he had genuinely hoped that being able to demonstrate a close relationship with the painter would help him towards this ecclesiastical objective. Michelangelo's refusal to share his glory with the upstart satirist by indulging him in this fantasy, and the consequent failure of Aretino's designs, would inevitably result in his increased bitterness towards the legendary artist.

☉☾

Aretino's relationship with the Venetian painter Jacopo Robusti, better known as Tintoretto, was at least in the initial years as troubled as that which he shared with Michelangelo. Tintoretto, who came from a large family, was observed by his father one day daubing the walls of the dyeing workshop where he carried on his trade. The daubings, which were quite accomplished for a boy his age, exhibited promise and so the father brought the son to Titian's studio to determine whether he could be enrolled as the master's pupil. This had been around the year 1533. Titian took the boy in but after just ten days the master sent Tintoretto home. The reason for this has been contested ever since by historians of art. The popular explanation is that Tintoretto had exhibited such promise for a youngster that Titian felt threatened and did not wish to train up his own future rival. Another variation on the same theme is that Tintoretto's style was too independent and so Titian judged that although the young man might make a great painter someday he would never make a particularly good pupil, therefore there was no point in keeping him on any further. Whatever the reason, Tintoretto was left largely to his own devices from that point forward, forced to develop his own artistic style and often reduced to selling his paintings on the streets and on the Ponte Rialto to make ends meet.

As a result he was cut off from the more aristocratic clientele of Titian and consequently, although Tintoretto always admired the older master, the two men were never friends and did not associate together. In order to make a living, Tintoretto quickly developed a new painting style called *prestezza* which enabled him to paint at a much faster rate than Titian, which in turn allowed him to fulfil a much wider demand for portraits amongst the bourgeoisie. Portraiture was a booming market around this time. From the fifteenth-century onwards, realistic and lifelike portraiture which captured the *haecceitas* (unique 'thisness') of the sitter became *de rigueur* amongst kings, queens and great nobles. As prosperity grew amongst the merchant and professional classes—doctors, lawyers, scholars, actors—the demand for individuals to be captured for posterity also grew in tandem. There arose a new confidence and an acceptance that private citizens, though not of the noble or royal classes, could nevertheless be recognised for their social and professional attainments; part of this revolution lay in changing habits of reflecting, representing and memorialising a person's unique features and bearing. During his 1542 visit to Venice, Giorgio Vasari observed that 'there are many portraits in all the houses of Venice, and in many gentleman's homes one may see their fathers and grandfathers back to the fourth generation, and in some of the more noble houses back further still'. Aretino himself exaggerated in 1545 that 'tailors and butchers' were appearing in portraits, whilst Giovanni Paolo Lomazzo, the art theorist, reproved portraitists for accepting commissions from 'plebeians and the base' (*'plebei e vili'*).[775]

As a result of his more efficient *prestezza* working method, Tintoretto's portraiture work actually began eroding the price for portraits in Venice despite the huge increase in demand. This was looked at askance by those who, like Titian and his supporters, had traditionally held the monopoly and kept prices high through deliberately slow and laborious working methods. Lodovico Dolce would later decry in the *Dialogo della Pittura, intitolato l'Aretino* that such rapid working methods as Tintoretto had pioneered sprang from *avarita*, 'greed', and the need to earn as much money as possible in as short a time as possible. Although Dolce did not mention Tintoretto specifically by name it was fairly obvious who was being referred to in these observations. Furthermore, since the *Dialogo della Pittura* was a thinly-veiled summation of Aretino's own personal views on art and art criticism, we can be confident that the satirist was, by extension, personally active in criticising Tintoretto's fast working methods, methods which seemed to be spoiling the art market for his close friend and associate Titian. Another of Aretino's literary circle who criticised Tintoretto in the 1540s for straying beyond the confines of acceptable good taste in art was Francesco Sansovino.

Interestingly, in 1538 in *Il Genesi con la visione di Noè*, Aretino had earlier written of the speed with which God had created the heavens and the earth, which was in effect being mimicked by Tintoretto's speed in painting God's creation with the rapid strokes of his brush. Neither had the élitist criticism of Tintoretto been limited to just Dolce, Sansovino and Aretino. In his 1556 guidebook to Venice, *Delle cose notabili che sono in Venetia*, Francesco Sansovino also criticised Tintoretto's inappropriately rapid painting technique.[776] Giorgio Vasari later joined in the chorus of criticism, decrying Tintoretto's practice of leaving 'as finished works sketches still so rough that the brush strikes may be seen'.[777] Tintoretto would, in a close-knit community like Venice, have been acutely aware of his contemporary's denigrations of his work. It cannot have been easy for a struggling young artist to maintain his morale in the face of such discouragement yet he evidently tried. A sign reportedly placed over the door of Tintoretto's studio read 'Michelangelo's design [*disegno*] and Titian's colouring [*colorito*]'.[778]

Due to the satirist's *sdegno* (disdain) Pietro Aretino can hardly be said to have been one of Tintoretto's early friends. And neither, for his part, did Tintoretto ever solicit Aretino's favour or patronage, as was certainly the case with other aspiring young painters. Tintoretto was a proud man and, though often poverty-stricken, simply refused to curry favour with the influential writer and proto art critic. Tintoretto worked diligently away from his house and *bottega* (workshop) beside a quiet canal in the mainly Jewish district of Cannaregio. Aretino continued to speak ill of Tintoretto whilst praising Titian to the skies. In the 1540s, Aretino would record a visit to Lake Garda, a landscape which, Aretino intimated, only Titian had the consummate artistry to capture adequately: 'I walked for miles, but my feet didn't move, behind hares and hounds, around clumps of mistletoe and netted partridges. Meanwhile I thought I saw something that I might have, but did not fear: beyond the dense undulating mountains, and hills full of game, were a hundred pairs of spirits obedient to the power and magic of art.'[779] Aretino was also not above praising the work of other aspiring young artists so long as they were not seen to threaten the status of his friend Titian. In his *Lettere* DCLXXI to Dolce, Aretino would for example praise the painting of Niccolò Gabrielli, the pupil of '*il miracoloso* Tiziano'.[780]

When the time finally came for the deadlock between the writer and the hard-done-by young artist Tintoretto to be broken, the artifice was provided by the latter. One day in 1544, Tintoretto slyly invited Aretino to visit his studio to have his portrait painted. Disarmed by the flattering gesture, the satirist accepted and came calling on the painter. Tintoretto seated him on a chair directly in front of his easel and then, to Aretino's shock, the artist drew out a large Italian dagger known as a *pistolese* which he then made a show of brandishing. The surprised Aretino naturally believed that Tintoretto, a hot-tempered individual, was seeking revenge for his many insults and cried out, asking the painter what he intended to do? Coolly, Tintoretto simply replied to the terrified satirist, 'Don't move one inch, I'm using this to take your measurements'. The famous incident was itself given an artistic treatment by later artists such as Alexandre-Evariste Fragonard and Jean Auguste Dominique Ingres in the eighteenth and nineteenth centuries; in the painting by Fragonard we see Tintoretto wielding a 'pistol' instead of a dagger, a common error in the story's retelling which lies in the confusion of the true meaning of the word *pistolese*. Regardless of the nomenclature ascribed to the weapon which the painter used in his clever practical joke, Aretino was suitably intimidated and never spoke badly of Tintoretto again and from that point forward they became firm friends. The following year Tintoretto painted Aretino's two ceiling frescos, in payment for which Aretino praised Tintoretto publicly in his published letters.

Aretino's February 1545 letter to the artist is redolent with enthusiasm for Tintoretto's work: 'My son, now that your brush bears witness with the present works to the fame that future ones are bound to acquire for you, let no time pass before you thank God, the goodness of whose mercies inclines your soul to the study of righteousness no less than to that of painting'.[781] In the same letter, Tintoretto's twin frescos *Apollo and Marsyas* and *Argus and Mercury*, painted on Aretino's bedroom ceiling, are praised for their speed of execution, something which Aretino (and Titian) had earlier criticised: 'You did them in less time than it took you to think out what you ought to put there. And since when we ask for rapid work in the things we desire, we also are asking for bad work, what a pleasure it was when you did the work swiftly and it was good work too!'[782]

It may well have been Aretino who was responsible for the adoption of Robusti's diminutive 'Tintoretto' since the satirist had addressed this 1545 letter to 'Iacopo Tintore' and the painter would later sign himself

'Jacomo Tentor'.[783] The nickname may have had its early origins in Aretino's desire to disparage the artist through reference to his father's lowly profession as a cloth dyer. The name, however, was uncannily apt in light of the fact that, like his father, Tintoretto made his living applying colour to the surface of woven cloth. Nevertheless, Tintoretto eventually made it his own and by 1551, when he was just coming to prominence as a city-wide painter of repute, the artist was actively referring to himself as 'Jacomo Tentorello', which is the version of the name when rendered in the Venetian dialect. In 1548, we find Aretino praising Tintoretto's triumphant painting The Miracle of the Slave, lauding 'your art, which is surpassing' ('*a vostra arte, che passa sì oltra*').[784] The work, which had been commissioned for the Scuola Grande di San Marco, had astonished both his critics and sceptics alike and was the artist's first public triumph with a major *scuola* (lay confraternity). Aretino cautioned the artist on getting too 'puffed up' and advised him to 'hold in check the careless haughtiness which so prevails over the wilfulness and swiftness of youth'.[785] He also warned Tintoretto about his general tendency towards *trascuratezza* or 'carelessness'.

There has been some suggestion amongst certain academics that, having at last established a degree of friendship and mutual understanding, Aretino and Tintoretto then fell out again around or just after the year 1548, an intermission which then continued into the 1550s. Several reasons are cited to support this such as the fact that after 1548 Tintoretto no longer appears in any of Aretino's published letters and neither is he mentioned in Lodovico Dolce's *Dialoguo L'Aretino*. Then, in January 1549, Aretino wrote to one of his *corrispondenti*, Domenico Boccamazza, alluding to a quarrel which had lately arisen between Tintoretto and Titian. 'Tintoretto, out of wickedness or folly, has broken his promise', Aretino writes, somewhat enigmatically, since the nature of the 'promise' is never disclosed.[786] Titian was at this time newly returned from Augsburg and was evidently unhappy to learn that Aretino had been singing his rival's praises while he was away, particularly in light of the fact that Titian had been acting as an advocate for Aretino to the Emperor and other important officials at the imperial court. He must have seen Aretino's behaviour as something of a betrayal. This, after Titian had immortalised Aretino in his earlier 1543 painting *Ecce Homo*, a resemblance which was first noticed by the artist biographer Carlo Ridolfi. The assumption here is that Aretino had subsequently been forced to sacrifice his newfound friendship with Tintoretto in order to preserve his longstanding relationship with Titian.[787]

Having said this, there is also reason to believe that any rupture, however serious, was not a permanent one. Marcolini alludes to the fact that Tintoretto painted Aretino's portrait in 1551 so the situation couldn't have been that fraught. (This was same year, incidentally, that both Tintoretto and Titian would witness the arrival of Paolo Veronese, a remarkably talented artist, who would seem to go from strength to strength in the years after his coming to Venice.) Tintoretto would also later pay tribute to Aretino by including the satirist's likeness in his great 1565 canvas of the *Crucifixion* which he completed for the Scuola di San Rocco. That said, unlike Titian's tribute, which placed Aretino front-and-centre as Pontius Pilate displaying Christ to the Jews, Tintoretto's *homage* would be altogether more discreet, relegating the satirist to a lesser role within the overall composition. Considering Aretino's fickle behaviour towards Tintoretto it was no better than he deserved.

☉☾

Friendly association with the well-connected art critic Pietro Aretino seldom did an artist's career or reputation any harm. When Rosso Fiorentino fled Rome after its sacking and pitched up in Venice he drew *Mars disrobed by Cupid and Venus disrobed by the Graces* for Aretino, which the satirist subsequently forwarded to King François I as an allegory on the Peace of Cambrai (1529). Rosso was subsequently invited to France in 1531, where he was one of the first prominent artists to work at the Chateau Fontainebleau as part of the 'First School of Fontainebleau'. He was soon joined by Francesco Primaticcio, a pupil of Giulio Romano's, who had been similarly recommended by the duke of Mantua. Aretino was also quick to praise new up-and-coming artists, like the miniaturist Jacopo del Giallo for example, to whom he wrote in May 1537: 'Your work is all design and all relief: yet everything is subtle and delicate as if done in oils'.[788] The paintings of Giovanni Antonio de' Sacchis, known as Pordenone, were also gaining attention in Venice during Aretino's stay and were praised especially for their three-dimensionality. In 1534, we find Aretino writing: 'Here is Pordenone, whose works make one doubt if nature gives relief to art or art to nature' (*'Ecco il Pordenone, le cui opere fan dubitare se la natura dà rilievo all'arte o l'arte alla natura'*.)[789]

At other times we find him commiserating with his artist and craftsman friends on apparent reversals in their fortunes, as in the case of the medal-maker Leone Leoni, whom Aretino tried to cheer up after he learned that his patron Pietro Bembo favoured his rival with an extravagant fee just for having sketched his portrait ('Titian and Sansovino are here with a group of other men of good taste. They have been talking about your achievements, and are astounded by them. Nor can I believe that Bembo will not do the right thing, or that he lacks the perception to know which is the better, you or that fellow.')[790] Likewise, Aretino offered his solicitous advice to the Croatian-born painter Andrea Schiavone, who was well-established in Venice by the 1540s. In April 1548, the satirist wrote to Schiavone: 'It is a cruelty by no means different from that which a son shows his father when he forgets the latter's love, that you do not come any longer as you used to before when you never painted anything lascivious or religious without having it brought to my house to show it to me; and the admirable Titian–no less dear to Charles V than Apelles to Alexander–knows how I have always praised the consummate quickness of your intelligent handling. Even that worthy painter was almost baffled by the experience which you display in brushing the sketches of your compositions, which are so intelligent and well organised that, if the haste of the sketching was changed into care for finishing the works, you too would confirm the excellence of my judgement.'[791]

Occasionally, Aretino's intervention was deemed unwelcome, especially when he critiqued artists who perhaps were not used to his very public style of evaluation. One such case seems to have occurred in August 1545 when Aretino writes to the sculptor Danese that his criticism of an unnamed artist was not intended in any way as malicious: 'It is because I love him, and not because I wanted to find fault with him, that I said what truth put upon my tongue when I saw the nude painted by that fellow who thinks he holds first place in excellence and perfect judgement in the matter of painting'. Aretino the art critic was quick to point out that more established masters were glad to have him assess their output: 'Titian does marvellous things, Sansovino is successful, and yet they always thank me for criticising their work, although the whole world knows that their genius is without equal.'[792] For the most part, Aretino's insights on art were penetrating and insightful, as when he wrote to the poet Francesco Coccio: '..art which is not based on life is like a man from Bergamo who has the tools of his trade in his hands, but has nothing to use them on. It is like a tailor who has neither cloth nor any other fabric to cut up yet he still brings his scissors to the shop.'[793]

The artist who benefitted most of all from his close friendship with Aretino, however, was Titian, on whom Aretino lavished page after page of admiring ekphrasis. The American art historian Bernard Berenson would later write in *The Venetian Painters Of The Renaissance* (1911) about how the influx of fugitive writers, poets and humanists to Venice following the sack of Rome and the Spanish ascendancy in Italy had 'for the first time [brought] Venetian painters … in contact with men of letters', adding that 'the relation of the man of letters to the painter became on the whole a stimulating and at any rate a profitable one … Titian would scarcely have acquired such fame in his lifetime if that founder of modern journalism, Pietro Aretino, had not been at his side, eager to trumpet his praises and to advise him whom to court.'[794] Aretino became, in effect, Titian's publicist in the modern sense of that word and, in doing so, he also arguably invented the literary discipline of art criticism.

It was the case of course that by the 1520s Titian's fame as a portraitist of international reputation was already, to a certain extent, established. Moreover, when Aretino arrived in Venice in 1527, Titian was already the Official Painter to the Republic of Venice, whom he had chosen to serve in 1513 as opposed to its rival Rome.[795] In 1523, the artist had painted the portrait of the duke of Ferrara, Alfonso d'Este; his painting style during this period showed that Titian was already fully cognisant of the overriding desire of subjects to be depicted as a persons of power, nobility, influence and prestige. In this sense Titian's portraiture was the visual counterpart of Aretino's eulogies to all the prominent personalities of the age. Aretino's friendship with Titian culminated that same year in the important commission to paint Aretino's own patron Federico Gonzaga. This would prove a regular source of income and patronage for Titian; between the years 1528 and 1540, Federico bought in total around thirty works from the artist. Three years later, through the good offices of Aretino's other patron, Cardinal Ippolito de' Medici, Titian would be invited to Bologna in 1530 to paint his (non-extant) first portrait of the Emperor Charles V. In 1533, Titian would be granted an imperial patent which bestowed upon him the privilege of painting imperial portraits and that same year a second portrait would be executed. In 1548, Aretino would praise the painting's qualities and subject matter in a sonnet:

Descending from the idea that Nature
Imitates in a divine and lifelike design
Comes the holy and dignified example of the great Charles,
No longer a sacred figure by Titian.

For he shows in his silent figure
How valour and genius are fused,
What by nature possesses within itself both imperium and rule,
And what thus offers to others both hope and fear.

In his eyes he possesses Justice and Clemency,
Between his eyebrows Virtue and Fortune,
Price and grace and wisdom.

His brow seems free from any clouds,
And where his proud heart makes its residence
A sun overshadows every Sultan's moon.[796]

The famous portraits of Francesco Maria della Rovere and his wife Eleonora Gonzaga followed in 1536. The paintings are an especially good example of the interweaving, common at this time, of the personal qualities of the portrait's subject along with the social roles and societal virtues which they are seen to embody. Francesco Maria is depicted as a proud, forceful individual, the epitome of the virile Renaissance *condottiere*, an interpretation which is quite inescapable given the array of phallic appurtenances stacked behind him in the painting. His wife, by contrast, is represented as a chaste, serene and poised duchessa and mother figure. Both sitters play their social roles to perfection for the benefit of the recording and memorialising artist, Titian. One year later, on 7 November 1537, Aretino would write to Veronica Gambara enclosing a pair of sonnets itemising the virtues of both subjects. The Duke of Urbino, for example, 'reveals the victories held within his heart' and Aretino speaks of the 'awesomeness between his brows' and the 'fiery spirit in his eyes' (*l'animo in gli occhi*).[797]

Such descriptions of Titian's paintings were at this time almost entirely new and unprecedented and introduce another of Aretino's attributes as one of the first modern art critics. Far from being merely a pictorial record and 'social document' of an important ruler or other personage, Aretino approached the portrait as a work of art in its own right. How far did the portrait capture the essence and concept (*concetto*) of the subject? Was the likeness a faithful one in artistic terms? Was the choice of setting and sitter's posture appropriate to the subject matter? Aretino's insightful monologues on Titian's canvases guided the viewer in discovering and better understanding the attributes of the artwork in relation to its subject.[798] Following Francesco Maria's assassination in 1538, his successor Duke Guidobaldo II continued his predecessor's patronage of Titian. In 1536 or 1537, Guidobaldo sent Titian a burnished, black suit of armour by Filippo Negroli for the artist to use in a painting of Claudius which had been commissioned by Federico Gonzaga.[799] This would mark the beginning of Guidobaldo's ongoing patronage of Titian, a relationship which would continue for the ensuing thirty-five years. During the 1540s, the duke of Urbino would commission Titian to paint portraits of himself as well as his young wife Giulia Varano.[800]

In 1538, Aretino commissioned Titian to paint his famous portrait of King François I of France, which the satirist proposed to send as a lavish gift designed to curry favour with the powerful monarch. There would also be a second painting, also probably commissioned from Titian on a devotional subject and Aretino wrote to François informing him that he could anticipate two gifts 'one magnifying the honour of man, the other magnifying the glory of god'.[801] Since François never sat for Titian in person, the artist painted him sight-unseen from a portrait on a cast medal by the silversmith Benvenuto Cellini. As a direct result of receiving these two paintings, Titian was cordially invited to come to France and work, an offer which he nevertheless politely declined since he was perfectly content to remain living and working in his beloved Venice.

Another benefactor who patronised both Titian and Aretino in the 1530s and 1540s was Alfonso d'Ávalos, the marchese of Pescara and del Vasto. In 1531, Alfonso applied to Aretino to have Titian paint a family group portrait of himself, his wife Maria d'Aragona and his two-year-old son Francesco Ferrante (disguised as Cupid) on the eve before he set out on a military expedition against the Turks in Hungary. Later, in 1540, d'Ávalos commissioned Titian to paint *The Allocution of Alfonso d'Ávalos, Marchese del Vasto to his troops*. The painting depicted d'Avalos rallying his troops during the Hungarian campaign of 1532. Standing at his side, holding his helmet, is his young son. The boy, Francesco Ferrante, now nine years older, is attired in what Aretino describes as ancient Roman costume derived from figures on Roman triumphal arches. From Aretino's letters to d'Ávalos we can ascertain that the picture was painted in 1540-41. On 22 December 1540 Aretino sent d'Ávalos, as a stopgap, a 'small painting' (since lost) to 'keep him amused while the larger canvas was being finished'. The completed painting was delivered in August 1541.

Alfonso d'Ávalos had been made governor of Milan in January 1538. His wife Maria d'Aragona then went about inaugurating her court in that great city of the Lombard Plain. Another celebrated sixteenth-century female patron of humanism and the arts, Maria corresponded not only with Pietro Aretino but also with other prominent writers including Bernardo Capello, Girolamo Muzio, Niccolò Franco, Bernardino Spina, Paolo Giovio and Luca Contile.[802] The Titian paintings of her husband were quite possibly also commissioned by Maria for her husband and young son. She was an avid Church reformer who kept in touch with reformist clerics like Bernardino Ochino, Galeazzo Florimonte and Pietro Carnesecchi (who would later be burned at the stake for his belief in the Protestant doctrine of justification by faith). Milanese court records show that Pietro Aretino was employed as one of the Milanese court *letterati* along with Luca Contile and Giovanni Alberto Albicante.[803] Titian had petitioned the marchese and his spouse for a benefice for his son Pomponio and the artist's pension was granted and duly paid from the imperial Milanese treasury.

In 1540, Titian would paint Pietro Bembo in the full ecclesiastical finery of a cardinal of Holy Mother Church. By this time the great poet, linguist, critic, collector and lover was seventy years old. He and Titian had been lifelong friends and the artist had already painted Bembo several times; the 1540 portrait was no doubt painted to commemorate Bembo's recent elevation to cardinal in March 1539. Titian presents us with a truly commanding presence attired in his scarlet regalia and gesticulating to some unseen interlocutor. Titian also flatters the subject by apparently presenting us with a far younger man than the septuagenarian. Bembo, Vasari tells us, 'took pains over a sonnet for months or even years' and this ponderous 'Petrarchan' way of working may well have influenced Titian's own style of working paint onto canvas. Unlike Tintoretto's faster, more fluid and improvisatory brushwork, at this time all the rage in Venice, Titian preferred to construct his subjects and his compositions with slow and painstaking care. Boschini in *La carta* quotes Titian's viewpoint in this respect, telling us that the artist never painted a figure all in one go because 'he who improvises [*canta all improviso*] cannot compose learned [*erudito*] or well-constructed verses'. The simile Titian uses here draws on the Horatian idea of the correspondence between the poet and the painter and underscores Titian's preference for a more meticulous, more laborious method of painting.[804] On the other hand, Titian's tardy style of working was sometimes criticised by his customers who experienced long delays in taking delivery of their commissioned works; under such circumstances no amount of citing 'Bembist' Petrarchan principles could have offered any consolation.

Between the autumn of 1545 and June 1546, Titian would be commissioned by the Farnese family during the artist's visit to Rome to paint *Pope Paul III and His Grandsons*. The Romans, and the Pope, welcomed the celebrated painter to their city. This visit and the commissioning of the Pope's portrait was due in part to Aretino's intervention. Tirelessly, from 1537 until the early 1550s, Aretino would trumpet the talent and originality of Titian over all other Italian painters; using psychology, Aretino had slyly informed the Romans that Titian had been invited to paint in Madrid but that his preference was to come to Rome instead. To Cardinal Salviati, the satirist had written that Titian's artistry in landscapes was far superior to Dürer's. In the *Dialogo della Pittura, intitolato l'Aretino*, Dolce would allude to Titian's celebrity and the fact that 'Nor was there ever a cardinal or other grandee in Venice who did not visit Titian's establishment to see his creations and have his own portrait painted'.[805]

The prestigious papal commission of the Farnese Pope came just after Titian's well-known 1545 portrait of Pietro Aretino which today hangs in the sali di Venere of the Palazzo Pitti in Florence, a portrait which Aretino described to Paolo Giovio as '*una si terribile meraviglia*' ('such an awesome marvel')[806] and which 'celebrates the figure of my natural semblance' ('*essaltando la figura de la mia naturale sembianza*').[807] When Aretino had branded this portrait as having been 'sketched rather than unfinished' to Cosimo I, and that this was due to Titian's miserly attitude at having been underpaid by the satirist, the comment betrayed a subtle and clever implied threat to Florence's ruler. If the great Titian could work in such a lacklustre way over a simple matter of money so too might Aretino's characterisation of Cosimo leave much to be desired if he did not receive his due in terms of gifts and pensions.[808]

The triumph of Titian's portraiture art would follow in 1548, when the artist painted his iconic *Equestrian Portrait of Charles V* during his visit to the imperial court of Augsburg. The Emperor is depicted on horseback at the Battle of Mühlberg fighting heroically against the Protestant Schmalkaldic League (1547), a case of barefaced artistic license since Charles, who was suffering badly from gout at the time, was in fact carried into battle on a litter rather than a great war horse. In a letter to Titian, Aretino found it hard to conceal his astonishment at how his friend had been granted so many private opportunities to meet and converse with the Emperor, concluding that it was due to his virtuous qualities that Charles paid him such heed. A letter written from Titian to Aretino two years later on 11 November 1550 show that their relationship was very much a two-way street, with the artist also acting as Aretino's advocate and promoter when the occasion presented itself. Titian informs Aretino of a conversation with Charles during which the painter alludes to the satirist's ambition to become a cardinal of the Church. Titian informs his friend that the Emperor had reacted favourably to a letter which Titian had earlier presented him from Aretino and 'shewed [sic] signs of pleasure in his countenance' when learning of Aretino's eagerness to serve him.[809]

Many such important commissions were a direct result of Aretino's lobbying or his giving 'good press' to Titian in his prolific written output. Aretino frequently paid tribute to Titian's artistry in his published collections of letters. To Count Massiminiano Stampa, for example, he wrote in October 1531 concerning a Titian canvas which had been delivered to the Count: 'Look at the softness of the curled hair and the pretty youthfulness of St. John. Look at the flesh tints so skilfully rendered that they are like snow tinted with vermillion, and seem animated by living pulses and warmed by the spirit of life. Of the crimson of the cloak and of the lynx fur with which it is lined, I will not speak. Although painted, they are real crimson and the skin of an actual lynx. They are alive.'[810] There is no mistaking the fact that the two men's relationship was one built on an almost brotherly trust and mutual affection which mirrored, in certain important respects, that of the satirist's earlier friendship with Giovanni delle Bande Nere. Difference of personality were seldom, for Aretino, any barrier to the striking of close lifelong friendships. Giovanni de' Medici had been the roustabout soldier yet Aretino could still love him for all the things that the satirist himself was not. Titian too differed in many significant respects from Aretino, being far more sensitive, serious and thoughtful and considerably less quick to anger than the hair-triggered writer. And they shared other tastes in common, particularly the company of charming young women, although Titian was considerably more discreet in his liaisons. The relationship was obviously far from being a mere marriage of convenience or one based on simple mutual profit. There was genuine affection and fellow feeling too.

Aretino helped Titian by offering advice and guidance to the painter's erring son Pomponio, chiding him about the state of his Hebrew, Greek and Latin and encouraging him to study harder ('I realise that old age is a fable to youth, just as youth is an extravagant fairy tale to old age', Aretino wrote to the wastrel, continuing, 'It is not right that the money amassed by the paint brushes, the skill, the labour, and the long journeys of Titian should be thrown away in riotous living … So go back to your books, and give up your licentious habits. You should be ashamed to have your laziness give birth to nothing but lewd doings.')[811] At the same time Aretino was writing to Titian and Sansovino expressing his understanding for the turbulence of youth: 'Pomponio and Francesco have carried on in such a way that you ought to deny them not merely luxuries, but bread, and that forthwith. But if it should come to pass that we oldsters were willing to remember what we did at the same age, we would forgive young people their faults and laugh at them, getting back one hundred percent what we spent by enjoying their amusements and their pleasures.'[812] Despite the friendly strictures from the family friend, Pomponio would however remain a sad disappointment to his father; preferring his riotous life to diligent study both father and son argued bitterly. Aretino's final prognostication was that the father's fame had proved too overwhelming for the ill-disciplined and weak-willed Pomponio. Titian's second boy Orazio, by contrast, remained at his father's side and assumed the management of Titian's affairs as the artist began to age. Always extremely careful with money, a legacy of his humble country origins, Titian worried and fretted constantly about the fees owed to him by both Charles V and King François I. This trait was often unfairly remarked upon by his royal debtors. Writing in regard to a payment of 400 *scudi* which was due to Titian over a two year period, the Spanish ambassador to Venice wrote to the Emperor that Titian, 'Being old, [he] is somewhat covetous'.[813]

Titian for his part painted Aretino's daughter Adria, who is the little girl depicted in his 1543 painting *Ecce Homo* who stands in front of Titian's own grown-up daughter Lavinia. In August 1530, Titian's wife Cecilia Soldani had died giving birth to Lavinia and his sister Orsa came to live with him as his housekeeper. Unlike Aretino, however, his life since the tragedy seems to have remained uncomplicated and he appears to have kept aloof from romantic entanglements (although the widower may simply have continued to be very discreet in his habits). Although he and Aretino might dine with notorious courtesans like Angela Zaffetta that was as far as things went. So close-knit was the so-called 'triumvirate' of Titian, Aretino and Jacopo Sansovino that the three men met almost every day. The satirist would write: 'While you, Titian, and you, Sansovino, on canvas and in marble display your art so that it is resplendent everywhere and the example of every pilgrim spirit: I with zealous heart bowed in homage paint and carve humbly on paper..'[814] All three were revolutionaries of their respective artforms, busily engaged in tossing out the old, outmoded aesthetic order. As such, they mirrored and reinforced one another.

The art critic Paolo Pino would write that the artist must transcend all static proportions, which meant by extension the art of the great Tuscan masters like Michelangelo, because the new type of artist paints in flourishes of movement and movement is the enemy of abstract proportion.[815] This is certainly visible in Titian's brushwork, although the iconoclastic sentiment which lay behind Pino's dictum may also be seen as being paralleled in Aretino's rejection of classical humanist literary forms. These three creators (Sansovino perhaps somewhat more literally than his two associates) were engaged in tearing down the established order and rebuilding it in their own image. In 1590, in *Idea del Tempio Pittura*, Giovanni Paolo Lomazzo would, describe Titian as 'the sun amidst small stars not only among the Italians but all the painters of the world', making reference to the final line of Dante's *Paradiso*.

CHAPTER 15

❧❦

Recognition

For look here is my name bandied about by every idle gossiper, and you read it upon the title page of romances which could not be sold in any other way. Look here you see me in lead, copper, silver and gold. I rejoice at all this–and not merely at this, but at the evil legends which the lady poets make up about me. I rejoice too because the midget-minded actually think they amount to something if they get into a quarrel with me.

Pietro Aretino to Francesco Marcolini,
January 1545

F or the carnival of 1542, Pietro Aretino was specially commissioned by a relatively new addition to the *Compagnie della Calza* known as the Sempiterni, which had been formed in March 1541, to write and help produce one of his signature bawdy comedies.[816] As we have seen, such 'Companies of the Hose' were renowned for staging often notoriously lascivious masquerades, ballets and theatrical performances, as well as for accompanying attractions such as the slaughtering of bulls and pigs for public consumption, or else daredevil performances which often featured agile Turks who walked tightropes and other acrobatic feats. The *Compagnie*, however, were not above price-gouging the general public for these various attractions and performances which were always well-attended.[817]

In response to the request from the Sempiterni, the satirist penned a new work entitled *La Talanta*, a sex comedy of manners loosely based on *Eunuchus* ('The Eunuch') by the Roman playwright Terence.[818] In Aretino's adaptation, the courtesan Talanta (who is closely based on Terence's character Thais) is beset by four suitors: Armileo, the young and handsome Orfinio (a regurgitation of the Phaedria character from *Eunuchus*), the worldly Capitano Tinca and the old Venetian miser

Vergolo. As in *Eunuchus*, at the start of the play Talanta/Thais bars her youngest and most earnest *innamoratus* Orfinio from her house, telling him that if he grants her leave to spend one day alone with each of her three other suitors she will reward him with ten long summer days alone with her. She also echoes Aretino's aging, practical-minded whore Nanna by asserting to the audience that love is little more than a business transaction.

With this initial scenario, Aretino loses no time in spiralling the plot into a complex, bewildering and often grotesque farce involving love, avarice, gift-giving, cross-dressing and all-round gender-confusion. Capitano Tinca offers Talanta the gift of a slave girl who is in reality a cross dressed man, Antino. Vergolo, who is Aretino's version of the stock character Pantalone (who represents 'money and social status' in the *commedia dell' arte*), meanwhile offers the courtesan a male Saracen slave who is in reality a cross dressed woman, Lucilla, who also happens to be Antino's sister. When Aretino introduces a third cross dressed 'slave' character named Oretta the comedy essentially devolves from there. The outcome is, as always, somewhat predictable with the courtesan opting after all is said and done for her dashing young lover Orfinio whilst the older suitors are humiliated and cheated of their gifts and possessions by the courtesan in collusion with her crafty servants. The production was perfect for the Venetian carnival, containing as it did just the right admixture of humour, vulgarity and the didactive elements of a morality play.

For the production of *La Talanta*, Aretino invited the thirty-one-year-old Giorgio Vasari to come to Venice to create the elaborate painted stage scenery and room decorations known as the *apparato*. 'I was summoned to Venice by M. Pietro Aretino, then a poet of renown and my fast friend' Vasari writes in his 1568 autobiography, 'As he greatly desired to see me I was obliged to go, and I was glad of the opportunity for seeing the works of Titian and others'. Vasari, a fellow countryman of Pietro's from Arezzo, had by this time lost his three most important Medici patrons: Pope Clement VII, Cardinal Ippolito de' Medici and Duke Alessandro de' Medici. He was at this time still a decade away from the renowned work which he would later complete for the Grand Ducal court of Cosimo I and, although by this time a highly accomplished painter in his own right, he had yet to establish his reputation and renown.[819] Vasari had visited Venice one year earlier in December 1541 and had remained until August the following year. Aretino's invitation to return to the maritime republic was nonetheless most welcome for the struggling young artist who had sworn 'that I would never again follow the fortune of courts, but only art..'[820] and who had been forced, following the young Duke Alessandro's

300

assassination, to look for alternative sources of patronage from amongst the various monastic orders.

Before arriving back in Venice, he took the opportunity to visit Antonio Allegri da Correggio in Parma and Giulio Romano in Mantua; the latter had acquired a house from the Ippoliti family in 1538 which he renamed the Casa Pippi and which he filled with classical art after the trend first set by Mantegna, redecorating throughout according to the latest architectural principles.[821] When Vasari passed through Ferrara he stayed with the Mannerist painter Benvenuto Tisi, who had earned his nickname *Il Garofalo* due to his habit of sometimes signing his work with a carnation (*garofano*). The staging for *La Talanta* was set up in an as yet uncompleted but spacious dwelling in Venice's Cannaregio district.[822] In a letter to Ottaviano de' Medici, who had previously served as Duke Alessandro's major domo of arts, Vasari described both the space and his staging creations for it:

'I tell you that the room where the *apparato* was located was very large, likewise the scenery, that is the perspective, depicting Rome, including the Arch of Septimus, the Templum Pacis, the Rotunda, the Coliseum, the Peace, Santa Maria Nuova, the Temple of Fortune, Trajan's Column, Palazzo Maggiore, the Seven Rooms, the Conti Tower, the Tower of the Milizia, and finally [the statue of] Maestro Pasquino, more handsome than he has ever been; in it there were the finest palaces, houses, churches, and an infinity of various things in Doric, Ionic, Corinthian, Tuscan, Rustic, and Composite [style] architecture.'[823]

Out of love for his daughter, Aretino asked Vasari to paint a personification of Venice as 'Adria' who was depicted as presiding over the deities of the ocean 'seated upon a rock in the midst of the sea, with a branch of coral in the hand'.[824]

As for Aretino's play, Vasari records that the 'comedy was played by these Magnificent Lords, young men of the nobility, and so many people attended that, between the lamps and the crowding, one could not withstand the great, suffocating heat'.[825] Overhead, the coffered ceiling incorporated four large panels allegorically depicting the four stages of day: Night, Dawn, Day and Evening, each of which was surrounded by a further six panels symbolising the corresponding six hours of time. Aretino and Vasari's collaboration on the production for the Sempiterni was a triumph and it helped establish the artist in business in Venice, where he also mingled with Leonardo Cungi, Cristofano Gherardi and other renowned painterly figures.[826] Lucrative commissions followed, including an important assignment to paint nine ceilings in the Palazzo Corner

Spinelli. For his host in Venice, Francesco Leoni, Vasari also completed a *Holy Family with St. Francis.*

Aretino, for whom his *palazzo* balcony window was his own private proscenium arch looking out over a rich and endlessly varied 'theatre' of real-life courtesans, nobles, diplomats, merchants, soldiers, tradesmen, ordinary folk and ne'er–do–wells all going about their daily business, would serve as an important influence on Giorgio Vasari, whose own most famous writings, the *Lives*, would in many ways come to mirror the *Lettere* of the great satirist himself. Aretino, Vasari and to a similar extent Cellini too would all self-aggrandize by casting themselves in their literature as the central figures in their respective stories, taking part in key historical events, meeting with important personages of note and undertaking significant activities or artistic commissions. For Cellini he was the man whose harquebus had shot and killed the Duke of Bourbon as he scaled the walls of Rome wearing his distinctive silver surcoat. For Vasari his own autobiography and his encounters with emperors, kings and popes was never far from his biographies of the great artists. Whilst for Aretino he enjoyed boasting about how horses, canals and even women had been named after him: 'I am a second Alexander, Caesar, Scipio', he wrote to Francesco Alunno, 'Nay more: I tell you that some kinds of glasses they make at Murano are called Aretines. Aretine is the name given to a breed of cobs–after one Pope Clement sent me, and I gave to Duke Federico. They have christened the little canal that runs beside my house the Canalozzo, Rio Aretino. And, to make pedants burst with rage, besides talking of the Aretine style, three wenches of my household, who have left me and become ladies, will have themselves known only as Aretines.' He then went on to affirm immodestly that 'So many lords and gentlemen are eternally breaking in upon me with their importunities ... I have come to be the Oracle of Truth, the Secretary of the Universe: everybody brings me the tale of his injury by such and such a prince or prelate'.[827]

For Aretino there was no sense of competition for Vasari was the younger man and still, as yet, relatively unestablished. The satirist could afford to be generous in his dealings with the ambitious young painter and besides they had known each other previously in Venice and were, as yet, entrenched in different fields. Aretino's feelings towards Vasari are captured in a letter to Andrea Udone in which the satirist flatters Vasari with the observation: '[F]or anyone who wants to see how clean [*netto*] and bright [*candido*] is his spirit, let him look at his face [*fronte*] and his house; let him look at them, I say, and he will see what calm and what beauty one can contemplate in a house and in a face'.[828] All in all, 1542 had been a productive year for Aretino as he had also sent another new play, *Lo Ipocrito*, to Duke Cosimo I in Florence. As the play's title suggests, the play, which is set in Milan, is about a cunning hypocrite who is called in to advise Messer Liseo on his problems. Liseo has a shrew of a wife, five daughters whom he cannot marry off, and moreover learns that a long-lost brother, Brizio, from whom he was separated in boyhood, has found him and now wishes to re-establish contact. The hypocrite advises Liseo to resign himself to his troubles and console himself with philosophy. As a result Liseo ends up as the ridiculous parody of a Stoic whom no problem can touch. The play was intended to have been performed during Florence's own carnival season but, as Cosimo explained to Aretino in a letter dated 23 February 1542, he received the manuscript too late and 'I did not stage it in this last carnival because time was too short, but it will be done another time with greater ease'.[829]

Just the year before on 25 March, Cosimo's consort Eleonora di Toledo had given birth to their first male child, Francesco, who would later become Cosimo's successor as Duke of Florence. Aretino had lost little time in sending his felicitations in April 1541, writing to the Duke: 'My lord, my heart is full of such rare and intense and sudden pleasure that I am beside myself with joy ... because the birth of a son to you means for Caesar the birth of loyalty, for Italy adornment, for Tuscany glory, for Florence unity, for the Medici stability, for their subjects an idol, for their adversaries a bridle, for the humble forgiveness, for the just a refuge, for the poor abundance, for the virtuous support, for praise breath, for honour dignity, for fame a subject and for the pen a theme.' Neither could Aretino resist a subtle reminder who the infant's grandfather had been: '..may the child grow in prudent valour and power, and may he achieve a harmonious perfection derived from the gentleness of your Highness and the ferocity of your great father'.[830]

As usual, Aretino had not paused to consider whether the Duke might possibly take it amiss to have his 'gentleness' contrasted with the martial prowess of his father. After all, that same year of 1542 Cosimo had embarked upon an aggressive three year long war of expansion in Tuscany which would see not only the subjugation of ever-hostile Siena but also the eventual acquisition (in 1548) of the island of Elba from Genoa. Cosimo intended to transform Elba into a naval base, thus transforming his duchy into a great seagoing power to rival Venice and Genoa. Giovanni delle Bande Nere may have been the greater soldier but Cosimo had done more to transform the map of Tuscany since coming to power. Where Giovanni had been a man of action, Cosimo was a man of strategy. Giovanni's energy had been unbounded and diffused, Cosimo's was focused and concentrated on his desired political ends. In the event, the son would complete the raw potential of the father. Aretino's great error in his ongoing dealings with Cosimo lay in not giving credit where credit was in fact due, as well as in the underlying assumption that the son would be content to remain forever in the shadow of the illustrious father.

November 1542 brought sad news as Aretino learned from his brother-in-law Orazio Vanotti that his beloved sister Francesca had died during childbirth. Hers had been a largely indigent lifestyle as her soldier-husband was always short of money. Aretino wrote to his bereaved brother-in-law in stoical vein: 'Certainly it was a very bitter blow, and yet I am not overcome by it because we have so few reasons to desire life and so many to long for death. After all, death is no other than an escape from the perils of life, and since living or dying we should never give up constancy and patience, let us comfort ourselves with the example of her virtues. Moreover, since a great sorrow often brings us something useful, let us hope that it must so happen to us.' Aretino then treated his brother-in-law to a rather pompous disquisition on the virtues of poverty '..since he who scorns riches is all the more worthy of God. Consider how nature can satisfy our modest needs with bread and water.' Finally, after consoling poor Orazio that Francesca was given all the honours that were her due both in life and death, Aretino managed to end his letter with a self-tribute: 'So complain no more, and be persuaded that my native city never gave me reputation or authority and that I have indeed given it honour and glory, in consequence of which Arezzo is more spoken of because of my doings than thanks to a thousand others'.[831] This, it has to be said, is not one of the crowning moments of Pietro Aretino's letter writing, although it does throw into sharp focus his pervasive and narcissistic tendency to view the trials and tribulations of others through the lens of his own life.

Neither does Aretino especially seem to have subsidised the poorer members of his family. In January 1545, we see a letter from Aretino to his relations stating: 'You complain because it seems to you that I am as rich as I really am poor and yet I don't send you any money at all from my income. But what greater treasure can a man leave his relatives than that of not having anything to leave anyone in the world? And that's what I haven't got.'[832] It is hard to know what exactly to make of Aretino's apparent parsimoniousness with regard to his blood relations when contrasted with his endless protestations that he is a constant source of munificence for complete strangers in Venice. There is a certain kind of self-made-man who, having received little material support from his family, feels disinclined to reward his immediate family members when he strikes prosperity; perhaps Aretino can be said to fall within this category. But again, his urging of penny-pinching habits on others whilst gleefully declaring to Jacopo Sansovino '..it irks me not to have it in my hands to squander in a single day ... Ah well, let us live it up. Nothing else matters'[833] is not perhaps one of the satirist's more endearing qualities.

On the other hand, Aretino was never exactly trying out for a sainthood either. Besides, he'd received little advancement from his own family when young.

⊙☾

I n stark contrast to the worldly and lascivious delights of carnival was the newly-instituted and greatly-feared Congregation of the Holy Office of the Inquisition. The Roman Inquisition was established by Pope Paul III's bull *Licet ab initio* on 21 July 1542, the same year as Aretino's latest theatrical triumph *La Talanta*. It was the Church's answer to the growing spread of Protestantism and was largely a defensive move by the papacy to preserve and enforce its authority. It had been established in the immediate aftermath of the Regensburg Colloquy in 1541, which had failed to achieve reconciliation between Catholics and Protestants in Europe, but instead saw numerous prominent Italian clerics either defecting to the Protestant side or else demanding Lutheran-style reforms of Church practices. The Inquisition, which was closely modelled on the feared Spanish Inquisition, was the brainchild of the hard-line Cardinal Gian Pietro Carafa, later Pope Paul IV, who was notorious for having reputedly stated 'Even if my own father were a heretic, I would gather the wood to burn him'.[834] It was charged with maintaining and defending the integrity of the Roman Catholic faith and of examining and proscribing errors and false doctrines and was the 'business end' of the Counter Reformation, which by now was beginning to gather momentum under the combined oversight of the Pope and the Emperor. Its activities made any reformist endeavours by the so-called *spirituali*, those Catholic churchmen who still hoped to effect a compromise with the Protestants, not only difficult but potentially hazardous in Italy. It would increasingly come to exert its authority in the moral and artistic sphere as well.

Venice was not immune from its reach or its power and, as the Inquisition gained ground, artists and writers would scarcely be invulnerable from charges of heresy. The Inquisition was permitted to enter Venice that same year of 1542 although the maritime republic's traditionally suspicious attitude towards Rome led to the Venetian *signori* working out a compromise arrangement. Instead of the Inquisition operating autonomously within Venice's sovereign lands a special local court known as the Holy Office was established with the power to act in the Inquisition's name.[835] However, due to the participation of three lay magistrates in this new ad hoc body, the so called *Savii sopra l'Eresia* (Wise Men Overseeing Heresy), the spirit of religious fervour behind the Inquisition's activities tended as a result to be somewhat blunted. Consequently, people of all religious persuasions still continued to come and go in Venice without let or hindrance.[836] Nevertheless, the admittance of the Inquisition was a breach of Venice's traditional policy of tolerance and liberty and a tacit recognition that the state was willing to act to suppress heresy if indeed it posed a serious threat to the political stability of Venice itself. By 1544, Monsignor Giovanni della Casa had arrived in the republic as papal nuncio and the Inquisition's chief representative. Under della Casa's auspices the authorities now began a series of arrests, trials, executions and banishments of spiritual reformers resident here. Four years later the nuncio would institute book burnings in the *piazza* of San Marco as well as near the Ponte Rialto. By 1549 he had published an *Index* of prohibited books which Venetian printers were meant to adhere to.

One of the first high profile victims of this new inquisitorial regime had a singular admirer in Pietro Aretino. This was the Church reformer Bernardino Ochino. Born in Siena, the son of a barber, Ochino had joined the Franciscan Order at the age of eight but later transferred to the Capuchins in 1534, eventually becoming that order's vicar-general in 1538. By this time he was a correspondent of such literary luminaries as Pietro Bembo, Vittoria Colonna, Pietro Martire and Pietro Carnesecchi. At Bembo's instigation, Ochino visited Venice in 1539 and delivered a series of nine sermons in which he showed some degree of sympathy for the heretical Protestant doctrine of justification by faith. He also exhibited in his own bearing a form of simple, austere, mendicant observance which had not really been seen since the days of Girolamo Savonarola in Florence. Aretino went to listen to Ochino preach at Santi Apostoli, his parish church which was located just behind his rented *palazzo*. The satirist was much moved by the experience, which led to him praise the friar publicly and it was also the beginning of a correspondence between the two men. So moved was Aretino in fact that he took up his pen and wrote to Pope Paul III: 'Moved by the trumpet tones, uttered by the Apostolic friar [Ochino], I yield to the admonitions of your Reverence. By means of this letter, as my substitute, I throw myself at the feet of your blessed Holiness, and ask pardon for the insults offered to your court by my foolish writings'.[837]

Father Ochino used the free Venetian press to publish fifteen of his sermons in 1541, the year of the Regensburg Colloquy, but was denounced for heresy that same year. Although no specific action was taken as a result of the denunciation, when the papal nuncio della Casa arrived in Venice the following year, Ochino found himself promptly issued with a summons to go to Rome. He set out in August 1542 but when he reached Bologna he encountered the reformist *spirituali* Cardinal Gasparo Contarini who was suffering from the effects of poison and the cardinal advised the Capuchin vicar-general not to continue his journey to Rome, asserting (according to Ochino's account) 'that the Cardinal lamented with him the proceedings of the court of Rome against good men'.[838] Ochino took the dying Contarini's advice and instead fled across the Alps to Geneva where he was cordially welcomed by one of the triumvirate of northern reformers, John Calvin. Upon learning of Ochino's apostasy, Pope Paul III was said to have been so enraged that he threatened to suppress the friar's entire Capuchin order. The friar himself met with a sad end, however. He had broken his Catholic priest's vows by marrying and his wife subsequently bore him four children; however, a life lived more or less permanently on the run from the imperial authorities eventually took its toll. With his wife and two of his children already dead, Bernardino Ochino eventually died in abject poverty and obscurity at Slavkov in Moravia, around the end of 1564.

But Ochino was not the only well-known apostate in Aretino's circle for there was also his good friend Pier Paolo Vergerio, the man who had earlier acted as Aretino's lobbyist to the potential patrons King Ferdinand and the Cardinal of Trent. Following his stint as papal nuncio to King Ferdinand in Austria and Hungary, Vergerio had gone on to appear alongside the reformist Cardinal Gasparo Contarini at the Colloquy of Regensburg and, like Contarini, he too had been accused of having conceded far too much ground to the Protestants. As a result, suspicion had been sufficiently awakened against him for Puritan allegations to surface and a formal denunciation to be lodged with Venice's Holy Office on 13 December 1544. Following his initial examination, Vergerio was released but his published work from this point forward took a markedly reformist, polemical and antagonistic tone towards the Church. Like the northern Protestants and humanist reformers, Vergerio began to accept that there was a palpable historical disconnect between the ancient and 'true' Christian Church of Jesus Christ and the monolithic, hyper-politicised Roman Catholic Church with its wealthy and worldly bishops, cardinals and inquisitors. These, Vergerio denounced as modern day Pharisees. When, as a result, della Casa ominously summoned him for a second time to appear before the Holy Office he prudently fled Italy. His trial was conducted in Venice *in absentia* and by 1549 Vergerio was convicted of heresy, deposed from his episcopal dignity and made subject to arrest.

Whilst at the court of King Ferdinand, Vergerio had encouraged Aretino to write more in the way of sacred works. 'This is the way, Aretino, to succeed in the world', Vergerio had advised the worldly and cynical satirist, 'for if you lose all the favour [of the world], Jesus Christ, Whom you have only recently begun to praise and then with your efforts, will find a way to succour and honour you. In short, it seems to me that with this work you have turned your precious ability into pure gold, when it was formerly in iron and other such despised metals.'[839] Aretino's obvious fondness for Vergerio is apparent from his letter dated 20 January 1534: 'It was with great consolation that I received Your Lordship's two letters, and they were all the more gratifying because unexpected; for when one begins mingling with prelates, he becomes like them, and it is all the greater miracle to find that Vergerio is the same Vergerio I used to know, and to perceive that he has not become, as I should have done, the apprentice and good fellow of the priests.' Aretino then continues: 'On the contrary, I discover the same gentle and lovable Pietro Paolo that you have always been, with me and with all; and so, I am glad, rather than sorry, for the transformation from the first profession to the second, since if self-preservation were the essence of good, I should have said you were better off at the Venetian than at the Roman court.'[840]

By 1543, however, before even Vergerio's first examination by the Holy Office, Aretino had become sufficiently frightened of the Inquisition's reach as to discontinue writing any more religious works from this point forward. One simply could not know which ideas would later be denounced as being undoctrinal or even heretical. It mattered not that earlier admirers had flattered Aretino that his sacrosanct scribblings united 'the subtlety of Augustine, the moral force of Gregory, Jerome's profundity of meaning, the weighty style of Ambrose'.[841] Those sacred writings which he had already penned were gathered together and published as a compendium in 1551 by the Aldine Press but, in other respects, the often imprudently outspoken satirist now considered it better to err on the side of caution where matters of faith were concerned and simple self-preservation now took sway over attempting to impress the Church establishment. Writing to the Pope in praise of the by now heretical Bernardino Ochino had also, upon reflection, been a hasty and imprudent act. Having said that, Aretino was still not one to abandon his friends. In May of 1548, when things were already getting very hot for Vergerio, we find Aretino still writing faithfully to him with words of moral support.

Aretino also persisted in committing potentially heretical thoughts to paper in his personal correspondence to secular figures. To Captain Francesco Faloppia, a sonnet-writing professional *condottiere*, Aretino wrote on 4 May 1542: 'I almost died laughing when they showed me the verses in which you say that if the three Magi had lived in my time, they would have had to pay tribute to me, just as—one might say—all the princes of the world already have done'.[842] Here was Aretino once more basking in a comparison between himself and Jesus Christ, a potentially dangerous exercise to say the least. August of that same year also finds Aretino writing to Marcolini heaping abuse on monks and friars, one of the satirist's favourite objects of derision: 'I couldn't care less, comrade, about these croaking friars who say that I am not fit to argue about our faith. At least I know better how to believe in Christ than they know how to talk about Him, and so from my discourses men are not led into the ways of doubt. I have made myself worship God in a silent heart rather than with a talkative mouth, wherefore I pay no attention to what these gentlemen gabble on about. As is obvious, most of them have put on the habit because they have been abandoned by Hope as well as by Fortune.'[843]

Also surprising, in light of the presence of the Holy Office in Venice, is Aretino's 1542 dedication of the second edition of the *Lettere* to the Protestant King Henry VIII. In August that year, Aretino wrote Henry one of his characteristically cloying letters in which he praised the arguably 'heretic' English King as having been produced by God 'not just by chance like other princes but with care and deliberation' before going on to eulogise: 'You are equal to the heavens; but in willing that men be freed from the obstacles of misery and want, you surpass them. I assert this, because they permit the insolence of malign influences, whereas you extirpate the iniquity of depraved wills. Thus the title of Godhead and the name of religion both befit you: you are rightly called divine, since all your deeds are immortal; and you bear the stamp of a priestly minister, considering that you always fulfil the duties of Christian worship, whose observance is integrity of purpose, testimony of goodness, fulfilment of the laws, and a sign of perfection.'[844] In return for Aretino's dedication, which had included the motto *Omnia vincit amor* ('Love conquers all') King Henry promised the poet *in compenso* 300 *scudi* but, as was usual with kings and their promises, the money never arrived. Two years before, in July 1540, the King had put to death his loyal and tireless Lord Chamberlain Thomas Cromwell. For the sake of continued good relations with King Henry, Aretino was of course willing to overlook the grisly affair and he had written at the time to Messer Antonio Carsidoni concerning Cromwell's downfall, attributing it not to King Henry but to the will of God: 'The terrible misfortune which has befallen my Lord Cromwell demonstrates, my good sir, how much more enduring are the gifts which come from everlasting God than those made by flighty fortune'.[845] To his credit Aretino nevertheless paused to acknowledge a debt to Cromwell: 'True, I lament his sad end. I received many benefits from him, although to be sure, it would have been good for his reputation if the courtesies he showed me at the command of the renowned Henry had been mixed with some generosities of his own. Be that as it may, I will never forget that I was once in his favour.'[846]

After Henry VIII had died in 1547, a rumour reached Aretino to the effect that the late King's ambassador Edward Harwell had pocketed the 300 *scudi* owed to him by the English crown. As usual Aretino took instant offence; without first seeking to substantiate the rumour with Harwell himself, the satirist took up his quill and published a libellous accusation that King Henry's envoy had stolen the money for his own personal enjoyment. Harwell, in a fit of pique, then waylaid the satirist in the streets with seven of his retainers and gave Aretino what the English would probably have described as a sound thrashing. Aretino, bruised and bleeding, was left face down in the gutter to ponder the results of his latest libel. The assault on Venice's most renowned resident playwright scandalised all of Venice, however, and Harwell, suitably embarrassed by his brutal and cowardly actions, called personally on the convalescent satirist at his *palazzo* to offer his sincerest apologies. He also paid him the long-withheld gratuity from Henry, which he may or may not have kept for his own uses earlier. Aretino, slow to bear a grudge once an apology and restitution had been made, received Harwell with great magnanimity and a show of forgiveness which impressed everyone in Venice.[847] The maestro of 'good press' had just earned himself a few more points in the esteem of his adoptive neighbours the Venetians. Remarked Aretino afterwards, he was 'glad to be given the opportunity of pardoning an affront.'

☉☾

On 12 July 1542, King François declared war on Charles V once again and a new phase in the Italian Wars now got underway. The ostensible reason given was the assassination by imperial soldiers the previous year of France's ambassador to the Ottoman court, Antoine de Rincon. This had occurred while de Rincon had been travelling through Italy in the proximity of Pavia. But as was always the case in the interminable conflict between these two monarchs, the real cause had been François's reluctance to surrender his claim to the duchy of Milan, the state which had been at the epicentre of the long series of wars stretching all the way back to 1494. An attempt to broker a lasting truce through the marriage of François's youngest son Charles, Duke of Orléans, to the Emperor's daughter Maria fell through when François refused to wait for the Dauphin to be given title to the Netherlands after the Emperor's death, demanding instead the immediate receipt of the Dutch territories in exchange for agreeing to relinquish Milan in perpetuity. François then resurrected his earlier alliance with the Turkish Sultan, who by April 1543 placed Khair ed-Din's Mediterranean fleet at France's disposal. All of Christendom was once more scandalised by this move. By the late summer of 1543, Charles V was making his way up through Italy on the way to the Brenner Pass en route to his German territories. High on his agenda was the need to extirpate the Lutheran heresy once and for all as a precursor to taking on François in this latest war.

Venice sent a high level delegation into the Veneto to welcome the Emperor as he passed through their territory. The late Francesco Maria della Rovere's son, the twenty-nine-year-old Guidobaldo II della Rovere, Duke of Urbino, was–out of deference to his father's longstanding relationship with the republic–assigned the honour of leading the delegation. A proud young man generally lacking in the literary accomplishments of Francesco Maria, he had expressed his eagerness to succeed his father visually, by having Agnolo Bronzino paint him in 1532 wearing an unabashedly enlarged red *braghetta* or codpiece, and standing with a massive hound, two very obvious and undeniable symbols of sexual potency. This had been a none too subtle hint that he was ready to rule in his own right, but he still had another six years to wait. After his father was assassinated in 1538, Guidobaldo had promptly shifted his residence from Urbino to Pesaro and began draining his duchy dry thanks to his extravagant living and high expenditure. Bartolomeo Campi of Pesari was commissioned to create his parade armour; Campi outshone even Filippo Negroli of Milan by devising an impressive cuirass of steel, gold, silver and brass, a year's work which he completed in just two months and which was much praised by Aretino.[848] Guidobaldo now renewed his father's past affiliation with Aretino by inviting the poet to accompany him on the prestigious mission to meet and greet the Emperor on Venetian soil. Aretino makes great play in a letter dated July 1543 to Titian of being unwilling to leave the comforts of Venice: 'For it is indeed true, brother, that the longing that I have for the Grand Canal is more than I can bear, nor do I ever put foot into stirrup without pining for the ease and comfort of a gondola ... And so if I get back there, if I crawl into my hole again, if I put all these emperors into their places, I won't ever again scurry off in such a mad hurry for all the treasures in the world. For all other places seem like hovels, huts and even dark caves when compared to my excellent and famous Venice.'[849]

For all his protestations, though, the opportunity to meet the most powerful paymaster in all of Christendom was too good to pass up and Aretino accepted the offer to go along. Their route from Venice would pass through Padua,[850] Vicenza and Verona[851] and the plan was to rendezvous with Charles at the hamlet of Peschiera on the banks of Lake Garda. Fittingly that same year, Aretino had already been immortalised in Titian's latest painting *Ecce Homo* as the representative of another emperor. In the canvas, Aretino had been depicted in a cameo portrait as Pontius Pilate, the governor of Judea under the Emperor Claudius. As already noted, Aretino had by now ceased writing anything of a religious stripe due to his deep-seated fear of the Holy Inquisition.[852] Whether, by depicting Aretino as the impartial Roman governor who gave Christ up to his fate, Titian was making some elliptical point about Aretino's apparent ambiguity when it came to matters of religion it is hard to say. But in his sky blue Roman armour Aretino certainly cuts a striking figure in Titian's painting. He would cut an equally impressive figure during his journey to meet the modern day Emperor. At Padua, Venice's university city, Aretino (who was greeted by his friends Nofri Camaiani and Giovanni dei Rossi) was acclaimed loudly by the townspeople, which according to the satirist included amongst their number '..a great crowd of scholars, moved more by natural curiosity than by any worth which I had'.[853] Passing through Vicenza and arriving in Verona, Aretino then described the scene which met his eyes: 'There, behold, there waited for us four ambassadors of the illustrious nobility, charming presence, and rare gravity. These men of judgement had been sent by the Republic [of Venice] to welcome reverently the august loftiness of Caesar.'[854]

When Aretino and Urbino's entourage arrived some distance from Peschiera and the black, double-headed eagles of the Habsburgs became visible on the road up ahead, Aretino was treated to the most prestigious reception of his entire life. A dark, solitary horseman rode out in advance of the imperial group asking who amongst them was Pietro Aretino. The inquisitive figure was none other than the Holy Roman Emperor Charles V. The Emperor's wife, Isabella of Portugal, had died in childbirth some four years earlier and to honour her memory Charles now always wore solemn black. The sombre figure, by now in his early forties, plain-speaking, his beard disguising his massive Habsburg chin, beckoned the cobbler's son from Arezzo to come forward 'commanding me with a nod to ride at his right hand'. Aretino did so, holding what the Barbary pirate Barbarossa had described as his 'magnificent head' high and proud. As the astonished courtiers and captains looked on, Aretino trotted at Charles's elbow, prattling on with some of his choicest flatteries and witty conversation while Charles obligingly listened, occasionally inclining his head towards the poet's prating mouth to better catch his remarks. 'At that point', records Aretino, 'my manifest unworthiness made me say to the true servant of God that he did not show himself toward me, an abject worm, to have other than the incomparable qualities of the sun. Nor did I err in saying this, for just as that mighty planet does not see any other luminary that equals it in radiance, so also its rays do not do other than bring life and reinvigoration to whatsoever wretched shepherd in his hovel.' Charles in turn regaled the 'abject worm' Aretino with 'the outcome of the disastrous expedition against Algiers' which caused the satirist to weep genuine tears of sorrow. Eventually the party reached the town of Peschiera, Charles having all this while 'consented to talk to me and listen to me in a sweetly intimate and friendly manner'.[855]

Later that evening, before the party entered the imperial pavilion for the ceremonial banquet, Aretino declaimed a long laudatory *capitolo* (a stanzaic *terza rima* or *'third rhyme'*) which he had prepared for the occasion: *Il capitolo e il sonetto in laude de lo Imperatore*[856]. When the party then went inside to dine it was Aretino, and not the head of the diplomatic mission Guidobaldo della Rovere, who was afforded the supreme honour of sitting at Charles's right hand and as they ate the two men engaged as equals in an entertaining tête-à-tête. Throughout the rest of his brief sojourn Charles treated Aretino with inordinate respect, acknowledging and greeting the poet with a smile whenever he encountered him. But when Charles was due to leave and proceed on his journey, the Emperor looked around in vain for Aretino, who had already departed the town without bidding Charles goodbye ('I did not follow him any further', the poet would write, 'The reason that I did not follow him was that it did not please God that I should'.) The Emperor despatched his courtier Niccolò Zeno to search for Aretino at his lodgings and the latter expressed his wonder to Giovanni dei Rossi how 'Even though his sovereign mind was still occupied with the revolts in Flanders, the rash conduct of Cleves, the potency of France, and the raids of Barbarossa, he still did not abstain from acknowledging with every possible sign of pleasure my devotions towards his deity'.[857]

Before the two men, one the most powerful man in Europe and the other a shoemaker's son made-good, had parted ways, the former had attempted in vain—as he had also been unsuccessful in the case of Titian—to persuade Aretino to come with him back to Germany and ultimately permanently to Madrid.[858] The offer was an enticing one which might conceivably even open the gates of heaven itself. Had not the lowly Sienese humanist Æneas Silvius Piccolomini been poet laureate to the Emperor Frederick III prior to his becoming a cardinal and then later ascending the chair of St. Peter? The same Piccolomini in fact who had earlier enjoyed a career as the writer of such titillating trifles as *The Tale of Two Lovers*? As tempting as the offer may have been to become to Charles V's court 'creature', Aretino could not find it in himself to accept. Unlike the more retiring and reclusive Titian, Aretino's personality would undoubtedly have been more than equal to the fawning Spanish courtiers surrounding the Emperor. It was not that. Aretino simply could not leave his beloved adopted home of Venice to chance fate and lose his freedom and independence in Charles's personal service. Duke Guidobaldo would later chide Aretino about the satirist's vow, telling him: 'When I thought that you might follow the Emperor I knew that I would have no peace of mind until I restored you to Venice'.[859] Though emperors wanted him in their service, Pietro Aretino was his own man always.

The Emperor was gracious about the poet's rejection of his offer. He commended Aretino to the Venetian ambassadors and bade them treat him well, telling them that 'Aretino's person is something very dear in my affection' ('*rispetto alla persona dello Aretino come cosa carissima alla mia affetione*').[860] To Giovanni dei Rossi the poet confessed: 'When the wise, learned and loyal secretary Rhamberti told me this, I was stunned, yet not so much so that I did not lift my hands to heaven, for my reputation esteemed it a higher privilege to keep alive this memory than my mortal body would have a permanent source of income which would take from it its needs'.[861] The poet's return to Venice was enthusiastically received as though he were an official ambassador of the republic returning from a successful diplomatic assignment.[862] Aretino had of course been famous well before the year 1543 but his triumph in meeting with the Emperor Charles had transformed him into one of the most celebrated men not just in Venice but indeed throughout all of Italy. It is from this point forward that Aretino's reputation as an early Renaissance celebrity or (to coin that modern expression) 'superstar' really took off. Some of the praise even bordered on the blasphemous: 'One might well say that you, most divine Signor Pietro, are neither Prophet nor Sibyl, but rather the very Son of God, seeing that God is the highest truth in heaven, and you are truth on earth',[863] remarked one of his correspondents. Pietro Aretino was by now larger than life.

The writer Girolamo Parabosco would later immortalise Aretino in 1551 in *I Diporti*, Parabosco's own quirky version of Boccaccio's *Decameron*. Parabosco's work tells the tale of a group of seventeen illustrious gentlemen, including Pietro Aretino, Sperone Speroni, Ercole Bentivoglio and Alessandro Lambertino, who are out for a hunting trip in one of the Venetian lagoons. As the inclement weather has not proven conducive to an enjoyable hunt they decide instead to tell each other stories and this intermission takes place over the course of three days. A fictionalised Aretino delivers one of these stories. We find Parabosco also composing a *capitolo* mentioning, amongst others, Aretino as attending the famous literary *salon* of Domenico Venier:

> I'll go ever so often to the Veniers' house
> Where I've never gone for four whole years
> Without learning about a thousand things.
> For eminent spirits are always there
> And folk reason divinely there
> Among that company of rare men.
> Who Badoer is you know, and who Molino is,
> Who the father of the stanza, and Amalteo,
> Corso, Sperone, and Aretino.
> Each one in the sciences is a Capaneus,
> Great, I mean, and so equal are they
> That if one is an Amphion, the other is an

Orpheus.[864]

Parabosco's work also in turn inspired imitations such as Valerio Marcellino's *Il diamerone* (1561),[865] which would depict both Parabosco and Aretino some years after they were already dead. Thus the poet entered the fictive imagination of other writers who now gladly paid homage to him in their work.

But this kind of fame also inevitably brought the naysayers out of the woodwork. As his renown grew, Aretino had no shortage of enemies and detractors, especially in the literary world ('the good things said about me are not growing more, and the spiteful things are not growing less'),[866] but he remained philosophical about their attacks on him. Neither did he expect others to stand up for him, no matter how well intentioned their motivation in doing so. To a fellow Aretine, Nofri Camaiani, he had written in April 1542: 'My son, when you take up cudgels on my behalf against those who say nasty things about my doings, you think you are defending me but you are really harming me. You see, all the hate that those bestial fellows have for me comes from my being what I am in spite of anything that they can do, and to pay any attention to what they say is like taking away from dogs the right to bark. Do not, then, say anything more to them about me, for, as I have said, you will harm me by defending me. The greatest glory anyone can have, is to have his merits envied.'[867] The secret of Aretino's insouciance towards his many detractors may perhaps be found in his letter to Marcolini dated March 1545 in which he writes: 'In my opinion, envy is nothing else but the dagger which the envied are forever thrusting into the heart of the enviers who die every day from these thrusts and yet do not ever die'.[868]

At the same time, Aretino seems to have been disinclined to offer his enemies any grounds for criticism which could hurt him and sometimes went out of his way to thwart his own interests simply to deny his naysayers any ammunition. Aretino would, for example, later write to his half-brother Francesco Bacci, affirming that the Emperor had wanted to bestow a knighthood upon him at Verona but that he had declined. The amusingly cryptic reason he gave for this was, to be sure, a typical Aretine witticism: 'It is true, brother, as many knights well know, that I refused the knighthood with which the Emperor wished to honour me. The reason is that it is more to my credit to have people going about trying to discover why I was *not* given such a rank than it would be to have them clamouring to find out why I *was* given it.'[869]

☉☾

As for the satirist himself he was thankful to be back in Venice again, had renewed his vow never to leave, and had not–above the usual Aretine chest-beating–allowed his experience with the Emperor to go unduly to his head. In a letter dated May 1544 to Titian, Aretino waxes lyrical over his beloved Venice, describing 'Infinite boats, some laden with foreigners and others with the people of our own city … moving about on the water. They diverted not only the onlookers, but the Grand Canal itself which diverts all those who plough its waves.' He goes on to describe some fun on the Grand Canal: 'In front of my eyes, two gondolas were having a race. Each was guided by a famous boatman and their contest gave great sport to a crowd of spectators, which thronged the Rialto Bridge, the fish markets, the Santa Sofia ferry landing, and the Casa da Mosto to see the regatta.'[870] To his printer and publisher Marcoloni we find Aretino writing in August that same year, bemoaning the abundance of new correspondents who have written to him in expectation of a personalised reply: 'I have heard the hullabaloo set up by those who complain that I never answer what they are forever writing me. But if it suited me to make reply to all those who send me letters, I would have to have the assiduous patience of the tribe of pedagogues who cement their back sides into the chairs of study. That is where the good-for-littles spend the total of their days and the sum of all their nights.'[871] In January 1545, Aretino writes again to Marcolini rehearsing once more those traits which have contributed to his fame and success: 'Take it, my good friend, as an inevitable consequence of my greatness that you should again hear it said that it is because of fear and not from love that the mighty give me presents every day'. But surely, isn't it better to be loved rather than feared? Aretino offers the procatalepsis: 'It is true that if I were a prince I would hold it more fitting to be loved than feared. But I am Pietro and count it a happier fate to have the lords tremble before me than I would call it good fortune to have them adore me.'[872]

Life for Aretino's friend Titian, meanwhile, was not so blessed. Doge Andrea Gritti had died in December 1538 and the painter had lost a staunch supporter who recognised in his talents an artist capable of glorifying Venice and those notables who served her. His replacement was Pietro Lando, an aging aristocrat who had earlier been forced to make a humiliating peace with the Ottoman Turks. His age and his exclusive preoccupation with political affairs made him a poor replacement for Gritti as a patron of the arts. Nevertheless Titian, as official painter, was obliged to paint his portrait, which he duly completed the following year together with a sister portrait of the doge's relative, Count Agostino Lando. To the latter, Aretino wrote on 15 November 1539, informing the Count that the esteemed artist 'continually sees you alive in the portrait, which is full of the spirit infused into it by the divinity of his pencil' and closed by affectionately thanking Lando for 'the anchovies you sent us; and the sweet ripe apples resembling the sweetness and suavity of your Lordship's conversation'.[873]

For the church of Santa Maria della Salute, Titian next painted the pendentives of the cupola, making the three violent stories of the Death of Abel, the Sacrifice of Abraham, and David and Goliath the central themes. Dispirited, Titian then drifted to Rome between autumn 1545 and June 1546 at the invitation of Cardinal Alessandro Farnese. He left his friend Aretino behind to suffer in the heat wave which was roasting Venice that summer ('..sweat has turned my person into, as it were, an alembic which distils away my living flesh and bones. Clad only in a shirt and without breeches, I toss this way and then that way, more like a dumb animal than a man,' Aretino wrote to Lodovico Domenichi.)[874] In cooler, but not much cooler, Rome, Titian was treated like visiting nobility and given sumptuous lodgings in the Belvedere Palace ('Nor could I be other than moved to the depths of my heart at the friendliness shown to you by the blessed Pope who is our lord', Aretino wrote to his absent friend in October 1545, 'But it is characteristic of the House of Farnese to abound in a great plenty of kindly deeds'.)[875] Giorgio Vasari, who had himself recently returned to Rome from Naples, was assigned to bring Titian around the city and keep the aging painter company.[876] Aretino chided his friend for not having gone to Rome sooner: 'I can well believe you, however, when you lament that the idea of betaking yourself to Rome did not come to you twenty years ago. For if you are astounded at it as you find it now, what would you have thought of it if you had seen it in the state in which it was when I left it? For you must surely know that this great city is now still in the confusion of her evil days, and that she is much like an egregious prince whom bad fortune has sent into exile. He is gripped by anguish, but he is still a prince in the virtue of his generous and royal nature.'[877]

Titian was commissioned by the Pope to paint him alongside his two grandsons Cardinal Alessandro and Ottavio Farnese the duke of Parma. The painting would pay homage to Raphael's earlier canvas depicting Pope Leo X with his two nephew cardinals Giulo de' Medici and Luigi de' Rossi. Titian's canvas, which has since provoked a good deal of controversy, depicted Pope Paul III being greeted by Ottavio, who is caught in the act of bending down to kiss the pontiff's slipper. Meanwhile, a watchful Cardinal Alessandro Farnese observes his relative's obsequious act with sacerdotal detachment. Many critics have noted the dynamic interplay between Ottavio's fawning insincerity and the Pope's own cunning and guarded reserve and the fact that the painting appears dramatically unfinished has even raised the suggestion that Titian was forced to abandon it because it caused offense to the subjects. Vasari's own statement that the portrait was 'all admirably executed to the great satisfaction of these lords' would however seem to contradict this assessment. In 1543, Titian had already painted an earlier portrait Pope Paul III which had been produced during the pope's visit to Northern Italy. At that time Aretino had written to Titian praising the painter for having declined the Pope's offer to make him *piombatore* ('But every masterpiece of yours, even though it be divine, has to take second place to what you did in scorning to accept something that any other painter would have called himself happy to have obtained' Aretino had remarked),[878] and there is hence little reason to imagine that the artist had subsequently placed himself under a cloud with the new painting.

While in Rome, Titian also had leisure to paint other commissions, including a Danaë for Cardinal Alessandro Farnese. While Titian was busy painting it, Vasari brought Michelangelo along to his studio to watch the Venetian painter at work. Both spectators offered Titian high praise for his latest canvas, however when they were out of earshot Michelangelo turned to Vasari and 'strongly commended him, declaring that he liked his colouring and style very much but that it was a pity artisans in Venice did not learn to draw well from the beginning and that Venetian painters did not have a better method of study'.[879] What Buonarroti was alluding to of course was the unique habit of Venetian painters to apply oils directly to the canvas without having worked up a great many drawings and cartoon sketches to first determine the basics of composition. Clearly, to his way of thinking, Michelangelo's central Italian school of painting, in which the fundamental problems of design had been fully resolved before brush had even touched canvas, was far superior to the Venetian method, where the painter proceeded empirically, experimenting with different compositions directly to the medium.[880] Under the circumstances it was hence a little ironic that Aretino was at this time urging Titian to study the work of others: 'Do keep in mind the accomplishments of every painter, and especially those of our friend, Fra Bastiano. Study carefully the wood carving of Bucino, and compare in your own mind the statues of our gossip, Messer Jacopo [Sansovino], with those carved by men who, since they compete with him without justification, are rightly criticised.'[881]

In January 1546, Aretino wrote again to Titian with news that one of Sansovino's buildings had collapsed and the architect himself had been arrested by the authorities 'whereupon the joyous pleasure which filled me upon having these words from you, was changed into sorrow and affliction as I learned of his misfortune'.[882] Aretino was referring to the structure facing the Doge's Palace in the Piazza San Marco which Sansovino was raising to house Venice's national library, whose librarian-curator was none other than Pietro Bembo. Whilst work was nearing completion the vault of the building had suddenly collapsed due to a severe frost. Afterwards, Sansovino had been clapped in irons as though he were some unreliable *condottiere* who had contravened his orders. The incident reminded Aretino of the vagaries of the wheel of fortune. 'You can imagine how I felt when the actual mishap made me realise that any evil can come true', Aretino wrote in the same letter to Titian. It was only through the satirist's considerable lobbying prowess that Sansovino was eventually released, having been obliged to cough up the expenses caused by the unforeseen structural mishap. 'And so our worthy friend is in the same happy state he was in before, and the person who committed the rash act of thinking he did well by arresting him, is in prison himself', Aretino had merrily concluded.

Titian had scarcely been back in Venice two years when he was called away once more, this time to Augsburg by the Emperor. Here, he was to paint several portraits commemorating Charles's recent victory over the Lutheran Schmalkaldic League at the battle of Mühlberg as well as the various glittering court personalities who had gathered in the German city for the Diet of Augsburg. Aretino lauded the Emperor's reliance upon Titian's genius: 'Neither Apelles, nor Praxiteles, not any of the others who of old carved statues or painted pictures of whatsoever Prince or King, can boast of having received rewards of gold or gems that even partly approached the reward that you have received from His Most High Majesty when he deemed that you alone were worthy to be summoned to him in the midst of such disordered times. He thus showed that he attached more importance to you than he does to all the leagues and the alliances which he is organising throughout the world.'[883] But the journey to fulfil his latest imperial commission was not easy for a man who was by now in his late fifties. With his ever helpful and loyal son Orazio, his nephew Cesare Vecellio and his student the Dutchman Lambert Sustris, Titian struggled over the freezing, wintry Alpine passes to Augsburg in January 1548.[884]

Titian spent his long months at Augsburg productively. In addition to the magnificent equestrian *Charles V at Mühlberg*, he would also paint a seated portrait of the Emperor which was perhaps designed to evoke the subject's divinity, since seated paintings were usually reserved almost exclusively for popes.[885] His work engrossed him so much that he became remiss in failing to keep up with Aretino's correspondence. This caused the disgruntled satirist to send him the following missive in April 1548, which began with a rebuke: 'Although I have had only one letter from you since you arrived at court, I cannot yet persuade myself that the favours of His Majesty have so inflated your ego that you no longer deign to notice your friends', but which signed off with the tender words, 'In the meantime Sansovino kisses you on the face and I kiss you on the forehead'.[886] Aretino's dear friend would return briefly to Venice to resume his usual convivial round of dinner parties at his large, commodious home in Cannaregio. The house still stands to this day, just off the quiet street called the Calle Larga dei Boteri in a small courtyard which is named for Tiziano. There is an unassuming gate bearing a plaque reading HANC DOMVM COLVIT TITIANVS VECELLIVS beyond which is what was once Titian's garden. The house, an imposing three storey affair, has in recent years been renovated by a former Cosmopolitan magazine model and her husband. It was here that Titian welcomed his friends Aretino, Sansovino and others like the humanist and philologist Francesco Priscianese, who has left us this delightful description of one of Titian's gatherings which was held one day in the year 1540:

'There were assembled with the said M. Tiziano, as like desires like, some of the most celebrated characters that are now in this city, and of ours chiefly M. Pietro Aretino, a new miracle of nature, and next to him as great an imitator of nature with the chisel as the master of the feast is with his pencil, Messer Jacopo Tatti, called *il Sansovino*, and M. Jacopo Nardi [a Florentine historian], and I; so that I made the fourth amidst so much wisdom. Here, before the tables were set out, because the sun, in spite of the shade, still made his heat much felt, we spent the time in looking at the lively figures in the excellent pictures, of which the house was full, and in discussing the real beauty and charm of the garden with singular pleasure and note of admiration of all of us. It is situated in the extreme part of Venice, upon the sea, and from it one seas the pretty little island of Murano, and other beautiful places. This part of the sea, as soon as the sun went down, swarmed with gondolas adorned with beautiful women, and resounded with varied harmony and music of voices and instruments which till midnight accompanied our delightful supper.'[887]

Following this all too brief idyll, Titian would be called away to Augsburg once more from November 1550 to May 1551, during which time he would complete a second full-length portrait of the Emperor's son Philip. An initial portrait which Titian had painted of Philip earlier in Milan in 1548 would be sent by the Prince's aunt, Mary of Hungary to Mary Tudor to assist in the dynastic marriage negotiations then ongoing between England and the Empire. Mary of Hungary passed the comment that 'Titian's pictures not bearing to be looked at too closely, it would enable the Queen, by adding three years to the Prince's age, to judge of his present appearance'.[888] Mary Tudor was, by all accounts, well pleased with the likeness of her suitor. Philip would become an important patron for the artist, especially after 1556. Aretino would be sorry to see his friend leave again so soon. Around this time we detect a certain mellowing in Aretino's attitudes towards material things and an admission instead that friendship is the most important thing in the world. To Jacopo Sansovino's son Francesco, Aretino writes in February 1550: 'He who deserves to have that which he does not have, is a worthy fellow like me. He who thinks he will enjoy the many things which he does not deserve, is a shabby one like you. So, instead of boasting about your possessions, you should keep still. Even if I have nothing else, I have friends, and since there are no jewels more precious than these, I find myself rich and you wretched, who do not even love yourself.'[889]

CHAPTER 16

Final Years

But ha! I laugh at the dream I dreamed last night while sleeping. Resting in my bed with my eyes shut, I saw a devil and an angel side by side. They said to me that, when it pleased God, my soul would go to the other world post-haste, and that it would spend one month in Hell, and another month in Heaven. "How so?" I asked. They answered that the praises given by me to great lords who did not deserve them, condemned me to the abyss as a liar, but that the rebukes with which I had buried them alive, won me Heaven and its joy.

Pietro Aretino to Giovanni Battista Coppola,
December 1554.

Aretino's circle at this time continued to be diverse, comprising both literary men as well as men of action. Sometimes, as in the case of Collaltino Collalto, the two qualities managed to be combined in a single person. Collaltino, a nobleman, landholder, soldier and poet from the Friuli region on the mainland, was an associate of Lodovico Domenichi, Lodovico Dolce, Girolamo Muzio and also Pietro Aretino, who was godfather to his brother Vinciguerra's child and to whom he wrote some of his *lettere*.[890] His secretary Giuseppe Betucci was the author of the acclaimed erotic work *Il Raverta* and Collaltino had attended the same literary salons as the celebrated poetess Gaspara Stampa. Stampa was the daughter of a Paduan jeweller who had been brought to live in Venice by her mother following her father's death. Both she and her sister Cassandra performed as virtuoso singers in the salons of the city's élite and this had been her introduction to Venice's cultural scene. In 1549, Gaspara–who was in love with Collaltino–had sent her beloved one hundred of her love poems, the famous collection known as the *Rime*, which she dedicated to her fickle lover. Sadly, however, her love would remain unreciprocated. Collaltino left Italy that same summer to offer his sword to the new King Henry II of France against his English adversaries at the siege of Boulogne-sur-Mer. The year 1554 found him back once more in Italy, fighting in various parochial conflicts pertaining to Parma, Bologna and Siena.[891] In 1558, an embittered Collaltino entered the territory of the Venetian Republic at the head of a private army with the intention of settling a family dispute with his relatives. For this violation of Venice's sovereignty he was pronounced exiled. A collection of Collaltino's mediocre poems was printed by Giolito in 1545 and again in 1549.[892] He would die in 1569. His admirer, Gaspara Stampa, died in April 1554, the year of the prodigal's return to Italy, 'from fever, colic, and matrix sickness'. Cassandra Stampa had her sister's poems published posthumously.

Seldom it seemed did the course of true love run smooth. In 1549, Aretino's daughter Adria was married to a minor nobleman named Diovatelli Rota, aged around thirty and from Bergamo, but who was at this time however a resident of the duchy of Urbino.[893] Adria herself was by now thirteen years old, but she had been advertised for betrothal some two years earlier at the age of eleven. Today we flinch at her youth but betrothal, if not actual consummation, at this age was a fairly common practice at the time. Diovatelli, who himself possessed property worth 5,000 crowns,[894] had been drawn to the generous dowry which Aretino had promised for his daughter, the sum of 1,000 ducats in all. But the profligate and spendthrift Aretino, who had no inheritance money or wealthy relatives to rely on to help assemble the dowry, was instead forced to depend upon patronage. Accordingly, 500 ducats of Adria's dot had been contributed by the cardinal of Ravenna, Benedetto Accolti, some of the remaining balance by Charles V's Spanish ambassador Diego de Mendoza, and the Duke of Florence had also agreed to contribute some 300 crowns from his own chest. Nevertheless the latter, knowing Aretino's legendary extravagance, would only agree to part with the money once Adria was safely married, and he wrote to Aretino: 'From your natural liberality, which is no vice, you might put the amount to some other use'.[895] The marriage ceremony finally took place in March 1549, but the conniving Diovatelli refused to leave the Palazzo Aretino until the entire dowry amount had been paid, at which point Aretino, who was still outstanding the sum promised by a diffident Duke Cosimo, peevishly threatened to pawn a gold collar gifted to him by the future Philip II of Spain just to make up the shortfall.

When the couple arrived at Urbino in June 1550, Duke Guidobaldo della Rovere graciously sent his guard cavalry to meet them eight miles from the city gates to escort them back. Upon arrival the couple found the entire city of Urbino lit up in their honour and the duke and duchess came to greet Adria and her new spouse in person. However, despite this highly auspicious beginning, the union would tragically prove to be an unhappy one. The reality was that Diovatelli had only ever been interested in Adria's considerable dowry and once this was in his possession he soon began neglecting his unfortunate young bride. By 1554, Duke Guidobaldo himself was begging Aretino to take the girl out of the marital home and repatriate her to Venice, which he duly did. In Venice, Adria had 'recounted the torments, the villainies, and the cruelties put upon her by her mother-in-law, her brother-in-law, her sister-in-law and all her relatives', a series of revelations which, Aretino recorded, 'reduced the worthy Titian to a state of anguish'.[896]

Diovatelli pursued his runaway bride back to Venice. In a tearful reunion he promised Adria that 'her mother-in-law had gone to a nunnery, his brother to a monastery forever, and that only an old family servant remained who would stay by her side and serve her'.[897] But sadly it was all soft soap designed to entice her back under the spousal roof. When Adria returned with him once more to Urbino her frightful in-laws immediately placed her under lock and key. Half-starved, the poor girl was then forbidden from wearing jewellery ('Who do you think you are?' her brother-in-law, an abbot, raged at her as though she were one of her father's *cortigiane*, 'Who do you think you will ever be? Take those off your wrists, you hussy! Take that off your neck, you bitch!')[898] Her husband 'the base-born Bergamasque' Diovatelli meanwhile gave her nothing to wear except 'a rag of sackcloth to cover her back' whilst bullying Adria to part with a valuable diamond which 'she wanted to keep as a remembrance' of her father, Aretino. In a letter to the Duke dated November 1554, Aretino pleaded with Guidobaldo to intercede with the cruel Rota family and extend his protection to his beloved Adria: 'take my modest little daughter under your protection until such time—may it be soon—that she is restored to me. Since you know that it is God who hath bestowed on us the light of His sun and of His moon and His stars, I know that you will not deprive me of so humble and so seemly a grace.'[899] This plea was duly granted and Adria would go to live under the shelter of the duchess of Urbino.

Aretino was most touching in his obvious devotion to his daughters Adria and Austria. Here is no trace of the man whom James Dennistoun would later decry as being 'destitute of moral or religious principle'. When Adria was eight years old he had described her as his soul ('*Adria mia figlia e anima*'). Soon after her birth he wrote to Sebastiano del Piombo, painting the picture of an indulgent *papa*: 'I must submit to being her plaything, for what are we fathers but our own children's clowns? The little innocents climb all over us, pull at our beards, beat our faces with their fists, and rumple our hair. It is for such coin that they sell us the kisses we imprint upon them and the hugs with which we bind them to us.

Nor is there any pleasure in the world that could equal the delight this brings us, if only the fear that something bad might happen to them did not constantly keep us uneasy of mind.'[900] For Adria he would commission a 45 millimetres diameter bronze medal with her mother Caterina depicted on one side and Adria on the other facing left, wearing a gown, a mantle secured at the left shoulder, an ear-ring and braided hair and with the inscription HADRIA DIVI PETRI ARETINI FILIA ('Adria, daughter of the divine Pietro Aretino'). The medal was an admission of paternity in lieu of any birth certificate or other legitimate notarised document and showed the lengths to which Aretino (the notorious fornicator) was prepared to go to acknowledge to the world that Adria was his natural daughter.[901] In light of her precarious marital situation and the abuse of the Rota family it was clearly done to help bolster her spirits and rally support around her during this most difficult time. Sadly, however, his beloved Adria did not live out the year in Urbino. Disillusioned and heartbroken by her experience of marriage to the cruel Diovatelli, Adria died in 1554 aged just seventeen. Aretino, as can be imagined, was devastated.

Around the same time that Adria was being married to Diovatelli Rota and going to live in Urbino, Rome and Christendom was transitioning to a new pope for Paul III had died on 10 November 1549 at the age of eighty-one. Aretino's close friends who had influence in Rome had lobbied Pope Paul throughout his pontificate to confer a cardinal's hat on the poet-satirist. The idea of the debauched Aretino garbed in the *pallium* or cardinal's mantle, the *biretum* or scarlet cap, and the *galerus*, the broad-brimmed tasselled hat, may on the surface seem vaguely ludicrous. But it was hardly unusual for literary figures, even those with distinctly worldly tastes and proclivities such as Pietro Bembo, who had only recently died in January 1547, or indeed Bernardo Dovizi de Bibbiena, author of that cross-dressing extravaganza *La Calandria*, to be made princes of the Holy Roman Church. Aretino's ambition in this regard cannot be so easily dismissed therefore as being merely some vague pipe dream. All depended on pleasing the Supreme Pontiff and obtaining his patronage. The late Pope's grandson, Ottavio Farnese the duke of Parma, had also lobbied Paul III on Aretino's behalf, telling him: 'Every day of your life, Holy Father, you make men who are poor and of low degree cardinals, for no other reason than that they have served our family faithfully at all times. You have acted wisely and laudably in so doing. But if such persons have seemed to you fit for such high promotion, what would you not gain by bestowing a similar advancement on Pietro Aretino?' Ottavio finished his missive by concluding that Aretino 'may be poor and baseborn. But he is on good terms with every prince in the world. If he should receive this dignity from you he would render you immortal'.[902]

Purchasing an eternity of 'good press' for the price of a cardinal's *biretum* might, according to anyone's conception of a bargain, have been regarded as a farsighted insurance policy. However, Paul III–a rather difficult and ungenerous character–had remained diffident towards Aretino and the latter had eventually relapsed into his usual stance of hurt and wounded pride. Aretino issued a scathing new sonnet from the relative safety of Venice which criticised the Pope's nepotism:

Dimmi, o Farnese mio, padre coscritto,
che con sì grande onor fusti sensale
del sangue tuo per esser cardinale,
qual stella t'ha fra noi papa prescritto?
Tu piggior sei ch'un Crasso al mondo scritto
e della fe/ nimico capitale,
superbo e vile inventor d'ogni male,
ch'n croce hai Cristo mille volte fitto.

('Tell me, my friend Farnese, conscript father, you who to your honour traded your own flesh and blood to become cardinal, what star has singled you out among us to be Pope? Everybody knows you are worse than Crassus and a mortal enemy of the faith, a proud and cowardly inventor of all evil, who has nailed Christ to the cross a thousand times').[903]

Titian had, as we have seen, already lobbied Charles V in person on Aretino's behalf throughout the whole of his first visit to Augsburg whilst carrying out portraits and other commissions for the Emperor. Titian's letter to Aretino on this very subject on 11 November 1550 came a year to the day after Pope Paul's death. From Titian had come the following encouraging report, not only concerning Charles, who regarded the application with favour, but also touching upon other important and influential personages too: 'Not a day passes but the Duke of Alva speaks to me of the Divine Aretino because he loves you much; and he says he will favour your interest with His Majesty. I told him that you would spend the world, that what you got you shared with everyone, and that you gave to the poor even the clothes on your back, which is true as everyone knows.'[904] Titian also includes the bishop of Arras and the English ambassador to the imperial court, Sir Philip Hoby, as being amongst those whom he has tirelessly lobbied on Aretino's behalf. Overjoyed at this encouraging news, Aretino replied to Titian: 'Who would not rejoice in his heart, when he heard with what affectionate benignity of grace His Majesty, as soon as he saw you, asked how I was, and whether you brought letters from me, and then added (after he had first read to himself and then aloud what I had humbly written him) that although he had not yet exerted his good offices with the Pope on my behalf, he would answer my letter immediately?'[905]

The new pope with whom Aretino would need to contend for his cardinal's hat was a fellow Aretine, Giovanni Maria Ciocchi del Monte, who assumed the name Pope Julius III. Born in 1487 in Rome, he had followed his father–an illustrious Roman jurist–into the law, following which he studied theology under the Dominican Ambrosius Catharinus. Later he became the bishop of Siponto in 1512 and then bishop of Pavia in 1520. During the Sack of Rome in 1527 he had very nearly lost his life. Held as a hostage for Pope Clement VII he had been strung up by his hair in the Campo di Fiori by the brutal German *landsknechts* but had been rescued by Cardinal Pompeo Colonna.[906] Aretino proceeded according to his customary form. Upon his elevation Aretino wrote the new pope a laudatory sonnet which included the lines '*Ecco pur, die in prò nostro, ha Dio converso, In Iulio Terzo, il Gran Iulio Secondo...*'[907] The lines were a great hit. Aretino received 1,000 gold crowns from Rome and was decreed a *gonfalonier* of his native town of Arezzo. Then, in June 1550, more honours and emoluments followed. Aretino was created *Cavaliere di S. Pietro*, a knight of St. Peter, a papal designation which came with a welcome pension of 80 *scudi* per year.

Whilst scooping these precious fees Aretino nevertheless continued to pompously praise 'the riches of poverty' to one of his correspondents, Luigi Caorlino, with whom he commiserated: 'I am very happy that since fortune has ruined you, taking from you your wealth but not your wits, you are making your sons learn how to be skilful in some art. It not only pleases me, but I praise it. For the arts are the richnesses of poverty and he who can follow one may have nothing, yet he possess enough.'[908] Caorlino was a member of the Cavorlini family, merchants of Venice and neighbours of Aretino who had fallen on hard times in recent years. To Titian and Sansovino, meanwhile, Aretino was expressing the contrary argument and praising conspicuous consumption: 'You should spend freely, and dress yourself lovingly in perfumed clothes. For there is no folly like that of one who amasses a fortune for his heirs, depriving himself of the smallest luxury and discovering that his great accumulation has made him hateful to his friends, to his relatives and to God.'[909]

Meanwhile, things seemed to be going well with Aretino's bid to reinvent himself as a cardinal. Messer Vicenzo di Poggio, whilst en route to Palestine, wrote Aretino when he passed through Rome: '..in the streets and houses of the citizens bets are offered and taken on the honours that await you. It is publicly said that His Holiness and his friends love and esteem you beyond measure, comparing you with the hydra which grows seven new heads in the place of every one cut off ... your old enemies now act and speak as if they were your fathers, sons or brothers

... at an assembly of the Knights of St. Peter I was surrounded by the members, who all asked for news of the lord Aretino, crying, "How is he and when will he be coming to Rome?"'[910] Duke Guidobaldo of Urbino now contacted Aretino, imploring him to join him on the road to Rome whence he needed to go to take up his new post as captain-general of the Church. Just as he had introduced Aretino to the Emperor some years earlier, he now offered to introduce the satirist to the new bishop of Rome. This was in February 1553 and Aretino was at first edgy about the prospect of leaving the safety of Venice for Rome after all these years. But he relented when he heard that if he were to venture to Rome the Pope would see to it that 'it would be like a second Jubilee because all the world would flock to see him'.[911] Writing in March to the duke of Urbino he begged for additional funds on top of the 100 gold crowns which Guidobaldo had already sent him: 'For, look you, half of the money I have received has already been laid out for a jerkin of velvet and satin which is no less seemly than it is handsome. And don't you realise that I will need four others to wear at our receptions and on the road? Nor have I even mentioned hosen, greatcoats, caps, shoes, slippers, riding boots, capes, valises and strongboxes, nor have I opened my mouth about liveries for my serving man..'[912] By May 1553, having dallied in Urbino just long enough to visit his unhappy daughter Adria under the Rota family roof, Aretino had set out from Urbino for Rome in the company of the Duke.

Upon arrival in the eternal city, Pope Julius III welcomed Aretino as 'fratello fraterna' (a fraternal brother),[913] even rising unsteadily from the papal throne to help the unwieldy satirist up from his knees, after which the Pope kissed him tenderly on the forehead. The datarius Gian Matteo Giberti was already long dead in 1543; so too was his odious creature and poet-lapdog Francesco Berni. Most of those now remaining in the eternal city were, unless he had attacked them personally over the years, reasonably well-disposed towards Aretino. The debonair satirist had every reason to imagine that his bid for a cardinal's hat might at last be realised. However, it was not to be. Julius III was, despite all appearances to the contrary, no easy touch. He had come to power partly at least due to the influence of Duke Cosimo I of Florence and yet the Pope was at that time being niggardly in granting Cosimo's eight-year-old second son Giovanni a cardinal's hat by way of gratitude.[914] If Pope Julius III could defy such a powerful former sponsor as Cosimo de' Medici, how much easier would it be for him to conveniently ignore the aspirations of a satirising serial blackmailer like Pietro Aretino? Throughout the long, hot summer of 1553, Aretino loitered in Rome's stifling heat. By August it was obvious to the writer that Pope Julius had absolutely no intention of raising him to the cardinalate and so, disappointed but perhaps for once in his life philosophical about the situation, he took his leave of Rome, this time forever.

☉︎☾

The satirist returned to Venice in September 1553 by way of Pesaro and Urbino, where he paused to declaim a new *capitolo* in honour of his patron Duke Guidobaldo. He later claimed that the cardinal's hat had in fact been offered to him but that he had refused to accept it, something that all his friends and acquaintances knew to be highly improbable. But this time he refrained from lambasting Pope Julius personally. He could so easily have done so for the Pope had laid a fertile ground for satirists. The Cupid and Psyche cycle painted in the Pope's apartment in the Castel Sant'Angelo by Perino del Vaga and Giulio Romano was reputedly based on the amatory frescos in the 'Room of Cupid' at the Palazzo Te. Vasari wrote of their richness of invention whilst diplomatically refusing to point out their lack of decorum as decorations befitting the papal living quarters.[915] Aretino could have effortlessly dispraised His Holiness's affinity for erotica if he'd wished to but there was no reason to. He was, after all, now in receipt of a papal pension as a Knight of St. Peter and it would have been foolhardy to jeopardise any new and much-needed sources of income.

In October of that year he was writing to Guidobaldo in praise of the Duke and describing himself as 'a good Christian' who 'has already done his ecclesiastical duty in abhorring both in private and with a loud voice the falsehood of the diabolical Lutheran beliefs'.[916] Perhaps it was due to his advanced age (he was by this time sixty-one years old, an age of decline for most people of the period) but Aretino's correspondence in 1553-54 after returning from Rome display a noticeable mellowness and resignation to the vicissitudes of life. To Titian, he wrote in December 1553 excusing himself for allowing his household servants to get away with liberties, which he dismissed as being trivial in the greater scheme of things.[917] To Sansovino that same month he described the age-old debate over the primacy of painting over sculpture as being 'madness that canonizes madness'[918] and to Sansovino's son Francesco he writes the following stoical lines: 'I hear ... that you have been robbed of I don't know how much valuable property, which leads me to observe to you that our worldly goods are filched from us without our having anything to do with it, but our time is never stolen from us without our own consent ... Certain it is that, when we die, we will weep for the years that we spent in vain, and say nothing about the reason that made us so waste them.'[919] Aretino is, it seems, aware that his own time will soon be drawing to an end and is endeavouring to assign meaning to how he has spent his own life. Perhaps most astonishing of all is Aretino's frank and confessional admission to Sister Arnulf in December 1553 that 'For when all is said and done, we must insist plainly that pomp is but a vapour, pleasure clay, and high living a sickness. Like time and death, in the end they destroy all. Time, as you know, eats up all beauty, and death extinguishes both life and breath. And in the shadows of the tomb, the worms who feast upon the bodies of the dead, do not make any distinction between the anointed bones of a king and the crumbling corpses of the mean and lowly.'[920]

Can it really be that Aretino had by this time, following his latest disappointments and frustrations in Rome, arrived at some deeper philosophical insight into life which now caused him to cherish all those things (such as friendship and 'time well spent') that mattered more than riches, fame and reputation? In his letter to Sister Arnulf he alludes to his younger daughter Austria, 'that delightful little soul of mine', and asks the nun to pray for both his daughters as well as for their mother Caterina. By now, Aretino's hopes and dreams were firmly affixed to the lives of his children. If his servants were sometimes cheeky with him it was no great matter. Not even the great and perennial questions of art moved him as they had formerly done. Aretino was instead acutely aware, as we can gauge from his words to Sister Arnulf as well as to Francesco Sansovino, that time erodes all man's vain endeavours. The failure to be appointed a cardinal must, by any stretch of the imagination, have come as a bitter blow for a proud man such as Aretino. However, disappointment is in the very nature of things.

Quite possibly, Aretino had already been prepared for his disappointment surrounding his bid for the cardinalate by earlier developments in Venice. At the beginning of 1551 he had already been taught another valuable life lesson concerning the ephemerality of existence and the constant nature of change. Aretino's landlord Domenico Bollani had, after twenty-two years, refused to renew the lease on Aretino's home, the Palazzo Bolani. The news had come as a shock to Aretino who had been supremely contented dwelling here since 1529 and who had happily raised his two daughters under its roof. During his tenancy he had also made certain improvements to the property, such as refurbishing the fireplace and replacing the floorboards.[921] To Bolani, Aretino composed an acerbic reply: 'Distinguished and honourable sir, I herewith return to you the keys of that house in which I have dwelt for twenty-two years, and to which I have given the same care that I would have if it had been my own'. Characteristically, he then pretends that it was he, and not Bollani, who is relinquishing the lease ('Nor will I give any other reason for doing this except that it is completely run down, and that I can no more repair its decrepitude than I can shore up my own old age') before treating Bolani to a lengthy disquisition on his tenant's fame and importance: 'I will not mention the little respect that you have shown to me–me, upon whose behalf the Emperor himself interceded, asking no less than four Venetian ambassadors to relate his goodwill toward me to the Venetian signory. I will not mention all this. I will say only that if you look into the room where I had hoped to live out my days happily, if you look at the figures on the ceiling, at the gracious balcony and at the decorations over my bed and over the mantelpiece, you will realise that I avenge even discourtesies with my courtesy. The daughters that have been born to me, the treasure everyone knows about, the works that all see, I have begotten, I have amassed, I have composed here.'[922]

Aretino had not succeeded in securing his cardinal's hat and furthermore he had been kicked out of his comfortable and prestigious home. He moved to new apartments on the Riva del Carbon owned by the Dandolo family which were twice as costly but far less satisfactory.[923] However, a leopard does not change its spots so easily. If his letter writing around this time evoked a new spirit of resignation and humility, his behaviour soon reverted to the curmudgeonly Aretino of old. The person Aretino chose to pick his next fight with was Duke Cosimo I of Florence, the son of his dearest friend, Giovanni delle Bande Nere. Cosimo's act of withholding Adria's dowry until she was married was never calculated to win Aretino's approbation, although it was intended to prevent the spendthrift writer from squandering the advance. To Aretino it was gratuitously discourteous and Cosimo had failed to show his client the respect which was his due as his late father's close friend. Aretino began making his feelings very publicly known to Florence's resident ambassador, the Reverend Pero Gelido of San Miniato. Affronted, Pero wrote to his master Cosimo, 'This ruffian deserves as many beatings a day as the Duke gives him ducats a year. He never shuts his loud mouth.'[924] Neither did Duke Cosimo feel especially indebted to this relic from his father's era; he had been just seven years old when Giovanni delle Bande Nere had died and his late father's friendships now meant very little to him. All his most crucial battles against his Florentine enemies had been his own victories, fought whilst standing on his own two feet. Likewise, his mother Maria Salviati, whom Aretino had always taken pains to flatter and cultivate, had already been dead for the better part of a decade. The plays which Aretino had once sent the Duke were by now long-forgotten. Gifts such as the perfumed money roll which Cosimo had once sent to Aretino were, by the same token, memories of the dim and distant past.[925]

The times were changing and so too was the old guard. Henry VIII had already died in January 1547 at the age of fifty-five, thus relieving Aretino of one patron who (through the persistent promise and then paucity of coin) was never especially advantageous to him. By July 1553, while Aretino was still awaiting word of his cardinal's hat in Rome, the English king's heir, Edward VI, had also died at the tender age of fifteen, to be succeeded for nine days by the ill-starred Lady Jane Grey before Queen Mary came to the throne later that same month. King Henry VIII had been followed to the grave just two months later by his lifelong rival King François I of France, with whom Aretino had had at best a love-hate relationship. The French king had died at the Château de Rambouillet on 31 March 1547 on his son and successor Prince Henry's twenty-eighth birthday. He was, at fifty-two, only slightly younger than Henry VIII. The court painter François Clouet made a wax death mask of the dead king's features for posterity. François's death created another gaping hole in the satirist's dwindling list of royal patrons. Aretino also continued to fall out with his friends, usually writers who had impinged upon his supremacy as Italy's Prince of Letters. 1549 found Aretino writing to Bernardo Tasso, author of the chivalrous romance *Amadigi*, scolding him for boasting to Annibale Caro that 'today there is no writer of letters who is fit to be used as a model–though without doubt you did hint, with your sly craftiness, that if anybody was worthy to be imitated, it was you'.[926] Aretino added a postscript to his letter to the effect that 'everyone is convinced that we will fight a duel. Should we do this, it is as certain that I will gain the victory as it is unlikely that you will fight at all. So I urge you to be wise and not to rage. But if anger has more power over your spirit than commonsense, I will give to you the choice of arms. I will let you name the place of combat too.'[927]

The cruellest blow of all, however, came in 1554 with the premature death of Aretino's daughter Adria. It is probably true to assume that his heart never mended from this great tragedy. The satirist's artist friends were still going strong, Titian, Tintoretto and Sansovino for example. Titian would be relieved of his position as official painter of Venice in 1556 when his hands began failing him. According to the gossip Vasari, he developed a fresh rivalry with an up-and-coming painter named Paris Bordone.[928] But otherwise Titian's career had another twenty-two years to run. Aretino's time, unbeknown to him, was however drawing to a close. Old and tired as he now was, however, Aretino's battles were still not quite yet at an end. The satirist who had made a lifelong career out of waging paper warfare with the likes of Broccardo and Franco and others had actually admitted in a 1539 letter to Giovanni Alberto Albicante that he disliked these petty squabbles. 'When one poet writes against another, it seems to me I see two butcher's dogs who tear the hide off each other with their teeth because they both want to gnaw on the same bone, and yet all this bone does is to blunt their teeth without satisfying the hunger that fills their bodies. But when they lie down together with their legs stretched out and licking each other, they bark at every stranger.'[929]

To an unnamed ambassador Aretino had earlier in 1545 expressed a similar opinion involving more or less the same canine metaphor concerning poets: '..as far as barking goes, poets are like dogs. Unbearable hunger is the evil friend which makes the latter bear their teeth and the former wag their tongues. But the pleasant after-effects of bread set before them at the right hour and time will quiet the rabies of one and smother the anger of the other.'[930] And yet Venice teemed with competitive, egotistical *huomini letterati* who demanded to be fed at regular intervals and who were seldom slow on self-congratulation. Jacopo Sansovino's son, the writer Francesco Sansovino published his *Dialogo di tutte le cose notabili e belle che sono in Venetia* ('Dialogue on all the notable and beautiful things in Venice') in 1556. In this work, which as its name suggests was a sort of guide book, one of the two interlocutors Forestiero states that Venice 'is a country of *virtuosi*' to which the other, Venetiano, affirms 'in fact the copiousness of excellent men here is great'.[931]

One such hungry *letterato*, Anton Francesco Doni, the sometime friend who had once jokingly compared the satirist to the Antichrist, now decided for reasons of his own to round upon his former patron and supporter. Since returning to Venice in 1548, Aretino had shown Doni every consideration. Born in 1513, the son of a scissor-maker in the Medici-dominated San Lorenzo district of Florence, Doni had begun his career as a Servite monk known by the name of Fra Valerio; he had then become a priest, a student of law at Piacenza, followed by a stint as a printer in Venice in 1544. Doni had probably first met Aretino at a party hosted at the Venetian home of the Marquess Annibale Malvicino.[932] Thereafter, he became a member of that tight-knit Aretine circle which also included Titian, Sansovino, Niccolò Franco, Lodovico Dolce and Lorenzo Venier. Doni's literary career had always been at best a mediocre one and remained largely unremarked in wider critical circles. Perhaps this lay at the root of Doni's animus towards the wealthier and more successful Aretino. Perhaps it was also to do with Aretino's own somewhat disparaging attitude towards his younger protégés, whom he often chided for depending for their success on their association with book sales and the printing presses. Aretino had written of such younger authors: 'The fools with their breeches down, up to their necks in a lake of ink blacker than the fumes of the printing press; there is no more absurd spectacle in the world'.[933] Lodovico Dolce would prove to be a particularly stark example of the type Aretino had dispraised. Despite publishing 112 books he would die in abject poverty. 'The sum and substance of our accomplishment is, then, that we will eat, drink, and be merry in the world to come, but in this one we must go hungry "as long as life endures"', had been Aretino's doleful remarks on the poetical existence.[934]

As for Anton Francesco Doni's work, it had a knack for invoking the low Tuscan of the Florentine lower classes: as a kind of early proto-socialist he enunciated the concerns of the labouring classes whilst censuring the selfishness of the Italian nobility.[935] Perhaps the ultimate closet cynic, his work *Libraria* (1550) contained the words: 'What happens today already has happened before, what is said now has been said and will be said again; what is going to be has taken place'. Another of his works, *I marmi*, is based on a conversation which Doni supposedly overheard on the steps of the Duomo in Florence between a poultry-seller, a merchant and an anonymous third party; after some deliberation the assemblage decide that the Liberal Arts are insufficient to teach men either wisdom or virtue. Like Niccolò Franco and other low-born writers such as Ortensio Lando and Girolamo Ruscelli, Doni nevertheless aspired to profit from and climb the ladder of the same social hierarchy which, in the guise of social warrior, he criticised in his barbed satires and epistles.[936] He also kept company with such comic poets as Alessandro Caravia and Pietro Nelli who both found in the lower orders a bottomless source of humorous material.

Doni had always sung the praises of his friend and benefactor Aretino, honouring him as a *poligrafo* - a writer who was able to tackle many different genres with aplomb, something which he himself always aspired to but largely failed at mastering. To the poet-satirist, Doni had flatteringly commented, 'your wisdom knew how to distinguish the tongue in which we should discuss Christ ... from that of the Dialogues on the state of women...'[937] Now, however, in the 1550s he decided like Niccolò Franco before him to sever his ties with the satirist who had nurtured and suckled him, decrying his former patron as both infamous and amoral. He published a defamation against Aretino under the title of *Il Terremoto*, which prophesied the satirist's death in 1556. From initially being his eulogist, Doni now joined the scurrilous Niccolò Franco in delivering a flurry of crude insults against Aretino. The aging satirist was ridiculed as 'the scourge of pricks' and 'Peter, writer of the vices of others', or else 'possessor of the most horrible, vituperous and ribald tongue ever born'.[938] Unfortunately Doni, whose literary efforts had never quite hit the mark before, would for once prove strangely prescient in predicting Aretino's death that year.

Aretino was drinking and dining in a tavern on the evening of 21 October 1556. One month earlier, he had lost another of his long-time patrons the Emperor Charles V, who in September 1556 had abdicated as Holy Roman Emperor in favour of his brother Ferdinand. He would retire into contemplative seclusion at the monastery of Yuste in Extremadura, although he would still correspond widely and maintain an ongoing interest in the affairs of the empire which he had just relinquished.

Aretino does not seem to have been unduly crestfallen that evening, however, at the loss of his latest patron. As was customary, he was in the loud company of a group of his friends, men drawn from all walks of life. At some point in the evening's festivities somebody uttered a vulgar joke or else an obscenity; one of the accounts handed down to us is that the story concerned his two sisters who allegedly once worked 'as prostitutes in a brothel in Arezzo'.[939] In appreciation of the lewd anecdote Aretino threw up his arms and leaned back to let loose his usual uproarious laughter. But this time, arrested by the sudden onset of apoplexy, the laughter never came. Instead, the chair, with its great sixty-four-year-old burden, crashed backwards against the hard flagstones and the satirist's huge bulk lay motionless where it fell prone on the tavern floor and breathing only with some difficulty.[940] The painter Anselm Feuerbach would later capture the scene of Aretino's collapse in his painting of 1854.

His friends struggled to carry his dead weight back the short distance to his home on the Riva del Carbon and they put him to bed. Aretino lay there delirious. A priest was sent for and when he arrived he proceeded to administer the Last Rites. Despite his condition Aretino managed to summon one final reserve of energy to confess and receive the Eucharist and Extreme Unction, which he did we are told, 'weeping very much'. As to his alleged deathbed exclamation: 'Now that I'm all greased up, don't let the rats get me', there is no way to confirm whether he actually said this, although the humour behind the remark would no doubt have appealed to him.

As dawn began to break the doctor announced that all life had departed from the massive body of the legendary poet-satirist Pietro Aretino. Word of the writer's passing quickly spread throughout Venice. His friends, foremost amongst them the painter Titian and the architect-sculptor Sansovino, were naturally heartbroken. His enemies, Francesco Doni (whose prediction of Aretino's death made him briefly famous), Niccolò Franco, Giovanni Alberto Albicante and a few others no doubt rejoiced at his passing. On 24 October 1556, Florence's ambassador Pero Gelido notified his master Duke Cosimo de' Medici: '*Il mortal* Pietro Aretino (no longer *Il divino*) on Wednesday at the third hour of the night was carried off into the next world by a stroke of apoplexy without any decent man being sorry to lose him. May God pardon him.'[941]

POSTSCRIPT

Since it is plain that being miserly is what the lords are lavish with, I kiss goodbye to that pension that brought me as much honour when it was taken away from me as it snatched away honour when it was given. We poor citizens, ah? We boorish bumpkins, eh? But we have a right to be born, I have always said. We have a right to be born, I say now. We have a right to be born, I will keep on saying in a loud and disrespectful voice.

Pietro Aretino To Antonio Boccamazza,
August 1554.

Pietro Aretino was buried in his local parish church of San Luca, built before 1072 by the Dandolo and Pizzamano families, and standing just a stone's throw away from his rented home on the Riva del Carbon. His great body was deposited in a new sepulchre located near the sacristy. The great gold chain of interlocking serpents tongues which Aretino had got from François, King of France, and of which he was always so proud, was reportedly pawned to pay the poet's funeral expenses. The church itself, aside from having been the satirist's parish church, is for the most part undistinguished. It is tucked away just off the Grand Canal along a smaller tributary canal called the Rio de San Luca towards which its main entrance faces. The orangey-pink Palladian façade which may be seen today is mainly the work of the eighteenth-century artist Sebastiano Santi, but inside the church Paolo Veronese's altarpiece, though by now a little worse for wear, can still be seen portraying *The Virgin appearing to St. Luke as he writes the Gospel*. The altarpiece was added to the church twenty-five years after Aretino's death in 1581, although Veronese himself had been in Venice during the last few years of Aretino's life and had known and socialised with the satirist during this time.[942]

That Veronese's art should preside over Aretino's final resting place was fitting for like the satirist he was also an irreverent man, a non-conformist who also pushed the envelope of his creative *daemon*. For his 1573 canvas, *The Feast in the House of Levi*, Veronese would have to answer to the Holy Office for having included likenesses of German soldiers, dwarves, and animals, subjects which were considered 'heretical' by the Church authorities in the context of any depiction of the most sacred event of the Last Supper. The church of San Luca was also later the parish church of Mozart's librettist, Lorenzo da Ponte, who was a priest here in the 1770s. Whilst living in a nearby boarding house he would meet Anzolletta Bellaudi, who became his mistress. As dissolute as da Ponte himself, Anzolletta would engage in mutual fondling sessions with handsome young men in public and sometimes even in church. In 1779, Lorenzo Da Ponte was tried for living a debauched life and he was banished from Venice for fifteen years. Aretino would, without a shadow of a doubt, have looked down from Heaven (or else glanced up from Hell, remember he predicted that he would alternate between the two places) and smiled at da Ponte's and Anzolletta's ribald carrying on.

Some years earlier a certain Francesconi had suggested the following epitaph for Pietro Aretino: 'Arezzo's hoary libeller here is laid, / Whose bitter slanders all save CHRIST essayed: / He for such slip this reason good can show, - / 'How could I mock one whom I do not know?' Hardly missing a beat, Aretino himself had shot back: 'Francescon, wretched rhymer, here is laid, / Who of all things save asses evil said: / His plea in favour of the long-eared race, / A cousinship that none could fail to trace.'[943] Francesconi's doggerel is quite possibly the origin for the erroneous legend of an epitaph which supposedly adorned the dead satirist's tomb: 'Condit Aretini Cineres lapis iste sepultos, Mortales atro qui sale perfricuit. Intactus Deus est illi, causamque rogatus Hanc dedit. Ille, inquit, non mihi notus erat.'[944] Loosely translated by John Harington the Latin inscription stated: 'Here lies the Aretine who did raile on priest and prince, and all but God, / And said (for his excuse) I doe not know him'.[945] Aretino's first biographer, Giammaria Mazzuchelli, denies that such an inscription was made on the tomb and with good reason. Though Aretino himself may have enjoyed it, his devout friends like Titian and company would never have permitted such a disrespectful epitaph. Neither either would the Church in all likelihood. There was no shortage of scurrilous *faux* epitaphs in the years following the satirist's death. On the wall of the church of San Luca in Arezzo were scrawled the words: 'Base-born Pietro Aretino rose / to such heights in the scourging of foul vice / that those who held the world in fee paid price / to him in fear of even fiercer blows'.[946]

In 1559, three years after Pietro Aretino's death, and at the instigation of Pope Paul IV, an *Index librorum prohibitorum* ('Index of prohibited books') was published with the intention of reinforcing the mission of the Holy Inquisition by suppressing the *opera omnia* of some 550 authors deemed to contain heretical, anti-clerical, lascivious or morally subversive notions.[947] It was the first time, with the exception of

Giovanni della Casa's 1549 *Index*, that the supreme spiritual authority of Roman Catholicism reached out and defined to all of Christendom which authors and which books Catholics were permitted to read.[948] A committee of cardinals appointed to carry out the scrutiny banned selected works by such authors as Boccaccio, Rabelais, Erasmus as well as the political writings of Aretino's former acquaintance Machiavelli. The *Index* also went back in time to ban two dialogues of the Greek satirist Lucian of Samosata and selected works of the medieval philosopher William of Ockham.

A later edition which appeared in 1564, the *Tridentine Index*, extended its prohibitions to other writers and contemporaries of Pietro Aretino's including Ludovico Ariosto, Pietro Bembo, Agnolo Firenzuola and Anton Francesco Doni to name only a few. As for Pietro Aretino's own books, all of them were banned by the index and his name appeared at the top of the blacklist. His works were publicly burned. Many Venetian booksellers protested the unprofitable ban on selling Aretino's highly popular works but the Church's response was to mount economic reprisals against them which ultimately forced them to comply with the ruling.[949] With the *Index librorum prohibitorum* and the *Tridentine Index* the Aretine age now officially drew to a close.[950] Under the counter, however, his work was still available throughout Italy by means of subterfuge. Often, for example, his and Machiavelli's works were printed under pseudonyms like Partenio Etiro or Amadio Niecollucci, their titles having also been slightly altered to disguise and obscure their true authorship. In 1601, Aretino's *Marescalco* was published as the *Cavallarizzo* and in 1610 *Lo Ipocrito* was printed under the title *Finto*, both presented as being the work of 'Luigi Tansillo' of Vicenza. By such clever means crafty publishers were able to circumvent the Church's prohibition and still turn an illicit profit from these ever-popular works, so long as they were extremely careful about it of course.[951]

It is conceivable too that Aretino's books were not banned primarily or exclusively because of their lewd content. It is plausible that his *opera omnia* was included on the list because the satirist—so the Church authorities privately determined—was also suspected of heresy, possibly even atheism, during his lifetime. Aretino lived a publicly dissolute life and unrepentant dissolution implied godlessness. Furthermore, as we have already noted, the dead writer was a known associate and correspondent of such religious reformers as those two Italian *spirituali* Bernardino Ochino and Pier Paolo Vergerio and he also corresponded with others who privately questioned their faith. These included individuals such as the painter Lorenzo Lotto, to whom Aretino wrote quite a well-known letter in April 1548 consoling Lotto on his lack of material success in the arts field. Aretino told Lotto not to be downhearted as a result of his artistic trials and tribulations for he had nevertheless neared the peak of achievement in his religious devotion.[952] Lotto's 1542 altarpiece *The Alms of Saint Anthony* for Venice's church of Santi Giovanni e Paolo depicts a wealthy and privileged Church hierarchy starkly separated from the common rabble and is an obvious statement of Lotto's own inner turmoil regarding such matters as clerical privilege.

There was also the fact that Aretino's own religious writings were faintly Protestant in flavour, combined with his tendency to innovate and editorialise, as in the case of *I sette salmi della penitentia di David* for which Aretino personally provided the translations from Hebrew.[953] One reformer who Aretino had read avidly was the Florentine Antonio Brucioli, a former associate of Machiavelli's who was famous for his vernacular Italian translation of the Bible, a work which was also placed on the Index of 1557. Like Aretino, Brucioli lived in exile in Venice for the remainder of his life, but assailed by heresy charges for most of this time, unlike the dead satirist, he ended his life under effective house arrest, eventually dying in extreme poverty in 1566 (coincidentally, that same year the word 'atheist' appeared for the first time in an English book, in John Martial's *A Replie to M. Calfhills Blasphemous Answer*).[954]

The Pope's *Index* of prohibited books did not of course prevent subsequent writers from touching upon sexual or lewd subjects or indeed having their work published. Thomas Stigliani's 1628 work *Mondo nuovo* ('The New World') featured examples of incest and bestiality for example. Meanwhile, the career of Ferrante Pallavicino in the seventeenth-century closely mirrored that of Aretino's (and the reformers of Italian Catholicism known as the *spirituali*) in its criticism of the deficiencies of the Catholic Church and the moral laxity of its clergy. As Aretino had spent several years on picaresque adventures with Giovanni delle Bande Nere, so too had Pallavicino participated in the Thirty Years War under the aegis of the imperial captain Ottavio Piccolomini. Pallavicino's scandalising, in his work *Il Corriero svaligiato*, of the nepotistic Pope Urban VIII and his family the Barberini clan echoed Aretino's earlier feud with Pope Clement VII and the Medici and landed him in a Venetian prison for six months. Pallavicino continued the Aretine's recurring theme of 'ignoring social and behavioural constraints' and, like the Aretine, preached that patronising prostitutes was far preferable for numerous reasons to the holy sacrament of marriage. Pallavicino's 1643 work *La retorica delle puttane* ('The Rhetoric of Whores'), in which an aged prostitute offers a wise disquisition to her naïve young apprentice, presents us almost with a facsimile of the *Ragionamento* and *Dialogo* between Nanna, Antonia, and Pippa. As with Aretino's work, *La retorica delle puttane* uses clever satire combined with healthy doses of scepticism to offer an inverted naturalistic morality. It is inverted because although the Venetian authorities might burn sexual deviants to ensure the grace of their souls, for Pallavicino spreading knowledge and dispelling ignorance on sexual matters is sufficient for ensuring 'grace'. According to his outlook, a surprisingly modern one, sexual activity is a perfectly healthy natural biological function just like other bodily function such as eating or slaking one's thirst and accordingly carnal desire and sexual contact with women is nothing to be shunned.[955]

This sentiment was echoed by other post-Aretine intellectuals of the day including, for example, Jacop Zabarella who taught philosophy at Padua from 1564 until 1589. Zabarella had argued that nature had created carnal desire out of the perfectly innocent and reasonable imperative to ensure the survival of the species, a disarmingly modern line of argument.[956] But whereas Aretino's Nanna is a wealthy, successful courtesan who imparts practical, efficacious self-help advice for her protégé-daughter to navigate the male sexual environment, Pallavicino's whore-teacher is aged, poor and sick and bemoans to her student the fact that she did not stop at using rhetoric (defined as the arts of simulation and dissimulation) to achieve her practical ends but instead veered into philosophy, which submerged her in an inconvenient emotional authenticity with regard her actual situation. Where Pallavicino perhaps went too far was in using *La retorica* to satirise the powerful new Jesuit Order in his tract, a reforming force which was at this time seeking to monopolise all European educational and intellectual life, as well as spearhead the punishment of heresy itself. His earlier work, *Il Divortio celeste* ('The Celestial Divorce'), had unfortunately depicted Jesus Christ as seeking to divorce himself from the Roman Catholic Church, otherwise known as the 'bride of Christ', because in Christ's eyes she had committed countless sins and adulteries. Pallavicino's days were, to a certain extent therefore, numbered once the Jesuits got wind of his activities.

If Aretino had commented upon the moral laxity of individual members of the Church such as priests and monks, he had always been careful not to openly criticise the Church itself. During the Counter Reformation era of Tridentine reform this would have been to sail too close to the wind. Betrayed by Charles de Breche, an agent of the papal Barberini family, Pallavicino was turned over to the papal authorities whilst crossing into France and the unfortunate satirist was beheaded in Avignon on 5 March 1644. Aretino had been living in an entirely different era from Pallavicino. Prior to the Council of Trent, the Catholic world was still caught on the back foot as Lutheran Protestantism exploded across Germany, England, the Netherlands and Switzerland. The papacy of Clement VII had been far too victimised by its own Catholic subjects Spain and the Empire to fight back against its more vocal critics north of the Alps. According to the historian George Haven Putnam, the century and a half from 1400-1550 had seen papal toleration of some of 'the most obscene books to be found in any literature' and even such a ribald writer as Aretino 'could aspire with fair prospects to the scarlet of a cardinal'.[957] But Pallavicino would not be the only pornographer of his generation. In 1660, a work entitled *Aloisiae Sigaeae, Toletanae, Satyra sotadica de arcanis Amoris et Veneris* was published by the Frenchman Nicolas Chorier. Like Aretino and Pallavicino, Chorier used as his literary vehicle the education of a young whore, in this case Ottavia, who is being 'instructed' by her older cousin Tullia, a twenty-six-year-old Italian woman who is married to Callias. Tullia confides in the girl: 'Your mother asked me to reveal to you the most mysterious secrets of the bridal bed and to teach you what you must be with your husband, which your husband will also be, touching these small things which so strongly inflame men's passion'.

By the end of the seventeenth-century, however, Italian libertine literature of that century had already withered on the vine. Whether this was a result of Tridentine Church suppression or else merely changing social attitudes towards sexuality and erotic literature in general is hard to ascertain. Literary libertinism would not enjoy a resurgence until the Enlightenment era of Casanova, Voltaire and the Marquis de Sade. Casanova was said to have never ventured out of doors without his copy of Aretino's *Sonetti lussuriosi* tucked in his coat pocket. Casanova's *Histoire de ma vie* placed straightforward Aretine sexual misbehaviour in the context of autobiography, a confessional genre which the merry and uncomplicated fornicator Samuel Pepys would also make uniquely his own. Casanova seems to have made frequent practical use of Aretino's sexual handbook. He mentions spending New Year's Eve 1753 in a convent near Venice with a young nun called Marina Morosini practising one of *I Modi's* sexual 'postures', the 'straight tree', a kind of standing '69' with the woman inverted and grasping a small wheel for mutual oral sex.[958] 'In that position I lifted her up to devour her chamber of love, which I could reach otherwise since I wanted to make it possible for her, in turn to devour the weapon that wounded her to death'–climax– 'without taking away her life.'

Another kissing cousin of Aretino's was Restif de La Bretonne, a French novelist who churned out hundreds of racy books during his largely impoverished life. The term 'retifism' meaning 'shoe fetishism' was named after him and Napoleon awarded him a place in his ministry of police but he died just before taking up the position. Restif de La Bretonne was perhaps the last gasp for this improper sort of literature and the experimentation and libertinism of the eighteenth-century would soon pass. Replacing it would be the narrow-minded puritanism of the Victorian era with its earnest tuberculosis-ridden poets striding inspired through the bracing moorland heather. This was a strait-laced era to which Aretino and his explicit sexual irreverence simply did not belong. With the greatest possible irony it was even dubbed the Romantic period. Pietro Aretino would not survive the prudery of the nineteenth-century. Unfortunately, the literary scholars and historians of that era could never quite see past their own sexual hang-ups to understand Aretino's true mission and purpose. It was during the nineteenth-century that the word pornography and its derivatives (with all the pejorative connotations these words now carry) first surfaced in the English language. *Pornographer* appeared in 1850, *pornography* in 1864, and *pornographic* in 1880.[959]

It was true, Aretino had adopted the image of the shameless and licentious satyr. Indeed, one of the most notorious representations that we have of him is on one of a number of bronze medals which the poet almost certainly had struck of himself. On the obverse of this medal Aretino is depicted, beard flowing magnificently, dressed in his splendid robes and wearing one of his heavy gold chains, accompanied by the inscription TOTVS IN TOTO ET TOTVS IN QVALIBET PARTE ('All in all and all in every part'). On the reverse is a depiction of the poet as a *bacchante* made up entirely from male phalli (*cazzi*) thus echoing Niccolò Franco's slur 'the scourge of pricks', which was a bowdlerization of Ariosto's description of Aretino as 'the scourge of princes'. Some have suggested that Franco himself or some other enemy of Aretino's could have commissioned the medal as a kind of post mortem visual insult, but the fact remains that medals were seldom used in this way, to denigrate. They were created to celebrate and commemorate, often (as in Aretino's case) one's own self. Furthermore, a cast bronze medal—hardly a cheap item to produce in the sixteenth-century—would have been an unusually expensive means of blackening a rival's reputation. We are therefore left with the realisation that the obscene phallic medal was commissioned by the satirist himself, probably from Leone Leoni, who had commemorated his likeness in other bronze medals, to celebrate how he for one saw himself.

The Arcimboldi-like head made up entirely from pricks is, unmistakably, Aretino's own unique way of identifying himself with the classical satyr. The head of cocks is Aretino's *impresa*, a visual image symbolising what the subject sees as being his principle virtue or calling in life.[960] This mythological beast lay at the heart of his self-image and his life's mission. To sixteenth-century scholars and philologists (incorrectly as it so happened, though this need not concern us here) the satyr was etymologically related to the satirist and the business of satire, a literary typology which had its forerunner in such classical Roman writers as Juvenal. Although uncivilised, coarse and prone to brutish and uncontrollable animal lusts, the satyr was nevertheless also an essentially 'innocent' creature. Although satyrs occasionally attacked mortal humans, either sexually or else vituperatively, the attack was quite often justified because in doing so the satyr drew back the veil of social pretence to expose the foul underbelly of human failings, vices and hypocrisies. This, by the way, was also the satirist's self-appointed mission.[961] Pietro Aretino, in depicting himself in this manner, was admitting that he may have been a *cazzo* (prick) but human society nevertheless called for somebody to play that unwelcome satyrical/satirical role. It just so happened that he was also unusually good at his trade, so good in fact as to become quite literally the first writer to earn a consistent and handsome living from his writing, of which satire obviously formed an important and central part.

When marquesses, dukes, grand dukes, princes, kings, popes and emperors shrunk from the pen of Pietro Aretino they were not only reacting to the possibility of having their darkest secrets revealed to the rest of the world. Aretino's writings constituted an alternative confessional to the Church's, one in which they recoiled from the sins and sordid acts which they themselves knew they had committed. Aretino was a human mirror held up to the great men of his day. Federico Gonzaga's act of making a cuckold of Count Giovanni Calvisano, as well as his other outlandish sexual exploits, might have caused him shame if he suspected that intimate details of his activities would be released to the public. Pope Clement VII may have secretly regretted not taking a harder line over Achille della Volta's potentially deadly attack on the poet. King François may have been embarrassed that his fine promises to Aretino usually never materialised into very much. He was perhaps still more embarrassed when Aretino publicly criticised his alliance with the godless Turks against the Emperor Charles V. Numberless other examples obtain. Whatever their acts, and their specific acts towards him, Aretino held them all to account regardless of their station in life. With his five editions of his published *Lettere*, affordably priced so that even a day labourer could manage to purchase a copy after just two or three days of toil (and assuming he could read), Aretino was the prototype of that familiar modern figure, the hard-nosed, investigative journalist subjecting preening and overpaid politicians to uncompromisingly tough questions in the full glare of televised public exposure. Astonishingly, Aretino simultaneously invented modern critical journalism in addition to its sister industry, public relations. His subjects and interlocutors were glad to pay handsomely for his 'good press' whilst being secretly relieved that they were not being placed awkwardly in his diamond hard spotlight. Jacob Burckhardt in his hugely influential book *The Civilization of the Renaissance in Italy* acknowledges that Aretino 'made all his profit out of a complete publicity, and in a certain sense may be considered the father of modern journalism'.[962] Burckhardt compares and contrasts Aretino's deliberately *public* mass circulation of his letters to the habit of his predecessors, who circulated their letters purely for their own private consumption and edification.

The fad which Aretino singlehandedly created for publishing letters to important intellectuals began a floodtide of imitators. From 1538 to 1627, no less than 540 volumes of letters were published in Italy. The more well-known authors of these volumes included, aside from Aretino himself, such writers as Pietro Bembo, Anton Francesco Doni, Nicolò Franco, Andrea Calmo, Annibal Caro, Stefano Guazzo, Claudio Tolomei, and Bernardo Tasso along with his poet son Torquato. To his former courtier friend Bernardo Tasso, Aretino had mockingly written: 'Thinking too highly of your own productions and too little of those of others, you exhibit the value of your judgement. In epistolary style you are but my copyist, and you follow me with naked feet. You can imitate neither my facility of phrase nor the splendour of my metaphors. They wither on your weary page; while on mine they appear full of life and vigour.'[963] Clearly, Aretino's innovation in this field was a touchy area for him and in many respects only he could have pioneered the genre. It required a sufficiently narcissistic personality to come forward and cast aside the usual decorum of writing and then publishing in the first person. The genre was also unabashedly self-promotional and Aretino dominated the landscape when it came to vernacular Italian letter collections until 1547, which was the year in which Andrea Calmo[964] and Claudio Tolomei[965] published their own best-selling epistolary anthologies.

Today his letters have sadly fallen into neglect and are practically unknown outside of the Italian-speaking world. Yet after nearly five hundred years they still speak out and resonate, surprisingly fresh, and the great spirit of the satirist is unmistakably there in its all-too-human failings. It is the voice of a talented man, a man of *virtù* and *sprezzatura*, making his way in the world with the only talent he had, his quill. Though often histrionic, traducing, magniloquent and turgid, his epistolary output holds a mirror up to the daily annoyances, frustrations and tribulations that are the lot of every ordinary, struggling person who is not born to great rank or magnificent fortune:

> 'I have read the sonnet which you made about me and against those who attack me more with the ill will of their malicious natures than with an effective style. But while thanking you, I would also like to request you–in case you should ever again take arms upon my behalf–to tell those who assert that I am gutter-born, that I honour my humble origin in the same way in which they dishonour their noble birth'.[966]

Here is the common ground on which we can approach and understand *the man* Pietro Aretino. 'We have a right to be born, I say now. We have a right to be born, I will keep on saying in a loud and disrespectful voice,' he would contend to Antonio Boccamazza. These are not the words of a man that is 'to the manor born' but of one of the *popolo minuto*, 'the little people'. And although he might occasionally try too hard and thunder to the world 'I AM PIETRO ARETINO!' he also enjoyed poignant moments of humility, not to mention prescience. To Lodovico Dolce, who memorialised his trailblazing ideas on art and art criticism, Aretino wrote on 25 November 1537, summing up his thoughts on his career up until that point: 'My dear friend, Glory's handmaiden lights up my obscure name with a tallow candle not a torch. I carry ignorance in the palm of my hand, and I pray only that I will at least do well enough to keep the learned from excommunicating me when moved by the presumption which every kind of person has within him I dip my pen into their sacrosanct ink.'[967]

APPENDIX 1

THE WORKS OF PIETRO ARETINO

POETRY

Opera Nova del Fecundissimo Giovene Pietro Pictore Aretino zoe Strambotti Sonetti Capitoli Epistole Barzellete et una desperate, 1512.
Esortazione de la pace tra l'Imperatore e il Re di Francia, 1524.
Laude di Clemente VII, 1524.
Canzone in laude del datario, 1524-25.
Sonetti lussuriosi sopra i XVI modi, 1524.
Dubbi amorosi & Altri dubbi amorosi 1526.
Dui primi canti di Marphisa (Only two cantos published), 1532.
D'Angelica due primi canti (Only two cantos published), 1535.
Stanze in lode di madonna Angela Sirena, 1537.
Tre primi canti di battaglia (three cantos of *La Marfisa*), 1537.
De le lagrime d'Angelica due primi canti (fragment of *La Marfisa*), 1538.
Abbattimento poetico del divino Aretino, et del bestiale Albicante, 1539.
Li dui primi canti di Orlandino, 1540.
Il capitolo e il sonetto in laude de lo Imperatore, 1543.
Ternali in gloria di Giulio terzo pontefice, et della maestà della Reina cristianissima, 1551.
Pasquinata di Pietro Aretino e anonime per il conclave di Adriano VI, 1891.

PLAYS

Il Marescalco, 1533.
La Cortigiana, 1534.
Lo Ipocrito, 1542.
Talanta, 1542.
Il Filosofo, 1546.
La Orazia, 1546.

OTHER WORKS BOTH SACRED AND PROFANE

Ragionamento della Nanna e della Antonia, 1534.
La passione di Gesù con due canzoni, 1534.
I sette salmi della penitentia di David, 1534.

I tre libri de la humanità di Cristo, 1535.
Dialogo nel quale la Nanna insegna alla Pippa sua figliuola, 1536.
Il Genesi con la visione di Noè, 1538.
Vita di Maria vergine, 1539.
Vita di Catherina vergine, 1540.
La vita di san Tomaso signor d'Aquino, 1543.
Dialogo nel quale si parla del giuoco con moralità piacevole (known as *Carte parlanti*), 1543.
Regionamento de le Corti, 1938.

LETTERS

Lettere I, 1538.
Lettere II, 1542.
Lettere III, 1546.
Lettere IV, 1550.
Lettere V, 1550.
Lettere VI, 1557.

APPENDIX 2

A NOTE ON BIOGRAPHICAL SOURCES

Mazzuchelli and Luzio are perhaps the best-known Italian language biographers of Pietro Aretino. Giammaria Mazzuchelli was an eighteenth-century Italian historian-biographer who completed numerous scholarly biographies of ancient and more modern authors. He had conceived of an ambitious plan to collect biographies of all the writers of Italy from the earliest times. To this end, he relied on the Queriniana library in Brescia, donated by the Cardinal Angelo Maria Quirini, as well as his extensive correspondence with the scholars of Italy and Europe. Mazzuchelli's biography of Pietro Aretino, the *Vita di Pietro Aretino* was first published in 1741 but was reprinted in Milan in 1830. Alessandro Luzio was a nineteenth-century Italian journalist and writer whose writings often covered Aretino's career. Luzio's *Pietro Aretino nei primi suoi anni a Venezia e la corte dei Gonzaga* (Torino, Ermanno Loescher, 1888) is a useful insight into the satirist's career at the court of Federico Gonzaga.

Francesco de Sanctis, author of the *Storia della Letteratura Italiana*, was meanwhile a leading nineteenth-century Italian literary critic and scholar of the Italian language. His monograph on Pietro Aretino, the *Biographical Essay*, is worth reading, though with the caveat that it is heavily biased against the poet and his lifestyle. The standard modern biography in the Italian language is Paul Larivaille, *Pietro Aretino* (Rome: Salerno Editrice, 1997).

The first major English language biography of Aretino was Edward Hutton's *Pietro Aretino The Scourge of Princes* (Constable, 1922). Hutton's book is essential reading, well documented with exhaustive footnotes and source references and provides a solid bare bones chronology of Aretino's life in addition to separate excursions into his relationships with the king of France and the Holy Roman Emperor, his secretaries, friends and his many lady friends. Thomas Caldecot Chubb's *Aretino, Scourge of Princes* (Reynal & Hitchcock, 1940) should also be included on the essential reading list although, like Hutton, it betrays the obvious stylistic limitations of the era in which it was written. Much of Aretino's output concerned sex and sexuality and 1922–1940 was an era in which a spade still could not yet be called a spade. Hutton, incidentally, also authored another book with a Venetian theme, *The Pageant of Venice* (John Lane, 1922), which incorporates illustrations by Sir Frank Brangwyn and is worth a read if you can only lay your hands on a copy.

A more recent English language biography is James Cleugh's *The divine Aretino, Pietro of Arezzo, 1492-1556: a Biography* (A. Blond, 1965). Cleugh's book is a more imaginative (and less prudish) visualisation of Aretino's life and times but tends on occasion to over-fictionalise and over-dramatise the material. Though a 'generalist' book that is clearly typical of its era, *The divine Aretino* is nevertheless a light hearted and engaging jaunt through Aretino's life and career. It also has the advantage of containing many excerpts of material which are otherwise difficult to find in English (Francesco Marcolini's published letter to Aretino being a good case in point). In the writing of this book I have, at times, drawn heavily on Cleugh's excellent quotes and translations of Aretino's correspondence as well as the correspondence of his friends to him (which is considerably less easy to fine).

In the sparse landscape of English-language criticism of the satirist's work, Raymond B. Waddington's *Aretino's Satyr: Sexuality, Satire, and Self-Projection in Sixteenth-Century Literature and Art* (University of Toronto Press, 2004), towers head and shoulders above what little else which is available out there. Waddington's thesis contends that Aretino's carefully cultivated public identity and 'scandalous persona', which was based on that of the satyr (the Renaissance origin of the word 'satire') came to eclipse the value of his writings, causing him to be denigrated both during and after his life as a pornographer and a blackmailer. Waddington also argues that Aretino's was the most famous face in Western Europe for a period, a claim which justifies to some extent the idea that Pietro Aretino was in certain important respects 'the world's first real celebrity'.

Christopher Cairns's book *Pietro Aretino and the Republic of Venice: Researches on Aretino and His Circle in Venice, 1527-1556* (University of California, 1985) meanwhile offers an interesting perspective on Aretino's life and work in the Venetian context. On the subject of Aretino's relationship with Titian see Luba Freedman's 1995 book *Titian's Portraits through Aretino's Lens* (Penn State University Press).

Finally, in the writing of this book I have made use of three main sources of English language compilations of Aretino's letters. These are as follows. *Pietro Aretino, The Works of Aretino: Dialogues - Letters and Sonnets [2 Vols.]* by Samuel Putnam (Covici Friede, 1933) includes letters which only goes up to the end of 1537. Thomas Caldecot Chubb's *The letters of Pietro Aretino* (Archon Books, 1967) is the most comprehensive selection of letters and goes up to the end of 1554. George Bull's *Aretino: Selected Letters* (Penguin Classics, 1976) cherry picks some of the most important letters and goes up to 1542. Since no compilation is completely exhaustive I have ransacked all three books for excerpts and quotations, not being a competent enough translator to make my own effort at this.

Putnam's translations from 1933 are obviously slightly more old-fashioned than Chubb's in 1967, and Bull's are the most modern of all. However, very often Putnam strikes the better turn of phrase or captures Aretino's meaning and nuance the best and so his translations have been used over and above the other two editors.

I make no apology for the difference in tone or phrasing that this may on occasion engender when different translators are placed side-by-side; the choice has been made purely based on my own personal preferences and what sounded right to my own ear. Meanwhile, for the most exhaustive compilation of the letters in the original Italian see *Le Lettere: Edizione nazionale delle opere di Pietro Aretino*, vols 1-6 translated and edited by Giovanni Aquilecchia and Angelo Romano (Rome: Salerno, 1997-2002).

BIBLIOGRAPHY

Ackroyd, P., *Venice: Pure City* (Vintage Books, 2010).

Alberti, L. B., (author), Romano, R. (editor), Tenenti, A. (editor), Furlan, F. (editor), *I libri della famiglia* (Einaudi, 1994).

Alberti, L. B., Watkins, R. N. (translator), *The family in Renaissance Florence* (University of South Carolina Press, 1969).

Andrews, R., *Scripts and Scenarios: the performance of comedy in Renaissance Italy* (Cambridge University Press, 1993).

Aretino, P. (author), Campbell, J. D. (translator), Sbrocchi, L. G. (translator), *Cortigiana* (Dovehouse Editions, 2003).

Aretino, P. (author), Roberto Di Marco (editor), *Dubbi amorosi, altri dubbi, sonetti lussuriosi* (Sampietro, 1966).

Aretino, P., *The letters of Pietro Aretino* (the University of Michigan, 2008).

Aretino, P., *Sonetti lussuriosi e dubbi amorosi* (castello volante, 2012).

Aretino, P. (author), Danilo Romei (editor), *Poem cavallereschi* (Rome & Salerno, 1995).

Aretino, P. (author), translator (anon.), *The Works of Aretino* (Rarity Press, 1931).

Arfaioli, M., *The Black Bands of Giovanni: Infantry and Diplomacy During the Italian Wars (1526-1528)*, (Pisa University Press, 2005).

Ashbee, H. S., *The Encyclopaedia of Erotic Literature: Being Notes, Bio-, Biblio-, Icono-graphical and Critical, on Curious and Uncommon Books, Volume 3* (Documentary Books, 1962).

Austern, L. (editor), Naroditskaya, I. (editor), *Music of the Sirens* (Indiana University Press, 2006).

Austern, L. P. (author), McBride, K. B. (author), *Psalms in the Early Modern World* (Routledge, 2016).

Avery, C. B., *The New Century Italian Renaissance Encyclopaedia* (Simon & Schuster, 1972).

Azzolini, M., *The Duke and the Stars: Astrology and Politics in Renaissance Milan (I Tatti studies in Italian Renaissance history)*, (Harvard University Press, 2013).

Baldini, N., *Raphael* (Rizzoli International Publications, 2005).

Bambach, C. (editor), *Leonardo da Vinci: Master Draftsman* (MetPublications, 2003).

Barnes, R. B., *Books Have Their Own Destiny: Essays in Honour of Robert V. Schnucker, Volume 50 of Sixteenth century essays & studies* (Truman State University Press, 1998).

Bataille, G., *Eroticism* (City Lights Books, 1962).

Bayer, A., *Art and Love in Renaissance Italy* (Metropolitan Museum of Art, 2008).

Beecher, D., *Renaissance Comedy: The Italian Masters, Volume 1* (University of Toronto Press, Scholarly Publishing Division, 2008).

Belozerskaya, M., *Luxury Arts of the Renaissance* (Getty Publications, 2005).

Berenson, B., *The Venetian Painters Of The Renaissance With An Index To Their Works* (G.P. Putnam's Sons, 1899).

Bergreen, L., *Casanova: The World of a Seductive Genius* (Simon and Schuster, 2016).

Bergreen, L., *Over the Edge of the World: Magellan's Terrifying Circumnavigation of the Globe* (Harper Collins, 2009).

Berni, F., *Il Primo Libro Dell'Opere Burlesche* (Leida, 1823).

Berni, F. (author), Virgili, A. (trans.) *Rime e poesi latine. Lettere edite e inedite* (Florence, 1885).

Bernstein, J. A., *Print Culture and Music in Sixteenth-Century Venice* (Oxford University Press, 2001).

Bernstein, J. A., *Music Printing in Renaissance Venice: The Scotto Press (1539-1572)*, (Oxford University Press, USA, 1998).

Black, R., *Benedetto Accolti and the Florentine Renaissance* (Cambridge University Press, 1985).

Black, R., *Machiavelli* (Routledge, 2013).

Boccaccio, G., *The Decameron* (Oxford University Press, 1998).

Boulting, W., *Tasso and His Times* (Haskell House Publishers, 1968).

Bouwsma, W. J., *Venice and the Defense of Republican Liberty: Renaissance Values in the Age of the Counter Reformation* (University of California Press, 1968).

Brand, P. (editor), Pertile, L. (editor), *The Cambridge History of Italian Literature Revised Edition* (Cambridge University Press, 1997).

Bruce, Y., *Images Of Matter: Essays On British Literature Of The Middle Ages And Renaissance: Proceedings Of The Eighth Citadel Conference On Literature* (University of Delaware Press, 2005).

Bruckman, P., *La Divina Commedia* (The Divine Comedy) Purgatorio (Xlibris Corporation, 2011).

Brundin, A. (author), Crivelli, T. (author), Sapegno, M. S. (author), *A Companion to Vittoria Colonna* (Brill, 2016).

Bull, G., (editor), *Aretino: Selected Letters* (Penguin Classics, 1976).

Bullard, M. M., *Filippo Strozzi and the Medici: Favour and Finance in Sixteenth-Century Florence and Rome* (Cambridge University Press, 2008).

Buonarroti, M. (author), Ramsden, E. H. (editor), *The Letters of Michelangelo, Volume 1* (Stanford University Press, 1963).

Burckhardt, J., *The Civilisation of the Period of the Renaissance in Italy* (Cambridge University Press, 2014).

Camesaca, E. (editor), Pertile, F. (editor), *Pietro Aretino, Lettere sull'arte, vol. 2, Vite lettere testimonianze di artisti italiani* (Milan: Edizioni del Milione, 1957).

Campbell, S. J., *The Cabinet of Eros: Renaissance Mythological Painting and the Studiolo of Isabella d'Este* (Yale University Press, 2006).

Campbell, J. D. (editor), Sbrocchi, L. G. (editor), *Cortigiana* (Dovehouse Editions, 2003).

Carney, J., *Renaissance and Reformation, 1500-1620: A Biographical Dictionary (The Great Cultural Eras of the Western World)*, (Greenwood, 2000).

Cartwright, J., *Isabella d'Este, marchioness of Mantua, 1474-1539; a study of the renaissance* (London: John Murray, 1923).

Cast, D. J., *The Ashgate Research Companion to Giorgio Vasari* (Routledge, 2016).

Castiglione, B. (author), Bull, G. (trans.), *The Book of the Courtier* (Viking Penguin, 1967).

Cawthorne, N., *Sex Lives of the Popes* (Prion, 2004).

Chamberlin, E. R., *The Sack of Rome* (Batsford, 1979).

Chastel, A., *The Sack of Rome, 1527*, trans. Beth Archer (Princeton, 1983).

Chubb, T. C., *Aretino, Scourge of Princes* (Reynal & Hitchcock, 1940).

Chubb, T. C., *The letters of Pietro Aretino* (Archon Books, 1967)

Cleugh, J., *The divine Aretino, Pietro of Arezzo, 1492-1556: a Biography* (A. Blond, 1965).

Clubb, L. G., *Pollastra and the Origins of Twelfth Night: Parthenio Commedia (1516) with an English Translation* (Ashgate Publishing Company, 2010).

Cohen, S., *Animals as Disguised Symbols in Renaissance Art* (Brill, 2008).

Cole, B., *Titian And Venetian Painting, 1450-1590* (Westview Press, 2000).

Collins, R., *Keepers Of The Keys Of Heaven: A History Of The Papacy* (Weidenfeld & Nicolson, 2009).

Connell, W. J. (editor), Zorzi, A. (editor), *Florentine Tuscany: Structures and Practices of Power* (Cambridge Studies in Italian History and Culture), (Cambridge University Press, 2004).

Conway, W. M. (editor), *Literary Remains of Albrecht Dürer* (Cambridge University Press, 1889).

Corretti, C., *Cellini's Perseus and Medusa and the Loggia dei Lanzi: Configurations of the Body of State* (Brill, 2015).

Cowan, Dr. A., Steward, Dr. J., *The City and the Senses: Urban Culture Since 1500* (Ashgate Publishing, Ltd., 2013).

Cox, V., *The Italian Renaissance* (I.B. Tauris, 2016).

Creighton, M., *A History of the Papacy from the Great Schism to the Sack of Rome, Volume 6* (Longmans, Green, and Company, 1919).

Cronin, V., *The Flowering Of The Renaissance* (Random House, 2011).

Crowe, J. A. (author), Cavalcaselle, G. B. (author), *Titian: His Life and Times: With Some Account of His Family, Chiefly from New and Unpublished Records, Volume 2* (J. Murray, 1877).

Dall'Aglio, S., *The Duke's Assassin: Exile and Death of Lorenzino de' Medici* (Yale University Press, 2015).

Davies, J., *Aspects of Violence in Renaissance Europe* (Routledge, 2016).

Dean, T. (author), Lowe, K. J. P. (author), *Crime, Society and the Law in Renaissance Italy* (Cambridge University Press, 1994).

D'Elia, U. R., *The Poetics of Titian's Religious Paintings* (Cambridge: Cambridge University Press, 2005).

Delph, R. (author), Fontaine, M. (author), Martin, J. (author), *Heresy, Culture, and Religion in Early Modern Italy: Contexts and Contestations* (Truman State University Press, 2015).

Dennistoun, J., *Memoirs of the Dukes of Urbino, Illustrating the Arms, Arts, and Litterature of Italy, from 1440 to 1630: In Three Volumes, Volume 3* (Longman, Brown, Green and Longmans, 1851).

Denton, C. *The War on Sex: Western Repression from the Torah to Victoria* (McFarland, 2014).

De Sanctis, F., *Storia della Letteratura Italiana* ('History of Italian literature'), (Morano, 2 Vols., 1870/71).

De Vries, J., *Caterina Sforza and the Art of Appearances: Gender, Art and Culture in Early Modern Italy* (Routledge, 2016).

Ditmore, M. H., *Encyclopaedia of Prostitution and Sex Work, Volume 2* (Greenwood Publishing Group, 2006).

Drummond, W., *The Poetical Works of William Drummond of Hawthornden, Volume 1* (Ardent Media, 1913).

Duppa, R., *Life of Michelangelo* (Bogue, 1846).

Durant, W., *The Renaissance: A History of Civilization in Italy from 1304-1576 A.D. (Story of Civilization, 5)*, (Simon & Schuster, 1953).

Dyer, G., *War: The New Edition* (Random House of Canada, 2010).

Elkins, J. (editor), Williams, R. (editor), *Renaissance Theory (The Art Seminar)*, (Routledge, 2007).

Emison, P. A., *Creating the "Divine" Artist: From Dante to Michelangelo* (Brill, 2004).

Erasmo, M., *Death: Antiquity and its Legacy* (I. B. Tauris & Company, 2012).

Ettore, B. (editor), *Opere di Francesco Algarotti e di Saverio Bettinelli* (Ricciardi, 1969).

Feerick, J. (editor), Nardizzi, V. (editor), *The Indistinct Human in Renaissance Literature* (Springer, 2012).

Feinstein, W., *The Civilization of the Holocaust in Italy: Poets, Artists, Saints, Anti-semites* (Fairleigh Dickinson University Press, 2003).

Fernando, A. (author), Silenzi, R. (author), *Pasquino Quattro secoli di satira romana* (Vallecchi, 1968).

Fiore, S. R., *Niccolò Machiavelli: An Annotated Bibliography of Modern Criticism and Scholarship (Bibliographies and Indexes in Law and Political Science)*, (Greenwood, 1990).

Finucci, V., *The Manly Masquerade: Masculinity, Paternity, and Castration in the Italian Renaissance* (Duke University Press, 2003).

Fletcher, C., *The Black Prince of Florence: The Spectacular Life and Treacherous World of Alessandro De' Medici* (Oxford University Press, 2016).

Forbes, B. H. R., *Studies in the History of Venice, Volume 2* (BiblioBazaar, 2009).

Franco, V. (author), Jones, A. R. (trans.), Rosenthal, M. F. (trans.), *Poems and Selected Letters* (University of Chicago Press, 2007).

Frantz, D. O., *Festum Voluptatis: A Study of Renaissance Erotica* (Ohio State University Press, 1989).

Freedman, L., *Classical Myths in Italian Renaissance Painting* (Cambridge University Press, 2015).

Freedman, L., *Titian's Portraits through Aretino's Lens* (Penn State University Press, 1995).

Freund, P., *Dramatis Personae: The Rise of Medieval and Renaissance Theatre* (Peter Owen, 2006).

Furlotti, B. (author), Rebecchini, G. (author), *The Art of Mantua: Power and Patronage in the Renaissance* (J. Paul Getty Museum, 2008).

Furlotti, B. (author), Rebecchini, G. (author), *The Art of Mantua: Power and Patronage in the Renaissance* (J. Paul Getty Museum, 2008).

Garin, E., *Renaissance Characters* (University of Chicago Press, 1997).

Gayangos, P., (editor), *Calendar of State Papers, Spain, Volume 3 Part 1, 1525-1526* (London, 1873).

Gaylard, S., *Hollow Men: Writing, Objects, and Public Image in Renaissance Italy* (Fordham University Press, 2013).

Geremek, B. (author), Birrell, J. (author), *The Margins of Society in Late Medieval Paris* (Cambridge University Press, 2006).

Getz, C. S., *Music in the Collective Experience in Sixteenth-century Milan* (Ashgate Publishing, 2005).

Giannetti, L. (editor), Ruggiero, G. (editor), *Five Comedies from the Italian Renaissance* (Johns Hopkins University Press, 2003).

Giannetti, L., *Lelia's Kiss: Imagining Gender, Sex, and Marriage in Italian Renaissance Comedy* (University of Toronto Press, 2009).

Gilbert, F., *The Pope, His Banker, and Venice* (Harvard University Press, 1991).

Gleason, E. G., *Gasparo Contarini: Venice, Rome and Reform* (University of California Press, 1993).

Glendinning, R., *Love, Death, and the Art of Compromise: Aeneas Sylvius Piccolomini's Tale of Two Lovers* in William C. McDonald (editor), *Fifteenth-Century Studies, Volume 23* (Camden House, 1997).

Gouwens, K., *Remembering the Renaissance: Humanist Narratives of the Sack of Rome* (Brill, 1998).

Grafton, A. (editor), Most, G. W. (editor), Settis, S. (editor), *The Classical Tradition* (Belknap Press, 2013).

Grafton, A., *Cardano's Cosmos: The Worlds and Works of a Renaissance Astrologer* (Harvard University Press, 1999).

Greenblatt, S., *The Swerve: How the World Became Modern* (W. W. Norton & Company, 2011).

Grendler, P. F., *The Universities of the Italian Renaissance* (Johns Hopkins University Press, 2002).

Grendler, P. F., *The Roman Inquisition and the Venetian Press, 1540-1605* (Princeton University Press, 2016).

Grillot, S. R (author), Z. P., Messitte (author), *Buon Giorno, Arezzo: A Postcard from Tuscany* (University of Oklahoma Press, 2016).

Guicciardini, F. (author), Brown, A. (editor), *Guicciardini: Dialogue on the Government of Florence (Cambridge Texts in the History of Political Thought)*, (Cambridge University Press, 1994).

Hajek, H. J., *Still a Rivalry: Contrasting Renaissance Sodomy Legislation in Florence and Venice* (2015).

Hale, J., *The Civilization of Europe in the Renaissance* (HarperCollins, 1993).

Hale, J. R. (author), Chambers, D. (author), Clough, C. H. (author), Mallett M. (author), *War, Culture and Society in Renaissance Venice: Essays in Honour of John Hale* (A&C Black, 1993).

Hale, S., *Titian: His Life* (Harper Collins, 2012).

Hall, M. B. (author), Cooper, T. E. (author), *The Sensuous in the Counter-Reformation Church* (Cambridge University Press, 2013).

Harrán, D. (translator), Sarra Copia Sulam (author), *Jewish Poet and Intellectual in Seventeenth-Century Venice: The Works of Sarra Copia Sulam in Verse and Prose Along with Writings of Her Contemporaries in Her Praise, Condemnation, or Defense* (University of Chicago Press, 2009).

Hayes-Healy, S., *Medieval Paradigms: Volume I: Essays in Honour of Jeremy duQuesnay Adams* (Springer, 2016).

Herlihy, D., *Women, Family and Society in Medieval Europe: Historical Essays, 1978-1991* (Berghahn Books, 1995).

Hickson, S. A., *Women, Art and Architectural Patronage in Renaissance Mantua: Matrons, Mystics and Monasteries* (Routledge, 2016).

Hoenselaars, A. J., *The Italian World of English Renaissance Drama: Cultural Exchange and Intertextuality* (University of Delaware Press, 1998).

Hope, C., *Titian* (London: Jupiter Books, 1980).

Hook, J., *The Sack of Rome: 1527* (Palgrave Macmillan, 2004).

Horodowich, E., *Language and Statecraft in Early Modern Venice* (Cambridge University Press, 2008).

Howard, D., *Jacopo Sansovino Architecture and Patronage in Renaissance Venice* (Yale University Press, 1975).

Hunt, J. M., *The Vacant See in Early Modern Rome: A Social History of the Papal Interregnum* (Brill, 2016).

Hunt, L., *The Invention of Pornography, 1500-1800: Obscenity and the Origins of Modernity* (MIT Press, 1996).

Hutton, E., *Pietro Aretino The Scourge of Princes* (Constable, 1922).

Hutton, E., *The Pageant of Venice* (John Lane, 1922).

Janin, H. (author), Carlson, U. (author), *Mercenaries in Medieval and Renaissance Europe* (McFarland, 2013).

Jones, R. (author), Penny, N. (author), *Raphael* (Yale University Press, 1983).

Jordan, P., *The Venetian Origins of the Commedia dell'Arte* (Routledge, 2014).

Karlen, A., *Sexuality and Homosexuality* (Norton, 1971).

Keizer, J (author), Richardson, T. (author), *The Transformation of Vernacular Expression in Early Modern Arts* (Brill, 2011).

Key, N. (editor), Bucholz, R. O. (editor), *Sources and Debates in English History, 1485 – 1714* (John Wiley & Sons, 2009).

Kidwell, C., *Pietro Bembo: Lover, Linguist, Cardinal* (McGill-Queen's Press - MQUP, 2004).

Kim, D. Y., *The Traveling Artist in the Italian Renaissance: Geography, Mobility, and Style* (Yale University Press, 2014).

Klein, H. M. (author), Marrapodi, M. (author), *Shakespeare and Italy* (Mellen, 1999).

Klein, R (editor), Zerner, H. (editor), *Italian Art, 1500-1600: Sources and Documents* (Northwestern University Press, 1989).

Kleiner, F. S., *Gardner's Art through the Ages: A Concise Western History* (Cengage Learning, Inc., 2016).

Kliemann, J., *Giorgio Vasari* (Oxford University Press, 2016).

Knecht, R. J., *Francis I* (Cambridge University Press, 1984).

Knecht, R. J., *Renaissance Warrior and Patron: The Reign of Francis I* (Cambridge University Press, 1996).

Lach, D. F., *Asia in the Making of Europe, Volume I: The Century of Discovery. Book 1.* (University Of Chicago Press, 1994).

Lamb, H., *Süleyman the Magnificent - Sultan of the East* (Read Books Ltd, 2013).

Landon, W. J., *Lorenzo di Filippo Strozzi and Niccolò Machiavelli: Patron, Client, and the Pistola fatta per la peste/An Epistle Written Concerning the Plague* (Toronto Italian Studies).

Langdon, G., *Medici Women: Portraits of Power, Love and Betrayal from the Court of Duke Cosimo I* (University of Toronto Press, 2006).

Larivaille, P., *Pietro Aretino* (Rome: Salerno Editrice, 1997).

Lawner, L., *I Modi: The Sixteen Pleasures : An Erotic Album of the Italian Renaissance* (Northwestern University Press, 1989).

Leavitt, D., *Florence (The Writer & the City)*, (Bloomsbury Publishing, 2002).

Legman, G., *Rationale of the dirty joke: an analysis of sexual humour, Volume 2* (Grove Press, 1975).

Leigh, L., *Shakespeare and the Embodied Heroine: Staging Female Characters in the Late Plays and Early Adaptations* (Palgrave Shakespeare Studies), (Palgrave Macmillan, 2014).

Lepschy, A. L., *Tintoretto Observed: A Documentary Survey of Critical Reactions from the 16th to the 20th Century* (Longo, 1983).

Levy, A. M., *Remembering Masculinity in Early Modern Florence* (Ashgate Publishing, 2006).

Lisa Pon, Raphael, Dürer, and Marcantonio Raimondi: *Copying and the Italian Renaissance Print* (Yale University Press, 2004).

Lowe, K. J. P., *Nuns' Chronicles and Convent Culture in Renaissance and Counter-Reformation Italy* (Cambridge University Press, 2003).

Lowenthal, A. W., *Joachim Wtewael: Mars and Venus Surprised by Vulcan* (Getty Publications, 1995).

Lytle, G. F. (editor), Stephen Orgel, S. (editor), *Patronage in the Renaissance* (Princeton University Press, 2014).

Lucchese, F. D. (author), Frosini, F. (author), Morfino, V. (author), *The Radical Machiavelli: Politics, Philosophy, and Language* (BRILL, 2015).

Luther, M. (author), Dillenberger, J. (editor), *An Appeal to the Ruling Class, in Martin Luther: Selections From His Writing* (Anchor, 1958).

Luzio, A. (author), Renier, R. (author), *Giornale storici della Letteratura Italiana, V* (1885).

Luzio, A., *La Famiglia di P.A. in Giornale Stor. della Lett. Ital, IV* (1884).

Luzio, A., *Pietro Aretino Nei Primi Suoi Anni a Venezia e la Corte dei Gonzaga* (Torino, 1888).

Machiavelli, N., *Discourses on Livy* (Dover Publications, 2007).

Machiavelli, N., *Discourses on Livy* (University of Chicago Press, 1996).

Machiavelli, N., *Machiavelli: The Chief Works and Others, Volume 2* (Duke University Press, 1989).

Machiavelli, N. (author), Milner, S. J. (translator), *The Prince and Other Political Writings* (Everyman, 1995).

Magno, A. M., *Bound in Venice: The Serene Republic and the Dawn of the Book* (Europa Editions, 2013).

Mallett, M. (author), Mann, N., *Lorenzo the Magnificent: Culture and Politics* (The Warburg Institute, 1996).

Marek, G. R., *The Bed and the Throne: The Life of Isabella d'Este* (Harper and Row, 1976).

Marrapodi, M., *Shakespeare and the Italian Renaissance: Appropriation, Transformation, Opposition (Anglo-Italian Renaissance Studies)*, (Routledge, 2014).

Marrone, G. (editor), Puppa, P. (editor), *Encyclopaedia of Italian Literary Studies: A-J* (Routledge, 2006).

Martin, J. J. (author), Romano, D. (author), *Venice Reconsidered: The History and Civilization of an Italian City-State, 1297–1797* (JHU Press, 2002).

Martin, J., *Venice's Hidden Enemies: Italian Heretics in a Renaissance City* (University of California Press, 1993).

Matarazzo, F. (author), Morgan, E. S. (trans.), *Chronicles of the City of Perugia 1492-1503* (J. M. Dent & Co., 1905).

Mayernik, D., *The Challenge of Emulation in Art and Architecture: Between Imitation and Invention* (Routledge, 2016).

Mazzuchelli G. of Brescia, *La vita di Pietro Aretino Scritta Dal Conte* (Padova, G. Comino, 1830).

McCormack, J., *One Million Mercenaries: Swiss Soldiers in the Armies of the World* (Leo Cooper, June 1993).

McDonald, W. C., *Fifteenth-Century Studies, Volume 23* (Camden House, 1997).

McNeill, W. H., *Venice: The Hinge of Europe, 1081-1797* (University of Chicago Press, 2009).

Meyer, G. J., *The Borgias: The Hidden History* (Bantam, 2013).

Michelson, P., *Speaking the Unspeakable: A Poetics of Obscenity* (SUNY Press, 1993).

Milano, D. (editor), *Vita di Pietro Aretino*, formerly attributed to Berni, in Bib. Rara (1864) (the '*Pseudo-Berni*').

Mitchell, B., *Rome in the High Renaissance: The Age of Leo X* (University of Oklahoma Press, 1973).

Monti, J., *The King's Good Servant But God's First: The Life and Writings of Saint Thomas More* (Ignatius Press, 1997).

More, T., Bacon, F., Neville, H., *Three Early Modern Utopias: Thomas More: Utopia / Francis Bacon: New Atlantis / Henry Neville: The Isle of Pines* (Oxford University Press, 1999).

Moulton, I., *Love in Print in the Sixteenth Century: The Popularization of Romance* (Springer, 2014).

Moulton, I., (author), Arsiccio (*Intronato*), *La Cazzaria: The Book of the Prick* (Psychology Press, 2003).

Moynahan, B., *The Faith: A History of Christianity* (Crown Publishing Group, 2007).

Muir, M., *Civic Ritual in Renaissance Venice* (Princeton University Press, 1981).

Müntz, E., *Michelangelo* (Parkstone International, 2012).

Murphy, P. V., *Ruling Peacefully: Cardinal Ercole Gonzaga and Patrician Reform in Sixteenth-Century Italy* (CUA Press, 2007).

Murray, W., *City of the Soul: A Walk in Rome* (Crown, 2003).

Murrin, M., *History and Warfare in Renaissance Epic* (University of Chicago Press, 1994).

Nagel, A., *The Controversy of Renaissance Art* (University Of Chicago Press, 2011).

Najemy, J. M., *Italy in the Age of the Renaissance: 1300-1550* (Oxford University Press, 2005).

Nichols, T., *Tintoretto: Tradition and Identity* (Reaktion Books, 2015).

Nissen, C., *Kissing the Wild Woman: Art, Beauty, and the Reformation of the Italian Prose Romance in Giulia Bigolina's Urania* (University of Toronto Press, 2011).

Northcote, J., *The Life of Titian* (1830).

Norton, R., *My dear boy: gay love letters through the centuries* (Leyland Publications, 1998).

Orgel, S., *Imagining Shakespeare: A History of Texts and Visions* (Palgrave Macmillan, 2003).

Ovid (author), Green, P. (translator, introduction), *The Erotic Poems* (Penguin Classics, 1983).

Ovid (author), Green, P. (translator, introduction), *The Erotic Poems* (Penguin Classics, 1983).

Paoletti (author), Radke, G. M. (author), *Art in Renaissance Italy* (Prentice Hall, 2005).

Pardoe, J., *The Court and Reign of Francis the First, King of France, Volume 2* (Richard Bentley, 1849).

Pattenden, Dr. M. (editor), Baker-Bates, Dr. P., *The Spanish Presence in Sixteenth-Century Italy: Images of Iberia* (Ashgate Publishing, 2015).

Penn, I., *Dogma Evolution & Papal Fallacies* (AuthorHouse, 2007).

Peterson, D. S. (editor), Bornstein, D. E. (editor), *Florence and Beyond: Culture, Society and Politics in Renaissance Italy: Essays in Honour of John M. Najemy (Essays and Studies, Volume 15)*, (Centre for Reformation and Renaissance Studies, 2008).

Pila, J. (author), Torremans, P., *European Intellectual Property Law* (Oxford University Press, 2016).

Plaisance, M., *Florence in the Time of the Medici: Public Celebrations, Politics, and Literature in the Fifteenth and Sixteenth Centuries* (Centre for Reformation and Renaissance Studies, 2008).

Pon, L., *Raphael, Dürer, and Marcantonio Raimondi: Copying and the Italian Renaissance Print* (Yale University Press, 2004).

Price, P. M., *Moderata Fonte: Women and Life in Sixteenth-century Venice* (Fairleigh Dickinson University Press, 2003).

Putnam, G. H., *Books and Their Makers During the Middle Ages: A Study of the Conditions of the Production and Distribution of Literature from the Fall of the Roman Empire to the Close of the Seventeenth Century, Volume 1* (Hillary House, 1962).

Putnam, S., *The Works of Aretino: Dialogues* (Covici Friede, 1933).

Putnam, S., *The Works of Aretino: Letters and Sonnets* (Covici Friede, 1933).

Pyhrr, S. W. (author), Godoy, J. A. (author), *Heroic Armour of the Italian Renaissance: Filippo Negroli and His Contemporaries* (Metropolitan Museum of Art, 1998).

Quaintance, C., *Textual Masculinity and the Exchange of Women in Renaissance Venice* (University of Toronto Press, 2015).

Rebecchini, G., *Private Collectors in Mantua, 1500-1630* (Ed. di Storia e Letteratura, 2002).

Reiss, S. E. (author, editor), Wilkins, D. G. (author, editor), *Beyond Isabella: Secular Women Patrons of Art in Renaissance Italy (Sixteenth Century Essays & Studies, V. 54)*, (Truman State University Press, 2001).

Reston, J. Jr., *Defenders of the Faith: Christianity and Islam Battle for the Soul of Europe, 1520-1536* (Penguin Books, 2010).

Reynolds, A., *Renaissance Humanism at the Court of Clement VII: Francesco Berni's "Dialogue against Poets" in Context* (New York, 1997).

Ridolfi, C., *The Life of Titian* (Penn State Press, 2010).

Roeder, R., *Renaissance Lawgivers: Savonarola, Machiavelli, Castiglione, and Aretino* (Viking Press, 1933).

Roskill, M. W., *Dolce's Aretino and Venetian Art Theory of the Cinquecento* (Renaissance Society of America).

Richard, A., *Scripts and Scenarios: The Performance of Comedy in Renaissance Italy* (Cambridge University Press, Cambridge, 1993).

Richardson, B., *Printing, Writers and Readers in Renaissance Italy* (Cambridge University Press, 1999).

Robin, D., *Publishing Women: Salons, the Presses, and the Counter-Reformation in Sixteenth-Century Italy* (University of Chicago Press, 2007).

Rocke, M., *Forbidden Friendships: Homosexuality and Male Culture in Renaissance Florence* (Oxford University Press, 1998).

Rosand, D., *Titian* (Abrams, 1978).

Rosenberg, C. M. (editor), *The Court Cities of Northern Italy: Milan, Parma, Piacenza, Mantua, Ferrara, Bologna, Urbino, Pesaro, and Rimini (Artistic Centers of the Italian Renaissance)*, (Cambridge University Press, 2010).

Rosenthal, M. F., *The Honest Courtesan: Veronica Franco, Citizen and Writer in Sixteenth-Century Venice* (University of Chicago Press, 1992).

Roskill, M. W., *Dolce's Aretino and Venetian Art Theory of the Cinquecento* (Toronto: University of Toronto Press, 2000).

Rosenthal, R., (trans.), *Aretino's Dialogues* (Stein and Day, 1971).

Rossi, V., *Dal Rinascimento al Risorgimento* (Florence, 1930).

Rossi, V., *Pasquinate di P. A. edanonime* (Palermo-Turin, 1891).

Ruggiero, G., *The Renaissance in Italy: A Social and Cultural History of the Rinascimento* (Cambridge University Press, 2014).

Russell, J. R., *Diplomats at Work: Three Renaissance Studies* (History/prehistory & Medieval History), (Sutton Pub Ltd., 1992).

Sanders, D., *Music at the Gonzaga Court in Mantua* (Lexington Books, 2012).

San Juan, R. M., *Rome: A City Out of Print* (University of Minnesota Press, 2001).

Sanudo, M, Labalme, P. H. (trans.), White, L. S. (trans.), *Selections from the Renaissance Diaries of Marino Sanudo* (JHU Press, 2008).

Satz, A. (editor), Wood, J. (editor), *Articulate Objects: Voice, Sculpture and Performance* (Peter Lang AG, Internationaler, 2009).

Saul, J. R., *Voltaire's Bastards: The Dictatorship of Reason in the West* (Simon and Schuster, 2013).

Scaglione, A. D., *Knights at Court: Courtliness, Chivalry and Courtesy from Ottonian Germany to the Italian Renaissance* (University of California Press, 1992).

Schmitt, C. B., *The Cambridge History of Renaissance Philosophy* (Cambridge University Press, 1988).

Schulz, J., *Venetian Painted Ceilings of the Renaissance* (University of California Press).

Schutte, A. J., *Pier Paolo Vergerio: The Making of an Italian Reformer* (Librairie Droz, 1977).

Scigliano, E., *Michelangelo's Mountain: The Quest For Perfection in the Marble Quarries of Carrara* (Simon and Schuster, 2007).

Serlio, S. (author), Rosenfeld, M. N. (editor), *Serlio on Domestic Architecture* (Dover Publications, 1997).

Servadio, G., *Renaissance Woman* (I.B.Tauris, 2016).

Sethre, J., *The Souls of Venice* (McFarland, 2003).

Setton, K. M., *The Papacy and the Levant, (1204-1571): The sixteenth century to the reign of Julius III* (American Philosophical Society, 1984).

Shaw, C., *Julius II: The Warrior Pope* (Blackwell, 1993).

Shephard, T., *Echoing Helicon: Music, Art and Identity in the Este Studioli, 1440-1530* (Oxford University Press, 2014).

Shepherd, W., *The life of Poggio Bracciolini* (T. Cadel, Jun and W. Davies, 1802).

Siena, K. P., *Sins of the Flesh: Responding to Sexual Disease in Early Modern Europe (Essays and Studies, Vol. 7)*, (Centre for Reformation and Renaissance Studies, 2005).

Skinner, Q. (author), Price, R., *The Prince (Cambridge Texts in the History of Political Thought)*, (Cambridge University Press, 2007).

Smarr, J. L. (editor), Valentini, D. (editor), *Italian Women and the City: Essays* (Fairleigh Dickinson University Press, 2003).

Smith, J. C., *Nuremberg, a Renaissance City, 1500-1618* (University of Texas Press, 1983).

Smithers, L. C., (trans.), Burton R. F. (trans.), *Priapea sive diversorum poetarum in Priapum lusus, or, Sportive Epigrams on Priapus* (1890).

Sohm, P. L., *The Artist Grows Old: The Aging of Art and Artists in Italy, 1500-1800* (Yale University Press, 2007).

Sokol, B. J., *Art and Illusion in The Winter's Tale* (Manchester University Press, 1994).

John T. Spike, *Young Michelangelo: The Path to the Sistine: A Biography Paperback* (Duckworth Overlook, 2011).

Stampa, G., *The Complete Poems: The 1554 Edition of the 'Rime', a Bilingual Edition* (University of Chicago Press, 2010).

Stewart, A., *Close Readers: Humanism and Sodomy in Early Modern England* (Princeton University Press, 2014).

Strocchia, S. T., *Death and ritual in Renaissance Florence* (The Johns Hopkins University Press, 1992).

Symonds, J. A., *Renaissance in Italy: Italian literature* (Henry Holt, 1888).

Symonds, J. A., *The Life of Michelangelo Buonarroti: Volume II: Based on Studies in the Archives of the Buonarroti Family at Florence* (University of Pennsylvania Press, 2002).

Tafuri, M., *Venice and the Renaissance* (MIT Press, 1995).

Talvacchia, B., *Taking Positions: On the Erotic in Renaissance Culture* (Princeton University Press, 1999).

Terpening, R. H., *Miserabile Et Glorioso Lodovic* (University of Toronto Press, 1997).

Thomsett, M. C. (editor), Thomsett, J. F. (editor), *War and Conflict Quotations: A Worldwide Dictionary of Pronouncements from Military*

Leaders, Politicians, Philosophers, Writers and Others (McFarland, 1997).

Thucydides (author), Finley, M. I. (editor), *The History of the Peloponnesian War* (Penguin Books, 2000).

Tinagli, P. (author), Rogers, M. (author), *Women in Italian Renaissance Art: Gender, representation, identity* (Manchester University Press, 1997).

Titian, *Delphi Complete Works of Titian (Illustrated)*, (Delphi Classics, 2015).

Turner, J., *Sexuality and Gender in Early Modern Europe: Institutions, Texts, Images* (Cambridge University Press, 1993).

Unger, M., J., *Machiavelli: A Biography* (Simon & Schuster, 2011).

Van Veen, H. T., *The Translation of Raphael's Roman Style* (Peeters, 2007).

Vasari, G., *Lives of the Painters, Sculptors and Architects* (Everyman's Library, 1963).

Vasari, G. (author), Bondanella J. C. (trans.), Bondanella, P. (trans.), *The Lives of the Artists* (Oxford University Press, 1991).

Vasari, G. (author), Lavin, M. A. (editor), Foster, J. (translator), *Vasari's Lives of the Artists* (Courier Corporation, 2012).

Vasari, G. (author), Pallen, T. A., (editor), *Vasari on Theatre* (SIU Press, 1999).

Vaughan, H., *The Medici Popes: Leo X and Clement VII* (Methuen & Co., 1908).

Verberckmoes, J., *Laughter, Jestbooks and Society in the Spanish Netherlands* (Springer, 1999).

Verstegen, I. (editor), *Patronage and Dynasty: The Rise of the Della Rovere in Renaissance Italy* (Truman State University Press, 2007).

Viladesau, R., *The Triumph of the Cross: The Passion of Christ in Theology and the Arts from the Renaissance to the Counter-Reformation* (Oxford University Press, 2008).

Viroli, M. (author) & Shugaar, A. (translator), *Niccolò's Smile: A Biography of Machiavelli* (Hill and Wang, 2002).

Viroli, M., *Machiavelli's God* (Princeton University Press, 2010).

Waddington, R., *Aretino's Satyr: Sexuality, Satire, and Self-Projection in Sixteenth-Century Literature and Art (Toronto Italian Studies)*, (University of Toronto Press, 2004).

Waddington, R., *Review of Talvacchia 1999. Sixteenth Century Journal 31, no. 3* (2000).

Weinstein, R., *Juvenile Sexuality, Kabbalah, and Catholic Reformation in Italy: Tiferet Bahurim by Pinhas Barukh Ben Pelatiyah Monselice* (Brill, 2009).

Wills, G., *Venice: Lion City: The Religion of Empire* (Simon and Schuster, 2002).

Michel Winock, *Flaubert* (Harvard University Press, 2016).

Young, C. C., *Apples of Gold in Settings of Silver: Stories of Dinner as a Work of Art* (Simon & Schuster, 2002).

Young Kim, D., *The Traveling Artist in the Italian Renaissance: Geography, Mobility, and Style* (Yale University Press, 2014).

NOTES

1 A distinction which Voltaire would later arguably inherit.
2 Patricia A. Emison, *Creating the "Divine" Artist: From Dante to Michelangelo* (BRILL, 2004), p. 273.
3 Edward Hutton, *Pietro Aretino, the Scourge of Princes* (Constable, 1922), p. 245.
4 *Sonetti lussuriosi*, Of Fireside Sports, II; in Samuel Putnam, *The Works of Aretino: Letters and Sonnets* (Covici Friede, 1933), p. 253.
5 Peter Michelson, *Speaking the Unspeakable: A Poetics of Obscenity* (SUNY Press, 1993), p. 4.
6 Quoted from *The Works of Thomas Nashe*, ed. R.B. McKerrow and Rev. F.P. Wilson, 5 vols. (Oxford, 1958), II: 264.
7 Richard Duppa, *Life of Michelangelo* (Bogue, 1846), p. 56.
8 James Dennistoun, *Memoirs of the Dukes of Urbino, Illustrating the Arms, Arts, and Literature of Italy, from 1440 to 1630: In Three Volumes, Volume 3* (Longman, Brown, Green and Longmans, 1851), pp. 270-271.
9 James Dennistoun, *Memoirs of the Dukes of Urbino, Illustrating the Arms, Arts, and Literature of Italy, from 1440 to 1630: In Three Volumes, Volume 3* (Longman, Brown, Green and Longmans, 1851), pp. 271-272.
10 Jacob Burckhardt, *The Civilization of the Renaissance in Italy* (The Floating Press, 2015), p. 136.
11 John Addington Symonds, Renaissance in Italy: Italian Literature (Library of Alexandria, 1906).
12 Pietro Aretino, *The Works of Aretino: Dialogues - Letters and Sonnets [2 Vols.]*, trans. Samuel Putnam (Covici Friede, 1933), p. 9.
13 Ibid., p. 280.
14 Marcia B. Hall & Tracy E. Cooper, *The Sensuous in the Counter-Reformation Church* (Cambridge University Press, 2013), p. 56.
15 Pietro Aretino, *The Works of Aretino: Dialogues - Letters and Sonnets [2 Vols.]*, trans. Samuel Putnam (Covici Friede, 1933), p. 290.
16 John Ralston Saul, *Voltaire's Bastards: The Dictatorship of Reason in the West* (Simon and Schuster, 2013), p. 467.
17 Georges Bataille, *Eroticism* (City Lights Books, 1962), p. 273.
18 Pietro Aretino, translator (anon.), *The Works of Aretino* (Rarity Press, 1931), p. 24.
19 Richard Andrews, *Scripts and Scenarios: the performance of comedy in Renaissance Italy* (Cambridge University Press, 1993), p. 66.
20 Pietro Aretino, *The Works of Aretino: Dialogues - Letters and Sonnets [2 Vols.]*, trans. Samuel Putnam (Covici Friede, 1933), p. 15.
21 Raymond Rosenthal (trans.), *Aretino's Dialogues* (Stein and Day, 1971), pp. 123-124; cited in Margaret F. Rosenthal, *The Honest Courtesan: Veronica Franco, Citizen and Writer in Sixteenth-Century Venice* (University of Chicago Press, 1992), pp. 35-36.
22 In an interesting and lively metaphor, Aretino would compare pedants who '..study, and studying concoct their fantasies with the same stubborn patience that ladies have when they bleach their hair upon the rooftops when the sun is burning hot'. Aretino references a common 'cosmetic' practice of Venetian women at this time. Quote is from Aretino's letter of Francesco Marcolini, July 1545, *Lettere* 110. The Vanity of Pedants, in in Thomas Caldecott Chubb, *The Letters of Pietro Aretino* (Archon Books, 1967), p. 206.

[23] The quote is from the chapter on Aretino by John Addington Symonds, *Renaissance in Italy: Italian literature* (Henry Holt, 1888).

[24] John Addington Symonds, *Renaissance in Italy: Italian Literature* (Library of Alexandria, 1906).

[25] Aretino to Boccamazza, August 1554, *Lettere* 255. A Right to be Born, in Thomas Caldecott Chubb, *The Letters of Pietro Aretino* (Archon Books, 1967), p. 319.

[26] Janet Sethre, *The Souls of Venice* (McFarland, 2003), p. 184.

[27] *'Il condottiero della letteratura'.*

[28] Luba Freedman, *Titian's Portraits through Aretino's Lens* (Penn State University Press, 1995), p. 66.

[29] Raymond B. Waddington, Aretino's Satyr: Sexuality, Satire and Self-projection in Sixteenth-century Literature and Art (University of Toronto Press, 2004), p. 92.

[30] Aretino to Danese, January 1553, *Lettere* 244. The Scion of a Lowborn Race, in Thomas Caldecott Chubb, *The Letters of Pietro Aretino* (Archon Books, 1967), pp. 306-307.

[31] Quoted by Alessandro Marzo Magno, *Bound in Venice: The Serene Republic and the Dawn of the Book* (Europa Editions, 2013).

[32] The quote is Bruce Cole's from *Titian And Venetian Painting, 1450-1590* (Westview Press, 2000), p. 138.

[33] Philip Lindsay Sohm, *The Artist Grows Old: The Aging of Art and Artists in Italy, 1500-1800* (Yale University Press, 2007), p. 91

[34] Pietro Aretino, *The Works of Aretino: Dialogues - Letters and Sonnets [2 Vols.]*, trans. Samuel Putnam (Covici Friede, 1933). All further references will be to this edition. See letter to Giovio written in May, 1545 (III, 141) in which he says he was in his fifty-fourth year; another written in July of same year (III, 153), in which he says he had reached the age of fifty-three years; and another written in November, 1552 (VI, 111), in which he says that he has passed his sixtieth birthday.

[35] Requoted by Robert Black, *Benedetto Accolti and the Florentine Renaissance* (Cambridge University Press, 1985), p. 5.

[36] Suzette R. Grillot & Zach P. Messitte, *Buon Giorno, Arezzo: A Postcard from Tuscany* (University of Oklahoma Press, 2016), p. 30.

[37] Requoted by Robert Black, *Benedetto Accolti and the Florentine Renaissance* (Cambridge University Press, 1985), p. 15.

[38] L. Cardella, *Memorie Storiche de' Cardinali*, 1793, iii., p. 450.

[39] See Alessandro Luzio, *La Famiglia di P.A. in Giornale Stor. della Lett. Ital*, IV (1884), 361, et seq., as cited in Edward Hutton, *Pietro Aretino, the Scourge of Princes* (Constable, 1922), pp. 5-6.

[40] Louise George Clubb, *Pollastra and the Origins of Twelfth Night: Parthenio Commedia (1516) with an English Translation* (Ashgate Publishing Company, 2010), p. 22.

[41] See Letter II, 158, as cited in Hutton, p. 9.

[42] Aretino to his brother-in-law Orazio Vanotti, November 1542, *Lettere* 95. The Death of a Sister, in Thomas Caldecott Chubb, *The Letters of Pietro Aretino* (Archon Books, 1967), p. 187.

[43] See Will Durant, *The Renaissance: A History of Civilization in Italy from 1304-1576 A.D. (Story of Civilization, 5)*, (Simon & Schuster, 1953), pp. 50-51.

[44] See John Hale, *The Civilization of Europe in the Renaissance* (HarperCollins, 1993), pp. 374-375.

[45] See James Cleugh, *The divine Aretino, Pietro of Arezzo, 1492-1556: a biography* (Anthony Blond, 1965), p. 27.

[46] See Hutton, pp. 9-11; 'You are an Antichrist, a limb of the Great Devil. One sees the picture of the Virgin Annunciate that you have in your rooms, the portrait painted by Messer Giorgio Vasari that he was made by you to copy because you said it was an effigy of your mother. So to all you say: This is my mother, showing the Madonna. Thus you compare yourself to Jesus Christ, just like Antichrist' (Doni, *Terremoto*, II, 204.)

[47] Cleugh, p. 27.

[48] See Francesco De Sanctis, *Storia della Letteratura Italiana* ('History of Italian literature'), (Morano, 2 Vols., 1870/71), regarded as the first truly complete, organic treatment of Italian literature.

[49] Aretino to Francesco Marcolini, July 1545, *Lettere* 110. The Vanity of Pedants, in Thomas Caldecott Chubb, *The Letters of Pietro Aretino* (Archon Books, 1967), p. 207.

[50] See Hutton, pp. 4-5.

[51] Cleugh, p. 28.

[52] The insulting information was contained in a letter from Medoro Nucci to Aretino which has been preserved in the *Archivio di Stato di Firenze*. See Hutton p. 6.

[53] Pietro Aretino, *The Works of Aretino: Dialogues - Letters and Sonnets [2 Vols.]*, trans. Samuel Putnam (Covici Friede, 1933), p. 18.

[54] See Hutton, p. 7.

[55] For an engaging account of Poggio Bracciolini and his influence on Italian Renaissance humanism and indeed the scientific era which followed see Stephen Greenblatt, *The Swerve: How the World Became Modern* (W. W. Norton & Company, 2011).

[56] See *The Penny Cyclopaedia of the Society for the Diffusion of Useful Knowledge. In fourteen volumes, Volume 2* (Charles Knight, 1833-1844), p. 304.

[57] The commander of the Ghibelline cavalry at the battle of Campaldino, Bonconte da Montefeltro, was killed in one of the Aretine attacks and his body was never subsequently found. This fate made a deep impression on Dante, who had fought with the Guelph cavalry during the battle. Consequently, Bonconte appears in the V canto of Purgatory and is accorded repentance *in extremis*. Buonoconte's widow and the friends he knew in life are all indicated as having forgotten about him, therefore he walks among the shades with his head bowed with sadness. See Paul Bruckman, *La Divina Commedia (The Divine Comedy) Purgatorio* (Xlibris Corporation, 2011), pp. 114-118.

[58] See William J. Connell & Andrea Zorzi, *Florentine Tuscany: Structures and Practices of Power (Cambridge Studies in Italian History and Culture)*, (Cambridge University Press, 2004), pp. 297-299.

[59] See Michael Mallett & Nicholas Mann, *Lorenzo the Magnificent: Culture and Politics* (The Warburg Institute, 1996), p. 230.

[60] See Miles J. Unger, *Machiavelli: A Biography* (Simon & Schuster, 2011), p. 113.

[61] For a graphic description of Piero de' Medici's lifestyle whilst in exile in Rome see Danny Chaplin, *The Medici: Rise of a Parvenu Dynasty, 1360-1537* (CreateSpace Independent Publishing, 2016), pp. 380-381.

[62] See Connell & Zorzi, Chapter 14, *Arezzo, the Medici and the Florentine Regime*, pp. 293-311 for a comprehensive account of the Arezzo rebellion of 1502.

[63] For details of the psychopathy of the two Vitelli brothers see G. J. Meyer, *The Borgias: The Hidden History* (Bantam, 2013), pp. 320-321.

[64] For a more detailed account of the respective roles of Vitelli, Bagliono and Cesare Borgia in the Arezzo rebellion of 1502 see G.J. Meyer, *The Borgias: The Hidden History* (Bantam, 2013), p. 330, p. 333, pp. 339-340, p. 343.

[65] See Carmen Bambach (editor) et al, *Leonardo da Vinci: Master Draftsman* (MetPublications, 2003) for an image of the sketch map which Leonardo drew of Arezzo, Siena and the surrounding towns of the Chiana valley. Da Vinci took up his post as Cesare Borgia's military engineer in May 1502, the same month as the Arezzo rebellion.

[66] See Louise George Clubb, *Pollastra and the Origins of Twelfth Night: Parthenio Commedia (1516) with an English Translation* (Ashgate Publishing Company, 2010) for a hair-raising account of the playwright Pollastra's escape from Arezzo, having sided with Vitelli, in the aftermath of the *Aretine* rebellion. Pollastra's long-lost Italian Renaissance comedy *Parthenio* was the foundation of Shakespeare's *Twelfth Night*.

[67] Niccolò Machiavelli, *Discourses on Livy* (Dover Publications, 2007), Book II, Chapter XXIII, 'That in chastising their Subjects when circumstances required it the Romans always avoided half-measures', pp. 215-219.

[68] James Cleugh says fourteen, p. 31; Edward Hutton says nineteen, p. 13.

[69] See Girolamo Muzio, *Lettere Catholiche* (Venice, 1571), p. 232., as cited in Hutton, p. 13.

[70] See Hutton, p. 14.

[71] See Roger Jones & Nicholas Penny, *Raphael* (Yale University Press, 1983), pp. 40-41. Also, see Quentin Skinner & Russell Price, *The Prince (Cambridge Texts in the History of Political Thought)*, (Cambridge University Press, 2007), pp. 117-118 for a discussion of Grifonetto and Gian Paolo's respective roles in the 3 July 1500 Perugia massacre.

[72] See Nicoletta Baldini, *Raphael* (Rizzoli International Publications, 2005), p. 106.

[73] See Skinner & Price, pp. 117-118.

[74] Miles J. Unger, *Machiavelli: A Biography* (Simon & Schuster, 2011), Chapter 5.

[75] See G. J. Meyer, *The Borgias: The Hidden History* (Bantam, 2013), p. 363.

[76] See John Addington Symonds, *The Life of Michelangelo Buonarroti: Volume II: Based on Studies in the Archives of the Buonarroti Family at Florence* (University of Pennsylvania Press, 2002), pp. 184-185.

[77] Niccolò Machiavelli, *Discourses on Livy* (University of Chicago Press, 1996), I. 27, p. 62.

[78] Ibid., p. 62.

[79] Ibid., p. 62.

[80] As paraphrased from Machiavelli by David Peterson & Daniel Bornstein, *Florence and Beyond: Culture, Society and Politics in Renaissance Italy: Essays in Honour of John M. Najemy (Essays and Studies, Volume 15)*, (Centre for Reformation and Renaissance Studies, 2008), p. 448.

[81] See Paul F. Grendler, *The Universities of the Italian Renaissance* (Johns Hopkins University Press, 2002), pp. 64-65.

[82] Christine Shaw, *Julius II: The Warrior Pope* (Blackwell, 1993), Chapter I 'The Papal Nephew'.

[83] Giorgio Vasari, *Lives of the Painters, Sculptors and Architects* (Everyman's Library, Vol. 4, 1963), p. 123.

[84] Franceso Matarazzo (author) & Edward Strachan Morgan (trans.), *Chronicles of the City of Perugia 1492-1503* (J. M. Dent & Co., 1905), Introduction, p. ix.

[85] Ibid., p. 4.

[86] See Aretino's letter to Firenzuola, 26 October 1541, *Lettere* 81. Bright College Years, in Thomas Caldecott Chubb, *The Letters of Pietro Aretino* (Archon Books, 1967), pp. 172-173.

[87] See David Leavitt, *Florence (The Writer & the City)*, (Bloomsbury Publishing, 2002), Chapter 3.

[88] Ibid., Chapter 3.

[89] Alan Stewart, *Close Readers: Humanism and Sodomy in Early Modern England* (Princeton University Press, 2014), p. 9.

[90] See Kevin Patrick Siena, *Sins of the Flesh: Responding to Sexual Disease in Early Modern Europe (Essays and Studies, Vol. 7)*, (Centre for Reformation and Renaissance Studies, 2005), pp. 199-200.

[91] See Donald Beecher, *Renaissance Comedy: The Italian Masters, Volume 1* (University of Toronto Press, Scholarly Publishing Division, 2008), p. 145.

[92] See Hutton, pp. 14-15.

[93] For a mannered, well-behaved nineteenth-century account of Bracciolini's life see William Shepherd, *The life of Poggio Bracciolini* (T. Cadel, Jun and W. Davies, 1802) or else Stephen Greenblatt's more frank appraisal in *The Swerve*.

[94] See Robert Glendinning, *Love, Death, and the Art of Compromise: Aeneas Sylvius Piccolomini's Tale of Two Lovers* in William C. McDonald (editor), *Fifteenth-Century Studies, Volume 23* (Camden House, 1997), p. 101.

[95] *'Plures vidi amavique feminas, quarum exinde potitus tedium magnum suscepi'* was the Latin phrase used by Piccolomini in his 1444 letter to Noceto. See Glendinning & McDonald, p. 115.

[96] Peter Brand & Lino Pertile, *The Cambridge History of Italian Literature* (Cambridge University Press, 1997), p. 271.

[97] Cleugh, p. 32.

[98] Ibid., p. 32.

[99] Ibid., p. 65.

[100] Aretino to Federico Gonzaga, 2 June 1531, *Lettere* 9. A Fan for Hot Weather, in Thomas Caldecott Chubb, *The Letters of Pietro Aretino* (Archon Books, 1967), p. 38.

[101] Machiavelli defined *virtú* as the attributes by which a man becomes a person of property and means, someone who takes an active role in self-government; also a protector of liberties and a self-actualized Renaissance man.

[102] See Hutton, p. 14-15.

[103] Carolin C. Young, *Apples of Gold in Settings of Silver: Stories of Dinner as a Work of Art* (Simon & Schuster, 2002), p. 46.

[104] Roger Collins, *Keepers Of The Keys Of Heaven: A History Of The Papacy* (Weidenfeld & Nicolson, 2009), p. 319.

[105] *Lettere*, I, 64; V, 271; VI, 114, cited in Hutton, p. 20.

[106] Peter Partner, *Renaissance Rome 1500-1559: A Portrait of a Society (Portrait of a Society 1500-1559)*, (University of California Press, 1980), pp. 117-118.

[107] Martin Luther (author) & John Dillenberger (editor), *An Appeal to the Ruling Class, in Martin Luther: Selections From His Writing* (Anchor, 1958), p. 429.

[108] The figure is cited (together with a brief discussion of prostitute demographics) in Peter Partner, *Renaissance Rome 1500-1559: A Portrait of a Society (Portrait of a Society 1500-1559)*, (University of California Press, 1980), p. 99.

[109] Quoted in Margaret F. Rosenthal, *The Honest Courtesan: Veronica Franco, Citizen and Writer in Sixteenth-Century Venice* (University of Chicago Press, 1992), p. 284.

[110] For a more detailed discussion the *cortigiane onesta* see Margaret F. Rosenthal, *The Honest Courtesan: Veronica Franco, Citizen and Writer in Sixteenth-Century Venice* (University of Chicago Press, 1992).

[111] Margaret F. Rosenthal, *The Honest Courtesan: Veronica Franco, Citizen and Writer in Sixteenth-Century Venice* (University of Chicago Press, 1992), p. 284; see also

Bronislaw Geremek & Jean Birrell, *The Margins of Society in Late Medieval Paris* (Cambridge University Press, 2006), p. 219.

[112] Montaigne, M. de. (1971). *Essays*. In *Great books of the western world* (vol. 25). Chicago: Encyclopaedia Britannica.

[113] Quoted in Courtney Quaintance, *Textual Masculinity and the Exchange of Women in Renaissance Venice* (University of Toronto Press, 2015), pp. 18-19.

[114] Gaia Servadio, *Renaissance Woman* (I.B.Tauris, 2016), p. 40.

[115] Ibid., p. 91.

[116] Quoted in Courtney Quaintance, *Textual Masculinity and the Exchange of Women in Renaissance Venice* (University of Toronto Press, 2015), p. 19.

[117] Ibid., p. 144.

[118] Peter Partner, *Renaissance Rome 1500-1559: A Portrait of a Society (Portrait of a Society 1500-1559)*, (University of California Press, 1980), p. 84.

[119] See G. Innamorati, *Aretino, Pietro, Dizionario Biografico degli Italiani* (Rome, 1962), pp. 89 and 91; as cited in Louise George Clubb, *Pollastra and the Origins of Twelfth Night: Parthenio Commedia (1516) with an English Translation* (Ashgate Publishing Company, 2010), p. 22.

[120] Luba Freedman, *Titian's Portraits through Aretino's Lens* (Penn State University Press, 1995), p. 10.

[121] Raymond Waddington, *Aretino's Satyr: Sexuality, Satire, and Self-Projection in Sixteenth-Century Literature and Art (Toronto Italian Studies)*, (University of Toronto Press, 2004), p. 133.

[122] Gaia Servadio, *Renaissance Woman* (I.B.Tauris, 2016), p. 41.

[123] Luba Freedman, *Titian's Portraits through Aretino's Lens* (Penn State University Press, 1995), p. 10.

[124] *Lettere*, I, 126, cited in Hutton, p. 24.

[125] Peter Partner, *Renaissance Rome 1500-1559: A Portrait of a Society (Portrait of a Society 1500-1559)*, (University of California Press, 1980), p. 153.

[126] Vasari, Life of Raphael.

[127] Gaia Servadio, Renaissance Woman (I.B.Tauris, 2016), p. 43.

[128] Henk Th. van Veen, *The Translation of Raphael's Roman Style* (Peeters, 2007), p. 36; also Tinagli, P. (author), Rogers, M. (author), *Women in Italian Renaissance Art: Gender, representation, identity* (Manchester University Press, 1997), p. 129.

[129] Hutton, p. 23.

[130] Herbert Vaughan, *The Medici Popes: Leo X and Clement VII* (Methuen & Co., 1908), pp. 120-121.

[131] Aretino's friend Lodovico Dolce argued that in order to speak refined and nuanced Tuscan one need not necessarily 'be' Tuscan, as was the case with Bembo who was a Venetian. In his *Osservationi nella volgar lingua* (Venice, 1550), Dolce had written that Bembo and others in Venice, 'who, writing often in this language, produce fruits worthy of immortality, such as [Bernardo] Capello, Domenico Venier, M. Bernardo Zane, Girolamo Molino, Pietro Gradenigo, and many others' (*'che in essa lingua, spesso scrivendo, producono frutti degni d'immortalità si come il Capello, M. Domenico Veniero, M. Bernardo Zane, M. Girolamo Molino, M. Piero Gradenigo Gentilhuomini Vinitiani, e molti altri'*).

[132] David Young Kim, *The Traveling Artist in the Italian Renaissance: Geography, Mobility, and Style (Yale University Press, 2014)*, p. 165.

[133] Stephen John Campbell, *The Cabinet of Eros: Renaissance Mythological Painting and the Studiolo of Isabella d'Este* (Yale University Press, 2006), p. 241.

[134] Patricius Schlager, 'Paulus Jovius'. Catholic Encyclopaedia (Robert Appleton Company, 1910).

[135] By Alan Stewart, Close Readers: Humanism and Sodomy in Early Modern England (Princeton University Press, 2014), p. 10. The line is: 'Qui giace Paolo Giovio Ermafodrito / Che seppe far da moglie, e da marito'; Mazzuchelli, Vita di Pietro Aretino, pp. 137-138.

[136] Michele Marrapodi, Shakespeare and the Italian Renaissance: Appropriation, Transformation, Opposition (Anglo-Italian Renaissance Studies), (Routledge, 2014), p. 240.

[137] V. Rossi, Pasquinate di P. A. edanonime (Palermo-Turin, 1891), pp. xxvii and 117; as cited in Hutton, p. 25.

[138] Aretino to Jacopo del Giallo, 23 May 1537, Lettere 20. A Painter of Miniatures, in Thomas Caldecott Chubb, The Letters of Pietro Aretino (Archon Books, 1967), p. 56.

[139] As quoted in Raymond Waddington, Aretino's Satyr: Sexuality, Satire, and Self-Projection in Sixteenth-Century Literature and Art (Toronto Italian Studies), (University of Toronto Press, 2004), p. 133.

[140] Melissa Meriam Bullard, Filippo Strozzi and the Medici: Favour and Finance in Sixteenth-Century Florence and Rome (Cambridge University Press, 2008), p. 73.

[141] Aretino's sonnet is published by Domenico Gnoli in Giornale storico della letteratura italiana, XXII (1893), p. 263; cited in Melissa Meriam Bullard, Filippo Strozzi and the Medici: Favour and Finance in Sixteenth-Century Florence and Rome (Cambridge University Press, 2008), p. 74.

[142] Felix Gilbert, The Pope, His Banker, and Venice (Harvard University Press, 1991), p. 109.

[143] Ibid., p. 109.

[144] Mario Erasmo, Death: Antiquity and its Legacy (I. B. Tauris & Company, 2012), p. 101.

[145] Leon Battista Alberti, I libri della famiglia, ed. Ruggiero Romano, Alberto Tenenti and Francesco Furlan (Einaudi, 1994), pp. 321-428; in English translation see Leon Battista Alberti, The family in Renaissance Florence, trans. Renée Neu Watkins (University of South Carolina Press, 1969).

[146] Leon Battista Alberti, I libri della famiglia, ed. Ruggiero Romano, Alberto Tenenti and Francesco Furlan (Einaudi, 1994), p. 58.

[147] Virginia Cox, The Italian Renaissance (I.B. Tauris, 2016), p. 113.

[148] For a more detailed exposition of the relational and collective aspects of individual identity and Renaissance norms of patronage see Virginia Cox, The Italian Renaissance (I.B. Tauris, 2016), pp. 110-131.

[149] Guy Fitch Lytle & Stephen Orgel (editors), Patronage in the Renaissance (Princeton University Press, 2014), pp. 4-5.

[150] Johan Verberckmoes, Laughter, Jestbooks and Society in the Spanish Netherlands (Springer, 1999), p. 169.

[151] Peter Jordan, The Venetian Origins of the Commedia dell'Arte (Routledge, 2014), chapter on Pietro Aretino.

[152] From the manuscript in the Museo Correr (Codex Cicogna 2673, fol. 2410v-241r) of Venice as published in Vittorio Rossi, Dal Rinascimento al Risorgimento (Florence, 1930), pp. 232-238. It was Rossi who first attributed this manuscript to Aretino. For a partial translation see T.C. Chubb, Aretino, Scourge of Princes (New York, 1940), pp. 50-51.

[153] V. Rossi, Pasquinate di P. A. edanonime (Palermo-Turin, 1891), pp. 151; as cited in Hutton, p. 28.

[154] Camillo Querno (1470-1530) was an Italian poet and author who moved to Rome around 1514, where he presented a poem of 20,000 verses called the *Alexiades*. He was crowned *Archipoeta*, a title that became his nickname. Aware of the poet's talent, Pope Leo X used him as part-poet laureate, part court jester and he was reputedly able to compose impromptu couplets on any topic that was proposed. In 1528, he committed suicide by slashing his abdomen with a pair of scissors.

[155] Cleugh, pp. 42-43.

[156] Andrea Bayer, *Art and Love in Renaissance Italy* (Metropolitan Museum of Art, 2008), p. 178; see also Op. cit. *"Rapture to the Greedy Eyes": Profane Love in the Renaissance*, pp. 43-59.

[157] Ed. G. Battelli (Lanciano: Carabba, 1914), p. 11, 14; cited in Aldo D. Scaglione, *Knights at Court: Courtliness, Chivalry and Courtesy from Ottonian Germany to the Italian Renaissance* (University of California Press, 1992), p. 250.

[158] J. Douglas Campbell & Leonard Gregory Sbrocchi (editors), *Cortigiana* (Dovehouse Editions, 2003), pp. 16-17.

[159] Giorgio Vasari, *The Lives of the Artists* (Oxford University Press, 1991), p. 498.

[160] Signori e collegi, deliberazioni, ordinaria autorita 113, 57r-66r (June 6-18, 1511); cited in Michael Rocke, *Forbidden Friendships: Homosexuality and Male Culture in Renaissance Florence* (Oxford University Press, 1998), p.229, 327.

[161] Sanudo, *I diarii*, cit., XX, p. 151.; cited in Maurizio Arfaioli, *The Black Bands of Giovanni: Infantry and Diplomacy During the Italian Wars (1526-1528)*, (Edizioni Plus-Pisa University Press, 2005), p. 23.

[162] Cleugh, p. 47.

[163] Maurizio Arfaioli, *The Black Bands of Giovanni: Infantry and Diplomacy During the Italian Wars (1526-1528)*, (Pisa University Press, 2005), p. XII.

[164] Tommaso Gar (author) & Eugenio Alberi (editor), *Le relazioni degli ambasciatori veneti al Senato (in Italian)*. Series 2, Volume III, Secolo XVI, Vol. 1. (Società editrice fiorentina, 1846), p. 64: '*Il cardinal de' Medici, suo nepote, che non è legittimo, ha gran potere col papa; è uomo di gran maneggio e di grandissima autorità; tuttavia sa vivere col papa, nè fa alcuna cosa di conto se prima non domanda al papa. Ora si ritrova a Fiorenza a governare quella città.*'

[165] Anthony Grafton (editor), Glenn W. Most (editor) & Salvatore Settis (editor), *The Classical Tradition* (Belknap Press, 2013), p. 694.

[166] Cleugh, p. 52.

[167] Rose Marie San Juan, *Rome: A City Out of Print* (University of Minnesota Press, 2001), p. 4.

[168] Aura Satz & Jon Wood, *Articulate Objects: Voice, Sculpture and Performance* (Peter Lang AG, Internationaler, 2009), p. 44.

[169] John T. Paoletti & Gary M. Radke, *Art in Renaissance Italy* (Prentice Hall, 2005), p. 408.

[170] See *Every Saturday, Volume 5 (Ticknor and Fields, 1868)*, pp. 207-208.

[171] Rose Marie San Juan, *Rome: A City Out of Print* (University of Minnesota Press, 2001), p. 4.

[172] John M. Hunt, *The Vacant See in Early Modern Rome: A Social History of the Papal Interregnum* (Brill, 2016), pp. 239-240.

[173] Cleugh, p. 53.

[174] Ibid., p. 53.

[175] Aretino to Gabriele Cesano, August 1545, *Lettere* 111. The Chieti Friars, in Thomas Caldecott Chubb, *The Letters of Pietro Aretino* (Archon Books, 1967), pp. 207-208.

[176] James Reston, Jr., *Defenders of the Faith: Christianity and Islam Battle for the Soul of Europe, 1520-1536* (Penguin Books, 2010), p. 91.

[177] Newton Key & R. O. Bucholz, *Sources and Debates in English History, 1485 – 1714* (John Wiley & Sons, 2009), p. 16.

[178] Mandell Creighton, *A History of the Papacy from the Great Schism to the Sack of Rome, Volume 6* (Longmans, Green, and Company, 1919), p. 221; as cited in Hutton, p. 42.

[179] Eugenio Garin, *Renaissance Characters* (University of Chicago Press, 1997), p. 79.

[180] Ibid., p. 79.

[181] Ibid., p. 79.

[182] Cleugh, pp. 56-57.

[183] Ibid., p. 58.

[184] Gaetana Marrone (editor) & Paolo Puppa (editor), *Encyclopaedia of Italian Literary Studies: A-J* (Routledge, 2006), p. 74.

[185] James Reston, Jr., *Defenders of the Faith: Christianity and Islam Battle for the Soul of Europe, 1520-1536* (Penguin, 2009), p. 107.

[186] Francesco Berni, *Il Primo Libro Dell'Opere Burlesche* (Leida, 1823), p. 108.

[187] John M. Hunt, *The Vacant See in Early Modern Rome: A Social History of the Papal Interregnum* (Brill, 2016), p. 207.

[188] Ibid., p. 203.

[189] Af Fernando & Renato Silenzi, *Pasquino Quattro secoli di satira romana* (Vallecchi, 1968), p. 224.

[190] William Murray, *City of the Soul: A Walk in Rome* (Crown, 2003), pp. 75-76.

[191] Sebastiano Serlio (author) & Myra Nan Rosenfeld (editor), *Serlio on Domestic Architecture* (Dover Publications, 1997), p. 2.

[192] William J. Landon, *Lorenzo di Filippo Strozzi and Niccolò Machiavelli: Patron, Client, and the Pistola fatta per la peste/An Epistle Written Concerning the Plague* (Toronto Italian Studies), p. 97.

[193] Niccolò Machiavelli, *Discorsi sopra la prima deca di Tito Livio, Opere, vol. 1*, Chapter 10, ed. Corrado Vivanti (Einaudi-Gallimard, 1997); cited in Maurizio Viroli (author) & Antony Shugaar (translator), *Niccolò's Smile: A Biography of Machiavelli* (Hill and Wang, 2002), p. 216.

[194] For a lively discussion of the (to coin a modern expression) 'brand' which Isabella d'Este established for herself see Virginia Cox, *The Italian Renaissance* (I.B. Tauris, 2016), pp. 118-120.

[195] C.M. Brown, 'The Decoration of the Private Apartment of Federico II Gonzaga on the Piano Terreno of the Castello di San Giorgio', in *Guerre Stati e città*, pp. 315-343 (324).

[196] Charles M. Rosenberg (Editor), *The Court Cities of Northern Italy: Milan, Parma, Piacenza, Mantua, Ferrara, Bologna, Urbino, Pesaro, and Rimini (Artistic Centres of the Italian Renaissance)*, (Cambridge University Press, 2010), p. 169.

[197] Julia Cartwright, *Isabella d'Este Marchioness of Mantua, 1474-1539. A Study of the Renaissance, 2 vols.* (E.P. Dutton & Co, 1905), 2:80; cited in Sally Anne Hickson, *Women, Art and Architectural Patronage in Renaissance Mantua: Matrons, Mystics and Monasteries* (Routledge, 2016), p. 103.

[198] Luba Freedman, *Classical Myths in Italian Renaissance Painting* (Cambridge University Press, 2015), p. 26.

[199] Paolo Giovio, *Delle imprese* (Lyon, Giulio Roviglio, 1559), pp. 123-125; cited in Sally Anne Hickson, *Women, Art and Architectural Patronage in Renaissance Mantua: Matrons, Mystics and Monasteries* (Routledge, 2016), p. 103.

[200] Baldassare Castiglione, *The Book of the Courtier*, trans. George Bull (Viking Penguin, 1967), p. 36.

[201] Peter Jordan, *The Venetian Origins of the Commedia Dell'Arte* (Routledge, 2014), pp. 106-107.

[202] Ian Frederick Moulton (author), Arsiccio (Intronato), *La Cazzaria: The Book of the Prick* (Psychology Press, 2003), p. 16.

[203] Peter Jordan, *The Venetian Origins of the Commedia Dell'Arte* (Routledge, 2013), p. 94.

[204] See Baschet, *Doc, inediti su P.A.* in *Arch. Stor. Ital. Serie* III, Vol. III, Pt. ii, p. 110.; as cited in Hutton, pp. 48-49.

[205] See Baschet, *Doc, inediti su P.A.* in *Arch. Stor. Ital. Serie* III, Vol. III, Pt. ii, p. 110.; as cited in Hutton, p. 49.

[206] Cleugh, p. 62.

[207] Ibid., p. 62.

[208] Ibid., p. 62.

[209] Ibid., p. 62.

[210] R. J. Knecht, *Renaissance Warrior and Patron: The Reign of Francis I* (Cambridge University Press, 1996), p. 112.

[211] For a comprehensive survey of syphilis within the court of Gonzaga see Alessandro Luzio and Rudolfo Renier in "Contributo alla storia del mal francese," *Giornale storici della Letteratura Italiana*, V (1885), pp. 408-432.

[212] See Sheryl E. Reiss (author, editor) & David G. Wilkins (author, editor), *Beyond Isabella: Secular Women Patrons of Art in Renaissance Italy (Sixteenth Century Essays & Studies, V. 54)*, (Truman State University Press, 2001), p. 116, note 26.

[213] See George R. Marek, *The Bed and the Throne: The Life of Isabella d'Este* (Harper and Row, 1976), pp. 166-169.

[214] Catherine B. Avery, *The New Century Italian Renaissance Encyclopaedia* (Simon & Schuster, 1972), p. 470.

[215] Paul V. Murphy, *Ruling Peacefully: Cardinal Ercole Gonzaga and Patrician Reform in Sixteenth-Century Italy* (CUA Press, 2007), p. 160.

[216] Paul V. Murphy, *Ruling Peacefully: Cardinal Ercole Gonzaga and Patrician Reform in Sixteenth-Century Italy* (CUA Press, 2007), p. 160.

[217] Judith Hook, *The Sack of Rome: 1527* (Palgrave Macmillan, 2004), p. 90.

[218] Cleugh, p. 63.

[219] Ibid., p. 64.

[220] Ibid., p. 64.

[221] Ibid., p. 65.

[222] John M. Najemy, *Italy in the Age of the Renaissance: 1300-1550* (Oxford University Press, 2005), p. 108.

[223] Sharon T. Strocchia, *Death and ritual in Renaissance Florence* (The Johns Hopkins University Press, 1992), p. 234.

[224] The theory that Giovanni de' Medici did not receive the name 'Giovanni of the Black Bands' until after his death is discussed at some length in Maurizio Arfaioli, *The Black Bands of Giovanni: Infantry and Diplomacy During the Italian Wars (1526-1528)*, (Edizioni Plus-Pisa University Press, 2005), p. xiii and also elsewhere.

[225] See Joyce de Vries, *Caterina Sforza and the Art of Appearances: Gender, Art and Culture in Early Modern Italy* (Routledge, 2016).

[226] Cleugh, p. 66.

[227] Pietro Aretino, *Lettere* (Verona, 1960), p. 569, letter to Gerolama Fontanella.

[228] Pietro Aretino (author) & Francesco Erspamer (editor), *Pietro Aretino, Lettere, Volume 2* (University of Michigan, 1995), p. 240; also Cleugh p. 67.

[229] Cleugh, p. 68.

[230] Ibid., p. 67.

[231] Aretino to Battista Strozzi, 16 November 1537, *Lettere* 1. Glory to Heel, in Thomas Caldecott Chubb, *The Letters of Pietro Aretino* (Archon Books, 1967), pp. 89-91.

[232] Appendix, Pietro Aretino, *The Works of Aretino: Dialogues - Letters and Sonnets [2 Vols.]*, trans. Samuel Putnam (Covici Friede, 1933), p. 22.

[233] Aretino, *Lettere*, vol. I, p. 468; cited in Maurizio Arfaioli, *The Black Bands of Giovanni: Infantry and Diplomacy During the Italian Wars (1526-1528)*, (Edizioni Plus-Pisa University Press, 2005), pp. 70-71.

[234] Aretino, *Lettere*, vol. I, p. 468; cited in Maurizio Arfaioli, *The Black Bands of Giovanni: Infantry and Diplomacy During the Italian Wars (1526-1528)*, (Edizioni Plus-Pisa University Press, 2005), p. 71.

[235] Michel Winock, *Flaubert* (Harvard University Press, 2016), p. 43.

[236] Christine Suzanne Getz, *Music in the Collective Experience in Sixteenth-century Milan* (Ashgate Publishing, 2005), p. 2.

[237] Cleugh, p. 70.

[238] Judith Hook, *The Sack of Rome: 1527* (Palgrave Macmillan, 2004), p. 19.

[239] Cleugh, p. 69.

[240] Chad Denton, *The War on Sex: Western Repression from the Torah to Victoria* (McFarland, 2014), p. 173.

[241] Abigail Brundin, Tatiana Crivelli & Maria Serena Sapegno, *A Companion to Vittoria Colonna* (Brill, 2016), p. 44.

[242] Giuliari, *Lettere di V.C.* (Verona, 1868), as cited in Hutton, p. 62. Also, see Alexander Nagel, p. 225.

[243] Peter Partner, *Renaissance Rome 1500-1559: A Portrait of a Society (Portrait of a Society 1500-1559)*, (University of California Press, 1980), p. 211.

[244] Hutton, p. 59.

[245] 'Marforio, che vuol dir che il tuo Pasquino, / Dal dì che fu costui Papa creato, È quasi muto affatto diventato, / Nè più riprende i vizi 1' Aretino ? ... / Pietro Aretino che sta tanto in favore / Come la rana fu preso al boccone / E talor canta, ma non vuol toccare / Dal maioringo, che sarebbe errore / Perchè lo fa sfoggiar come un' barone...' in Hutton, p. 59.

[246] Antonio Pigafetta, *Magellan's Voyage: A Narrative Account of the First Circumnavigation* (Courier Corporation, 2012), p. 15.

[247] Giorgio Vasari famously refers to as the 'Palazzo del T'.

[248] The Palazzo Medici is better-known as the 'Palazzo Madama', which took its new name from the Dowager Duchess Margaret of Austria, the widow of Duke Alessandro de' Medici of Florence, who acquired the property as part of her settlement from Cosimo I de' Medici around 1538. Margaret's popular soubriquet was simply 'Madama'.

[249] See Vasari's *Life of Giulio Romano*.

[250] See Ibid.

[251] See Ibid. (2:136); cited in Barbara Furlotti & Guido Rebecchini, *The Art of Mantua: Power and Patronage in the Renaissance* (J. Paul Getty Museum, 2008), p. 116.

[252] Barbara Furlotti & Guido Rebecchini, *The Art of Mantua: Power and Patronage in the Renaissance* (J. Paul Getty Museum, 2008), p. 116.

[253] Carol Kidwell, *Pietro Bembo: Lover, Linguist, Cardinal* (McGill-Queen's Press - MQUP, 2004), p. 19.

[254] See Vasari's *Life of Giulio Romano* (2:126); cited in Barbara Furlotti & Guido Rebecchini, *The Art of Mantua: Power and Patronage in the Renaissance* (J. Paul Getty Museum, 2008), p. 132.

[255] Barbara Furlotti & Guido Rebecchini, *The Art of Mantua: Power and Patronage in the Renaissance* (J. Paul Getty Museum, 2008), p. 170.

[256] Francesco Algarotti, *Lettere sull'Eneide del Caro (Lettere V)*, in *Opere di Francesco Algarotti e di Saverio Bettinelli*, ed. Ettore (Ricciardi, 1969), pp. 304-305.

[257] See Vasari's Life of Giulio Romano.

[258] Courtney Quaintance, *Textual Masculinity and the Exchange of Women in Renaissance Venice* (University of Toronto Press, 2015), p. 5.

[259] Ibid., pp. 5-6.

[260] Guido Rebecchini, *Private Collectors in Mantua, 1500-1630* (Ed. di Storia e Letteratura, 2002), pp. 45-46.

[261] For an in-depth discussion of the Renaissance revival of classical pagan modes of eroticism see Bette Talvacchia, *Taking Positions: On the Erotic in Renaissance Culture* (Princeton University Press, 1999), pp. 49-70.

[262] Ovid (author) & Peter Green (translator, introduction), *The Erotic Poems* (Penguin Classics, 1983).

[263] For a fairly comprehensive discussion of *I Modi* refer to Lynne Lawner, *Sixteen Pleasures* (Northwestern University Press, 1989).

[264] See Fred S. Kleiner, *Gardner's Art through the Ages: A Concise Western History* (Cengage Learning, Inc., 2016), p. 274. Also refer to Justine Pila & Paul Torremans, *European Intellectual Property Law* (Oxford University Press, 2016), p. 12, which, interestingly, describes the ruling of the Emperor Maximilian granting a monopoly on the publication of Dürer's work to his widow.

[265] For a highly detailed discussion on this topic see Lisa Pon, *Raphael, Dürer, and Marcantonio Raimondi: Copying and the Italian Renaissance Print* (Yale University Press, 2004).

[266] See Vasari's Life of Marcantonio Raimondi.

[267] See John T. Paoletti & Gary M. Radke, *Art in Renaissance Italy* (Prentice Hall, 2005), p. 37.

[268] See Vasari's Life of Marcantonio Raimondi.

[269] B. J. Sokol, *Art and Illusion in The Winter's Tale* (Manchester University Press, 1994), p. 108.

[270] *Ekphrasis*, from the Greek for the description of a work of art produced as a rhetorical exercise, is a graphic, sometimes dramatic, verbal description of a visual work of art, either real or imagined. In ancient times, it referred to a description of any thing, person, or experience. The word derives from the Greek *ek* and φράσις *phrásis*, 'out' and 'speak' respectively, and the verb ἐκφράζειν *ekphrázein*, 'to proclaim or call an inanimate object by name'.

[271] Anne Reynolds, *Renaissance Humanism at the Court of Clement VII: Francesco Berni's "Dialogue against Poets" in Context*, New York, 1997, p. 125; Raymond B. Waddington, *Review of Talvacchia 1999. Sixteenth Century Journal 31, no. 3* (2000), p. 886.

[272] Aretino, *School of Whoredom*, 2003 (ed.), p .39; cited in Andrea Bayer, *Art and Love in Renaissance Italy* (Metropolitan Museum of Art, 2008), p. 54.

[273] B. J. Sokol, *Art and Illusion in The Winter's Tale* (Manchester University Press, 1994), p. 106.

[274] Lynne Lawner, *I Modi: The Sixteen Pleasures : An Erotic Album of the Italian Renaissance* (Northwestern University Press, 1989), p. 80.

380

[275] Nicolaus J. Hajek, *Still a Rivalry: Contrasting Renaissance Sodomy Legislation in Florence and Venice* (2015), p. 2.

[276] Letter to Battista Zatti, 18 December, 1537; *Lettere*, 1957-60, vol. I, pp. 110-111, no. LXVIII, quoted in translation in Waddington 2004, p. 26.

[277] Valeria Finucci, *The Manly Masquerade: Masculinity, Paternity, and Castration in the Italian Renaissance* (Duke University Press, 2003), p. 55.

[278] Boccaccio, *Decameron*, 9.3; English translation by George Henry McWilliam in *The Decameron* (Penguin, 1972), p. 560.

[279] Christine Corretti, *Cellini's Perseus and Medusa and the Loggia dei Lanzi: Configurations of the Body of State* (Brill, 2015), p. 64.

[280] *Priapeia* 4; L. C. Smithers & R. F. Burton, *Priapea sive diversorum poetarum in Priapum lusus, or, Sportive Epigrams on Priapus* (1890).

[281] Suetonius, *Tiberius* 43, quoted in Bette Talvacchia, *Taking Positions: On the Erotic in Renaissance Culture* (Princeton University Press, 1999), p. 193.

[282] Peter Michelson, *Speaking the Unspeakable: A Poetics of Obscenity* (SUNY Press, 1993), p. 2.

[283] J. Feerick (editor) & V. Nardizzi (editor), *The Indistinct Human in Renaissance Literature (Springer, 2012)*, p. 192.

[284] Vasari, *Vita di Antonio Da Correggio*.

[285] See Vasari's Life of Marcantonio Raimondi.

[286] Vasari, *Le vite*, 1568/1906 (ed.) vol. 5, p. 418 (Vita of Marcantonio).

[287] For a detailed discussion of Giberti's role in the suppression of *I Modi* and the jailing of Raimondi, see Alexander Nagel, *The Controversy of Renaissance Art* (University Of Chicago Press, 2011), pp. 224-226.

[288] The surviving nine fragments of *I Modi* are in the care of the British Museum (BM catalogue number: 1972,U.1306-1314. The provenance of the fragments is from Ralph Willett's sale catalogue, 1812. Willett is said to have come into possession of them from Mariette's collection, although Mariette's 1775 auction catalogue does not contain any item which corresponds exactly (quoted from BM website).

[289] As cited in Paola Tinagli (author) & Mary Rogers (author), *Women in Italian Renaissance Art: Gender, representation, identity* (Manchester University Press, 1997), p. 127.

[290] Letter to Battista Zatti, 18 December, 1537; *Lettere*, 1957-60, vol. I, pp. 110-111, no. LXVIII, quoted in translation in Waddington 2004, p. 26; as also cited in Hutton, p. 64.

[291] See Vasari's Life of Marcantonio Raimondi.

[292] Letter to Battista Zatti, 18 December, 1537; *Lettere*, 1957-60, vol. I, pp. 110-111, no. LXVIII, quoted in translation in Waddington 2004, p. 26; as also cited in Hutton, pp. 64-65.

[293] Letter to Battista Zatti, 18 December, 1537; *Lettere*, 1957-60, vol. I, pp. 110-111, no. LXVIII, quoted in translation in Waddington 2004, p. 26; as also cited in Hutton, p. 65.

[294] Hutton, p. 62.

[295] Two of Aretino's modern biographers, Hutton and Cleugh, specifically state that Giovanni delle Bande Nere was at Fano on the Adriatic in August 1524 when he summoned Aretino from Arezzo to be with him. Hutton cites Aretino's Letter (15 July 1537) to Mario Bandini in which he states: 'I was with the great Giovanni de' Medici at Fano, when he swore to me that if Jesus ever did him a favour, it was in blessing him with me...' however this in no way supports the assertion that Giovanni was at Fano in mid-1524 (Cleugh does not adduce any sources for his own claim and is probably merely following Hutton's lead in this). There is a major problem with the Hutton/Cleugh timeline, however. Catherine Mary Phillimore in *The Warrior Medici:*

Giovanni delle Bande Nere (London Literary Society 1887), p. 76-77, contradicts this account by stating that Giovanni only came into possession of Fano sometime after the Battle of Pavia and his initial wounding by harquebus fire (i.e. after February 1525), when his wife Maria Salviati travelled to Rome in some desperation to beg Pope Clement VII to provide her and her husband with a fief and an income sufficient to meet the costs of paying his troops. At some point Giovanni was definitely at Aulla for a short time and had indeed purchased this fief legally. Phillimore, however is unclear on when specifically Giovanni was at Aulla (she seems to give the impression that it was shortly after Giovanni's intervention at San Secondo on behalf of his half-sister Bianca in mid-1523). Hutton and Cleugh, by contrast, say nothing whatsoever about Giovanni's tenure of Aulla at all. For the purposes of this narrative we place Giovanni, and consequently Aretino also, at Aulla in August of 1524.

[296] Again, there is controversy over the genesis of the Brunella Fortress at Aulla. The three theories basically are (1) that the building dates to the end of the fifteenth-century century and is attributed to Jacopo Ambrogio Malaspina, Lord of Aulla at that time; (2) that the fortress was built by Giovanni delle Bande Nere, who came to Aulla in the first half of the sixteenth-century who may have entrusted Antonio da Sangallo il Vecchio with the project; and (3) that the builder was one Adamo Centurione, a merchant from Genoa who became the owner of the estate of Aulla in 1543. For the purposes of our narrative I have favoured hypothesis (2).

[297] John T. Spike, *Young Michelangelo: The Path to the Sistine: A Biography Paperback* (Duckworth Overlook, 2011), p. 58.

[298] *Opere di Macliiavelli*, Vol. VIII., p. 479; see also Villari, *Niccolò Machiavelli e i suoi Tempi*, Vol. III. p. 335.

[299] See Will Durant, *The Renaissance: A History of Civilization in Italy from 1304-1576 A.D.* (Story of Civilization, 5), (Simon & Schuster, 1953), p. 657.

[300] *Nè potea Dio terreno / Ritrovar mai tra l' universa gente / Miglior Datario et ei miglior Clemente.*

[301] See Will Durant, *The Renaissance: A History of Civilization in Italy from 1304-1576 A.D. (Story of Civilization, 5)*, (Simon & Schuster, 1953), pp. 654-655.

[302] The nefarious copy by Andrea del Sarto today resides in the Capodimonte Museum in Mantua.

[303] Cleugh, p. 83.

[304] Ibid., p. 84.

[305] Ibid., p. 84.

[306] Ibid., p. 85.

[307] Mandell Creighton, *A History of the Papacy During the Period of the Reformation* (Cambridge University Press, 2011), p. 251.

[308] Edmund Spenser, Edwin Almiron Greenlaw, Charles Grosvenor Osgood, Frederick Morgan Padelford & Ray Heffner, *The Works of Edmund Spenser: The faerie queene Vol. 3* (Johns Hopkins Press, 1934), p. 338.

[309] The German *landsknechts* had come to prominence around the turn of the century as mercenary pikemen from the lowlands of Swabia and fought in similar fashion to the Swiss pikemen, except for certain stylistic differences – the Swiss fought with their pikes held level whilst the *landsknechts* held their own pikes slanting slightly upwards. See John McCormack, *One Million Mercenaries: Swiss Soldiers in the Armies of the World* (Leo Cooper, June 1993), p. 42.

[310] Hunt Janin, Ursula Carlson, *Mercenaries in Medieval and Renaissance Europe* (McFarland, 2013), p. 155.

[311] Aretino to the King of France, 24 April 1525, *Lettere* 1. To the King of France, in Thomas Caldecott Chubb, *The Letters of Pietro Aretino* (Archon Books, 1967), p. 19.

[312] Aretino to the King of France, 24 April 1525, *Lettere* 1. To the King of France, in Ibid., p. 19.

[313] Aretino to the King of France, 24 April 1525, *Lettere* 1. To the King of France, in Ibid., p. 21.

[314] Quoted in Vincent Cronin, *The Flowering Of The Renaissance* (Random House, 2011).

[315] Requoted in by Joycelyne G. Russell, Diplomats at Work: *Three Renaissance Studies (History/prehistory & Medieval History)*, (Sutton Pub Ltd., 1992), p. 95.

[316] Yvonne Bruce, *Images Of Matter: Essays On British Literature Of The Middle Ages And Renaissance: Proceedings Of The Eighth Citadel Conference On Literature* (University of Delaware Press, 2005), p. 127.

[317] Pietro Aretino, *The Works of Aretino: Dialogues - Letters and Sonnets [2 Vols.]*, trans. Samuel Putnam (Covici Friede, 1933), p. 255.

[318] Quoted from Stephen Orgel, *Imagining Shakespeare: A History of Texts and Visions* (Palgrave Macmillan, 2003), p. 114; as requoted in L. Leigh, *Shakespeare and the Embodied Heroine: Staging Female Characters in the Late Plays and Early Adaptations* (Palgrave Shakespeare Studies), (Palgrave Macmillan, 2014).

[319] *Opere burlesche* in 3 Vols. (Firenze, 1723), I, p. 174.

[320] Federico Gonzaga's letter to Guicciardini regarding della Volta's assassination attempt on Aretino is quoted in Alessandro Luzio, *Pietro Aretino Nei Primi Suoi Anni a Venezia e la Corte dei Gonzaga* (Torino, 1888), p. 61, Doc. I.

[321] Giammaria Mazzuchelli di Brescia, *La vita di Pietro Aretino Scritta Dal Conte* (Padova, G. Comino, 1830), p. 25; 'trovatolo solo, gli diede con un pugnale cinque ferite nel petto, storpiandogli eziandio le mani'. The same basic story is repeated by the *Pseudo-Berni* attributed to Francesco Berni (Perugia, 17 August 1538).

[322] Alessandro Luzio, *Pietro Aretino Nei Primi Suoi Anni a Venezia e la Corte dei Gonzaga* (Torino, 1888), p. 33.

[323] Ibid., p. 33.

[324] Ibid., p. 90, Doc. XXVIII. The fact that Giberti seems to fully comprehend Gonzaga's insinuation is also discussion in Hutton, p. 74.

[325] *XVIII. Sonetti contro a Pietro Aretino* by Francesco Berni (full text).

Tu ne dirai e farai tante e tante,
lingua fracida, marcia, senza sale,
che al fin si troverà pur un pugnale
meglior di quel d'Achille e più calzante.

Il papa è papa e tu sei un furfante,
nodrito del pan d'altri e del dir male;
hai un pie' in bordello e l'altro in ospitale,
storpiataccio, ignorante e arrogante.

Giovan Mateo e gli altri che gli ha appresso,
che per grazia de Dio son vivi e sani,
ti metteran ancor un dì in un cesso.

Boia, scorgi i costumi tuoi ruffiani
e se pur vòi cianciar, di' di te stesso:
guàrdati il petto, la testa e le mani.

Ma tu fai come i cani,
che, dà pur lor mazzate se tu sai,
come l'han scosse, son più bei che mai.

Vergognati oramai,
prosontuoso, porco, mostro infame,
idol del vituperio e della fame,

ché un monte di letame
t'aspetta, manegoldo, sprimacciato,
perché tu moia a tue sorelle allato;

quelle due, sciagurato,
c'hai nel bordel d'Arezzo a grand'onore,
a gambettar: "Che fa lo mio amore?"

Di quelle, traditore,
dovevi far le frottole e novelle
e non del Sanga che non ha sorelle.

Queste saranno quelle
che mal vivendo ti faran le spese,
e 'l lor, non quel di Mantova, marchese;

ch'ormai ogni paese
hai amorbato, ogni omo, ogni animale:
il ciel, Iddio, il diavol ti vol male.

Quelle veste ducale,
o ducali, acattate e furfantate,
che ti piangon in dosso sventurate,

a suon di bastonate
ti seran tolte, avanti che tu moia,
dal reverendo padre messer boia;

che l'anima di noia
mediante un bel capestro caveratti
e per maggior favor poi squarteratti;

e quei tuoi leccapiatti
bardassonacci, paggi da taverna,
ti canteran il requiem eterna.

Or vivi e ti governa;
ben che un pugnale, un cesso, o ver un nodo
ti faranno star queto in ogni modo.

384

[326] Bonner Mitchell, *Rome in the High Renaissance: The Age of Leo X* (University of Oklahoma Press, 1973), p. 107.

[327] This will be the 1534 edition of *La Cortigiana* published by Giovanni Antonio de Nicolini da Sabio for Francesco Marcolini; See J. Douglas Campbell & Leonard Gregory Sbrocchi (editors), *Cortigiana* (Dovehouse Editions, 2003), p. 11.

[328] Quoted in Richard Andrews, *Scripts and Scenarios: The Performance of Comedy in Renaissance Italy* (Cambridge University Press, 1993), p. 56.

[329] Pietro Aretino, J. Douglas Campbell & Leonard Gregory Sbrocchi (translators), *Cortigiana* (Dovehouse Editions, 2003), p. 82.

[330] Ibid., p. 82.

[331] Hutton, p. 83.

[332] Sanudo, I *diarii*, XLIV, pp. 99-105.; cited in Maurizio Arfaioli, *The Black Bands of Giovanni: Infantry and Diplomacy During the Italian Wars (1526-1528)*, (Edizioni Plus-Pisa University Press, 2005), p. 29.

[333] Joycelyne Gledhill Russell, *Diplomats at work: three renaissance studies* (A. Sutton Publishing, 1992), p. 95.

[334] Maurizio Viroli, *Machiavelli's God* (Princeton University Press, 2010), p. 189.

[335] Pietro Aretino, J. Douglas Campbell & Leonard Gregory Sbrocchi (translators), *Cortigiana* (Dovehouse Editions, 2003), p. 109.

[336] Vitello Vitelli was married to Angela de' Rossi, daughter of Giovanni delle Bande Nere's half-sister Bianca de' Rossi.

[337] Philip Thody, *French Caesarism from Napoleon I to Charles de Gaulle* (Springer, 1989), p. 136. The line is from the character Petit-Jean in Racine's *Les Plaideurs*.

[338] E. R. Chamberlin, *The Sack of Rome* (Batsford, 1979), p. 119.

[339] Matteo Bandello, *Novelle* I, 40.

[340] Aretino to the Grand Master [King François I of France], 8 June 1537, *Lettere* 25. My Sword is My Pen, in Thomas Caldecott Chubb, *The Letters of Pietro Aretino* (Archon Books, 1967), p. 63.

[341] Quoted in Cleugh, pp. 99-100.

[342] Nicollò di Bernado dei Machiavelli, *Machiavelli: The Chief Works and Others, Volume 2* (Duke University Press, 1989), p. 1004.

[343] Ibid., pp. 1004-1005.

[344] Ibid., p. 1005.

[345] Aretino to Francesco degli Albizzi, 10 December 1526, *Lettere* 2. The Death of a Hero, in Thomas Caldecott Chubb, *The Letters of Pietro Aretino* (Archon Books, 1967), p. 28.

[346] Ibid., p. 28.

[347] *Opere burlesche* in 3 Vols. (Firenze, 1723), III, p. 11; quoted by Hutton, p. 90; 'Sotto Milano dieci volta, non ch' una / Mi disse: Pietro, se di questa Guerra / Mi scampa Iddio e la buona fortuna / Ti voglio impadronir della tua terra'.

[348] *Opere burlesche* in 3 Vols. (Firenze, 1723), III, p. 11; quoted by Hutton, p. 90.

[349] Cleugh, p. 95.

[350] I. Moulton, *Love in Print in the Sixteenth Century: The Popularization of Romance* (Springer, 2014).

[351] Gershon Legman, *Rationale of the dirty joke: an analysis of sexual humour, Volume 2* (Grove Press, 1975), p. 740.

[352] Pietro Aretino, *Sonetti lussuriosi e dubbi amorosi* (castello volante, 2012), Risoluzione XXV.

[353] Wiley Feinstein, *The Civilization of the Holocaust in Italy: Poets, Artists, Saints, Anti-Semites* (Fairleigh Dickinson University Press, 2003), pp. 115-116.

[354] For a more extensive discussion of Aretino's anti-Semitism as exhibited in his works, see Wiley Feinstein, *The Civilization of the Holocaust in Italy: Poets, Artists, Saints, Anti-Semites* (Fairleigh Dickinson University Press, 2003), pp. 111-116.

[355] Francesco Maria Molza (1489-1544). 'A poet of some ability and charms, but better known for his indiscriminate amours, to pursue which he abandoned his wife and children and squandered such little fortune as he had. The ladies ranged from the low-born Beatrice Peregia to the noble, beautiful and witty Camilla Gonzaga. He was once stabbed almost fatally and finally contracted the French disease which brought about his death after a long and lingering illness' (quoted from Chubb, *Lettere*, index p. 349).

[356] Aretino to Bernardo Tasso, 21 October 1537, *Lettere* 37. More Numerous than Flakes of Snow, in Thomas Caldecott Chubb, *The Letters of Pietro Aretino* (Archon Books, 1967), p. 83.

[357] Aretino to Messer Elias Alfan, 16 July 1542, *Lettere* 90. We Could Learn to be Christians, in Thomas Caldecott Chubb, *The Letters of Pietro Aretino* (Archon Books, 1967), p. 179.

[358] Cleugh, p.98.

[359] Pietro Aretino, J. Douglas Campbell & Leonard Gregory Sbrocchi (translators), *Cortigiana* (Dovehouse Editions, 2003), p. 103.

[360] 'Spain: September 1526, 1-10', in *Calendar of State Papers, Spain, Volume 3 Part 1, 1525-1526*, ed. Pascual de Gayangos (London, 1873), pp. 870-892.

[361] H. M. Vernon, *Italy from 1494-1790* (Cambridge University Press, 1909), p. 41.

[362] Quoted in Cleugh, p.93.

[363] Quoted in Cleugh, p.99.

[364] Michael Murrin, *History and Warfare in Renaissance Epic* (University of Chicago Press, 1994), p. 124.

[365] Ibid., p. 125.

[366] Ariosto, *Orlando Furioso* 14.1-2; quoted in *History and Warfare in Renaissance Epic* (University of Chicago Press, 1994), p. 126.

[367] Judith Hook, *The Sack of Rome: 1527* (Palgrave Macmillan, 2004), p. 110.

[368] Aretino to Francesco degli Albizzi, 10 December 1526, *Lettere* 2. The Death of a Hero, in Thomas Caldecott Chubb, *The Letters of Pietro Aretino* (Archon Books, 1967), pp. 22-28.

[369] Aretino to Francesco degli Albizzi, 10 December 1526, *Lettere* 2. The Death of a Hero, in Ibid., p. 23.

[370] Ibid., p. 23.

[371] Ibid., p. 24.

[372] Ibid., p. 24.

[373] Ibid., p. 25.

[374] Ibid., p. 26.

[375] Luba Freedman, *Titian's Portraits through Aretino's Lens* (Penn State University Press, 1995), p. 17.

[376] Aretino to Francesco degli Albizzi, 10 December 1526, *Lettere* 2. The Death of a Hero, in Thomas Caldecott Chubb, *The Letters of Pietro Aretino* (Archon Books, 1967), p. 28.

[377] Ibid., p. 22.

[378] Cleugh, p. 110.

[379] Federico Gonzaga's younger brother Ercole Gonzaga would be formally named as cardinal in Pope Clement VII's Consistory of 3 May 1527. The ostensible objective of naming five new cardinals during this consistory was to raise badly-needed funds for

the defence of Rome against Frundsburg and Bourbon. Federico's mother Isabella d'Este would travel to Rome to obtain the cardinal's the *biretum* or scarlet cap and be trapped in the city throughout the infamous Sack of Rome.

[380] Cleugh, p. 110.

[381] Ibid., p. 110.

[382] Ibid., p. 111.

[383] E. R. Chamberlin, *The Sack of Rome* (Batsford, 1979), p. 126.

[384] Paolo Giovio, *Lettere*, vol. 1, p. 116; cited in Maurizio Arfaioli, *The Black Bands of Giovanni: Infantry and Diplomacy During the Italian Wars (1526-1528)*, (Edizioni Plus-Pisa University Press, 2005), p. 177 (Appendix 1).

[385] Cleugh, p. 111.; also Hutton, p. 99; *Sett' anni traditori ho via gettati / Con Leon quattro e tre con ser Clemente, / E son fatto nemico de la gente / Più per li lor che per li miei peccati / Et non ho pur d' intrata dui ducati / Et son da men che non è Gian Manente, / Onde nel c …. se ponete mente / Ho tutte le speranze de papati. / Se le ferite vacasser ne havrei / Per diffender l'honor d miei patroni / Motu proprio ogni dì ben cinque o sei. / Ma benefici, offici et pensioni / Hanno bastardi et furfanti plebei / Che i Papi mangeriano in duo bocconi. / E i suoi servitor buoni / Muojon di fame, come che facc' io / Cosa da renegar Domeneddio; Cod. Marciano*, Cl. XI, it. No. LXVI, ac. 255 r. Cf. Luzio, p. 4.

[386] Monica Azzolini, *The Duke and the Stars: Astrology and Politics in Renaissance Milan (I Tatti studies in Italian Renaissance history)*, (Harvard University Press, 2013), p. 73.

[387] Stephen John Campbell, *The Cabinet of Eros: Renaissance Mythological Painting and the Studiolo of Isabella D'Este* (Yale University Press, 2004), p. 245.

[388] Ibid., p. 239.

[389] Anthony Grafton, *Cardano's Cosmos: The Worlds and Works of a Renaissance Astrologer* (Harvard University Press, 1999), p. 226.

[390] Code Marciano cl. xi. it. No. LXVI, c. 255, and Luzio, op. cit., p. 8; cited in Hutton, p. 103.

[391] Cleugh, p. 112.

[392] Ibid., p. 106.

[393] The paraphrase belongs to John Addington Symonds in his chapter on Aretino in *Renaissance in Italy: Italian literature* (Henry Holt, 1888).

[394] *La Cortigiana*, Act III, Sc. 7.

[395] John Martin, *Venice's Hidden Enemies: Italian Heretics in a Renaissance City* (University of California Press, 1993), p. 3.

[396] Giovanni Boccaccio, *The Decameron* (Oxford University Press, 1998), pp. 265-266.

[397] See Manfredo Tafuri, *Venice and the Renaissance* (MIT Press, 1995), p. 113.

[398] For a detailed discussion of the *cerretani* see Giancarlo Petrella, *Ippolito Ferrarese, a Travelling 'cerretano' and publisher in sixteenth-century Italy* in *Print Culture and Peripheries in Early Modern Europe: A Contribution to the History of Printing and the Book Trade in Small European and Spanish Cities* (BRILL, 2012), p. 201.

[399] *Lettere* I, 274-5; cited in Hutton, p. 108.

[400] Pericles' funeral oration, 2.35-46; Thucydides (author) & M. I. Finley (editor), *The History of the Peloponnesian War* (Penguin Books, 2000).

[401] Peter Ackroyd, *Venice: Pure City* (Vintage Books, 2010), p. 50.

[402] Quoted in Garry Wills, *Venice: Lion City: The Religion of Empire* (Simon and Schuster, 2002), p. 181.

[403] Quoted in Ibid., p. 181.

[404] John Hale, *Civilization of Europe in the Renaissance* (Simon and Schuster, 1995), p. 168.

[405] The Rialto bridge at this time was not, as yet, the iconic bridge designed by Antonio da Ponte and completed between 1588 and 1591. Prior to this the Rialto had been of wooden construction, however it had been destroyed by fire in 1310, had collapsed in 1444 and 1524 and had again been burned in 1574. In 1551, the authorities requested proposals for the renewal of the Rialto and da Ponte's structure continued the previous design, which featured two inclined ramps leading up to a central portico, with the covered ramps carrying rows of shops on either side of the portico.

[406] Like Maestro Abraham Arié, the Jewish surgeon who had operated on Giovanni delle Bande Nere.

[407] Quoted in Garry Wills, *Venice: Lion City: The Religion of Empire* (Simon and Schuster, 2002), p. 182.

[408] William Martin Conway (editor), *Literary Remains of Albrecht Dürer* (Cambridge University Press, 1889), p. 51.

[409] P. Barocchi (editor), Giogrio Vasari, *Le Vite* (Pisa, 1994), p. 501; cited in Dr Alexander Cowan & Dr Jill Steward, *The City and the Senses: Urban Culture Since 1500* (Ashgate Publishing, Ltd., 2013), p. 29.

[410] Aretino to Messer Francesco Bacci, 25 November 1537, *Lettere* 44. Rome and Venice, in Thomas Caldecott Chubb, *The Letters of Pietro Aretino* (Archon Books, 1967), p. 96.

[411] Ibid., p. 96.

[412] Ibid., p. 97.

[413] For a good discussion of Andreas Osiander's *A Wondrous Prophecy of the Papacy* see Jeffrey Chipps, Smith, *Nuremberg, a Renaissance City, 1500-1618* (University of Texas Press, 1983), p. 167.

[414] Aretino to His Serene Highness, Andrea Gritti, Venice 1530, *Lettere* 8. Refuge for the Nations, in Thomas Caldecott Chubb, *The Letters of Pietro Aretino* (Archon Books, 1967), pp. 35-37.

[415] Cleugh, p. 117-18.

[416] Alessandro Luzio, *Pietro Aretino nei primi suoi anni a Venezia e la corte dei Gonzaga* (Torino, Ermanno Loescher, 1888), p. 65.

[417] The Black Bands and the Pontifical Swiss Guard had in fact clashed, leading to the deaths of 20 soldiers. See Judith Hook, *The Sack of Rome: 1527* (Palgrave Macmillan, 2004), p. 160.

[418] Pietro Aretino, *Lettere*, cit., vol. I, p. 469; cited in Maurizio Arfaioli, *The Black Bands of Giovanni: Infantry and Diplomacy During the Italian Wars (1526-1528)*, (Edizioni Plus-Pisa University Press, 2005), p. 177 (Appendix 1).

[419] Quoted in Stephen John Campbell, *The Cabinet of Eros: Renaissance Mythological Painting and the Studiolo of Isabella D'Este* (Yale University Press, 2004), p. 241.

[420] From 'Confessione di Mastro Pasquino a Fra Mariano Martire e Confessore' in *Pasquino e dintorno. Testi pasquineschi del cinquecento*, ed. Antonio Marzo (Rome, 1990), p. 31.

[421] Gwynne Dyer, *War: The New Edition* (Random House of Canada, 2010), p. 165.

[422] James Monti, *The King's Good Servant But God's First: The Life and Writings of Saint Thomas More* (Ignatius Press, 1997), p. 137.

[423] André Chastel, *The Sack of Rome, 1527*, trans. Beth Archer (Princeton, 1983), p. 108.

[424] Gwynne Dyer, *War: The New Edition* (Random House of Canada, 2010), p. 165.

[425] For a harrowing account of the cruel extortions perpetrated upon the Roman public by the Imperialist troops see E. R. Chamberlin, *The Sack of Rome* (Batsford, 1979), pp. 176-181.

[426] Will Durant & Ariel Durant, *The Story of Civilization: The Renaissance; a history of civilization in Italy from 1304-1576 A.D* (Simon and Schuster, 1953), p. 631.

[427] Requoted from Guicciardini in Jonathan Davies, *Aspects of Violence in Renaissance Europe* (Routledge, 2016), p. 56.

[428] Nigel Cawthorne, *Sex Lives of the Popes: An Irreverent Exposé of the Bishops of Rome from St. Peter to the Present Day* (Prion, 1996), p. 234.

[429] Judith Hook, *The Sack of Rome: 1527* (Palgrave Macmillan, 2004), p. 121.

[430] Francesco Maria della Rovere's wife Eleonora Gonzaga was Isabella d'Este's oldest child and Federico Gonzaga's older sister.

[431] Julia Cartwright, *Isabella d'Este, marchioness of Mantua, 1474-1539; a study of the renaissance* (London: John Murray, 1923), pp. 265-266.

[432] Will Durant, *The Renaissance: A History of Civilization in Italy from 1304-1576 A.D.* (Simon and Schuster, 1953), p. 633.

[433] Deborah Howard, *Jacopo Sansovino Architecture and Patronage in Renaissance Venice* (Yale University Press, 1975), p. 9.

[434] See Vasari's Life of Sebastiano del Piombo.

[435] Sadly, Sebastiano del Piombo's 1526 portrait of Aretino, the remnants of which are now owned by the Museo Statale d'Arte Medievale e Moderna in Arezzo, was subsequently ruined.

[436] Kenneth Gouwens, *Remembering the Renaissance: Humanist Narratives of the Sack of Rome* (Brill, 1998), p. 149.

[437] Hutton, p. 113.

[438] Sheila Hale, *Titian: His Life* (Harper Collins, 2012), p. 281.

[439] Dr Miles Pattenden & Dr Piers Baker-Bates, *The Spanish Presence in Sixteenth-Century Italy: Images of Iberia* (Ashgate Publishing, 2015), pp. 31-32.

[440] See Elisabeth G. Gleason, *Gasparo Contarini: Venice, Rome and Reform* (University of California Press, 1993), pp. 42-43.

[441] Aretino's sending of the portrait to Federico Gonzaga is adduced in Aretino's letter to Federico dated 6 October 1527 (II).

[442] That the second, accompanying painting mentioned by Aretino refers to a depiction of Girolamo Adorno is, at least, the theory of some. See: Delphi Complete Works of Titian (Delphi Classics, 2015); also Hans Tietze, Titian: The Paintings and Drawings with Three Hundred Illustrations (Phaidon Press, 1950), pp. 24 & 390; also George Bull, Venice: The Most Triumphant City (M. Joseph, 1982), p. 33.

[443] Cleugh, p. 142.

[444] *Lettere*, I, 10; cited in Hutton, p. 112.

[445] Aretino to the marquess of Mantua, 6 August 1527, *Lettere* 5. A Statue for a Lord, in Thomas Caldecott Chubb, *The Letters of Pietro Aretino* (Archon Books, 1967), p. 32.

[446] Ibid., p. 33.

[447] Ibid., p. 33.

[448] Alessandro Luzio, *Pietro Aretino Nei Primi Suoi Anni a Venezia e la Corte dei Gonzaga* (Torino, 1888), p. 79.

[449] Cleugh, p. 143.

[450] Ibid., p. 143.

[451] Hutton, p. 141.

[452] Arno Karlen, *Sexuality and Homosexuality* (Norton, 1971), p. 108.

[453] Alessandro Luzio, *Pietro Aretino nei primi suoi anni a Venezia e la corte dei Gonzaga* (Torino, Ermanno Loescher, 1888), p. 23.

[454] Rictor Norton, *My dear boy: gay love letters through the centuries* (Leyland Publications, 1998), p. 52.

[455] Ibid., p. 55.

[456] Alessandro Luzio, *Pietro Aretino nei primi suoi anni a Venezia e La Corte dei Gonzaga* (Turin: Ermanno Loescher, 1888); English translation by Rictor Norton, *My dear boy: gay love letters through the centuries* (Leyland Publications, 1998).

[457] *Ragionamenti*; quoted in Cleugh, pp. 127-128.

[458] *Lettere*, 28 November 1537; cited in Michael C. Thomsett (editor) & Jean Freestone Thomsett (editor), *War and Conflict Quotations: A Worldwide Dictionary of Pronouncements from Military Leaders, Politicians, Philosophers, Writers and Others* (McFarland, 1997), p. 53.

[459] Thomas More, Francis Bacon & Henry Neville, *Three Early Modern Utopias: Thomas More: Utopia / Francis Bacon: New Atlantis / Henry Neville: The Isle of Pines* (Oxford University Press, 1999), p. 101.

[460] Aretino to Signora Girolama Fontanella, 6 July 1539, *Lettere* 70. Swords and Ladies, in Thomas Caldecott Chubb, *The Letters of Pietro Aretino* (Archon Books, 1967), p. 146.

[461] *La Cortigiana*, Act v.

[462] Pietro Aretino, *Aretino's Dialogues*, translated by Raymond Rosenthal (Stein and Day, 1971), p. 244.

[463] Aretino to the Emperor, 20 May 1527, *Lettere* 3. The Goodness and Piety of Charles V, in Thomas Caldecott Chubb, *The Letters of Pietro Aretino* (Archon Books, 1967), pp. 28-29.

[464] Ibid., p. 29.

[465] Ibid., p. 30.

[466] Aretino to Clement VII, 30 May 1527, *Lettere* 4. Your Holiness Should Turn to Jesus, in Thomas Caldecott Chubb, *The Letters of Pietro Aretino* (Archon Books, 1967), pp. 30-31.

[467] Ibid., p. 31.

[468] Ibid., p. 31.

[469] Ibid., p. 32.

[470] Quoted in Cleugh, p. 132.

[471] The *strappado* was the characteristic interrogation method of the Florentine republic. Raised several meters into the air by his wrists, which were bound behind his back, the victim was then dropped, his fall then being arrested just short of the floor, which usually tore the victim's shoulder blades out of their sockets. The process was repeated several times in succession until the prisoner admitted guilt or passed out. The friar Savonarola had famously been subjected to an especially long and agonizing session of *strappado* in order to induce him to sign a damning confession of guilt.

[472] Niccolò Machiavelli, *The Prince and Other Political Writings*, trans. Stephen J. Milner (Everyman, 1995), pp. 115-116 (ch. 18).

[473] Quoted in Imma Penn, *Dogma Evolution & Papal Fallacies* (AuthorHouse, 2007), p. 192.

[474] Maurizio Viroli (author) & Antony Shugaar (translator), *Niccolò's Smile: A Biography of Machiavelli* (Hill and Wang; 2002), p. 258.

[475] Will Durant, *The Renaissance: A History of Civilization in Italy from 1304-1576 A.D.* (Simon and Schuster, 1953), p. 657.

[476] Donald Sanders, *Music at the Gonzaga Court in Mantua* (Lexington Books, 2012), p. 31-32.

[477] Alessandro Luzio, *Pietro Aretino nei primi suoi anni a Venezia e la corte dei Gonzaga* (E. Loescher, 1888), p. 65.

[478] Ibid., p. 66.

[479] Holger Michael Klein & Michele Marrapodi, *Shakespeare and Italy* (Mellen, 1999), p. 432.

[480] Brian Richardson, *Printing, Writers and Readers in Renaissance Italy* (Cambridge University Press, 1999), p. 94.

[481] Laurence Bergreen, *Over the Edge of the World: Magellan's Terrifying Circumnavigation of the Globe* (Harper Collins, 2009), p. 405.

[482] Kenneth M. Setton, *The Papacy and the Levant, (1204-1571): The sixteenth century to the reign of Julius III* (American Philosophical Society, 1984), p. 294.

[483] Ibid., p. 292.

[484] Hutton, p. 117.

[485] Quoted in Cleugh, p. 141.

[486] The quote is from the chapter on Aretino by John Addington Symonds, *Renaissance in Italy: Italian literature* (Henry Holt, 1888).

[487] R. J. Knecht, *Renaissance Warrior and Patron: The Reign of Francis I* (Cambridge University Press, 1994), p. 445.

[488] Elizabeth Cropper, *Pontormo: Portrait of a Halberdier* (Getty Publications, 1997), p. 49.

[489] Quoted in Cleugh, p. 144.

[490] Quoted in Cleugh, p. 145.

[491] Letter to the duke of Mantua, 2 June 1531, Pietro Aretino (author), George Bull (editor), *Selected Letters* (Penguin Classics, 1976), p. 68.

[492] Quoted in Margaret F. Rosenthal, *The Honest Courtesan: Veronica Franco, Citizen and Writer in Sixteenth-Century Venice* (University of Chicago Press, 1992), p. 39.

[493] David O. Frantz, *Festum Voluptatis: A Study of Renaissance Erotica* (Ohio State University Press, 1989), p. 99.

[494] Quoted in Margaret F. Rosenthal, *The Honest Courtesan: Veronica Franco, Citizen and Writer in Sixteenth-Century Venice* (University of Chicago Press, 1992), p. 45.

[495] The office of Procurator of San Marco (Italian: *Procuratore di San Marco*) was the second most prestigious life appointment in the Republic of Venice (the position of Doge of Venice being the most prestigious). It is unclear however whether Angela La Zaffetta was the daughter of the exalted *Procuratore* or else was merely the daughter of a sergeant of the law, *un birro*, or in Venetian dialect, *un zajjo*, which would account for her being given the name 'La Zaffetta'.

[496] 'Rape prosecution was also most sensitive to a woman's age and status. The victimisation of children (puellae) was treated with a stern hand. Wive, though much less important, were more valued than widows by the measure of penalties. Unmarried girls of marriagable age, however, found their rapists penalised with little more than a slap on the wrist. When rape struck down the social hierarchy, it could virtually disappear as a crime ... Rapes that crossed social boundaries upward, however, were quite another matter and entailed penalties of unique severity'; Cited in Margaret F. Rosenthal, *The Honest Courtesan: Veronica Franco, Citizen and Writer in Sixteenth-Century Venice* (University of Chicago Press, 1992), p. 38.

[497] The translation of Aretino's letter to Angela Zaffetta is taken from Janet Sethre, *The Souls of Venice* (McFarland, 2003), p. 156. Another translation is: 'I give you the palm, among all those that ever were, for knowing how to put upon the face of lasciviousness the mask of decency..." being *Lettere* CXIII, Pietro Aretino, *The Works of Aretino: Dialogues - Letters and Sonnets [2 Vols.]*, trans. Samuel Putnam (Covici Friede, 1933), p. 237.

[498] S. Hayes-Healy, *Medieval Paradigms: Volume I: Essays in Honor of Jeremy duQuesnay Adams* (Springer, 2016), pp. 60-61.

[499] R. J. Knecht, *Francis I* (Cambridge University Press, 1984), p. 218.

[500] In what was a conscious decision, the Emperor Charles V's younger brother Ferdinand had been crowned King of Bohemia in St Vitus' church in Prague, Bohemia, three years earlier on the exact same date of 24 February (1527), which was Charles' birthday.

[501] Quoted in Cleugh, p. 135.

[502] Quoted in Cleugh, p. 135.

[503] Quoted in Cleugh, p. 136.

[504] Quoted in Cleugh, p. 136.

[505] Quoted in Cleugh, p. 136-37.

[506] Description of Andrea Gritti taken from Marino Sanudo, Patricia H. Labalme (trans.) & Laura Sanguineti White (trans.), *Selections from the Renaissance Diaries of Marino Sanudo* (JHU Press, 2008), p. 64.

[507] Quoted in Cleugh, p. 131.

[508] Quoted in Cleugh, pp. 137-138.

[509] Giorgio Vasari (author), Marilyn Aronberg Lavin (editor) & Jonathan Foster (translator), *Vasari's Lives of the Artists* (Courier Corporation, 2012), p. 226.

[510] Bruce Cole, *Titian and Venetian Painting, 1450-1590* (Westview Press, 2000), p. 101.

[511] Bruce Cole, *Titian and Venetian Painting, 1450-1590* (Westview Press, 2000), p. 100.

[512] Titian, *Delphi Complete Works of Titian (Illustrated)*, (Delphi Classics, 2015).

[513] Quoted in Cleugh, p. 138.

[514] *Lettere* VIII, Pietro Aretino, *The Works of Aretino: Dialogues - Letters and Sonnets [2 Vols.]*, trans. Samuel Putnam (Covici Friede, 1933), p. 61.

[515] Luzio, Doc, XLII, XLIII.

[516] Aretino to Federico Gonzaga, 2 June 1531, *Lettere* 9. A Fan for Hot Weather, in Thomas Caldecott Chubb, *The Letters of Pietro Aretino* (Archon Books, 1967), p. 38.

[517] *Lettere* IX, Pietro Aretino, *The Works of Aretino: Dialogues - Letters and Sonnets [2 Vols.]*, trans. Samuel Putnam (Covici Friede, 1933), p. 62.

[518] Peter Ackroyd, *Venice: Pure City* (Vintage Books, 2010), p. 51.

[519] Aretino to Giovan Battista Dragoncino, 24 November 1537, *Lettere* 43. The Muses Need Money, in Thomas Caldecott Chubb, *The Letters of Pietro Aretino* (Archon Books, 1967), p. 95.

[520] Catherine Fletcher, *The Black Prince of Florence: The Spectacular Life and Treacherous World of Alessandro de' Medici* (Oxford University Press, 2016), p. 213.

[521] Ibid., p. 65.

[522] Ibid., p. 70.

[523] Alessandro Luzio, *Pietro Aretino nei primi suoi anni a Venezia e la corte dei Gonzaga* (Torino, Ermanno Loescher, 1888), p. 52.

[524] Francesco Berni (author) & Antonio Virgili (trans.) *Rime e poesi latine. Lettere edite e inedite* (Florence, 1885), p. 133.

[525] Julia Pardoe, *The Court and Reign of Francis the First, King of France, Volume 2* (Richard Bentley, 1849), pp. 24-25.

[526] Abigail Brundin, Tatiana Crivelli & Maria Serena Sapegno, *A Companion to Vittoria Colonna* (Brill, 2016), p. 50.

[527] Ibid., p. 44.

[528] Quoted in Raymond B. Waddington, *Aretino's Satyr: Sexuality, Satire and Self-projection in Sixteenth-century Literature and Art* (University of Toronto Press, 2004), p. 99.

[529] John Addington Symonds, *Renaissance in Italy: Italian literature* (Henry Holt, 1888), p. 503.

[530] Raymond B. Waddington, *Aretino's Satyr: Sexuality, Satire and Self-projection in Sixteenth-century Literature and Art* (University of Toronto Press, 2004), p. 99.

[531] Hutton states that *La Marfisa* was published in 1535 (Hutton, p. 127), whereas Cleugh states that 1532 was the publishing date, p. 147. *The Encyclopaedia of Italian Literary Studies: A-J*, edited by Gaetana Marrone states, however, that *Dui primi canti di Marphisa* was published in 1532.

[532] At forty-six cantos and 38,736 lines, Ariosto's *Orlando Furioso* is one of the longest poems in European literature.

[533] Author of the *Rime*, published posthumously in 1538.

[534] Janet Sethre, *The Souls of Venice* (McFarland, 2003), p. 184.

[535] *Lettere*, I, 211-12; cited in Hutton, p. 140.

[536] Ronnie H. Terpening, *Miserabile Et Glorioso Lodovic* (University of Toronto Press, 1997), p. 176.

[537] Raymond B. Waddington, *Aretino's Satyr: Sexuality, Satire and Self-projection in Sixteenth-century Literature and Art* (University of Toronto Press, 2004), p. 84.

[538] Benedetto Varchi, *Orazione funebra sopra la morte del reverendissimo Cardinal Bembo* (Florence: Anton Francesco Doni, 1546).

[539] Ettore Camesaca and Fidenzio Pertile (editors), *Pietro Aretino, Lettere sull'arte, vol. 2, Vite lettere testimonianze di artisti italiani* (Milan: Edizioni del Milione, 1957), 2:392-3.

[540] According to Titian biographer Sheila Hale the present day structure of Aretino's palazzo has since had one additional floor added to it since the satirist's day (see Hale, *Titian: His Life*, p. 247).

[541] *Lettere*, III, 144; cited in Hutton, p. 133.

[542] Lettere LXXX, Pietro Aretino, *The Works of Aretino: Dialogues - Letters and Sonnets [2 Vols.]*, trans. Samuel Putnam (Covici Friede, 1933), pp. 180-181.

[543] Ibid., p. 181.

[544] Quoted in Elizabeth Horodowich, *Language and Statecraft in Early Modern Venice* (Cambridge University Press, 2008), p. 108.

[545] Ibid., p. 108.

[546] Lettere LXXX, Pietro Aretino, *The Works of Aretino: Dialogues - Letters and Sonnets [2 Vols.]*, trans. Samuel Putnam (Covici Friede, 1933), p. 181.

[547] Aretino to Messer Girolamo Agnello, 11 November 1529, *Lettere* 6. A Keg of Wine, in Thomas Caldecott Chubb, *The Letters of Pietro Aretino* (Archon Books, 1967), p. 33.

[548] Lettere CI, Pietro Aretino, The Works of Aretino: Dialogues - Letters and Sonnets [2 Vols.], trans. Samuel Putnam (Covici Friede, 1933), pp. 212-213.

[549] Ibid., pp. 212-213.

[550] Jane A. Bernstein, *Print Culture and Music in Sixteenth-Century Venice* (Oxford University Press, 2001), p. 132.

[551] *Lettere*, II, 35; cited in Hutton, p. 133.

[552] Tintoretto's *Contest between Apollo and Marsyas* may be found today at the Wadsworth Atheneum Museum of Art in Hartford, Connecticut.

[553] Aretino had written to Tintoretto: '*E belle e pronte e vive in vive, in pronte e in belle attitudini da ogni uomo ch'è di perito giudicio sono tenute le due istorie: una in la favola di Apollo e Marsia, e l'altra in la novella di Argo e di Mercurio, da voi così giovane quasi dipinte in meno spazio di tempo che non si mise in pensare al ciò che dovevate dipingere nel palco de la camera, che con tanta sodisfazione mia e d'ognuno voi m'avete dipinta.*' Pietro Aretino, *Lettere*, Paris, III, 1609, 110, no. 161;

idem, Lettere sull'arte, ed. E. Camesasca, Milan, 1957-1960, II, 52, no. ccxi. As cited in Juergen Schulz, *Venetian Painted Ceilings of the Renaissance* (University of California Press), p. 177.

554 The artist Sebastiano Luciani's later acquired surname 'del Piombo' alludes to his 1531 elevation to the office of *piombatore papale* (keeper of the papal seal), that is, the office of Sealer of Briefs of the apostolic chamber. When the office had become vacant, Sebastiano Luciani, hitherto a relatively poor man, and Giovanni da Udine both competed for the office. Sebastiano was awarded the highly lucrative appointment with the proviso that he should pay out of his emoluments 300 *scudi* per annum to Giovanni da Udine. To take up the post Sebastiano became a friar, despite having a wife and two children at the time.

555 Manfredo Tafuri, *Venice and the Renaissance* (MIT Press, 1995), p. 4.

556 The words are those of John Addington Symonds, Renaissance in Italy: Italian literature (Henry Holt, 1888).

557 Not the original marble bust which stood in the entrance to his home but another of Jacopo Sansovino's busts of Pietro Aretino, this time in bronze, *Ritratto di giurista* ('Bust of a jurist'), can today be found in the collection of the National Gallery of Art, Widener Collection, Washington (DC).

558 *Lettere*, III, 48; cited in Hutton, p. 136.

559 *Lettere*, III, 48; cited in Hutton, p. 137.

560 *Lettere*, III, 48; cited in Hutton, p. 137.

561 See Sheila Hale, *Titian: His Life* (Harper Collins, 2012), p. 128.

562 Aretino to Count Manfredo di Collaltino, 10 October 1532, *Lettere* 11. Of All Fine Birds the Thrush, in Thomas Caldecott Chubb, *The Letters of Pietro Aretino* (Archon Books, 1967), p. 39.

563 Ibid., p. 40.

564 See Janet Sethre, *The Souls of Venice* (McFarland, 2003), p. 184; Aretino was especially missing out on the fish of the Venetian lagoons which comprised of 'sturgeon, trout, turbot, tench, sea pike, goby, *megla barbone, scarpena, lucena, variolo*, gilthead bream, plaice, chub, sole...'

565 Aretino to Brother Vitruvio dei Rossi, 6 September 1537, *Lettere* 33. Antipasto of the Gods, in Thomas Caldecott Chubb, *The Letters of Pietro Aretino* (Archon Books, 1967), pp. 76-77.

566 Aretino to Madonna Maddalena Bartolina, 10 December 1537, *Lettere* 53. Olives, in Thomas Caldecott Chubb, *The Letters of Pietro Aretino* (Archon Books, 1967), p. 117.

567 Aretino to Count Manfredo di Collaltino, 10 October 1532, *Lettere* 11. Of all Fine Bird the Thrush, in Thomas Caldecott Chubb, *The Letters of Pietro Aretino* (Archon Books, 1967), p. 39

568 Aretino to Francesco Marcolini, 3 June 1537, *Lettere* 23. The Flowers that Bloom in the Spring, in Thomas Caldecott Chubb, *The Letters of Pietro Aretino* (Archon Books, 1967), pp. 60-61.

569 Sheila Hale, *Titian: His Life* (Harper Collins, 2012), p. 250.

570 'I assure you that I do not believe that from the udders of all the herds of cattle and the flocks of sheep that Apollo ever looked upon, would have come, in their whole lifetime, enough milk to make a cheese as enormous as the one that your and my Gian Tomaso Bruno made me a gift of in your name', quoted in Aretino to Count Ludovico Rangone, December 1550, *Lettere* 234. An Enormous Cheese, in Thomas Caldecott Chubb, *The Letters of Pietro Aretino* (Archon Books, 1967), p. 300.

571 Aretino to Messer Girolamo Sarra, 4 November 1537, *Lettere* 53. To Salads, in Thomas Caldecott Chubb, *The Letters of Pietro Aretino* (Archon Books, 1967), p. 87.

[572] Janet Sethre, *The Souls of Venice* (McFarland, 2003), p. 183-84.

[573] Aretino to Lord Ranieri of the Marchesi dal Monte, April 1545, *Lettere* 106. Easter Gifts, in Thomas Caldecott Chubb, *The Letters of Pietro Aretino* (Archon Books, 1967), p. 202.

[574] Paola Malpezzi Price, *Moderata Fonte: Women and Life in Sixteenth-century Venice* (Fairleigh Dickinson University Press, 2003), p. 76.

[575] Courtney Quaintance, *Textual Masculinity and the Exchange of Women in Renaissance Venice* (University of Toronto Press, 2015), p. 69.

[576] Aretino to Parabosco, October 1549, in the Edizione nazionale delle opera di Pietro Aretino, vol. 4, pt. 5 (Rome: Salerno editrice, 1992), p. 281; quoted in Courtney Quaintance, *Textual Masculinity and the Exchange of Women in Renaissance Venice* (University of Toronto Press, 2015), p. 69.

[577] Hutton, p. 136.

[578] His pleading to Michelangelo for one or two of the artist's sketches would, however, fall on deaf ear, leading to Aretino's ungracious retaliatory attack on *The Last Judgement.*

[579] Christopher Nissen, *Kissing the Wild Woman: Art, Beauty, and the Reformation of the Italian Prose Romance in Giulia Bigolina's Urania* (University of Toronto Press, 2011), pp. 68-69.

[580] Christopher Nissen, *Kissing the Wild Woman: Art, Beauty, and the Reformation of the Italian Prose Romance in Giulia Bigolina's Urania* (University of Toronto Press, 2011), pp. 68-69.

[581] Philip Freund, *Dramatis Personae: The Rise of Medieval and Renaissance Theatre* (Peter Owen, 2006), p. 148.

[582] Hutton, p. 138; also see the letter Aretino writes in 1551 when leaving his house (*Lettere*, VI, 37).

[583] Pietro Aretino, *The Works of Aretino: Dialogues - Letters and Sonnets [2 Vols.]*, trans. Samuel Putnam (Covici Friede, 1933), p. 228. La Cortigiana, Act III scene 7.

[584] With his usual meanness of spirit where Aretino is concerned, the moralising Victorian critic John Addington Symonds in his *Renaissance in Italy: Italian literature* (Henry Holt, 1888) dismisses the poet's generous nature with the following words: '..while squandering money first upon his vices, he paid due attention to his reputation for generosity. The bastard of Arezzo vanuted he had been born in a hospital with the soul of a king. Yet he understood nothing of real magnanimity; his charity was part of an openhanded recklessness, which made him fling the goods of fortune to the wind as soon as gained – part of the character of the grand seigneur he aspired to assume.'

[585] Quoted in Cleugh, pp. 122-123.

[586] Aretino to Don Lope de Soria, 20 March 1542, *Lettere* 83. Why I Die of Hunger, in Thomas Caldecott Chubb, *The Letters of Pietro Aretino* (Archon Books, 1967), pp. 174-175.

[587] *Lettere* all' Aretino, I, ii, 347; cited in Hutton, p. 146.

[588] Sanudo, *Diarii*, Vol. LVII, 102 (No. 1532); Luzio, in *Giornale Stor. delta Lett. It.*, XIV, 367); cited in Hutton, p. 145.

[589] *Lettere*, I, 100, 16 May 1537; cited in Hutton, p. 145.

[590] *Lettere*, I, 24; cited in Hutton, p. 146; also *Lettere*, I, 17, and V, 116. See also Luzio, XXXII, p. 94.

[591] In the *Marescalco*, Act III, Sc. 5, Aretino says it weighed 8 lbs., but in *Lettere*, I, 28, he says 5 lbs.

[592] Aretino to the King of France, 10 November 1534, *Lettere* 12. A Lie from my Mouth, in Thomas Caldecott Chubb, *The Letters of Pietro Aretino* (Archon Books, 1967), p. 41.

[593] Ibid., p. 41.

[594] *Lettere* XII, Pietro Aretino, *The Works of Aretino: Dialogues - Letters and Sonnets [2 Vols.]*, trans. Samuel Putnam (Covici Friede, 1933), p. 67.

[595] Ibid., p. 68.

[596] The quote is from Harold Lamb, *Süleyman the Magnificent - Sultan of the East* (Read Books Ltd, 2013).

[597] *Lettere*, I, 26 and 30, cited in Hutton, p. 148.

[598] Lettere XIII, Pietro Aretino, *The Works of Aretino: Dialogues - Letters and Sonnets [2 Vols.]*, trans. Samuel Putnam (Covici Friede, 1933), p. 69.

[599] The quote is from Harold Lamb, *Süleyman the Magnificent - Sultan of the East* (Read Books Ltd, 2013).

[600] *La Cortigiana*, Act III, scene 7, *Pietro Aretino, The Works of Aretino: Dialogues - Letters and Sonnets [2 Vols.]*, trans. Samuel Putnam (Covici Friede, 1933), p. 229.

[601] *Lettere* all', A., I, i, 261 and 263; cited in Hutton, p. 148.

[602] *'per esser io non Pietro, ma un miraculoso mostro degli uomini'*.

[603] A reference to Cicero's Catalinarian: *Sit inscriptum in fronte unius cuisusque quid de republica sentiat.*

[604] Lettere XIII, Pietro Aretino, *The Works of Aretino: Dialogues - Letters and Sonnets [2 Vols.]*, trans. Samuel Putnam (Covici Friede, 1933), p. 69.

[605] Quoted in Cleugh, p. 150.

[606] Quoted in Cleugh, p. 152.

[607] A.S., *A Corrupt Tree: An Encyclopaedia of Crimes committed by the Church of Rome against Humanity and the Human Spirit* (Xlibris Corporation, 2014), p. 216.

[608] Barbarossa's letter to Aretino is quoted in *The Works of Aretino: Dialogues - Letters and Sonnets [2 Vols.]*, trans. Samuel Putnam (Covici Friede, 1933), p. 285, Appendix I.

[609] Gaetana Marrone (editor) & Paolo Puppa (editor), *Encyclopaedia of Italian Literary Studies: A-J* (Routledge, 2006), p. 83.

[610] Patricia A. Emison, *Creating the "Divine" Artist: From Dante to Michelangelo* (Brill, 2004), p. 141.

[611] Mark W. Roskill, *Dolce's Aretino and Venetian Art Theory of the Cinquecento* (Renaissance Society of America), p. 32.

[612] Sheila Hale, *Titian: His Life* (Harper Collins, 2012), p. 50.

[613] Nigel Cawthorne, *Sex Lives of the Popes* (Prion, 2004), p. 232.

[614] Anne Jacobson Schutte, *Pier Paolo Vergerio: The Making of an Italian Reformer* (Librairie Droz, 1977), p. 66.

[615] *Lettere* XIV, *The Works of Aretino: Dialogues - Letters and Sonnets [2 Vols.]*, trans. Samuel Putnam (Covici Friede, 1933), p. 71.

[616] *Lettere* XV, *The Works of Aretino: Dialogues - Letters and Sonnets [2 Vols.]*, trans. Samuel Putnam (Covici Friede, 1933), pp. 72-73.

[617] Ibid., pp. 72-73.

[618] George B. Parks, *The Pier Luigi Farnese Scandal: An English Report* in *Renaissance News*, Vol. 15, No. 3 (University of Chicago Press, 1962), pp. 193-200.

[619] Jacob Burckhardt, *The Civilization of the Renaissance in Italy* (The Floating Press, 2015), p. 138.

[620] *Lettere* LXXXVIII, *The Works of Aretino: Dialogues - Letters and Sonnets [2 Vols.]*, trans. Samuel Putnam (Covici Friede, 1933), pp. 195-196.

[621] Aretino to Messer Ferraguto di Lazzara, 12 August 1541, *Lettere 80*. A Light Lady, in Thomas Caldecott Chubb, *The Letters of Pietro Aretino* (Archon Books, 1967), p. 170.

[622] The quote is from the chapter on Aretino by John Addington Symonds, *Renaissance in Italy: Italian literature* (Henry Holt, 1888).

[623] Linda Phyllis Austern & Kari Boyd McBride, *Psalms in the Early Modern World* (Routledge, 2016), p. 9.

[624] K. J. P. Lowe, *Nuns' Chronicles and Convent Culture in Renaissance and Counter-Reformation Italy* (Cambridge University Press, 2003), p. 325. See also Mary Laven, *Sex And Celibacy In Early Modern Venice*, The Historical Journal, Volume 44, Issue 4 (December 2001), pp. 865-888. It is worth noting that Priuli's nervous outburst was born of a specific context: a few weeks earlier, Venetian troops had suffered a humiliating defeat at the battle of Agnadello.

[625] Raymond Rosenthal (trans.), *Aretino's Dialogues* (Stein and Day, 1972), p. 158.

[626] Brian Richardson, *Printing, Writers and Readers in Renaissance Italy* (Cambridge University Press, 1999), p. 95.

[627] The *Works of Aretino: Dialogues - Letters and Sonnets [2 Vols.]*, trans. Samuel Putnam (Covici Friede, 1933), p. 59, Translator's Note.

[628] Raymond Rosenthal (trans.), *Aretino's Dialogues* (Stein and Day, 1972), p. 42.

[629] Ibid., p. 102.

[630] Ibid., p. 102.

[631] Ibid., p. 25.

[632] Requoted in Margaret F. Rosenthal, The Honest Courtesan: Veronica Franco, Citizen and Writer in Sixteenth-Century Venice (University of Chicago Press, 1992), p. 45.

[633] Aretino to Messer Gabriello Cesano, 21 December 1538, *Lettere 67*. The Sweat of My Ink, in Thomas Caldecott Chubb, *The Letters of Pietro Aretino* (Archon Books, 1967), pp. 143-144.

[634] For a superb discussion on Aretino's recurring economic themes and metaphors in the *Ragionamenti* please refer to Ian Frederick Moulton, *Whores as Shopkeepers: Money and Sexuality in Aretino's Regionamenti* in Diane Wolfthal, Money, Morality, and Culture in Late Medieval and Early Modern Europe (Routledge, 2016).

[635] Margaret F. Rosenthal, *The Honest Courtesan: Veronica Franco, Citizen and Writer in Sixteenth- Century Venice* (University of Chicago Press, 1992), p. 11.

[636] Melissa Hope Ditmore, *Encyclopaedia of Prostitution and Sex Work, Volume 2* (Greenwood Publishing Group, 2006), p. 515.

[637] David Herlihy, *Women, Family and Society in Medieval Europe: Historical Essays, 1978-1991* (Berghahn Books, 1995), p. 18.

[638] See Sheila Hale, *Titian: His Life* (Harper Collins, 2012), p. 35.

[639] Melissa Hope Ditmore, *Encyclopaedia of Prostitution and Sex Work, Volume 2* (Greenwood Publishing Group, 2006), p. 515.

[640] See Sheila Hale, *Titian: His Life* (Harper Collins, 2012), p. 148.

[641] Veronica Franco (author), Ann Rosalind Jones & Margaret F. Rosenthal (trans.), *Poems and Selected Letters* (University of Chicago Press, 2007), p. 3.

[642] For a first-rate account of the life and times of Veronica Franco refer to Margaret F. Rosenthal, *The Honest Courtesan: Veronica Franco, Citizen and Writer in Sixteenth-Century Venice* (University of Chicago Press, 1992).

[643] Veronica Franco (author), Ann Rosalind Jones & Margaret F. Rosenthal (trans.), *Poems and Selected Letters* (University of Chicago Press, 2007), p. 4.

[644] Ibid., p. 2.

[645] More more details on Franco's *Terze rime*, see Sara Maria Adler, *Veronica Franco's Petrarchan Terze rime: Subverting the Master's Plan*, Italica 65: 3 (1988): 213-33.

[646] Veronica Franco (author), Ann Rosalind Jones & Margaret F. Rosenthal (trans.), *Poems and Selected Letters* (University of Chicago Press, 2007), p. 34.

[647] John Jeffries Martin & Dennis Romano, *Venice Reconsidered: The History and Civilization of an Italian City-State, 1297–1797* (JHU Press, 2002), p. 436.

[648] James Turner, *Sexuality and Gender in Early Modern Europe: Institutions, Texts, Images* (Cambridge University Press, 1993), p. 115.

[649] Jacob Burckhardt, *The Civilization of the Renaissance in Italy* (The Floating Press, 2015), p. 450.

[650] 'Franco returns a friend's advice to him in adversity', Veronica Franco (author), Ann Rosalind Jones & Margaret F. Rosenthal (trans.), *Poems and Selected Letters* (University of Chicago Press, 2007), p. 29.

[651] Aretino to Biagio Spina, 1544, *Lettere* 100. Rosaries, in Thomas Caldecott Chubb, *The Letters of Pietro Aretino* (Archon Books, 1967), p. 197.

[652] University of California, Los Angeles. Dept. of Italian, *Carte italiane* (1980), p. 46.

[653] Aretino to Messer Luigi Anichini, 23 November 1537, *Lettere* 42. O Brother, This Love!, in Thomas Caldecott Chubb, *The Letters of Pietro Aretino* (Archon Books, 1967), p. 94.

[654] *La tariffa delle puttane di Venegia*, reprinted in *Donne o cortigiane?: la prostituzione a Venezia : documenti di costume dal XVI al XVIII secolo* (Bertani, 1980), p. 173; cited in Elizabeth Horodowich, *Language and Statecraft in Early Modern Venice* (Cambridge University Press, 2008), p. 177.

[655] Christopher Nissen, *Kissing the Wild Woman: Art, Beauty, and the Reformation of the Italian Prose Romance in Giulia Bigolina's Urania* (University of Toronto Press, 2011), p. 174.

[656] Aretino to La Zufolina, March 1548, *Lettere* 169. To a Light Lady, in Thomas Caldecott Chubb, *The Letters of Pietro Aretino* (Archon Books, 1967), p. 249.

[657] Aretino's letter cited in Allison Mary Levy, *Remembering Masculinity in Early Modern Florence* (Ashgate Publishing, 2006), pp. 63-64.

[658] Aretino to La Zufolina, March 1548, *Lettere* 169. To a Light Lady, in Thomas Caldecott Chubb, *The Letters of Pietro Aretino* (Archon Books, 1967), p. 249.

[659] Ibid., p. 249.

[660] Henry Spencer Ashbee, *The Encyclopaedia of Erotic Literature: Being Notes, Bio-, Biblio-, Icono-graphical and Critical, on Curious and Uncommon Books, Volume 3* (Documentary Books, 1962), p. xxviii.

[661] *Lettere* 4.295 cited in Christopher Nissen, *Kissing the Wild Woman: Art, Beauty, and the Reformation of the Italian Prose Romance in Giulia Bigolina's Urania* (University of Toronto Press, 2011), p. 258.

[662] *Lettere* 4.275.

[663] Sheila Hale, *Titian: His Life* (Harper Collins, 2012), p. 250.

[664] Aretino to Sebastiano del Piombo, 15 June 1537, *Lettere* 26. My Little Daughter, in Thomas Caldecott Chubb, *The Letters of Pietro Aretino* (Archon Books, 1967), p. 64.

[665] Aretino to Messer Giorgio Vasari, April 1549, *Lettere* 206. Don of Arezzo–and Tita, in Thomas Caldecott Chubb, *The Letters of Pietro Aretino* (Archon Books, 1967), pp. 275-276.

[666] Aretino to Sebastiano del Piombo, 15 June 1537, *Lettere* 26. My Little Daughter, in Thomas Caldecott Chubb, *The Letters of Pietro Aretino* (Archon Books, 1967), p. 64.

[667] Cleugh, p. 161

[668] 'God knows if she is his', Berni, Daelli, Milan, II, 191; cited in Hutton, p. 11.

[669] Aretino to La Sandella, December 1547, *Lettere* 153. Nurse and Governess, in Thomas Caldecott Chubb, *The Letters of Pietro Aretino* (Archon Books, 1967), p. 238.

[670] Aretino to Caterina Sandella, December 1547, *Lettere* 165. How to Bring Up a Daughter, in Thomas Caldecott Chubb, *The Letters of Pietro Aretino* (Archon Books, 1967), p. 246.

[671] Aretino to Ambrogio degli Eusebi, 1 June 1537, *Lettere* 22. Neither Marry Nor Burn, in Thomas Caldecott Chubb, *The Letters of Pietro Aretino* (Archon Books, 1967), pp. 58-59.

[672] Ibid., p. 58.

[673] Ibid., pp. 59-60.

[674] Aretino to Monsignor Zicotto, 15 September 1537, *Lettere* 34. A lovely and Lively Girl, in Thomas Caldecott Chubb, *The Letters of Pietro Aretino* (Archon Books, 1967), p. 77.

[675] Count Ludovico Rangone of Spilamberto was the younger brother of the papal captain Guido Rangone.

[676] Cleugh, p. 164.

[677] Aretino to Monsignor Zicotto, 15 September 1537, *Lettere* 34. A lovely and Lively Girl, in Thomas Caldecott Chubb, *The Letters of Pietro Aretino* (Archon Books, 1967), p. 78.

[678] *Lettere* LXVII, Pietro Aretino, *The Works of Aretino: Dialogues - Letters and Sonnets [2 Vols.]*, trans. Samuel Putnam (Covici Friede, 1933), pp. 160-163.

[679] *Lettere* CX, Pietro Aretino, *The Works of Aretino: Dialogues - Letters and Sonnets [2 Vols.]*, trans. Samuel Putnam (Covici Friede, 1933), pp. 231-232.

[680] Aretino to the Count of San Secondo, 24 June 1537, *Lettere* 28. That Devil, Love, in Thomas Caldecott Chubb, *The Letters of Pietro Aretino* (Archon Books, 1967), p. 67.

[681] Ibid., p. 67.

[682] Ibid., p. 67.

[683] Aretino to Pierina Riccia, 2 September 1537, *Lettere* 32. A Proverb for Little Girls, in Thomas Caldecott Chubb, *The Letters of Pietro Aretino* (Archon Books, 1967), p. 75.

[684] *Lettere*, II, 115; cited in Hutton, p. 163

[685] Cleugh, p. 168.

[686] Ibid., p. 168.

[687] Ibid., p. 169.

[688] *Lettere*, III, 187; cited in Hutton, p. 164.

[689] Aretino to Marietta Riccia, September 1545, *Lettere* 116. The Death of Pierina, in Thomas Caldecott Chubb, *The Letters of Pietro Aretino* (Archon Books, 1967), p. 214.

[690] Cleugh, p. 172.

[691] *Stanze di Messer Pietro Aretino in lode di Madonna Angela Serena*, no. 15, in Pietro Aretino, *Poesie Varie*, ed. Giovanni Aquilecchia and Angelo Romano (Rome: Salerno Editrice, 1992), 1:230; also Linda Austern & Inna Naroditskaya (editors), *Music of the Sirens* (Indiana University Press, 2006), pp. 143-144.

[692] Cleugh, p. 173.

[693] Aretino to Francesco Macasola, November 1547, *Lettere* 152. Life Begins At Sixty, in Thomas Caldecott Chubb, *The Letters of Pietro Aretino* (Archon Books, 1967), p. 237.

[694] John Addington Symonds, *Renaissance in Italy: Italian Literature* (Library of Alexandria, 1906), p. 332.

[695] Ibid., pp. 332-33.

[696] *Lettere* XVII, Pietro Aretino, *The Works of Aretino: Dialogues - Letters and Sonnets [2 Vols.]*, trans. Samuel Putnam (Covici Friede, 1933), p. 75.

[697] *Lettere* XX, Pietro Aretino, *The Works of Aretino: Dialogues - Letters and Sonnets [2 Vols.]*, trans. Samuel Putnam (Covici Friede, 1933), p. 82.

[698] *Lettere* XXV, Pietro Aretino, *The Works of Aretino: Dialogues - Letters and Sonnets [2 Vols.]*, trans. Samuel Putnam (Covici Friede, 1933), p. 91.

[699] Aretino to the King of France, 1536, *Lettere* 15. Neither King of France Nor Free, in Thomas Caldecott Chubb, *The Letters of Pietro Aretino* (Archon Books, 1967), pp. 45-47.

[700] See John Addington Symonds, *Renaissance in Italy: Italian Literature* (Library of Alexandria, 1906), p. 368.

[701] *Lettere* XXX, Pietro Aretino, *The Works of Aretino: Dialogues - Letters and Sonnets [2 Vols.]*, trans. Samuel Putnam (Covici Friede, 1933), pp. 100-103.

[702] Filippo Strozzi to Francesco Vettori, Bologna, 20 January 1537; cited in Stefano Dall'Aglio, *The Duke's Assassin: Exile and Death of Lorenzino de' Medici* (Yale University Press, 2015), p. 82.

[703] Stefano Dall'Aglio, *The Duke's Assassin: Exile and Death of Lorenzino de' Medici* (Yale University Press, 2015), pp. 13-19.

[704] *Lettere* XXIX, Pietro Aretino, *The Works of Aretino: Dialogues - Letters and Sonnets [2 Vols.]*, trans. Samuel Putnam (Covici Friede, 1933), p.99.

[705] *Lettere*, 3:124, cited in Stefano Dall'Aglio, *The Duke's Assassin: Exile and Death of Lorenzino de' Medici* (Yale University Press, 2015), p. 83.

[706] Aretino to Captain F., Venice, February 1548; cited in Stefano Dall'Aglio, *The Duke's Assassin: Exile and Death of Lorenzino de' Medici* (Yale University Press, 2015), pp. 175-176.

[707] Gabrielle Langdon, *Medici Women: Portraits of Power, Love and Betrayal from the Court of Duke Cosimo I* (University of Toronto Press, 2006), p. 23.

[708] Aretino to Signor Gianbattista Castaldo, 12 March 1537, *Lettere* 16. A Robber Robbed, in Thomas Caldecott Chubb, *The Letters of Pietro Aretino* (Archon Books, 1967), pp. 50-51.

[709] Aretino to Agostino Ricchi, 16 May 1537, *Lettere* 19. Ten Thousand Crowns, in Thomas Caldecott Chubb, *The Letters of Pietro Aretino* (Archon Books, 1967), p. 55.

[710] *Lettere* XXXIV, Pietro Aretino, *The Works of Aretino: Dialogues - Letters and Sonnets [2 Vols.]*, trans. Samuel Putnam (Covici Friede, 1933), p. 107.

[711] Jacob Burckhardt, *The Civilization of the Renaissance in Italy* (The Floating Press, 2015), p. 139.

[712] *Lettere* LXVI, Pietro Aretino, *The Works of Aretino: Dialogues - Letters and Sonnets [2 Vols.]*, trans. Samuel Putnam (Covici Friede, 1933), p. 159.

[713] Aretino to Francesco dal' Arme, 15 May 1537, *Lettere* 18. My Talents Grow Lazy, in Thomas Caldecott Chubb, *The Letters of Pietro Aretino* (Archon Books, 1967), p. 54.

[714] Aretino to Francesco Marcolini, 22 June 1537, *Lettere* 27. To a Publisher, in Thomas Caldecott Chubb, *The Letters of Pietro Aretino* (Archon Books, 1967), p. 66.

[715] Brian Richardson, *Printing, Writers and Readers in Renaissance Italy* (Cambridge University Press, 1999), p. 92.

[716] Aretino to Francesco Marcolini, 22 June 1537, *Lettere* 27. To a Publisher, in Thomas Caldecott Chubb, *The Letters of Pietro Aretino* (Archon Books, 1967), p. 66.

[717] Robin Bruce Barnes, *Books Have Their Own Destiny: Essays in Honor of Robert V. Schnucker, Volume 50 of Sixteenth century essays & studies* (Truman State University Press, 1998), p. 140.

[718] Quintilian, *Institutio oratoria*, translated into Italian by Orazio Toscanella and dedicated to Domenico Venier in 1566; cited in Veronica Franco (author), Ann Rosalind Jones & Margaret F. Rosenthal (trans.), *Poems and Selected Letters* (University of Chicago Press, 2007), p. 8.

400

[719] Filippo Del Lucchese, Fabio Frosini & Vittorio Morfino, *The Radical Machiavelli: Politics, Philosophy, and Language* (BRILL, 2015), p. 150.

[720] Aretino to Messer Giorgio the Painter, 22 September 1537, *Lettere* 36. Your Renown, Not My Honour, in Thomas Caldecott Chubb, *The Letters of Pietro Aretino* (Archon Books, 1967), p. 82.

[721] Aretino to Messer Agostino Richi, 10 July 1537, *Lettere* 30. Winter and Summer, in Thomas Caldecott Chubb, *The Letters of Pietro Aretino* (Archon Books, 1967), p. 72.

[722] Aretino to Niccolò Franco, 25 June 1537, *Lettere* 29. Advice to an Author, in Thomas Caldecott Chubb, *The Letters of Pietro Aretino* (Archon Books, 1967), pp. 68-71.

[723] Aretino to Francesco Marcolini, 22 June 1537, *Lettere* 27. To a Publisher, in Thomas Caldecott Chubb, *The Letters of Pietro Aretino* (Archon Books, 1967), p. 65.

[724] Susan Gaylard, *Hollow Men: Writing, Objects, and Public Image in Renaissance Italy* (Fordham University Press, 2013), p. 126.

[725] Brian Richardson, *Printing, Writers and Readers in Renaissance Italy* (Cambridge University Press, 1999), p. 94.

[726] *Lettere* LI, Pietro Aretino, The Works of Aretino: Dialogues - Letters and Sonnets [2 Vols.], trans. Samuel Putnam (Covici Friede, 1933), p. 135.

[727] Ariosto, *Satira*, VI, ll. 25-7; cited in Trevor Dean & K. J. P. Lowe, *Crime, Society and the Law in Renaissance Italy* (Cambridge University Press, 1994), p. 74.

[728] Rictor Norton, *My dear boy: gay love letters through the centuries* (Leyland Publications, 1998), p. 54.

[729] Arsiccio (author), Ian Frederick Moulton (translator), *La Cazzaria: The Book of the Prick* (Psychology Press, 2003), p. 75.

[730] Laura Giannetti, *Lelia's Kiss: Imagining Gender, Sex, and Marriage in Italian Renaissance Comedy* (University of Toronto Press, 2009), pp. 163-164.

[731] See Richard Palmer, *The Church, Leprosy and Plague in Medieval and Early Modern Europe* (Ecclesiastical History Society, 1982), pp. 79-99.

[732] Alan Stewart, *Close Readers: Humanism and Sodomy in Early Modern England* (Princeton University Press, 2014), p. 9.

[733] Nicolaus J. Hajek, *Still a Rivalry: Contrasting Renaissance Sodomy Legislation in Florence and Venice* (2015), p. 7.

[734] Nicolaus J. Hajek, *Still a Rivalry: Contrasting Renaissance Sodomy Legislation in Florence and Venice* (2015), p. 8.

[735] *Lettere* LXX, Pietro Aretino, The Works of Aretino: Dialogues - Letters and Sonnets [2 Vols.], trans. Samuel Putnam (Covici Friede, 1933), p. 169.

[736] Ian Verstegen (editor), *Patronage and Dynasty: The Rise of the Della Rovere in Renaissance Italy* (Truman State University Press, 2007), p. 163.

[737] The murder of Francesco Maria della Rovere, which had been instigated by the Duke's brother-in-law Luigi Gonzaga, became the basis for The Murder of Gonzago, the story-within-a-story which, in the guise of the play 'The Mousetrap', is recounted in William Shakespeare's play *Hamlet, Prince of Denmark*.

[738] Jane A. Bernstein, *Print Culture and Music in Sixteenth-century Venice* (Oxford University Press, 2001), p. 131.

[739] Christopher Nissen, *Kissing the Wild Woman: Art, Beauty, and the Reformation of the Italian Prose Romance in Giulia Bigolina's Urania* (University of Toronto Press, 2011), p. 259.

[740] Cleugh, p. 180.

[741] *I sette salmi della penitentia di David* (The Seven Psalms of David, 1534), *I tre libri de la humanità di Cristo* (The Humanity of Christ, 1535), and *Il Genesi con la visione di Noè* (The Story of Genesis, 1538).

[742] Aretino to Lodovico Dolce, 7 October 1539, *Lettere* 71. Portrait of a Scoundrel, in Thomas Caldecott Chubb, *The Letters of Pietro Aretino* (Archon Books, 1967), p. 150.

[743] Pietro Aretino, *The letters of Pietro Aretino* (the University of Michigan, 2008), p. 149.

[744] Coppialettere di Margherita Paleologa, 3 January 1541, cited in Sally Anne Hickson, *Women, Art and Architectural Patronage in Renaissance Mantua: Matrons, Mystics and Monasteries* (Routledge, 2016), p. 99.

[745] See John Rigby Hale, David Chambers, Cecil H. Clough & Michael Mallett, *War, Culture and Society in Renaissance Venice: Essays in Honour of John Hale* (A&C Black, 1993), p. 132.

[746] *Lettere*, p. 595, no. 124 (to Lodovico Dolce, 7 October 1539); cited in John Rigby Hale, David Chambers, Cecil H. Clough & Michael Mallett, *War, Culture and Society in Renaissance Venice: Essays in Honour of John Hale* (A&C Black, 1993), p. 132.

[747] Cleugh, p. 185.

[748] *Lettere*, III, 285; cited in Hutton, p. 193.

[749] Cleugh, p. 185.

[750] Ibid., p. 185.

[751] First published in Rome only in 1569.

[752] Lynn Hunt, *The Invention of Pornography, 1500-1800: Obscenity and the Origins of Modernity* (MIT Press, 1996), p. 345.

[753] Luigi Tansillo, Niccolò Franco & Carlo Clausen, *Il vendemmiatore, poemetto in ottava rima di Luigi Tansillo; e la Priapea, sonetti lussuriosi-satirici di Niccolò Franco* (J.C. Molini, 1790), p. 83, poem XXXII.

[754] Quoted in Don Harrán (trans.) & Sarra Copia Sulam (author), *Jewish Poet and Intellectual in Seventeenth-Century Venice: The Works of Sarra Copia Sulam in Verse and Prose Along with Writings of Her Contemporaries in Her Praise, Condemnation, or Defense* (University of Chicago Press, 2009), p. 395.

[755] *Lettere* XLI, Pietro Aretino, The Works of Aretino: Dialogues - Letters and Sonnets [2 Vols.], trans. Samuel Putnam (Covici Friede, 1933), p. 118.

[756] Hutton, p. 166.

[757] Letter to Michelangelo, 15 September 1537, Pietro Aretino (author), George Bull (editor), *Selected Letters* (Penguin Classics, 1976), p. 109.

[758] Ibid., p. 111.

[759] Michelangelo Buonarroti (author), E. H. Ramsden (editor), *The Letters of Michelangelo, Volume 1* (Stanford University Press, 1963), p. 3.

[760] Anne W. Lowenthal, *Joachim Wtewael: Mars and Venus Surprised by Vulcan* (Getty Publications, 1995), p. 69.

[761] Richard Viladesau, *The Triumph of the Cross: The Passion of Christ in Theology and the Arts from the Renaissance to the Counter-Reformation* (Oxford University Press, 2008), p. 180.

[762] Eugène Müntz, *Michelangelo* (Parkstone International, 2012), p. 134.

[763] Aretino to Titian, October 1545, *Lettere* 120. Titian in Rome, in Thomas Caldecott Chubb, *The Letters of Pietro Aretino* (Archon Books, 1967), p. 219.

[764] Aretino to Buonarotti, April 1545, *Lettere* 107. A Gift of Drawings, in Thomas Caldecott Chubb, *The Letters of Pietro Aretino* (Archon Books, 1967), p. 204.

[765] Eric Scigliano, *Michelangelo's Mountain: The Quest For Perfection in the Marble Quarries of Carrara* (Simon and Schuster, 2007), p. 293.

[766] Ibid., p. 330.

[767] Letter to Alessandro Corvino, July 1547, Pietro Aretino (author), George Bull (editor), *Selected Letters* (Penguin Classics, 1976), pp. 226-227.

[768] The phrase, appropriate though anachronistic, is from Eric Scigliano, *Michelangelo's Mountain: The Quest For Perfection in the Marble Quarries of Carrara* (Simon and Schuster, 2007), p. 330.

[769] Letter to Alessandro Corvino, July 1547, Pietro Aretino (author), George Bull (editor), *Selected Letters* (Penguin Classics, 1976), pp. 226-227.

[770] Ibid., p. 227.

[771] Lodovico Dolce, *Dialogo della Pittura*, C. Teoli (editor), Edgar Wind (translator), (1863), p. 51; cited in Edith Balas, *Michelangelo's Medici Chapel: A New Interpretation*, Volume 216 (American Philosophical Society, 1995), p. 33.

[772] Marcia B. Hall & Tracy E. Cooper, *The Sensuous in the Counter-Reformation Church* (Cambridge University Press, 2013), p. 83.

[773] Lodovico Dolce, *Dialogo della pittura* (1557), Linda and Peter Murray (translators), (New York, 1968); cited in Edith Balas, *Michelangelo's Medici Chapel: A New Interpretation*, Volume 216 (American Philosophical Society, 1995), p. 32.

[774] The quote is by William James Bouwsma, *Venice and the Defense of Republican Liberty: Renaissance Values in the Age of the Counter Reformation* (University of California Press, 1968), p. 298.

[775] Joanna Woods-Marsden, 'Theorizing Renaissance Portraiture', in James Elkins and Robert Williams (editors), *Renaissance Theory (The Art Seminar)*, (Routledge, 2007), p. 362.

[776] Tom Nichols, *Tintoretto, prestezza and the poligrafi: a study in the literary and visual culture of Cinquecento Venice*, Renaissance Studies, Vol. 10, No. 1 (March 1996), pp. 72-100.

[777] Robert Klein & Henri Zerner, *Italian Art, 1500-1600: Sources and Documents* (Northwestern University Press, 1989), p. 91.

[778] Tom Nichols, *Tintoretto: Tradition and Identity* (Reaktion Books, 2015).

[779] Quoted in Sheila Hale, *Titian: His Life* (Harper Collins, 2012), p. 18.

[780] Luba Freedman, *Titian's Portraits through Aretino's Lens* (Penn State University Press, 1995), p. 11.

[781] Anna Laura Lepschy, *Tintoretto Observed: A Documentary Survey of Critical Reactions from the 16th to the 20th Century* (Longo, 1983), p. 16.

[782] Aretino to Jacopo Tintore, February 1545, *Lettere* 104. Art is Calling, in Thomas Caldecott Chubb, *The Letters of Pietro Aretino* (Archon Books, 1967), p. 200.

[783] Aretino, P., *Lettere sull'arte di Pietro Aretino*, vol. I, pp. 55-56.

[784] Pietro Aretino, *Lettere sull'arte*, ed. Camesasca (Milan: Edizioni del Milione,1957), II, CCXI, pp. 52-53.

[785] Aretino to Jacopo Tintore, April 1548, *Lettere* 171. The Miracle of St. Mark, in Thomas Caldecott Chubb, *The Letters of Pietro Aretino* (Archon Books, 1967), pp. 251-252.

[786] Anna Laura Lepschy, *Tintoretto Observed: A Documentary Survey of Critical Reactions from the 16th to the 20th Century* (Longo, 1983), p. 17.

[787] Mark W. Roskill, Renaissance Society of America, *Dolce's Aretino and Venetian Art Theory of the Cinquecento* (University of Toronto Press, 2000), p. 31,

[788] Aretino to Jacopo del Giallo, 23 May 1537, *Lettere* 20. A Painter of Miniatures, in Thomas Caldecott Chubb, *The Letters of Pietro Aretino* (Archon Books, 1967), p. 56.

[789] Pietro Aretino, *Commedie, nuovamente riv. e corrette, aggiunta L'orazia* (Milan: Sonzogno, 1888), pp. 117-118, cited in Furlan, *Pordenone*, p. 34.

[790] Aretino to Leone Lioni, 25 May 1537, *Lettere* 21. Advice to an Artist, in Thomas Caldecott Chubb, *The Letters of Pietro Aretino* (Archon Books, 1967), p. 57.

[791] Aretino's letter to Andrea Schiavone in L'Aretino, *Lettere sull'arte*, ed. Flora, Pertile, and Camesasca (Milan, 1957-1960), 4 vol, II, p. 221; cited in Robert Klein & Henri Zerner, Italian Art, 1500-1600: Sources and Documents (Northwestern University Press, 1989), pp. 55-56.

[792] Aretino to Danese, August 1545, *Lettere* 115. Art Critic, in Thomas Caldecott Chubb, *The Letters of Pietro Aretino* (Archon Books, 1967), pp. 213-214.

[793] Aretino to Coccio, September 1547, *Lettere* 150. Definition of Art, in Thomas Caldecott Chubb, *The Letters of Pietro Aretino* (Archon Books, 1967), pp. 236-237.

[794] Bernhard Berenson, *The Venetian Painters Of The Renaissance With An Index To Their Works* (G.P. Putnam's Sons, 1899), p. 45.

[795] Luba Freedman, *Titian's Portraits through Aretino's Lens* (Penn State University Press, 1995), p. 11.

[796] Sonnet reproduced in Carlo Ridolfi, *The Life of Titian* (Penn State Press, 2010), pp. 85-86.

[797] Tim Shephard, *Echoing Helicon: Music, Art and Identity in the Este Studioli, 1440-1530* (Oxford University Press, 2014), p. 148.

[798] For a more detailed examination of Aretino as art critic see Luba Freedman, *Titian's Portraits through Aretino's Lens* (Penn State University Press, 1995), pp. 8-10.

[799] Stuart W. Pyhrr & José-A. Godoy (authors), *Heroic Armor of the Italian Renaissance: Filippo Negroli and His Contemporaries* (Metropolitan Museum of Art, 1998), p. 148).

[800] Ian Verstegen (editor), *Patronage and Dynasty: The Rise of the Della Rovere in Renaissance Italy* (Truman State University Press, 2007), p. 163.

[801] R. J. Knecht, *Renaissance Warrior and Patron: The Reign of Francis I* (Cambridge University Press, 1994), p. 445.

[802] Diana Robin, *Publishing Women: Salons, the Presses, and the Counter-Reformation in Sixteenth-Century Italy* (University of Chicago Press, 2007), p. 246.

[803] Christine Suzanne Getz, *Music in the Collective Experience in Sixteenth-century Milan* (Ashgate Publishing, Ltd., 2005), p. 42.

[804] See Tom Nichols, *Tintoretto: Tradition and Identity* (Reaktion Books, 2015).

[805] Luba Freedman, *Titian's Portraits through Aretino's Lens* (Penn State University Press, 1995), p. 12.

[806] Giorgio Vasari, *Vita di Tiziano* (Edizioni Studio Tesi, 1994), p. xi; also David Rosand, *Titian* (Abrams, 1978), p. 20.

[807] Luba Freedman, *Titian's Portraits through Aretino's Lens* (Penn State University Press, 1995), p. 67.

[808] Philip Lindsay Sohm, *The Artist Grows Old: The Aging of Art and Artists in Italy, 1500-1800* (Yale University Press, 2007), p. 91.

[809] Luba Freedman, *Titian's Portraits through Aretino's Lens* (Penn State University Press, 1995), p. 141.

[810] Aretino to Count Massiminiano, 8 October 1531, *Lettere* 10. A Painting by Titian, in Thomas Caldecott Chubb, *The Letters of Pietro Aretino* (Archon Books, 1967), pp. 38-39.

[811] Aretino to Pomponio Vecelli, September 1550, *Lettere* 228. A Dissolute Young Man, in Thomas Caldecott Chubb, *The Letters of Pietro Aretino* (Archon Books, 1967), pp. 295-296.

[812] Aretino to Titian and Sansovino, September 1550, *Lettere* 227. Crabbed Age and Youth, in Thomas Caldecott Chubb, *The Letters of Pietro Aretino* (Archon Books, 1967), pp. 294-295.

[813] Joseph Archer Crowe & Giovanni Battista Cavalcaselle, *Titian: His Life and Times: With Some Account of His Family, Chiefly from New and Unpublished Records, Volume 2* (J. Murray, 1877), p. 312.

[814] *Lettere* II, 249; cited in Hutton, p. 110.

[815] Janet Sethre, *The Souls of Venice* (McFarland, 2003), p. 97.

[816] David J. Cast, *The Ashgate Research Companion to Giorgio Vasari* (Routledge, 2016), p. 173.

[817] See Edward Muir, *Civic Ritual in Renaissance Venice* (Princeton University Press, 1981), pp. 170-176 for a more indepth description of Venetian carnival activities during this time.

[818] A. J. Hoenselaars, *The Italian World of English Renaissance Drama: Cultural Exchange and Intertextuality* (University of Delaware Press, 1998), p. 280.

[819] David J. Cast, *The Ashgate Research Companion to Giorgio Vasari* (Routledge, 2016), p. 172.

[820] Ibid., p. 172.

[821] Guido Rebecchini, *Private Collectors in Mantua, 1500-1630* (Ed. di Storia e Letteratura, 2002), p. 214.

[822] Giorgio Vasari (author), Thomas A. Pallen (editor), *Vasari on Theatre* (SIU Press, 1999), p. 35.

[823] Ibid., p. 35.

[824] Quoted in Raymond B. Waddington, *Aretino's Satyr: Sexuality, Satire and Self-projection in Sixteenth-century Literature and Art* (University of Toronto Press, 2004), p. 83.

[825] Giorgio Vasari (author), Thomas A. Pallen (editor), *Vasari on Theatre* (SIU Press, 1999), p. 35.

[826] See Julian Kliemann, *Giorgio Vasari* (Oxford University Press, 2016).

[827] Quoted in Vincent Cronin, *The Flowering Of The Renaissance* (Random House, 2011).

[828] Aretino's letter to Andrea Udone is quoted in David Mayernik, *The Challenge of Emulation in Art and Architecture: Between Imitation and Invention* (Routledge, 2016), p. 53, which also goes into interesting detail on the house which Vasari was building for himself around this time in his hometown of Arezzo, the Casa Vasari.

[829] *Lettere scritte a Pietro Aretino*, 3:11 (letter of 23 February 1542); cited in Michel Plaisance, *Florence in the Time of the Medici: Public Celebrations, Politics, and Literature in the Fifteenth and Sixteenth Centuries* (Centre for Reformation and Renaissance Studies, 2008), p. 121.

[830] Letter to Duke Cosimo I de' Medici, April 1541, Pietro Aretino (author), George Bull (editor), *Selected Letters* (Penguin Classics, 1976), pp. 205-206.

[831] Aretino to his brother-in-law Orazio Vanotti, November 1542, *Lettere* 95. The Death of a Sister, in Thomas Caldecott Chubb, *The Letters of Pietro Aretino* (Archon Books, 1967), p. 187.

[832] Aretino to his relatives, January 1546, *Lettere* 130. To My Relatives, in Thomas Caldecott Chubb, *The Letters of Pietro Aretino* (Archon Books, 1967), p. 226.

[833] Aretino to Messer Jacopo Sansovino, 1545, *Lettere* 127. If The Pyramids of Egypt, in Thomas Caldecott Chubb, *The Letters of Pietro Aretino* (Archon Books, 1967), pp. 222-223.

[834] Brian Moynahan, *The Faith: A History of Christianity* (Crown Publishing Group, 2007), p. 440.

[835] Guido Ruggiero, *The Renaissance in Italy: A Social and Cultural History of the Rinascimento* (Cambridge University Press, 2014), p. 572.

[836] William H. McNeill, *Venice: The Hinge of Europe, 1081-1797* (University of Chicago Press, 2009), p. 174.

[837] Aretino's letter to Pope Paul III is cited in M. Young, *The life and times of Aonio Paleario, or, A history of the Italian reformers in the sixteenth century, Volume 1* (Harvard University, 1860), p. 568.

[838] Beccatelli, *Vita del Card. Contarini.*

[839] Vergerio to Aretino, 10 December 1534, in Landoni (editor), *Lettere scritte a Pietro Aretino*, p. 286, no. 177; cited in Anne Jacobson Schutte, *Pier Paolo Vergerio: The Making of an Italian Reformer* (Librairie Droz, 1977), p. 66.

[840] *Lettere* XIV, Pietro Aretino, *The Works of Aretino: Dialogues - Letters and Sonnets [2 Vols.]*, trans. Samuel Putnam (Covici Friede, 1933), pp. 70-71.

[841] Quoted in Vincent Cronin, *The Flowering Of The Renaissance* (Random House, 2011).

[842] Aretino to Captain Francesco Faloppia, 4 May 1542, *Lettere* 88. An Agent of the Sophy, in Thomas Caldecott Chubb, *The Letters of Pietro Aretino* (Archon Books, 1967), p. 177.

[843] Aretino to Francesco Marcolini, 18 August 1542, *Lettere* 92. The Croaking of the Friars, in Thomas Caldecott Chubb, *The Letters of Pietro Aretino* (Archon Books, 1967), pp. 180-181.

[844] Letter to King Henry VIII, August 1542, Pietro Aretino (author), George Bull (editor), *Selected Letters* (Penguin Classics, 1976), p. 163.

[845] Aretino to Antonio Carsidoni, 15 July 1540, *Lettere* 74. Eviction, in Thomas Caldecott Chubb, *The Letters of Pietro Aretino* (Archon Books, 1967), pp. 161-162.

[846] Aretino to Antonio Carsidoni, 15 July 1540, *Lettere* 74. Eviction, in Thomas Caldecott Chubb, *The Letters of Pietro Aretino* (Archon Books, 1967), pp. 161-162.

[847] Vincent Cronin, *The Flowering Of The Renaissance* (Random House, 2011).

[848] Stuart W. Pyhrr & José-A. Godoy, *Heroic Armor of the Italian Renaissance: Filippo Negroli and His Contemporaries* (Metropolitan Museum of Art, 1998), p. 283; also Marina Belozerskaya, *Luxury Arts of the Renaissance* (Getty Publications, 2005), p. 160.

[849] Aretino to Titian, July 1543, *Lettere* 96. A Horse is not a Gondola, in Thomas Caldecott Chubb, *The Letters of Pietro Aretino* (Archon Books, 1967), pp. 187-88.

[850] *Lettere.* III, 40; cited in Hutton, p. 197.

[851] *Lettere*, III, 41 and 28, cited in Hutton, p. 198.

[852] Simona Cohen, *Animals as Disguised Symbols in Renaissance Art* (Brill, 2008), p. 191.

[853] Aretino to Messer Giovanni dei Rossi of Pisa, October 1543, *Lettere* 98. The August Loftiness of Caesar, in Thomas Caldecott Chubb, *The Letters of Pietro Aretino* (Archon Books, 1967), p. 190.

[854] Aretino to Messer Giovanni dei Rossi of Pisa, October 1543, *Lettere* 98. The August Loftiness of Caesar, in Thomas Caldecott Chubb, *The Letters of Pietro Aretino* (Archon Books, 1967), p. 190.

[855] Aretino to Messer Giovanni dei Rossi of Pisa, October 1543, *Lettere* 98. The August Loftiness of Caesar, in Thomas Caldecott Chubb, *The Letters of Pietro Aretino* (Archon Books, 1967), p. 191.

[856] *Lettere*, III, 30-4; cited in Hutton, p. 199.

[857] Aretino to Messer Giovanni dei Rossi of Pisa, October 1543, *Lettere* 98. The August Loftiness of Caesar, in Thomas Caldecott Chubb, *The Letters of Pietro Aretino* (Archon Books, 1967), p. 194.

[858] *Lettere*, V, 280; cited in Hutton, p. 199.

[859] Aretino to Messer Giovanni dei Rossi of Pisa, October 1543, *Lettere* 98. The August Loftiness of Caesar, in Thomas Caldecott Chubb, *The Letters of Pietro Aretino* (Archon Books, 1967), p. 195.

[860] *Lettere*, III, 43, and VI, 37; cited in Hutton, p. 199.

[861] Aretino to Messer Giovanni dei Rossi of Pisa, October 1543, *Lettere* 98. The August Loftiness of Caesar, in Thomas Caldecott Chubb, *The Letters of Pietro Aretino* (Archon Books, 1967), pp. 194-195.

[862] *Lettere*, III, 44; cited in Hutton, p. 199.

[863] Quoted in Vincent Cronin, *The Flowering Of The Renaissance* (Random House, 2011).

[864] *Andarò spesso spesso a ca' Venieri,*
Ove io non vado mai ch'io non impari
Di mille cose per quatr' anni intieri;
Et ivi fassi un ragionar divino
Fra quella compagnia d'huomini rari.
Chi è il Badoar sapete, e chi il Molino,
Chi il padron della stanza, e l'Amaltèo,
Il Corso, lo Sperone, e l'Aretino.
Ciascun nelle scienze è un Campanèo,
Grande vo' dire, et son fra lor sì uguali,
Che s'Anfion è l'un, l'altro è un
Orfeo.

[865] Courtney Quaintance, *Textual Masculinity and the Exchange of Women in Renaissance Venice* (University of Toronto Press, 2015), p. 74.

[866] Aretino to Messer Giovanni dei Rossi of Pisa, October 1543, *Lettere* 98. The August Loftiness of Caesar, in Thomas Caldecott Chubb, *The Letters of Pietro Aretino* (Archon Books, 1967), p. 189.

[867] Aretino to Nofri Camaiani, 12 April 1542, *Lettere* 86. The Greatest Glory Anyone Can Have, in Thomas Caldecott Chubb, *The Letters of Pietro Aretino* (Archon Books, 1967), pp. 176-177.

[868] Aretino to Francesco Marcolini, March 1545, *Lettere* 105. In My Opinion, Envy, in Thomas Caldecott Chubb, *The Letters of Pietro Aretino* (Archon Books, 1967), p. 201.

[869] Aretino to Francesco Bacci, March 1546, *Lettere* 135. A Knighthood Refused, in Thomas Caldecott Chubb, *The Letters of Pietro Aretino* (Archon Books, 1967), p. 231.

[870] Aretino to Titian, May 1544, *Lettere* 99. Sunset in Venice, in Thomas Caldecott Chubb, *The Letters of Pietro Aretino* (Archon Books, 1967), pp. 195-196.

[871] Aretino to Marcolini, August 1544, *Lettere* 102. The Printing Presses would not have Time, in Thomas Caldecott Chubb, *The Letters of Pietro Aretino* (Archon Books, 1967), p. 198.

[872] Aretino to Marcolini, January 1545, *Lettere* 103. The Consequences of Greatness, in Thomas Caldecott Chubb, *The Letters of Pietro Aretino* (Archon Books, 1967), p. 199.

[873] Aretino's letter to Agostino Lando is quoted in James Northcote, *The Life of Titian* (1830), pp. 182-183.

[874] Aretino to Lodovico Domenichi, July 1545, *Lettere* 109. Heatwave, in Thomas Caldecott Chubb, *The Letters of Pietro Aretino* (Archon Books, 1967), pp. 205-206.

[875] Aretino to Titian, October 1545, *Lettere* 120. Titian in Rome, in Thomas Caldecott Chubb, *The Letters of Pietro Aretino* (Archon Books, 1967), p. 218.

[876] For Vasari's fascinating account of Titian's 1545-46 visit to Rome, see G. Vasari, *The Lives of the Artists*, trans. J. and P. Bondanella (Oxford, 1991), pp. 500-501.

[877] Aretino to Titian, October 1545, *Lettere* 120. Titian in Rome, in Thomas Caldecott Chubb, *The Letters of Pietro Aretino* (Archon Books, 1967), pp. 218-219.

878 Aretino to Titian, July 1543, *Lettere* 97. A Good Name More Than Ample Revenues, in Thomas Caldecott Chubb, *The Letters of Pietro Aretino* (Archon Books, 1967), p. 189.

879 G. Vasari, *The Lives of the Artists*, trans. J. and P. Bondanella (Oxford, 1991), pp. 500-501.

880 For a fuller elucidation of the Venetian verus Florentine methods of painting see Bruce Cole, *Titian and Venetian Painting*, 1450-1590 (Westview Press, 2000), pp. 144-146.

881 Aretino to Titian, October 1545, *Lettere* 120. Titian in Rome, in Thomas Caldecott Chubb, *The Letters of Pietro Aretino* (Archon Books, 1967), p. 219.

882 Aretino to Titian, 1546, *Lettere* 133. Sansovino in Trouble, in Thomas Caldecott Chubb, *The letters of Pietro Aretino* (Archon Books, 1967), p. 228.

883 Aretino to Titian, December 1547, *Lettere* 157. Be Satisfied with Enough, in Thomas Caldecott Chubb, *The Letters of Pietro Aretino* (Archon Books, 1967), p. 242.

884 Bruce Cole, *Titian and Venetian Painting*, 1450-1590 (Westview Press, 2000), pp. 147-148.

885 Ibid., pp. 152-153.

886 Aretino to Titian, April 1548, *Lettere* 176. The Hands of Ambition, in Thomas Caldecott Chubb, *The Letters of Pietro Aretino* (Archon Books, 1967), p. 256.

887 For Priscianese's description of Titian's house see Joseph Archer Crowe & Giovanni Battista Cavalcaselle, *Titian: His Life and Times: With Some Account of His Family, Chiefly from New and Unpublished Records, Volume 2 (J. Murray, 1877).*, II, p. 40.

888 For the full text of Mary of Hungary's letter see Joseph Archer Crowe & Giovanni Battista Cavalcaselle, *Titian: His Life and Times: With Some Account of His Family, Chiefly from New and Unpublished Records, Volume 2 (J. Murray, 1877).*, II, p. 209.

889 Aretino to Titian, February 1550, *Lettere* 218. I Have Friends, in Thomas Caldecott Chubb, *The Letters of Pietro Aretino* (Archon Books, 1967), p. 288.

890 Janet Levarie Smarr & Daria Valentini, *Italian Women and the City: Essays* (Fairleigh Dickinson University Press, 2003), p. 44.

891 Gaspara Stampa, *The Complete Poems: The 1554 Edition of the 'Rime', a Bilingual Edition* (University of Chicago Press, 2010), pp. 11-12.

892 Collaltino Collalto and Gaspara Stampa would at least be lyrically united in 1738 when eleven of Collattino's poems were published together with Stampa's *Rime* in an edition edited by Bergalli.

893 Aria's husband's name is spelled Diovatelli by both Hutton. It is spelled Diotalevi by both Cleugh and Chubb and Diotallevi by Raymond B. Waddington and the British Museum (which has the bronze Adria Sandella medal commissioned by Aretino). My personal preference here is for the more Italian-sounding Hutton spelling, Diovatelli.

894 Cleugh, p. 236.

895 Ibid., p. 230.

896 Aretino to the duke of Urbino, *Lettere* 257. The Woes of Adria, in Thomas Caldecott Chubb, *The Letters of Pietro Aretino* (Archon Books, 1967), p. 321.

897 Ibid., pp. 321-322.

898 Ibid., p. 322.

899 Ibid., p. 323.

900 Aretino to Sebastiano del Piombo, 15 June 1537, *Lettere* 26. My Little Daughter, in Thomas Caldecott Chubb, *The Letters of Pietro Aretino* (Archon Books, 1967), pp. 64-65.

901 Raymond B. Waddington, *Aretino's Satyr: Sexuality, Satire and Self-projection in Sixteenth-century Literature and Art* (University of Toronto Press, 2004), p. 89.

902 Cleugh, p. 237.

903 Peter Brand & Lino Pertile, *The Cambridge History of Italian Literature* (Cambridge University Press, 1997), p. 273.

904 Titian to Aretino from Augsburg, 11 November 1550 in *Lettere all' A.*, I, i. 244; cited in Hutton p. 225.

905 Aretino to Titian from Venice, November 1550, *Lettere* 232. His Majesty's Benignity of Grace, in Thomas Caldecott Chubb, *The Letters of Pietro Aretino* (Archon Books, 1967), p. 298.

906 Frank W. Thackeray & John E. Findling (editors), *Events That Formed the Modern World: From the European Renaissance through the War on Terror [5 volumes]: From the European Renaissance through the War on Terror* (ABC-CLIO, 2012), p. 289.

907 Quoted in Hutton, p. 222.

908 Aretino to Luigi Caorlino from Venice, September 1550, *Lettere* 231. The Riches of Poverty, in Thomas Caldecott Chubb, *The Letters of Pietro Aretino* (Archon Books, 1967), p. 298.

909 Aretino to Titian and Sansovino from Venice, September 1550, *Lettere* 227. Crabbed Age and Youth, in Thomas Caldecott Chubb, *The Letters of Pietro Aretino* (Archon Books, 1967), p. 295.

910 Cleugh, p. 238.

911 *Lettere*, VI, 113 and 160; cited in Hutton , p. 226.

912 Aretino to the duke of Urbino, March 1553, *Lettere* 247. 100 Crowns, in Thomas Caldecott Chubb, *The Letters of Pietro Aretino* (Archon Books, 1967), p. 298.

913 *Lettere* VI, 174; cited in Hutton, p. 227.

914 See Judith Bryce, *Cosimo Bartoli (1503-1572): The Career of a Florentine Polymath* in Issue 191 of *Travaux d'humanisme et Renaissance* (Librairie Droz, 1983), pp. 73-74.

915 David J. Cast, *The Ashgate Research Companion to Giorgio Vasari* (Routledge, 2016), p. 258.

916 Aretino to the duke of Urbino, October 1553, *Lettere* 248. To the Most Holy Roman Church, in Thomas Caldecott Chubb, *The Letters of Pietro Aretino* (Archon Books, 1967), p. 312.

917 Aretino to Titian, December 1553, *Lettere* 249. Ill-mannered servants, in Thomas Caldecott Chubb, *The Letters of Pietro Aretino* (Archon Books, 1967), pp. 312-313.

918 Aretino to Sansovino, December 1553, *Lettere* 250. Madness that Canonizes Madness, in Thomas Caldecott Chubb, *The Letters of Pietro Aretino* (Archon Books, 1967), pp. 313-314.

919 Aretino to Francesco Sansovino, December 1553, *Lettere* 251. The Years We Spent in Vain, in Thomas Caldecott Chubb, *The Letters of Pietro Aretino* (Archon Books, 1967), p. 314.

920 Aretino to Sister Arnulfa, December 1553, *Lettere* 253. In Praise of Holiness, in Thomas Caldecott Chubb, *The Letters of Pietro Aretino* (Archon Books, 1967), pp. 315-317.

921 Sheila Hale, *Titian: His Life* (Harper Collins, 2012), p. 247.

922 Aretino to Domenico Bolani, January 1551, *Lettere* 235. Eviction, in Thomas Caldecott Chubb, *The Letters of Pietro Aretino* (Archon Books, 1967), pp. 300-301.

923 Luba Freeman, *Titian's Portraits through Aretino's Lens* (Penn State Press, 1995), p. 11.

924 Cleugh, p. 243.

925 Jacob Burckhardt, *The Civilisation of the Period of the Renaissance in Italy* (Cambridge University Press, 2014), p. 129.

926 Aretino to Bernardo Tasso, October 1549, *Lettere* 213. My Own Praises, in Thomas Caldecott Chubb, *The Letters of Pietro Aretino* (Archon Books, 1967), p. 281.

[927] Ibid., p. 284.

[928] Titian, *Delphi Complete Works of Titian (Illustrated)*, (Delphi Classics, 2015).

[929] Aretino to Signor Albicante, 2 July 1539, *Lettere* 69. The Fury of Poets, in Thomas Caldecott Chubb, *The Letters of Pietro Aretino* (Archon Books, 1967), p. 145.

[930] Aretino to an Ambassador, October 1545, *Lettere* 117. Poets and Dogs, in Thomas Caldecott Chubb, *The Letters of Pietro Aretino* (Archon Books, 1967), p. 215.

[931] David Young Kim, *The Traveling Artist in the Italian Renaissance: Geography, Mobility, and Style* (Yale University Press, 2014), p. 165.

[932] Jane A. Bernstein, *Music Printing in Renaissance Venice: The Scotto Press (1539-1572)*, (Oxford University Press, USA, 1998), p. 303.

[933] Tom Nichols, *Tintoretto: Tradition and Identity* (Reaktion Books, 2015).

[934] Aretino to Giovan Battista Dragoncino, 24 November 1537, *Lettere* 43. The Muses Need Money, in Thomas Caldecott Chubb, *The Letters of Pietro Aretino* (Archon Books, 1967), p. 95.

[935] Joost Keizer & Todd Richardson, *The Transformation of Vernacular Expression in Early Modern Arts* (Brill, 2011), p. 110.

[936] John Martin, *Venice's Hidden Enemies: Italian Heretics in a Renaissance City* (University of California Press, 1993), p. 78.

[937] Anton Francesco Doni, *La Libraria*, in Pietro Aretino, *La Cortigiana*, ed. Angelo Romano (Rizzoli, 1989), p. 28.

[938] Niccolò Franco, *Rime contro Pietro Aretino con la Priapea in Antonio Vignali, La Cazzaria*, ed. Pasquale Stopelli (Editioni dell'Elefante, 1984), p. 14. & Anton Franceso Doni, *La Vita dello infame Aretino*, ed. Constantino Arlia (S. Lapi, 1901), pp. 25-26, 32.

[939] Hendrik van Gorp & Ulla Musarra-Schrøder, *Genres as Repositories of Cultural Memory, Volume 5; Volume 15* (Rodopi, 2000), p. 23.

[940] The story of Aretino's fit of laughter over the dirty story concerning his sisters, and his subsequent backward fall in his chair and apoplectic fit is mentioned first in Antonio Lorenzino's 1603 book on laughter, *De risu*. Lorenzino apparently copied the story about Aretino's sisters from a scabrous anecdote from Francesco Berni. For a more detailed discussion on the historiographical origins of this account of Aretino's death see Hendrik van Gorp & Ulla Musarra-Schrøder, *Genres as Repositories of Cultural Memory, Volume 5; Volume 15* (Rodopi, 2000), pp. 23-24.

[941] Gaye, *Carteggio*, Vol. II, 337; cited in Hutton, p. 229.

[942] Raymond B. Waddington, *Aretino's Satyr: Sexuality, Satire and Self-projection in Sixteenth-century Literature and Art* (University of Toronto Press, 2004), p. 156.

[943] *Memoirs of the Dukes of Urbino, Illustrating the Arms, Arts, and Litterature of Italy, from 1440 to 1630, Volume 3* (Longman, Brown, Green and Longmans, 1851), p. 273.

[944] William Drummond, *The Poetical Works of William Drummond of Hawthornden, Volume 1* (Ardent Media, 1913), p. 380.

[945] J. Feerick & V. Nardizzi, *The Indistinct Human in Renaissance Literature* (Springer, 2012), p. 192.

[946] Cleugh, p. 247.

[947] Brown Horatio Robert Forbes, *Studies in the History of Venice, Volume 2* (BiblioBazaar, 2009), p. 70.

[948] C. B. Schmitt, *The Cambridge History of Renaissance Philosophy* (Cambridge University Press, 1988), p. 45.

[949] Paul F. Grendler, *The Roman Inquisition and the Venetian Press, 1540-1605* (Princeton University Press, 2016), pp. 116-122.

[950] The papal Index of prohibted books would go on to prohibit such authors as Balzac, Casanova, Sade, Hugo, Flaubert and the modern existentialist author Sartre, before it was ultimately abolished in 1966, a belated victory for the forces of free speech.

[951] See A. Gerber, *All of the Five Fictitious Italian Editions of Writings of Machiavelli and Three of those of Pietro Aretino Printed by John Wolfe of London (1584-1589). III* (Modern Language Notes, 1907).

[952] Aretino, *Lettere*, 4:10-11, *Lettere sull'arte*, 2:218-19; cited in Ronald Delph, Michelle Fontaine & John Martin, *Heresy, Culture, and Religion in Early Modern Italy: Contexts and Contestations* (Truman State University Press, 2015), p. 29.

[953] Linda Phyllis Austern & Kari Boyd McBride, *Psalms in the Early Modern World* (Routledge, 2016), p. 9.

[954] *English recusant literature*, 1558-1640, Volume 203 (the University of California), p. 49.

[955] Roni Weinstein, *Juvenile Sexuality, Kabbalah, and Catholic Reformation in Italy: Tiferet Bahurim by Pinhas Barukh Ben Pelatiyah Monselice* (Brill, 2009), p. 172.

[956] Trevor Dean & K. J. P. Lowe, *Crime, Society and the Law in Renaissance Italy* (Cambridge University Press, 1994), p. 82.

[957] George Haven Putnam, *Books and Their Makers During the Middle Ages: A Study of the Conditions of the Production and Distribution of Literature from the Fall of the Roman Empire to the Close of the Seventeenth Century, Volume 1* (Hillary House, 1962), p. 333.

[958] Laurence Bergreen, *Casanova: The World of a Seductive Genius* (Simon and Schuster, 2016), p. 177.

[959] John Ralston Saul, Voltaire's Bastards (Simon and Schuster, 2012).

[960] *Studies in iconography, Volume 5* (University of California, 2007), p. 133.

[961] For a fuller exposition of the prick medal and a discussion of the satyr's relationship to satire see Andrea Bayer, *Art and Love in Renaissance Italy* (Metropolitan Museum of Art, 2008), pp. 221-223.

[962] Jacob Burckhardt, *The Civilization of the Renaissance in Italy* (The Floating Press, 2015), p. 137.

[963] William Boulting, *Tasso and His Times* (Haskell House Publishers, 1968), p. 11.

[964] Venice: Comin di Trino, 1547.

[965] Venice: Giolito, 1547.

[966] Aretino to Pilucca, the Academician, December 1546, *Lettere* 146. My Humble Origin, in Thomas Caldecott Chubb, *The Letters of Pietro Aretino* (Archon Books, 1967), p. 235.

[967] Aretino to Lodovico Dolce, November 1537, *Lettere* 45. A Tallow Candle, in Thomas Caldecott Chubb, *The Letters of Pietro Aretino* (Archon Books, 1967), p. 97.

Made in the USA
Monee, IL
19 March 2021